This was written by a clerk in Base Operations. It was designed
as a "razz" on the 509th Composite Group. Subsequent events proved
the old adage "He who laughs last ------."

NOBODY KNOWS

Into the air the secret rose,
Where they're going, nobody knows.
Tomorrow they'll return again.
But we'll never know where they've been.
Don't ask us about results or such,
Unless you want to get in Dutch.
But take it from one who is sure of the score.
The 509th is winning the war.

When the other Groups are ready to go.
We have a program of the whole damned show.
And when Halsey's 5th shells Nippon's shore.
Why, shucks, we,hear about it the day before.
And MacArthur and Doolittle give out in advance.
But with this new bunch we haven't a chance.
We should have been home a month or more,
For the 509th is winning the war.

Many thanks to the National Archives, Smithsonian Air and Space Museum,National Atomic Museum, and Archives at Los Alamos for their extensive photo collections

Library of Congress Cataloging-in-Publication Data

The 509th remembered : a history of the 509th Composite Group as told by the veterans themselves, 509th anniversary reunion, Wichita, Kansas October 7-10, 2004 / edited by Robert and Amelia Krauss.— [2nd ed.]

p. cm.

Includes index.

ISBN 0-923568-66-2

1. United States. Army Air Forces. Composite Group, 509th—History. 2. World War, 1939-1945—Regimental histories—United States. 3. World War, 1939-1945—Aerial operations, American. 4. World War, 1939-1945—Personal narratives, American. 5. Nuclear warfare—History—20th century. 6. Veterans—United States—Biography. 7. Bomber pilots—United States—Biography. I. Krauss, Robert, 1943- II. Krauss, Amelia.

D790.253509th .A16 2005

940.54'4973—dc22

2005010355

To Jeffery Shaw – good luck

THE 509TH REMEMBERED

A History of the 509th Composite Group As Told by the Veterans That Dropped the Atomic Bombs on Japan

Dutch Van Kirk

Navigator – Enola Gay

Hiroshima – 6 Aug. 1945

Robert and Amelia Krauss, Editors
366 E. Wagner Rd.
Buchanan, MI 49107
Revised 2010

DEDICATION

For the veterans and families of the 509th Composite Group,
my wife, Amelia, and son, Robert

TABLE OF CONTENTS

509th Organization
During 1944 - 1945

The 509th consisted of eight units with a combined roster of about 1770 men. The number of men of Project Alberta on Tinian was 53.

509th Composite Group Headquarters was established as the formal command center of the group at the time of activation 17 December 1944. In addition to the office of the Group Commander, Colonel Paul W. Tibbets, Jr. several functions vital to achieving the goals set for the group were represented at 509th Headquarters. Among these were: Intelligence, Operations, Armament, Weather, Photo Interpretation, and Personnel. Also included were Group Bombardier and Navigator.

Headquarters had the responsibility of organizing the component units of the group and seeing that all were working together toward the common objectives.

390th Air Service Group

The 390th Air Service Group was activated as an adjunct to the 509th, originally incorporating the 603rd Air Engineering Squadron and the 1027th Air Material Squadron as well as having its own Headquarters and Base Services Squadron.

The 390th and its components were initially manned mostly from units already stationed at Wendover Field when the 509th arrived. Later, the 603rd and the 1027th functioned as largely independent squadrons within the 509th, while the Headquarters and Base Services Squadron of the 390th continued to provide close support to the 509th Headquarters.

393rd Bombardment Squadron (VH - Very Heavy)

The 393rd Bomb Squadron, chosen to be the Combat Unit of the 509th commanded by Lt. Col. Thomas J. Classen, had completed two-thirds of its training in the 504th Bomb Group (VH) at Fairmont Field, Nebraska and was starting to prepare for movement overseas, when word came they were going to Wendover, Utah.

There were originally 20 B29 flight crews. It was determined that only 15 crews were required to carry out the 393rd mission. The men of the remaining five crews were given the choice of transferring to other groups of the Second Air Force or remaining at Wendover and being assigned to the 320th Troop Carrier Squadron. The members of the five crews who qualified for positions within the 320th opted to remain.

320th Troop Carrier Squadron

The 320th started operations in September 1944 although not officially activated as part of the 509th until 17 December 1944. Initially, several twin engine C46s and C47s were utilized to carry cargo and passengers between key points throughout the US. These planes were gradually phased out after four engine C54s were acquired starting in November.

Flights were made throughout the US. The "milk run" to and from Kirtland Army Air Force Base in Albuquerque (closest to Los Alamos) linked Wendover and Los Alamos. Frequent trips were made to Naval Test Stations in California. Flight plans were often deliberately misleading for security reasons. Cargo almost certainly included fissionable materials produced at Oak Ridge, Tennessee and Hanford, Washington. Many atomic scientists and technicians of the Manhattan Project as well as members of the Military were among the passengers. The 320th provided logistical support for the 393rd when they trained at Batista Field, ferried crews of the 393rd to pick up the "Silver Plate" B29 at Martin-Omaha Plant, air lifted personnel and equipment of the 509th and Project Alberta from the US to Tinian.

603rd Air Engineering Squadron

On December 17, 1944, the 603rd Air Engineering Squadron was activated. A survey of all the shops was made and only the most highly skilled men were selected to form this new squadron. A large percentage of the personnel had been at Wendover for some time as part of the 216th Base Unit. They had been working as a team, thus eliminating months of training.

It was the 603rd's responsibility to see that the third and fourth echelon repair and maintenance on the B29s of the 509th was of the highest caliber. The squadron was so organized that even a major overhaul could be accomplished with factory precision.

Tech Supply procured aircraft parts, flying equipment and issued mechanic's clothing, tools and other equipment needed to properly maintain the aircraft. Mobile repair units were formed that could go from plane to plane repairing minor damage or removing a major portion or component requiring shop work.

Specialized shops performed work on propellers, instruments, electrical equipment, bombsights, automatic pilots, armament, radar systems and trainers, auxiliary power units (put-puts) communication and office equipment, and parachutes and other lifesaving equipment. The shops augmented line maintenance.

The sheet metal shop repaired or rebuilt any damaged surface of a wing or other metallic structure brought to it by the mobile unit. At Wendover, this shop was busy modifying the early models of the B29 to meet the special requirements of the 509th such as turret and blister removal.

1027th Air Material Squadron

The mission of the 1027th was to anticipate, procure, and issue all air corps, quartermaster, signal, chemical warfare, and ordnance supplies and equipment for the 509th Composite Group. Time of activation was December 17, 1944.

1395th Military Police Company (Aviation)

Activated December 17, 1944, the 1395th was to provide for security of personnel and equipment. They went through a rigorous training program to enable them to meet any situation.

1st Ordnance Squadron Special (Aviation)

Activated in March 1945, the 1st Ordnance Squadron Special (Aviation) was formed to bring overseas the men, skill and equipment needed to assemble the atomic bombs. The men had been working with top scientists on the Atomic Bomb Program for over nine months. The technical and military security requirements for the squadron were so exacting that only twenty percent of those having basic qualifications were accepted.

The men were subjected to loyalty and background checks. Once they were accepted and commenced operations, they were placed under military secrecy and no transfers were permitted. They were not allowed to inform their families or anyone not connected with the squadron including other members of the 509th as to the type of work they were doing. No conversations between men were permitted outside the restricted area within which they worked both at Wendover and Tinian. When troop movements commenced for overseas destination, the men were accompanied by members of the Military Intelligence Department. While traveling by troop train, the men were not permitted to mix with other travelers. No other passengers, military or civilian were allowed to enter dining cars while these men were eating. Many men traveled to overseas destination by air and they were also segregated from other personnel at all island stops.

Project Alberta

Project Alberta was established in March 1945 as a separate element of the Manhattan Project at Los Alamos for the purpose of unifying the various activities concerned with the preparation and combat use of atomic bombs. Its three main tasks were (1) design, procurement and assembly of bombs complete and ready for use with active materials (2) continuation of the Wendover W47 Test Program (3) preparation for overseas operation against the enemy.

Activities at Wendover Associated with the 509th

216th Army Air Force Base Unit (Special)

The 216th AAF Base Unit was at Wendover prior to the arrival of the 509th and continued there after the 509th moved to Tinian. It was an umbrella organization over various units and activities at the base. Two of the units were established and operated as test facilities under the direction of the Los Alamos Weapon Development Laboratory of the Manhattan Project. There was a Flight Test Section and Special Ordnance Detachment, both formerly within Squadron A of the 216th. There was close interaction between these units and joint operations.

Flight Test Section, 216th Base Unit

Operations began as early as March 1944 dropping a large number of dummy bombs (test units) from high altitude at various instrumented ranges, including Naval facilities at Muroc Dry Lake, Salton Sea and Inyokern, California as well as a range on the Salt Flats near Wendover.

Special Ordnance Detachment, 216th AAF Base Unit

Worked closely with scientific and engineering personnel from Los Alamos, assembled and loaded numerous Little Boy, Fat Man and Pumpkin test units.

Additional B29 Crews at Wendover

Two additional B29 Crews came to Wendover after the 509th moved to Tinian. Special order number 184 was cut at Topeka Army Air Force Base Headquarters diverting two crews to the 216th AAF Base Unit at Wendover Field. The first crew was commanded by Donald C. Rehl, the second by Elwin G. Kirby.

Wendover Air Base, 1944

Fairmont AAF Paper

FAAF NEWS

VOL. 1, NO. 8   Official Publication Of Fairmont Army Air Field

FAAF, GENEVA, NEBRASKA.

SATURDAY, AUGUST 26, 1944

Voting is the privilege and duty of every citizen.

ANNOUNCE CONTEST

Gurney Group Arrives; Is Welcomed To Base

Lt. Col. Carl Springer, Executive Officer, In Command Pending Arrival Of Col. Gurney

After a long, hot, and dusty troop train ride from Dalhart, Tex., the ground echelon of our new Bomb Group arrived on the field Tuesday, August 15. For some undisclosed reason, the group desires to be known as "Colonel Gurney's Group," named after the Group Commanding Officer, Colonel Samuel C. Gurney, Jr., who is still with the Air Echelon, in training presently at another base.

A welcome, complete with band playing, was accorded the new group upon their arrival at the Fairmont station. Preparations for their arrival had been completed by an advance echelon of the group, which arrived three weeks ago. Lt. Col. Carl Springer, executive officer, and acting Commanding Officer, said at an interview this morning: "We are very happy to be here and want to express our appreciation for the warm welcome which we received. We expect to begin training very soon.

Assisting Colonel Springer in the organization of the new group

(Continued on Page 2, Col. 5).

EM Receive Still More Promotions

Forty-Seven Announced On August Twenty-First

It was announced Monday that the following EM have been promoted to grades indicated:

To Master Sergeant—George C. Bellude, Michael J. Komeski, Kenneth H. Moe.

To Tech Sergeant—Challance A. Maloney, Warren P. Stanley, Charles W. Goddard, George V. Ward, Leo M. Wasner.

To Staff Sergeant—Frank V. Potts, Russell M. Weyrauch, Robert E. Little.

To Sergeant—Jerome Luke, Thomas G. Curran, Andrew Halls, Manfield J. Holland, Thadeus P. Juszczak, Howard J. Kotker, Clarence A. Dickey.

To Corporal—Robert V. Curry, Kenneth Nimphius, Charles F. Haviland, Barron J. Shores, Cecil L. Bohn, Henry Chudofsky, Edward W. Croft, William M. Fisher, Harry M. Hafelen, Samuel A. Hallyburton, Gordon H. Hart, James W. Jordan, Alexander F. Kowalski, Henry J. Krystopowics, John W. Macy, Jr., Reynaldo J. Ortiz, Harry Pardoll, Emmitt G. Schaefer, Robert W. Schmidl, Frank D. Steel, Jr., Clyde G. Trout, Jr., Orville J. Uadhjem, Lavern J. Zacharas, Dallas E. Boeken, Eldren C. Carlson, Gary H. Edmunds, Robert E. Ormston, Oliver J. Alanen, Bob B. Manns.

NCO Party At Lincoln Is Success

Plan For Another Party Within Three Weeks

BY PVT. P. W. LORIS.

Last Sunday, August 20, 250 members of the base unit enjoyed a Sunday afternoon and evening at the Hillcrest Country Club in Lincoln, Nebraska, made possible by the FAAF NCO Club.

Beer and refreshments were free to all that attended. Dancing started at 2:00 p. m. and ended at 11:00 p. m. with lovely girls for everyone. A steak dinner was served with potatoes, gravy, sweet

(Continued on Page 2, Col. 4).

For further information about soldier voting, consult Lt. Milton Litvak, soldier voting officer, at the legal boards and claims office in base headquarters. Phone 214.

Ladies Entertain At Base Hospital

A group of ladies from Grafton, Nebraska, entertained the patients at the Fairmont Army Air Field Hospital on Sunday evening, August 20th, with a program of music and cake. The ladies, who are members of the Catholic, Congregational, and Lutheran Churches at Grafton, are organized to put on this entertainment, in conjunction with the Red Cross, by Mrs. P.

(Continued on Page 2, Col. 1).

Deprey New Camera Club Vice-Pres.

Committee To Purchase "Darkroom" Supplies

The FAAF Camera Club held its regular meeting in the Special Service Office in Base Headquarters at 1930 Tuesday, 22 August 1944. Pvt. Arthur Woodnick presided. Sgt. Leland Kay read the minutes of the last meeting which were approved and made a matter of record.

"Announcement as to the exact location of Club rooms will be made in a very short time"—according to President Wodnick.

(Continued on Page 2, Col 4)

Happy Winners Of "Cross-Country Flight"!

BEST CREWS OF THE WEEK

Pictured in the upper Shot is the 393th "Crew of the Week." Standing—Capt. J. L. Gist, Airplane Commander; 2nd Lt. W. E. Welsh, Pilot; 2nd Lt. C. R. T. Barstad, Bombardier; 2nd Lt. R. F. Ready, Navigator; S/Sgt. E. W. Demlow, Flight Engineer. Kneeling—Pfc. F. T. De Vane, Gunner; S/Sgt. A. A. Sloan, Radio Operator; Pvt. W. E. Streissguth, Pvt. D. E. Innis, Cpl. G. Fallon, Gunners. and Pfc. D. C. Di Cammillo, Gunners. The lower left picture is of the 393rd winners. Left to Right: Standing—2nd Lt. E. B. Smith, Airplane Commander; F/O W. J. Desmond, Pilot; 2nd Lt. V. I. Mann, Navigator; F/O J. R. Soboleski, Bombardier; 2nd Lt. E. S. Grenning, Flight Engineer. Kneeling— Pfc. P. L. Marcello, Radio Operator; Pfc. A. J. Becker, Gunner; Cpl. B. Mitchell, and Cpl. Y. E. Baggett, Gunners. The lower right shows the 421st "Crew of the Week." Left to Right: Standing—2nd Lt. M. M. Doyle, Airplane Commander; 2nd Lt. C. B. Egger, Pilot; F/O R. E. Comer, Bombardier; J. Cipolla, S/Sgt. A. A. Zelt, Pfc. E. L. Smith, Pfc. W. A. Irwin, and Cpl. E. V. Cherven, Kneeling—Pfc. S. Zelt, Pfc. P. D. Murphy, Radio Operator.

Prizes To Be Awarded Insignia Contest Winners

War Bond Award for First And Second Best Design Submitted To Director Of Sta. Ser.

A contest to obtain a new Fairmont Army Air Field insignia which will represent the field, serve as a morale booster and identify the field's airplanes has been launched.

The contest which will close on September 9 is open to all enlisted personnel and the winner will be presented with a $25 war bond; the runner-up will receive one of the new $10 "GI" bonds! A board composed of officers and enlisted men will decide which suggestion is best.

The adoption of an insignia is authorized and subject to approval of the commanding general of the Army Air Forces.

The insignia selected will be used for painting on aircraft permanently alloted to the base unit as a patch for wear on pocket or flight jacket, field or work jacket, coveralls, and work uniforms; for decoration of recreational buildings, barracks, mess halls, etc.; and for unofficial stationery.

The insignia will serve as an identification device. It may either be of caricature design or classic heraldic style, and must in good taste. Under no circumstances will the design be copyrighted to any nations or persons approved, designs will not be

Each insignia will be of simple design and will

(Continued on Page 2, Col. 3)

Another USO Show At Theater Sunday

Tomorrow night, Sunday 27, August, the 21st Bombardment Wing Special Weekly USO Show "Space About" will be presented at this field featuring the following people: Billy Burke as Emcee and comedy Music; The New Yorkers, who do a Comedy Juggling act; Alice Kavin, dancer; the Kelly Sisters, Trio Singers; the Gilberts, who are Comedy Acrobats. Members of our own Base Band, under the direction of Warrant Officer Thayer, will accompany this troupe.

Don't miss the USO Show at the Base Theatre at 1830 (6:30) or 2000 (8:00) Sunday.

NCO's Hold Election Of Officers

Discuss Plans For Enlargement Of Club

The Non-Commissioned Officers club held a special meeting at 1700 on Thursday evening, August 17, at the Base Theater at which time an election of officers was held. The secretary of the club, T/Sgt. Joseph Nudelman, served as temporary chairman in place of ex-president S/Sgt. John Barker who has been transferred from the field.

The following new officers were elected: President, S/Sgt. John Clancy; vice president, S/Sgt. William J. Brennan, and a board of governors consisting of the following members was elected to

(Continued on Page 2, Col. 3).

P-47 Pilot On Carpet At Bruning

Courtmartialed For "Buzzing" Of Beatrice

Second Lt. Alvin J. Luongo, 20, of New York City, a P-47 instructor pilot at Bruning Army Air Field, is about to be court martialed at Second Air Force Headquarters. He has been sentenced to dismissal from the service forfeiture of all pay and allowance due and to become due.

Citizens of Beatrice, Nebraska, testified the Officer on July 15, led a flight of three ships, piloted by students, in a 30-minute "buzzing" of the town at low altitude.

The case will go before Major

(Continued on Page 2, Col. 3).

GI Insurance Totals $117 Billions

Washington (CNS) — The Veterans' Administration has become the world's largest life insurance company; it has policies of $117,000,000,000 outstanding for men and women in the service.

Lee Palmert at Fairmont

3

*Col. Tibbets, 509th
Commanding Officer
North Africa, 1942*

*Tom Classen, Deputy Commander, 509th,
Wendover, 1944*

Main Gate

One of many signs

WHAT YOU HEAR HERE—
WHAT YOU SEE HERE—
WHEN YOU LEAVE HERE—
LET IT
STAY HERE!

Stateline Hotel

Housing Project
Wendover Air Base, 1944

Lt. Tom Costa, Bombardier, Crew B-7
in front of building on approach to town of Wen-
dover with future wife Jacqueline Shoemaker

Inside 2006 Wendover AFB, 1944
Leo Czaja, 603rd

Mont Mickelson,
603rd Engineering Squadron
Wendover AFB State Line 1944

Wendover AFB, 1945
Wajeskie (left); Leo Czaja (right)

Harold Glick and
Mont Mickelson, 1945

Wendover AFB, 1945

Edward Costello entertains at
Wendover Air Base Service Club

Chapel at Wendover

*Wendover Air Base Photo Group
preparing for gas attack*

*Alex Schiavone with snowman
outside Wendover Photo Lab*

Staff of Wendover Air Base Post Office

Top Row L-R: William Carroll (delivered mail by Jeep on Tinian), Richard Shaw, Unknown
Row 2: George Wagner, Unknown
Row 3: Lt. Schafer, Fred Elbers (driver for Lt. Schafer)
Row 4: Mrs. Schafer
Row 5: Kathryn Murphy, Roy Roberts

Arriving at Wendover in February 1943, I was in the 7th Airdrome Squadron. I was born with an eye defect that I could use either eye but only one at a time. So I was moved to the 216th and left at Wendover. I had finished mechanics school but my eye doctor said it was too dangerous for me to be around the planes so I was put in the small squadron mail room. While making trips to the main military post office, I met the postal officer, Lt. Schafer. He seemed to like me and after a few weeks he asked if I would like to work at the main post office and work for him. After most of the men were transferred to other bases, I was put in charge under Lt. Schafer.

About a year later, Lt. Schafer was transferred and the post office was put under the base adjutant. The next morning when we opened, Capt. Pearson was waiting to see me. He told me I was in charge and I had permission to sign his name anytime it was necessary. He said he knew nothing about the post office and expected me to run it; but if he got chewed out, he would be coming to see me.

Kathryn Murphy was the first lady to be hired and later when we had only four men left, they sent twenty women to help us. Kathryn was a big help as she trained the ladies.

ROBERTS, ROY SR.
216 Base Unit

One of the first five Silverplate versions delivered to Wendover, April 1945.
This plane was identified in Sheldon Dike's report as one of the B-29s used in the Los Alamos drop testing program. Records show assignment to the 509th, but it was assigned to the 216th Base Unit.

For Your Information

Voting
Is the Privilege and
Duty of Every
Citizen
Use It

WENDOVER FIELD
SALT TABLET

By And For The Men Of Wendover Army Air Base
Published Semi-Monthly At Wendover Field, Utah

Vol. 3 No. 30

For Voting Information

Consult
Capt. Walter L. Budge
Base Voting Officer
Building 204
Phone 149

A 'Suggestion' Week Planned

By Pfc. Russell Naughton

To promote efficiency and improve working procedures at Wendover Field, October 7 through 14, 1944, will be designated as "Suggestion" Week. During this week, all military and civilian personnel will be encouraged to submit any suggestion that will improve the day's work, increase safety or improve the morale of personnel.

A special AAF Suggestion Committee was named last week. Serving on this committee are: Major John P. Porter, chairman; Captain John S. Fulton; Lt. Frank E. Washbourne and Mr. Lafayette H. Anderson, recorder.

It will be the function of this committee to act on all suggestions submitted and make awards based on the importance of the ideas suggested.

In general, favorable consideration will be given when a suggestion results in—a. Conservation of manpower, material, time or space. b. Elimination of unnecessary processes or improvement of existing methods. c. Improvement in conditions affecting safety and health. d. Increased productivity. e. Elimination of excess, tooling or equipment. f. Improvement of quality. g. Invention or mechanical device. wh'h, when adapted, proves to be of value. h. Conservation of critical material and the utilization of material previously scrapped.

Civilian awards for suggestions adopted will range from $5.00 to $250.00, while military awards will include—a. Recommendation for the Legion of Merit. b. Consideration for promotion. c. Letter of Commendation.

Suggestion boxes are located at S & M Hqs. Slide (116): Civilian Personnel Office (2004): Post Engineers (8204); Hospital Adm. Bldg. (2624); and the General Supply Office (405).

Thursday, Oct. 5, 1944

A Message From The C.O.

TO: All Personnel.

In the short time that I have been with you at Wendover Field, there has already come to my attention several instances of loose talk emanating from this base. Let me take this opportunity to ask the cooperation of all personnel, military and civilian, towards safeguarding military information of all kinds. The easiest way to accomplish proper precaution is for each and every one of us to STOP TALKING SHOP the minute we go through the gate.

Every effort of the nation is being bent toward bringing the war to a rapid conclusion with the least possible cost to our armed forces. That any of us here at Wendover should defeat or delay this purpose by careless talk is unthinkable, and yet that is just what can happen if we don't watch our step!

Nothing could be more false than the idea that the enemy is interested only in our plans and activities in the theaters of operation. Our military efforts in this country, your and my efforts right here at Wendover, all have as their primary purpose preparation for the support of active operations abroad. Don't take a chance! Don't talk!

No individual among us is qualified to judge just what piece of information will be helpful to the enemy. A statement which taken alone seems perfectly harmless may be combined with several others like it to give an amazingly clear over-all picture of major importance to our opponents. And don't forget that actual experience has proven that the enemy has effective means of collecting such bits of information. Don't try building yourself up by telling that pretty blonde on the bus all you know—she may be looking for just one scrap of information and you may be the one to supply it.

Army Regulations regarding the safeguarding of military information will be strictly enforced at this base and any violations will result in severe disciplinary action. The full cooperation of all personnel is demanded, both in preventing and in reporting such violations.

LT. COL. CHARLES E. TROWBRIDGE,
COMMANDING OFFICER.

Bids Major Farewell

Lt. Col. C. E. Trowbridge (left), base commander, bids farewell to Major Clark Pardee, former director of supply and maintenance here as latter left for a new Second Air Force assignment. Major Pardee had been stationed at Wendover since February 1943. A party in his honor was held at the Officers club.

Served 30 Months In Pacific
Former Civil Engineer Now Here

After serving 30 months in the southwest Pacific, 17 months of which were spent in the rugged battlefields f New Guinea, S-Sgt. Edwin J. Carroll of Beaumont, Mississippi, recently returned to the States, arriving at Wendover Field on September 20.

As a member of a service squadron, Carroll did 3rd echelon repairs in the bush country of New Guinea where often the temperature rose to 140 degrees. With their workshop set up under the trees in the swamps, they had to do most of their work at night, especially during the early months of the campaign as the enemy continually harassed them with daily bombing and strafing. Knee-deep in water and muck, Carroll's outfit did heroic duty in keeping American aircraft in top-top condition; a job which aided materially in turning the favorite of the campaign in our favorite.

Formerly a civil engineer employed by the State of Mississippi, Carroll wears the Asiatic-Pacific Theater ribbon with 2 stars for major campaigns in the Coral Sea battle and the Bismarck Sea engagement; and has been awarded the Presidential Unit Citation.

Lt. Col. Bean Is New Director

Lt. Col. Gerald E. Bean has been assigned as director of station services, according to an announcement by base headquarters last week.

Commissioned in 1930 as a second lieutenant in the infantry and an ROTC graduate of Rhode Island State college, Col. Bean's first post was at Fort Adams, R. I.

During a 10-year period in the infantry he served at various installations in the first, eighth and ninth corps areas. These included assignments in Oregon and Wyoming.

In 1940 he was detailed to duty with the Air Corps at Randolph Field, Texas. He held the rank of first lieutenant.

He was promoted to captain in October, 1941, and received his majority in January, 1943, while he was serving in Headquarters AAF Washington in the military personnel division where he had been assigned in March, 1942.

He went overseas and saw service in the CBI theater before returning to the states. He was promoted to lieutenant-colonel in June, 1944.

His wife and 20-months-old son are with him at Wendover.

Major Porter Takes New Post At Base

Major John W. Porter of Mackinaw, Ill., has been named Director of Maintenance and Supply relieving Major Clark E. Pardee, it was announced here last week. Major Porter left for a new assignment.

The new director of M&S is a graduate of the University of Illinois where he received his BS degree in 1941. He had 14 years of ROTC in College and was a cost accountant at the Carnegie Illinois Steel Corp., prior to entering the service.

Soldier Here Flew A Grand Total Of 75 Combat Missions

By Sgt. William Petro

With 75 combat missions to his credit as an aerial gunner, including the daylight bombings of both Rome and Berlin, Tech Sergeant Kurt J. Hermann II, of Long Island, N. Y., hopes his next stop will be somewhere in the general vicinity of Tokyo. A grand slam in aerial warfare—100 missions and the bombing of all three Axis capitals.

The indefatigable gunner's extended tour of combat service has taken him over the Italian capital to blast the vital railway lines that were feeding supplies to the German army in southern Italy; over Bizerte in Tunis to hammer the fleeing Nazis, and as a waist gunner on a Flying Fortress, he has taken part in the Eighth Air Forces daylight bombing of strategically important industrial and military objectives in Germany and Nazi-dominated Europe. During his combat career with the British-based Fortresses and has been over Berlin four times, and has participated in successful daylight bombing attacks on Nazi targets.

Hermann flew his first mission in the European theater on December 20, 1943. Besides his trips to Berlin, he was in on an assault on a Nazi aircraft production center. On that occasion, Hermann blasted a Nazi plane out of the sky during a running battle with 14 enemy fighters downed during his tour in Africa. This victory raised his bag to a total of five.

"After we got back, I knew what they meant when they referred to 'Big League de aerial warfare'," Hermann declared. "It was really rough. The enemy fighters came in at our ship four and five abreast. My top turret sent one down in flames, and on the very next attack, I managed to put another one away. A heard later that there were more than 300 fighters in the air against us that day."

Flew Night Mission

A short time later, Hermann obtained permission to go on a

T/Sgt. Kurt Hermann

night mission with the RAF. Flying as a gunner, he found the night operation "thrilling—so was an eerie experience to watch the searchlights and flak seeking us out through the clouds," he says. "It was like flying in a black pit, with no lights inside or outside the ship. I returned from that mission with a lot of respect for the RAF boys."

Then came the first attack on Berlin.

"The Berlin mission was a huge success," Hermann said. "We hit the Nazi capital a terrific whack. The flak was very intense—the heaviest I have ever seen—but the Jerry fighters made a very poor show in defending their principal city that day."

During his tour with the 8th, the oldest B-17 Flying Fortress group in Britain, Hermann won the Distinguished Flying Cross for "extraordinary achievement" in combat and four Oak Leaf Clusters to the Air Medal. He won the Air Medal for

Continued on Page 4

Cpl. Reid Joins 'Winged Victory'

Cpl. Joseph Reid o' the base squadron left last week for Santa Monica, California, to join the AAF production staff of the Winged Victory Unit. Practically born in the theater, Reid has been connected with show business since he was 13 years of age.

A native of New Jersey, Reid has been connected with the Schuberts in various capacities from an extra to property man and production manager. He got his start as prop boy in the famous Broad Street theater in Newark, N. J., over 26 years ago.

Cpl. Joseph Reid is proud of his theatrical backgro'nd. Both his parents were connected with the theater and his cousin, Wallace Reid was reigning matinee idol of a decade ago. Reid numbers among his personal friends the Barrymores, Katherine Cornell, Helen Hayes, George Jessel, Eddie Cantor, Sophia Sanderson, William Gillette, Madge Bellamy, Ruth Chatterton, Ethel Merman and many others.

Pringle New Head Of Base NCO Club

Tech. Sgt. John C. Pringle of the medical detachment at Wendover Field was elevated to the presidency of the NCO Club last week to fill a vacancy caused by the transfer of master Sgt. Charles E. Searcy to the AAB at Alexandria, La. Pringle has been vice president of the club.

The Wendover Field Paper

Matchbook

Postcard

*393rd Weld Shop,
civilian boss car
in front*

*603rd Air Engineering
Building
Skip Marcheese (left) and
James Johnson (right)*

ACKERMAN, CARL
393rd Bomb Squadron, Pilot

History of the 509th is a challenge because of the secret nature of our project. Some things were recorded; some were not.

I graduated from Aviation Cadet Pilot training in February 1944 at Albany, Georgia, then went to Lockbourne, Ohio for B17 training. In June, I was sent to Lincoln, Nebraska where our crews were formed. We went to B29 training at Fairmont, Nebraska as the 393rd Squadron of the 504th Bomb Group. I was rated a B29 pilot on July 19, 1944.

Survival Training in Nebraska

The survival training took place at Geneva, Nebraska because it was Major Keith Merrill's crew. Merrill was Airplane Commander (AC); I was Pilot; Stewart Williams, Bombardier; James Elder, Flight Engineer; Harold Rider, Navigator; Leander Baur, Radio; Neil Corey, Gunner and Gerald Clapso, Gunner. When the 509th was organized, it was decided the group had too many high ranking officers so they shipped out Majors Merrill, Sheldon and others. Merrill's crew met with Col. Tibbets requesting they ship out with Merrill because they had a good crew. Tibbets refused their request. Major Merrill became Squadron Commander with a group on Saipan and was shot down on the Kochi raid losing his entire crew.

In the summer of 1944, two of our crews were taken by a 6x6 to a nearby swimming pool to learn how to operate a five man life raft. Now you know what happens when you take young people to a swimming pool, a lot of cavorting, splashing and dunking. The instructor ordered everyone out of the pool and said, "Those of you that have that much energy can pump up this raft with a hand pump and save Uncle Sam some money by not using the CO2 cylinder that inflates this raft". It was hard work. We finally launched the raft in the pool and practiced turning it over, one side was blue, the other

yellow. The blue side up if in enemy territory, the yellow side up if in friendly territory. It takes a group effort to turn over a five man raft. All the people have to work on one side because if anyone is on the other side, he will be covered up when the raft flops over. You can see the possibility of some kind of game and soon the cavorting, splashing and dunking became more vigorous and someone accidently tripped the CO2 cylinder. Now this was serious because the raft was already inflated and was rapidly growing in size. Some of the men were frantically looking for some kind of a pressure relief valve and still that ominous hissing noise from the cylinder. The sides became too high for anyone to get inside the raft and I thought this was a good time to vacate the pool, which I did expecting a huge explosion. Some of the guys stayed with the ship which it was by now. It was enormous and still the hissing sound. Finally with a disappointing plop, it blew up and sank to the bottom of the pool.

On September 10th, the 393rd was taken out of the 504th and shipped to Wendover, Utah where we became the 509th Composite Group.

Wheels

While we were at Wendover, Major Merrill's crew flew a cross country navigational training flight in a B17. The B17 had a unique landing gear design in that the wheels did not retract completely into the nacelle and the bottom of the tire was in the slipstream which caused the wheel to spin in flight sometimes causing a vibration.

As we were flying along, Merrill asked me "What's wrong? The airplane is beginning to vibrate". I replied, "The wheels need balancing". He gave me an odd look and chuckled thinking it was one of my corny jokes. As the vibration worsened, he asked me "What's making this plane shake all over. I said, "The wheels need balancing". He said, "Now come on". I said, "Step on the brakes and see". He stepped on the brakes. There was a thud and the vibration stopped.

The major started laughing and said, "I thought you were kidding me". I said, "Oh no, I wouldn't do that".

That winter I went to Batista Field near Havana, Cuba. Capt. Stanley Zahn was the Airplane Commander for our crew. I have two photos from Sloppy Joes which I treasure highly because this was the remainder of

OFFICER'S PAY DATA CARD

LAST NAME—FIRST NAME—INITIAL	SERIAL NUMBER	GRADE	ARM OR SERVICE
ACKERMAN, CARL G.	0823518	2nd Lt	AC

PAY PERIOD	LENGTH OF SERVICE	DATE YEARS COMPLETED
1st	OVER 0 YEARS	—

PAY AND ALLOWANCES	AMOUNT	TOTAL
Monthly Base Pay and Longevity	$ 150.00	
Additional Pay for Flying	75.00	
Rental Allowances		
Subsistence (30-DAY MONTH)	21.00	
Date 1 March 1945		$ 246.00

PAY RESERVATIONS				SUBTOTAL
Allotments, Class E	$	$	$	$
Insurance		X	N	6.50
War Bonds, Class B				
Allotments, Class X				
Other Deductions (SPECIFY)				
SUBSEQUENT CHANGES IN ABOVE DATA WITH DATES				$ 6.50
			NET	$ 239.50

DEPENDENTS (STATE NAMES AND ADDRESSES)
NONE

W. D., A. G. O. FORM No. 77 (29 June 1944)   5633 NSC 12-29-44 120M
This form supersedes W.D., A. G. O. Form No. 77, 26 March
1942, which will not be used after receipt of this revision.

Merrill's first crew. We wanted crew pictures and agreed to meet at Sloppy Joes at a certain time. Zahn was reluctant to go to an establishment that served drinks but he said he would come to have the photo taken. He didn't come at the time agreed on, so we decided to have the photo taken without him. We waited a little longer, drank more beer, Zahn finally arrived and the second photo was taken showing before and after. Zahn was the only one that had his eyes completely open.

When we returned to Wendover, the crews were already formed and I served as a replacement pilot wherever needed in both the 393rd and 320th.

Ground School

On June 12, 1945, we arrived on Tinian Island and were informed we had to go to ground school instructed by the 313th Wing. This presented a problem because our planes were not the standard B29s. The problem was compounded because most of the differences were top secret.

We had our own ground school but Wing insisted we had to take their courses. The very first course was about Hamilton Props which we didn't have. We had Curtis Electric Reversible Pitch Props which was one of the top secret items.

I was given the job of getting twenty people to attend the class with the understanding no one ever mention Curtis Props. Most of the people I contacted agreed to go, some thought of it as a joke to play on Wing. The course lasted one week.

When we asked for the test papers back, Wing refused. This caused another confrontation because it was 509th policy to return the test papers to the people for their own review.

When we finally did get the papers back, we discovered many of our people made 100% and the rest scored high marks. After that we received word from Wing we should resume our own school.

I was really proud of our guys, not only for their good grades, but for the good character they displayed. In that whole boring week, not one ever mentioned we had Curtis Electric Props.

We flew three pilots on long missions. I was credited with four combat missions. I did not appear in any photos because they were taken of crews and I was not assigned to any crew. The day the photos were taken, Elbert Smith and I flew to Guam in a C54 to get supplies.

(L-R)
Carl Ackerman, Harold Rider, Leander Baur, Stewart Williams, Neil Corey, Gerald Clapso, Raymond Allen, Phillipe the Cuban Guide

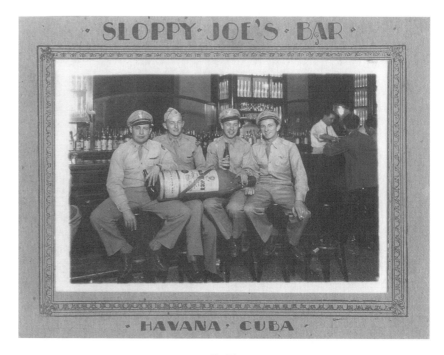

(L-R)
Harold Rider, Herman Zahn, Stewart Williams, Carl Ackerman

I never heard or knew anything about the Atomic Bomb until President Truman announced it publicly. I was discharged at Roswell, New Mexico in November.

ALBURY, CHARLES D.
393rd Airplane Commander, Crew C-15

My first impression of Wendover - What a desolate place this is. I flew in with Paul Tibbets to inspect the airport to see if it was usable for B29s. Paul decided we could always take off to the south or the east and maybe use the west runway. On our flight to Wendover, Paul Tibbets asked if I would like to go overseas with the outfit he was going to form. I said, "Yes, of course" because I had a lot of respect for him and his abilities.

We had just bought a 1939 Ford convertible coup, dark green, in Pratt, Kansas. When my transfer came in, Roberta and I piled our entire possessions in the rumble seat and started for Wendover. At the outskirts of Salt Lake City, on our way to Wendover, we stopped for breakfast. Roberta being about three months pregnant, spotted waffles with strawberries and whipped cream and ordered it several times. We made that 125 mile trip for that same dish.

At Wendover, just being the two of us, we were given housing, single room, single bed, at the civilian dormitories. What a deal, pregnant wife and me 155 pounds on a single bed.

Our 1st Christmas together was at Wendover. We finally found a small Christmas tree and set it up in our room with a few home made tinsels and paper chains and really enjoyed it.

Eating at the Officers Club mostly - Saturday night roast beef dinner and camaraderie with other members of the fledgling 509th Composite Group.

Playing pool at the club - Tom Ferebee getting mad because the ladies played pool and took up the pool table. There was also a tar paper building (restaurant) that you had to go down like a cellar which had the best steaks I've ever had.

Hand ball at the gym - Playing Beahan, Ferebee, Tibbets (who took no pity on anyone), Jerry Sluskey, Bob Lewis, Van Pelt, Van Kirk, and others. Bunking in the BOQ with Beahan (his snoring) being buddies. Also

duck hunting on the reservation on a small warm water lake fed by a warm spring coming out of the side of a high rock. Using shot guns (govt. issue) and skeet shot. Not too many dead ducks, but what we did get we took to officers' club for duck dinners. Slusky, myself, Bob Lewis, Dora Dougherty; we really enjoyed ourselves.

Poker playing in BOQ - Tom Ferebee getting provoked because of wild cards and jacks or better to open. The one that got him the most was one eyed kings wild.

There are many more memories, too many to mention. It did bring the whole group together and I believe most of us enjoyed being with each other.

Roberta Albury with British racing green 1939 Ford

Albury crew practicing with life raft at Wendover Pool

ANGELI, RUSSELL F.
320th Troop Carrier Squadron, Airplane Commander

It was great to get moving after marking time in Lincoln, Nebraska, waiting for assignment. The air base seems nice but where are the B29s? We were flying training flights in B17s, getting acquainted with crew, and learning navigation from roommate and navigator, Fred Hoey. This came in handy later on cross ocean trips. Just about all of our training was in B17s. Finally, got B29s - early flights, long takeoff runs, cylinder head temps all at red line, engineer opening cowl flaps to decrease temps, pilot closing cowl flaps to increase speed, climb above tops of corn field but not quite to pattern altitude, eventually get on down wind with one engine feathered, final approach with two engines feathered, landing - another successful flight! Engine problem was corrected on later B29s.

Recreation in York, Nebraska, was a nice town, friendly people, country club swimming pool, horse back riding, and other small town activities.

On To Wendover - 509th Composite Group!

FIRST IMPRESSIONS; Desolate, God forsaken, you name it. For me it was a first time in the mountains so I found the mountains majestic and impressive.

RECREATION: Not much to do except play cards. Some exciting jeep drives out on the desert, flying was safer. Best though was Salt Lake City "One More Time".

FLYING: Shortly after we got the B29s our crew was broken up. Our Pilot, Major Sheldon and Bombardier, Butterworth, were transferred out and

SECURITY: After listening to Col. Tibbets talk and hearing about transfers to Alaska, you believed and it stayed with you for remainder of war and then some!

the rest of the crew reassigned. I went to 320th Troop Carrier Squadron.

Every flight a story in itself. Most of our flying was in C46s and were pretty much all over the United States. Winter flying in the mountains was challenging. Most fun was low altitude cross country flights spooking the wild horses. We got the C54s about the time the 393rd went to Cuba and started round trips to Tinian in February 1945.

Whether the flight was local or across the ocean, Wendover was coming home - it grew on you. I guess that's why I so enjoyed the two reunions we have had at Wendover!

ALLEN, RAYMOND E.
393rd Bomb Squadron Tail Gunner Crew C-12

Written By His Wife, Dorothy Allen

It was a time of gasoline, food, shoe and tire rationing, Khaki, olive drab and blue uniforms, three day passes, two week furloughs and all the other things that come to mind from that period of time called the Fighting Forties, especially of World War II.

My story begins in August of 1944 when my future husband called from Denver to say that he had a ten day delay enroute to his next assignment at Fairmont Army Air Force Base in Nebraska and did I want to get married during that time. I really can't remember what I said but by the time he arrived in Wichita on the following Saturday morning, plans for the wedding were going full steam ahead. The wedding took place just six days after the phone call and, for such short notice, was very nice with my sister and brother-in-law as our attendants and girl-

friends serving as ushers and providing the music in a nearly full church. There was even time for a few of them to have a shower for me.

Ray, my husband by then, went ahead of me to Nebraska and a few days later I followed. Our sojourn in Nebraska was short, but while there, we stayed at Dan's Hotel in Geneva, Nebraska. Housing was hard to come by in those days as all available places to rent were full. Dan's Hotel was nothing to write home about – small rooms and one bathroom on each floor. If I thought that was bad, it was well that I didn't know what was in store for me.

Shortly after I arrived in Nebraska, my husband received orders his squadron was being sent to Wendover, Utah, where a new 509th Composite Group was being

Dorothy & Ray Allen, sitting on coal storage unit behind their Wendover apartment

but during the next day, the train wound through the Colorado Rockies. The Aspen trees were just beginning to turn a brilliant golden yellow. This was my very first train ride and the scenery was breathtaking with pine trees interspersed with Aspen and no sign of life anywhere.

I really don't know what I expected but it wasn't what I saw upon arrival. Wendover was a town located on the Utah/Nevada line with one hotel, one drug store, one grocery store, I'm sure a filling station or two, some house trailers, a few houses and a population of 103 which did not include the military people and their dependents on the base. It was 130 miles west of Salt Lake City and nearly that from Elko, Nevada, the only places of any size.

There were mountains but not the kind I saw coming through the Rockies. They were just bare rock with no vegetation whatsoever growing. All roads were dirt except the highway going through town. All heating was done with coal which makes it impossible to hang out washing.

I found out later my husband's reason for not telling me anything; everything was top secret. When I arrived, no one met me and I had trouble getting information. The train tracks ran parallel to the fence surrounding the base so I walked until I came to a sentry post. I was told to go to the main base entrance which was not easy walking on the rocks with a suitcase.

Finally, I was allowed inside the Provost Marshall's Office. Here I was, 19 years old, never been away from home, just married three weeks, didn't have any identification showing my name was Allen, so they said they would try to locate my husband and I could go to the Enlisted Mens' Club a half block away. Someone escorted me there to wait until Ray came. Was I ever glad to see him.

Needless to say, it took some adjustment living in a place where everyone wanted to be somewhere else. I got a job on the base so we could live in one of the apartments provided for military personnel and their families. We made friends that we still have contact with today and some of our happiest memories were made there.

formed. There was nothing to do but come home to Wichita and wait until he sent word I could join him.

In early September, word came that it was all right to go west so after making a reservation on the old Missouri Pacific train and getting things needed to set up housekeeping packed into a footlocker, I sent a telegram with my Wendover arrival time asking to be met. Apparently the telegram did not arrive and now comes the rest of the story.

The trip across western Kansas was made at night which was just as well as there isn't all that much to see,

ASHWORTH, FREDERICK L.
U.S. Navy Commander, Project Alberta

My first recollection of Wendover had nothing to do with the 509th Composite Group or the atom bomb. It goes back to the summer of 1924 while I was traveling with my Mom and Dad in our nineteen twenties vintage of an air-cooled Franklin, four door sedan, from the east coast to the west and return. One day in July, we left Salt Lake City heading west. By evening we had arrived at the small town, Wendover, Utah. We pitched our camp for the night on the eastern outskirts of town. Camped, literally, that is, for we pitched a tent each night, cooked all meals on a gasoline Coleman stove and slept on collapsible double deck bunks that my Dad had devised, which could be stowed beneath the running boards of the car.

Although the next morning I suppose we had seen the town as we traveled on westward, I recognized nothing when the Manhattan Project brought me there twenty years

later. That was during the month of December, 1944. Things were different there then; there was nothing separating the town from the North Pole but a barbed wire fence!

I had been ordered to report to the Manhattan District and proceed to the Army Air Force base at Wendover. I don't know who I was supposed to report to there, but almost as soon as I arrived I was met by Dr. Norman Ramsey from Los Alamos, driven by him in an Army staff car out into the salt flats well away from prying ears and was told that I would be involved in the development of an atom bomb.

Even in that short time, I learned that Wendover was no place for my wife and our two very small children. Wasn't there somewhere else that we could be stationed? Ramsey told me that he would try to have me located at Los Alamos, wherever that was, but I was sure that it would be better than their current plans; and that is the way it turned out.

My job at Los Alamos was to supervise and coordinate the work of engineers in the testing at Wendover of bomb components then being developed at Los Alamos. I don't know who thought the Los Alamos people needed supervising and coordinating by a young commander, U.S. Navy. But I was able to run interference for them with the Base Commander, Colonel Heflin, and I think in useful ways. That wasn't difficult either because Colonel Heflin was one fine Air Force officer.

The engineers to conduct the test work and I would fly from Kirtland Field in Albuquerque to Wendover each week for the next five months. The tests would be carried out, mostly using Major Shields' or Chuck Sweeney's B29 detachment placed there for that purpose. Late Friday, after that week's work was finished, we would fly back to Kirtland to prepare for the next set of test work the following week. That is, the engineers would, but more often than not, I found myself leaving the Hill on Saturday mornings for Washington or wherever my gofer duties were to take me, returning usually on the red eye flight to be ready to leave for Wendover Monday morning. That went on for most of the next four months when the 509th Group and Los Alamos Project Alberta people left for operations on Tinian.

There are a few incidents that happened during those days that may be worth recollecting.

There was the day Chuck Sweeney apparently wanted to try out his new reversible propellers. Reversing thrust about ten feet off the ground isn't exactly the way they were intended to be used. He found out the B29 was a pretty rugged aircraft!

We were attempting to see whether or not the detents that prohibited the uranium projectile from joining the uranium target in the gun barrel of Little Boy, would function as designed as a result of impact with the ground.

The test B29 was proceeding to the drop area when Captain Roark apparently reached beyond the Bombardier and flipped a switch. Upon release of the bomb, to land where no one ever learned, Captain Roark reported by radio to the ground, "This is Private Roark. We just inadvertently dropped the Little Boy test bomb somewhere in southern California".

Frederick Ashworth at Annapolis

It turned out those tests were not very useful because anywhere the test models were dropped and subsequently located, the things had penetrated so deeply into the ground they were not recoverable. But not to worry!

When informed of this problem, Naval Ordnance Training Station (NOTS) at China Lake offered the use of their ranges when they had located an area where it was guaranteed the bomb would not penetrate more than a few feet.

Chuck Sweeney loaded up a Little Boy and carried it to China Lake. The bomb was dropped into the selected area, and then the digging began. Some thirty-five feet deep later and more than $135,000 worth of digging, the test bomb was finally recovered. The detents had worked exactly as designed!

And so it went. Charley Beggs First Ordnance Squadron (Special) performed excellently to provide the man power to assist the Los Alamos personnel prepare bomb components for testing. Chuck Sweeney's B29 support detachment delivered the units on target, mostly, that is, or to the Navy's ballistic test range at Salton Sea. Unfortunately, the Officers' Club burned down but someone saved most of the bar supplies. The Bachelor Officers Quarters were lively, the Salt Lake City imports probably enjoyed their adventures and it is my recollection that all hands had a great time!

TINIAN AND SILVERPLATE

In February 1945, I was designated to carry a top secret letter to Guam and hand it personally to Admiral Nimitz. The letter would inform him, for the first time, there was under development an Atomic Bomb which would be available to him, in the Pacific, about the first of August 1945. Although, I am sure this letter was written by General Groves, was addressed "Dear Nimitz" and signed "King". It informed Nimitz of the bomb's explosive yield, that support of his staff would be required and he was authorized to inform only one officer on his staff. It also said, the bearer of this letter would be able to answer any questions and directed Admiral Nimitz to give me any support I might need in selecting a site for the operation.

Frederick Ashworth, Torpedo Squadron 11, Guadalcanal, 1943

Identification of Fat Man Components by Frederick Ashworth

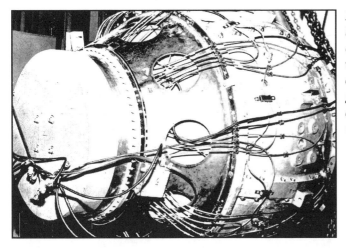

Photo #1. *(left)* This is a picture of a Fat Man type atom bomb under assembly. Seen to the left, the massive cylindrical component, is the "X- Unit", the bank of four condensers that would be charged to about 5000 volts. It provided the electrical energy to all 32 "handlebar" (from their shape with two leads going into the detonator) detonators. To the right is the assembled explosive sphere with the conical mounting structure for the X-Unit.

Photo #2. *(right)* This is a photo of a Fat Man bomb under assembly. At the left is shown the assembled explosive sphere with the X-Unit attached. Note the co-axial cables from the X-Unit leading to the detonators. Note the circled "handlebar" detonator. To the right is the front section of the outer case of the bomb ready to be moved to the left to cover the front half of the explosive sphere.

Photo #3. *(left)* This is photo of the assembled Fat Man bomb explosive sphere. None of the ancillary parts such as the X-Unit shown in Photos #1 and #2 have been assembled to the sphere.

Photo #4. *(above)* This is a photo of the front section of the outside case of the bomb. It shows at the bottom of the case, the "bath tub fittings" that are used to join the front and rear sections of the bomb case. Bolts will be used to connect the bath tub fittings together on each section of the case.

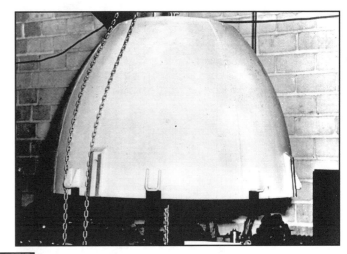

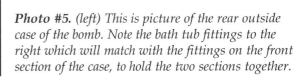

Photo #5. *(left)* This is picture of the rear outside case of the bomb. Note the bath tub fittings to the right which will match with the fittings on the front section of the case, to hold the two sections together.

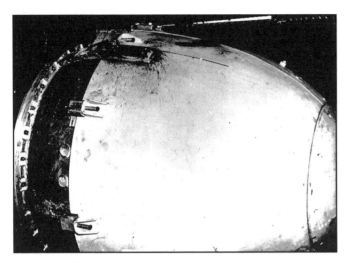

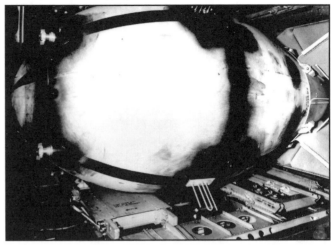

Photo #6. (left) This is another picture of the front outside case of the bomb. The nose plate is attached. Note the bath tub fittings with the connecting bolts mounted in the fittings. The blackened uneven "blob" (upper left) is probably the mounting plate for the "Yagi" type antennas used by the radar type fuses.

Photo #8. (below) This picture shows the unmounted box tail of the bomb, looking at the part that would be attached to the rear section of the outer bomb case. Not easy to distinguish, but this also shows the baffles that were placed in the box tail for a "parachute" effect, which smoothed out completely the ballistic anomalies and made stable and reproducible bomb ballistics flight possible.

Photo #7. (above) This shows the assembled bomb with the box tail attached , to the right. Note at the bottom (center) the "Yagi" antenna attached to its mounting plate that is seen in photo #6. Also at the very top (right center) note another `Yagi" antenna. There were four antennas, one for each radar fuse. Four were used for reliability through redundancy, and any two functioning would be adequate to initiate the fuse action. Also note mounted on the front section of the outer bomb case, and to the left in the photo, two contact fuses. There were four of these M219 fuses mounted on the front case to explode the bomb on contact with the ground, should the radar fuses fail to function.

Photo #9.
(right) This photo shows the box tail of the bomb attached to the rear section of the bomb outer case. In the upper extreme right can be seen again one of the bath tub fittings joining the two sections of the outer bomb case.

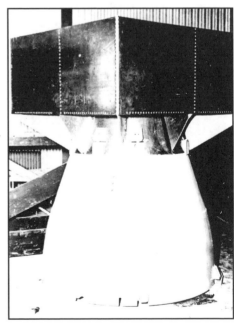

Photo #10. (above) This photo shows the four bomber aircraft tail warning radars that were converted for use as the four radar fuses for the fat man bomb. (And also for the Little Boy.) For the Fat Man, the devices shown in this photo were mounted on the explosive sphere opposite to the X-Unit. The conversion changed these radars from use as radars to warn bombing aircraft of fighter attack from astern, into radar altimeters which would measure the height of the atom bomb above the ground after release, and as it fell. When the pre-selected height above the ground was measured, the fuse would provide the signal to detonate the bomb, resulting in an above ground explosion.

I had traveled from Washington direct through to Guam wearing the ordinary cotton Khaki uniform of the period. I carried the letter in a money belt around my waist next to my skin. After the long trip, needless to say, the money belt was a bit worse for wear and its contents a little stained and damp from sweat, but in good enough shape for the Admiral to open and read.

General Groves had been given the highest priority throughout the Army and Navy in the procurement of people and supplies for his project. In order to implement this priority in the Air Corps, General Arnold, Chief of Staff of the Army Air Corps, established the code name "Silverplate" and directed that at any time a responsible official used the code word, that official's needs would have the highest priority of any programs in the Army Air Corps.

The selection of the island was easy. Guam was too far south, Saipan was furthest north, but did not have the air operations facilities that were available on Tinian. I asked for transportation to Tinian. When I arrived on the island, I reported to the Island Commander, Brigadier General Kimble, Army Air Corps, and told him that in connection with a "Silverplate" project I wanted to stake out some real estate on his island for a special operation. He recognized the significance of "Silverplate" and said he was at my service. He suggested if it was an air project, the north end of the island would be most appropriate for there were extensive B29 operations going on there. We rode in his jeep to the north end of the island, I indicated the areas I thought would be satisfactory and asked him to hold that area for future use.

Weaponeer - That term was dreamed up by Captain Parsons to try to define, in a title, the duties of the Los Alamos Representative of General Groves, who would be on board the bomb carrying aircraft. General Groves was concerned over the possibility of crises coming up during the actual bombing operations that would require decisions to be made and by someone who could evaluate the situation from a technical and tactical point of view, tactical because it was possible the situation might dictate deviations from the tactical plan. Captain Parsons and I were the only regular officers at Los Alamos that fit General Groves requirements. Groves placed great importance on the matter of being a regular officer and he preferred Service Academy graduates. Parsons was the obvious choice for this important job because no one in uniform was as well acquainted with the technical aspects of the bomb. It was always General Groves policy to have spares of everything throughout the project. Since I met his criteria, I became the spare for Captain Parsons. General Groves felt I had sufficient knowledge to make the decisions he expected might be required. Just before the Hiroshima operation, he told us we would alternate on each tactical operation.

The Black Box and the Flashing Red Light

Both of the atomic bombs, the Little Boy and Fat Man were designed to be self sufficient when released from the bomb shackle in the B29 bomb bay and the arming wires extracted as the weapon fell away from the aircraft. By self sufficient it was meant that the weapon had its own power supply thus requiring no input from the aircraft electrical system and that it would function as designed. Prior to being released, the bomb would take its power from the aircraft electrical system and the readiness to function of the various components, for example, the Safe Separation Timers, the Barometric Switches and the Radar Fuses could be monitored from inside the aircraft by means of an Umbilical Cord connected to the bomb and attached to the Black Box.

Photo showing race track – Kermit Beahan's aiming point

Black Box is sort of a common generic name for any instrument box containing switches, electrical meters and indicator lights. If my memory serves me correctly, these boxes were indeed painted black.

Since these systems that were being monitored were complex electrical devices, monitoring their performance required a highly trained officer who had participated in their design and development. He was a member of the aircraft crew and had been designated as the Electronic Assistant for the Weaponeer. Lt. "Dick" Jeppson was this crew member aboard Enola Gay. Lt. "Phil" Barnes was that crew member aboard Bockscar. During training operations and during the operational missions to the designated targets, Hiroshima and Nagasaki, the Electronic Assistant ran readi-

Fred Ashworth receives Silver Star for Nagasaki mission from General Arnold

ness tests on the bomb electrical components by means of the Black Box.

On board Bockscar, Lieutenant Barnes conducted several monitoring tests, the first, shortly after takeoff and when well clear of the Base on Tinian. During one of these tests later into the flight, a white indicator light illuminated which indicated a major circuit in the bomb had closed connecting the fusing system to the firing system and therefore the bomb was fully armed. Theoretically, a spurious signal from the fuse section could detonate the bomb. As was my duty as Weaponeer, I reported to the Aircraft Commander, Major Sweeney, that it appeared we had a major problem with the bomb. In recent stories about the mission, this event has been glamorized by referring to this as a "flashing red light" which became, as one might expect, the major point of concern of the entire flight crew.

Suspecting this might be only a monitoring box failure and not a serious problem in the Fat Man, Lieutenant Barnes unpacked his set of wiring diagrams for the box, removed the top and sides and proceeded to analyze circuits to see if possibly an error had been made either in the box connections or in his setting of the various switches. After several minutes of this examination, he noted that certain switches were in the wrong position and if so the false indication would result. He reset the switches properly, the indicator light went out and the crisis was over. Needless to say this problem was corrected after we returned to base.

Commentary on the Nagasaki Mission

Delay at the Rendezvous - I am on record that this was a bad mistake and very nearly cost us the mission. The preflight briefing instructions were to spend no more than twenty minutes at the rendezvous. The only reason for the stay so long was to try to get all three planes together and make the mission perfect. I

was not in a position to tell which plane had apparently joined. After about fifteen minutes, I went up to the flight deck and told Sweeney that I particularly wanted the instrument plane to accompany us to the target. Apparently, everybody but me knew Fred Bock arrived with the instruments. After some more minutes, I went up and told Sweeney "We have to get out of here and get going". It was at least thirty minutes. After that, we went ahead to Kokura. All that time, John Kuharek knew we were using up precious gasoline. Fred Bock's engineer proved later there was no reason why the fuel could not have been transferred. It was a mistake not having Fred Bock's flight crew go with his plane. They knew how to work the systems, which in the case of the fuel system, Kuharek found more temperamental than he was used to.

Immediately after all three B29s landed at Yontan in Okinawa, I collected the pilots, Bock, Sweeney and Hopkins and Kermit Beahan, bombardier, and while looking at a target map tried to figure out where the bomb had actually gone off. During this discussion, I recall clearly that Beahan said he had synchronized the bomb sight on a "race track" and the bomb was released aiming at it. That is pretty good bombing for the short time Kermit had to synchronize the sight and satisfy himself that he had a good target. I am confident Beahan had studied, very carefully, the entire target area prior to the operation, as any good bombardier would do. He knew exactly where the "race track" was in relation to the general area of the city. He probably had it in his mind, at that time, the race track would make an ideal target to aim at. He may have even realized he was aiming at a better part of the city to attack than the central "downtown" area.

After my meeting with the pilots, Sweeney and I commandeered a jeep with its driver and I directed we be taken to the local Air Forces Communications Headquarters. I needed urgently to send a message to General Farrell and Captain Parsons on Tinian to clarify the incomplete coded strike report I had composed and was transmitted from the aircraft after the attack. I was told at the Communications Center they were too busy to send my message, whereupon I asked to be directed to General Doolittle's office. This was a double pyramidal tent. I knocked on the door and was invited in by General Partridge, Doolittle's Chief of Staff. I told him of my need to communicate with Tinian, but he told me I should talk to General Doolittle first. I went to his half of the tent, laid out the target maps, showed him where the designated aiming point was in the urban area of the city and where we concluded the bomb actually hit. After studying the maps for a moment, he said, "General Spaatz will be much happier the bomb went off over the industrial part of the city". There will be far fewer casualties. With that, he called the Communications Center and told them to send my message.

BADALI, JOSEPH A.
216th Base Unit, Atomic Bomb Assembly, Aircraft Armament Specialist

One day in early 1944 at Dover, Delaware, the captain called me into his office and told me they were going to have a special award ceremony on the field to give medals to several of the returned men who had earned them on active duty overseas. He said the commanding officer asked him to pick out two armorers to receive aircraft armament specialist awards. The captain chose me and Steven Gregg to receive the award. This did not seem very important at the time, but it proved to be so later.

A few days later, the first sergeant took me to the field headquarters building to be interviewed by a major who asked me a lot of questions dealing with security. He told me that I was being considered for a top secret program. He then questioned Steven.

Top Secret Project

The major called Mitchell Field and told them as far as he was concerned, we could pass the top security requirements. We cleared the field that afternoon and took a train from Philadelphia to Wendover, Utah. Steve and I were excited about going to Wendover to work on a top secret project.

When we got to Wendover, we saw the field and the endless Salt Flats. We were very disappointed and hoped we would not stay at Wendover very long. We were assigned to a barracks and told by the first sergeant that we could not leave the base. If we went anyplace on the base, we had to let him know. We spent most of our time at the PX drinking 3.2 beer.

About two weeks went by before the first sergeant took us up to field headquarters where I was told to go into an office. A man in civilian clothes was sitting at a desk. He told me to sit down and relax. He then looked at some papers on his desk and said I had been investigated by the FBI. The agents had visited Bassett Junior High School and Boardman Trade School to inquire about me. They also talked to some people I had worked with at C. Cowels & Co. He told me all the inquiries were satisfactory. He then asked me, "Can you keep a secret"? I replied, "I think so". He stood up and leaned forward and pounded the desk with his fist and said very loudly, "Can you keep a secret, yes or no"? I replied, "Yes". He then told me, "If you reveal to anyone the program that you will be working on you will be shot"! He scared the hell out of me. I could feel the hair on the back of my neck standing up. He continued, "If you write to anyone, tell them you are an aircraft armorer on B29s. Your mail will be censored. Do not drink outside of your barracks. (We could keep liquor in our barracks). Do not

associate with anyone not working on the program. Do not discuss the program with anyone outside the work area. If you go into Salt Lake City, Utah, you must tell your first sergeant and you may not drink alcoholic beverages. There are several FBI agents on the base and in Wendover and in Salt Lake City that will be watching you." This all sounded very scary to me, but my curiosity was so aroused that I could hardly wait to find out what this top secret project was all about. He then told me to go out the side door from his office and wait in the hall while he interviewed Steven. About an hour later, Steven came out of the office and said, "Joe, what the hell are we getting into"?

The Atomic Bombs

The FBI agent came out of his office and we were driven to an area south of the field to some fenced-in buildings. We had to get out of the car and walk through a security check gate. We went into a building where we were introduced to Captain Les Rowe and Lieutenant Westrip. They took us to one of the buildings that they called the Mechanical Assembly Building. As soon as I entered into the building, I saw several large bombs. We were told the smaller bombs were called Thin Man (Little Boy) and the larger bombs were called Fat Man. We were introduced to the men working there and we were assigned to work with Sergeant Cerace, who took us over to one of the Fat Man bombs. He patted the bomb and said, "If this Fat Man atomic bomb were to explode, there would be a big hole in the ground where Utah used to be". He then said, "You do not have to worry about any of these bombs exploding because

Bomb Assembly Crew, Wendover
Back Row (L-R): Sergeant Murphy, James Imbesi, Joseph Badali,
Al Larson, Steven Gregg, Unknown, Harold Kirby
Front Row, (L-R): Joe Cerace, Michael Paparo, Robert Nelson, Coleman

they do not have any atomic material in them. These bombs are being assembled for testing purposes. We will be putting explosives in some that we will be assembling, so you will have to learn how to handle and assemble these explosive blocks that go into the bomb."

The Little Boy bomb was a black powder cannon that fired a uranium 235 slug down a 5" cannon tube into the front end of the bomb, which was called the target and contained another uranium slug. When these two slugs came together, they formed a critical mass that caused the atomic explosion.

The Fat Man bomb was completely different. The center of the bomb contained a pit that had plutonium in it. When the explosive blocks were detonated by fuses that were spaced all around the outer sphere, this crushed the pit inward, causing a nuclear explosion, This crushing action caused the bomb to implode at the center. The Fat Man bombs were much more difficult to assemble.

We had a very busy schedule during June and July assembling Thin Man and Fat Man test bombs. July was the busiest month. We were loading some of the test Fat Man bombs with the high explosive blocks, but without the plutonium that caused the nuclear explosion.

Thin Man Bomb

In July, we assembled four Thin Man bombs. The last bomb we assembled was the most important one. While we were assembling this bomb, a photographic team took pictures for General Groves. We asked to have a group picture taken of the assembly crew and if each of us could get a copy of the print. General Groves approved this request. The bomb was then taken out to the loading pit and loaded on a B29, which flew to Tinian Island (where the 509th was stationed). We learned later that the uranium slugs were put into the bomb at Tinian. The projectile slug was not put into the breech until the plane had taken off again from Tinian.

We had been told the Little Boy bomb would be dropped on Japan in a short period of time after it left Wendover. We

each took turns listening to a radio that was in the guard shack at the gate into our area. On August 6th, the announcement came over the radio. Col. Tibbets had dropped the Little Boy on Hiroshima. We started to celebrate in the assembly building with some liquor that we had been able to smuggle into the building. We had it hidden up on one of the beams that the hoist was mounted on. One of the men climbed onto the beam and dropped the bottles down to us while shouting, "Bombs Away".

Captain Rowe and Lt. Westrip came into the building and sent us back to the barracks area. They told us to stay there and not to discuss the bombing with anyone. They told us they would arrange a party for that evening.

Fat Man Bomb

The Fat Man bomb was first assembled in the mechanical assembly building where I worked. Many of the parts had to be modified and hand-fitted to get them to go together. The bomb was then taken to the high explosive building, which had a copper covered floor to prevent static electricity. There it was disassembled and the high explosive blocks, the pit with the plutonium,

Sandia Base, Albuquerque, New Mexico

A group of men left Wendover in September to go to Albuquerque, New Mexico, to start setting up our new location at Sandia Base. Shortly after, a sec-

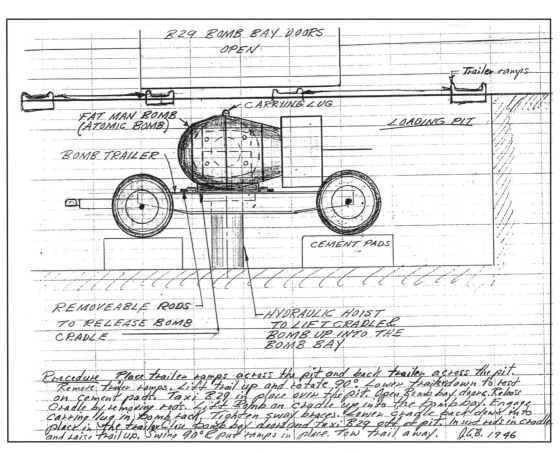

Fat Man Sketch by Joe Badali

ond group flew down. The rest of us that were left at Wendover disassembled the mechanical assembly building to ship it and all the bomb parts to Sandia Base.

In November, the rest of the 216th transferred to Sandia Base. When we arrived there, we were put to work re-assembling the mechanical assembly building and setting up the rest of the new tech area. When we completed the assembly building, we started to assemble more test bombs. I enjoyed the work very much, but I was anxious to be discharged and go home. I wanted to attend college and get on with my life.

Many of the men were being discharged. The draftsman was discharged and Captain Rowe saw in my records that I was a draftsman and asked me to take over the job. He told me there was very little drafting work being done so I could still work in the assembly building. He would let me know when he needed any drafting to be done. I only had to work on a few modifications to some drawings.

Some of the pit crew that loaded the bombs into the B29s were discharged, so Captain Rowe assigned me and another assembly crew member who we called "Scony" to work with the pit crew when a bomb had to be loaded. When we assembled a test bomb, we took it over to Kirtland Field and worked with the pit crew learning how to load the bomb into the B29. The bomb was hanging on the hoist when it was completely assembled. It was then lowered onto the bomb trailer and transported to the pit at Kirtland Field. Two

ramps were positioned over the pit. Then the trailer was backed over the pit. The hydraulic hoist was then raised to lift the trailer off the ramps. The ramps were removed and the trailer was then swung around so that it could be lowered down into the pit where the wheels sat on four cement pads.

The B29 was then taxied up to the left side of the pit until the right landing gear tires were on the center of a turntable. The right brakes were then locked so that the right wheels would not move. The engines in the left wing were revved up so that the plane would swing around until the nose wheel was centered with the pit. The bomb cradle was disconnected from the trailer and the bomb was raised up into the bomb bay. The carrying lug was engaged into the sear on the bomb rack and the sway braces tightened to prevent the bomb from moving. The cradle was then lowered back down into the trailer where it was re-engaged to the trailer. The B29 taxied off the pit and trailer was raised up and swung crosswise over the pit. The ramps were positioned under the wheels and the trailer was hooked up to the truck and pulled back to Sandia Base. I got to raise the bomb up into the bomb bay and hook it to the bomb rack several times.

Captain Rowe told me he was re-enlisting for another year to train a new crew on how to assemble bombs and he asked me to re-enlist and work with him until our replacements were fully trained to do the work. He told me I would be sent to Officers Training School and would become a 2nd Lieutenant. He also told me they needed men to go to Kwajalein to load bombs for tests that would be carried out at Bikini Atoll and I could do this if I wanted to. I told him I just wanted to be discharged and go home and get on with my life.

Just before I was going to be discharged, Captain Rowe told me that after I was discharged I could come back and work as a civilian on the project. I also turned down this offer and was discharged in February 1946.

An Intermediate phase Fat Man Bomb at Wendover being readied for a Drop Test at Sandy Beach. Note that there are no Nose Fyzes, Antennae, Bath Tub Fittings over the Case Bolts, Rubbing Blocks on the Tait Flanges, No pull-out wires, etc. This model would be about Autumn, 1944.
509th Composite Group, Wendover Air Base, Utah. (W-47)
Harlow W. Russ, 1st. Tech. Svc. Detach., Project Alberta.

Intermediate phase Fat Man bomb

Little Boy configuration bomb being lowered into pit by 216th B.U. at Wendover

Little Boy Drop Model #7 in pit at Wendover

"This is a photo of a "High Bed Transport Trailer", sometimes called a "Flatbed" or a "Float," at Wendover, with an early model of a "Pumpkin" being readied for loading into a B-29 at Wendover for a drop test at "Sandy Beach".
The Pumpkin has only three contact nose fuzes, M-103, instead of four that later model pumpkin and "Fat Man" bombs had. The Pumpkins had no fuze antennae, and the tail is an early Fat Man type, with no rabbing plates and no drag plates to keep the tail aligned during a test drop.
The Fat Man Type Nose Cap could be removed for pouring High Explosive material into a near spherical container that held about 5,000 lbs. of explosive material.
Final design Pumpkin and Fat Man bombs had 4 contact Nose Fuzes.

Harlow W. Russ
1st. Tech. Svc. Detach.
509th Composite Group,
(W-47), Wendover, Utah
1994.

Fat Man on trailer

Fat Man test unit at Muroc

24

Working on Fat Man housing with 45° angle parachute drag plates at Muroc Bombing and Gunnery Range

Thin Man test units, front; Fat Man housings, rear at Muroc

Loading of Fat Man by 216th B.U.

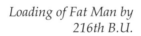

Loading Thin Man bomb into pit at Muroc using prototype silver plate B-29 for drop test

Little Boy Drop Model inside B29, Wendover

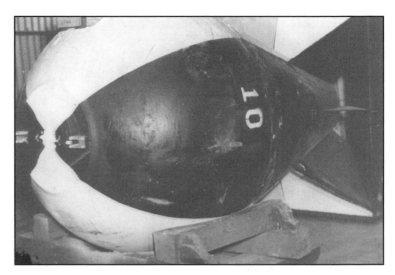

Fat Man Test Unit

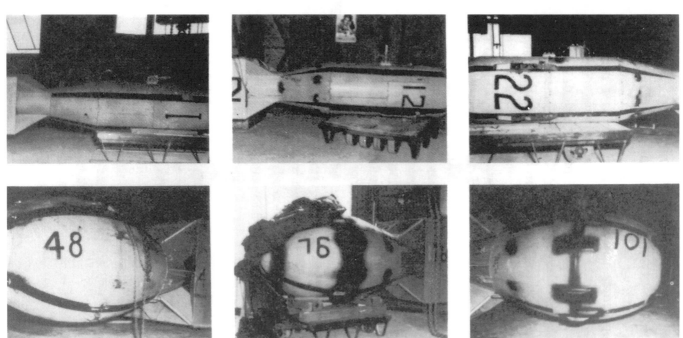

The spread of test numbers.

26

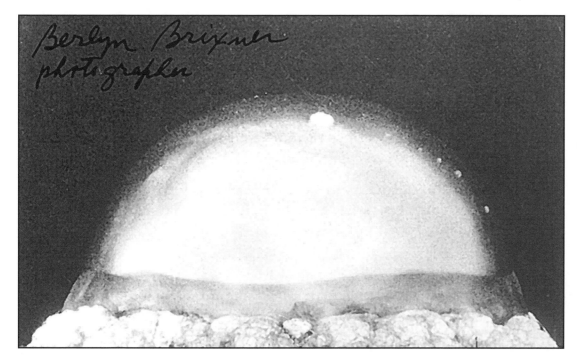

Berlyn Brixner
photographer

Photo by*
Berlyn Brixner,
Chief Photographer:
mushroom cloud
forming at
Los Alamos,
July 16, 1945

Berlyn Brixner photographing experimental bomb drops with
Mitchell 35mm cameras

Berlyn Brixner, photographer,
using mitchell 35-mm cameras
to photograph dummy bomb
drops on the Nevada desert,
1945.

I was very pleased when I was assigned the job of photographing the
early bomb drops. I don't remember the
bombers ever hit the targets in the early
drops. So I moved my camera station
close to the target and don't remember
that any of the drops came close to me.
Those were very exciting times.

BRIXNER,
BERLYN
Manhattan Engineering District
Photographer

Berlyn Brixner
Photographer

Berlyn Brixner photographing
experimental bomb drops

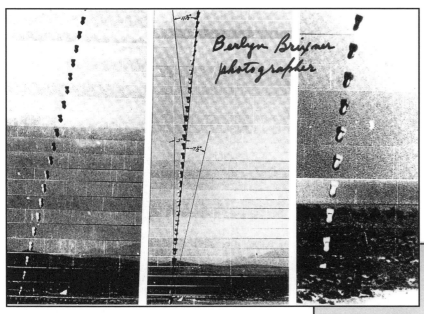

Fat Man drop tests

Naval Photo Unit

Observation Post, experimental bombings, Navy photographers

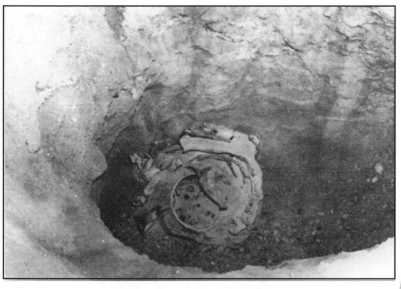

Wreckage of unexploded Fat Man test unit at bottom of bomb crater

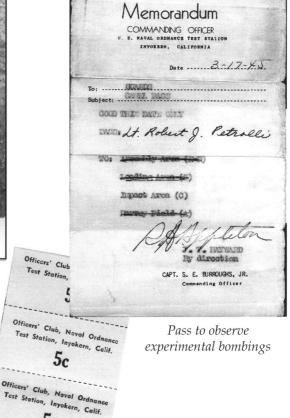

Pass to observe experimental bombings

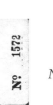

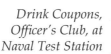

Drink Coupons, Officer's Club, at Naval Test Station

BARNEY, WILLIAM C.
393rd Bomb Squadron, Radar Operator, Crew C-13

When I first went into service, I was given a job of inspecting meat in a packing house and at army bases. I did not like this at all, so I applied for cadets.

In January 1944, I was sent to Miami Beach and was informed they had all pilots, bombardiers and navigators they needed. They still had openings for gunners, so I went to gunnery school for B24s. After completing this, I was given an opportunity to go into B29 gunnery. I jumped at this chance and completed another school. We then went to Lincoln, Nebraska, where we were assigned to different bases. I was asked if I would like to become a radar operator. That was how I became a radar operator on B29s.

In summer of 1944, eleven men met on an airfield outside Fairmont, Nebraska. That was the start of our air crew. We trained there for a couple of months and were getting ready to go overseas. A notice came in on the bulletin board that 393rd Radar Squadron was to be at Wendover Air Base by a certain date.

The first time I saw Wendover I couldn't believe that any plane could be in such a desolate place. Being from the midwest, I was used to looking about and seeing homes and other buildings over the country side.

My first trip to the Stateline Hotel is well remembered; eating dinner on the Utah side and then walking through the door to the Nevada side and seeing all the gambling and other things that went on.

While in Wendover, we met Colonel Tibbets and were told some of what was to follow. Our crew was cut to nine men as they were doing away with all the guns except those in the tail. This was when we became known as Crew 13.

Life was quite different in Wendover. We were out in the middle of nowhere. We did a lot of additional training and spent a month in Cuba.

Bill Barney

We picked up our new planes in May 1945 and again prepared to go overseas. This time we made it.

On August 9th, we were flying the Great Artiste. Our own plane, the Bockscar, was being flown by Chuck Sweeney and his crew. Our purpose on this mission was to drop three small monitoring units to measure the power of the bomb blast. My regular job was Radar Operator. On this particular day I had a second job to generate a recorder to gather information from one of the monitoring units. Larry Johnston, a Lieutenant, was operating one of the other units. We had to stay with the units for several minutes after the bomb blast which was over by the time we could get to a window to see anything. We were a good many miles away by this time. It was kind of hard to see much with four people looking out an 8 inch window. The rest is history.

The thing I remember most about Wendover is, that is where our Crew C-13 really got to know one another and became close. We have remained that way through many years since. I feel very privileged to have been a member of Crew C-13.

It was also a great feeling to know the plane we took overseas, flew in combat and brought home, is now in the Air Force Museum in Dayton, Ohio. This is the "Bockscar" named after our pilot Fred Bock.

Nagasaki cloud photo taken from Great Artiste

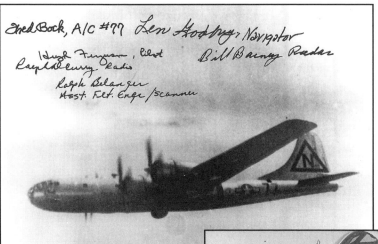

Bockscar in flight over Tinian. Note Nagasaki mission markings on plane and noseart.

Crew C-13 at Wendover
Charles Levy (left), Rod Arnold (right) did not autograph photo.

30

BEAHAN, KERMIT B.
393rd Bomb Squadron, Bombardier, Crew C-15

From Original Notes Owned by Joseph Papalia

August 9, 1945 is the unforgettable date I flew aboard the B29 Bockscar as Bombardier on the second atomic bomb mission during World War II. Our takeoff from North Field on Tinian, a small island in the Mariannas group in the West Pacific was uneventful. However, while climbing enroute to Japan, our Flight Engineer advised that due to a fuel pump failure, 500 gallons of fuel in the rear bomb bay was trapped. At the time, this did not seem to be a problem as the flight plan indicated ample fuel would still be available.

We proceeded to our rendezvous point, a small island off the coast of Japan, where we met with the instrumentation aircraft almost immediately but we could not link up with the photographic aircraft both of which were to accompany us over the target. We circled the island for some length of time consuming considerable fuel in the process. It was decided to proceed with the flight without the photographic aircraft. As we approached the selected primary target, Kokura, site of the largest arsenal in Japan, it was completely obscured by clouds and industrial haze. We had strict orders the bomb must be released visually, that is the Bombardier must be able to sight the target through his bombsight. We made three approaches from different directions hoping to sight the target from a different angle of view. Fuel supply was now becoming a matter of concern.

We proceeded to take a direct course to the secondary target, Nagasaki. Enroute, it was determined that enough fuel remained for only one bomb run. Visibility over the Nagasaki area was very poor, eight to nine tenths cloud cover prevailed. The decision was made, if necessary, we would drop the bomb by radar in spite of the edict stipulating visual release only. We proceeded on the bomb run under radar control until about twenty to thirty seconds from bomb release when I saw a hole developing in the clouds over the target area. I took control of the aircraft and selected an aiming point in the Nagasaki in-

Note: Beahan not in crew photo

dustrial valley. Fortunately, the radar team had made an excellent initial bomb approach and in the very brief time remaining, I was able to synchronize the cross-hairs of the bombsight on the target and released the bomb visually with good results being achieved. It was as if a great weight had been lifted from our shoulders since we did succeed in following the order "visual drop only!"

Fuel was now critical with only enough left for one landing attempt so we made a bee line to our emergency landing site in Okinawa. We landed OK and as we taxied to the airfield ramp both outboard engines sputtered to a stop - fuel starvation! It was really a "sweat job".

Only after returning to Tinian and being debriefed did I realize it was my 27th birthday - we celebrated into the night.

EDITOR'S NOTE -
Story as Related by Ben Jordan

Ben Jordan worked on staff of Maj. Gen. Curtis E. LeMay, Deputy Commander 20th Air Force and was Flight Engineer for the 20th Air Force. He was also Project Officer for eight to nine B29s from the 315th Wing that flew to Chitose Air Base Hokkaido, Japan. These planes were equipped with the APQ7 Eagle Wing Radar Antenna between bomb bays. It was approximately thirty feet long and three feet wide; (509th Planes used APQ13 Radar).

Three of the B29s were placed heading into the wind at Chitose Air Field and the bomb bay tanks were topped off with fuel. The next morning it was discovered the landing gear had gone through the concrete. Steel landing mats had to be flown in so the planes would have a thousand feet of runway for takeoff. The purpose of this flight, piloted by Curtis LeMay, Maj. Gen. Emmett J. (Rosie) O'Donnell and Lt. Gen. Barney Giles (Spaatz' Deputy Commander) was to set a nonstop record from Japan to Washington. Barney Giles ordered all three planes to land at Chicago to refuel.

Approximately three days later, General Armstrong and two combat pilots accomplished the record mission.

Kermit Beahan was a passenger on the flight of B29s.

BEAUDETTE, DONALD D.
393rd Bomb Squadron, Crew Chief, Straight Flush, Crew C-11

Written by Faye Beaudette

Don Beaudette on scooter at Wendover

When we went to Wendover, Don and I were already married and had a four month old daughter. I followed him in the service; wasn't easy but I managed OK. We lived in the housing in Wendover. Our neighbors were the Millers from Connelville, Pennsylvania and the Freys from Tulsa, Oklahoma.

We burned coal in our stove for heating and cooking. We lived on the end of the housing not too far from the State Line Hotel. Some of the guys went up there to gamble once in awhile but nobody had much money to spend.

Don had a scooter he rode around on. We went up in the foothills of Wendover on it and he would bring groceries in it. I think he gave it to someone when he went to Tinian.

I lived with my parents on a farm in Nebraska. He wired home for money probably to play the slots in the State Line Hotel. Not much else to do when we all went home.

Family housing at Wendover

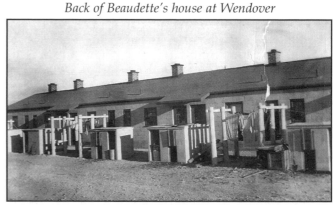
Back of Beaudette's house at Wendover

Don Beaudette on left in front of hut by plane on flight line

Engine change

Engine change – Note tail markings from Hiroshima
mission on plane

Engine change

BESER, JACOB
393rd Bomb Squadron, Radar Countermeasures Officer

(Reprinted from Hiroshima & Nagasaki Revisited, Global Press 1988)
Permission Granted by Sylvia Beser

On the afternoon of September 10, 1944, the commandant of Fairmont Army Airfield published general order no. 254. Paragraph 7 of that order was a bombshell. All personnel of the 393rd Squadron were ordered to depart not later than September 15th to Wendover Field, Utah, for temporary duty, complete with all organizational equipment. The inclusion of all organizational equipment and the statement that no per diem would be paid while at Wendover, and authorization for dependents to accompany were all clues to the fact that the 393rd was never going to rejoin the 504th.

Friday, September 15,1944, the troop train that carried the bulk of the men of the 393rd from Fairmont to Wendover had been sitting in a freight yard in Salt Lake City, Utah, since about 0400 hours. It was on the track adjacent to a load of Italian prisoners of war. Both trains were awaiting new engines and crew before proceeding further towards their destinations; we were about 120 miles from ours.

As the men on both trains began to wake up, they began talking back and forth between the trains; many of the POWs were quite fluent in English, and some of our Brooklyn boys spoke the language of their fathers. One thing was obvious to us, as far as creature comforts were concerned, the train supplied to the POWs had it all over ours. Both trains had "kitchen cars" set up and the troops on either train prepared their own food. If you have never been involved in a large troop movement, you cannot appreciate the miracle of hot food. Uncle Sam, in those days at least, supplied good food and if the cooks didn't ruin it, one could eat reasonably well. This was nothing compared to the way those Italian boys were fed. The hot breakfast pastries that they were served made our hot GI bread almost medicinal. There was one redeeming circumstance,

Jacob Beser in Wendover

however, we had American cigarettes in quantity, and for these, the Italians would have traded their mothers. Their pastries were just superb.

At about 1000 hours, a new engine was hooked to our train, we moved out of the yard, and once again headed west.

The scenery from Fairmont, Nebraska, to eastern Colorado had been flat and unimpressive. It got interest-

33

ing from Denver to Laramie, Wyoming, and continued that way on into Salt Lake City. Now on the last leg of our trip, we were being set-up for Wendover. The Bonneville Salt Flats are just plain dreary. Off in the distance, in almost any direction, one can see a blue haze, some of the steepest mountains in the entire U.S., and some of nature's finest scenery. You just knew from what you had learned in school that this was "the land where the buffalo roam and the deer and the antelope play".

Just before noon, the train began to decelerate and slowly came to a stop. One look to the right side of the train and there was the highway, a gas station complete with restaurant attached, several other stores and little else. The whole thing was nestled into the side of a brown mountain. Out the left side of the train, one could see at the base of the mountain an airfield and a collection of assorted barracks and shops. There were several large hangars and a chapel. My first impression of this place has endured for over forty years; if the North American Continent ever needed an enema, the tube would be inserted here at Wendover.

The rest of the day was spent getting the train unloaded, getting assigned to quarters, and finding the bar at the officers club. We also discovered that Wendover, Utah, lay across the Utah-Nevada border, and the Stateline Hotel on the Nevada side of the border had a bar and casino. There would be ample opportunities for recreation right here. If you were the outdoors type, hiking, hunting and fishing in glacial mountain lakes were all present in abundance and could fill your leisure hours, when and if you had them. For the rest of the people, there was the restaurant, Spike's, and the hotel to provide other types of recreation. On base, there was an officer's club, a non-coms club, and a large recreation hall for the enlisted men. On the base, a theatre showed the latest first-run movies and an occasional traveling USO show stopped in.

Although our orders indicated that this was to be a Temporary Change of Station, no one believed it. The married men were sure that this was temporary since wives were not initially encouraged, even though our orders authorized their inclusion in the movement.

We began to see some strange faces almost from the start, officers and enlisted men. We began to set ourselves up almost immediately. I staked out a space and an office in the engineering hangar where Lt. Elroy Homa and myself set up our squadron electronics facility. Since the radar equipment was classified, our shop would require a twenty-four hour guard. It was assigned a post number and this duty was performed as a routine interior guard duty. Our men began the task of making test benches and equipment mock-ups immediately and within a week Sergeants Lathrop and Richardson had our two sections in full operation.

By the middle of our first week at Wendover, strangers had become numerous. No one seemed to know where they were coming from and what they would be doing.

An answer to all of the unknown was not too long in coming. On Monday, September 25th the entire squadron was called to the base theatre at 0900 hours. Not only our own people were there but most of the new strangers were showing up at the theatre at the same time.

The meeting was called to order and a short fellow, wearing the silver leaf of a Lieutenant Colonel and command pilots wings introduced himself to us. He was L/C Paul Tibbets and he said he was our new commanding officer. We were selected to form the cadre of a new type of combat group; one that would be self sufficient and could operate anywhere in the world. We would be asked to carry out a mission, that if successful would bring the war to a rapid conclusion. We must trust him, because we would not be told what our mission was until we were ready to actually perform it. We are going to be asked to do a lot of hard work over the next few months in order to bring our skills and performance to the highest possible level. We are to be reorganized and some new people will be coming in. Security is of the utmost importance. WHAT YOU HEAR HERE, WHAT YOU SEE HERE, WHEN YOU LEAVE HERE, LET IT STAY HERE. There will be no second chances where security breaches are concerned. "Gentlemen, much is going to be expected of you. If it all works out, it will have been worth it." Then the bombshell was dropped. "For the next two weeks, the entire 393rd Squadron will be on furlough, including most of your officers. Those who are required to be here to help in the reorganization have already been notified."

The days at Wendover became weeks, and the weeks became months. New people came, some stayed and some went. Gradually, we became the unit that was to eventually go overseas. The squadron got a set of new B29s from Martin, Omaha, and each crew was assigned its own aircraft. Training missions were flown almost daily and every man was scored, from the airplane commander to the lowest ranking mechanic on the flight line.

The 320th Troop Carrier Squadron was activated and began to provide logistic support immediately, initially under the command of Chuck Sweeney and later under the command of John Casey.

The various other ground elements of the 509th came into being in this time period and all of them underwent intensive training, as individual elements and as functioning components of the group. All of this was overseen by Col. Tibbets and his staff.

In January and February of 1945, the air crews were all sent to Batista Field, outside of Havana, Cuba, where a training task force had been established for extensive long range over water flying.

Time was running out on our training program. In January, the ground echelon had been "shipped out". They would proceed by surface vessel from Seattle, Washington, to Tinian, Marianas Islands.

Our aircrews were given extensive training in drop and breakaway procedures. A lot of this was done while at the same time the ballistics of the weapon were being studied. Engineering flights were also training flights. We literally wore out one set of airplanes.

Once the final configuration of our airplanes was established, a new set was prepared at the Martin Plant at Ft. Crook, Nebraska, just outside of Omaha and on the present site of the headquarters, Strategic Air Command.

All guns except the tail turrets were left off. The latest engine and propeller designs were used. The bomb bays were modified to carry their new loads. The crews of the 393rd trained up until the time they were ready to leave.

Monday 6 August 1945, the general briefing for the Hiroshima Mission was started at 2300 in the Combat Crew Lounge for the crews that would precede us to the Empire. These crews would proceed to three separate respective target areas to look at weather conditions. At about 0900, they would contact us in the strike aircraft while we were en route and give us the results of their observations.

The strike mission general briefing began at midnight and was a closed briefing. Only those directly involved were permitted to attend. Colonel Tibbets thanked everyone for their help and cooperation in getting us this far and that tomorrow the world will know the 509th helped end the war. Other details were covered by Operations and Intelligence; then Captain Parsons rose to speak. He said he had brought a movie of the weapon test in New Mexico which would give an idea of what to expect. The movie projector malfunctioned and we were not able to view the movie. He then gave us a tutorial lecture and chalk talk mentioning the equivalent of 20,000 tons of TNT and drew a picture of a mushroom cloud describing the color display that would come with it. Finally, Chaplain William Downey delivered his prayer. The briefing was over at 0030 and we headed for the mess.

William Laurence, the Senior Science Editor of the *New York Times* had been loaned to the War Department to do all the releases on our project. He was short of stature, had a boxer's flattened nose and spoke with a very heavy Russian, Jewish accent. He was disappointed he could not go along on this trip, but was promised a spot on the next one. He just sat in the mess and marveled at the way we youngsters packed away our food.

We arrived at the flight line at about 0200 just in time to see the weather planes take off the hardstand where our airplane was parked. It gave all the appearances of a Hollywood opening. There were Kleig lights and movie cameras in abundance. This was all done by the Military. The Civilian Press was represented by William Laurence. The airplane now had a name. Colonel Tibbets had his mother's name, Enola Gay, painted on the nose in plain block letters. In later years, Bob Lewis, who was the assigned Airplane Commander to that airplane but would fly as copilot this time, used to claim how upset he was about this naming, but he sure didn't show it that night.

Just prior to boarding the airplane for takeoff, Ed Doll handed me a small piece of rice paper, not much larger than a postage stamp, that had four radio frequencies on it. His instructions were to "eat it" before you bail out. These frequencies were the measured operating frequencies of the modified APS-13s that were being used as proximity devices on the weapon which was in the region of 400-420 MHG. What I was supposed to do in the target area was to monitor from approximately 390-430 MHG, which I did with an AN-RPR Receiver with the appropriate tuning unit installed. It also had attached to it a panoramic adapter which, set to the proper band with scan, allowed me to examine incoming signals and their adjacent side bands. I could differentiate various types of signals such as pulse radar code. A thermal paper recorder was attached so I could make a permanent record of any incoming signals. I also had a hand built prototype direction finding device which I could use to deter-

mine the direction from which the incoming signal was coming. I could then triangulate and locate the source of the signal.

To be alert for enemy fighters, I had an AN/ARR-5 Communications Receiver used to scan the Japanese fighter control frequencies. My headset had a modified two channel device with a special built junction box which allowed me to select two receivers or one receiver or the aircraft interphone channel. On the way to Hiroshima, I used the APR-4 to scan the active Japanese radar frequencies and kept track of radar that might be tracking us. In the event it would become necessary, I carried two jamming devices AN/APT-1 and AN/APT-4. I did not have a Chaff dispenser (Chaff was metal strips that when dispensed outside the plane would confuse the enemy radar).

At about 0300, we loaded into the airplane for takeoff. About five and a half hours later, we approached the Island of Iwo Jima. It was here we would rendezvous with the other two airplanes. Right on schedule, at about 0900, the weather reports began coming in. Buck Etherly and his crew were over Hiroshima and reported one-tenth cloud cover, essentially wide open. Ralph Taylor and John Wilson had gone to Kokura and Nagasaki; their reports were equally as good. Since Hiroshima was briefed as the Primary Target, the decision was made, then and there on the Enola Gay, to go to Hiroshima.

From Iwo Jima, we headed straight for Hiroshima. As we neared Japan, I began to detect the familiar Japanese early warning radar. Soon it was locked on us. Then another radar picked us up. At the same time, but on different frequencies that we shared with the Navy, I detected considerable activity off the coast. The Fifth Fleet was in full operation that morning and the radio chatter of the pilots made fascinating listening.

As the range to Hiroshima began to close, I made an intensive search in that part of the spectrum where our proximity devices would operate; I found the area was clear. Several minutes before 0815, I heard the navigator inform the bombardier we were over our Initial Point; that landmark from which we formally begin the bomb run. With that call, the bomb bay doors were opened and a radio tone signal was activated. This signal alerted Sweeney and Marquardt that we were about to bomb. They now made ready to do their jobs; release instruments and take photographs. At precisely 0815:15 Hiroshima time, the tone signal stopped. The bomb was on its way.

Wednesday 8 August 1945 was to be a day of "worries" for everyone concerned with the mission due to depart at 0330 the next morning. The weather over Japan had deteriorated in the past forty-eight hours and the forecast for the next twenty-four hour interval was somewhat "iffy". Major Charles Sweeney and his crew had been named as strike crew for this mission. He was Squadron Commander had the option of selecting any of the squadron crews for this job; so he chose the Don Albury crew since he had most of his experience with them and had accompanied us to Hiroshima. Except for Ralph Taylor and Claude Etherly who led the squadron in missions flown, they were right up there with the best. Major Sweeney had been selected by Paul Tibbets based on prior experience with him in the B29 Test Program and not on prior combat experience. Although we all liked Chuck and had confidence in his ability as a B29 Pilot, there were those of us in the original cadre of the 393rd who felt based on combat experience and demonstrated valor, Tom Classen, our original Squadron Commander, would have been a more logical choice. This was not to be as Tom was on his way back to the States on a "special mission" for Colonel Tibbets.

Thursday 9 August 1945, I made my way to the flight line in a jeep driven by Paul Tibbets in the company of William Laurence and Fred Ashworth who would be the Weaponeer and representative of General Groves on this flight. As had happened several nights previously, Dr. Ed Doll gave me another slip of rice paper with the operating frequencies of the four proximity fuses; once again with instructions to eat it if need be.

The assembly on the flight line this night in no way resembled the scene prior to departure for Hiroshima. I was beginning to feel the effects of lack of sleep so I just sat on the hood of the Colonel's jeep until it was time to go. Major Sweeney, who would be our Pilot that night, came over to Paul several times, removed themselves from our presence and had several animated discussions. I determined from one of the enlisted men there were two concerns: one, the weather over Japan was not clearing as expected and two, there was some kind of problem with the bomb bay fuel transfer pump. Sweeney and Captain James Van Pelt came back to the jeep with their slide rules and maps and evidently worked out a new flight plan which Paul Tibbets and Fred Ashworth agreed was OK and we were given the signal to load up.

The takeoff was routine and uneventful and in less than three minutes the wheels were up. The weather en route to Japan was somewhat worse than forecast, although expected to clear by the time we reached our target area. We reached our rendezvous at 0900. By 0912, The Great Artiste, under the command of Captain Fred Bock arrived. Yet to arrive was Major James Hopkins in V-90. We waited forty-five minutes but could wait no longer. The weather reports had been received from Charles McKnight and George Marquardt and were about the same for both Kokura and Nagasaki. Since the Industrial Center at Kokura was briefed as our Primary Target, we proceeded there.

Jacob Beser, wearing officer's hat, on deck of USS Deuel

When we arrived in the target area, it was obvious that visual bombing was going to be a problem. Yawata, the steel industry center for Japan, had been fire bombed the night before and was still burning. Situated a few miles west of Kokura, it was sending smoke and haze over our target, compounding Kermit Beahan, the Bombardier's problem. After approximately two thirds of a run, we heard Kermit say "no drop"; he could not get a clear sight of his briefed aiming point. We circled the area to try a second run. This time we not only didn't drop, but we were now receiving antiaircraft fire. Couple this with a deteriorating fuel situation and the situation became more tense. There was considerable conversation on the flight deck concerning fuel remaining and alternate flight plans. It seemed to me that Chuck and the Flight Engineer had a difference of opinion as to what the alternatives should be. But a cool head prevailed; I heard Fred Ashworth very clearly enunciate what he felt we should be doing and especially not doing. There was no time for lengthy debate. We were burning fuel at a rate of 400 gallons per hour. We should make one more pass at Kokura and if we don't drop then head for Nagasaki. If we are unable to make it visually at Nagasaki, then he, Fred Ashworth as General Groves Deputy on this flight, would make a radar run. From there we would head down the coast of lower Kyushu for an emergency landing at Okinawa.

While all the above was going on, I began to detect activity on the Japanese fighter control frequencies. In a few moments, it became obvious they scrambled some fighters and before long they would be looking for us. We made our third pass at Kokura without success. We headed across the Shimonosaki Straights, followed the coastline down and then across to Nagasaki. As we left the Kokura area, after about one hour and several power cycles of turning on and off the weapon in our bomb bay, our tail gunner announced he could see fighter aircraft breaking through the clouds below. As luck would have it, the Japanese fighters must have had a different target in mind, because they never came after us.

We headed for our new target and found the weather was no better there than at Kokura. If anything, slightly worse. We were on a radar run to the city. Fred Ashworth, in an unpublished memoir, states that commensurate with his responsibility, he paid close attention to the navigator's radar scope to be sure it was Nagasaki we were approaching. He was monitoring the navigator/bombardier talk-in procedure we were following. The navigator tracks the target on his scope and verbally gives the bombardier the data he would have otherwise acquired visually with his bombsight.

Approximately twenty seconds before the bomb would have been released, we heard Beahan say, "I've got it". A hole opened up in the clouds and he saw what we thought was our briefed aiming point. The airplane lurched as the bomb was released and Sweeney put it into a tight turn to the left to give us distance from the explosion. Within forty-five seconds came the now familiar bright flash and the rapidly ascending mushroom cloud. This time we felt three shock waves. We reasoned the first wave was from the explosion itself; the second was a direct reflection under the airburst and the third had to be from a wall of hills. This told us we had hit the Urakami Valley and missed our target, the city of Nagasaki, by at least a mile and a half. There was not enough fuel to go back and take another look. The flight engineer's latest calculation, after we set up reduced power glide from altitude, was that it would be close, but we just might make it to Okinawa. In the interim, our radio operator had alerted the Air-Sea Rescue Unit of our intentions.

After the bomb burst over Nagasaki, Major Hopkins, who until then had not been seen or heard from by us, put out a radio call in the blind, "Chuck, where the hell are you?" This startled all of us, but once the bomb had been dropped, the need for radio silence no longer existed. Hopkins was told we were en route to Yontan Airstrip on Okinawa and if there was any way, try to catch up with us there. It seemed when we realized he missed his rendezvous with us, he decided to loiter somewhere between Kokura and Nagasaki in the hopes of finding us. When he was about to abandon his wait to go to Okinawa to refuel, he saw the mushroom cloud rise above Nagasaki and decided to give a call.

As we neared Okinawa, the radio traffic was horrendous. They had a raid of B24s returning from Japan along with their fighter escorts. Chuck broadcast a MAY-DAY-MAYDAY distress signal which theoretically should have cleared the air, but it didn't. He told the navigator to fire the appropriate flare with the Very Pistol. This brought no results either. In desperation, he told the navigator to fire everything, which he did. This had two results; in the back of the plane, we thought a major fire had broken out from the amount of smoke coming out of every duct and two, some pilot in the traffic pattern sensed we were in trouble and peeled off. Those in the pattern behind him followed suit and we were able to land. We came in high and fast and when we touched down, it was a "controlled crash". We came to the end of the runway still rolling fast; our options were to go over the cliff or make a ninety degree turn. We opted for the latter. As we followed the "follow me" jeep to the hardstand to park the airplane, the two inboard engines drained their tanks and stopped.

When Fred Bock and his crew arrived at Okinawa, they confirmed to us we had indeed hit the Urakami Valley and the large Mitsubishi Plant was the most likely target we hit. We waited for James Hopkins to arrive and had to get out of there before the afternoon Kamikaze raid came in.

Our flight back to Tinian was five hours arriving late at night. We were taken to the Intelligence Quonset. Before the interrogation crew arrived, Rear Admiral Purnell, in discussing our "miss" with Fred Ashworth, pointed out this was a fortunate happening; for if we had hit the city,

the loss of life would have been greater. He also described for us the concern of General Farrell when we were overdue. He had "tossed his cookies". That was real concern and we appreciated his feelings for us.

10 August 1945 After our return from Nagasaki, our Flight Engineer John Kuharek noted; "check bomb bay tank hookup. Lower tank works erratic. Appears booster pump at fault." Note that John never said he could not transfer fuel. When I asked Cecil King about John Kuharek, he had nothing but praise for John and his ability and integrity. The Bockscar Crew Chief, Fred Clayton, told me he had personally conducted the preflight inspection of the airplane and he was satisfied the transfer system was operational. He noted some sluggishness in the fuel flow system and said he talked to John about this before they left. He says when he was ready, just turn the pumps on and leave them on. Full flow would be established and the fuel successfully transferred.

The airplane is on permanent display at the Wright-Patterson Airforce Base Museum, Dayton, Ohio. They have, in their files, all of the airplane records.

Jacob Beser at Roswell, New Mexico

37

BIEL, RAYMOND P.
393rd Bomb Squadron, Pilot, Crew A-1

From the Lincoln, Nebraska pilot pool, several B17 pilots and I were transferred to Fairmont, Nebraska to serve as copilots for the B29 program just starting. We were assigned to the 393rd Bomb Squadron and I became a member of Capt. Ralph Taylor's crew. We transitioned to B29s and in September 1944 were sent to Wendover, Utah for duty in the 509th Composite Group. There we were trained in long range navigation, high altitude bombing accuracy and radar techniques. Our crew was sent to Inyokern, California to test drop pumpkins on the California desert.

The highlight at Wendover was to visit the Boeing assembly plant in Omaha and pick up a new aircraft specially equipped for a top secret mission; like driving a new Cadillac off the showroom floor.

By June of 1945, our crew had trained into a close knit unit in our new airplane and flew to Tinian via Hawaii and Kwajalein with our ground crew and several passengers. There we were assigned to mosquito infested tents for a few weeks and eventually to Seabee quonsets as permanent quarters. Our food was always excellent to good, except for the Australian goat on occasion. On Tinian, we flew several missions carrying Fat Man bombs to Japan. We felt we were pretty successful hitting our assigned targets.

Takeoff for a bombing mission to Japan was usually early in the morning so our bomber could be over our target shortly after daybreak. Our 10,000 pound Fat Man inside the bomb bay, loaded with high explosives, required us to drop it visually on an assigned target from 30,000 feet.

A mission to Japan began with posting of orders on the squadron bulletin board for crews to report for briefing at a certain time, usually three hours before liftoff.

Pre-flight briefings were truly in depth. We knew where we were going, how to get there and exactly what our mission was all about. Flights were long, anywhere from 12 to 14 hours airborne.

One sought a few hours sleep before reporting to the quonset hut for details of the anticipated flight. Navigators gathered together; also the bombardiers, pilots, copilots and flight engineers met in another area. Gunners, radar men and radio operators met separately. All the minute details of the mission were discussed and explained by intelligence officers.

Gathered together, the crew members were informed of assigned targets. Altitudes and courses were mapped out on the strike orders. Locations of Navy Rescue Ships along the flight path and off the coast of Japan were pointed out. Briefing concluded, crews were dismissed and the religiously inclined met at the theater for a short chapel service. Trucks soon arrived to transport the men to their individual aircraft.

Walk around pre-flight procedures checked the exterior of the plane for any problems or oil leaks. Propellers were pulled through several rotations on the giant engines to disperse lubricant into the pistons and the crew climbed aboard with their flight gear. The ground crew

Ray Biel in cockpit

chief started the auxiliary power unit in the rear of the fuselage, and the ship became alive as electricity activated the complex instruments and systems aboard.

"Start number three" sounded over the intercom. The starter engaged and within seconds, the engine roared to life with a cloud of white smoke. Numbers one, two and four soon followed and the words "ready to taxi" came. The B29 slowly began to roll off her parking pad onto a taxi strip. Just off the runway, all four engines were individually brought to full power and double checked for proper operation. Given tower clearance, the ship entered the runway, full power was applied while the brakes kept the ship from moving. Upon release, the plane roared down the runway and was quickly airborne into the dark night.

Enroute to Iwo Jima at twenty-five hundred feet, warm outside air ventilated the cabin until it was time to slowly climb to bombing altitude. Flight instruments, compass headings and engine operation was constantly monitored as the ship flew on autopilot. Crewmen checked their parachute locations, donned side arms and heavy flight clothing as pressurization of the cabin began. The ship headed for her assigned target. Off to the east, the sky was showing the first signs of dawn. Down below, the small Island of Iwo Jima, with its single runway, stood alone in the vast expanse of ocean.

On the slow ascent to bombing altitude, radar constantly searched for signs of opposition. The flight crew monitored their instruments as the bombardier and navigator compared strike orders.

Nearing the coastline of Japan, the rising sun behind the plane began to illuminate the ocean below and major landmarks on the strike maps were identified on the coastline. Cities were recognized and the bombardier and navigator checked for wind directions and velocity at 30,000 feet. Soon the target was identified and the bomb run began. The pilot and copilot checked engine gauges, altitude and air speed critical for a proper drop. Then a bomb run under control of the bombardier. Cross hairs on the bomb sight were centered on our target. With a sudden snap, the hydraulic bomb bay doors opened, and within an instant, five tons of dead weight was freed from its shackle in the bomb bay. The ship jumped upward and was quickly brought under control by the aircraft commander. Visually, the bombardier watched as the huge, tear-drop shaped casing fell free. High resolution automatic cameras in the tail, photographed the long drop, and eventual explosion on the ground.

With a sharp turn to the right, the plane was put on a course to home base. Departing the coast, power was reduced and a long, slow descent to a lower altitude began. With lessened weight due to expended fuel and the bomb gone, speed increased. Crewmen sought a space to curl up and sleep, usually in the tunnel above the bomb bay as the tension of potential Japanese opposition ended.

Approaching the Island of Tinian, landing instructions were acknowledged and touchdown was a routine maneuver. On her hardstand, the aircraft was parked and engines shut down. After nearly thirteen hours of roaring engines sounding in our ears, keeping us airborne, the sudden quietness seemed unreal.

Debriefing was usually short, with a shot of government issue bourbon to relax one, and within minutes it was sack time to catch up on lost sleep. The next mission could be a day away or several days off until the crew number reappeared on the squadron bulletin board. In the interim, for the air crews, it was poker, baseball, beaches or just goofing off.

Mechanics and other ground crew personnel serviced the B29s keeping them in top condition for the next mission. Everything worked perfectly when it had to and was first class. Any speck of oil on the engine cowling or wings was immediately checked out and corrected before leaving the hard stand on a mission.

August 6th we were assigned to weather reconnaissance over Nagasaki and radioed conditions back to base. Target was clear with 3/10ths cloud cover,

Ralph Taylor at controls of "Full House".
Fred Hoey on right.

bombing conditions good, but Hiroshima reported the same and was bombed. On our return to base, a beer bash was in progress and word that a Jap city was gone was reported. We knew the war would soon be over.

It was a great time to be young, 22, and piloting a B29 accompanied by a fantastic flight crew. Other crews on the base formed a baseball league and had frequent softball games. One afternoon, we cleared a quonset of all beds and had a football scrimmage from one end to the other. Some were former football stars and the game got a little rough but no score was recorded. We forgot to count due to high alcoholic content of time out refreshments.

An outstanding event was loading our B29 for return to the states with a bevy of passengers. Over Johnston Island, we observed a tremendous show of St. Elmo's fire. All the propellers were a glowing circle of light.

Control tower on Tinian.
509th plane can be seen through window

Crew A-1 prepares for take off

V-83 after atomic missions with square P marking on tail.

Ray Biel at controls while Glen Mahugh (pointing) directs plane onto hard stand after Hiroshima mission

Plane after August 6th mission, flight and ground crew.

BIVANS, JACK
393rd Bomb Squadron, Asst Flight Eng/Scanner, Crew C-11

Prior to enlisting in the Air Corps in 1943, I had been a juvenile radio actor since 1939 on several thousand network radio shows originating from Chicago during dramatic radio's heyday. This was before there was television. One of the daily kid shows I was on for several years was Capt. Midnight, in the role of the juvenile lead named Chuck Ramsey. I acted on as many as five different network programs each day before and after my service.

I was 17 years old when I enlisted in the Army Air Corps Air Cadet Program. The deal was you wouldn't be called to active duty until up to six months past your 18th birthday. I reported for active duty on February 3, 1944. At the time, the Capt. Midnight cast gave me a fine, water-proof hack watch as a going away gift. I wore it daily throughout my two years in service. I gave up my radio acting career out of patriotism. Also, I wanted to

beat the draft and enter the branch of service of my own choosing.

After basic training, the Air Corps decided they didn't need anymore Cadets and washed 40,000 of us out of the program. I was then sent to gunnery schools (B17, B24 and B29) and after that ended up in Wendover as Assistant Flight Engineer on Buck Eatherly's crew of the Straight Flush.

On payday, my friends and I would go to the State Line Hotel's Nevada side to do a little gambling. Before long I would lose my entire paycheck and would hock my Capt. Midnight watch with the guy who was the manager until next payday when I would get it out of hock only to turn it back in to him a few hours later.

On one of our trips to Salt Lake in Eatherly's car, we pulled along side another car also containing friends from the 509th. The road between Salt Lake and Wendover was straight as a die and the two lane highway, one lane

40

to go in and the other coming out, was about 120 miles long situated along side the salt flats. You could see for about 15 miles down the road if any traffic was coming toward you, so for our two cars to be running along side each other was comparatively safe from running into an oncoming car. The only dangerous part of the trip was at 60 or 70 miles per hour, both cars rolled down their windows and began passing a fifth of whiskey back and forth for swigs. At that time we were approximately three feet apart leaning out our windows. It was a wild ride!

Another time we were practicing bombing on large bulls eyes painted on the salt flats, I heard Eatherly on the intercom saying to someone, "Isn't that the girls in my car down there?" He was referring to his wife and another crew member's wife he knew driving into Salt Lake City for the day. The next thing I heard was Eatherly saying, "Let's scare them"! With that, he turned our plane around and dropped to a very low altitude and screeched across the top of the wife's car. He repeated it again before returning to the bomb practice range. Just full of fun!

The scariest time we ever had on the bomb range was one day when Eatherly became bored and I heard him on the intercom say, "Kenny", our bombardier, "let's dive bomb the target on the next go around". So when we were far enough away to complete the dive bombing and starting at the right high altitude to make it work, Eatherly put our plane in a steep dive toward the target on the salt flats and, at the right time, Kenny released the bomb and Eatherly immediately started climbing. However, an instant after he started to pull out of the dive, we heard a sound in the back, where I was sitting with other crew members, similar to our tail having touched ground for a split second. Then we started for our Wendover home base field. When we landed, Eatherly, Kenny and other officers came down their front ladder and joined those of us who had gotten out first from the rear ladder, standing under and looking up at the tail section. It had salt on it! Eatherly snapped, "Get that salt off there before Classen or Tibbets sees it"! Someone from our crew started wiping all the salt off the tail and we never heard another word about the incident.

It wasn't until we left for Tinian that I had full time possession of my watch and could wear it every day. On Tinian, I traded a bottle of cheap whiskey for a stainless steel watchband made by a Seabee to fit that watch. I'm very proud of it for sentimental and historical reasons and even wear it once in a while today. It still has that stainless band and still keeps perfect time!

After the war, the War Bond people set us up for appearances in several different venues to plug buying bonds. We were being interviewed during half time of a Chicago Bears football game when Irv Kupcinet introduced us to Olsen & Johnson right after their interview. Tallulah Bankhead came over to see her friends Olsen & Johnson do "Hellzapoppin" and after meeting Al and me insisted we join her backstage after her performance the following night. About 11 pm Monday night, the three of us pranced down Michigan Avenue to her hotel suite in the Stevens (now Hilton) for a party she threw in our honor with her two ex-husbands present. Room service arrived with food and booze and we ate, drank, played cards and laughed until 4am. When leaving, she asked what I wanted to do after service and I told her be a movie star. She asked me if I could act so I told her about my radio experience and training on the Captain Midnight show. As we thanked her for a wonderful evening, she took my phone number saying she would make an appointment with her agent at the William Morris Agency.

True to her word, Tallulah telephoned a few days later with instructions to go to the Agency on Michigan Avenue for an appointment with the head man. Her last words were "Goodbye, Jack, and good luck"!

The following day as I said my name and the person I had an appointment with, it became apparent the staff was aware Tallulah had an interest in me. The man took me to his office where he ordered coffee and asked me to give him some background, professional experience and training which I summarized in about fifteen minutes. At this time, he said I was about a year too late because all the top players and stars in the service were being discharged and returning to their studios to resume their unfulfilled contracts.

(L-R): Al Barsumian, Jack Bivans, and Ralph Belanger at Alta Ski Resort, Wasatch Mountains, north of Salt Lake, January 1945

I thanked him for taking time to see me that I would be returning to my contract with the Captain Midnight show and going to attend Northwestern University School of Speech which I did. I wrote Tallulah a warm thank you note telling her the outcome of the meeting. It was a very nice and memorable time of my life.

The photo of Al Barsumian and me at age 19 in Olsen and Johnson's dressing room after a performance of their "Hellzapoppin" in Chicago. "Ole" Olsen is on your left as you view the photo taken during a War Bond tour 11-1-45 / 1-30-46. I'm peering over Chic Johnson's back. The woman wearing the mink coat in the center is Tallulah Bankhead, the nation's premier stage actress during her Chicago run of "Private Lives".

BOCK, FREDERICK C.
393rd Bomb Squadron, Airplane Commander, Crew C-13

Fred Bock entered the Army Air Corps on July 10, 1941, as an Aviation Flying Cadet. He had the distinction of flying a basic training airplane at Moffett Field, California, and when he landed, he learned about Pearl Harbor. On the last day of the war, he and his crew dropped a bomb that was a direct hit on the Toyota Factory.

He completed his primary and basic training on the West Coast, and trained with the 34th Bomb Group at Pendleton, Oregon. In April of 1942, he went to the China Burma India Theatre of war as a B17 Pilot and remained there for sixteen months. While stationed in India, we were re-equipped with B24s. He completed a full combat tour, after which he entered the B29 program becoming part of the 393rd Bombardment Squadron.

As part of the 393rd, he was training to go overseas, when in Sept. 1944, he was given orders to go to Wendover Field, Utah. "We had the best record of available B29 Squadrons in the United States. The B29 was a giant step forward; it had a pressurized cabin, no oxygen mask or heavy suit at high altitudes, 200 horsepower, 18 cylinder engines, and bigger bomb load capacity.

Wendover was a training base for other groups. We were the only unit there - Salt Lake was a distance away. It had spartan accommodations but served the purpose. We had B17s in addition to B29s. The emphasis being on high altitude, daylight bomb testing. We flew missions working with Los Alamos people testing bombs of different configurations. The Los Alamos people were constantly redesigning the bomb casings based on tests we made.

At Inyokern, California, there were people on the ground so they could trace trajectory.

We spent two to three weeks in Cuba. That part of the Caribbean and Atlantic was similar to the Japanese approach to Japan. The emphasis was the use of radar to pick up the coastline and long range navigation. We made simulated bomb runs while stationed at Batista Field.

Many other air crews were confined to base, but we were allowed to visit Havana. There were always security people with us looking for leaks.

In the early part of July, all the airplane commanders were questioned, one at a time, by Manhattan District Security people. Col. Pere DeSilva was in charge of security at Los Alamos. He later came to Tinian and conducted interviews of airplane commanders about the nature of the weapon.

"Major Hopkins, Group Operations Officer and Major Sweeney, 393rd Squadron Commanding Officer, had been briefed because of rank and position; the others had not been briefed. When I was asked, I was quite specific, I said, "Uranium 235 - you could hear a pin drop. I had been at the University of Chicago in 1939 and it was openly discussed, at that time, in the University newspaper. I had that background and was aware that many of the people that came and went were physicists. Even at Wendover, I was certain what the nature of the weapon had to be.

A BOMBING MISSION AS EXPLAINED BY FRED BOCK

Pumpkin Strike Against Sumitomo Plants at Niihama on Shikoku

Special Bombing Mission No. 5, 509th Composite Group, 24 July 1945

A prime example of the combat operations of the 509th Composite Group in which precision targets on the Japanese home islands were attacked using 10,000 pound pumpkin bombs is provided by the strike against chemical and nonferrous metals plants of the Sumitomo Company at Niihama, Shikoku, on 24 July 1945. Sumitomo, founded in the 17th century as a refiner of copper and other metals, later diversified and became one of Japan's largest corporate groups (zaibatsu), although mining and metallurgy remained central. The company expanded greatly during World War II. Its activities during the war included heavy involvement in the unsuccessful attempt to develop an atomic weapon. Among other materials, it has been reported that thorium, an element considered as a possible alternative to uranium in the route to a fission bomb, was produced by Sumitomo at Niihama. However, no evidence has come to light that Allied intelligence was aware of this aspect of Sumitomo's contributions to the Japanese war effort.

The city of Niihama is located on the north coast of the island of Shikoku, facing the Inland Sea. The complex of Sumitomo plants at Niihama, situated partly on a man-made peninsula that juts out on the east side of the harbor, was the fourth largest producer of chemicals (sulphuric and nitric acids, ammonia, ammonium nitrate, calcium superphosphate, methanol, formalin, etc.) and one of the largest producers of aluminum in Japan, with a rated capacity of 25,000 metric tons per year. The Sumitomo Rayon Plant was another component. This complex was se-

Fred Bock

lected by the Twentieth Air Force for attack by the 509th because its output could help sustain Japan in the war. It encompassed precision targets and it had not been damaged by other Air Force units. Another important factor was the relatively close proximity to Hiroshima, across the Inland Sea, since it was deemed mandatory to familiarize the 509th combat crews with the general areas in which the cities reserved for possible atomic attack were located. (The four reserved cities at the time were Kyoto, Kokura, Hiroshima and Niigata.) The assumption by intelligence and mission planners was that the main plants at the Niihama site were the Sumitomo Copper Refining Company of Sumitomo Chemical Industries.

The plan for Special Bombing Mission No. 5, according to Operations Order No. 24, of the 509th Composite Group and the Tactical Mission Report of the Twentieth Air Force, specified three Silverplate B29s with nine-man crews and the primary targets. *See Table below* (The original low Victor or tactical numbers on the B29s were later changed to those in brackets.)

A tenth man, Jacob Beser, Radar Countermeasures Officer of the 393rd, was on board Full House. On this occasion each crew flew its "own" B29. The three planes happened to be the second, third and fourth of those made by Martin-Omaha that were in the 393rd Bomb Squadron on Tinian.

Each B29 carried in the forward bomb bay a 10,000 pound high explosive Pumpkin bomb that had three AN-MK219 instantaneous contact nose fuses. About half of the bomb's mass consisted of the HE charge. These bombs were externally and ballistically virtually identical to the Fat Man Atomic Bomb later dropped at Nagasaki. The tail gunners had 1,000 rounds of 50 caliber ammunition per gun in the twin gun turrets. A vertical strike camera and radar scope camera were mounted in each plane.

The one-way great circle distance from Tinian North Field to Niihama is 1,520 statute miles; the actual route to and from Niihama was via Iwo Jima, about halfway. The distance traveled, taking into account the bomb run, was thus somewhat longer than 3,040 miles. The main

Airplane Serial No.	Victor No.	Name	Airplane Commander	Crew	Primary Target within the Sumitomo Complex
44-27298	13 (83)	Full House	Taylor	A-1	Copper Refining Co.
44-27299	6 (86)	Next Objective	Devore	A-3	Copper Refining Co.
44-27297	7 (77)	Bockscar	Bock	C-13	Aluminum Co

BI7E and crew, Allahabad, India, July 1942
Flew from Florida to India, April 1942
7th Bomb Gp, 10th Air Force, China-Burma-India Theater
436th Bomb Squadron
To Bob Knauss
Fred Bock copilot

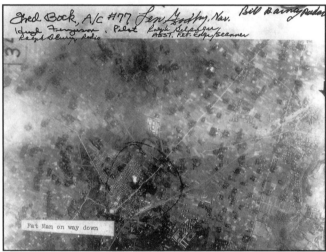

Fred Bock, A/C #77   Len Godfrey, Nav.   Bill Barney, radar
Hugh Ferguson, Pilot   Ralph Belanger, Asst. Flt. Eng./Scanner
Ralph Curry, Radio

Fat Man on way down

Photo taken from V-77 Pumpkin Bomb, Tokyo-Musashino
(Nakajima Aircraft Engine factory), July 29, 1945

and the aft bomb bay tanks were full and there were 250 gallons in the center tank, for a total fuel load of 7,000 gallons, somewhat below the maximum capacity.

Dates and 24 hour clock times will refer to Tinian (zone K). Religious services for the crews were held at 1900 and 1930 on 23 July. The general briefing for the mission took place in the Combat Crew Lounge of the 509th compound at 2100. The special briefing for navigators, bombardiers and radar operators was at 2200 in the Officers Mess. Special briefings for Airplane Commanders (ACs) and pilots, radio operators, gunners and flight engineers were at four different locations (Combat Crew Lounge, Communications, Library, Officers Club Annex, respectively) at 2300. Mess was at 2330.

Trucks left for the airfield at midnight. Scheduled takeoff time was 0200 with Elbert Smith, John Lundgren and James Anderson as flag men and George Marquardt in the control tower. The reason for that number of flag men and a 509th man in the control tower was there were two other 509th missions on 24 July taking off at about the same time: four crews with ACs Westover, Lewis, Ray and Albury had primary targets in the Kobe area (Special Bombing Mission No. 6); three crews with

ACs Price, McKnight and Eatherly had primary targets in the Yokkaichi area (Special Bombing Mission No.7).

The actual times of the night takeoffs on Mission No. 5, using the 8,500 foot runways at North Field, were from 0201 to 0212. The takeoff gross weight was about 130,200 pounds. Once airborne, the three planes flew to Niihama, bombed and returned to Tinian individually.

At takeoff, there were scattered low clouds. From base to a little north of Iwo Jima, there was 5/10 to 6/10 cumulus cloud cover below the flight level of 8,000 to 10,000 feet, with a few scattered middle and high clouds. A frontal zone extending roughly 250 miles was then encountered with 10/10 clouds, including cumulonimbus, in layers to 30,000 feet. Beyond, until landfall on Shikoku, there was 4/10 cumulus with a few high clouds. On the return, there was little change in the weather pattern except the frontal zone had moved south to Iwo.

Before reaching the south coast of Shikoku, the planes climbed to the briefed bombing altitude of 28,000 feet. They must have passed near the port of Kochi where, on a B29 incendiary mission earlier that month (3-4 July) by the Saipan based 73rd Wing, Major Keith Merrill and his whole crew were lost. The remains were recovered after the war. Merrill had been an AC in the 393rd Bomb Squadron at Fairmont, Nebraska but transferred to the 497th Bomb Group of the 73rd Wing after the 393rd moved to Wendover.

All three crews flew over Shikoku to reach the north coast and identified Niihama. Weather over the target area was 6/10 stratocumulus, topping out at 8,000 feet. Winds at bombing altitude were 335 degrees at 45mph. Each crew made a bombing run from its initial point and dropped a pumpkin visually on a Sumitomo installation. The times of bomb release were 0845 to 0921. No enemy fighters or antiaircraft fire were seen.

After recrossing Shikoku and leaving the south coast, the planes gradually descended but per standard operating procedures, were still at or above 18,000 feet passing Iwo to prevent alerting the defenses there. Average airspeed was about 25% faster on the return, the B29s being lightly loaded and going "downhill", than on the way to Niihama. The first landing back at North Field was at 1408, the last at 1505. The planes had been in the air an average of 14 ½ hours.

The results were uniformly reported as "excellent" at the crew debriefings as reported by 509th Group Combat Intelligence.

Strike photographs were rushed to 313th Bomb Wing for interpretation, and also reached higher headquarters. The results of this mission and the two other missions by the 509th on the same day, confirmed by examination of the strike photos, led the Commanding General of the 313th Bomb Wing, Brigadier General John Davies, to send a TWX message to the Commanding Officer of the 509th Composite Group, Colonel Paul Tibbets. The commendation reads:

Interpretation of strike photos taken on your mission yesterday, 24 July, reveals outstanding bombing capabilities. Such results as these are indicative of an organization with good leadership, high degree of training and determination to achieve outstanding results. Congratulations to you and your men.

Two of the Pumpkins, those dropped from Full House and Bockscar, scored direct hits on their primary targets. The Pumpkin from Next Objective hit an alternate target, the Sumitomo Rayon Plant, the primary target being obscured at the time of the bomb run.

Two of the strike photographs were taken from Bockscar at Niihama by a K18 or K22 camera of 24 inch focal length, vertically mounted in the aft unpressurized compartment. The film, nine inches wide, was automatically advanced and exposed by an intervalometer that was switched on by the bombardier about the time of the drop. The plane was flown straight and level, continuing the bomb run, which was upwind from southeast to northwest, until after bomb impact, with the camera running.

A team from the US Strategic Bombing Survey spent six days at Niihama in November 1945 studying the effects of two of the three Pumpkins: the one dropped from Full House by Crew A-1 with Ralph Taylor as Airplane Commander and Michael Angelich as Bombardier; and one dropped from Bockscar by Crew C-13 with Fred Bock as Airplane Commander and Charles Levy as Bombardier. The study confirmed the evidence of accurate bombing and substantial damage that was provided by the strike photos. The

(L-R): Fred Bock, Dr. Young, Lou Allen, Franklin MacGregor

bomb from Full House fell in the area where the Sumitomo Copper Refining Company was supposedly located, actually a cluster of chemical plants and caused about 70,000 square feet of structural damage to buildings and 48,000 square feet of lesser damage. The bomb from Bockscar caused about 38,000 square feet of structural damage and 72,000 square feet of lesser damage to the Aluminum Company buildings.

BONTEKOE, JACOB Y.
393rd Bomb Squadron, Pilot, Crew B-8

Like most men of the 393rd Bomb Squadron, I was ordered to Wendover in September, 1944, from Fairmont Air Force Base (AFB), Geneva, Nebraska, where we had trained in B29s under Col. Tom Classen. There was some secrecy at Fairmont but nothing compared to Wendover. It hit us from every side. We could see little to cause such secrecy, but no one opened his mouth except with extreme caution, especially after at least one base officer who reportedly talked at the wrong time and place, left the outfit suddenly and without goodbyes.

The Wendover wives did some speculating among themselves. One day a group of them was at our apartment and among other priceless bits of base gossip came this from Billy DeVore: "I'll bet the guys are going to drop a big new bomb!" I don't know if my wife was naive or, in view of all the secrecy, thought the matter shouldn't be discussed, or just wanted to argue, but at any rate, she replied: "Oh, I don't think so, Billy!" Actually, I doubt she gave the matter any very serious thought because her mind was pretty well occupied with taking care of our son, Steven who was born at Fairmont Oct. 11, 1944. The two of them had arrived in Wendover via train, plane, and bus early in November. We lived in the first housekeeping apartment we had occupied since I went into Cadets in January 1943. A lot of the fellows hated Wendover because of its isolation, but we thought it was great and often hiked up into the mountains in back of our apartment carrying Steve in a basket affair Betty rigged up out of cardboard, lathes, clothesline cord and other odds and ends and only weighing a couple pounds. Our backyard was one giant flower garden

Jake Bontekoe and Charles McKnight

Betty and Stephen Bontekoe, 1945

Jake and Stephen Bontekoe, 1945

when the desert bloomed. Maybe it was because of the isolation but people got well acquainted with each other and a lot of life-long friendships were formed there. The wives were left to their own resources much of the time because we were often away from the base, sometimes weeks at a time.

In March of 1945, three B29 crews including ours, went to Inyokern, California, which was a naval base, to test the ballistics of what we called pumpkin bombs — actually the same type of bomb that was soon to be dropped on Nagasaki, but without the high-powered components, although we didn't know that. It was called Fat Boy. Several such bombs were dropped. A Navy fighter plane followed each one down to take pictures, recording its fall. One crew would drop one one day and get to watch the next day when a different crew would make the drop. Scientists were much in evidence watching the procedure. Proving my ignorance of the project with which we were involved, one day I asked one of the scientists why we were messing with this bomb when all we got was a barn sized hole in the ground. He replied, "See that group of buildings over there?" They were three miles away. "This is going to knock every window out!" That was an eye-opener, indicating we weren't witnessing the final product.

That fact became even more plain to me the day we went to a place in the desert where high dirt banks surrounded the entire site, and we were shown half a bomb, a cross section of one. I could see that in its complexity it was literally an engineering marvel and it bore no resemblance to the interior of an ordinary bomb.

Being in a top secret VHB (Very Heavy Bomb) Group, it was obvious to everybody, that we would either be involved in different bombing methods, a very secret strike, or a more powerful bomb, but it wasn't until the experiences at Inyokern that it finally dawned on me that we were dealing with something truly momentous. We all knew that we were in that war until the United States won it and everybody hoped and prayed for an early victory, but I'm sure it never occurred to very many of us at Wendover, until Inyokern, that our outfit would play a decisive role in bringing it about. However, we all remained very leery of any verbal speculation regarding the group's purposes and I never heard the words, atom or atomic, uttered until after the Hiroshima bombing, when it appeared in the newspapers.

I don't think anyone in our crew will ever forget the night training flight we made for Jack Widowsky, navigator. It was in the spring of 1945; we took off from Wendover

and were flying at about 31,000 feet over San Francisco, which was such a fantastic sight that we called back to Jack, who had been taking star shots from the tunnel, to come up and look at the lights. Mac, Charlie McKnight, had also been in back with Jack. Both reached the front of the plane just an instant before we had a decompression explosion and a huge hole opened in the floor over which they had just walked.

Although our group's planes had been built to accommodate them, they had no gun turrets and the turret hole was covered with metal. It was this covering which blew out and it was a pure miracle that Jack wasn't sucked out along with the oxygen equipment, regulators, parachutes, the plane's kitchen and a ladder, all of which fell on San Francisco that night.

Jack had left his navigation instrument in the tunnel, but it flew forward and clobbered him on the head, knocking him coo-coo. Bleeding, he tried to fight his way back to his navigator's position on the other side of the hole. It took all George Cohen and I could do to keep him from it. Of course he didn't have on a parachute, but even if he had he was in no condition to pull the cord. With junk and insulation flying around inside the plane, Mac descended at about 1500 ft. per minute while we struggled with Jack. There was blood all over the three of us and the cockpit. Lloyd Reeder, the radio operator, sat in his little chair right beside the hole; it was five miles straight down through that gaping hole. Why the kitchen blew out and Reeder didn't, I'll never know. But he continued to operate his radio, without oxygen, just as though nothing had happened.

Jake Bontekoe in test flight of V-82 observes V-84

46

That explosion was heard for thirty miles around, but the scanners, tail gunner, and radar operator in the back of the plane, didn't even feel it, except for the loss of oxygen, but they had masks and used them. We landed at Hamilton Field. An ambulance met the plane and took Jack to a hospital where they sewed up his head.

Since ours was a secret plane, no one could board it from the base and there were special orders for dealing with such planes by the ground personnel. The only person who knew where those orders were was a Sergeant who was at home sleeping, so Mac, I and somebody else went in a staff car with an Army driver to find the Sgt. and get those orders. It was a mad drive and a lot scarier than the decompression explosion. A cop stopped us. We told him it was an emergency and since we were all covered with blood, he let us go. Eventually, the Sgt. and orders were located, the plane was towed to the other side of the field, a piece of plywood was secured over the turret hole and we flew back to Wendover at low altitude. We were all well aware that but for the Grace of God, Jack, Mac, and Reeder, any or all, could have been lost that night on a routine flight.

Our crew left Wendover with a brand new B29 named Top Secret on June 6th arriving on Tinian the 9th or 10th. For a few days we occupied tents, then we moved into Seabee (CB) Quonsets which were comfortable. We flew quite a lot but didn't drop any bombs until July. I have in my records that we flew July 1, 2, 3, 4, 5, 8, 9, 14, 18, 20, 22 (2x), 24, 29. About this time, Tokyo Rose complained that we had dropped new bombs. Our flights were considered to be training flights.

On August 6th, 1945, our crew went to Iwo Jima where our plane served as standby for the Enola Gay. If anything had gone wrong with the Enola Gay, the Big Stink would have delivered the bomb to Hiroshima.

On August 9th, ours was weather ship for the Nagasaki bombing. We went to Iwo Jima and listened for the strike report, then got orders from Tinian to go to Okinawa. Halfway there, we got other orders to return to Tinian, where everyone anticipated an early end to the war.

We made one more bomb drop on Japan at Korome, on the 14th of August.

When we got the news of the surrender, there were some Generals present and we formed ranks to listen to one of them make a speech. I have no recollection who he was or what he talked about, and I don't think anyone else did either. Afterward, we were ordered to pass in review, but that review fizzled; everybody had had enough of Army regulations and orders, and the war was over, so all the men walked right off the runways. We figured our job was done, we felt like civilians again, and I guess we thought we were.

However, we had to keep on flying all through September and October. Somebody forgot we were still there, and we didn't get back to the States, Roswell, New Mexico, until November 8th. We all made it home for the holidays, and I was discharged in April, 1946, from Fort Bliss, El Paso, Texas.

The 393rd was one outfit where one principle duty was to not know what anyone else was doing, unless you happened to be in G2 where you had to know what everyone else was doing, at all times!

Written by Betty Bontekoe

When the men left Wendover June 6, 1945, some of the wives who had jobs there may have stayed on, but I had eight month old Steve and as soon as Jake's plane left the ground, destination unknown as far as we were concerned, I went back to our apartment and threw everything we owned into a footlocker Jake had made for us. Very early the next morning, someone drove us to the train station and we headed home for Michigan. I think the trip took me longer than it took Jake and it was no picnic.

My parents were dairy farmers and my Dad had just bought what was one of the first newly invented hay balers in our county. It was haying season when I got home and my Mother and I took on new roles: she took over most of baby Steve care and I got on the tractor and drove the baler all summer. My Dad had the miserable job of sitting on the baler itself to keep check on the finicky knotter that wasn't perfected till a few years later. We did all our own hay plus we baled the neighbors hay for miles around. The baler was paid for by fall, which in post depression and war era was awesome. Everyone was doing everything possible to help win the war and we were doing our part.

V-95 and V-72 in flight over Tinian

BRABENEC, GEORGE L.
393rd Bomb Squadron, Flight Engineer, Crew C-14

Memories begin with the Classen-Hopkins transition from Nebraska to Wendover and wind up with the Tibbets-Sweeney days from Wendover to Tinian. At Wendover, we met each other, we met the B29, we trained together, we lived together, and we depended on one another. The fun times and bonding times were usually our frequent ball games - especially on Tinian.

As a flight crew member, we depended so much on all the support groups - especially our excellent ground crew. Not one of our planes had to abandon a single bombing mission due to mechanical failure. Not one plane was lost. Thank you, all support groups.

Late on a lonely, frigid Christmas night at Wendover, the chapel PA system sounded out the music and words to the song "The Holy City". It was a clear, cold, star-filled night. All was quiet, smoke came up from the chimneys of every barrack, and I felt God was near our 509th; and He was, for throughout our training and combat missions, not one man was lost. Above all the support groups, my thanks to God for His safe physical deliverance to all of us, and to all of you in our "Wendover Family".

BYSOM, CLYDE L.
393rd Bomb Squadron, Tail Gunner, Crew B-7

The range was a two-burner coal stove that provided the heat, hot water and a way to cook in the two room cement block apartments near the highway. Luckily, it didn't get too cold because the ranges had minds of their own. Kindling was needed to start the fire and there were no trees for miles. As I remember, some resourceful GIs salvaged wood shipping crates, cut them into small pieces and sold small bundles for kindling for fifty cents. Finding an empty, waxed, milk carton while walking to and from the base was like finding a five dollar bill. They were great for starting a fire.

Married enlisted men with wives who could perform secretaries' duty on the base were eligible for the apartments and Pauly was employed in the Air Inspector's Office. Getting ready for work in the mornings was many times frustrating when the fire refused to start and we left without hot water or coffee. We would return later to find the fire had started and boiled the coffee pot dry. After much trial and error, we mastered the use of the range and learned to prepare gourmet meals and desserts. We took turns sharing with other couples in adjoining apartments. Eating out was above our means. We did see and enjoy every movie about twice a week for ten or fifteen cents - a far cry from current movie prices.

Pete Powell, a radio operator with the Troop Carrier Squadron, organized the 509th Jazz Band, eight pieces pictured in our album and we played for Red Cross dances, Noncommissioned Officer (NCO) dances and even a couple bars in downtown Wendover. The highlight of musical happenings was a dance with a professional traveling band and the girl vocalist was a high school friend of my copilot. He invited Pauly and me to join them for the dance and a good time was had by all.

Our few visits to Salt Lake City were enjoyable with a stay at the Hotel Utah and on Sunday hearing and seeing the great Mormon Tabernacle Choir and organ. Our crew trip to Batista Field, Cuba, for over water flight training was a bonus. Sight seeing and shopping in Havana, with side trips to some of the smaller towns, was really great and enlightening. After a few days of tanning in the sun, I was asked if I was a Cuban. The cloth covered tobacco fields were neat and, at that time, I enjoyed the smell of tobacco.

All our schooling and training flights over Lake Tahoe, Grand Canyon and simulated bomb runs over distant cities kept us interested. One run stands out above the others when engine trouble grounded us in the desert and we visited Las Vegas.

Tom Costa Bombardier #84 'SOME PUNKINS' Wendover, Utah November 1944

James N. Price Jr. Airplane Commander

Clyde Bysom Tail Gunner

Enola Gay Welcome Party

Life on Tinian had its ups and downs. It was hot, humid and clothes never dried. After hanging in the hut for a few days, they were still damp. Hanging them outside for a few more days didn't help much so we wore them damp. Green mold had to be scraped off our shoes and rain was almost a daily occurrence. Movies were outside and raincoats were needed at least one time during a movie. Sometimes the movies were interrupted by air-raid sirens and flood lights when a strange plane was observed.

We enjoyed a super USO stage presentation of "South Pacific". Another time, comedian Peter Lind Hayes brought a group from Saipan featuring a small band led by Joe Bushkin, piano and trumpet, and harmonica virtuoso Harry Adler to our group theater.

When we were through flying missions, we reactivated our 509th Jazz Band, pictured in the "Recreation on Tinian" section of our album and entertained at theaters and the enlisted men's coffee shop. I had a tenor sax checked out from Special Services by W.O. Jack Teagarden, Jr. son of famous big band leader Jack Teagarden. He looked like his dad, played trombone and led the 313th Wing Jazz Band, a fifteen piece dance band of accomplished musicians. The officers had erected a few nice clubs and the band played for their dances. When one of the sax players left for the States, I was asked to join the band. I had played with the piano player in Wichita, Kansas and our lead trumpet player was Thad Jones, who on returning to the US would play, arrange and compose music for the Count Basie Band. I enjoyed being a part of the band until I returned to the US. Because of the small number of nurses and Red Cross workers, we saw the same ladies at every dance.

When time permitted, swimming and playing tennis provided some exercise. Trips around the island to bombed out bunkers and Old Tinian Town helped us understand the history of the island. The main crop had been sugar cane and remains of narrow gauge railway trains and tracks were scattered around some areas. Vegetation was lush and in the bombed out town yards where homes had been beautiful orchids, gardenias and pineapple plants were still growing. One of the beaches had a level stretch where water was about three feet deep for some distance out to the breakers. With diving goggles, we could look through cracks in the ocean floor and see beautiful colored fish swimming below. Sometimes a small octopus could be seen on adjoining reefs. A swimming hole had been set up on the other side of the island

with deep water and diving boards. Also, from there, one could swim to coral reefs and formations - beautiful but dangerous.

Exploring caves could also be dangerous. One of our crew members brought back a shell, later took it outside to detonate and steel fragments bounced off the walls of the Quonset Huts making lots of noise. Luckily, only one soldier received cuts on his hand that required medical attention.

When K and C Rations appeared on the scene, most of the huts grew a little kitchen on the back side. With cookies, food stuff from home and the rations, a welcome change from mess hall food was enjoyed by all.

JACK TEAGARDEN'S
313 WING - 20TH AIR FORCE
SPECIAL SERVICE BAND
OCT. 1945

BRASS	SAXES
TEAGARDEN - TROMBONE	GENE CHANEY - ALTO
THAD JONES - TRUMPET	JACK BROWN - ALTO
JOHNNIE ARCH - TRUMPET	CLYDE BYSOM - TENOR
JERRY EKLUND - TRUMPET	RAY PRICE - TENOR
	ARTHUR BRUNO - BARI

WILLIAM JOHNSON - PIANO, MELIS LAVELLA - BASS
JOHN MURRAY - DRUMS

CAIN, WILLIAM R. "BOB" JR.
320th Troop Carrier Squadron, A & E Mechanic

I was one of the group that did not get to Tinian. I was transferred into the 320th Troop Carrier Squadron on May 25, 1945 from the base group at Wendover where I had been working in sub depot in the B29 engines build up section. I was assigned to Eugene Krause's crew and C54 and was told to ship a barracks bag on the next flight to Tinian and would fly over there in a couple of weeks. When it was time to go, I was told "not enough room" or "I was needed in Wendover". We pulled 100 hour inspections and then the engineering hop. The C54 was then loaded with personnel and materials, etc. and then took off for Tinian. Our C54 made a few trips to station "X" and would return covered with red dust. When we asked where station "X" was, we were told "down the road a piece".

At Wendover I went on one of the engineering hops, Captain Casey was the Pilot and he rushed through the check list. On take off he said the plane was hard to handle and something was wrong. Flight Engineer Eugene Krause said, "Captain, your automatic pilot is on". Of course, after the captain turned off the switch, everything was OK. Thank goodness, as we were headed for the water tower.

Our plane and Parke Miller's plane had enough hours that a complete engine change was required. We finished ours first and on the test hop, we flew to southeastern Utah, then the Grand Canyon and at times you could look out and see the sides of the canyon, then look up and see the top. We circled Hoover Dam and Las Vegas and back to Wendover in 3 1/2 hours. We fell in and helped Miller's crew finish their engine change. This test hop took us to Yakima, Washington, the home of CWO Mathison. This was a 2x4 field of the Navy. On take off, we hung the tail over a barbed wire fence, set the brakes, wound up the engines and took off. From Yakima, we flew to Eureka, California, the pilot's home town which we buzzed a couple of times (you could have reached out and touched the top of the pine trees).

During the time we were at Wendover, those who worked on the line in the hanger consumed $2,700 of K-Rations during our coffee breaks. The breakfast rations were the best.

We were told by some of the flight crews that every time they landed at Kwajalein, they were fed stew that tasted like it had been eaten before. We talked them into bringing us some. They did (a gallon can), and sure enough, it did taste as if it had been eaten. Afterwards, trying to change the taste with all kinds of seasonings, it still tasted the same. I think it was Australian Lamb stew. It tasted terrible!

Another time, Robbie Roberson and I decided that we were going to break the bank at the Stateline Hotel. One night as we walked back to the base gate, we threw the mills (a Nevada tax receipt) that were left in our pockets into the air leaving us flat broke.

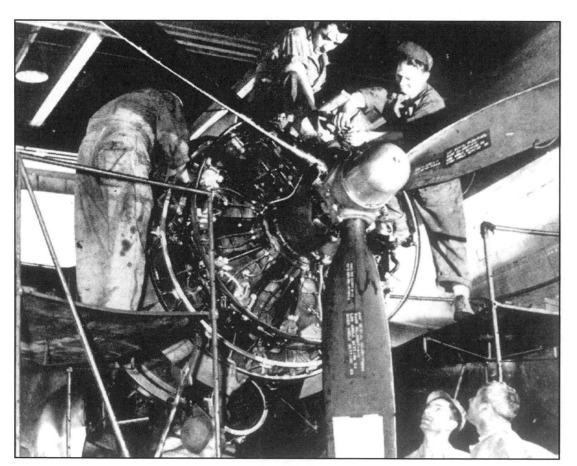

Engine change, C54

Top, (L-R): Robby Roberson, Parke Miller, Eugene Krause
Bottom, (L-R): Bob Cain, Newton Mahon, Harry Zimmerman

CANNON, RICHARD F.
393rd Bomb Squadron, Radar Operator, Crew C-14

At the age of eighteen, I was the last of four sons to leave for the service. It was on the eve of my oldest sister's wedding day that I left for Fort Dix, New Jersey. After a week at Fort Dix, I went to Greensboro, North Carolina for basic training. From there to Aerial Gunnery training in Panama City, Florida. Next I was sent to an assignment center in Lincoln, Nebraska where the group I was with went to Central Fire Control in Clovis, New Mexico. I was then sent back to Lincoln for reassignment to the 393rd Bomb Squadron of the 504th Bomb Group located at Fairmont Air Force Base in Geneva, Nebraska. There we prepared to go overseas. Midway through our training it was announced we were being transferred to Wendover Field, Utah, which became the training base for the 509th Composite Group.

After about a month there, a special meeting was held introducing us to Colonel Paul Tibbets who would be the new Commanding Officer (CO). Tibbets explained we were on a mission of the utmost secrecy. FBI Agents addressed us as to what we could or could not say.

In the process of training, I became Radar Operator of Norm Ray's crew. We completed training after about three months and started training all over again. When we questioned the repeat of what we had already done, we were never given an answer. Later we found out they had not exploded the first atomic bomb at the Trinity site yet.

On Tinian, we had training sessions to establish flying procedures for combat missions. On our combat flights to the Empire, we would drop five-ton bombs, the same as the atomic bomb would be. We did this on the missions both before and after the two A-Bombs were dropped. The targets we trained for were Kokura and Nagasaki.

When we rendezvoused at Yakushima, the other two planes were not there. We stayed for our agreed forty minutes, then went on to the primary, Kokura. At this point our pilot, Major James Hopkins (Norm Ray was ill) told

everyone on board to get near any blister seat to watch for the other two planes. My normal position after radar was to take the left scanner seat where I hoped to see the other two aircraft. Due to cloud formations, we realized no one could have bombed it.

We went on to Nagasaki which was south and slightly west of Kokura. As we passed over Nagasaki, we could tell it had not been bombed. We continued farther south when our tailgunner, Martin Murray, broke in on the intercom and yelled, "There she goes!" Our pilot made a sharp left turn where I had a perfect view of the bombing from the left blister seat. We continued to Nagasaki where the bomb cloud had risen to about 20,000 feet coming up fast. At about 30,000 feet it began to form the mushroom. Our plane circled around the cloud taking pictures. On the second go around our pilot turned toward our Navigator, Stan Steinke and said, "Give me a course for Okinawa."

When I talked to our Flight Engineer, George Brabenac, a few years ago regarding the amount of fuel left, he said they took a reading on the ground at Okinawa and we had a little over two hundred gallons remaining.

(L-R): Mike Bohon, Dick Cannon, Thomas Bunting, Martin Murray, Francis Dolan

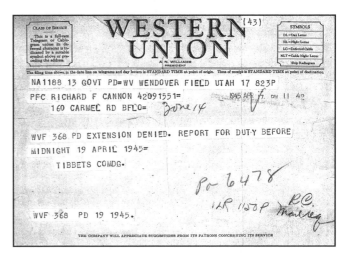

51

CARLSON, EDWARD G.
Project Alberta, Chemist

Letter Home

August 10, 1945

Hello Darlings,

Today was a day off for us so I went swimming in the blue Pacific! The only trouble was it wasn't possible to swim farther than twenty feet without running into rocks that nearly came out of the water. My feet are hot and sore from trying to walk on sharp coral and rocks, slipping off that stuff into water about hip deep and climbing out again. Even the sand is sharp be-

Alice and Edward Carlson

cause it isn't like ordinary sand but is only finely broken coral. We weren't allowed to go beyond the reef where the only deep water is.

Anyhow, I saw some odd looking fish. There were some small bright blue ones the size of minnows and some vivid black and yellow fish swimming in the shallows. Some of the odd coral growths are lovely. Nearly all coral is a dirty white color with a little dirty yellow thrown in. The occasional pretty stuff is lavender and pink and it's not quite so pretty out of water. In the water, it's the cause of considerable sulfurous language because it's so sharp.

One fellow with underwater glasses and a spear hit the jackpot when he got a small octopus with a tentacle spread of two to two and a half feet. That, of course, drew a big crowd. The octopus could change color to suit his surroundings and did. On the beach he was a dirty white color but in the water near brown rocks, he turned from white to brown and white in irregular streaks. The suction cups under the tentacles were small but fairly strong. When let out into the water, he squirted out some brown stuff - Lights out cut me off last night. Anyhow, the ink was darn good camouflage for him. He moved in

spurts and did so by drawing water in an opening at his rear and expelling it through two ports near and underneath his eyes, or so they tell me.

I laid on the beach for about fifteen minutes to get my front side tanned a little and I found that it was enough. I have two white spots where dog tags were against my skin. One leg is starting to peel now from the burn I got the second day here. Oops, time to go. Love, Poppy

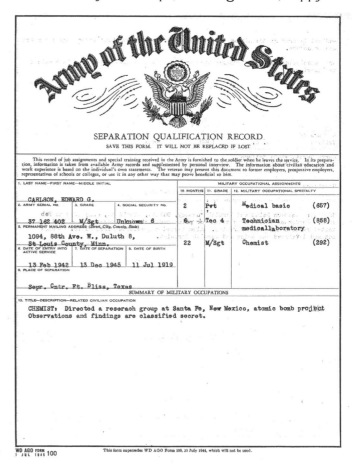

Separation papers classified secret

Enlisted men's beach

Envelope for letter home – still censored after bomb drop

CHAUSSY, PERN
1st Ordnance Squadron, Special Aviation

I arrived at Wendover in late May of 1945 having been transferred as a 2nd Lieutenant from the Army Ordnance Dept. Proving Ground in Aberdeen, Maryland where I was a Proof Officer testing rockets and launchers. The three day trip by train was downright miserable, no air conditioning and windows that would not open. My first impression of Wendover was WOW! Why would a base be located in such a desolate area? I will always remember the glare and heat. Secrecy and security were all around. I realized then I was destined for some high power secret assignment.

We, five of us, were escorted by MPs to individual rooms and told we would be taken to dinner and then interviewed later that evening. I was beginning to feel like a prisoner. Later, I was interviewed by a number of top brass officers and civilian security and intelligence personnel. They asked about my Army experience, education and background. I found out later they had already contacted my parents and neighbors in my home town of New Orleans, Louisiana. I informed the board I had recently received my Bachelor of Science (BS) degree in Mechanical Engineering from Louisiana State University in Baton Rouge. I covered my experience as a Proof Officer and was very familiar with the handling of classified information. Later that evening, I was told I had been accepted and would be working on top secret aircraft bombs. I was not told they were atomic. Security and secrecy were top priorities and I was not to discuss my assignment with fellow officers. The next morning I began training on the Little Boy bomb.

After about 2½ weeks at Wendover, I was told I would be shipping out by plane the next morning at daybreak. Our first stop was in California where I received secret orders to be opened in flight outside Continental US. This was the first time I learned we were going to Tinian in the Marianas Islands.

We stopped at Pearl Harbor and about four islands before arriving at Tinian. We were welcomed by Captain Combs and informed immediately not to rush a suntan as it will come fast enough. On Tinian, I was trained for two major jobs; one, the assembly of the Fat Man bomb minus the critical material, and second, the loading of both type bombs from a submerged pit into the bomb bays of B29s. At the time the two atomic bombs were dropped, Bill Long and I were the loading officers.

After bombs were dropped in August 1945, we spent a lot of time packing for our return to the States. We dumped a lot of equipment into the Marianas Trench off the coast of Tinian. Since my Military Occupational Status (MOS) as an enlisted man was in auto mechanics, I was asked to teach a brief course in auto engines to the men of the 509th. We shipped out by boat in early November arriving in Oakland, California and then traveled by train to Roswell, New Mexico.

My stay on Tinian was pleasant and very enjoyable. My friends in the First Ordnance Squadron and my job experience will always be remembered.

1st Ordnance Quonset Hut #1

Rear (L-R):
Lt. Bill Long,
Lt. William Burgmeier,
Lt. Curt Havekotte
Front (L-R):
Lt. William Shropshire,
Lt. Kenneth Roebuck,
Capt. Harvey Piepho,
Lt. Richard Podolsky,
Lt. Pern Chaussy,
Lt. Bruce Corrigan

CHILDS, RAYMOND
1395th Military Police Company

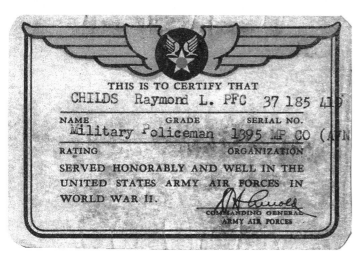

Honorable Discharge ID Card

Raymond Childs

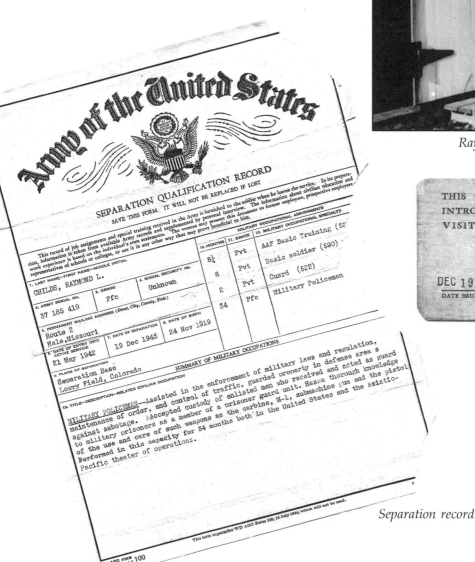

Separation record

COHEN, GEORGE H.
393rd Bomb Squadron, Flight Engineer , Crew B-8

I was a newly winged 2nd Lieutenant Flight Engineer on McKnight's crew in the 393rd when we were designated Crew of the Week. COW was not a term to be found in Air Corps regulations. So far as I know, it was unique to the 393rd while we were in training at Fairmont, Nebraska, although it is possible that the other squadrons in the 504th Bomb Group participated also. What did we do to earn this distinction? I sure don't know. During the week of August 6, 1944, we flew a night mission in a B17F on Wednesday and on Thursday we lost a turret cover on a pressurized flight in B29 #4224476. I have no recollection of the details of this incident, but obviously it was far less dramatic than the time we blew our lower front turret cover over Oakland, California on December 4th. Perhaps our COW designation was more random than meritorious.

The standard COW award was a weekend flight to any city in the US. Our crew flew to Washington, DC which coincidentally happened to be the home of our Airplane Commander. Since B29s in flying condition were precious, we flew the six hour trip to Bolling Field in B17F #423460 on Saturday, August 12, 1944. The crew scattered on arrival. Mac went home of course, Frank MacGregor, our Bombardier, took the opportunity to go to Long Island and get married. Jack Widowsky, our Navigator, went home to nearby New Jersey. Jake Bontekoe and other crew members toured Washington. I hopped on a train and went to New York City (NYC) to visit friends from my high school. I returned to Washington on a train that left NYC at 0350 Sunday morning. I guess none of us required much sleep in those long ago days. Despite a gas leak on #3 engine, we arrived safely back at Fairmont Sunday, after a six and a half hour flight, tired but happy.

It was agonizing to say the least, to send a telegram on 7 Sept 44 to my fiancé in Tacoma: "Do not come to Fairmont to be married. Will explain later." We had just gotten word that we were going to Hell instead of overseas. Wendover turned out to be more like paradise

than Hell when we were married in Salt Lake City on 24 Sept. and had a glorious ten day honeymoon trip to San Francisco. Then instead of going overseas, we spent eight wonderful months in paradise for reasons that we could not understand at the time. Doris Mae and I remember Wendover fondly.

I enjoyed the training flights we made all over the USA and especially the time we spent at Batista Field in Cuba. It did seem, however, that I had to feather engines much too frequently for oil leaks, high cylinder head temperatures, etc. When we finally got B29s with fuel injection, reversible props and no turrets, I felt we were on top of the world.

The turret removal produced my worst experience of the war on 4 December. We were flying at 25,000 feet over Oakland when the riveted cover over the lower forward turret well blew. The explosive decompression blew out parachutes, meal container, my slide rule, our radio operator's oxygen mask, and other things which were near the gaping hole in the floor. Mac, with his consummate flying skill, performed the fastest descent and landing on record at Mills Field, which was a Navy Base. The only one hurt was Jack Widowsky, our Navigator, who was hit in the head by his sextant when air from the rear compartment propelled it from where he had left it in the tunnel under the astrodome. Next day, the local paper reported the things which fell into Oakland came from an Army plane which was reducing weight in preparation for landing!

We had many fun times at the Officers' Club eating, shooting pool, dancing, and loafing. Doris Mae sang in the chapel choir and when we visited Wendover in February 1990, it was poignant to see the chapel converted to a dance hall, as one of the few buildings remaining. We climbed Macgregor's Peak, named after our bombardier, to get a good view of the scenic Salt Flats. Doris Mae and I met on a ski trip near Mt. Rainier in Jan '44 when I was at Boeing B29 school. We really enjoyed skiing at Alta near Salt Lake City and have returned there many times and found it has retained its charm, great skiing, and low prices.

B-8 Crew of the Week, Fairmont AAF
(Note B17 in background; August 12, 1944)

So many times I have been asked the ubiquitous questions, "Do you really think dropping the bomb was the right thing to do?" and "Is it true that many of your Group went crazy after the war?" My answers of "Yes!" and "No!" resound loud and clear. I am certain we helped save the lives of millions of Americans and Japanese.

Crew B-8 being awarded prize for
Crew of the Week

Charles McKnight and Crew, Wendover

(L-R): McKnight, Bontekoe, Widowsky, MacGregor, Cohen, Reeder, Cole, Sherman, Legg

COSTA, THOMAS F.
393rd Bomb Squadron, Bombardier, Crew B-7

After graduating Bombardier School in June 1944, I was sent to Fairmont, Nebraska, went through processing, received equipment; parachutes, gas masks, etc. but at that time was not assigned to a particular crew. I met our navigator, Bill Collinson at one of the meetings. Afterwards, we walked to the aircraft line, got into the nose, I in the bombardier seat, Bill in the pilot seat. We were checking out the equipment, Nordon Bombsight, etc. and the group of officers outside operations milling around. We found out later they were looking at planes assigned to their crews. I said to my navigator, "Look at that young man over there. I wonder how he obtained clearance to get on the field. He sure looks young and small amongst the big aircraft. He's bound to get hurt. I hope he's not our pilot". With that, the young man, in flight coveralls, started walking toward us, clipboard in hand, making notes on his pad. He came to the plane, gave us a wave and when we got out to meet him, he introduced himself as Jim Price our pilot and crew mate. We swallowed hard as he did not fit the picture we had in mind of someone to take us into combat.

As I found out later, this man was a combat veteran of Guadalcanal, had probably 30-40 missions over there, many hours of combat and used a B17 not only as a bomber but for strafing. My understanding was during one of the battles, he and two other planes flew over a Japanese cruiser, planted two bombs right on deck and between the three aircraft sank the cruiser.

After flying with Jim Price for three or four missions, we learned quickly this was a man who knew what it was

Lt. Tom Costa standing in front of crew's quonset hut. Railings, adirondack chair and bike garage made by Tom when not flying missions

all about. We found he was an instructor in B17s and was waiting for transition to B29s which he did with ease.

My crew had never had any experience dropping the Little Boy test configuration bomb, however, we dropped some Fat Man configuration bombs at Inyokern Range, California, Wendover Range nearby and Salton Sea area in California. I understand the special ordnance people would locate the bombs dropped at Wendover Range and dig thirty feet down in the ground to retrieve

August 14th mission to Nagoya (Arsenal Factory). Fat Man bomb can be seen in lower part of photo

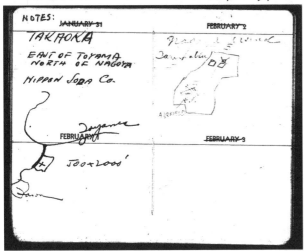

Tom's notes from August 14th mission

them. The practice pumpkins did not contain high explosives but were filled with concrete to the right weight. It also contained a quantity of black powder spotting charges which would detonate on impact. In bombardier training, they rigged the practice bombs to have a black powder receptacle in the end of the bomb and on impact an inertial driven pin would strike a shot gun shell which in turn would blow up the black powder creating heavy smoke for spotting the hit. The hit would be observed from above and photographed by the large aircraft camera. When we were scheduled for pumpkin drops, our plane was previously loaded at the loading pit and the plane was put on the line ready for flight. Every phase of loading was kept from us due to tight secrecy.

My navigator, Bill Collinson and I, had a great part in turning our pilots reddish blond hair white. After the war had been declared over, we were on a flight to slow time an engine in the process of getting rid of a lot of equipment no longer assigned to us. Sgt. Herbert Norder in charge of bombsight maintenance, called me over to ask if I would do him a favor on my next flight. He said, "I have this extra bombsight head we scrounged for parts, it's not on my list, cannot be taken to the States so would you deep six it next time you are over the Pacific?" He gave it to me in a bag and I brought it back to our barracks. Bill Collinson saw it and we agreed it was too good to let go of without making something of it. We developed a scenario to replace the head of our present bombsight with this one. When we were slow timing the engine, I started my theatrics of being fed up with the war, wanting to go home and not dropping anymore bombs. Bill opened the bomb bay doors, I took the replaced bombsight, walked past the pilot, copilot, and navigator and threw it out!

1st Lt. Tom Costa, Bombardier, V-84 'Some Punkins'

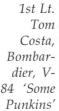

(L-R) Christine Croft, Beverly Croft, James Price, Tom Costa, Jacqueline Shoemaker. The convertible belonged to Jim's girlfriend Beverly. She named the car Pocahontas. Beverly also dated Everist Bednorz, co-pilot.

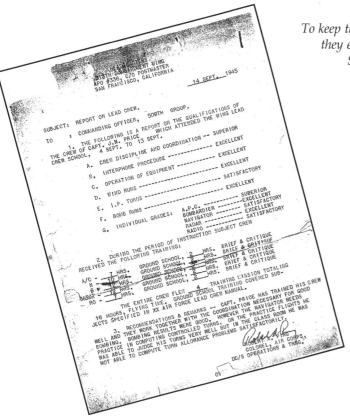

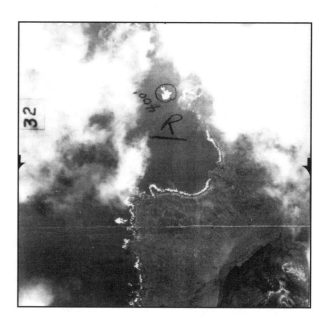

*To keep the 509th flight crews busy on Tinian,
they experienced Lead Crew Schooling,
September 4 to September 13*

DE CUIR, LAWRENCE
1st Ordnance Squadron, Special Aviation

I was in Berkeley at the University of California. In October 1942, I enlisted in the Air Cadet Program, Armament as that was the only option available. Later, I switched from Armament to Engineering.

I was called up in April 1943 to Boot Camp as an Aviation Cadet in Boca Raton, Florida. I went to Yale University where I successfully completed communication training and was commissioned in the reserves with my Military Occupational Status (MOS) in Communications. I was asked if I would like to attend Radar School, was sent to Harvard, upon completion received a certificate, then went on to Massachusetts Institute of Technology (MIT).

From there I went to Lincoln, Nebraska and Dalhart, Texas, both intermediate staging areas; then to Great Bend, Kansas where I was assigned to a bomb group in the Radar Maintenance effort for either the group or squadron level. I along with some enlisted men worked with them several months successfully setting up a complete first and second level eschelon that could service the effective elements and train people, if needed, for the Radar Maintenance Station at Borinquen Field in the northwest corner of Puerto Rico.

I went back to Great Bend and was sent to a Miami school to learn another radar system, the ANAPQ7 that had a small wing protruding from the bomb bay. Upon completion, I returned to Great Bend where there was no opening for me, so the Administrative Officer suggested an opportunity with my background at Wendover Field Utah. I talked to several people and officers who suggested I "grab it" as this place was very political.

In April 1945, I went to Wendover, reported to Major Charles Begg, Commander of the 1st Ordnance Squadron, who is one of the best officers I worked for in the military. He said they were one of the best electronics supports for a program he couldn't tell me about. Tucker told me it was an Atomic Bomb. Security was impressed on me.

I remember an officer in the 1st Ordnance Squadron that worked for Begg at the Salton Sea Ground Station acquiring and transmitting data associated with the dummy bomb drops. He happened to speak in a bar about working on a unique program that would have a major effect on the course of the war - He vanished to Alaska with his stuff still in Wendover. I remember Major Begg showing me a letter from him requesting to come back from Alaska. Major Begg looked at me, shook his head and said, "He knows better than that." O'Keefe said it was of such importance that if Hitler had this he could win the war. It had no significance to me at the time; they both told me this was something you did not talk about at any time to anybody. I did not want to go to Alaska.

I remember sitting in the officers' club when a flight crew member, navigator, said, "I know what we are working on, it's an Atomic Bomb isn't it?" I was sitting there; I had to respond. "That's an interesting speculation, we will have to wait and see, won't we?" He shook his head and walked away. I made sure my face had no expression.

Major Begg gave me some material to assemble for a future operation involving equipment attached to bombs dropped in the Salton Sea. They were instrumented to determine what the characteristics were so bombardiers could accurately set their bombsights. I had no interaction with technical activities other than instru-

menting the dummy bombs. I worked three or four weeks, then prepared general electronic tools, equipment, supplies and spares, while Los Alamos prepared material to go into the bomb for shipment overseas to Tinian in early June or July via the Green Hornet.

Occasionally, someone would call me from Los Alamos saying they were getting really noisy signals. I'll never forget suggesting they mount a telemetry transmitter using Zeus fasteners so it wouldn't shake all over. (A Zeus fastener isolates the physical mounting of the equipment itself to the carrier and the thing it attaches to with rubber that prevents any shock or harsh movement on the back plate of the dummy bomb.) If you want to instrument some aspects of the bomb's air motion, you need a transmitter sending information to the ground that won't shake to pieces. You physically isolate the transmitter from the shaking device holding it. A week later they called at 10:30 pm wanting me to be their technical contact at Wendover.

The purpose of the signals on the dummy bomb was to tell the people on the ground what was happening to the bomb physically. Was it shaking, tipping, filming the bomb's movement, was it a continuous frame by frame signal? If you send telemetry, it is a continuous signal on strips going up and down with no gaps enabling you to process, evaluate, make changes and see how well things are working based on what you see. Changes may have been made to fins looking at the basis of the telemetry. Then they would drop another bomb to see if the characteristics they were concerned with were improved. I worked on the Fat Man Bomb in charge of the X-5 Unit which was only on that bomb.

I was defined as the physical interface to Archie Combs. Whatever the Los Alamos Group on Tinian wanted, I got it. Everything pending they asked me to do had to be worked through the Administrative Organization rather than instantly. I did not make regular progress reports. The technical aspects

Our Tinian home

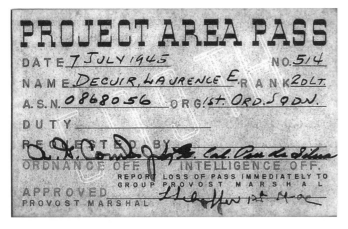

We were able to buy one bottle ration every month, so we had excess for a party.
(L-R): Larry De Cuir, Phil Barnes, Dick Jeppson, George Koester

of the unit; the clock box, archies and other devices that would set off the bomb, were run by Dr. Ed Doll from Los Alamos. Stevenson of Los Alamos was responsible for the X-5 Units.

The flight crew guys were always speculating; I remember one night on Tinian there was a blackout with everything shutdown for quite a few hours. There was a suspected air raid. This was before the bombs were dropped. The marines did not take the island and we were warned there may be Japanese who would swim over at night, so don't go out. If you walked off the designated areas, there were tennis shoes, all over the place, with foot bones in them from Japanese soldiers killed on the island. If you kicked a shoe, you could hear the foot bones rattle.

We had selected the site for our tent not too far from the latrine and got the OK from Major Begg and Captain Archie Combs. I drew a sketch of the tent layout and where it was in respect to the Quonset Huts the other officers of the bomb group lived in. We all joined in and made our individual contributions. Of course, we hung out together from early days at Wendover, so it sort of fell into place.

I remember Smitty, Leon Smith, did the major effort of getting the tent and shipping crates that formed the floor of the tent and the attached screened in patio. He and I negotiated on the supports under the floor so that it would not sag, buckle, or bounce when we were all in there. Needless to say, it was a great success and the envy of the other officers. I remember reading in one of many books about the 509th where Jake Beser made some jealous remarks about the elite quarters we had.

I had a refrigerator in the X-5 building where we had support ice and mixes for adult beverages we served to our distinguished guests as documented in numerous pictures of our screened in patio. The most fun I had was to hop into a jeep, drive to the X-5 building, get a drink with ice and sit in our screened in porch.

When Lt. Shropshire and I were getting ready to shut down the operation in the X-5 assembly Quonset hut, we received a copy of an official Army Air Corps Tech Manual (TM) that explained the process of assembling and testing the X-5 units. Shortly before our return to the states, we were advised, by phone, to destroy all of this material, which we did. About five years after I was discharged, I was contacted by phone, at my place of employment, to verify this had been accomplished. I answered in the affirmative and referred the caller to my associate Lt. Shropshire.

A party in our tent, July 1945
Bruce Corrigan, Project A person, Phil Barnes, Larry De Cuir, Security man, Morris Jeppson, George Koester

DESMOND, WILLIAM
393rd Bomb Squadron, Pilot, Crew A-4

I remember the Sloppy Joe pictures were taken using a manganese flash. The powder was in a tray and a spark would ignite it filling the room with smoke after a good flash.

From the time we were told of a strike tomorrow, usually late afternoon, meetings were held for all bombardiers together, all navigators, all pilots, etc. till 10 pm. Planes were checked, we had a visit to the chaplain, supper, midnight, then dressed and were driven with our gear, in trucks to the flight line to our individual plane pad.

Individual tasks were performed on the aircraft and by 2:30 am, we were rolling down the taxi ways. Planes took off every 3-5 minutes. We were flying missions in June. Not all 393rd planes were at Tinian until August.

Our plane V-73 was in the first group of three departing from Wendover. Our first mission in late June was to Nagoya; Mitsubishi heavy steel industry. Before this, we were practicing on local islands. One mission for us was cancelled; the bomb fell out of the bomb bay onto the coral pad. I had been under the bomb checking the

air pressure to close the bomb bay doors (1250# / in 2). Ordnance personnel had been called to check the hanging mechanism. No one was hurt, just scared.

DOANE, PHILIP E.
1st Ordnance Squadron, Special Aviation

I received orders to travel to Wendover Field, Utah, in early 1945 from Casper, Wyoming Air Base where I had been assigned to the base machine shop. I was working with the maintenance crews in maintaining the B24 Bombers that were used in training for overseas duty. Some of the crews that came through were boys from my home town I had gone through basic training with.

When I arrived in Wendover Field, Utah, I reported to the assigned office and was interviewed by Captain Archie G. Combs, Jr. In our preliminary discussions, he asked me what I knew of Silver Plate. Having never heard of the Silver Plate Project, I answered that as a machinist I was familiar with the process of silver plating as well as cadmium plating. He told me I was being considered to work on a project that would require secrecy. He seemed to be satisfied with my answer about silver plating. Considering what I later found out about the Silver Plate Project that seemed quite reasonable.

I furnished the names of several people that could vouch for me as to my character and past activities. In the meantime, Captain Combs indicated I would be assigned to the 603rd Squadron for quarters and rations since the First Ordnance Squadron was not yet formally activated. He cautioned against talking to anyone about the project and said Secret Service personnel are apt to be listening to any conversation that I might have. He

indicated the references I had provided would be contacted and when this had been completed, I would be cleared to work as a machinist on the project. After about a week or ten days, clearance came through and I was issued the passes that permitted me to work in the section of the base that had been set aside for the work we were to do. Our work area was a part of the desert that extended out from the main base area. Our own security forces guarded the gates leading into the work area but we did not have any patrolling inside the gates. When we had a mockup bomb ready for a practice drop, a heavy canvas covered the gadget as we called it, for transport to the loading pit near the runways the bomb crews used.

The First Ordnance Squadron, Special Aviation was activated and we were assigned to crews. I was assigned to Assembly Crew #3 and most of my work was on the Fat Man Bomb. We struggled to fit the various castings together to make the complete assembly of the unit.

After I had been working for several weeks and progress was being made toward taking the 509th Composite Group overseas, I was told by Sergeant Freddie Denton I was going to be granted a furlough. I boarded one of our flights to Oklahoma City on a C47 and made my way to Shattuck, Oklahoma, where my mother met the train about forty miles from home.

One of the first questions she asked me was, "Did you get that secret job"? I asked her what she was talking about and she told me an Army Colonel had been to see our neighbor Ed Parvin and had told him he was checking on Philip Doane because he was being considered for a secret job. I told her I could not tell her anything which was the truth. She indicated that Ed Parvin told her the Colonel told him he should not tell anyone about his visit and questions because it was supposed to be kept secret. Ed said to my mother, "You are his mother and I don't want to know anything about your son you don't know so I am going to tell you about this anyway". Good American that she was, she never mentioned it again.

She did inform me another neighbor had a visitor, an Army Colonel, who was looking for information about Philip Doane but didn't say why. There was speculation that the Doane Boy had gone Away Without Leave (AWOL) because the Army was looking for him. I found out later my high school mathematics teacher had received a visit by an Army Colonel who was looking for information about Philip Doane. She was in the Elk City, Oklahoma hospital to give birth to her first born son and was interviewed in her hospital room just prior to delivery.

Among other references I had given was one by my former high school basketball and football coach, Hack Witherspoon, who had left coaching and had taken a position with the Oklahoma Highway Patrol. I know he was visited but I never heard any comments other than he had received a visit by an Army officer regarding my reference to him. I assume he got a good report, otherwise my future would have changed at that point.

Lots of activity indicated a major move was to occur and most of the 509th Composite Group shipped by rail to Seattle for transport to what proved to be our final destination, Tinian Island in the Pacific. I was not sent by sea but was kept behind to help train other personnel that would continue to function on the project. We did not question any of the reason for any activity that was occurring because it was obvious something pretty important was in the works. We never heard the word atomic although I do remember on one of our three day passes into Salt Lake City, in

a hotel room where a group of us had gathered, we heard someone report he had heard our gadget was a weapon that, if successful, would destroy a city the size of Salt Lake City.

The following is an account which I wrote in a little notebook in 1945 when I flew to Tinian Island from Wendover Field, Utah on a C54 509th Aircraft piloted by Lt. Henderson. We began our flight July 16, 1945 the date of the first atomic explosion in the New Mexico desert.

It took 2 1/2 hours to fly from Wendover Field, Utah to Hamilton Field, California where we spent 7 1/2 hours for processing. We flew across the Pacific Ocean taking 12 1/2 hours to reach Hawaii staying 5 hours while the C54, Wendover Special, was serviced and refueled for takeoff to Johnston Island.

In 1939, the Navy was awarded a construction contract to build a Naval Base on Johnston Island which was nothing more than a lot of ocean bottom composed of coral dragged up from the reefs. They completed it in August 1941 in time for the Japanese to bomb during their December 7th raid on Pearl Harbor.

Upon our arrival, it looked like an airplane carrier from the air but proved to be quite a large field where we spent 1 1/2 hours for an Air Transport Command (ATC) stop. Since it was meal time, we went into the Naval Mess Hall or galley whatever they call it, for chow. The traffic was tremendous because the flow of material from the European Theater of Operations (ETO) and USA was just getting up its impetus. Now it is one very important island inasmuch as it is strategically located for servicing Air Transport Command Craft and Naval Craft.

Assembly Crew #3
Top Row (L-R) 1) Buford L. Locke; 2) Harold W. Kirby; 4) Philip Doane.
Bottom Row (L-R) 2) John P. Nagy; 3) Howard Rosenthal

The next stop for us was Kwajalein. We arrived there in the middle of the night and as soon as we stepped down the ladder from the plane it began a downpour of rain that sent us back after our raincoats, though it stopped very quickly. We thought this island was much more desolate than even Johnston, small as it was. Mud, no water to drink, heat that was stifling, and very poor food. We were there about an hour and were glad to get into the air where it was nice and cool.

I suppose we were all wondering if the next island would be better than Kwajalein as we knew it would be for a longer duration. Most of the outfit was already at Tinian having been gone for over a month from Wendover. Part of them had left by air and part had shipped out by boat at the time the outfits supplies and material had been sent. The ones who had gone by air had been there a month and the others a shorter length of time since it took them two weeks traveling by water.

Since it was dark and would be until we arrived at our final destination, we all tried to get some sleep. There were ten of us besides the crew who kept pretty much to themselves in the cabin ahead. Seven of us were enlisted men and the other three were officers. The wheel was with us along with his wheel which made quite a bit of brass on board. Colonel Paul Tibbets was with us.

Tinian at last! By the lights that shown up at us, we could tell it was quite a large island. There were still a couple hours before daylight so we couldn't tell much about it. The plane was met by several officers who had come over before so we all piled into jeeps, weapons carriers, and trucks heading for the mess hall to get a bite to eat before it became light enough to unload the plane. Driving along the two or three miles to the barracks, we could smell the green vegetation as it had just finished raining. The men were waiting by the vehicles when the officers came out of the mess hall to go to the plane. The Colonel on down to us privates pitched in and soon we had all our bags, packages, firearms, field packs and some freight unloaded.

By this time our old gang of transportation men were there with Military Police (MPs) and guards to take the freight. They questioned us about what we had brought and in turn we were curious about fishing in the ocean, whether there was any fresh water fishing on the island, how many Japs there were and innumerable other questions.

When we went back, it was full daylight and we could see the area was right on the edge of the ocean. The men were coming back from chow carrying their gear back to their huts and tents. We saw a lot of our buddies that had been sent over ahead of us and I especially looked for the one that owed me $10 so I could send a cable home since I had only $1. However, I was informed by the 1st Sergeant, the quickest way to get a message home was an Air Mail letter and even that took seven or eight days.

DOUGHERTY, DORA JEAN (McKEOWN)
WASP (Woman Airforce Service Pilot)

At the time the 509th was started, Col. Tibbets arranged for me to fly cargo out of Wendover for him. My fellow WASP (Woman Airforce Service Pilot), Mary Helen Gosnell was with me. Her boy friend had just proposed to her before leaving and instead of a ring, gave her a puppy. The puppy was on a diet of warm milk and pablum. She took a thermos with warm milk, pablum, and the puppy in a zippered bag and put it the radio compartment of a C47. As passengers, we took turns in the copilot seat. We were at 10,000 feet when she went back to feed the dog and forgot what happens in a vacuum at altitude. She unplugged the thermos and had warm milk and pablum explode all over the compartment and us when we arrived at Wendover (DWV) on October 23, 1944 at 23:00 hours. We spent the night in the "Guest House" in the hospital. The nurses' barracks were to become our permanent Wendover home for the two months we would be stationed at Wendover.

Next morning, we had our first daylight view of the base. The cold Utah mountain air greeted us and I saw my first mountain. There it was at the end of the runway, dark and brooding. We officially reported in and as we became acquainted with the base, we saw the warning sign: WHAT YOU HEAR HERE, WHAT YOU SEE HERE, WHEN YOU LEAVE HERE, LET IT STAY HERE!

The need to obey those signs was emphasized, we knew not why.

I was assigned to the Base Unit as a Civilian Pilot. Everything was so secret, I can't tell you exactly what I did. I had a mission flying a C47 with a bunch of men in the back. I was told to fly at a certain altitude, certain heading, climb; we went all over the desert doing these things. I learned in later years from a man at Los Alamos that I was flying the "Dipsy Doodle", probably practicing bomb fusing.

Dora Dougherty, WASP 43-3

Mary Helen Gosnell

Before the days of pictorial navigation devices, you could tune your radio to a frequency for a given airport radio range and it would spell out the three letter designation in Morse Code. That way, you would know you had the correct radio aid to navigation. Wendover would be -.., .—, ...- (DWV). If you heard that combination of "dits and dahs", you would know you were tuned to Wendover. All flight crews had to know the code in those days.

When I left Wendover on 20 December 1944, it was because the WASP program was disbanded. I cleared the post and turned in all my "gear" there. I caught a ride with a flight leaving Wendover and heading to the East Coast. They stopped in Chicago to let me off.

DOWNEY, JOHN L.
393rd Bomb Squadron, Bombardier , Crew A-2

On a bright sunny day, June 10, 1944, a group of Aviation Cadets, mainly washed out pilot aspirants, marched to the San Angelo Bombardier School post theater just outside the city. After a number of speeches related to what a fine group of patriotic, potentially heroic and without doubt the finest to ever graduate from the school, we were transformed from Cadet status to Flight Officer or 2nd Lieutenant (Lt.) and magically became Officers and Gentlemen. What we didn't know at the time, it was a carefully guarded secret, was from midnight June 9 till we accepted our commission about noon June 10, we were discharged from service as Cadets, were civilians and could have gone home. Another opportunity lost. As a reward for having achieved such an honor, we were given a fifteen day delay enroute to our next duty station that I spent traveling from Texas to Columbus, Ohio for my first leave in over two years of servitude. If you think that's an improper choice of words you were never a Cadet. After re-introducing myself to my family and convincing them I was really their long lost son, they permitted me to stay with them till it was time to head for Lincoln, Nebraska for assignment to a Combat Crew Training Station.

We were presented with orders to proceed without delay to Fairmont Air Force Base where our crew was formed in mid 1944 at Fairmont, Nebraska, as the 504th Bomb Group, 393rd Bombardment Squadron. The Operations Officer advised that I was to become a member of Capt. Costello's crew and to check in with him at the morning daily briefing. I arrived early to eyeball my new leader and request a change in assignment if needed. However, Captain Edward Costello looked OK so I reported to him in my best military manner, you remember, "Reporting as ordered, Sir", complete with salute. His response was to stick out his hand, "Glad you're here, we've been waiting for you. Come meet the rest of the crew."

We trained in B17s, flying cross-country, dropping bombs, shooting landings, flying night missions, high altitude missions, getting to know each other, our jobs and learning to backup each others duties. This along with some infantry training in small arms practice, joined the

Air Force to avoid this sort of thing, was a pretty busy period with little off duty time, just as well as Fairmont's night life consisted of milking cows and rolling up sidewalks. Just kidding, there were no sidewalks.

At the end of our training, with bags packed, loaded aboard the troop ship, apparently we were judged combat ready and were waiting for orders. Our 393rd Squadron orders were cancelled on the scheduled day of departure with the 504th consisting of the 421st, 398th and us. About 10 pm that day, we were issued new

orders stating the 393rd was no longer part of the 504th but now a part of the 509th directing us to proceed without delay to Wendover Air Force Base, Utah.

I had a 1930 Ford Model A Coupe and along with others loaded my B4 bag starting a long 1000 mile odyssey drive. A fellow bombardier who also graduated in class 44-8DR, assigned to the 393rd, joined me in the trip, driving straight through to Salt Lake City without incident and completing the journey to Wendover the next day.

I Remember:

The hill at the west end of the east / west runway which required a circuit around it to get enough altitude to get over the mountains; the German Buzz Bombs being test flown; the local Sheriff with his Lincoln-Zephyr Squad Car, shades of the Green Hornet; when an engine prop reversed on final approach; the night the Officers Club burned; Destination I and the dropping of the first live bomb; Dave Semple and the first time I experienced a store drop on Salton Sea as a passenger with a flight / test crew; a four ship formation flight to Cuba with Tibbets, Taylor, Costello and ?; shooting ducks at the hot lakes; Kenny Wey being encouraged to name his new daughter Bombsa; Wherry housing - back in the early days of the draft, many troops were being moved about the country and those with wives and families were hard pressed to find any housing at all, let alone reasonably priced. To alleviate the situation and no doubt to ensure his reelection, Senator Wherry introduced a bill in Congress that resulted in the government funding the construction of housing units at bases across the country. Wendover had two types of housing, just west of the main road into the base were a series of barracks type buildings each containing about 20 one bedroom apartments while to the east and just north of the base's perimeter were a group of buildings each made up of 4 two bedroom units shaped in a quad arrangement. All these buildings were to be occupied by both enlisted and officer personnel. You had to get on a waiting list but the rents were reasonable.

During the tour at Wendover, our crew was scheduled to participate in a three airplane formation flying practice with Col. Tibbets as lead, another crew as left wing and we at right wing position. As this was our first opportunity to try out formation flying, we were all looking forward to the experience. The other two planes took off, started to form up and orbit while waiting for us to join up. Getting tower clearance to start our takeoff roll, throttles were opened, we picked up speed, raced down the runway, all was normal, we lifted off and started our climb out to join the other two ships.

Just another day at the office, then the gremlins made their appearance; when gear and flaps were up, power was reduced at least on three of the engines but number two continued to roar mightily at full military power. This situation is not good either for the engine or flying formation. Being unable to correct the problem which turned out to be a broken throttle linkage, an emergency was declared and we started a 180 degree turn back to the runway we had just left, making a straight in approach for a downwind landing. The landing was smooth but quite fast and we were eating up landing space rapidly. The A/C yelled to the Flight Engineer to cut all four engines but communications weren't all they should have been and he cut number four instead which added to the pull of the runaway engine on the other side. He immediately saw the error of his ways and cut the remaining three engines. To overcome the impending ground loop at a rather destructive speed, both pilots stood on their left wheel brake pedal along with pulling strenuously on the emergency brake handle and were successful in bringing the B29 to a shuddering halt out on the blacktop runup area at the end of the runway. But wait, that's not the end of the story.

As we all breathed a sigh of relief and started to unbuckle our seat belts, the A/C saw a huge cloud of black smoke pouring from the left wheel well and assuming the plane was on fire from the jammed throttle, rang the emergency bell to tell everyone to abandon ship as quickly as possible. As he stood in the aisle by his seat saying "Everyone out, I'm last", he didn't realize he was blocking me from leaving the bombardiers position in the nose and as a result, I was the last to depart. I wasn't concerned since by then I figured nothing else could happen, everything that could already had. Wrong!

Once on the tarmac, we could see the smoke was from the overworked, overheated brake linings and the plane was not on fire. At that time the crash crew and fire trucks arrived from the far end of the runway, where they had expected us to be and would have been if we had flown the pattern and landed into the wind. They grabbed fire hoses, ran to the wheel well and prepared to wet down the superheated landing gear, but were restrained by the A/C and belated common sense. We never did get to practice formation flying.

As part of our B29 training, we practiced flying missions utilizing different power settings, various bomb loads, at different altitudes, under differing climatic conditions to maximize the radius of Siverplate airplane action and it was under these simulated combat conditions the following adventure occurred.

Our crew was sent to Eglin Field, Florida to perform a mission flying over both land and water for an extended period with a conventional bomb load in a typical combat mission environment. Piece of cake. Early one morning we collected our flight gear, met at the airplane, got our mission briefing from the A/C, preflighted the plane (remember pulling 16 blades of each of the 4 props through?), boarded the plane, settled in our various positions, started engines, proceeded to takeoff heading east out over the water for our first check point which was Bermuda, turned north after passing the island and flew our assigned power settings, monitoring fuel consumption until we reached the midpoint of the flight.

At this time, we were at scheduled bombing altitude and dropped our bomb load on a white cap, the bombs were dropped safe so we didn't harm any ocean life. We then continued our flight to Bangor, Maine where we turned southwest and headed back to Florida over land and at a lower altitude. Soon we had used up our daylight, it was dark outside and we were all feeling the effects of having been immobile for hours, so when we reached the Mason-Dixon line, we were groggy and wishing the trip was over.

We could see ahead of us a towering cumulus thunder storm with bright flashes of lightning, however, everything was running smoothly and there was no great concern. I was laid back in the nose compartment with my feet propped up on the metal of the nose glass, about half asleep, when I was disturbed by a light, so I looked over my shoulder to see if the copilot was using his flashlight, when I saw that he was also relaxed. Looking back to the nose, I saw there was a little ball of fire on the end of the temp gage that stuck out through the glass and there were little streaks of blue light flickering back and forth across the nose glass from metal to metal. I immediately removed my feet from said metal and became quite alert. Then I realized I was experiencing St. Elmo's fire, a static electricity generated by the electrical storm we were in at the time.

As time passed and fuel was consumed, it became obvious that distance to home and remaining fuel were on equal footing, a not too desirable situation in case of a problem. For insurance, we tried to contact other fields along our path but were unable to do so since the storm wiped out our radio communications. We were also unable to contact Eglin Field.

Things were getting a little tense, so we decided on two plans of action; Plan A was to proceed to Eglin and if possible land; Plan B was to put the ship on autopilot headed out to sea and bail out over Florida if Eglin was socked in. We had reached the point of no return when we finally made contact with the tower at Eglin and requested a weather status. The tower responded, "I'll contact the weather officer" whereupon he was mildly directed to look out the window and see if we could get in, his response was "I guess so".

Fate smiled, we got a small break in the clouds and were able to spot the runway just ahead but close in. A steep approach put us over the end of the runway, as the copilot started to flare and cut power, I could see from the nose position that we were still about 10 to 15 feet in the air and advised him we weren't on the ground. He replied, "Yes we are, I felt the gear touch." My response was, "Wait and see". We dropped in but didn't bounce and no damage was done since we were so light from having used up all our fuel. It was the most welcome landing to date.

The next day, it was found the fuel tanks didn't have enough fuel in them to wet the dip stick. It seems that whomever set up the power settings, altitudes and other mission criteria, cut the safety margin pretty slim.

At Wendover, we trained in B29s developing bomb delivery techniques; spent some time in Cuba for over water training, spent more time dropping inert pumpkins on a target anchored off shore at Salton Sea and Destination I which was Naval Ordnance Testing Station (NOTS) Inyokern, California. Since they had instrumented bomb ranges, we were the only airforce on the Navy Base. Our crew dropped the first bomb that had the explosive blocks in it. Part of the reason for spending eighteen months at Wendover was waiting for the bomb to be developed.

Finally as the development phase was nearing completion, the 509th started its move to Tinian. Ground and support troops went by ship and the air troops flew their planes to Tinian via Hawaii and Kwajalein.

During this time period, the need arose for some crews to wait at Wendover until three more stores were ready for use. Our crew, Capt. Zahn's and a flight test crew

from the 216th Base Unit, each in turn went to Albuquerque to load a store in the front bomb bay and from there to Mather Field, Sacramento, California for part of aerial embarkation.

Also during this time frame, Capt. Costello, Lt. Davis and myself were sent to New Mexico to witness the Trinity Test, collect all appropriate data and deliver it to Col. Tibbets on Tin-

(L-R): Tom Brumagin, Harry Davis, John Downey

ian. As it turned out, the UC45 we were flying was low on fuel and we landed at Kingman, Arizona to refuel only to find the civilian employees had gone home for the day and there was no way to get fuel. So we spent the night and went on to White Sands the next day, thus, missing the Trinity Test. However, we did collect all the necessary data.

This is a story of coincidence and relates an incident that took place sometime in June 1945. Captain Costello and crew had been dispatched on a training mission to practice cruise control procedures which required being away from home base for several days and it was during this mission that we were staying overnight at an Air Force Base in Florida. We had finished supper at the mess hall and retired to the Officers Club for dessert. While sitting at the fountain, I was aware that close by was an officer, in an unfamiliar uniform, who was giving the clerk a request as follows, "Vanilla cream with chocolate sauce, please", in a marked British accent. The clerk asked that the order be repeated, and the officer responded as before. I could see from the clerks puzzled expression that he was not sure what he should prepare and that he didn't really want to ask again. I caught his eye and said quietly, "A chocolate sundae." The British Officer turned to me with a thank you and that was the start of a friendly conversation. It developed that he, a Major in the Royal Air Force and Group Captain Cheshire were on an official visit to the States and were returning to England the next day. We were joined by Group Captain Cheshire, met with the rest of the crew and chatted awhile in the lounge, getting acquainted and swapping flying experiences. Later, we ended up playing low stakes poker through most of the night and enjoyed a great evening of learning about the British way of life in the Royal Air Force (RAF), as well as their poker playing techniques. We parted company with each group going their own way, back to England and we, back to the mission, with best wishes all around and no further thoughts about our meeting.

About a month later, we landed on Tinian, having transported the Fat Man bomb from the states. We dismounted from the airplane and were greeted by the other crews already on the island. We were quite surprised to find among the personnel, none other than Group Captain Leonard Cheshire. We renewed our acquaintance and were both amazed at our meeting again under such different circumstances. He had joined the RAF at the outbreak of WWII and by August 1942 was promoted to squadron commander. In March 1943, he became the youngest group captain in the RAF at age 25. In November 1943, he commanded the 617th Squadron, the Dam Busters. In 1944, he was awarded the Victorian Cross (VC) for completing 100 missions over Germany. Upon his return to England, he was designated, by Sir Winston Churchill, as the official British observer of the atomic bomb dropped on Hiroshima. He was then the official representative of the new Prime Minister Clement Attlee. He was created Lord Cheshire in 1991. He founded over 240 homes in 50 countries over the world for the care of people with physical or mental disabilities, this stemming from his deep shock of seeing the effect of the atomic bomb. Lord Cheshire died on 31 July 1992 of Motor Neuron Disease.

On July 24, 1945, Capt. Costello and our crew departed from Wendover AFB under sealed Top Secret orders in B29 V-95 fully loaded and ready for overseas

V-95 in flight over Tinian – Nagasaki weather plane markings still on tail.

duty. Upon reaching altitude, the orders were opened and we were directed to Kirtland Field in Albuquerque, New Mexico. Special personnel took our aircraft to a remote site to load a Fat Man Special Store #F31 into the front bomb bay; a complete store contained 10,500 pounds without the trigger mechanism. We departed for Mather Field, which was our aerial port of embarkation for the Pacific Theater landing there July 28, 1945. Mather was under jurisdiction of the Air Transport Command (ATC) and although our airplane was brand new with only 11 hours of flight time, all emergency gear and survival equipment had been thoroughly inspected, we had to permit Mather personnel to check everything. This created an awkward situation since we were under strict security measures and no one but our crew could enter the airplane.

Mather personnel were allowed to open the external storage bays near the top of the fuselage just above the wing. The contents were removed, inspected and repacked in the bay. The door to the area was hinged at the bottom and latched at the top. The door had to be safety wired from inside the airplane. Since Mather people were not allowed inside the airplane to safety wire the latch, the task was turned over to our people, but unfortunately and nearly fatally, no one passed the word from the base personnel through several other security paths to our folks.

About noon July 29th, we were ready to depart Mather Field for John Rogers, Hawaii. We had a fully loaded airplane; 19 people on board, crew, ground crew, security agent, bomb in front bay, rear bay full of luggage and other material we were transport-

Loading 50 cal. guns on V-95

ing to Tinian, plus full fuel tanks. With a takeoff gross weight of 136,000 pounds, we were quite overweight. We had filed a spurious weight and balance form to guard the security of our cargo, but takeoff was normal.

At about 30 to 50 feet in the air after lift-off, the gear had just started to retract when a loud "Whap" noise was heard and felt by the pilot through the control column. Immediately the airplane started to shake violently and started to nose down. Pulling on the wheel and rolling in trim tab wasn't helping and the pilot called to the copilot, "Help me Harry". Harry was 6 foot 3, weighed 220 pounds and in good physical shape which made the difference. As was soon discovered, the inside, unwired, emergency equipment bay door had been sucked open by the slipstream over the wing and all the survival gear had ejected; the 7 man raft had inflated and was wrapped around the right horizontal stabilizer and other items had struck the tail ripping the fabric being torn loose by the air flow. The jammed control was barely moveable and the turbulence caused by the debris on the tail was causing the plane to vibrate uncontrollably.

Being in a climb out attitude, still building air speed accentuated the problem and the pilot believing a crash landing was eminent, turned to the left about 10 degrees to line up with a better crash site. In doing so, the raft was dislodged and the violent shaking somewhat lessened.

As soon as we could reach a safe altitude, attitude and airspeed, the tower was contacted and advised of an emergency landing. When asked our weight, they directed us to fly till 120,000 pounds was reached taking about 5 hours. We responded we were coming in now. The landing was hot but uneventful with both pilot and copilot on the controls. Rollout was controlled by the reverse pitch props that aided with the excessive landing speed caused by our weight. The entire event only took about 15 minutes of real time, seemed to be much longer but resulted in the most welcome landing of them all.

The aircraft was repaired and we took off about midnight arriving on Tinian August 1, 1945. Capt. Zahn and a flight test crew also carried bombs; one damaged and unusable, one disassembled and sunk in the Marianas Trench after the war and the one we carried was dropped on Nagasaki.

I believe the reason we were assigned the responsibility of carrying the bomb was our crew was reliable, had the best rating for performance, our commander was a West Pointer and followed orders to a T. Colonel Tibbets knew he could depend on us to carry out the mission successfully.

DRAINER, WILLIAM C.
393rd Ordnance, Radar

Wendover's location, which was about 100 miles from anywhere, proved also to have some positive effects on people. In my four years in the Air Force, there was a feeling of respect and closeness for each other that I never experienced anywhere else. Now, as a psychologist, I can understand why! The subconscious mind guided each person toward the security of others as a reaction of one's survival instinct. To compound this instinct was the fact that the selection of personnel was super - a collection of truly fine people.

There are many wonderful memories of Wendover. One, however, was not too pleasant.

Since I flew on Colonel Tibbet's original crew and he didn't fly that often, I had to fly with other crews sometimes to achieve my monthly flying time.

On one of the other crews, after the practice bombing run, and as we were returning to Wendover, the No.1 engine - which had been running rough - burst into flames. Soon the flames were streaming back of the engine to almost touching the tail. We finally landed at Wendover and came to a screeching stop. Everyone was excited and ran - fearing an explosion!

We heard a thud and looking back, the engine had melted from its position and had fallen to the runway. Soon the Fire Safety Team arrived and quickly had everything under control.

This is my best memory of Wendover! There are others—Leaving Wendover for Tinian, on the Enola Gay, was comparable to the time I left home and family in West Virginia in 1942. I had that same feeling as I looked down at the airfield and thought that life wouldn't be that nice again!

DULIN, JOHN W.
393rd Bomb Squadron, Navigator, Crew A-4

A couple of brief incidents while in Batista, Cuba: Major Jim Hopkins made it mandatory for aircrew members to do some type of physical exercise on days that did not involve flying. It appeared that most of us were having a little too much fun on our off time. Havana was a great place to party and the price of alcoholic beverages was really cheap.

During one of our exercise days, at least two crews were in the workout area, Hopkins and McKnight. Five Cuban Air Force biplanes, I forget the nomenclature, flew in. They were supposed to play the base softball team. It seems the base team was on the southern end of the island with the exception of the pitcher. In effect, the potential game could not be cancelled after all the Cubans did to get to Batista Field. It wasn't. The 393rd crew members filled in all the positions except for the pitcher. The Cubans had full softball uniforms and equipment. The 393rd guys looked quite raunchy, GI boots, some shirts, partial fatigues, and perhaps the need of a bit more rest from the night before. The Cubans were good players, but not too hard to hit. Our guys had a ball. It was fast pitch and the Cuban pitcher was pretty accurate, but not very fast. Our pitcher must have been a graduate of the summertime municipal games where the fast pitch was really required. He was fantastic, both accurate and hot. I did the catching and rarely had to do anything but catch the ball and throw it back. I also had two wads of extra padding in the mitt to lessen the sting. I don't remember the score, but it was one-sided. We were all hitting. We all shook hands at games' end, watched the Cuban team climb back in their biplanes, still in softball uniforms, and waved them off. It was a very unique and enjoyable afternoon. Hopkins allowed that we had our workout and could hit the showers.

While on the TDY tour to Batista Field as Hopkins' navigator, I dated a Cuban lady who worked on the base. We went out several times, always accompanied by a chaperone. On one of the dates, I was taken up to a very nice apartment to meet my dates' grandmother. She had no knowledge of English, nor did I of Spanish. She wanted to know what I did in the military. The term navigator did not mean much to her, but after many tries and the assistance of my date, the grandmother suddenly exclaimed aloud, "Ah—Navigatoro!" It sounded good enough to me. I never saw the grandmother again, but thinking of her now and then brings up a pleasant memory.

1945 Tinian

Referring to the early bomb release. Crew A-4 was scheduled for a mission. We were on the hardstand. I had just finished my preflight. It was dark and the airplane was on putt-putt power. I was standing with my radar operator, Bill Cotter, perhaps 60 feet from the starboard side of the fuselage when we heard a loud click and physically felt a thud on the ground. The bomb bay doors were open. There was a moment of total silence and then a few personnel started running. We just stood and looked. Why run? Bill Desmond had left the bomb bay just before the drop. He was lucky. We were obviously cancelled. Most of us got our gear and were returned to quarters. I don't know how or what caused the release or how they put the bomb back into the plane.

The skull, no crossbones, was an actual skull along with a sign on top of our hut. The skull was actually found on Tinian. Nationality is unknown but it's not hard to figure.

Referring to Destination I is Inyokern, California, for test bombing. I offered you fine quarters, fine clubs, fine food, lots of Navy Waves, soft schedule, friendly atmosphere and direct involvement in a highly motivating project for the crew members, yet very classified. "One more time, Yes Sir!"

Another bonus. Upon departure, we were given permission to buzz the Navy Base. Treetop is a good description. But there were no trees. Just above ground level was more appropriate.

Referring to the piece of shrapnel. I'm holding it as a keepsake. Crew A-4 observed what I think was the first drop of the 10,000 pound bomb for ballistics and other requirements. The piece of shrapnel came from the resulting crater. The metal was still warm when I picked it up. Crew A-4 made the follow-up drop. McKnight's crew was at Inyokern when we were. His crew probably made the drop.

John Dublin, Navigator
#13 Strange Cargo
D9th Composite Grp.
Havana Fab/1945

Carmen: —
Convent educated in Kansas —
Excellent family —
Introduced to her Grandmother as a "Navigator" —
all dates chaperoned —

Letters Home:

August 29, 1943

Dear Hilda, Here it is Sunday and already nearly time for lights out. Yours truly is plenty tired but completed my low pressure test and passed with flying colors. That means I'm eligible for high and long distance bombing. Hot Dog! I originally wanted to be a bomber pilot but now I'm a cinch to get a bomber. Here's the statistics on the pressure chamber:

1330 - Started for preliminary jump to 5000 feet
1340 - Came down, one man couldn't clear ears
1342 - Started up again
1350 - Hit 18,000 and stayed for 10 minutes without oxygen. Atmosphere is cut to 1/2 (7.3 pounds per square inch). Anoxia, a numbing of the brain, ears and eyes from lack of oxygen, begins to hit all 19 of us.
1360 / 1400 - Put on oxygen masks; it became brighter, things were easier to concentrate on and could hear much better. Started up again.
1419 - Hit 38,000 feet (7 miles up). Atmosphere is 1/5 that at sea level. Breathing 100% oxygen. Eyesight normal, hearing not so good. Sound passes very poorly in thin atmosphere. Nothing is unusual. Feel swell. Two fellows with gas pains. Stomachs bloated out, but came out OK.
1519 - Started down. Everything swell. Ears were easy to clear.
1530 - Stopped at 18,000 feet. One man can't clear his ears. Pain is Terrific for him. Jumped up 3,000 feet in one second! Hard on us, but it helped the guy clear his ears.
1549 - Hit sea level. Everything in the pink.
There you have it. I had no trouble whatsoever. Only two had trouble in our bunch. However, in the bunch

(L-R): William Desmond, Paul Gruning, Grumersindo Oro, John Dulin, Lou Allen

following us, seven men had to be carried out. So you see, it's not just another test. It determines a heck of alot. All in all, it was a swell experience.

December 20, 1943

Dear Lydia, Frank and Gang.

I received your swell cards today. Thanks loads to all of you. I really appreciate them.

At present, I'm up at Indian Springs for my first week of flying. This morning, we were supposed to take off at 0700 but were rained out, fogged out and clouded out. Some weather for a desert, huh? Tomorrow, we'll try again.

We're supposed to get six missions in while up here, but now because of the weather, it's already been cut down to five. We'll be doing all our flying in B17s and will fly from four different positions. They are: the waist guns on either side, upper turret, lower ball turret and the newly mounted chin guns operated from the bombardier's seat. Our flying is divided into three different types of shooting. The first is; air to air, second; high altitude, third; air to ground.

In the first type at 10,000 feet, we shoot at a target that we pass or that passes us at varying speeds. There we'll be using the waist guns and the upper turret along with the ball turret. In the second type at 20,000 feet, we get up fairly high in order to check our oxygen equipment and get acquainted with it while shooting. There we shoot, with the upper turret and waist guns, at a target that crosses over us at various angles. In the third type at 200 feet, we fire from the ship into targets on the ground. Our gunnery class is the first to be taught any type of strafing whatsoever. In fact, it's so new that last Saturday was the first time the instructors had a crack at it! We'll use the chin turret, ball turret and waist guns for that stuff. We'll only be 200 feet off the ground, so it should be a lot of fun.

We're located about 60 miles out of Las Vegas which is exactly in the middle of nowhere. The usual desert and mountains are the scenery. A few of the mountains have snow on them. We live in 14 x 14 foot

tents with six men in each. The tents have a wooden floor and are boarded up halfway. In the center is the little GI stove which is usually blazing away whenever we are in the tent.

The food around here is straight GI but is plenty good. Our shower rooms etc. are about 1 1/2 blocks away. It reminds me a lot of basic training at Jefferson Barracks, It's a lot easier now though, because we've learned how to take care of ourselves.

Say, I've been told that a few of you have the flu. Let's not have anymore of that stuff! That's an order from a potential officer. That's what they tell us. But seriously, take good care of yourselves. If my delay enroute comes through, I don't want to see anyone in bed unless he or she is just sleeping.

That's about all there is to say about this place. We'll head back for Las Vegas on Christmas Eve and conclude our training with one more week of flying.

Please write soon, that is when you're all feeling better. I'll be waiting anxiously for a letter per usual. Love, John

August 14, 1945

Dear Lydia, Frank and Gang,

You'll have to excuse the stationery and pencil because I'm afraid it's the best I can do under the circumstances. You see, at present Crew A-4, of which I claim to be navigator, is on its way to Japan for a raid. We're 400 miles northwest of Tinian on our way to Iwo Jima which is used as a navigation check point on all raids. Our altitude is only 6,000 feet but will go higher as we hit the Empire. So far the trip has been smooth except for weather we are attempting to dodge. In fact, dead ahead of us is a small line of thunderstorms we'll have to go through. You can probably note the difference in writing because of the cloud's turbulence. This one is a very light one in comparison to others. Some tend to flip you over and that's when it's time to worry. Speaking of worry, you've saved me an awful lot of it by all your prayers. Incidently, it's raining like mad right now. Some of it is hail and is making itself really heard on the glass.

Just for your information, it's 2100 hours or 9pm on 13 August over here. We were dragged out of bed around 0500 this morning and were notified of this mission. We had thought we were all finished with all the peace offerings, etc. going around but it looks as if we were definitely

wrong. Of course, it's only our fourth mission so it doesn't bother us much yet.

You're going to have to skip the incoherence of the letter because it is just picked up and lengthened at odd and spare moments.

Have just picked up Iwo Jima by radar, our ground speed is 230 knots or 265 miles per hour. We passed Iwo Jima at 1306, my estimated time of arrival (ETA) was off a few minutes but my course was perfect.

It is a good hour later now and we had a little amusement for ourselves. I went to drop a smoke bomb to read drift but the darn thing went off before it got completely out of the plane. As a result, yours truly has a new name, Golden Boy. It so happens that the bomb gives forth a golden powder and this plane is just one mass of gold inside. Oh well, anything to break the monotony. Right now we are at 13,000 feet and still going up.

We have just sighted the Japanese mainland and are now putting on our chutes, etc. We have no flak suits in the front of this ship, somebody forgot them.

We just passed by Osaka and it is smoking from an earlier raid. Now we are up to 32,000 feet and funny as it may seem, my feet are getting cold. Lou Allen, our bombardier, has just spotted the target. The bomb run is over and Lou made a beautiful hit. We are now going up to see if our last mission was successful. We are going to take pictures of it to determine the amount of damage done. We got some good pictures. We are

Off to work

leaving Japan after flying over it for 1:07 hours. You probably wondered if we saw any flak, etc. That is something we are not allowed to say yes or no about.

Iwo Jima is next in our path of flight again. it is straight ahead. We have just been buzzed by two P51s and a mess of Corsairs. Our altitude is now 18,000 feet. I'm going to straighten out my leg and go to sleep. We have been flying over nine and a half hours so far.

Back again. I slept for one and a half hours. We are only about half an hour from Tinian but they woke me in order to give the radio operator a position report because they had seen ten shots of tracer ammunition go up into the air. It is probably someone in a life raft as a result of a bailout or crackup. Soon planes and boats will be out scouring that area. You can see they take pretty good care of us.

The sky is full of B29s now, all returning. You can't see them but their formation lights make their presence known. It looks like a rat race.

I'll conclude this imitation of a letter on normal stationery.

We got down OK after Joe Westover, our pilot, jockeyed around awhile for a landing position. After interrogation, we were given doughnuts, coffee and lemonade by the Red Cross. Then we went to the mess hall for a real meal about 2400 hours or midnight. This was followed by a quick shower and a nose dive into the sack for eight solid hours of sleep. We woke up this morning at 0900 just in time to hear the announcement of the end of the war. Needless to say, everyone was happy. Our only regret was we got so few missions to our credit. At 1100 this morning, we had Mass for the Feast of the Assumption and tomorrow we will have a solemn field Mass in thanksgiving for the war's end.

Well, I guess that brings us pretty much up to date, so I will close for now. Who knows, maybe I will be home before long. Will be waiting to hear from. Yours, Johnny. PS: Deane Churchill, my old copilot, says hello. You don't know him but he has heard a lot about you. At present, he is slightly happy celebrating the war's end.

8 September 1945

Well, she's all over for sure now. MacArthur just took up housekeeping in Tokyo today. More power to him. I will take up my keeping back in St. Paul. As to

Capt Joe Westover
Airplane Commander
#73 Strange Cargo

when that will be, the Lord only knows. The points for a second lieutenant are now up to 85 and at that rate, I will be in the Army quite a while because I'm still a comparative rookie as far as time goes especially overseas. I've been over here for three months and have only four missions to my credit and that doesn't begin to compare with the mess of veterans we have here. Remember Johnny Pearson, the one I met in the park during our picnic in Minneapolis last summer? He has twenty-two missions to his credit. He would have had more but was sent back to the states for a few months to a lead crew school. A lead crew is one that leads a formation over the target and determines the dropping position for bombs away for the whole formation, especially in radar bombing.

All of our fifteen crews were rated lead crews upon our arrival. Despite that, we had to go through a school over here. Now that the war is over, we are going to it again. Why, I don't know. Maybe it is because most of the 20th Air Force is slightly peeved at our good luck. By good luck I mean our outfit stands a good chance of getting home before the majority of the outfits, despite our newness. This time I know why, I think. It is probably because the 509th is the outfit with the atomic bomb that you may have heard a little about. The bomb was the reason for our staying in the States for so long a time. I think the time spent was pretty well justified in the end. As a result, they may try to keep us together as a group for a while yet.

If a few improbable miracles were pulled off, maybe I would be able to get home in time for your vacation, Frank. Once I get settled at home again, you will find you have an intruder on your hunting trips. The Army gunnery school, November through December 1943, tried to teach me how to use a shotgun and at present, I think I can still hit about 50% of what I aim at. At least that is much better than before I came into the Army. Too bad I can't get buckshot for a .45. I am an expert with that gun, according to the Army ways of marking. Wouldn't I look cute blasting away at a pheasant or rabbit with a .45? But enough of

John Hubeny and Joe Westover confer before mission

this, I only hope I'm not being too optimistic in reserving a spot at home for Christmas.

Our ship has been named Strange Cargo which is appropriate if you remember page 2 of this letter. The name is depicted by a hard working stork carrying a baby girl in the traditional diaper. The odd thing is, the girl seems to have aged about twenty years and has her share of attractions. Her appearance is very presentable to everyone, including the Chaplain. We are pretty proud of that gal of ours. Quite a few Seabees and Sailors have come around to have their pictures taken by her and I can't blame them. Speaking of pictures, I should have quite a few of them by the time I get back. The trouble is that over here, we haven't too much in line of facilities for developing so we'll have to wait until I get back to see them. I have one roll of Archbishop Spellman of New York, taken during a Mass here on Tinian, when he stopped during a tour. He is the head of Catholic Chaplains in the Armed Forces.

Guess that's all for now; so wishing all good relations with my favorite gang, I'll close hoping to hear from you again real soon. Love, John

Standing (L-R)
Fred Hoey, Ralph Taylor, Michael Angelich,
Raymond Biel, Charles McKnight, John Dulin, Louis
Allen, Jack Widowsky, William Desmond, George Cohen,
Jacob Bontekoe, Franklin MacGregor, Robert Donell,
Joe Westover

(L-R)
Front Row: Ralph Taylor, Fred Hoey, John Dulin,
Louis Allen, Franklin MacGregor, Robert Donell,
Joe Westover, Jacob Bontekoe, Back Row: Michael
Angelich, Raymond Biel, Charles McKnight, Jack
Widowsky, William Desmond, George Cohen

EASTON, WILLIAM L.
393rd Bomb Squadron, Pilot, Crew A-3

One night at Wendover, I received an assignment to go to one of the shacks on the high hill. When I entered, I was told I was going to sit and listen to telephone calls. It was a long shack with a lot of telephones and lines and I was to be the only person there. I had a tablet to record the calls and answers for which I had very little data. A typical call would be "John called Mary asking Mary for a date in Salt Lake".

I think to frame it properly, we were getting ready to move overseas. I think I was prompted to listen to anybody who might be talking about ship dates and move dates. It was a great assignment. I never met anyone else assigned to this task.

On Tinian, I traded a bottle of whiskey to a Seabee for a scooter that he had made. I added a couple of gears on it so it would run better. Leon Cooper, our bombardier and Fred Olivi had one and we ran around the island a lot. There was a lot of bartering going on.

Wiliam Easton relaxes in Cuba

EIDNES, KENNETH L.
393rd Bomb Squadron, Computer Specialist

I had always liked airplanes and when the war broke out, I wanted to become a pilot. I studied and learned as much about aircraft as I could. Taking the tests for both the Navy and Army pilot training, I passed with good grades. When it came to the physicals, I could not pass them; low blood pressure and over weight.

So on November 17, 1942, I enlisted in the Army Air Corps, given the serial #16143854 and sent to Camp Grant, Rockford, Illinois, for processing. Sent to Sheppard Field, Texas, for basic training and testing and by mid December, I was sent to Lowry Field, Denver, Colorado.

I was scheduled to attend the Norden Bombsight School but as that class was full, I was sent to Power Operated Gun Turret School. It was here that I would meet George Robert (Bob) Caron, who became my best buddy. After finishing that school, Bob, Herb Prout and I were asked if we would like to attend a new school on Central Fire Control System made by General Electric Co. Finding out that this was a new system of gun control for a new aircraft yet to be built, we decided it would be a good deal. Upon completion June 19, 1943, at Lowery Field, Denver, Colorado, we were sent to Boeing Aircraft Plant at Wichita, Kansas, and attached to the 58th Bomb Wing at Marietta, Georgia. At Boeing, we developed the targets and system to harmonize the guns and the sights. This system was then used by all B29 armament men. We learned how the planes were put together, spent much time in the altitude chamber learning how lack of oxygen would affect us in case we lost pressure. At this time, only two B29s were in condition to fly; the XB29 at Seattle and the YB29 #36954, the first production ship built at Wichita.

The story of how Eddie Allen, test pilot, died in a fiery crash of the XB29 was out and it did not help to get volunteers to fly the first YB29 #36954 on it's maiden flight on June 26, 1943. We drew straws and I was picked to fly as scanner to watch the engines and report any fires or other troubles. No one was to know that the plane would fly that day, but the whole town of Wichita came to the field to see if that big bird could get off the ground. Soon after takeoff, I reported a large amount of smoke coming from #3 engine. The flight lasted only about 10 minutes and we made an emergency landing. I had always thought it was a fire that day but

Kenneth Eidnes

found out many years later that an oil ring was left out during assembly and caused a very large oil leak.

Wichita was a busy town; open 24 hours a day, so our social life was full.

Col. Tibbets saw that we had time to enjoy the pleasures of the town.

As this aircraft was a new conception, there was much testing to be done and the Army Air Corps was assigned to do a lot of it. An officer was put in charge of testing and came to Boeing at this time. Lt. Col. Paul Tibbets had just returned from England where he had completed a tour of combat flying B17s. We took the second YB29 #36955 to Pratt, Kansas, where I was attached to the 40th Bomb Group, 25th Bomb Squadron. We flew many hours testing all the components of the aircraft, the fire control system, recommending changes to be made and testing the changes that were made. It is well known that the biggest problem was the engines.

While at Pratt, I got a three day pass to visit a friend in Wichita. This was a lady I knew that had a young son about a year old. This day she could not get a baby sitter so as we were going to a movie, we took the boy with us. While walking down the street holding the baby, we met Col. Tibbets. He said, "Ken I did not know your wife was here, you better take the week off and show her the town." It was years later when he found out that I was never married and we had a good laugh over that.

October 1, 1943, I was assigned as Director of Armament Tests for B29 Aircraft. I worked with Cliff Woodward, engineer from General Electric Co. setting up the equipment. We had bombing and firing ranges in Kansas that we used very much. The only problem was that Kansas had open range laws and we were killing too many cattle that had roamed onto the firing range. This was NOT done on purpose but flying at high altitudes, you could not see what was on the ground. To correct this, we took our plane and on October 25, 1943, we left Kansas and went to the Air Forces Proving Ground at Eglin Field, Florida, to continue the testing of our B29. On board with me were Tom Pake and Herb Prout. This was to be temporary duty but it lasted until 1945.

We were joined there by Col. Tibbets and Bob Caron who had flown the XB29 #118335, the third one built, from Seattle, Washington. It was equipped with a Sperry Hydraulic Armament System and we were to compare this with the General Electric System we were using on the other plane. The Sperry System had a periscope you sighted your target with. It went out the top and the bottom of the plane and in tracking a target, it would flip from top to bottom when the target passed the horizontal. The image in the scope would flip over and appear to be upside down. Very confusing. That plus the fact at high altitude the oil would freeze up caused us to reject it. The GE System proved to be very accurate, getting 75% hits at 1000 yards.

While at Eglin Field, I flew and worked with the following people: Paul Tibbets, Bob Lewis, Bob Caron, Wyatt Duzenbury, Charles Sweeney, Charles Albury, John Kuharek, Albert "Pappy" Dehart, Ray Gallagher, John Wright, Abe Spitzer, Charles "Herb" Prout and Tom Pake. All these men ended up in the 509th Composite Group.

We flew many times to see how long we could stay up or how much weight we could carry. We tried to make the flights as much like a combat mission as possible. I recall one flight where we were to drop our bombs and fire the guns over a bombing range out over the ocean east of Newfoundland. It was hard to tell if any ships were down there but we dropped on the range. Soon they let us know they were there, as anti-aircraft fire soon burst out in front of us. Another was to be made with maximum load.

The runways at Eglin were too short so we went to Pine Castle Airfield near Orlando, Florida, which had 11,000 foot runways. Paul wanted the ship in top shape and all the valve clearances checked. As only we were

allowed to work on the plane, I took the valve covers off, Paul checked the valves and I put the covers back on. He was as full of grease as were the rest of us. We used every inch of the runways to get off with the full load. I often think of this in later years when Bob Lewis said that Tibbets did not have experience in flying heavy loads.

In extended firing, the guns would get hot and could "cook off" by themselves. This happened once while flying over the Gulf of Mexico. Both #1 and #2 engines were hit so the pilot told us to put on our chutes. Henry Ellis, in putting on his chest pack, pulled the rip cord and the chute opened in the plane. We rolled it up and told him to hold it in his arms and that he was lucky as he knew his would open. We made it back and landed on two engines OK.

About this time, the plants that made or modified B29s were having trouble getting help to properly install the armament systems in the planes. The whole system had to be perfectly level with the plane body for it to be accurate. Col. Tibbets then put some of us enlisted armament men in the plants to teach the workers the right way to install the equipment. As we lived in hotels, we were paid $7 a day living expenses for 30 days. After that, it went down to $5 a day. So Paul Tibbets would rotate us so we would always collect the $7. One of the plants wanted us to return after we had been there so Paul Tibbets made a deal with them. In addition to the money we got from the Government, the company would pay us another $7 a day plus the hotel bill, free meals in the CO Cafeteria and furnish us with an automobile for our use. Col. Tibbets really took care of us as by March 1944, we had been promoted to T/Sgts on flight pay, our total income was $591 per month. That was a lot of money in those days.

When we flew from plant to plant, Col. Tibbets carried a Cushman Motor Scooter aboard the plane. As the plants were large, he could get around real well. We told the female workers, we also had coke machines and bunk beds on board. They did not believe

Exploring the island – (L-R): Jack Wright, George Caron, Sidney Bellamy, Charles Prout

Ken Eidnes

us but in reality, the first YB29s did have four bunk beds in the rear compartment.

In Florida, the nearest town of any size was Pensacola, a Navy town. Air Force personnel were not welcome there. So one day, Col. Tibbets said to us, "Go get cleaned up, bring some extra clothes with you and meet me down on the flight line". He loaded us in a B17, flew to Atlanta, Georgia, and dropped us off. He said, "I'll be back in four days so have a good time".

March of 1944, the 58th Bomb Wing was to leave to go to the CBI. The B29s were in sad shape as all of the modifications had not been done and they were not ready for combat. President Roosevelt had promised the Chinese that the planes would be there. So came "The Battle of Kansas". We were working in a plant in Birmingham, Alabama, when we were ordered to get to the airport pronto. All the passengers were taken off the airliner, including an officer of general rank and our bunch of GIs got on board. The general was hot until we showed him our orders to perform an emergency war mission. We flew to Chicago and after refueling went on to Pratt, Kansas. There for three days and nights, we worked on the planes and as we finished the crews got on board and left for India. This was sad for me as this was the outfit that I was a member of. When all the planes were done, we were allowed to get some rest. We slept for 24 hours without getting up at all.

May 18, 1944, we went on a practice mission, full bomb load, full ammo and gas. We dropped the bombs and fired the ammo over the ocean. Got a call to take the plane to Boeing in Seattle, Washington, for modifications so we could do some heat tests as the planes in India were having engine cooling troubles. We left Seattle June 16th to fly to Muroc Lake, California. On the way, we hit a down draft over the mountains falling 5,000 feet before we recovered. The bombsight came loose and smashed the nose glass, tow bar fell and broke the leg of our

navigator, tools flew all over the place and punched holes in the skin of the plane. We had to make an emergency landing at Hammar Field, California. As the B29 was still a secret plane, we were told to tell people at the airfield nothing. We had to remove the bomb arming wires, empty out the fired and unfired ammo. This along with the damage to the plane got the people wondering and they started to ask questions. That afternoon President Roosevelt told the people in a broadcast that B29s had bombed Yawata, Japan, from the base in Shangrila. The people thought we had been on this raid and we were treated like kings. Steak dinners, fresh eggs for breakfast and anything we asked for was given to us. We did not let them know anything different. After the plane was repaired and the tests were run, we headed back to Florida. From California to Florida we set a transcontinental speed record, 7.05 hours and we could not even brag about it as no info on B29s was given out.

Just to let you know how many hours I spent in B29s, here are flight times for some months: May 1944 - 48.25 hours; June 1944 - 52.00 hours; Aug 1944 - 22.30 hours; Sept. 1944 - 35.05 hours.

In the Fall of 1944, I went home on furlough and when I got back to Florida, the rest of the guys had all gone to a new outfit, the 509th Composite Group. I was to remain at Eglin and continue my work. I worked on testing the B32 Bomber, radar controlled tail guns on a B29 and most fun was using JATO units on the B29 so we could overload the planes with big bombs, one of which was the British Grand Slam weighing in at 10,000 pounds. On October 25, 1944, I signed up to attend a computer school in Denver, Colorado. These are the computers used on the B29 armament system.

Several times Col. Tibbets and Lt. John Wright came down on business and I was told when I joined them that I would be home as a civilian by Thanksgiving of 1945 as they were working on a project that could end the war. I did make it home the day after Thanksgiving so they were almost correct.

On July 16, 1945, Col. Tibbets came to Eglin Field flying one of the 509th C54s. I told him I was glad he was now a Bird Col. He asked me if I would like to join the old gang overseas. I told him yes but my commanding officer won't let me go. He went in and talked to him and when he came out he said go in and ask for a transfer. In my best military manner, I went in and asked for a transfer, his reply was to go pack your things as your orders are being cut right now.

I went home for a few days to tell my folks I was going overseas and they would know when I got there as they would hear about it on the news. I was only kidding but when the news was that an atomic bomb had been dropped, my Father said he knew I was a part of that outfit.

*Ken Eidnes outside his Quonset Hut
on Tinian*

I went by train from Chicago to Wendover, Utah, got on a C54 and flew over to Tinian. Very boring flight over the ocean so we played blackjack that cost me $13. On Tinian, I lived in a Quonset Hut with the enlisted men of the Enola Gay and the Great Artiste, who were mostly my old friends from Eglin. It was like going home to be with them again. I got to fly three practice missions on the Enola Gay with Bob Lewis and crew. Bob Lewis would like to spend time in our hut and would often bring over a bottle of whiskey to share with us. We would use Coke as a mix. After the war ended, he went to Japan with Tibbets and brought back some Sake for us to try. He also gave us some Japanese money that we had the crew members of both atomic missions sign. My money with signatures on it is in The Air Force Museum at Dayton, Ohio. When Sweeney found out that Lewis was spending time with us, he told him it was not proper for officers to spend time with enlisted men. So that ended that.

We had much free time as the war ended, swimming, exploring the island and just enjoying ourselves. Rats infested our huts; food or candy could not be left out as they would eat it. The noise they made was loud and we would get up and chase them, using brooms or clubs, we would try to kill as many as we could. Many evenings were spent down in the Enola Gay with Dick Nelson listening to Tokyo Rose on the radio. She would say that the fighter planes would be waiting for the Black Arrow Squadron planes. She played good old American music so it was worth while.

The food that was served to us was top grade with plenty of it. The only time I would not eat was when Australian mutton was served. It had a terrible smell. Speaking of smell, the Japanese civilians lived in camps that were enclosed with barbed wire. They saved their "night soil" to use on the gardens which gave the camps a very strong odor. Still many GIs were treated for barbed wire cuts on their backs.

Receiving mail was the high point of the day. Our outgoing mail was censored so we could not tell what we were doing until one day it was said that mail would not be censored anymore. We wrote and let it all pour out; several days later the mail was returned to us and we were told to write it over as the censorship was back on.

On the island, we were allowed one bottle of 3.2 beer a day and 3 cokes a week. As I did not drink beer, I had many friends that would take over my ration.

To give us some idea of what we had been using (atomic bombs), we were given lectures on the theory and construction of the units. It was quite basic but did not let us know all the problems that were involved in the making of the different bombs. This did not last very long and was soon stopped.

I left Tinian in October 1945, on an APA Troop Transport. We stopped at Saipan to pick up customs men who wanted to search all our baggage. Col. Tibbets was there to greet us and set the customs people straight. We passed through without anyone looking at our stuff. We got on a train and went right to Roswell, New Mexico. I was discharged from the service on Nov. 21, 1945, having spent 3 years and 4 days in the service of my country.

I might add that during our testing, Paul Tibbets included the enlisted men in all the plans. He would explain what we were trying to accomplish and what he expected from us. In our opinion, he was and still is a fine gentleman and we are proud to have served with him.

FELCHLIA, ALBERT O.
320th Troop Carrier Squadron, Navigator

The mission of the 320th was to transport needed 509th personnel and material. Many of the service people and civilians were scientists assigned to the "Manhattan Project" involved with development and delivery of Atomic Bombs. The 320th planes flew all over the United States, Cuba and overseas to Tinian. Many local flights returned to Wendover the same day, but most were overnight or several days temporary duty (TDY). By the time I joined, flights to Cuba were being phased out.

The 320th Troop Carrier Squadron with Major Charles Sweeney as Commanding Officer (CO) had five airplanes; two C54s and three C47s that were replaced with C54s before we flew overseas. In March or early April, Major Sweeney became CO of the 393rd Bomb Squadron and Captain John Casey became CO of the 320th.

When the 393rd Bomb Squadron, comprised of twenty B29s with crews, was transferred to the 509th, it was reduced to fifteen crews plus additional flight personnel brought in by Colonel Tibbets leaving some of the 393rd crew members without a job. Some were assigned to 509th Headquarters, others transferred to the 320th including: Gold, McKinney, Mills, Angeli and Henderson became Airplane Commanders; Bruenger, Churchill, Ames and Delaney were Pilots; Lyon, Mann, Sheer, Waggoner and Wasz as Navigators. Six Pilots, three Navigators, some

Flight Engineers and Radio men were later added to complete the flight crew requirements.

Overseas flight crews consisted of three Pilots: Airplane Commander, Pilot and Copilot; two Navigators, first and second; two Radio men and one Flight Engineer. They were oversized to cut down on the ground time enroute to Tinian and back to the States.

On the C54 flight deck, the Pilot had left seat, Copilot the right; Radio man sat behind the Pilot; I, Navigator, sat behind the Copilot facing the side of the plane. There was a small window over the deck allowing for some side vision. The Celestial Bubble (for shooting stars and sun) was over the walkway beside the Navigator's area where I would slide my stool to stand on when taking a shot.

The C54 had a crew room just aft of the flight deck with two bunks and a third over a 500 gallon gas tank in the tank compartment. The latter was my favorite since it was darker and cooler. A crew storage cabinet was over the 2nd 500 gallon gas tank (one tank on each side of the plane). The tank compartment was between the crew room and the passenger/cargo compartment. Thirty or more passengers sat on collapsible canvas seats along the sides of the airplane. If freight was hauled, the seats were folded and the entire deck was available for cargo. The deck was fitted with recessed tie-down stations to secure all cargo from shifting or breaking loose.

Prior to starting overseas flights for 509th support, the 320th C54s were decorated and received the nickname "Green Hornet Line". A green stripe was painted on each side of the fuselage starting aft near the tail as a point, growing to a width a little wider that the windows, continuing the length of the fuselage just past the front window. From this point was drawn a large wing that terminated in a circle containing a Walt Disney type winged Burro with saddle bags flying between two Pacific Atolls, under the Pilot's window. These decorations were unusual for the time and received considerable notice wherever our planes flew. A small black replica of the Burro was painted just forward of the logo each time the plane flew to Tinian and returned to Wendover. In addition, a small green winged circle with a white numeral was painted on the tail.

At Wendover, most of the buildings were covered with tar paper, including Bachelor Officers Quarters (BOQ), Officers Club and Enlisted mens Barracks. Each BOQ room comfortably heated with a coal furnace had two occupants with standard Army cots. The administrative buildings and quarters, sided and painted, were for the permanent party (personnel assigned to operate the base and provide support for the 509th missions). Special passes were issued to off limits areas housing top secret activities with special agents on guard. The only one we could identify was Major Uanna, Chief of Security, who was probably OSS or FBI. Security was stressed! We were not to speculate, write or talk about the group's mission or activities to anyone. Since my education was high school level not centered on sci-

Inside C-54, setup for transporting passengers

Inside C54 setup for transporting wounded on stretchers

ence, I had no clues about the mission of the 509th, but later heard some had guessed to themselves until the results were known.

The B29s were classed top secret because of their equipment and crew members along with maintenance workers were the only ones allowed near them. It was a known fact that Lieutenant Colonel Leutcke, Deputy Commander of the 393rd, flew one of the B29s on an unauthorized pleasure trip to Dallas, gave his father a tour which was against regulations and was shipped to Alaska within sixty minutes of his return to Wendover. From his time of takeoff, the Special Security Forces had him under surveillance documenting all movements. The manner in which this incident was handled made a lasting impression on everyone.

Many flights from base were kept secret by getting clearance for one airport then, when out of radio range, changing destination to designated area in our orders which were alphabetically coded such as Los Alamos was A; Naval Test Station at Inyokern, California, was I and so on. The flights to and from Tinian varied slightly by going to Johnston Island from Hawaii or directly to Kwajalein. After leaving Wendover, our first stop was Hamilton field, a distance of about 600 miles (air miles based on nautical miles) or three hours; a port of entry and exit. It took four to six hours to go through formalities. We were then cleared to fly to Hickham Field, Hawaii, a distance of about 2100 miles in 10½ to 13 hours, depending on wind speed and direction. After staying six or more hours, we left for Johnston Island 600 miles and 4½ hours to service the plane and eat. From Johnston Island, it was about 1400 miles and 8½ hours to Kwajalein. From Hawaii to Kwajalein, it was 2100 miles and took 11 to 13 hours. From Kwajalein, we flew to Tinian about 1300 miles and 7 hours to complete our trip. The return trip to Wendover was in reverse. The fastest time for a round trip was 4 days, 18 hours or 114 hours total.

Johnston Island was man-made used as a landing stop to refuel when winds were favorable with enough additional area for the Navy personnel needed to operate the base. Kwajalein, a fair sized island with more facilities than Johnston, was a Japanese Naval Base before US Marine takeover that needed all food and material brought in from the States and Australia as did all the islands.

We found the USO at Hickham Field kept a full bowl of fresh, ripe pineapple chunks for all servicemen that we ate in excess the first day, only to find the high acid content made our mouths raw. We would arrive in Hawaii late in the evening just in time to be served breakfast and stay long enough to get into Johnston in time for breakfast again. Food quality west of Hawaii declined in proportion with the distance traveled. Somehow we managed to time our arrival at Kwajalein to get breakfast once more. I think as soon as they ran out of the evening menu, they started breakfast.

We carried twenty-five to thirty passengers with inflatable rafts, rather than parachutes, hoping the pilot would set us down in water with time to inflate them before sinking. Upon return to the States, we carried servicemen from Tinian or Saipan, bound for discharges or reassignment.

Control tower, Chofu Airport, Tokyo base of operations, October 6, 1945

I missed the big celebration on Tinian when the bombs were dropped because we were in Wendover for the first one and enroute to Tinian for the second one. I picked up several newspapers at Hamilton Field and delivered them to the group on Tinian who were the first to arrive after Hiroshima. As a rule, we stayed on Tinian one to three days, then returned to the States. On October 6, 1945, we flew to Japan landing at Chofu Airport whose thirty square foot tower was constructed of wood with a hipped roof and an open twelve foot square observation tower in the roofed area. The area was open and you could see several old Japanese planes none of which appeared in flying condition. We stayed until October 8th at the Dai Ichi Hotel. The first evening we found a guide to take five or six of us, in a Jeep all armed with .45 Auto Pistols, on a ride in a city that had just been officially captured three weeks earlier. On October 13th, we left Tinian for the last time arriving at Wendover on the 15th. Special orders #290 PAR 16 dated 26 October 1945 issued by Headquarters Wendover Field transferred the remaining 509th personnel from there to Roswell Army Air Field, New Mexico.

Our last flight from Wendover occurred November 3rd when all five of our C54s left for Roswell, New Mexico. Our pilots decided to give the new base personnel an air show by flying over the base in formation, something they had never tried in the C54s and had last practiced as B29 Pilots back in 1944. It sounded like a good idea but I had never been exposed to formation flying and was not aware how close planes were to each other when flying like this. Looking out the window and seeing how close our wing was to the other fuselage, my desire to be elsewhere was immediate. I had complete trust in these pilots' abilities, but I think this was the only time I was truly scared while flying.

FREDLUND, RONALD D.
390th Headquarter Squadron, Finance Unit

I arrived at Wendover in September 1942 because of a transfer from the Salt Lake Army Air Base Finance Office to the Wendover Field Finance Office. I was a T/4 (sergeant) at the time. Two others were transferred at the same time - Dick Parshall and Tom Nevinger. We weren't too happy about it! Lt. Phil Sturtevant was the finance officer, and there were only about four other enlisted men, including Dave Chelnik (later to be in the 509th). The finance office was in a small section of the headquarters building at the west end of Wendover Field. Later in September, four new privates arrived from Fort Dix, and two more from California. These included Art Femmel and Wes Peterson, who were later to be in the 509th. With all the new people, our Finance Unit moved to another section of HQ.

(L-R): T/Sgt Dave Chelnik, S/Sgt Wes Peterson, T/Sgt Ron Fredlund

The Wendover area was pretty grim, and the base was rather austere. The barracks were un-insulated, one-story buildings with pot-belly stoves at each end. Latrines were in nearby separate buildings. There was no enlisted men's service club, and the PX had minimal services.

In early 1943, a new finance building was erected next to HQ. An outdoor swimming pool was built about a block south of HQ. The pool was reserved for officers and enlisted men on alternate days. A new enlisted men's service club and a cafeteria were completed the same year. By this time, a succession of B17 and B24 groups were at Wendover for training before going overseas. At one time, a P47 Fighter Group was there.

A slow-moving tram circled the base from the Mess Hall and Medics at the east end to HQ on the west end. Because of the isolation of Wendover, monthly three day passes to Salt Lake City or Elko, Nev., were sometimes available. Likewise, ten day furloughs were a welcome diversion. There was bus service on nearby US 40, and the Western Pacific Railroad had once a day service.

The Wendover location did not attract civilian employees to come there, so servicemen's wives were welcome as employees. I was married in July 1943 and my wife, Thelma, returned to Wendover with me. By November, we were able to rent an apartment newly completed for civilian employees. Many officers and enlisted men's wives did likewise.

When the Silver Plate project was made known in late 1944, many of the base personnel had an opportunity to join the 509th. Our finance group of about 12 was a part of the 390th HQ and Service Squadron.

As our troop train departed from Wendover in April 1945 for the Seattle Port of Embarkation, I reflected on the 2½ years spent at Wendover, including the first 1½ years of happy married life, and the contrast to the bleak arrival day in September 1942.

FRY, RALPH D.
603rd Air Engineering, Instructor: Driver & Motor Maintenance

My time spent at Wendover gave me a multitude of memories; some good, some bad.

I can remember being sent to that desolate part of the U.S. in mid summer. My wife and I shared a small cottage built from railroad ties, with an Hispanic couple.

During August of '43, my father became gravely ill and I was granted a special leave to be with the family. Ironically, I missed being shipped to England.

During my time there, I was an instructor in Drivers Maintenance School under Capt. Purdam. I can remember driving out into the Salt Flats, after training plane crashes, to retrieve bodies and salvageable items. Also, helping with clean up, just east of Wendover, after a plane crashed on the highway then into a freight train, causing it to crash. It still haunts me.

In December '43, we averaged the loss of a plane and crew a day; B17s and B24s. Salt Flats became covered with water. We went out to target areas to replace jeeps after some of the fighter pilots got trigger happy and shot them up.

The winters were cold and we had to fire the coal heaters in the barracks to get warm.

I still have a menu from the mess hall; fortunately for me, that I did not attend. Many suffered with and needed hospitalization after eating Thanksgiving Day

Wendover Field

dinner there. A significant number, who did, suffered with food poisoning.

Jack Dempsey and Max Baer giving boxing lessons at the base is still vivid in my mind. I still have their autographs.

The first jet planes to come to Wendover were unbelievably noisy.

Sharing that time at Wendover, with buddies from all walks of life, is among my most treasured memories. I feel it was a privilege and an honor to have been a part of the entire operation.

B24 engine at Wendover, from crash

GACKENBACH, RUSSELL E.
393rd Bomb Squadron, Navigator, Crew B-10

Early in my military career, I enlisted in the Aviation Cadet Program. At that time, there was a huge demand for pilots and I was sent to pilot training. As I was unable to solo within the allotted time, I was washed out. Thereupon, I was sent to navigators school; here I was successful and received a commission and a rating as a navigator. Prior to joining the 393rd, I successfully completed two courses in radar at Boca Raton. Thereafter, I was rated as a navigator-radar operator.

Upon being assigned to the 504th Bomb Group, AAF, Fairmont, Nebraska, I arrived on base in early July, 1944. Two days later, I was assigned to the 393rd Bomb Squadron and after processing, I was finally assigned to a flight crew. As a new arrival, I was totally unfamiliar with the base and the proper procedures. I was on my own. A day or so later and after an early dinner, an orderly informed me there was to be a night training mission. Up to this time, I had not met any of the crew and was not familiar with the location of the briefing room. Therefore, I was late in arriving at the briefing that was already in session. It was an embarrassing way to meet the crew and later the chief navigator.

After the general and navigators briefings, I met the crew and we proceeded to the assigned B17, made the required checks and took off. We followed the flight plan as ordered. As we neared the air base on the return, we were early and I directed the pilot to continue the present heading for another 15 minutes. He did as directed and called the bombardier. He asked the bombardier if I knew where we were and if I knew what I was doing. The bombardier checked with me and replied to the pilot in the affirmative. The pilot then requested a new heading for return to base. Another embarrassing situation.

After landing and debriefing, the pilot confronted me and inquired about my actions. I explained that in the navigators briefing, we were told we should arrive back at base no earlier than 10 pm. Since we were early, I decided to continue on our present heading. In no uncertain terms, he informed me that, in the future, this was to be his decision and not mine. After this misunderstanding, the crew and I got along fine and, except for

the bombardier who was replaced, we stayed together for the duration.

At Wendover, the officers were encouraged to understudy each other so that we would be better able to carry out our eventual mission. As a result of ground and aerial training, I became acquainted with the Norden Bombsight and, in an emergency, would be able to drop our bombload. However, I had little experience in the front seat of the pilot or copilot.

One of our training missions was for the gunners. As there was a crashed P47 in the area, this was the target

for the day. The pilot flew on the deck and the gunners took their turn with the tail gun. Then it was the officers turn; the pilot and the copilot along with the flight engineer, crawled through the tunnel. This left me in the pilot's seat, the bombardier in the copilot's seat and the assistant engineer crawled forward and occupied the engineer's seat.

While we continued to fly the deck, engine #3 suddenly conked out and was windmilling. Immediately, I went on the microphone and told the pilot to come forward, that we were feathering the engine, going to increased throttles and climbing to 10,000 feet.

When the pilot got forward, I started to rise out of his seat. He put his hand on my shoulder and held me in the seat. He asked what was wrong; my reply was that I did not know. He then asked what I was going to do about it. Thereupon, I told the assistant engineer to run an engine check. It was discovered that engine #3 ran out of fuel; fuel was transferred and the other engine tanks were checked. The pilot still would not let me out of his seat. He asked if this was the place and the condition the plane was in when I took over. He had the assistant engineer and me start the engine and return the plane to the deck.

After this, the rule was that at no time was both the pilot and copilot to be away from the flight deck at the same time. Needless to say, neither the bombardier nor I had a chance to fire the tail gun.

Shortly after the 393rd BS arrived at Wendover Field in October 1944, the CO of the new group called all members, officers and enlisted men, to a meeting. The meeting was held outdoors near the main gate and within reading distance of a large sign that stated, "What You Hear Here - What You See Here - When You Leave Here - Let It Stay Here".

This was our initial meeting with the new CO of our group, Lt. Col. Paul W. Tibbets, Jr. He informed us of the purpose of our transfer and about our special mission which would be employing a new weapon that, if successful, would shorten the war. He stated that a lot of hard work would be required; he also impressed on us the need for a high degree of secrecy. Then to our amazement, he announced that all were to be given a ten day furlough. After our return, we would begin training for our new assignment.

Inside V-88 -- Back Row (L-R): James Corliss, Russell Gackenbach.
Front Row, (L-R): James Anderson, George Marquardt

Photos taken by Russell Gackenbach showing various stages of V-88's nose art. Plane was named after Bombs were dropped

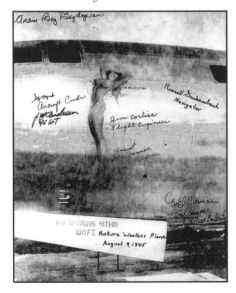  

James Anderson and I, copilot and navigator on crew B-10, remained on base and spent some of the time in Salt Lake City. One evening as we were strolling down the main street, we were stopped by two officers. They asked where we were stationed and inquired if we knew of Silver Plate. We replied that we could not tell him our base and denied any knowledge of Silver Plate. We suggested that they might inquire at Fort Douglas MP headquarters on South Temple Square East.

Yes, Andy and I were tested by security agents. Later, we found that many others were tested and investigated during the furlough.

Crew B-10 was sent to Cuba for training in long distance over-water flying and nighttime celestial navigation. Shortly after leaving Wendover, the plane developed engine trouble. The pilot and flight engineer did all they could to diagnose the problem; the engine was shutdown and the prop was feathered. Finally, it was decided that engine replacement was required and we proceeded to nearby Tinker Air Force Base, Oklahoma for repairs.

Our needs were disclosed to the proper base authorities. They informed us that an engine change could not be done immediately since the hangar was full; we had to wait our turn. After some hassle with base personnel, Capt. Marquardt called a special number that was given to him and to be used only for emergencies. A short time later, the planes were shifted around; our B29 was moved in and repairs were started.

We were not cordially welcomed by the base authorities. First of all, we refused to tell them where we came from and where we were going. Secondly, they did not like the way they were ordered to change our engine. Lastly, they did not like that all work had to be done under security measures. At all times, an officer and an enlisted man were in the plane keeping careful watch and preventing unauthorized work and unauthorized personnel from entering the plane. The interior doors to the bomb bays were blacked out. In addition, the base was requested to post two MPs around the perimeter.

The first evening James Anderson and I went to the Officers Club for dinner. While in the cafeteria line, all eyes were upon us and the Club was abuzz as we were in suntans during February. A colonel started to approach us to admonish us for being out of uniform. A major intercepted him and informed him we were associated with the newly arrived B29 in the hangar and it was best to leave us alone. After that no crew was challenged. When engine change was completed, we continued on our way to Cuba.

In preparation for going overseas, each person received a series of shots. After dinner on the day I received my shots, I was paged in the Officers Club. I answered the call. The caller did not identify himself but ordered me to listen and answer several questions. Mainly, the caller was inquiring about my health. Since I did not suffer any ill effects from the shots, I was told to change into flying clothes and get my navigation equip-

(L-R) James Strudwick Bombardier, Russell Gackenbach after Hiroshima mission

ment ready that an MP would pick me up in 15 minutes.

I was taken directly to the flight line and to a waiting C54. When aboard, an unidentified colonel told me to go directly to the navigator's desk. On the desk was a blank Mercator Map with two marked positions - Wendover and the final destination. After landing at the final destination, I was ordered to stay put and pay no attention to what was going on. However, I noticed some personnel got off and others got on. Also, some crates were brought aboard.

The way back to Wendover was uneventful until the last hour; we encountered turbulence, severe turbulence. The aforementioned colonel became sick over the navigator's table and made further work impossible. I was in a quandary as to what action to take; the usual rule was, he who gets sick also cleans up. I needn't worry; an unknown officer came to my rescue. He told me to leave everything as is and offered me another seat. He also gave me a card which authorized me to receive new equipment when the card was presented to base supply the next day.

The card was honored and new equipment was received. However, squadron operations did not recognize the previous night's flight as I could not produce proper papers authorizing me to fly. I never received credit in my Flight Record.

At the final briefing on August 5, our crew was told an additional observer was to be aboard our plane. I, as navigator, was told to cooperate with him and to give him the information he needed to complete his job. The observer was to oversee the operation of a Fastax Camera.

After takeoff and upon reaching level flight, the observer came to the navigator's compartment and introduced himself as Major Bernard Waldman. He informed me of the data that was needed when over the target area and at the time of the drop of the special bomb; this data was needed for the interpretation of the final film.

When our task was completed, he inquired if I was a Pennsylvania Dutchman. This came as a surprise; it was my guess he detected an unusual accent in my speech. I replied I was born and raised in Allentown, PA. Then, he wanted to know if I knew the area called Mountainville. My answer was I was familiar with the area and took Boy Scouts camping in the vicinity at Big Rock. To my further surprise, he inquired if I knew the location of East Rock Road. Again, I answered in the affirmative. I stated there was no water available at Big Rock and my troop had permission to get water from the well at the last house on that street. His reply shocked me. He asked, "Isn't the well kept locked?" To which I replied, "the well was kept locked but I knew where to find the key."

As it turned out, this house on East Rock Road was the home of his parents. Major B. Waldman was Dr. Waldman, a Nuclear Physicist from Notre Dame, assigned to Project Alberta.

I will never forget the sight of the initial atomic explosion. The three strike planes, Enola Gay V-82 bomb; Great Artiste V-89 instrument; Necessary Evil V-91 photographic; joined up at the assigned rendezvous point and proceeded to the IP (initial point). At the IP, Tibbets and Sweeney continued toward the target while Marquardt made a time controlled 360 degree turn before heading to the target. Thus, when the bomb exploded, our plane was about 15 miles from the target. At the time of the blast, the two lead planes were turning away from the blast and cloud area whereas our plane faced the explosion. I was standing on the flight deck between the pilot and copilot seats and thus had a front row view.

My first reaction was one of being awestruck and astonished; I was not prepared for the scene in front of me; it literally took my breath away; I could not take my eyes from the sight. In the meantime, there was almost complete silence on the flight deck of the Necessary Evil.

From a small, very bright red-orange fireball, there developed a boiling, dirty, purplish-gray cloud that expanded and rapidly rose as it turned into a mushroom shape. The light was so intense, even with our special goggles, I could have read the fine print of a pocket Bible.

Before hand, we were warned not to go through the cloud. By the time we arrived closer to Hiroshima, the cloud was off to our right and at a slightly higher altitude, about 35,000 feet, and still rising. As we left the area, it was evident the city of Hiroshima was destroyed. All around the edges of the mushroom cloud, we could see destruction and ruin.

All of us on the Necessary Evil were stunned and we had trouble contemplating the awesome power of his new bomb and the complete destruction it caused. On the way back to Tinian, the intercom remained relatively quiet. During the first 20 minutes, the stillness was broken by an occasional report from the tail gunner the billowing cloud was still visible.

Prior to going overseas, some adventurous officers made a midnight requisition and acquired several cases of glasses from the Officers Club. These were transported to Tinian, probably by B29 or C54. After the war was over, these same cases were returned to Roswell Army Air Field. In mid-January, George Marquardt as pilot, I as navigator and others flew a C54 to Wendover to return said glasses to the Officers Club which, in the meantime, had burned down under suspicious circumstances.

At the time of our arrival at Wendover Army Air Field, only a skeleton staff consisting of a captain and several enlisted men were on the airbase. After signing for the glasses, the captain said he didn't know what to do with them under the circumstances. Marquardt replied he could use them for target practice or another activity of his choosing.

After lunch and prior to departure for Roswell, a B29 appeared overhead. It was the B29 that Marquardt was flying when it caught fire on final approach in Spring 1945. It was repaired and was being flight-tested for air worthiness. The test crew had made several attempts but none were successful; the plane tended to fly in an erratic manner. Evidently, the heat of the fire warped the fuselage; the one wing was higher than the other and at a different angle of attachment. Eventually, the plane was scrapped.

It is worthy to note there were four navigators; James Duva, Russ Gackenbach, Len Godfrey and Bob Petrolli in the 393rd Bomb Squadron that were members of Navigation Class 44-2. We were trained by Pan American Airways instructors at the University of Miami, Coral Gables, Florida. We flew Consolidated Commodore flying boats out of Coconut Grove. All of our flying was over water and depended on celestial navigation. The four of us received our wings as rated navigators and commissions as Second Lieutenants on February 12, 1944.

GALLAGHER, RAYMOND G.
393rd Bomb Squadron, Assistant Flight Engineer, Crew C-15

As a boy, I became interested in aviation by building Balsa Wood models of airplanes. In December of 1943, I met Colonel Tibbets at Eglin Field, Florida. He had four B29s with four different types of guns that he was testing. I was sent there as an electrician. There were about twenty-five of us there.

When Colonel Tibbets received another order, he said, "I'm leaving, who wants to go?" About ten of us joined him. Wherever he went, we went. He knew our capabilities. When you become an aircrew member, you get 50% more base pay. He made us all aircrew members. He never put rank first. If he flew into a town with no base or barracks, he would take us to a hotel.

I attended many schools: mechanics, electrical, gunnery and Boeing School for B29 Engineers. We picked up from one another, each others skills. When Colonel Tibbets assigned us, he knew our capabilities. When we arrived at Wendover, the Florida fellows Sweeney, Albury, Dehart, Kuharek, all ended up on one crew. The officers knew these men.

I'll never forget standing on the chow line at Wendover; you could hear the bombs drop at Salton Sea. The bomb sounds like a freight engine, a rumble and a whistle. You couldn't see them, but you could hear them.

I was home on furlough December 1944. My niece, Margaret, asked "Uncle Ray, do you want my doll"? I said, "No, I can't take her", but she insisted. The doll's name was Mary Ann. I hung Mary Ann on a nail behind me in the barracks. Everywhere I went, I took Mary Ann with me. I had two pockets in my flight suit, one on each leg. I carried her in my flight suit and hung her up in the ship. Mary Ann went with me on both Atomic Missions.

Photo taken inside hut on Tinian.
Ray is looking at Mary Ann on Ed Buckley's knee,
while Abe Spitzer points to headline.

GASSER, ADOLPH
390th Air Service Squadron, Camera Technician

I had my own camera store at the age of 27 and a reputation for doing fine camera repair work. After the war started, I had a continual clientele of military personnel going out to the Pacific to have their equipment tested and checked by my shop. During the latter part of 1943 a Naval commissioned officer asked me if I would be interested in accepting a commission in the US Navy where my talents as a camera technician could be well used. In the course of discussion, it was necessary for me to reveal I had been unable to get a college education due to the financial hardships of my family and he said unfortunately we cannot offer you a commission because of that. This started me thinking I wanted to serve our country.

One of the professional photographers in the Air Transport Command I had known prior to the war, came to my shop every few months with his equipment, had it repaired and told me about where he had been. In the course of this conversation, I was approached to see if I was interested in entering the service with the Air Transport Command. He had checked with his captain at Hamilton Field and they were interested in acquiring my services and technical knowledge. The result was I took a voluntary induction, that way Uncle Sam took care of my wife, mother and two children. I left them in good financial shape because I had our

Camera Techs on Tinian – (L-R): Adolph Gasser, Harold Dube,
Ed Berg, Joe Gayeski – the quonset was on the line so they could
service the aerial cameras

home paid for, money in the bank and I felt I could be away from them for a while. I shut our shop down to just one elderly person not subject to the draft.

On arriving in the Monterey Presidio where draftees and inductees were processed, I found they had no information at all from Hamilton Field as to my induction and possible orders to report to them and I was just in the Army. I had the name of base personnel who were in San Francisco. I looked him up, told him about my technical background and he said he could get me in the Air Corps who definitely needed people with my talents but that was the extent he could help. As a result, I was assigned to the Air Force, sent to Buckley Field Denver, Colorado for basic training where our unit was being processed and was told I would be trained as a gunner on a B17. I explained in civilian life I was a professional camera technician and knew the Air Corp needed them. He looked it up and I was assigned 947 Camera Technician.

Most of the other inductees were eight to ten years younger than I but I was in good physical condition. Upon completion of basic training, I was given a short leave to go home, was later assigned to a pool in Lincoln, Nebraska where I volunteered to accept responsibility for keeping records of approximately 200 people a day being reassigned to various parts of the Air Corp, then known as the Army Air Force.

After a couple of months with no word from Air Transport Command, I was assigned to a Colorado Springs, Colorado unit training and being formed into a 2nd 20th Air Force. I met the photo officer Capt. Jerome Ossip who told me after Officers Training School he hadn't the slightest idea of photography when appointed photo officer. I gave him my background and was able to solve many problems he had run into, establishing my knowledge of the business. Capt. Ossip was gone a few weeks to apply for Photo Officer of another unit, was accepted and asked me to join him. About a month later, orders came for me to report to Wendover, Utah where I was assigned to the 509th Composite Group.

One of the first projects was Capt. Ossip asked me to check aerial cameras not showing pictures when flying training missions to Salton Sea Naval Base dropping simulated bombs. I disassembled the K22, a 9x9 aerial camera with 20 inch lenses, made several small adjustments, finding it in good working condition. I asked Capt. Ossip what procedure was followed once the B29s were airborne and he said the main camera switches were turned on about fifteen minutes before hitting the target. He told them to turn them on when they left the ground in order to keep heaters going and they began to get very interesting pictures. I suggested a change in bracket design so cameras pointed more toward the rear to get the bombs dropping from the bomb bay as well as see strike points on the ground. I also made a camera to fit a radar scope still giving a viewing screen so they could get pictures.

About this time, the 509th Group was headed to the west coast for embarking to Tinian

and Capt. Ossip gave me permission to stay back and finish working on the camera. He said I could fly over several weeks later with the lab group and the balance of our unit. They were having problems getting the pictures approved by base command so I immediately flew from Wendover to Hamilton Field, Hawaiian Islands, Johnston Island, Kwajalein and on to Tinian. Upon arrival, Capt. Ossip had me examine the photographs and I found the negatives were badly overexposed, so I made some changes in the exposure settings and the pictures turned out excellent. Our jobs were camera technicians on the flight line, loading the cameras with film, mounting them into the planes and keeping them in good working order. We had an excellent reputation as our cameras came back with good photos.

The fateful day had finally arrived with the Enola Gay poised and ready on her runway with all preparations triple checked. As a final thought, Capt. Jerome Ossip asked me to preset and load a K20, 5x5 hand operated camera for Bob Caron the tail gunner as he would have the best view. The pictures he took were the only ones recorded from the plane of the Hiroshima A-bomb blast.

When I returned to the United States, some men were given Rest and Recuperation (R&R) leaves while others were being discharged. At one point, I told Colonel Tibbets I had a small business, wife, two small children and a mother at home to support and would he grant me a dependency discharge. He agreed, so I worked in the office preparing discharge papers until my dependency discharge came through. I was home on November 27, 1945.

Photo unit on Tinian
Front row (L-R): Dominik Iosco, Floyd Ross, Jerome Ossip, Adolph Gasser, Harold Dube; Foreground: Abe Spitzer, Secret Service Agent, Nickname "Wimpy"
Back row (L-R): Ed Berg, Paul Lentz, Harold Weiss, unknown Secret Service, Alex Schiavone, Arthur Josephson, John Vandervoort; Middle: Edward Burgess, Robert Mulvey

GEORGE, HARRY H.
393rd Bomb Squadron, transferred to 6th Bomb Group

I entered the Army Air Force as an aviation student at the age of 22 and embarked on a long train ride to a hotel on Miami Beach at the exact site of the now internationally known South Beach!

Upon completion of my pilot training (B17 checkout) at Lockborne Army Air Field, Columbus, Ohio, in early 1944, my class was divided, one half was assigned to head a combat crew on a B17 to fly to Europe and the other half assigned to a B29 Unit.

In the summer of 1944, I arrived at the 504th Bomb Group in Fairmont, Nebraska, and was assigned as copilot to 1st Lt. Paul Monroe on one of the last crews formed in the 393rd Bomb Squadron. In what turned out as a possible deciding factor in my future, I was delayed joining my fellow Lockborne pilots due to an emergency leave (loss of my uncle). I was not pleased with my assignment with Paul Monroe. While an excellent pilot with European combat experience, he lacked what I believed to be officer qualities. In September 1944, the 393rd Squadron was transferred en masse to Wendover, Utah.

In early October, Lt. Col. Paul Tibbets gathered us in the base theater, told us we would be at Wendover for awhile and to make arrangements to bring our wives. Having a girlfriend back in Philadelphia that had been very dear to me for the past six years, I felt this was the time to cement the relationship. Immediately after the theater meeting, I dispatched a telegram from the Wendover WX Office to tell her I was coming home with marital intentions. I remember the words I used, "Hang on to your hope chest, I'm coming home"!

The trip from Wendover to our homes back east was with Monroe in his car along with my Lockborne B17 pilot friends Harry Davis, Art Henderson and Bob Bell. Together, we bummed gas ration coupons from truckers, finally separating in Ohio. I went on to Philadelphia by train where I became engaged to Skeet and returned to Wendover intending to marry later and bring my wife to the base. Upon return from leave, I contacted my flight commander, Ralph Taylor, and told him of my concern about Monroe as our aircraft commander. I remember Ralph's reply, he stated it several times, "I know just what you mean". I felt relieved and awaited results. This conversation occurred during the first week of October 1944. The next week on Friday the 13th of October, I was handed a set of Special Orders directing me to report to the 6th Bomb Group in Grand Island, Nebraska on Monday. I searched in vain for someone to give me reason why but all were gone for the weekend. I had no choice but to depart Wendover.

At Grand Island, I was assigned to the crew of the Anne Garry III as copilot replacing John Jennings (later president of the 20th Air Force Association in 1992). After flying outbound over the Golden Gate Bridge in January 1945, I flew 29 missions as copilot and then became an

Harry and Skeet, 1945

aircraft commander for the last few missions of the war in August and September of 1945 (combat, POW and show of force).

By April 1945, the 393rd had arrived and parked near us on Tinian. Their planes had the 6th Bomb Group's circle R on tails so they would not have any distinguishing markings. I took my long time good friends, Harry Davis and Jim Price of the 509th along with me on a "show of force" mission over Korea after the end of the war. I jokingly chided them that I was the (former) member of the 393rd who had the most missions over Japan - 30.

Remaining in the service, I met Colonel Tibbets again at Eglin in 1956 when he assumed command of the 3200th Test Wing. I was a test pilot and his material officer. My wife, Skeet, that I married upon my return from Tinian, and I visited Col. Tibbets in his base quarters at his invitation. I retired from the USAF in 1965 and have met Paul several times again at different B29 association reunions. I always consider him to be a fine gentleman. He will always have my admiration and respect.

Since my retirement, we have contacted Colonel Tibbets asking for his opinion as to what the reason might have been for my transfer. His reply of November 13, 1984, in part was, "I remember only wanting fifteen B29 crews and, I think, seven C54 crews and that we had a surplus of pilots. Consequently, I can only believe that you were a 'victim of the draw'. I can assure you, it had nothing to do with security or disciplinary action. There were three of those that I handled and they went to the 'rest' camp in northern Canada."

GODFREY, LEONARD
393rd Bomb Squadron, Navigator, Crew C-13

After an unsuccessful experience at a primary pilot training school, I was offered a choice of bombardier or navigation schools. I chose navigation that turned out to be a wise decision. Instead of being sent to an Army school, I was sent to Coral Gables, Florida and the University of Miami where Pan American Airways had trained their navigators for their commercial trans-Pacific flights. We flew in a 1929 flying boat called a Commodore that cruised at 90 knots. All our training in the air was over water with the octant, astro compass and chronometer as our tools and the sun and stars our guiding lights. This stands in sharp contrast to the experiences the students in the Army schools were having where pilotage and dead reckoning (looking out a window, seeing a place on the map and knowing where you were) were emphasized and celestial navigation seemed secondary.

There were not many maps between Tinian and Japan so I had an advantage. They sent us to Colorado Springs for Celestial Navigational training where I met Ted Van Kirk who got on my case. My test scores were too high so he ordered me to stay and retake the test a couple days later. Ted said, "I don't know how you do it, you must be cheating".

Eventually after months of further training, I was assigned to the 504th Bomb Group, 393rd Bomb Squadron stationed at Fairmont, Nebraska where I became a member of Crew C-13. The 393rd Squadron was split off from the 504th Group and sent to Wendover, Utah. After a short leave, we returned to Wendover and found a whole new chain of command. We were given a chance to leave the group or stay and become part of a highly trained group being organized for a special mission. Paul Tibbets became Group Commander and Charles Sweeney, Squadron Commander. Under this regime, correctly and understandably, Ted (Dutch) Van Kirk replaced Bill Wright as top group navigator.

To this day, I do not know what in my past records suggested I cheated on previous check flights. My Aircraft Commander, Fred Bock was to accompany and observe my performance. We flew in a twin engine cargo type aircraft with the astrodome as the only available window to the outside world. I tracked our flight on a plain Mercator Map which had just horizontal and vertical lines with no configuration, just lines and latitude. Van Kirk said, "I don't know how you did it, you got that fix right over the bend of a river. How do you explain that?" I could not. The plain map, the fact I had no view out of the aircraft, along with the testimony of Fred that I couldn't have cheated, cleared my case.

Fred Bock was the most methodical, careful, thoughtful Pilot you can imagine. Our crew went to Omaha to pick up at least two, possibly three finished Silverplate airplanes. We did a test flight there as passengers with the factory crew and then flew it back to Wendover. When I gave Fred a course setting, it would take three or four minutes and he would be right on it until I told him to move. If Hugh Ferguson were flying and I gave him a five degree correction, he would go right to it with things flying off the table. They were perfect together and great Pilots.

Claude Eatherly, was a good friend and marvelous Pilot. I liked the whole crew, Eatherly, Weatherly and Wey. I flew on training missions, not combat, with them and whomever I was assigned to. I can hear them now. It would start in the back, moving forward in the plane, singing the instructions: "Putt-putt's on the line, Sir, Putt-putt's mighty fine, Sir".

The crews shared the same Quonset Hut. Eatherly really took care of his men. He would trade with the Seabees a 5th of whiskey for a case of beer to give to his enlisted men. I would never gamble but Eatherly would play poker. When he won, he would stick the money in my shoe. He would call me Chuck, why I don't know; did he think he was talking to Chuck Levy, no, because I slept across from him. In the morning he would ask me how much money had he won last night, I would say, "I don't know, it's all right there".

Life in Wendover for a married couple and a mongrel dog named Spooky was difficult. While I was in Coral Gables, Florida, I had crawled under a porch to get a puppy that was part Chow and part Pit Bull. The owners were upset; they had a Pit Bull used in fights that got mixed up with a Chow resulting in Spooky. We had taken our puppy from place to place as we moved from base to base. In Wendover, we lived in a dormitory type housing just off base where no dogs were allowed. All we had was one little room with two single beds. We slept on one and took the other one apart. This gave us more room and under the bed a space where Spooky could and did hide. The central section of this building provided the amenities (necessities), showers, toilets, etc. that made dorm life possible. Spooky would go everywhere we went no matter how hard we tried to prevent it; he was a problem!

Spooky at Wendover

Mary was playing cards with Mrs. Trowbridge, Wendover's Commanding Officer's wife and two other people when she mentioned something about Spooky. Mrs. Trowbridge answered, "Oh, Trow loves Spooky" so then we were in. He would go on his own to the Officers' Club and movies. In the theater, people would call, "Here Spooky" and he would go all over looking for us. If we left him home tied with a rope, he would chew through it in seconds and be waiting for us at the Officers' Club. He also learned where the airplane hardstands were because I went there three or four times a week and after seeing me take off on a training mission, he would wait right there until we came back. Fred Bock talked about taking Spooky in the plane, but I said, "No". Most of his time was spent between the dorm, Officers' Club, theater and the flight line. Some people said he was homely but everyone seemed to like him. When we departed for our overseas destination, Spooky waited at the flight line for our aircraft to return. Mary had to go and pick him up.

Behind the seat in our 38 Ford Coupe, there was a shelf that extended the full width of the car where Spooky and small packages rode when we traveled. One day, I had Spooky with me and I picked up Chuck Levy. We visited the PX, did some other errands and returned to the base. Chuck suggested we stop at the Officers' Club for a game of pool; he was an excellent pool player. We took off our hats, threw them in the car and went in to play pool. When we returned to the car, we discovered Spooky had entertained himself chewing on the leather brim of Chuck's hat but mine was untouched. He never forgave either of us.

Putting this together has brought back many happy memories reminding me how very fortunate I was to be a member of the 509th Composite Group, 393rd Bomb Squadron and Crew C-13. Our crew could have been considered unlucky but with an aircraft victor number of V-77 and an Aircraft Commander like Fred Bock, I was a very lucky guy.

GORECKI, WALTER M.
390th Air Service Group, Rail Transportation Officer

I arrived at the 5th Regiment Armory on the morning of 3-20-41 for physical examination and induction into the US Army. Exam completed, I was then sent to Fort Lee, Virginia, and entered quartermaster school and basic training for a period of 12 weeks. Upon completion of training, went to Key Field, Meridian, Mississippi, to rail transportation office on a temporary basis and part-time in field with troops. Upon completion of the company being formed, the entire outfit was transferred to McDill Field in Tampa, Florida, to prepare for overseas duty. The entire company was sent to Walla Walla, Washington, Air Force Base for several months before the outfit was ready to go to Port of Embarkation in Seattle, Washington.

While at Walla Air Force Base, I noticed a large number of high ranking officers. One of whom was Captain Shepherd in charge of rail transportation whose position I filled while he traveled to various satellite bases. Colonel Cusack of Quartermaster Corp. suggested that since I was doing most of the work in rail transportation and being an enlisted man, I should take an examination for Warrant Officer which I did and was promoted to Warrant Officer in charge of rail transportation.

In the interim period, my entire outfit was shipped overseas, leaving me behind to take care of shipments. The offices were in two large freight warehouses. While at Walla Walla Air Base, I noticed that shipments of freight going in and out were extremely active. Also, numerous personnel were being brought in and out. We not only took care of freight in and out of Walla Walla Air Force Base, but we were also sending out various shipments surrounding the same area including two satellite bases (Redmond and Madras, Oregon). After a while, personnel was thinned out and decision was made to close Walla Walla Air Force Base leaving only a few soldiers to attend to housekeeping duties.

I was sent to Boise Air Force Base, Idaho, which also housed the 17th Bomb Wing. Short time thereafter, re-

ceived orders to transfer to Wendover Field, Utah, the latter part of 1943 and assigned as rail and assistant motor transportation officer as well as ration officer. Things were quiet for a very short time until 509th Composite Group arrived. I recall the first car of freight for the group and its arrival. I opened the car and looked inside, everything was normal there. Lt. McClenahan, Intelligence Officer, questioned me regarding opening of said box car and I replied, "I always open to see where freight is to be sent." At this time, it was unusual material. He further stated that if anything arrives for the 509th or any organization attached to the 509th, do not open cars until someone from said group would be present. From that point on, we were extremely busy. Numerous shipments were coming in and out. I remember things extremely weird. I recall a shipment of approximately 200 to 300 octagon shaped boxes with rope handles. Some seemed to be empty, some had contents and other things that were very unusual, too numerous to mention.

The 509th requested some shipments to arrive by Railway Express which was more expensive than by rail. Therefore, a code name was used requesting authority from the Chief of Transportation in Washington, DC. Code name

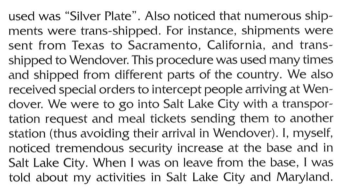

used was "Silver Plate". Also noticed that numerous shipments were trans-shipped. For instance, shipments were sent from Texas to Sacramento, California, and trans-shipped to Wendover. This procedure was used many times and shipped from different parts of the country. We also received special orders to intercept people arriving at Wendover. We were to go into Salt Lake City with a transportation request and meal tickets sending them to another station (thus avoiding their arrival in Wendover). I, myself, noticed tremendous security increase at the base and in Salt Lake City. When I was on leave from the base, I was told about my activities in Salt Lake City and Maryland.

When the group was ready to be shipped for overseas duty, I was immediately assigned to the 509th Composite Group.

While I was on Tinian, I was assigned to an important position, given a new military occupational specialty and number. It was the best kept secret in all my years.

In conclusion, I can truthfully say that I was not aware that our group was to drop an atomic bomb on Japan. I always thought they were to be some sort of missiles that would end the war. This was the best kept secret for which Colonel, now "General" Tibbets deserves all the credit.

GRIFFIN, FRANCIS E.
320th Troop Carrier Squadron, Pilot / Operations Officer

I have no idea why I was chosen to serve in the 509th. I was the last of four brothers to join the Army Air Force. We served in all theaters of World War II. Not all of us returned!

Before joining the Air Corps, I served in two branches of the service. In 1941, I was engineer on production of B17 aircraft engines. My work required that I pass top security clearance.

I was originally assigned to the infantry after induction to the Army. My goal in transferring to the Air Corps was to become a single engine fighter pilot. After completing single engine training, as is typical of the military, I was transferred to multi-engine training in B17s. If it had to be multi-engine, the B17 was my first choice. However, I never lost my love of the single engine planes, and I still regret the lost chance. If not for the transfer, I would never have been considered for the 509th.

It was while I was at Lincoln, Nebraska, waiting for crew assignment that I received orders to report to Wendover, Utah. Upon arrival, we were briefed about the strong security requirements. We were also asked if we wanted to volunteer for this unit or return to our former units. Colonel Tibbets asked us if our prefer-

ence was B29 or C54. He also said the 509th Group would have a big impact on the ending of the war! There was no more information about the 509th's true mission until the bomb was dropped.

I was assigned to the 320th Troop Carrier Squadron. Shortly afterwards, Major Sweeney was transferred from being the Commanding Officer of the 320th to the Commanding Officer of the 393rd Bomb Squadron. Captain John Casey was promoted from Operations Officer to CO of the 320th. Captain Elbert Smith became the Operations Officer of the 320th for a short period. He also requested transfer to the 393rd to fly B29s and his request was honored.

It was after much discussion with Col. Tibbets and Capt. Casey that I was persuaded to take the responsibility of being the Operations Officer of the 320th. My inexperience at this management position made this job very difficult at the start. But, it was with the help of the enlisted personnel that I was able to carry out my responsibilities.

However, my duties as Operations Officer curtailed my flying time. I was only able to occasionally assign myself to flight. The 320th provided flights to all points

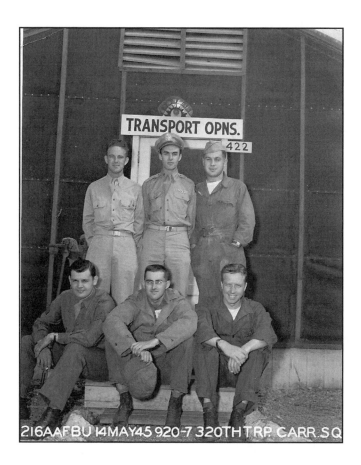

216AAFBU 14MAY45 920-7 320TH TRP CARR.SQ

of the United States for a wide variety of personnel and freight.

In May 1945, the 320th began flights to Tinian, ferrying both personnel and freight. Many crews flew over seven flights before August 6th. About half of the operations personnel were moved to Tinian, while the remainder was left behind at Wendover. Captain John Casey stayed behind and was in charge of the command at Wendover while I was in charge of the operations on Tinian. I was the only flight officer assigned to the permanent station at North Field on Tinian. The entire group was returned to the US and was stationed at Roswell, NM. We were given the opportunity there to re-enlist or request a discharge. I chose the latter and returned home in time for Thanksgiving.

Operations Office, Wendover

(L-R) Front Row: Sgt. Bayuk,
Corp. Cloepfil, Pfc Bradley
(L-R) Back Row: Pfc Weyland,
2nd Lt. Griffin, Corp. Schlessel

GRIFFIN, THOMAS REESE, 1ST LT.
393rd Bomb Squadron, Engineering

I arrived from the Salt Lake City Personnel Center in April 1944 and was assigned to the 393rd Bomb Squadron, 504th Bomb Group with Lt. Col. Tom Classen commanding. In early May, made a flight in an old B17 to Stevens Point, Wisconsin, with Lt. Col. Classen and several other people. I only remember Jim Galbreath. On return, many people from town came out to watch "their home town boy" take off. The airfield was grass and very small. In late May, I was sent to the Boeing B29 School in Seattle. Came back to Fairmont in August. Then, in late August, I went home on leave to Newark, Delaware. I saw some strange man across the street from our house that I thought was a security person. Although I graduated from Boeing's B29 Aircraft Engineering School in August 1944, my primary responsibility at Wendover was safety; parachutes, life rafts, oxygen systems, etc.

I came back to Fairmont in early September and was told not to unpack, the 393rd was moving. We boarded a troop train heading west and kept going forever. I had to abandon my old Model A Ford at Fairmont. I especially remember what a wonderful person, officer and pilot Tom Classen was. During my time with the 393rd, I flew eight of fifteen B29s. At Wendover, I especially remember the great people. Deer hunting in Nevada the fall of 1944 with Charlie Perry and though we didn't see a deer, learned that a 1903 Springfield Rifle could shoot through an old abandoned car engine. Almost running out of gasoline with

Mac McKinney's car on the way back from Salt Lake City one Sunday evening; Jack Benny was on the radio.

In January 1945, I flew in one of our C47s with many others from Wendover to Batista Field. I recall that I slept most of the way. Little things I remember about Batista were: light bulbs turned on in closets to keep clothes from mildew; Charlie Perry making fried egg sandwiches one night, first time I liked eggs; in the cemetery by the airfield, the open storage shed that contained piles of skulls and

bones. Apparently, if families didn't keep up payments on their plots, skeletons were disinterred. Visited the base hospital to see Sgt. Leo Morawa; heard a voice in the next bed say "Hi Tom". It was Sgt. Red Hogan who was with another group. Red was a University of Delaware fullback who went on to the University of Kansas after the war and made 1st team All American. He was only one of several people from home that I met in Cuba, Seattle and Wendover. One fraternity brother who I met at Wendover was at Los Alamos. I made one trip to Havana with Cecil King. Watched Fred Krug, our fine meteorologist and poker player, in a big poker game in the Operations building at Batista. Fred was dealt two pair of 8s and 6s. He threw away the 6s and drew another pair of 8s - what an ending!

In February 1945, I was sent back to Wright-Patterson Army Air Force Base, Dayton, Ohio, for a one week special course. Had to fly back to Wendover to get winter clothes; found snow in Dayton. Upon completion of the course, I returned to Wendover.

The most memorable event: Flew back to Batista Field with Lt. Col. Tom Classen and crew in one of our B29s. Over the Gulf of Mexico, we ran into a bad storm. Saw St. Elmo's fire on the wings and fuselage of our plane. Lt. Col. Tom Classen elected to turn around and go into Galveston Army Air force Base. We stayed overnight and then prepared to take off in the morning; had a very heavy fog. I think the tower raised the ceiling for our takeoff because a Lt. Col. Tom Classen was pilot. We got into the air and were immediately in dense fog. Lt. Col. Tom Classen was correctly flying by his instruments. I felt the plane slowing as did others. Then Lt. Col. Tom Classen looked over at the copilot, Bill Rowe's instrument panel and realized his instruments (electric vs. vacuum) were not working. He dropped the nose and increased power. Lt. Col. Tom Classen had a few drops of sweat on his forehead as he turned and said something like, "that was close". Apparently, we were almost in a stall!

In April 1945, going into the Salt Lake City Airport with McKinney and crew in a C47 to pickup Major Tom Ferebee. On the way back, McKinney let me fly the C47. Tom growled at him asking if I was going to land the plane. I never did tell Tom that I learned to fly and land after the war.

The active part I played in the "Great Wendover water fight" in the late Spring of 1945 - or the last P call. This historic event occurred in late May or very early June 1945 at Wendover Air Base, Utah in the BOQ Bldg. 408 diagonally across from the Officers' Club which later burned down.

The participants included Tom Griffin, I.D. "Mac" McKee, Charlie Levy, Hugh Ferguson, across the hall; Fred Bock, Lou Allen, room next door; Carl Ackerman, Carl Garner, Ira Weatherly and Stew Williams, all down the hall toward the front of the building. These were the 393rd Good Guys. The names of the Bad Guys or Wild Ones shall remain unknown.

Some of our illustrious buddies, i.e. the Bad Guys, with the intense training program winding down and everyone feeling we would be shipping out soon, were going up to the Old State Line Hotel in the evening for some relaxation and happy times. Returning about 1 am, the time the Officers' Club typically closed if the manager could get them to leave, and unfortunately most still had as much or more energy than when they

Deer Hunting, Fall 1944 (L-R): Tom Griffin, Charles Perry

arrived, went down our BOQ hallway banging on and throwing open each door to loudly announce P call.

Mac and I were in the last room on the left at the back end of the hallway, the room with the patriotic red and blue paint with the yellow trim. After several nights of being rudely awakened at 1am, I told Mac we were going to put a stop to this. Understand the 393rd Good Guys were all straight shooters who went to bed early.

The next night I went across to the men's room and got one of the large water fire extinguishers with a T pump handle. There were several of these large water extinguishers hung up and down the hallway for fire emergencies. Remember these buildings were wood, wall board and tar paper with iron potbelly coal stoves for heat. They were not the beautiful brick buildings with modern fire equipment as shown in the movie Enola Gay.

Anyway, we put the water container behind our door and went to sleep. Sure enough, about 1 am the Wild Ones came back from the State Line Hotel and started down the hallway, banging on each door, throwing it open and announcing P call. Little did they know what was waiting for them. Mac and I were up, standing behind our door with the pump handle in the up position. Finally, the Wild Ones reached our door, pounded on it and threw it open. Before P call could be announced, a stream of water hit them. I don't remember who was pumping and who was aiming the hose, but we soaked them. Then Mac and I were overcome and we got soaked. By this time, most of the rest of the BOQ was up and armed with additional waterpump extinguishers and joined the battle. When truce was finally declared about an inch of water was all over the floor. Remember, the room walls were about 4 inches off the floor. When the Great Wendover Water Fight was over, we got mops and cleaned up the floor.

GRILL, I. PATRICK
390th Air Service Group, Base Signal Office

I had arrived in Wendover shortly before the formation of the 509th. My squadron was the 390th Air Service Group. Those of us there were apparently carefully screened before being assigned, as a report came back to me of a check up of my character from my high school in Bloomer, Wisconsin. Our specific location at Wendover Field was known as the Base Signal Office. It was the center and hub of all communications in and out of this isolated place on the edge of Utah and Nevada borders. The adage was: "No one was counted as AWOL (absent without leave) for three days as the Salt Flats allowed one to be seen for that amount of time.

The office itself was a building not shared with any other unit of the field. Our job was dealing with high security as our constant and frequent teletype messages, often times in code, were carefully handled. We were aware of the highly secret nature of many messages about Manhatten Project, General Groves, Alamogordo, Los Alamos, Colorado Springs, Air Corp II, Colonel Tibbets, Silver Plate, etc. My work, along with about 6 to 8 others, was Teletype Operator, Western Union, and handling the front counter for military people to send and receive telegrams and other communications. Men I recall who worked with me were Scoggin, Peterson, Clemens, Kotoff and Larramore. We were open 24 hours a day with our Western Union Printer, two teletype printers, a phone switchboard, and a cryptographer operator named DeDemarco. He worked separately from us as his was highly secret with coding and decoding messages we received or sent on teletypes to various places; such as, Colorado Springs, Alamogordo, New Mexico, Washington DC, etc. Our messages were so long and complex that two teletypes were often going full time. We also saw Colonel Tibbets often as he personally came to the office to send private messages either by teletype or Western Union Telegram.

Colonel Tibbets gathered the whole group at a hanger meeting in December 1944 to announce the immensity of our project. It was so highly secret, he did not disclose it was a weapon that would "End the War". We were warned that "What you Hear here, What you See here, When you leave here, Let it stay here". For sure, the Base Signal Office personnel never violated that trust. All we knew was our outfit was highly secret and being quiet about it was no problem.

We were closely affiliated with civilian office of MT States Bell, and WW Sackman, General Mgr. of the Wendover Office. Col. Tibbets had asked Mr. Sackman for permission to have phone lines in and out of Wendover monitored for purpose of preventing leaks of a military type - Mr. Sackman said he was not able to allow that. Col. Tibbets then said, "Who is your boss and where is he located"? The answer was Salt Lake City. Tibbets said to get aboard the airplane and both flew to Salt Lake to get the necessary permission for his request - which they did.

As our teletype connections were made through Bell in Salt Lake City, I became acquainted with a lady, Jackie Paquette, in Salt Lake. She became my wife of 47 years

until her death in 1991. My then new wife and myself moved in and out of the Stateline as our residence of only 10 days at a time were allowed during this shortage of rooms - so we were forced to move around frequently, renting rooms at other motels until we finally found a room to rent in a private residence near the field. While moving around was an inconvenience, we had accumulated little material things in the early months of our marriage, so a few hardships was a normal thing and few of us complained.

Entertainment was mostly at the Stateline Hotel where gambling was legal and a meal of steak at Spikes on occasion with our own 509th band playing the songs of the 30s and 40s, still holds captive a large group of generations since. Girls were bussed in from Salt Lake and Elko, Nevada, for the USO dances. Jitter-bugging was big in those days of Glenn Miller, Tommy and Jimmy Dorsey and many others of music fame.

The 509th life on Tinian was a cultural shock from that in Wendover. Hot, humid climate and an oriental smell was evident especially as one passed the "Gooks Camp". Locals and Japanese prisoners (of which few were Japanese) were located enroute to our local 509th camp from Tinian Town and the ships docking area. The Seabees (CBs) who largely built the base after fierce battles a year earlier (1944), laid it out similar to Manhattan in New York City - even to naming streets, etc.

Because of the uncomfortably hot, humid weather, almost over night, most personnel had cut pants to shorts and nearly every day had to take a shower or two. A day in the ocean digging for shells was a welcome experience, but you had to avoid cutting your feet on the rocks. Sometimes we would drive into the wild jungle which was a dangerous thing to do as a number of Japs were hiding and reports of gun shots made this a very scary thing. Best of all was mail call that cheered us up as often there were many letters stacked up. Our letters were highly censored and my wife in Salt Lake City could only guess where we were in the Army Post Office San Francisco war location.

The food, well, when hungry enough, you didn't mind waiting for the Australian Mutton (not lamb chops), powdered milk (skim) and dried (green) eggs, because there was the Tinian Tavern where you could buy a beer. Most of us smoked and found solace in the nicotine habit even though they tasted musty and stale in the high humidity.

The drone of B29s was constant, including those returning with critical damage. We watched some crews bail out in parachutes. The world's largest airport was on North Field Tinian, in 1945. The big beer party on the airfield, when the crew emerged from the Enola Gay upon its return, was most memorable. We just knew, now the Japanese had to give up, which they did after Hiroshima and Nagasaki. The results of our weapons on August 6th and August 9th, 1945, which ended the war are well known and noted.

Then the wait to return home. Finally. I received that teletype which ordered the 509th to "lift off" the Island of Tinian and return to the USA on October 6th. The ship returning under the Golden Gate Bridge in early morning, I believe a Sunday, and hearing San Francisco radio as we approached, was a thrill to all of us aboard. Docking in Oakland and then boarding a train to Roswell, New Mexico, where it was already mid November, the humidity quickly took care of all the tropic scum and itch of which many of us were victims on Tinian.

Finally, that discharge for me on November 17, 1945, was one of the happiest moments of my life after 4 years, 8 months and some days. I was drafted for one year on April 3, 1941, nine months before "Pearl Harbor" - a day to remember!

GRUNING, PAUL WAYNE
393rd Bomb Squadron, Bombardier, Crew B-6

In 1942, I was falling timber in Blue River, Oregon, the old fashioned way. We were cutting old growth as big as seven feet in diameter!

The story of my days in the service and how I ended up in the 509th is long and complicated. It all started February 17, 1943, when I arrived at Portland, Oregon, the farthest I'd ever been from home. From there, I got sick on the train and was taken off at the Pocatello Air Base. At Buckley Field (Denver), I was left behind as my squadron of 150 guys went on their way. I think it was Grand Forks, North Dakota, I spent the whole night, the only person in a whole row of barracks. I was then sent to Hays, Kansas, where I was put in a new group, sent to San Antonio for classification, got a form of pneumonia and spent some time in the hospital. After I got out, was put in another group to go to Ellington Field, Houston, Texas, for bombardier preflight training. After graduation, I went to Laredo, Texas, for Aerial Gunnery School, then to Midland for bombardier training. Out of 150 guys, six were sent to Monroe, Louisiana, for navigation training but when we arrived were sent on to Boca Raton, Florida, for radar training. From there to Lincoln, Nebraska, where I was put in the 504th Group at Fairmont. We trained for a while in B17s (made the trip to Detroit in one of those). You all know the rest of the story from there.

My most interesting experience was being left behind by myself at Buckley Field, Colorado. I suspect that I had as many "snafus" as anyone in the Air Corps.

After the Hiroshima mission, we were one of two crews sent back to the States to finish the war at Wendover and Salt Lake City, arriving on August 10, 1945, and never going back to Tinian where the rest of the group spent almost three months. Our plane was wrecked at Chicago (Midway), the only one that was destroyed. I wasn't on it - I was home on leave at this time. I feel like the whole story is unusual but I suppose others have had a like experience.

We usually had a short group meeting of bombardiers before a mission to get information regarding aiming point and the IP, the point at which you start a bombing run. We had maps and sometimes photos. Often the target would be obscured and we would have to seek a target of opportunity. This was difficult because other bomb groups had destroyed major targets like Tokyo and Osaka. The bombsight was no longer secret so it stayed in the plane. I had some tools for the bombsight, screw drivers, stop watch, etc. but never had to use them. Maintenance on our bombsights was excellent. Also had a file of bombing information. I had to preflight it before a mission and it was so hot in the front of the plane that sweat just poured. Coral rock runways reflect a lot of light and heat. We had our parachute, C-1 vest, Mae West and 45 automatic, plus something to eat. Took our equipment with us because we might use another plane. What we used for bathrooms was already on the plane.

All practice missions carried conventional bombs. All missions to Japan were the pumpkin, except to Kokura when we carried none. The arming pins on conventional bombs are all left behind when the bombs leave the bomb bay. In the Marcus Island picture, you'll see 20 explosions from the twenty 500 pound bombs we carried. On our Guguan mission, we carried six 1000 pound bombs.

There was a big hook at the top of the bomb bay that held the Fat Man bomb. Things happened electronically then, as it does now, but more primitive. There is so much information it takes a lot of pages. I have a list of our missions when we were at Fairmont, Nebraska, and on through August 10th. I still have the notes describing

the practice bomb dropping on Guam Island into the boiling lava of the crater. It was in plane #12 and #72 on July 19, 1945. There are so many interesting things that happened.

A Close Call

July 4, 1945, we flew a practice bombing mission to the Island of Rota, between Guam and Tinian. The Japanese still held the island, but we were instructed to drop bombs on the runway, not where the enemy lived.

We carried six 1000 pound bombs and made bombing runs that carried us over Guam. These bomb runs were over a hundred miles long. The bomb bay doors had to be left open because they were pneumatic and could be opened and closed only three times. As we approached the target, everything looked good, the bomb was seconds short of dropping when suddenly there was a large bump, tumbling the bombsight gyro. At this moment, a plane came under us. I could see the crew members up front. Our pilot, John Wilson, had seen the other plane just in time to pull back on the control columns and avoid a disastrous collision. We continued our long loop for another run. I can't remember who that crew was but I do know we were only a few feet from changing the history of our group - no planes or crew members lost in all our operations.

Wilson, dedicated to doing the right thing had previous Caribbean experience on submarine patrol, like McKnight. He was down there quite awhile with two planes; Jabit, a B18 and Jabit II, a B25. That's why our plane was Jabit III; name came from his name John Abbot Wilson, a great guy and liked by all.

Crew B-6 in briefing room, Wendover, December 15, 1944, after practice navigation and bombing mission to the Boeing plant in Seattle.

(L-R): Joe Buscher, Donald Rowe, Jim Davis, Glen Floweree, Wayne Gruning, Jim Duva, Elsworth Carrington, John Wilson, Dr. Young, Chet Rogalski

Leather jacket patch worn by John Wilson Crew

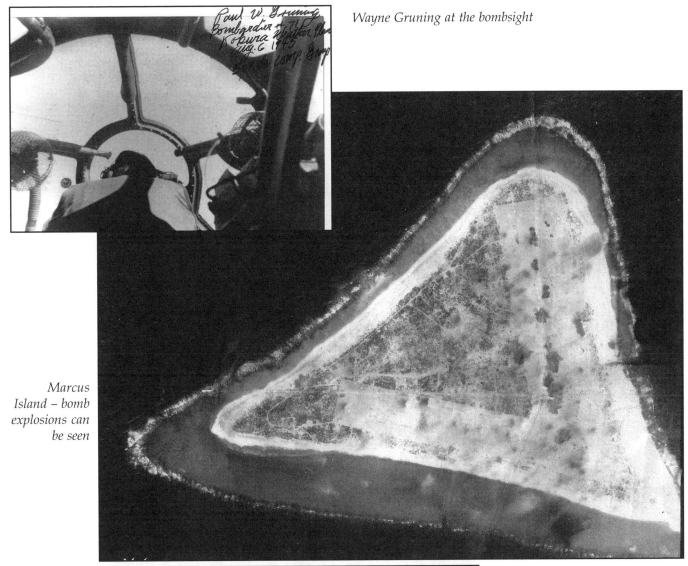

Wayne Gruning at the bombsight

Marcus Island – bomb explosions can be seen

UBE July 29, 1945
3 hits, 3 planes

Left smoke - Ralph Taylor crew

Center circle - John Wilson crew

Right smoke - Ralph Devore crew

Gruning - missed target 800 feet

13 hours of flying, no enemy opposition, bad weather over empire

John Wilson Crew on Tinian. Photo was carried in John Wilson's wallet for many years.

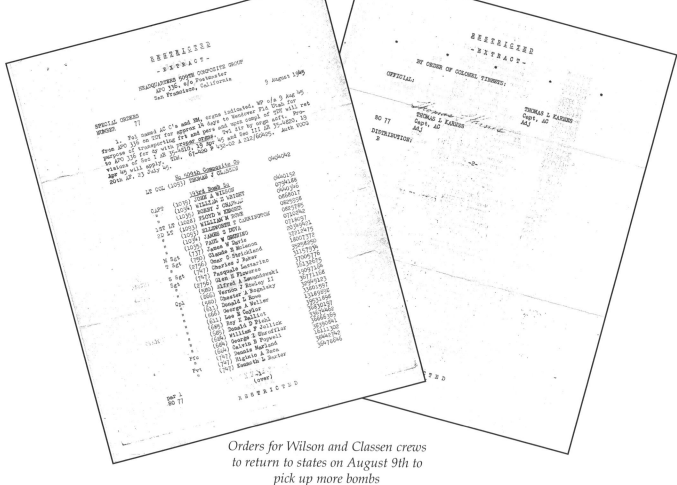

Orders for Wilson and Classen crews to return to states on August 9th to pick up more bombs

HALBUR, EDWIN
1395th Military Police Company

In 1944, I was transferred from Smoky Hill Army Airbase at Salina, Kansas to Wendover, where I became part of the 1395th MP Company, 509th Composite Group.

At Wendover, I was part of the training in preparation for overseas duty, which included posting guards at necessary posts, main gate checking passes, and Staff Noncommissioned Officer (NCO) assisting the Officer of the Day (OD). Part of our training was learning to fire all forms of fire arms, either fixed or side arms.

In May, we were moved to Seattle via troop train and boarded the USS Cape Victory for our trip to Tinian. After stops in Hawaii, we finally arrived at Tinian. One of the first duties was to aid in the escort of the material which was unloaded from the USS Indianapolis. A few days later, the ship was hit by torpedos from the Japanese submarine I-58 and sunk.

Other duties were posting guards at various posts on the Island. I was assigned to the gate entering into the bomb construction area making sure the people entering had the proper pass for any of the three buildings. Ray Driscol, a civilian with Civil Intelligence Corps (CIC), now known as CIA, was checking civilian personnel passes.

After the war ended, it was the usual job such as getting detail to police the area, pulling Charge of Quarters (CQ), guarding all night, and helping everyone to prepare for the trip back to the States.

October 15, 1945, we boarded the USS Deuel to return to the States. A long and sometimes rough trip, but nineteen days later, we arrived in Oakland and went by troop train to Roswell, New Mexico. After a 45 day leave, I returned to Roswell. On January 16, 1946, I was transferred to Lowrey Field, Colorado and received my discharge on January 21, 1946.

left to right: Ed Halbur, Ray Driscoll, CIC. Gate and Bomb Area

HENDERSON, ARTHUR D.
320th Troop Carrier Squadron, Airplane Commander

SEPTEMBER '44 - Car trip from Fairmont, Nebraska (504th Headquarters Group) to Wendover in Harry Davis' 1933 Pontiac - Col. Tibbet's address to the new 509th, "Secrecy and Security"!

OCTOBER '44 - Duck hunting (killed coyote) in Nevada - Halloween party!

NOVEMBER '44 - Began 320th Troop Carrier flights for "Silver Plate" project to "everywhere".

CHRISTMAS '44 - C46 grounded in Champaign, Illinois.

JANUARY, FEBRUARY '45 - Five trips to Cuba - Flying civilians over Salt Flats for testing a "strange" device.

MARCH, APRIL '45 - Week of bomb dropping (copilot) with Ed Costello's B29 crew in Inyokern, California, desert - C54 training school at Homestead, Florida. I flew as an extra crewman on an ATC (Air Transport Command) C54 from Wendover to the Marianas for the purpose of becoming familiar with the overseas routes I was expected to be flying in the months to come. On the return trip from Guam, we picked up an airman attended by several medics. He was completely bandaged, not unlike a mummy, as I recall. This airman while on a B29 mission over Japan had gone into the bomb bay and released a stuck burning fire bomb saving the crew and plane. He was the only 20th Airforce Airman to receive

the Congressional Medal of Honor. Name: M/Sgt Henry "Red" Ervin.

MAY, JUNE, JULY '45 - Back and forth from Wendover to Tinian - At the time the picture of my crew was taken, I was still a 2nd Lt., my promotion was about a month away. The trips between Wendover and Tinian were about 70 hours air time, with stops at Kwajalein, Johnston Island, Hickam Field Oahu and Hamilton Field San Francisco; one round trip per crew or plane approximately every 15 days. ATC personnel at Hickam named 320th, the "Green Hornets" - Visited "ole" 504th buddies on Tinian. They were "seasoned" combat pilots, made one feel like a civilian - Returned to Wendover to find Officers Club burned to ashes, must have been some party!

AUGUST, SEPTEMBER '45 - Flew ordnance party to Iwo Jima in advance of Col. Tibbet's Hiroshima mission for possibility of switching A-Bomb to Charley McKnight's B29. My flights with General Farrell's party began on Tinian about August 19th and continued until September 18th. We left General Farrell's party at Nagasaki and returned to Tinian via Atsugi. Other C54 crews including General Tibbets group took over Farrell's group. We had layovers at Okinawa and Atsugi before going to Nagasaki. Flew General Farrell's party to Okinawa and Japan after surrender. Saw the destruction of Nagasaki and Yokahama by foot and other large cities of Japan by air. The B29s had done their job!

OCTOBER '45 - Return to Wendover and Roswell, New Mexico - Flight to Los Angeles to pick up Glen Gray's Orchestra - Flight to Washington DC with Williamsburg (home) "flyover"!

NOVEMBER '45 - The end of my great adventure!

Photo taken at U.S. Navy Hospital on Guam of S/Sgt. Henry E. Erwin (in bandages), the only 20th Air Force serviceman to receive the Congressional Medal of Honor.

(L-R) – Sgt. Widmayer, 1st Lt. Liesch, Capt. Simeral, Lt. Col. Strause, Maj. Gen. Hale

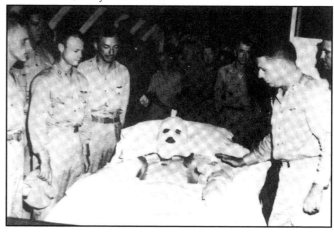

HULSE, WILLIAM T. "PAPPY"
393rd Bomb Squadron, Flight Engineer, Crew A-3

Letters To His Mother

September 17, 1944

Well, here we are in Utah! We left Nebraska last Tuesday morning and arrived here Friday noon. We had a very nice trip coming out and more or less took our time. We spent nearly a day and one night in Denver and a half a day and a night in Salt Lake City. The car ran very nicely except for heating up a little bit in the mountains, it did OK.

We are really out in the sticks here at Wendover. We are right on the Utah-Nevada State line; 126 miles west of Salt Lake City. We are on the eastern slope of a range of mountains and to the east there is nothing but desert and salt flats. We have an apartment (3 rooms) which is a Federal Housing Project.

It is real nice and hope we can hold on to it. Had quite a job getting it. Most of them are for civilian defense workers.

Our eating so far is rather light because we haven't any dishes or cooking equipment to speak of. We have a coal range and a refrigerator which is larger than yours at home. We cook on the coal range and it also heats our hot water.

Sketch of Wendover apartment

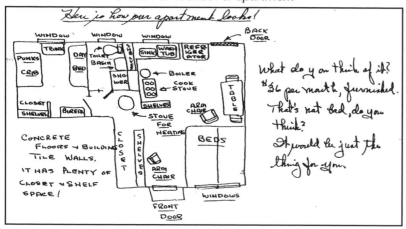

We bought 5 lbs of sugar and the girl forgot to ask for the ration stamps so we are ahead alot. I was out roaming the hills around here this morning and had a lot of fun. I scared up a couple of big Jjack rabbits and they sure were big fellows! Their ears stand about 12 inches high and they are pretty fast on their feet too. We just put the new shelf paper on the kitchen shelves. It has a blue check in it that matches our oil cloth.

February 27, 1945

Haven't done much as far as flying is concerned since I've been back from Cuba. Flew one hour today just to slow-time a new engine which had been installed. We went to Salt Lake City last Friday to do some shopping. Had two flat tires and broke my jack. What a Day! I've gotten two new tires since I've been here, have an application in for another one and have one in Salt Lake being recapped. So maybe I'll get fixed up yet.

Tinian - July 8, 1945 Sunday Afternoon

Dear Mom, I got real ambitious this morning and built myself a lawn chair out of some old bomb boxes. Sure is nice sitting out here under the trees with a breeze blowing. From where I sit, I can see the ocean and Saipan not far away.

Have been pretty busy lately, so haven't much time to write. Have been getting up at 2:30 and 4:30 in the morning and tomorrow have to get up at 1:30! That is before breakfast if you ask me, but then I would just as soon fly during the daytime while it is hot because it is so nice and cool up in the air.

The nights are nice and cool so it isn't too bad for sleeping. The biggest problem around here is to find something cold to drink. Boy, when I get home I'm going to sit down

Party inside Tinian hut

(L-R): William Hulse, Bobby Chapman, Elbert Smith

Touring Cuba

(L-R): Frank Wimer, William Hulse, Locke Easton, Leon Cooper

and eat about a gallon of ice cream! If a lot of the people back home realized how much a bottle of coke, beer or fruit juice meant to somebody over here, they might not find it so hard to get along without it.

We have been bombing a little Japanese held island near here lately but to me it was rather a disappointment. No flak at all to speak of. Probably it will be different when we start going against the Empire. I sure am looking forward to it.

July 14th Saturday Afternoon

Dear Mom, Have just come in from flying and found your letter here. It seems to be rather cool here today. We have 90 to 95 degrees temperature here everyday so that is nothing new to us.

When we were at Mather Field California on the way over, I bought a couple of fifths of whiskey. I swapped one of them for a bed with a spring made of strips cut from an innertube. I also got a mattress so I sleep pretty comfortable now. Money doesn't mean anything over here, but for a quart or two of whiskey, you can get most anything you want.

A couple of days ago, we moved out of the tents into quonset huts in a much nicer area and everything doesn't get all wet each time it rains which is quite frequently. It rained this morning while we were taxiing to take off.

Sketch done by William Hulse of officer crew.

Kermit Beahan and James Hopkins – Hulse sketch can be seen on wall behind Kermit

The radio is talking about US Battleships shelling Japanese Home Islands. I hope things will begin to happen before long because I'm ready to come home anytime now even though I've only just gotten here.

July 31st Saturday Morning

Dear Mom, You asked about Tinian Island. Have you looked it up on the map? It is small, with steep, rocky, coral hills covered with lots of trees, coconut palms, grass, weeds, bushes, sugar cane, corn etc. that grow very fast and hide many caves that the few remaining Japanese hide in. There are no nice sandy beaches such as we have at home. The roads are coral and were rebuilt by the US since they moved in. There are four lane divided highways with traffic circles and names of streets in New York, such as, Broadway, Post Road, 8th Avenue, 42nd Street etc.

The other night I went to see the show "This is the Army" made up of an all Army cast that travels all over the world. It sure was good. A few nights ago I saw a USO show.

Well, I have three missions over the Empire and so far they have been uneventful. I hope they stay that way. I wish the darned Japanese would give up. They just don't know when they are beaten.

September 24th Tuesday Morning

Dear Mom, I have been building a tool chest to bring home my model airplanes. We received another battle star yesterday for bombing Marcus Island; that makes two now at five points each. I should have seventy points at the end of the month. The 504th Bomb Group is hauling engines to Kwajalein to have ready in case any B29s need one changed on their way home. I haven't flown for a couple of weeks so we'll probably go sometime soon since it is better to use them from time to time. I don't know whether I told you the name of old 86 but it is "Next Objective". We have a picture of a red headed gal on the side of it.

October 27th

Dear Mom, It is very quiet around here these days. I flew a couple of hours Tuesday morning but have done very little since then. I am on our back porch writing this while watching a few planes taking off. Some of the boys are pitching horseshoes in the yard. I have 72 or 73 points now and I'm hoping to get out of the Army pretty soon after I get back to the States. I wish they would give us some definite date when we would be leaving but I guess I can't complain as I'm being paid about $408 per month to just sit around over here. I would just as soon be home with my family and only making half that amount.

Love and Kisses, Bill

HURST, FARR L.
603rd Air Engineering Squadron, Machinist

Early in June 1945, we sailed on the SS Cape Victory, a Merchant Marine Liberty Ship, to Tinian in the Mariana Islands. While at sea, we were told if we slept on the ground, the next morning we would find a bunch of scorpions under our beds or ponchos. Needless to say, we never did that! Also, we should always wear shoes outside because hookworms were very prevalent. These little creatures could enter your body through your toes and cause real havoc with your health. The islands had been sprayed with DDT to get rid of mosquitos so we didn't have to sleep under netting. Unfortunately, it killed the honey bees too leaving spiders and hornets whose sting would hurt for days.

While on board ship our hair grew pretty long, so Clarence Peterson, the tailor, also our camp barber, cut everyone's hair. I had him give me a crew cut and in the morning it was easy to just wash my face and hair at the same time. Clarence was a good guy and I corresponded with him at Christmas time.

Upon arrival, we boarded trucks that transported us to North Field. Our first detail was to put up our own 12 men squad tents. Once we got our tents up, we put up our camp cots. We were given two blankets and no pillow, so we doubled one of the blankets and used it for a pillow. After our sleeping quarters were squared away, we had a little free time and decided to do some exploring of our surroundings. We found an open-air theater close by, so we decided to go there that evening. As Mont Mickelson, Harold B. Glick and I left the tent, I decided to take along a raincoat, just in case. While we were watching the movie, all at once it started pouring. Since no one else had brought a raincoat, we all crawled under mine. You could hardly hear or see the movie because of the noise. We laughed about that and made sure we all took them with us after that as we soon learned it would rain unexpectedly, quite often and very hard.

It became so hot during the daytime, we hired Clarence for the reasonable cost of a quarter or fifty cents per item, to cut off our shirt tails, long sleeves to just below the shoulders, and pants to shorts. After getting both sets of suntans modified, we were much more comfortable and didn't sweat so much. Having our own tailor worked out great.

Prior to heading for chow, I went to the PX for a couple candy bars, returned to our tent and put them on my foot locker. After chow, I found one bar totally covered with sugar ants and they had started on the second! Not wanting to eat any chocolate covered ants, I threw them away. After that, I found a tin box with secure lid to put all edible stuff in. Some of the guys put little oil filled cups under the cot legs to keep the ants from crawling up onto the bed. They were miserable little things.

In our tent, I slept in the bunk next to one of the cooks. A little Korean girl had made a cloth doll for him. My mother was a doll collector, so I talked him into selling it to me for $3. He had it deloused with some type of spray not wanting to have any disease go with it. I mailed

it home to my mother and she was so thrilled to receive it, she named it Tinianna.

General LeMay started splitting up our composite group into different units. My group of machinists was assigned to a shop in a quonset hut not far from our camp. Sheet metal workers were assigned to repair damaged B29s from missions over Japan. The mission of the 509th was so secret that even the General did not understand it's formation. After Col. Tibbets told him, he backed off and we remained as we were.

We soon learned that taking a shower was an adventure! The stalls were fed through a gravity system with large water tanks at the top of the building allowing water to run down into different stalls. Trucks pumped the water back into the tank to keep it filled. Sometimes, just as we would get lathered up, the tank would run dry and we would have to wait till the trucks filled it back up.

One outfit built their own washing machine by taking a water filled 55 gallon drum rigged with a paddle in it that was attached to a windmill. When the wind caught the windmill, it would turn the paddle causing the water to churn the clothes. Our outfit never had anything like that, but the Korean women would wash our clothes at the rate of two cents for stockings or a nickel for a shirt. I did my own laundry. I bought soap at the PX, got a little bucket, washed, then hung them out to dry which didn't take long because it was very hot in the afternoons. I showered every day after work. Our hours were from about 9am to 5 pm every day, so we had a lot of free time, especially on Sunday. Then we would go swimming and shell hunting with a little glass bottom box to put in the water and see the fish and seashells.

We also visited Tinian Town which was inhabited mostly by Koreans the Japanese had brought before the war to work in the sugar cane fields. They had free run of the island until we arrived and put them all in one big area with armed guards to provide security for our B29s and for their own safety. They didn't have access to showers like we did and when you approached the town someone would usually comment, "We must be close to Tinian Town" as you could smell the village from about a mile away. The cement houses had all the roofs caved in because we had shelled them so much during the invasion. Hugh spiders could be seen crawling up and down inside, some carrying egg sacks as big as a large marshmallow.

Sometimes from a little knoll, we'd watch planes take off on bombing missions one right after the other. They would dip down skimming the water to increase flying speed. As they went over Saipan, they would lift up, gain altitude, join the others in formation and head for Japan. Occasionally, a plane with it's heavy bomb load wouldn't make it and in the morning we'd see a tail sticking up at the end of the runway. When that happened, a crane would pull them back onto the runway.

One night we were watching a movie when a large squadron returned, circled, and took turns landing. If a plane had wounded aboard, they would shoot off a red flare to be first to land. The engines were so loud and the lights so bright we could no longer hear or see the movie, so we gave up and went back to our tents never knowing how the movie ended! There was a stage right in front of the screen and occasionally the USO would put on a variety show with people playing instruments, or a demonstration pitching horse shoes, sometimes blindfolded, making a ringer every time. A brochure was distributed periodically describing the events at different locations, so we would make our decision, get a truck and drive to the appropriate place.

When we first arrived, we were instructed to always offer a ride to any military person walking no matter what outfit they were in. This was one way the positive camaraderie among the troops kept us watching out for each other.

One time, the three of us Glick, Mickelson and I saw this little hut on top of a hill. We found Korean people making souvenirs using seeds and other things available along with necklaces and other types of jewelry. The MPs told us we weren't allowed there, it was for officers only. We started to leave but Mickelson told us to walk real slow. Pretty soon the MP called to us and said, "Hey you guys, go on in and get whatever you want". So we went back to buy a bunch of trinkets to mail home. As we

returned to our tent, Mont said, "In the next war, I'm going to be an officer!"

Another time walking down the road, we passed by several Korean women herding some cows. The cows' udders were swinging back and forth just brimming with milk. I thought to myself, "Boy I'd like to milk one of those and get me a nice glass of fresh milk." That's one thing I missed most was real milk. We drank powdered but it's just not the same. It was a tempting thought but we never did it.

On Sunday mornings, we would go to church. One of the services was provided for the members of The Church of Jesus Christ of Latter-day Saints (Mormon) with Gerald Ericson as chaplain for the whole island. We not only had good speakers at our services but shared experiences we had while there. One time, in our dress suntans, we hitched a ride hanging onto the sides of the uncovered water truck. The driver went around a corner too fast, spilling water all over, soaking us to the skin. Fortunately, by the time we arrived at chapel, we were pretty much dried off. We all had a good laugh seeing each other dripping wet on the way to church.

They had an officers' beach called yellow beach which was just for them and their girlfriends. Some of the Red Cross nurses would fraternize with the officers but not with us enlisted men. We would sneak over there, look through the trees and watch them swim and kiss each other once in a while. Our beach was for enlisted men with a guard on a stand to make sure none of us were carried out to sea.

One time, about ten of us went to a secluded beach area. Glick had his glass bottom box and was hunting for seashells. A riptide came in and started sweeping us out to sea. It was really tough trying to get back but I finally made it. William Giguere was way out from shore and we could see he was in trouble hollering for help. I started out but knew I couldn't swim that well. Next we saw him go under. We thought we lost him! Before long, he came back up and swam crosswise of the current finally being able to get back to shore. We realized later, the reason he went under water was to take his shoes off so he could swim better. That was a harrowing experience, some of us could have drowned that day. We were fortunate all made it back to shore safely. We stood there awhile watching the water go back out underneath creating an undertow sweeping everything back out to sea that isn't glued down! When we got ready to leave, we noticed

CAPE VICTORY 1945

Glick had left his little box near the water and it had floated about half a mile out into the ocean. He didn't care as he had no use for it any longer.

On July 24th, all of North Field celebrated Utah Day in commemoration of having been stationed in Wendover, Utah for so long. We all went to a central location where the Red Cross women put on a banquet including potato salad, lunch meat, etc. to celebrate the Mormon pioneers first arrival in Utah. It was enjoyable to reminisce with all the Utah men who were stationed on the island.

After we dropped the bombs on Hiroshima and Nagasaki, the entire 509th had a field day; a big beer bust! My friends and I never indulged in the beer, but we had a lot of fun playing softball, games and different contests. They had a guitar player and other musical performances on stage. It was a great celebration. We thought the war was going to be over, but a rumor went around, the Japanese were going to counterattack by invading the Mariana Islands by submarine. Captain Casey gave me a magazine of ammunition and my .30 caliber M1 rifle with instructions to go down to the beach and repel any invaders coming in. I had never been trained for that, just metal butchering. I didn't know if I should go, but I finally stood guard, ready to shoot, hoping nothing came my way from the sea. We could hear Moaning Minnie, an air raid siren, that put a little scare into me. In high school, they had air raid drills all over the city in Ogden.

I thought it was the real thing, not a practice drill. I wondered now if the Japanese would come, but they didn't, although we were told a few invaded Saipan where the guards corralled them.

One evening we were watching a movie, From Pillar to Post. The film stopped and the operator announced over the loudspeaker the Japanese had unconditionally surrendered August 15th! Boy, everything on the island broke loose! Everyone was celebrating. People were running, driving Jeeps around, drinking and shooting flares all over the beach fronts. It was finally over.

About two weeks later, we took down our tents, loaded into trucks and were taken to the harbor to board a Navy Personnel Attack Ship, the USS Deuel that had been used to carry Marines in the Iwo Jima invasion. We sailed to Saipan where we picked up more ground troops, Air Force personnel and spent the night. It was so hot, I took my blanket topside to a corner of the ship where it was a little cooler and finally fell asleep. The next morning, we sailed back to the US. When we returned from Tinian, landing in Oakland Bay, one of the first things Mickelson, Glick and I did was to head for the dairy bar. I drank a whole quart of cold, fresh, delicious milk, just glug, glug, glug. It really felt good to do that. Most of the guys went looking for liquor stores, but I was totally satisfied with my bottle of fresh milk.

Members of the 509th on the ship USS Deuel, November, 1945

102

JEPPSON, MORRIS R.
1st Ordnance Squadron, Special Aviation, Weapon Test Officer

Sometime in the winter of 1944-45, I was ordered to make a trip to a place that proved to be Los Alamos, New Mexico. I believe there were three of us. We boarded one of the 509th's C54s. These planes were not pressurized and were certainly not fitted out like a present day airliner. We arrived at Albuquerque where a car met us and drove off - somewhere. It was night and the drive took about an hour.

The driver briefed us, "We will stop in Santa Fe where you will be further briefed by Security and where you will exchange your Air Force insignia for Army Ordnance. Where you are going, people are not to know the Air Force is preparing to use weapons they are developing."

Santa Fe was a pretty place. I remember the Security Office was a small shop across the street from a black iron decorative fence enclosing park like trees in a snow scene.

Then the car was driven another hour to a place in the mountains, through a guard gate and what looked like a military complex in a forested setting. It was still dark. Our final destination was a lodge like building. The accommodations were sparse, but the service was delightful - attractive Navajo girls and ladies in the dining room.

Next day I remember another security gate, and a wooden barracks type building where bomb fuzing developments were located. Some areas were off limits to me, but I was able to go to a small library in the technical area. I was planning a career in Physics, so I wanted to learn more about this project we were working on. In the library, I found a well worn section of a book on Atomic Physics, an account of the discovery of the fission of uranium by Hahn and Strassmann in 1938.

The weather was stormy on the return flight. We asked the pilot how he would get down through the clouds to land at Wendover. The procedure he said,

was to fly out over the level Salt Lake basin, let down through the clouds until the ground showed up, then look for the field. We watched out the windows and suddenly we could see snow covered mountains on both sides of the plane. They were higher than we were! It was an interesting trip.

The 509th used a Navy installation on the shore of the Salton Sea in the Southern California desert. A target offshore was used for testing the fuzing system designed to detonate an atomic weapon.

I flew on a testing mission in the Spring of 1945. Over the intercom came the usual report, "approaching town of Calipatria on downwind leg of bombing run". Suddenly, an upward jerk of the B29. The five ton bomb had fallen out of the bomb bay and we were approaching the town of Calipatria! Turned out we were flying at 30,000 feet so the bomb trajectory carried it over the town. It was buried in a field beyond. Security took over.

(L-R): Dr. Norman Ramsey sitting on Morris Jeppson's bunk, Captain Parsons, Col. Kirkpatrick, Ed Doll, on right, Commander Frederick Ashworth

On Tinian, our tent with a rear screened in porch, faced northward towards North Field with reflections through the screen that resembled B29 tails. Three of the guys sitting on my bunk are enjoying a rare cocktail treat. The flooring is salvaged wood panels from Fat Man bomb crates. Phil Barnes, sawing, was architect and best craftsman. We built this four man structure complete with electricity, but no plumbing.

Enola Gay was on the ground on Tinian 6 August 1945 after the Hiroshima mission. When I returned to my four man tent with porch, there was Navy Lt. Jack Scott, a childhood through college very good friend. Jack flew PBYs from the other end of Tinian Island on missions that included fishing B29 crews from the ocean between Marianas and Japan.

Jack had a jeep and suggested we drive back to his base where they had a good mess and plenty of booze. I said nothing about a flight to Japan.

The Navy club was quite different from ours and dinner was a special treat. There were about seven officers at the table talking about their activities and women. One finally said, "What does your outfit do"? The Navy, I gathered, looked down a bit at the Air Force. I took a shot, "We ended the war today". This was greeted with some laughs, friendly tolerance I think. I left it at that with no elaboration.

After a great visit, Jack drove me back to the 509th area.

(L-R): Morris Jeppson, Phil Barnes, Leon Smith

View of north field from weaponeer tent

Morris Jeppson, Phil Barnes

JERNIGAN, NORRIS N.
393rd Bomb Squadron, Intelligence Office Clerk

In March 1944, a small group of us arrived at Fairmont Army Air Base and were told we were to become part of a bomb group that would fly the B29, a new and very large bomber. Shortly thereafter other personnel began arriving including flight personnel, but no B29s, only B17s. The number of men rapidly increased and by the middle of April 1944, we were assigned to squadrons 393, 398, and 421, and I became part of the 393rd Bomb Squadron, 504th Bomb Group (VH).

At Fairmont, my original assignment was with the motor pool, however, Dick Tigner, my later to become friend in the orderly room, in reviewing personnel files, noticed I had just come out of the Army Air Corps Cadet program which included one semester at Denver University. He contacted me and asked if I would be open to a different assignment, in view of my training, to which I readily accepted. He directed me to report to Sgt. Francis Bell in the Squadron Intelligence Office where I remained until discharged from the service in March 1946.

Shortly after the squadrons were formed, training commenced with the flight crews flying B17s. One by one B29s began showing up to replace the B17s and we were on our way towards preparation for overseas duty. The 393rd was showing excellent results of our training and looking forward to getting into the action when rumors started circulating that our whole squadron had some other destiny apart from the 504th Bomb Group.

By the middle of September 1944, it became a reality - the 393rd Bomb Squadron was transferred to, of all places, Wendover, Utah, for additional training. Little did we know.

When the 393rd arrived at Wendover, the enlisted men working in the Orderly Room, Operations, and Intelligence Offices were assigned to a barracks across the street from the Orderly Room building. All of our barracks were in the older section of the base, single wall construction, with no insulation and painted an ugly green. Our particular one had a good sized room at one end of it with a potbellied stove located in the middle. We all agreed it could be furnished and become our own private Day Room. With the help of Mrs. Merrill, the Base Day Room Hostess, later to learn she was part of security, furniture was brought in and the room was transformed into a reasonably attractive Day Room which we named Happy Dale, from the movie Arsenic and Old Lace, and enjoyed by all during our days and cold nights at Wendover. I think it was the only barracks on the base with a private Day Room. Many times during that cold winter 1944-45, someone would over-stoke the old potbellied stove with the cheap, powdery coal the base provided for heating, and it would suddenly fill up with thick yellow smoke with no flame. If it wasn't noticed soon enough, it would spontaneously ignite and blow the stove door open requiring a hasty cleanup of coal dust mixed with live burning coal particles. Fortunately, we never did burn the place down. I think the building is still there, however, I don't think it would have been any great loss if it had burned down.

A day or so after arriving at Wendover, and still under the shock of it all, we were called to assemble near the orderly room for orientation. When assembled, a stranger to us, stepped up into the bed of a truck and introduced himself as Lt. Col. Paul Tibbets. He told us we had been selected to be part of a secret mission to deliver a new weapon that, if successful, should shorten the war by two years. He further instructed us that high security was in effect and any breach of same would have dire results for the person responsible for same. We were not to discuss anything with anyone. He then dismissed us to commence a ten day leave.

After returning from leave, the specialized training began, especially for our flight crews, for this new mission. In December 1944, the 393rd Bomb Squadron became the bomb squadron for the newly formed 509th Composite Group. By the end of April 1945, with training completed, the 509th began the move to Tinian and the rest of the story is history.

Norris Jernigan shaking hands with Ed Schlesinger as Robert Keister looks on from train leaving Wendover

JOHNSON, ARTHUR J.
390th Air Service Group Headquarters, Sergeant Major

In May 1943, I was transferred from Hill Air Force Base to Wendover and was assigned to Headquarters 216th Army Air Force Base Unit (AAFBU) (FPTS). Lt. Col. A.W. Kellond was Station Commandant at this time. This was a P47 Fighter Training Base and was being phased out.

The summer of 1944, I was assigned as the Base Sergeant Major at Wendover Air Force Base. The P47 fighter program had been phased out and the base was available for the organization of the 509th Composite Group. The isolation of Wendover was ideal for the security necessary for this group.

By September 8, 1944, Lt. Col. Tibbets had set up headquarters. Security was one of the first priorities and a group of about 30 special agents commanded by William Uanna arrived. Security was very tight and all key personnel had background checks. I was transferred from my assignment as Base Sergeant Major to the 509th Composite Group as Headquarters Sergeant Major.

By December 17, 1944, the group organization was complete and officially activated. Along with most of the personnel selected to serve with the 509th Composite Group, I was granted Christmas leave. When changing trains in Butte, Montana, I first realized that a security agent was keeping track of me. As I walked the depot platform for some exercise, he was standing at the end of the building all alone and smoking. I think he realized that I knew who he was; no words were exchanged. Upon my return, Mr. Uanna reminded me that one of his agents had kept track of me the entire two weeks. It must have been a real lonely Christmas for this agent spending two weeks during the holiday season in a small eastern Montana town in midwinter.

I was a member of the advance party who were flown to Tinian on one of our own C54 planes called the Green Hornets. We left Wendover AFB on May 15,

1945, under secret orders and with a security agent through Hamilton AFB, California. When we left there, well before midnight, each of us was given a sealed envelope containing our secret orders and revealing our destination. We were not permitted to open them until we had passed the point of no return on our way to Hickam Field, Hawaii. At last we knew we were going to Tinian Island.

Later in the night, we lost one engine and it became questionable if we would make it. We were asked to prepare to jettison our luggage. It never got to that point and as dawn broke, Diamond Head came into view. Group Chaplain Downey was aboard and when we deplaned at Hickam Field he remarked, "I have never prayed so hard or smoked so many cigarettes in my life". I replied, "I firmly believe if you want something done right, leave it to the professionals."

We spent a week in Hawaii for an engine to arrive from the continent and to be installed. That was an enjoyable week - my first time in Hawaii. It turned out to be a great Rest and Recuperation (R and R) between duty at Wendover and Tinian. Once again we were on our way with a refueling stop on Johnston Island. While there, we saw the stage play Arsenic and Old Lace starring Boris Karloff.

Not many hours later, we landed on North Field, Tinian Island, and settled in to do our duties as members of the advance party. Ground troops arrived on Cape Victory, May 29th and debarked Memorial Day, May 30, 1945. The 393rd Bomb Squadron and 320th Troop Carrier Squadron arrived about the same time.

Those several months in the 509th were the highlight of my military service and I cherish the memories of service with the many fine officers and enlisted men in this elite group.

JOHNSTON, LAWRENCE H.
Project Alberta

I would guess that each person who participated in the events in WWII launched from Tinian Island feels that it was a very special time in world history and perhaps he personally was meant to be part of that history. That is certainly how I feel.

In the Fall of 1940, I was a beginning graduate student at Berkeley University, California studying Nuclear Physics under a very bright Professor Luis Alvarez. The big program going on at Berkeley was the development of the cyclotron, a powerful atom smasher, and its use to make a large number of discoveries about atomic nuclei. The inventor of the cyclotron and the charismatic leader of this development, was Ernest Lawrence. One of my early experiences there was the award of the Nobel Prize to Lawrence for his work made by the Swedish Ambassador, rather than the King of Sweden on the Berkeley Campus rather than in Stockholm, because the War was already going on in Europe. It made a deep impression on me and my fiancee, Mildred Hillis, now my wife of many years.

I soon discovered that Lawrence had also become a statesman for national science policy. The National Defense Research Council (NDRC) had been formed with him as a prominent member. Many scientists had spent time in Berkeley learning how to build cyclotrons and they appreciated Lawrence's leadership. He was able later to recruit many of them for work in a number of critical wartime laboratories.

About October, Alvarez told me that Lawrence wanted me to go to an important meeting at Massachusetts Institute of Technology (MIT) and I would have to take over his class in which I was the teaching assistant, while he was gone for two weeks. But within a few weeks, I got a telegram from him saying he was going to stay at MIT and I was needed there too. So I went to Cambridge, Massachusetts about New Year's time 1941. At MIT, I was to find the radiation laboratory, room 4-133. Radiation Laboratory! That must mean it was a project in nuclear physics!

When I inquired for room 4-133, everybody knew where it was. I found a corridor had been blocked off and a friendly guard with a gun sat at a desk in front of the door. I told him I was to see Alvarez and he phoned him. Alvarez soon appeared and took me inside giving a nod to the guard. Security was not a common word in those days. Each person taken into this super secret laboratory was vouched for personally by someone on the staff who had been vouched for by someone else. Only later did a formal clearance process begin to take shape.

Then came the surprise. Alvarez told me this lab had been set up in a big hurry to work on microwave radar! What was radar? He explained saying it could be an important part of the war effort. The big breakthrough was Watson-Watt in Britain had invented the microwave cavity magnetron, now the power generator in everyone's microwave oven, and the magnetron suddenly gave us many kilowatts of microwave power, enough to use for

an effective microwave radar system. Britain had decided to share their most basic secrets with the US. We were already sending massive lend lease shipments to help them in resisting the Axis powers. The Tizard Mission had just recently brought the first magnetron to the US. I was present when our first magnetron was powered up and connected to a coaxial cable. A fiery discharge came out the open end. Edwin MacMillan quickly took out a cigarette and lit it, saying "The first cigarette lit by microwaves!"

I worked on several projects in the Radiation Laboratory (Rad Lab), but soon Alvarez had a bright idea. He was full of them. If radar was capable of directing gunfire to shoot down attacking airplanes even in fog, then radar should be able in bad weather, to provide enough information to bring friendly airplanes into a safe landing at an airfield. So he made me project engineer of his blind landing system, later called Ground Controlled Approach (GCA). That system should be familiar to most of the airmen in the 509th. The idea was simply that a high resolution radar truck would sit beside a runway at the airfield and a controller on the ground would be able to see a plane on the screen to be landed. He would give the pilot verbal instructions over his plane's radio to make the maneuvers needed to bring it down the ideal glidepath. No special equipment would be needed in the airplane beyond the usual military radio channels. After several false starts and more bright ideas, the system took shape in working prototype form. By early 1944, the prototype had spectacular wartime experience in Britain and

Larry Johnston in front of Japanese monument

106

was in production by the Gilfillan Radio Company in Los Angeles. The patents on the system were taken out jointly to Alvarez and me, but of course, our patents were assigned to the US Government!

In late 1943, Lawrence phoned Alvarez that he was now needed by Oppenheimer at Los Alamos on the ultra secret bomb project. It is of interest that General Groves had appointed Oppenheimer as director of Los Alamos at the recommendation of Lawrence. Oppenheimer had a reputation for being involved in Communist causes and it took Lawrence's assurance he knew Oppenheimer well enough that it would be worth the risk to have him in this very sensitive post. Oppenheimer did a tremendous job, partially fueled by his Jewish background and hatred of Hitler's holocaust of the German Jews.

After Alvarez had been at Los Alamos awhile, he phoned me I should stop to see him at the new Argonne Laboratory in Chicago where he was visiting. This I did. He took me in to see the world's second historical nuclear reactor and they started it up for us. Here was a real nuclear chain reaction going on! Could that reaction be used to make a bomb? He told me I was needed at Los Alamos to work with him. No more persuasion was needed for me, but it was a different story for the MIT Rad Lab director, Lee Dubridge, to let me go. It took some arm twisting by James Conant, head of the NDRC and Karl Compton, President of MIT, to persuade him I was needed more at Los Alamos than at the Rad Lab. It is of passing interest that the heads of all NDRC sponsored laboratories seem to have known the national picture of other secret projects going on.

On May 8, 1944, I got off the train in Lamy, New Mexico fifteen miles down from Santa Fe, to be met by Alvarez and George Kistiakowski, our new boss and head of the Explosives Division. Kistiakowski had been a professor of chemistry at Harvard, specializing in explosives. We left the station in an Army vehicle driven by a woman in Women's Army Corps (WAC) uniform. On the way, they briefed me on what they were doing. The Explosives Division was in charge of developing the implosion concept of the Fat Man bomb, required to utilize the plutonium metal that was being produced in the new nuclear reactors at the Hanford site in Washington State. The Fat Man was the type of bomb so successfully tested at Alamogordo, New Mexico and the one dropped not so accurately on Nagasaki.

First we stopped in Santa Fe at an office at 109 East Palace Street maintained to process new personnel and handle all mail for people on the hill. Post Office Box 1663, Santa Fe, New Mexico was to be our address. Dorothy McKibbin registered me and gave me a badge to wear and a billfold pass card with a Q clearance, the highest level for people working in the Manhattan Project. Then we drove across the Rio Grande, up a winding road through sagebrush, higher through thin pine forest, to the site of Los Alamos at 7500 feet elevation. At the entrance gate, we all showed our badges and passes. They dropped me and my bags off at Fuller Lodge where I stayed until my wife and child arrived several weeks later.

Fuller Lodge was a magnificent rustic log building two stories high. It had served as a lodging place for parents who were visiting their sons at the Los Alamos Ranch School for boys. The institution had been rudely removed to provide a hideout in the mountains for the nuclear bomb work. They gave me a room upstairs and a very agreeable roommate, Duncan Macdougal. I found out later Macdougal was a well known explosives expert. The downstairs was an elegant rustic dining room where I ate.

The first morning, I went to see Alvarez whose office was in the tech area. To get into the tech area, you had to show your pass card and display your badge at all times. Mine was a two inch round white button with a number. Secretaries and technicians wore blue badges.

Alvarez brought me up to date with the project. There were two main bomb types being worked on. The gun method for using Uranium 235 was coming along well. In this method, a large bore gun shot a six inch slug of Uranium into a hollow cylinder of Uranium making a super critical assembly start a fission chain reaction for the full effect of the nuclear bomb explosion. At that time, there were only small amounts of U235 available; but it's full production was underway at the Oak Ridge, Tennessee facility where magnetic spectrograph racetracks were separating one percent of the rare U235 from U238. This gun type bomb called Little Boy was dropped on Hiroshima.

Alvarez soon identified a problem for me to work on. The implosion type bomb was more efficient in its output energy of fissionable material than Little Boy, but it had some very challenging problems. This bomb used a large sphere of high explosives about four feet in diameter. At the center was a five inch core of Plutonium to be fired. The high explosive sphere had to be initiated all over its outer surface at the same time to create an imploding explosive wave that would finally reach the core and compress it to make a supercritical nuclear explosion.

The explosives experts had divided the outer surface of the sphere into 32 patches similar to a soccer ball. On each patch was an explosive lens to focus a point detonation into an imploding explosive wave. These lenses were a great invention and critical to success. But unsolved was the problem of initiating the focal points of each of these 32 lenses simultaneously so the waves of all the lenses would join to create the entire implosion wave. They had tried using a harness of 32 lengths of primacord as a means of producing this simultaneous detonation of the lenses, but the primacord was too variable in its speed of explosive propagation to produce the simultaneity required.

Alvarez asked Kistiakowski why they did not use 32 electric detonators fired simultaneously to do the job. Kistiakowski said that electric detonators had an intrinsic delay of several milliseconds in firing which would spoil the simultaneity. Timing of all the lenses was required simultaneous to within less than one microsecond. Alvarez then decided there was no basic physical law which would require this amount of delay if you could put enough electrical energy fast enough into the right design of an electric detonator.

So he gave me the job of designing a detonator and electric firing system that would have no substantial delays in initiating a high explosive. This was a far cry from doing nuclear physics but not so far from build-

ing equipment for doing physics experiments. I had always enjoyed the Fourth of July for shooting firecrackers. If only I had protected my ears while doing those explosive experiments at Los Alamos! I now have a deep hearing loss, which gradually showed up in later years.

At Los Alamos you could get things and services fast if you were working on a high priority project. Within two days, I had a portable building set up on lonely South Mesa, two miles from the main tech area. Also a big workbench, some stools, a gasoline driven generator, a few electric cords, an assortment of mechanical and electronic tools, an electronic power supply giving up to 5000 volts DC, an assortment of high voltage capacitors, a large roll of primacord, a gasoline blowtorch, some chemical glassware, some matches, a box full of DuPont electric blasting caps of the usual kind, and an olive drab colored automobile to get me around.

THE EXPLODING BRIDGEWIRE DETONATOR IS BORN

My first setup for trying to made a fast detonator was to suddenly discharge a high voltage capacitor through a very fine short wire, an electric current of thousands of amperes. The resulting explosion of the poor bridgewire, embedded in high explosive, should produce such a rapid buildup of high temperature and pressure that the explosive might be almost instantly launched into a full exploding mode. The explosive was PETN, the same explosive used in primacord. In fact my supply of the explosive was to cut open a length of primacord and pour it into a detonator capsule.

The first experimental shot was soon readied; it produced a loud bang and the disappearance of the detonator parts. All I could find outside the building was the frayed ends of the wires giving me the encouragement that we were on the right track. All this was within a week of my arrival at Los Alamos. I jumped into the car and drove in to the Tech Area and told the result. Alvarez was an instant believer, but Kistiakowsky could think of negative explanations of my results.

We set up a regimen of tests that would show the timing of such detonations beyond reasonable doubt. Within several more days and some failures, I was firing pairs of detonators and showing they fired simultaneously within two microseconds. The explosives experts showed us a very simple and clever way of measuring this. The two detonators to be compared were connected to op-

posite ends of a short piece of primacord and fired. If the two fired at the same instant, the two detonation waves would meet in the exact middle of the piece of primacord. The place of meeting was shown by a metal plate taped to the primacord. Where the two explosions meet there is an extra high pressure produced, which makes a well defined nick in the plate. If there was a small difference in the timing, the nick would be found off center on the plate. One eighth (1/8) inch off center represented a timing difference of one microsecond.

Kistiakowski was now convinced and we launched a program for full scale development and tests. Other groups who were making experimental implosions started using our detonator system and soon we had another large building on South Mesa for fabricating detonators. A number of Indian women were hired, from neighboring pueblos, to do the work of soldering the bridgewires and assembling the detonators including the explosive. They did a great job. The explosive experts were able to give valuable ideas for making the detonators perform better, soon giving timing of tenths of a microsecond. Advanced civilization came to South Mesa when we also had a pair of outside privies and electric lighting, but no running water.

COMMUNITY LIVING AT LOS ALAMOS

Living conditions were considered primitive by some at Los Alamos, but to us who enjoyed camping and outdoor experiences, it was a paradise. A walk of two blocks from our apartment took one to the edge of the Mesa and into pine forest. But there were no nightclubs, no bars, no fashion shops and no golf courses. There was a movie theater, a grocery store and a large cafeteria where you could eat. Most of the single people ate there. Each day there was a single standard meal, few choices. But periodically the word would get around that tonight would be steak night. The place would be crowded with people for three reasons: The chef was a great cook, it came out the way you ordered it; the meat was very high quality; and meat was rationed, but no meat stamps were required for eating those steaks; a great morale builder. Ration stamps were required for sugar and butter at the store.

If you wanted wider shopping, there was a daily bus to Santa Fe. They said Santa Fe merchants soon recognized people from The Hill because they were in a hurry and had currency in large denominations. Everybody in Santa Fe knew there was something big going on at the former Ranch School and many rumors went around. Some of the rumors were probably planted as counterintelligence by our agents. One rumor was that Los Alamos was now a sanctuary for pregnant Army women.

We lived in a four-plex apartment house along the main road that led West toward the nearby mountains, then turned South toward South Mesa and the outlying sites where explosives were cast from which several times a day you would hear pretty loud explosions. Also out along that road was Sawyer Hill, a skiing place where they had set up a rope tow.

Our upstairs apartment had two bedrooms, a livingroom, a bathroom with shower and a kitchen. For cooking, there was one of those Black Beauty wood stoves and a supply of firewood. There was also a two burner electric hotplate. We later were able to buy an electric roaster. The building was heated by a hot air furnace, also fueled by burning wood. Spanish American men came by several times a day and night to keep it burning.

There was a Sunday church service in the theater run by the Army Chaplain, who was Episcopalian. There were also Sunday school classes taught by volunteers. The Chaplain also encouraged us to start a Sunday evening fellowship group which was the highlight event of the week for us. We met in one of the schoolrooms that had a piano, so singing was a big part of it. Each Sunday someone would bring a message. Quite a few of the soldiers came, many were homesick for their families and home churches. We also had picnics on weekends. One of the soldiers enjoyed holding our young daughter as he had a baby at home about that age.

When Easter time 1945 came, we asked the chaplain if he was planning an Easter Sunrise service. He said his seminary had not taught them anything about such things, but encouraged us to organize one and he would promote it. So we had a big one with wonderful outdoor singing of Easter hymns and a message by James Roberts, a physics professor from Northwestern University.

There was a small hospital with several beds and good medical service. The doctors and nurses were Army staff. Many of the young scientists were having babies so that was one of the major occupations of the hospital. One of the nurses told Millie she was disillusioned. She had enlisted as a nurse in the Army expecting to be on a battle-front tending wounded soldiers and here she was acting as a midwife and baby nurse for civilian women in the USA. We had our second child there; Margaret was born in April 1945. Her attending physician was James Nolan who later went to Tinian with Project Alberta. Millie stayed in the hospital for a week as was standard practice in those days.

HOW I BECAME INVOLVED IN THE TINIAN EXPERIENCE

Early in 1945, our detonator work was taken over by the group of engineers who were producing the overall design of the Fat Man bomb. Germany was out of the war and it became apparent that Japan would become the theater in which the bomb would be used. Alvarez went to Oppenheimer and asked him if there were any jobs where he might be needed in that effort. Oppenheimer said there was one thing he had not taken care of and that was to have measurements made of the total energy put out by the bombs that were dropped on Japan. This information would be needed by the military to compare with the damage seen on the ground after the bombing.

He gave Alvarez this challenging job to fly on the bombing missions and make such measurements using whatever methods he could devise. Alvarez asked to have a separate B29 for use in doing the job and started to think of how he could come up

Above: Larry Johnston in front of Officer's Club

Right: Larry Johnston in front of Tinian Tavern

with a number, the number of kilotons of TNT equal to the output of the atomic weapons. He came up with the following scheme: He would make detailed measurements of the shape and size of the blast pressure wave produced by the bomb. In talking with the theorists, he found a shock wave such as this would produce a pressure waveform that would propagate for long distances and the duration of the shock wave would be closely related to the total energy. This meant the wave could be measured from the 30,000 foot elevation of the bombing group and the results would not depend critically on knowing the exact distance from the bomb explosion to the measuring point.

In terms of hardware, he would use a special linear microphone to listen to the blast wave and record that waveshape in his B29. But the microphone could not be mounted on the airplane because of the engine noise. He thought of having the microphone hang from a parachute in free open air to pick up the wave. This would require a radio transmitter also be hanging from the parachute to send out the information to be received in the airplane, by then several miles away, and recorded for later analysis.

So Alvarez recruited a small group of scientists and Special Engineering Detachment (SED) soldier technicians to do the job. I was one of the scientists. Time was short for getting it together. From his having visited many wartime laboratories, he was able to locate many of the components he would need. In particular he knew of a system at Caltech that had a linear microphone which could be modified for our use. This came with an FM telemetering transmitter and an FM receiver to go into the plane; so this was the core of his system. From our GCA days, he had friends at the Gilfillan Radio Company who agreed to quickly manufacture the several dozen copies of this system that would be needed. For each bombing mission, he decided he would have three independent measuring systems in case one or two of them failed. My job was to design the recording equipment to go in the plane.

We were looking for an opportunity to test our equipment and procedures to get us ready for our missions over Japan. That came when the Trinity test of the Fat Man bomb was planned for Alamogordo, New Mexico. Alvarez arranged for us to have a B29 take us on a flight over the test at 30,000 feet altitude when the Fat Man was to be

Walter Goodman in Tinian Tavern after beer party

exploded. We arranged to take off from Kirtland Air Force base near Albuquerque, but Oppenheimer called Alvarez at the last minute. He had cold feet about how big the explosion might be. If it was ten times what they had calculated, we might be in danger. He ordered us to be at least twenty miles away from the bomb when it exploded. Alvarez was very angry about this because it would make our measurements much weaker than would be expected. But we had no choice especially when we cooled down and realized Oppie might know something we did not.

We took off before dawn on July 16 and flew around listening to the countdown coming from the main bunker at Alamogordo. I started the recording system. We opened the bomb bay doors and at count zero dropped our parachute gauges. There was a flash as the bomb went off and we prepared for the shock wave to reach our microphones hanging in the air from the parachutes to be recorded. The flash was pretty bright, even at twenty miles. The white light lit the ceiling of our plane, faded to orange and disappeared.

My immediate reaction was Thank God, my detonators worked! There were so many new kinds of systems that had to work, I imagine each person there who was responsible for one of the systems had the same kind of thoughts. We circled around the rising mushroom cloud awed by the magnitude of the effects we were seeing that we had caused. The implosion bomb was a success! Nobody there doubted the Little Boy bomb would succeed, but the much simpler Little Boy required Uranium 235 which would be very costly compared to the Plutonium soon to come plentifully out of the Hanford reactors. When we got back to Los Alamos, we could not talk to our family or others about what had happened, but there certainly was noticeable joy in the town. The patent office got busy at this point and got people to patent various features of the bombs. I prepared the patent application on the Exploding Bridgewire Detonator and Alvarez decided they should take it out in my name. There were several other patents also concerning our work.

We now had only a few days to get ready for the bombing missions from Tinian. The Tinian event was called Project Alberta in Los Alamos code. I could not tell my wife where I was going but she guessed it must be overseas somewhere because I was getting immunizing shots.

On July 20, we and our boxes of equipment boarded one of the C54 twin engine Green Hornet airplanes. The Green Hornet fleet was a complete airline created for Col. Tibbets for service to his 509th Composite Group. We flew to Wendover code named Kingman at Los Alamos, where we were processed for our mission. We took off all our clothes and were issued standard military gear; underwear, shirts, pants, socks, some wonderful hiking boots and handkerchiefs, all military drab. Our civilian clothes and billfolds were put in a bag and delivered to our families without any explanation. Millie found out from Gerry Alvarez that she had received such a bag too and did not seem worried.

We were issued standard military identification cards, AGO cards from the Adjutant General's Office. My card said I was a captain in the air force. Alvarez was a colonel. We were each given a packet of mimeographed orders which would enable us to buy any goods or transportation needed to carry out our mission. My orders were not very specific, just that I was to go on a special military operation in the Pacific Theater. We were supposed to give a signed copy to any agent who supplied us things. We looked at each other and decided we were a pretty good-looking outfit.

We got into another Green Hornet for the series of hops to the Tinian Island base Alberta; first to Hamilton Field near San Francisco, then the longest hop to Hickam Field in Hawaii. We sat strapped into bucket seats along the sides of the plane, our cargo stored in the central aisle. We ate box lunches provided. We could wander around. The pilot was listening to an AM broadcast station in Honolulu and seemed to be homing in on the signals. Finally, we saw the outline of Diamond Head and landed. We stayed half a day at Hickam and took off for further hops to Johnston Island and Kwajalein. On this long hop, we crossed the International Date Line, Alvarez took out a dollar bill and wrote Short Snorter Luie and passed it around for all of us to sign. He said this is the standard practice on transpacific cruises; an initiation into the elite club of Short Snorters. Anyone who cannot produce a Short Snorter bill from previous crossings is initiated with ceremonies on deck. So we all did the same. I still have my Short Snorter bill somewhere. From Kwajalein, we flew to Saipan and then a short hop to Tinian. There was opportunity to eat at a mess hall at each station while the plane was being refueled.

On Tinian at last, we were impressed by the four mile long, parallel runways of our airfield. The runways were made of crushed coral mined from the hillside, they were kept wet with saltwater and rolled frequently. They were as smooth as good concrete and there were two such airfields in addition to others on nearby Saipan. Squadrons of B29s from these fields, 1800 miles from central Japan, had been bombing Japan for some time. The 509th had its own almost independent base, with the idea of improving security. We were given half a square mile of real estate with our own mess hall, diesel power station, latrines, outdoor shower, orderly room, officer's club, outdoor theater and a special parking line along the southernmost runway for our B29s.

The 509th planes had been practicing for the A-bomb missions by dropping on Japanese targets, bombs that simulated the Little Boy and Fat Man in their ballistics. They were filled with simple high explosives. The Fat Man, pumpkins, had five tons of explosive in them making them the heaviest bombs being used in that war zone.

We were housed in sleeping tents about fifteen feet square with about eight metal cots in each. I shared a tent with Henry Linschitz, a chemist who I later learned was part of the explosives assembly team for the Nagasaki Fat Man bomb. We were the only occupants of the tent.

They gave us a nice air-conditioned Quonset Hut in which we could work on our instruments. This was well planned since we had not considered high humidity in building our equipment. At one end of that hut was stored the plutonium core for the bomb. It was kept in a cast aluminum close fitting case with a thermometer sticking out of the top. I'm not sure what the purpose of the thermometer was except to reassure us that the plutonium was inside giving off alpha particles and staying several degrees above room temperature. A guard was posted 24 hours a day to watch that box, only the guards had no idea why it was so important. They were freaked out when they found out later the little box they had been guarding was the active part of a bomb that would destroy a city.

Our airplane for these missions was made available to us out on the lineup of B29s; it was labeled V-89, The Great Artiste. Its commander was Charles Sweeney and he had his own aircrew and a groundcrew for maintenance. We started installing our equipment in it in our modified rear compartment directly behind the bomb bays. I installed the telemetering receivers on their special metal table along with my pressure recording units all in triplicate. Others installed our parachute gauges in the rear bomb bay and the receiver antennas which were arranged so they could be thrust down into the airstream when they were needed. Alvarez spent a lot of his time in the officers club talking to the pilots and to our other scientists. He had an abiding interest in flying, having flown small planes before the war and having invented the GCA Radar Blind Landing System. I did not go into the officers club any more than I had to

Walter Goodman in front of diesel power station, Tinian Valley Authority.

Jesse Kupferberg at orderly room

because it reeked of cigarette smoke and was poorly ventilated to preserve the air conditioning.

We were told to prepare for our first mission on August 2nd and we were able to meet that deadline. On August 3rd, we were told we would go that night, but weather conditions made them call off the mission late that evening. We were constantly getting weather reports from our planes returning from missions over Japan and they also made special weather reconnaissance flights for our particular targets when they had been selected. Again on August 5th, we were alerted and got ready. About 8 o'clock our people gathered at the bomb pit where the Little Boy bomb was being loaded into the bomb bay of the Enola Gay. We were given opportunity to write messages on the bomb itself. I wrote, in black marker "To the people of Japan, from my friends in China" recalling the atrocities the Japanese Army had committed in its rape of Nanking. Army photographers were taking flash pictures of the loading and of the crew. One of the pictures that has survived shows Agnew, Alvarez and me beside the Enola Gay during the loading.

About midnight, we went to a briefing for the mission. The target city was announced as Hiroshima and there was probably a secondary target not announced. The weather officer gave a favorable report, the crews were told what armaments were to be taken and how much fuel to load. The three planes to fly were the Enola Gay V-82 piloted by Paul Tibbets, carrying the Little Boy bomb; the Great Artiste V-89 piloted by Charles Sweeney, carrying our instruments and scientists; and Necessary Evil V-91 piloted by George Marquardt, carrying Bernie Waldman as operator of the Fastax camera. The Chaplain prayed for the men on the mission and for an early end to hostilities.

Then we were told to pick up our protective gear: A parachute, an inflatable rubber life raft, a steel helmet, a vest with emergency supplies - eating rations, shark repellent, fishing line and a very heavy flack suit loaded with steel plates. We climbed up the ladder into our back compartment of the plane. It wasn't easy carrying all that weight and bulk of gear which would hopefully not be

Inside of Quonset Hut for group. Calendar for August 1945 with the days crossed off through the 16th. At far end are two blast gages.

needed. We took it all off inside the plane and I placed the flack suit under my chair. We needed freedom of action. We had Alvarez, Harold Agnew and myself back there. We strapped ourselves into our bucket seats and the plane took off at 2:45 am for Japan. The plan was to fly at low altitude, 5000 feet, to save fuel and rendezvous the three planes over an island off Japan for the strike formation.

At altitude, Agnew and I started testing our equipment. Alvarez was very tired from burning the midnight oil. He soon climbed up into the padded tunnel and went soundly to sleep. Agnew switched the power on to the pressure gauges in the bomb bay. Before the drop, these gauges were powered from the plane's power system. When they were dropped out of the bomb bay, they would change over to their internal batteries for the few minutes they performed their task of telemetering their pressure data. I picked up the telemetering signals on the three FM receivers and tuned the receivers to the signals. I loaded film into the three movie cameras and checked their focus on the bright spot on the CRT tubes. I calibrated the voltage sensitivity of the CRT tubes, wrote

Below: (L-R): Harold Agnew, Luis Alvarez, Larry Johnston, Bernard Waldman in front of bombed-out Japanese Administration Headquarters.

Above: Red Cross lady who provided recreational gear.

(L-R) top row: Harold Agnew, Luis Alvarez
(L-R) bottom row: Larry Johnston, Bernard Waldman
with parachute blast gage on Tinian

Before August 6, 1945 flight to Hiroshima
(L-R): Larry Johnston, Luis Alvarez, Harold Agnew

the calibration data in my large notebook and everything else I could think of.

But then I had a disturbing realization: Our group had not discussed how large an explosion we were expecting from the bomb. It was a gamble. If I set the gain of the system too high, the pressure spikes would go off scale on the film and be impossible to measure. If I set the gain too low, the signal would be small on the film and would not give good accuracy in the measurements.[1]

This called for a high level policy decision, but I hated to wake up our leader. So I decided to leave the setting until we were near Japan when he would need to be awake anyway. When it started to get daylight on our approach to Japan, I decided the time had come. I woke him up and told him what we needed. He was furious for being disturbed and told me to decide myself where to set it. He calmed down when he saw we needed to get active. We heard over the intercom phones that we would soon be climbing to altitude of 30,000 feet and we should start pressurizing. The tail gunner, who had been sitting with us monitoring the intercom phones, went back to his station. To do so, he had to go through an unpressurized section of the plane to his pressurized station. Agnew thrust the three receiver antennas down into the airstream.

Our planes got into the planned strike formation: First, the Enola Gay with the bomb, followed by our Great Artiste and then the observer's plane. Weather reports came in on the radio that our target was open. Our planes had been on orders of radio transmission silence all the way from Tinian in order not to give away the mission. Alvarez took over the intercom phones. Our planes approached Hiroshima on a planned path and we started the bomb-

ing run. Alvarez got a signal to that effect. I started the movie cameras running and tweaked up the receiver tunings. Then Agnew and Alvarez sat beside me and we each took over the tuning of one of the three receivers as indicated by a zero centered meter on their receiver. We heard the wind rushing as the bomb bay doors on our plane opened and a continuous tone transmitted by the Enola Gay ended, indicating the bomb had been dropped. Simultaneously, our bombardier dropped our parachute gauges which would slowly descend while the bomb dropped to its target, exploded and the pressure wave traveled up to our high altitude. The receivers needed constant tuning as the parachutes descended to slightly higher pressures. Then we saw the flash of the bomb explosion, as a white flash coming up through our small window made a bright disc on the ceiling of the plane that faded to orange. The Little Boy had worked! We kept tuning until a big swing on our meters indicated our microphones had seen the pressure wave and hopefully it had been recorded on my recording system and movie cameras.[2]

Then we felt a double jolt as the shockwave hit our plane. We relaxed and exulted together. Everything was going as planned! The war would soon be over! Captain Parsons, the Technical Weaponeer, sent a coded message back to Norman Ramsey on Tinian: "Clear cut results in all respects successful. Exceeded TR test in visible results. Normal conditions obtained in aircraft after delivery was accomplished. Visual attack on Hiroshima at 052315z with only one tenth cloud cover. Flack and fighters absent." We circled around while the mushroom cloud rose. We took turns looking out through the single nine inch window at the scene and then our planes headed back toward Tinian.

---

[1] The most basic calibration of the overall system was provided by a clever addition to the microphone itself. As soon as the canister was hanging freely in the air, two small pistons would snap into and out of the microphone cavity providing small positive and negative absolute pressure changes that would register on the record.

[2] Harold Agnew reminded me recently, March 2003, that the receivers he and I tended gave good results, but that Alvarez's film did not show any activity.

Many people have asked me if I was praying for the Japanese people who were dying at that time. No, I was not. I had done all that praying before starting on the mission, including the prayer for guidance whether I should be part of it. I was all prayed up and convinced that God was having mercy on the Japanese and on us in getting the wartime killing and waste stopped. I was thanking God that I could be and had been part of the process.

I started up the recording cameras and did all the calibration procedures again. We rested on the way back to Tinian. I wrote some more in my notebook including a letter to my two year old daughter, Ginger, which I expected her to read in later life. On Tinian, there was a big crowd waiting. General Spaatz was there and he awarded Col. Tibbets the Distinguished Service Cross. The air force had brought in a number of reporters and they interviewed us. A reporter from the Los Angeles Times interviewed me and that interview also appeared in the Hollywood Citizen News, my hometown newspaper.

The New York Times head science reporter, William Laurence, had been officially chosen early on to document the project and was given military clearance to spend time at Los Alamos where Alvarez had been assigned the job of educating him about the bombs. On Tinian, he spent hours in the officer's club talking to the fliers and scientists. By the time President Harry Truman announced the Hiroshima bombing, Laurence had the story of the whole Manhattan Project written up for the world's press. He had the "scoop" most reporters dream of.

We naively assumed that Japan would now surrender and the war would be over. Would we need to deliver another bomb? That question was soon answered when we were alerted to get ready for another mission August 9th. This was to be the Fat Man bomb that used my detonators and we had tested at Trinity. I had a proprietary interest in it. A question arose about who in our group should go on this mission. We had been told before we went to Tinian that no scientists were to go on the flights over Japan. But Alvarez had gotten an exception to that order from General Groves. He wanted to make sure our system worked and worked with us on the scene. But now that dropping A-bombs seemed to be getting routine, he decided it was not a good idea to expose our scientists to further dangers. We had our SED soldiers

William Laurence, Science Editor, New York Times. He erroneously reported the Great Artiste dropped the Nagasaki Bomb.

there and they could handle it. He asked me whom I had trained to do my job of handling the cameras, recording equipment and calibrations. I replied, "I had not heard we were supposed to train others to do our jobs and I had not trained anyone." Alvarez said, "Would you mind going again and doing it?" I had expected to do it anyway, so I said, "Fine with me". He chose soldiers, Walter Goodman and Jesse Kupferberg to go with me. He then thought a minute and remarked that if I went this time, I would be the only person who had witnessed all three of the wartime bomb explosions. We knew this was the only remaining bomb on the island and no more were scheduled to arrive soon from Los Alamos. That evening, Alvarez got together with Bob Serber and Phil Morrison with an idea. To help the Japanese military recognize the devastation they faced from nuclear bombs, they would take advantage of the parachuted canisters on that mission, to send a special delivery letter to a Japanese physicist at the University of Tokyo, whom they had known when he had made a visit to Berkeley. Alvarez wrote the final draft and we taped a copy in his handwriting, onto each of the three canisters which would be dropped along with the bomb. Here is the text of the message:

Headquarters
Atomic Bomb Command

August 9, 1945

To: Prof. R. Sagane
From: Three of your former Scientific Colleagues during your stay in the United States

We are sending this as a personal message to urge that you use your influence as a reputable nuclear physicist, to convince the Japanese General Staff of the terrible consequences which will be suffered by your people if you continue in this war.

You have known for several years that an atomic bomb could be built if a nation were willing to pay the enormous cost of preparing the necessary material. Now that you have seen we have constructed the production plants, there can be no doubt in your mind, all the output of these factories working twenty-four hours a day, will be exploded on your homeland.

Within the space of three weeks, we have proof fired one bomb in the American desert, exploded one in Hiroshima and fired the third this morning.

We implore you to confirm these facts to your leaders and to do your utmost to stop the destruction and waste of life which can only result in the total annihilation of all your cities if continued. As scientists, we deplore the use to which a beautiful discovery has been put, but we can assure you that unless Japan surrenders at once, this rain of atomic bombs will increase manyfold in fury.

Preparations for the mission went about the same as for the first. But this time, there was no big picture taking as the bomb was loaded into the strike plane Bockscar V-77. The pilot, instead of Fred Bock, was Charles Sweeney. Bock was assigned to pilot our plane the Great Artiste. For this mission, there was no lack of important people who wanted to fly on the third plane, the observation plane, since things had gone so smoothly on the

Hiroshima flight. On board were two distinguished Britons, Sir William Penney and Group Captain Leonard Cheshire of the Royal Air Force. The plane was Full House V-90 and the pilot was Major James Hopkins. William Laurence rode in the pilot compartment of our plane.

At the briefing, we were told the target would be the city of Kokura. I do not remember Nagasaki being mentioned as a secondary target. We took off as planned and flew to our rendezvous point, Yakushima, off the coast of Japan, only to find the observer plane was not there. Radio communication would have easily clarified the problem but we were on radio silence. We circled for an hour burning precious fuel waiting for them to come. Finally, we gave up and Bockscar followed by our plane, headed for the target Kokura. Goodman, Kupferberg and I prepared to drop our parachute canisters to make recordings. As we approached Kokura, it was evident the weather had gotten cloudy while we were circling. Sweeney started a bombing run on radar hoping to complete it visually since we were under orders not to drop our bomb except by visual contact. Our bombardier could not make that contact, so they decided to go back and make the run again, but again we were not able to penetrate the clouds over the city. Each attempt took us about fifteen minutes. After a third attempt to bomb Kokura, it became clear that Bockscar was running low on fuel. In addition, Kokura was well defended by antiaircraft guns and each time we flew over, the gunfire became more accurate. We felt our plane bouncing around from the bursts.

Sweeney decided we should go for Nagasaki, the secondary target and he told his bombardier if necessary he should drop the bomb by radar. With that five ton bomb aboard, his plane was consuming fuel rapidly and there was no way he could carry the bomb back to Tinian. We approached Nagasaki by the shortest path from Kokura and not along the planned bombing approach. We again prepared our instruments in the Great Artiste. We heard the tone start which meant we were on a bombing run and we opened our bomb bay doors. The tone stopped, the bomb had been dropped and so had our parachute gauges. We saw the white flash come in through our window. My detonators must have worked again! We did not stay around long to see what happened on the ground but our tail gunner had an amateur movie camera and he took pictures of the huge mushroom cloud that rose up.

Bockscar was now hopelessly short of fuel to return to Tinian so we headed for Okinawa with its airstrip which had recently been taken from the Japanese. He radioed the ground station he needed to refuel there, but the station radioed back the strip was much too short for a B29 to land. Sweeney said he had no choice, he was coming in anyway and he fired his emergency flares to indicate the emergency. The reason he was able to land safely on Okinawa was our B29 had a new secret device, reversible pitch propellers, which could brake the plane's forward motion very effectively. He was lucky he had enough gas left to run the propellers! We landed there a few minutes after Bockscar and got some food while the planes were refueled. Nobody seemed to dare ask us how we were able to stop safely on the runway. We only took on enough fuel to take us back to Tinian so we were

light enough to be able to take off again. That runway was mighty short!

Later, we learned what the observation plane, the Full House had done. They apparently mistook another island for the rendezvous place and waited for us to join them. After awhile, they decided we must have aborted the bombing mission for some reason and they broke radio silence telling Tinian we were probably on our way home. Tinian took them at their word and called back the emergency rescue planes that were supposed to be waiting to rescue us in case we were hit and had to ditch in the sea off Japan, or in case we ran out of fuel! This was a terribly botched mission but we had delivered the Fat Man bomb and returned safely. When we landed on Tinian, there was no big welcome. Someone came from the mess hall to tell us they had saved us some food.

Now we surely expected to hear Japan had surrendered, but that only came on August 14th. The news did not cause much surprise. Alvarez was anxious to get back to Berkeley because he had some big ideas about new kinds of particle accelerators, atom smashers, which he wanted to build. He cabled General Groves to get permission for us to leave Tinian but Groves replied we were not to leave until the surrender was signed and enough troops had occupied Japan to ensure their compliance. That would take several more weeks.

So we had some time on our hands. We got a jeep and did some sightseeing on the island. There were a number of things that remained from the Japanese era: a ceremonial arch, the blasted concrete Japanese military headquarters and some statuary. We did some swimming at a coral beach. I got a painful spike in my foot from stepping on a sea urchin. Alvarez spent a lot of time in our air-conditioned hut playing hearts with his buddies and poker games at night. Someone drew a calendar on the white air-conditioning cabinet and crossed off the days like a prisoner might in his prison cell. I spent some time with William Laurence often on worldview themes. He was a convinced Atheist, who could not see any ultimate meaning to life. I wish I had known then a lot of scientific facts which have now become prominently evident: The Big Bang origin of the Universe; the Anthropic Principle; the stubborn elusiveness of a scenario for an accidental origin of life; the availability of Information Theory for calculating probabilities of accidental synthesis of biomolecules; the Cambrian Explosion of multicelled animals with a number of different complex body plans. We parted good friends. Laurence certainly made a reputation among journalists from his coverage of the events at Los Alamos and at Tinian.

One time when I visited the post exchange, I noticed they sold necklaces of beautiful cowry shells. They told me they were from the tide pools around the island. That took me back to my childhood experiences with tide pools at LaJolla. The tides were not very pronounced in the mid Pacific, only a couple of feet. But there was plenty of life evident: Snails, sea urchins, hermit crabs, star fish, one moray eel. There was a kind of small fish which seemed to dislike the water; I think it was a kind of goby. These fish sat on the rocky edges of tide pools, I guess to catch the insects that flew around. If you came too close, they would skip across the water and hop up on the other side of the pool. They only went into the water if you really threatened them. Strange; but I did not see any cowries there.

There was a recreation office run by the Red Cross; they would loan you things like baseballs, bats and swimming aids. I checked out a face mask that would enable me to see clearly underwater and tried it out at one of the sites I had been exploring. What a revelation! Just like you see on TV nowadays! There were many colored fish, great coral formations, sea fans and lots of sea urchins. Finally, I spotted one of those cowries. The reason they were hard to see was when they were happily living on the sea floor, they spread their fleshy mantle completely around their beautiful shell. They looked like a meatball. They only pulled into their shell when they were disturbed. That explained why their shell had such a beautiful shiny polish; they were continually building it up by adding thin layers of shell material (lime?) to their exterior surface!

I brought several of these animals back to my tent to show them off, but there was a problem, they had a bad odor when the animal inside died. The ants got into them and would have eventually cleaned out the shells, but by popular request I knew I would have to move my mortuary somewhere else.

I continued to explore waterfront sites and dived at one site where the cowries were especially plentiful and sleek. The reason; I soon found out this was a place where garbage was dumped into the ocean providing plentiful nutrients for creatures in an ocean where competition was very keen. I collected a goodly number of those cowries and then started thinking about what to do with them. I decided to let the ants do their thing at this location in the sugarcane fields, so I went back about fifteen feet into the field and spread the cowries out.

When I came back the next day, I was distressed to find only a few of the cowries where I had left them. There were only a few ants around. Who stole my cowries? Looking further, I began to find more cowries and those shells had been cleaned out of all organic materials. Soon I discovered the culprit; Hermit Crabs! The

Hermit Crabs that usually live in the tide pools and take over the empty shells of sea snails keep growing until they cannot find any snail shells large enough to accommodate them. These crabs have very tender hindquarters which are normally protected by the snail shells, so when they find themselves homeless, they are very vulnerable to attack from any hungry predator, especially from other crabs. These creatures had found a solution: to leave their natural home in the ocean and move onto the land in the cane fields. They could keep their gills wet from the rain on the island and grow to a size at least four inches long. I have no idea what they normally ate there, but they evidently found the cowry meat tasty. They served me well in cleaning out the shells. I left Tinian with several hundred beautiful cowries of two very different species: One a dark mahogany brown with light colored spots on its back, about an inch long; and the other smaller ones were a cream colored variety with a yellow greenish back and 3/4 of an inch long. Both kinds later made nice necklaces with silver chains.

Alvarez found a way to get cowries without getting wet; trading with the natives. Agnew had brought a lot of small soap bars along for this very purpose and we elected Alvarez as head of a cowry cartel that would do the trading. He soon had saturated the market among the natives for soap and distributed the cowry dividends within our community.

The Green Hornets again carried us on the trip back to the USA. On Hawaii, a big party was thrown for Alvarez which almost made him miss the flight with the rest of us back to the States and to Albuquerque. I soon left Los Alamos for Berkeley to resume my graduate studies and get on with my career. I found there was a great interest among the populace to hear authentic information about the fantastic new bomb that had suddenly ended the war. The Extension Department at the University acted as agent to set me up for a number of talks to various civic groups, including the San Francisco Commonwealth Club. I must have given twenty or thirty such talks. Some of them gave me an honorarium afterwards which helped to feed my growing family. After my talk to the Commonwealth Club, the chairwoman presented me with an envelope. When I opened it afterwards, it explained that their club, as a matter of policy, never paid its internationally known speakers. I guess they considered it such an honor to be asked to talk to them that money would demean their reputation. However, the envelope also contained an engraved card saying they were making a contribution in my name to a charity! How wonderful! A number of churches also asked me to talk, including our own church First Presbyterian of Berkeley.

During my graduate studies, the Radiation Laboratory, now the Lawrence Berkeley Laboratory, had lots of funding from the Manhattan District. They paid me as a research assistant to help build Alvarez' big accelerator idea, the Proton Linear Accelerator. This accelerator was a great success and I did my PhD thesis, 1950, as an experimental study in Nuclear Physics, performed with the proton beam from this machine. This launched me on my academic career in physics.

Luis Alvarez with bomber equipped with his invention "Eagle" radar set for blind bombing. An extremely high-gain antenna for radar looked like an extra wing under the bomber. It saw only one use during the war, but performed admirably.

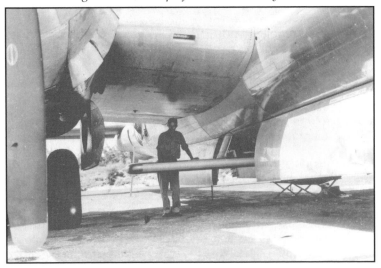

KARNES, THOMAS L.
509th Headquarters Adjutant, Base Classification Officer

The Army Air Corps established Wendover Field as an air base in 1940. Located on the edge of the Bonneville Salt Flats at the Utah, Nevada state line, its terrain and isolation provided a perfect location for the training of aerial gunners and bomb crews.

Originally designed in 1941 as a sub depot to Ft. Douglas, the nearly 2 million acres of salt and scrub persuaded the Army Air Corps to make the place the world's largest bombing and gunnery base. In August 1941, the eleven men stationed there began setting up targets on the salt flats that had ruined the famous Donner party. At its longest, the base stretched 36 miles. (103 people lived in the town!) The first bomb group appears to have arrived in April 1942, but Wendover was not officially activated as an Army Air Corps base until August 1942.

Fresh out of Officers Candidate School (OCS), I was assigned to Wendover in April 1943 straight from Adjutant General OCS as Base Classification Officer. For the next year, I took part in the classification and training of hundreds of crews, mostly B17s, B24s and even P47 pilots.

Virginia and I arrived in Wendover on April 19, 1943 too late in the day to get a room for her. We had to settle for meals in a Wells, Nevada hotel that could have held John Wayne (and straight out of Psycho), a room in a shack with no facilities and one stark light bulb hanging from the ceiling. I reported for duty just in time to learn of a court martial by the base commander of one of his officers. I never knew why nor the result, but Colonel Dippy scared me.

My worst memory was of a crash that must have occurred in the winter of 1943-4. It took place before the 509th was formed. We were training B24 crews then. One crew, on final approach, tried to avoid a small private plane. Instead it cartwheeled into the ground, probably killing the whole crew instantly. On crashing, the bomber hit the Southern Pacific Rail Line and spread the tracks. By awful coincidence, within seconds, a freight train hit the spread tracks, derailed and piled all the cars on end like dominoes, within sight of the B24. Eight or ten box cars caught fire.

As soon as headquarters learned of the wreck, I, as part of an investigation team, drove out the few miles to the carnage. The place was already swarming with Gis looting freight cars which were loaded with beer and clothing for the Pacific. In sum, all the plane crew were dead and several of the freight crew badly hurt. Most of the boxcars were demolished and their load gone. It was Wendover's worst accident and the worst I've ever seen.

I count at least fourteen bomb groups who were trained there from April 1943 when I came, until April 1944. One estimate is that hundreds of aerial gunners and a thousand crews were trained at Wendover on B24s and B17s. Probably most of them went to the 8th Air Force. Many of us were baffled when the bomb crews were replaced by some sixty P47 trainees in May 1944. At the end of June, sixty more followed them.

Colonel Arthur Kellond was base commander during the P47 era. I remember him well for his easy command style, for taking me to an expensive dinner in Colorado Springs and for his little spaniel that followed him everywhere. In August or September, the last fighters left, all of them finding it necessary to buzz the field on their way out.

I have fond memories of a base volleyball team.

Thomas and Virginia Karnes Wendover, 1943

Wendover was frequently visited by an inspection team led by General Travis (who also brought his Dalmatian along). Travis had a powerful team that humiliated most 2nd Air Force base teams. After much recruiting and practice, we whipped an irate Travis; he called off the inspection and returned in a huff to Colorado Springs.

Then in August 1944, the last trainees left and only the permanent cadre and a half dozen administrative airplanes remained. The base no longer had any function and many of us wondered if the base were about to be closed. Higher ranking officers were gradually being transferred elsewhere or went on leave and I was holding several acting positions in base headquarters.

During this strange period, a lone B29 arrived at the base and its pilot came to headquarters to declare his desire to inspect the general facilities. Although only a captain, I was the ranking headquarters officer at the time, so it fell upon me to greet the visitor. He was Lt. Col. Paul Tibbets. He asked a few questions, toured the base, thanked me and left. I gave the episode no particular thought until a few weeks later when Tibbets returned.

Again we had a conversation about the base and more directly, about base personnel. But this time, he offered me a job. He said he was organizing an unusual bomb group that would have a large number of men with rare qualifications, but he thought many of the base cadre could be utilized as the nucleus of the group. It seemed logical to him that I would be suited to arrange for their transfers. In short, I would still handle base personnel while serving him as group adjutant. I was delighted to accept on the spot. The job sounded great. Paul Tibbets and I were about the same age. His air of quiet confidence impressed me immediately as it must have the generals who selected him to command the 509th and I was eager to work for him. I remember asking a small favor; wherever we were to go, could I go by airplane as I had heard too many tales of troop ships. No problem. (In retrospect, one of the smartest moves I ever made in the service. Ask any of the men who went to Tinian by troopship.) Only much later did I learn from his crew some of Tibbets' experiences in the European Theater. His words to me were he had a lot to do and could not afford to spend time on paperwork. I told him that I could.

In its early days, Wendover was pretty primitive. Wives could stay but only if they had jobs on base. They lived in dorms for women only.

I spent the next few months transforming much of the base into the 509th and locating specialists from all over whom someone in the group badly needed. We got some already in the Air Force, Army, Navy, from college faculties and other civilians.

One early episode taught me the seriousness of our security measures. Paul directed me to arrange the transfer of one of our officers, a lieutenant colonel (to the Aleutians)! He was on Tibbets' staff and his crime was talking too much in a bar. Rank meant nothing when it came to security.

The sameness of the Wendover climate made it necessary to read the Salt Tablet or go to Salt Lake City to find out what season it was. It is still one of my favorite cities. The wide streets with clean water running down the gutters always contrasted with dryness of the salt flats. The theaters were air conditioned, a great change.

I also fondly recall the Hotel Utah where Virginia and I luxuriated on rare occasions. Nothing nicer than watching the sunrise over the Wasatch range when you don't have to get up. There was no air conditioning and you got a shock every time you pushed an elevator button. The dry, hot air caused the Deseret News to disintegrate in your hands while you read. That great hotel is now an office building, I think.

If you had enough gas ration coupons, you might drive to the city, much of the way being a straight sixty mile stretch of nothingness. The rail lines closely paralleled the highway and one long night en route to Salt Lake City, we drove barely able to see, mile after mile with the blazing freight train head lights in my eyes. I had no idea where the road was but just didn't turn. If you rode the bus, you had the fun of having your baggage exposed to everyone on the bus while Louis Schaffer's efficient MPs searched for something or other.

Tinian

In the Spring of 1945, I left for Tinian on one of our C54s as part of the first echelon to ready the base for the thousand plus men coming by ship.

Bill Downey, Chaplain, and I often swam together. Close to shore the coral was awful and would cut your feet to shreds. So the Seabees cleared a path out to deep water and anchored a float on which you could loaf or dive off for swimming. One day, Bill dove into the water, then instantly resurfaced screaming at lungtop. I helped him to shore, then drove to the hospital for treatment. Seems he had landed smack on a Portuguese man-of-war whose tentacles spread all over the surface, stinging Bill in a hundred places. He was OK in a few days but never swam again on Tinian.

Tibbets often rewarded 509th men for small jobs well done. A few days after Nagasaki, some scientists needed jeeps to visit the place. Our C54s of the 320th were the only transportation immediately available, so one of our C54s was assigned the job of taking two jeeps to Tokyo. Out of the blue, Paul asked Chuck Perry, mess officer, and me if we wanted to see Tokyo. (We had been tent mates early that summer.) Of course we went. The jeeps pretty well filled the cargo space so Chuck and I stretched out on the jump seats. Chuck nearer the tail than I. Somewhere over the Japanese Empire, the plane dropped about 1000 feet (according to the pilot later). I bounced up in the air several inches and as I was falling back, I saw Chuck about two feet above the seats and in a perfectly flat prone position. Just as suddenly, the plane caught up with him and with a whump he was back in the saddle again. For several minutes, neither of us had anything to say, each probably praying the gas loaded jeeps would stay put.

We cruised over the emperor's palace, took some pictures and spent a brief uneducational moment at the Tokyo airport. Jeepless we returned to Tinian.

After the August 1945 bombings, many scientists made inspection trips to Hiroshima and Nagasaki. Part of my job as adjutant of the 509th Bomb Group was to arrange for their meals and transportation from Tinian Island to the Empire and back. One of these officers clearly stood out by his rank, colonel, his age, about fifty and his scholarly demeanor. A C.Aubrey Smith type, if you are old enough to remember "old" movies. By coincidence, I returned home for discharge on the same plane as the colonel. Packed into one of the 509th C54s loaded with men like myself, we were seat mates on the long flight to San Francisco.

The colonel was Stafford Warren, Chief Radiation Officer of the Manhattan Project, responsible for protecting all of us in the project

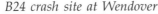
B24 crash site at Wendover

from radiation. He was also Dean of the School of Medicine at UCLA and shared with me some of his observations about atomic radiation and the value of graduate school, my own particular concern then.

In Hawaii, we were annoyed to learn we must pass through American customs, a slow process made worse by the quantity of Japanese souvenirs many of us carried. When it was our turn, the colonel and I placed our bags on the examining table and one of the agents zipped open Colonel Warren's bag first. Lying on top of the colonel's clothing lay a very dead rat, the largest I had ever seen. The customs man jumped back, cursed and demanded an explanation from my new friend. In his calmest professorial fashion, Colonel Warren pointed to me and said, "The captain and I have just returned from Hiroshima where the radioactivity is dangerously high; I have no idea what else you may find in our bags". ZIP! With a single, swift motion, the speechless agent closed the bag, waved all the remaining 509th men through unchallenged and fled to the hospital.

This Segment by Virginia P. Karnes - Wendover, Utah, April 1943

When we arrived, it consisted of desert, an isolated air base, Stateline Hotel and very little else. Barracks for military personnel were located on the base, but female civilian employees lived in barracks just off the base. Unless one was employed on the base, there was no housing for military families. As a result, my husband, new 2nd Lieutenant Thomas L. Karnes lived a few hundred yards from me. Tom had wanted to be stationed in the West, but our first impression of Wendover was, it was a very poor choice. Like every wife who followed her husband, I made the decision to live in the present. Too soon we knew the time of separation would come. For Tom and me, it came in May 1945 when he said goodbye to me and our eleven month old son.

The words bleak and barren come to mind when describing Wendover, brought to life only by the hundreds of young people and the airplanes. In contrast Salt Lake City was a clean, beautiful city (everything that Wendover was not) with wide streets and an abundance of greenery and color. A special joy to me was the line of large Lombardy Poplar Trees growing at a right angle to the road approaching the city. I felt as if my eyes were suddenly refreshed after being parched by the desert landscape.

Wendover weather was either very hot, gradually getting colder, or very cold gradually getting warmer. There was no vegetation except for a few scrubs to mark the changing seasons and no air conditioning to make summer more comfortable. As a bookkeeper in the Finance Office, I continually brushed sand from the pages in the summer when the windows were open and not quite as much in the winter when they were closed.

As the base population grew, there was demand for more civilian housing and concrete block apartments were built. We were able to move into one where I learned some unwelcome lessons from the big iron stove in our kitchen. First, how to start a fire. Anticipating a nice warm kitchen, I put in several tightly rolled

newspapers, some coal and a match. The result was not a cozy, warm fire, but a smoke filled room. One learns quickly from such an experience and we soon became adept at building a good fire.

One of my few cooking utensils was a glass frying pan (all iron was used for the war effort) which was useful for cooking eggs. At least it was until, lacking cake pans, I tried to bake a cake in it. The cake cooked beautifully, but before I could reach the table to put it down, the glass became too hot to handle. I dropped the pan, it shattered on the cement floor and the cake was destroyed.

While serving as the Personnel Officer at Wendover Field during WWII, my husband became good friends with the base Chaplain. In an effort to be highly visible and easily approachable to the men, the Chaplain, a very friendly, gregarious person, made it a practice to call on the various offices each day. During many of these visits, my husband noticed that if their conversation was interrupted by the telephone or business with one of his men, the Chaplain would surreptitiously - and improperly - satisfy his great curiosity by scanning the personnel orders on the desk, in spite of the handicap of reading upside down.

Later, my husband decided to provide the Chaplain with some really interesting news and enlisted a sergeant-conspirator to draw up a set of fake special orders. These orders pretended to transfer the Chaplain to a particularly undesirable base in the Aleutian Islands and were placed on my husband's desk in a normal fashion.

On his next visit to the office, the Chaplain quickly discovered his "transfer" and abruptly departed. Days passed with the anxious officer frequently raising the question of transfers, but never daring to mention his own. Finally, his guilt overcome by his anxiety - even fear - , the Chaplain claimed to have heard a rumor of his transfer; was it true? My husband inquired as to where he had heard such a rumor; transfers were supposed to be secret. Sheepishly, the Chaplain confessed to his sin; would he be going to the Aleutians and when?

The nervous officer was mercifully reassured he would not be shipped out. Then, like Moses, my husband pronounced a new commandment: "Chaplain, henceforth, thou shalt not read papers on desks upside down. Go and sin no more"!

There is one more vignette that belongs in these remembrances. It's a vivid picture of a proper young lady, just arriving at Wendover, perched high on an open GI truck. On her head was a straw hat, with ribbons, held in place by a white gloved hand. On her face was a look of bewilderment, but her posture remained erect and her attire looked clean and crisp down to the white pumps on her feet crossed correctly at the ankle. Should you be reading this now, I want you to know that I, as well as many others, gazed upon you in awe and admiration as you traversed the base. One never felt quite that immaculate and well groomed because of the sand constantly sticking to clothes and hair, but newly arrived, you showed us how it could be.

KING, CECIL N.
393rd Bomb Squadron, Aircraft Maintenance Officer

I have many memories of Wendover, as I spent time in the 2nd Air Force at Gowen in Boise, Idaho. Crews that trained there were very thankful not to have been assigned to Wendover and as B24 cadres quit being formed, Wendover was closed.

I was the first of 393rd personnel to arrive there with the assignment to select location of living quarters and maintenance facilities. Only a small base protection personnel group was there. The 2nd Air Force had stopped training in Wendover.

When the personnel arrived approximately a week later, I was told I was dismissed and should look for an assignment elsewhere. Subsequent events changed that order - I stayed with the squadron.

I remember the arrival of a "bird" colonel, his speech to the assembled, and a mass exodus of furloughs.

I remember that the "Colonel" had an entourage that was looked upon with great suspicion. A great bit of comic relief occurred when my Cocker Spaniel, a favorite of the line mechanics, lifted a leg and watered the dress pants of a rather pompous Captain, who was a part of the "Colonel's" group. The death of that dog was a sad moment for us during a cold winter.

My best memory is that my wife told me she must have a washing machine for diapers or she would not come, so a search began on base. The remains of a double tub machine was found and my sheet metal crew (Wagner and Bishop) fabricated an agitator for one of the tubs. My wife and two month old son arrived, the unit was put in service, and Jappie hung diapers on a line back of our unit. She reported occasionally seeing Mrs. Tibbets doing the same, but in the winter that became "taboo", too cold, and frozen diapers didn't work, so drying "in house" was done.

She did well cooking meals on a wood-burning stove. It was also our heat supply. We were young, healthy, in love and in a high adventure.

Cecil King on forklift loading 320th plane

Maintenance Office, Wendover

There were only a few who knew. In the last days in Cuba with missions ended and planes being prepared to return to Wendover, a broken connection at an intake to a filter canister in a vacuum system was discovered. This canister was located in the aft bomb bay (those planes were standard, thus two bomb bays). We had limited tools and supplies in Cuba and this break was in a solder connection with only minimum stress on the tube when in place. What to do? Take off was tomorrow morning. No solder or iron available. So, put the unit in place according to the shape of the break and make the seal with chewing gum, wrap it with tape for security and let it go. We didn't think it necessary to advise the air crew. The plane made the journey with all systems working and that repair was still in place, as far as I know, when the plane was retired from our group.

KING, JOHN A.
393rd Bomb Squadron, Executive Officer

You will all recall that when we first arrived on Tinian, we were subsisting on C-rations.

I was sitting in the rain, on a rock by the side of one of the island roads, eating my cold C-rations out of a can. A jeep, with a naval officer driving, came along the road and the Navy type stopped to say "hello". In the course of our conversation, he registered surprise at the fact we were on C-rations and invited me to eat at his mess where, he assured me, I would dine on something other than C-rations.

The next evening, a jeep from the Navy installation picked me up and took me to the Navy Officers' mess. I was escorted into the mess by the officer who invited me, and was taken to meet the Navy Captain who was the commander of the Navy installation. Upon being introduced to the captain, he said, "I must apologize to you. In my 30 years service in the United States Navy, this is the first time my guests have had to use paper napkins". I assured him that after sitting on a rock in the rain eating my dinner out of a can, it was no hardship to have to use a paper napkin.

The meal, of course, was excellent.

KOPKA, FREDERICK D.
1027th Air Material Squadron

My partner, Jim Wells, and I were ordered to report by bus to Wendover from the Salt Lake City Air Base. Upon arrival at Wendover, the bus driver looked out over the base and said, "What did you fellows do to deserve this". He laughed - we didn't.

After awhile, Wendover became to me like any small town in the USA.

Col. Tibbets said that if we could find a place to live off base, those of us who were married could have our wives join us. My wife purchased a nice house travel trailer in Lorain, Ohio, and brought it all the way to Wendover. She was a very courageous woman because she had many problems to overcome considering we had a three year old daughter among other things.

My job at Wendover was to run the Sales Commissary. Thru it, I was able to meet a good number of people on the base. A Captain in the Medical Corp, who I shall not mention by name, volunteered to visit our daughter the day before Christmas in a Santa Claus suit that he had acquired.

My trailer was located off base by the 1st-3rd Graders Club. The electrical supply to the base Power Plant operated on direct current. The Post Engineers had made a wooden walk to the door of the trailer to prevent being shocked when wet or damp.

When Santa Claus arrived at the trailer, he had made several previous calls and had been rewarded with several cups of cheer. Inadvertently, he got off the wood walk and was grounded when he took hold of the handle of the trailer. He had enough juice going thru him to light up half of Wendover. His false white beard stuck straight out and he looked more like Father Time than Santa Claus. From inside the trailer, I yelled for him to get on the wood walk after which his lights dimmed quite considerably. He went back to the North Pole more sober than when he arrived.

Wendover had no drunks - we all took turns.

Group Photo, 1027th Air Material Squadron, March 17, 1945, Wendover

PRAYERS of THANKSGIVING

Though the greater part of the year is spent in asking, let us on this day raise our hearts and minds in Thanksgiving. Let us lay aside our burdens and cares for a few hours to join our voices with those of the heavenly court in everlasting praise.

Freedom! What a priceless word! We fight for it; we die for it. But is it not to be found in Thee from Whom all good does come. Truly then are we to be thankful that Thou hast seen fit to bless us during these trying days of strife and hatred. May our hearts re-echo that glorious hymn of praise; Holy! Holy! Holy! Lord God of Hosts.

Nash P. Geany
Chaplain

Lord God of Hosts, we give Thee our humble Thanksgiving...for cattle on a thousand hills...for lands extending from sea to sea..for the harvest and the seasons for the hills and the plains, for the fields and the grain ...for a land of Freedom, of hope, justice...for the rivers that roll through this our land and the seas that wash upon its shores...for cities, tall and straight...for the rain and the winds...for prayers that were uttered at Valley Forge and Gettysburg...for prayers that from a million hearts seek Thee out at Thy throne of Grace... Father Almighty, keep us ever faithful to our heritage and to Thy blessings...keep us ever faithful, lest we forget, lest we forget. Almighty God, hear our prayer.

Amen.

William B. Downey
Chaplain

THANKSGIVING
NOVEMBER 30
1944

CONSOLIDATED
MESS

WENDOVER FIELD, UTAH
Charles E. Trowbridge
Lt. Colonel Air Corps
Commanding

MENU

Turkey Broth du Noodles

Crisp Crackers

Celery Hearts   Pickles   Olives

Roast Young Turkey

Giblet Gravy   Cranberry Sauce

Savory Dressing

Whipped Potatoes   Buttered Peas

Boiled Onions

Waldorf Salad

Parker House Rolls   Bread

Butter

Pumpkin Pie   Hot Mince Pie

Ice Cream

Fruit Punch   Coffee

Assorted Candy   Assorted Nuts

Fresh Fruits

whiskey   Cigars   Cigarettes   Rum
Dinner Music by the 593rd AAF Band   wine

THANKSGIVING MEMORIES
WENDOVER 1944

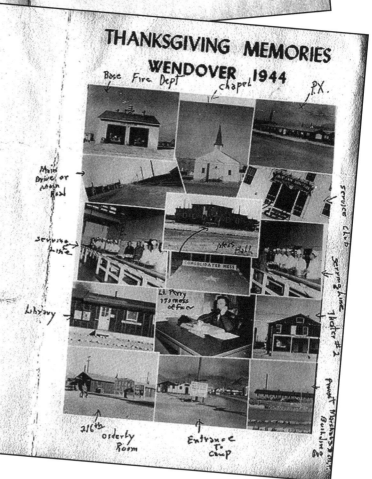

COME HITH-ER, YE FAITH-FUL

Peace on earth to men of good Will

William B. Downey
Chaplain

Nash P. Geany
Chaplain

CONSOLIDATED MESS
WENDOVER FIELD, UTAH

Christmas 1944

MENU

Turkey Broth

Crisp Crackers

Celery   Olives   Pickles

Roast Young Turkey

Giblet Gravy   Cranberry Sauce

Savory Dressing

Whipped Potatoes   Buttered Peas

Boiled Onions

Waldorf Salad

Hot Dinner Rolls   Bread

Butter

Pumpkin Pie   Hot Mince Pie

Ice Cream

Fruit Punch   Coffee

Assorted Candy   Assorted Nuts

Fresh Fruits

Cigarettes

Dinner Music by the 593rd AAF Band

The Officers Of Wendover Field Wish You A

Merry Christmas

and a

Happy New Year

With the sincere hope that the coming Year will bring us Final Victory and an Enduring Peace

Charles E. Trowbridge
Lt. Colonel, Air Corps
Commanding

Charles Perry in officer's uniform waiting to greet families for Christmas Dinner

The Wendover Field Salt Tablet, *Thursday, December 14, 1944*

Christmas Dinner at Wendover

*Christmas Dinner
at Wendover
1st Sgt. Seay on left*

By Lt. Col. Charles E. Trowbridge, Commanding Officer, Wendover Field

Christmas in the midst of world conflict holds a deep significance for all of us. This Christmas, whether it finds our men on the battle fronts of Europe or in the far Pacific, brings thoughts of home and the fireside to each and every one of us in the armed forces of the United States.

Their deeds have been an inspiration to their millions of countrymen. They will go on to undying glory. And when the day of final victory comes, the heartfelt prayers of those on the home front go with those in the front lines far away from the homeland.

*Christmas Dinner
at Wendover*

KRAUSE, EUGENE
320th Troop Carrier Squadron, Crew Chief / Flight Engineer
Privately Published 1990

We were returning to Wendover. After flying most of the night, we decided to land at one of the many fields across Nebraska. We picked Henderson Field to set down until morning. We called Henderson, gave our position and got clearance to land. We saw a big Airforce Base coming up and called, "We're on our downwind leg". The tower replied, "We don't see you". We put the gear down and lined up to land. The tower still didn't see us. After we taxied, we found we were on a different field. The tower was still complaining about not seeing us. The disgusted pilot snapped the radio off.

When we landed at Bolling Field, Washington, DC, Col. Tibbets, who had an important meeting, (maybe with Pres. Truman) happened to remember he needed his "ribbons". He sent me back to the plane for them. When I reached for the cargo door, I heard a rifle bullet being slammed into the chamber and a command "HALT!". A second sentry also echoed his terse command. I pleaded with the officer as he was leading me away, but to no avail. I told him I had just landed in that plane. It took Col. Tibbets to get me back again.

We were flying a C54 back to Wendover from Bolling Field, Washington, DC, when an engine with a shorted out ignition harness was giving us a bad time. As we neared Cheyenne, we were given clearance to land there. Col. Tibbets knew the manager of United Airlines there. When we inquired if we could get one put on, he found out they had just put the last one on that afternoon.

A Marine asked if he could hitch a ride to Salt Lake City. We decided to try to make it in with a bad engine, so he threw his barracks bag on. We went to the end of the runway to run up the engines. When we mag tested the bad engine, (we decided to use it and feather it after take

Ted Van Kirk poses at Wendover

off), it banged and backfired with a blue and orange flame. Just as we started to roll, I noticed the "cargo ajar" light flashed on. I went back to the cargo area just in time to see that marine throw out his bag. As he ran, he yelled, "I got through the war - I'm not gonna die in this damn wreck"!

On a night flight enroute to Wendover from Havana, Navigator, Dutch Van Kirk, was shooting Jupiter with his sextant. He came down from the dome with a puzzled look. Two other navigators on board also appeared puzzled and double checked their findings. At our Galveston, Texas, hotel, the next morning's paper contained an article which seemed to settle the big question on their minds. We read "Jupiter goes behind the moon - first time in 200 years". I assure you that we'll be old men next time it does that again.

LEMLEY, FLOYD
603rd Air Engineering Squadron

Here is a list of names I was associated with, or came in contact with, dealing with B29s, starting at Smokey Hill Air Force Base, probably in July 1943:

Col Tibbets	Ray Gallagher	Bob Hennes	Maj Sweeney
Abe Spitzer	George Caron	Lt. Lewis	Fred Michaels (Ala)
Henry Ellis	Lt Slusky	Wade Wolfe	Melvin Jones (Utah)
Roy Lockart	Capt Van Sciver	Joe Stiborik	Capt Dillon
Stan Tecoma	Roy Carrigan	F/O Brubaker	Hughes
Ed Buckley	Lt Hozenapfel	Bill Hoodak	Al Dehart
Capt Casey	John Kuharek	Capt Iller	Eugene Krause
Brown	Kermit Beahan	Bill Knatt	Wyatt Duzenbury
Marten	Chas Albury	Bob Siedel	McMurtrie
Tom Ferebee	Joe Fay	Lieberman	Van Pelt
Joe Gagnon	Bliven	Van Kirk	Krutch
Brantley Kay	Col Moseley	Paulson	Baker
Maj Smith	Ralph Lunn	Murray	Maj Grace
Mario Villareal	Frank Ortiz	Didi Moorman	Dora Dougherty

Floyd Lemley (left) on Tinian

From there, I went to Eglin Field, the Bell Bomber Factory at Marrieta, Georgia.

This assignment, February 18, 1944, came sometime after I had joined Colonel Tibbets' group at Eglin Field in October 1943. Here he had assembled a crew of men of various classifications; some I assumed had worked with him on previous occasions. He told some of us we were being farmed out to other bases, but would be regrouped later for a special project. Fred Michaels, Paulson and I were sent to McCook Field, Nebraska. I was assigned duties as a crew chief, flight engineer, electrical specialist or whatever the occasion called for. It was quite a career change from P39, P40, P51 to B29 in-line engines to radial corncobs.

On Friday, February 18, 1944, Lieutenant Slusky informed some of us we were leaving the next day. Roy Lockhart and myself were on the list. Saturday, we waited until 12:30 before takeoff due to bad weather. It was a rough trip in an overloaded RB34 but Colonel Tibbets handled it well. We were forced to land at Lawson Field, Fort Benning, Georgia. From there we had to take a GI bus to Marietta Army Air Corps base arriving about 1:30 am Sunday. We had chow and slept on the floor of the supply room without bedding since the supply sergeant was already asleep. We went to work at 13:00hrs when Captain Dillon gave us the low down about General Hap Arnold talking to Bell Aircraft Corporation and wanting 40 B29s by March 1st. Bell Aircraft Corporation said it was impossible, but Hap said it wasn't and that is why we were there.

Our job, the Army boys, was to take the ships as they came off the assembly line, fly them a couple hours and fix all the malfunctions we could find. I was put in charge of electrical on days; Roy Lockhart for nights. Our shifts were 12 hours; mine was from 06:00 to 18:00. This was going to take care of any off time recreation. There were a lot of inexperienced men and women working on the assembly lines accounting for many problems we were to encounter. Rumor was if they had changed a light bulb or an electrical outlet, they were qualified electricians.

We, four of us, had a nice little hut to sleep in. It had a small coal or wood stove in the center that really put out the much needed heat as it was very damp and cold here compared to Florida.

My first day was spent finding out why the bomb bay doors and nose wheel wouldn't retract. Located the door trouble just as we changed shifts. This was a minor introduction of problems to come and an incentive to get things right was to accompany the crew on test flights. Some were cancelled because of too many problems; such as generators not generating. One flight, I took two parallel generators, three were out due to faulty wiring. On one ship you would turn on an interior light switch that would blow a warning horn. There were faulty fuel relay switches, warning lights not working and direct electrical shorts burning up wiring and insulation. One direct short, as I watched it burning toward me like a fuse, caused a lot of smoke and commotion as five firemen came running with fire extinguishers while smoke poured out the escape hatch with my head sticking out for air. Luckily a fuse blew and the heat stopped.

Daily problems that required patiently eliminating items one by one, sometimes were solved quickly, others took all day and night. Some as serious as an engine starter switch turning over the wrong engine or cowl flaps not functioning. One good note came through all this was about March 10, 1944, I received word I had been promoted to Tech Sgt. This boosted my base pay to $114 a month, plus 5% longevity, plus 50% for flying time; made a nice income. Also word was a Gen. Saunders had written a complimentary about our crew and wanted all the names; never heard anymore about it.

Things were getting caught up about the middle of the month, we were working shorter shifts, giving us a little time to socialize and do a bit of sight seeing. So it was not all work and no play anymore. We were invited to a few parties and dances by the lady inspectors and workers at the plant. A popular hangout for socializing was the Shangri-la in Atlanta.

It was at the Brown Derby on the night of March 14, 1944,

(L-R): Didi Moorman, Paul Tibbets, Dora Dougherty

that Roy Lockhart found three of us with instructions to take fifteen days furlough, starting the next day. It was great for the guys living on the east coast with a twenty-six hour train ride to home for probably their first furlough. My home was in California so I asked Maj Grace for a five day extension, no soap. It would use ten days of my time for travel so after arriving, I wired for an extension which was approved by Capt Van Lear. Most travel was by hopping military flights, frequently getting bumped by officers also hopping flights, making for longer journeys.

While still working at Bell, some of the fellows like Stan Tecoma, Bill Hughes, Bob Seidle, Joe Fay, Roy Lockhart, Cpl Hoodak and Krutch were assigned to new B29 outfits off our lines and came to say farewell as they headed overseas. Some I visited later on Saipan and Tinian, never saw or heard from them again; gone but not forgotten.

A plus to this work was I gained a great amount of valuable maintenance and repair experience on major B29 operating systems which proved very helpful in future assignments with Col Tibbets' group.

When my leave was over, I returned to Eglin Field, rejoined the old group and resumed where we left off, lot's of work and cross country flights, reassignments, and split ups.

My Wasps Encounter and The Ladybird

It was June of 1944, some 4 ½ years into my time in the Air Force. The last year of this I was assigned to Col Tibbets nomads, working out of Eglin Field. We didn't have a group name to my knowledge. Wherever we went, we would be attached to some outfit for quarters and rations only. This day, after returning to Eglin from a high altitude 28,000 ft bombing run in B29 #42-6413 with Capt Van Sciver, Pilot, me as Flight Engineer, F/O Brubaker, Gallagher and Wolfe, were told to repack again for a new assignment. We were off to Birmingham, Alabama with Col Tibbets in his B34. Accompanying us were two WASPS (Woman Air Force Service Pilots) Dora Dougherty and Didi

(L-R): Didi Moorman, Dora Dougherty, Paul Tibbets, Dean Hudson

Moorman. We stayed at the Redmond Hotel. Col Tibbets told us he was going to train and check them out as pilots in a new B29; then we were going to tour the West to wherever B29s were stationed. The WASPS, Dora and Didi, were going to check out pilots in the B29 and our crew of Gallagher, Wolfe, Duzenbury, Ellis and I were going to check out engineers and mechanics. Rumors were flying that the B29 was a high risk plane to fly and this demonstration was to bolster the confidence and morale of future men B29 pilots.

After several days of takeoffs, landings and familiarization flights, Dora and Didi became quite competent and confident. I flew a few flights with Dora, once to Eglin; a trip to Patterson Field at Dayton, Ohio; then ending at Eglin. The crew spent two days getting B29, #42-6453, The Ladybird, ready for the tour of the West. We left probably 27 June 1944 at 1500 hrs and the first stop was Oklahoma City. From there, we went to Clovis Air Base, New Mexico. The maintenance of their planes was pretty poor. They had

Crew of the Tibbets-trained Lady Bird, Eglin Field

(L-R): Lt. Col. Tibbets, Dorothea Moorman, Dora Dougherty, Ray Gallagher, Wyatt Duzenbury, Floyd Lemley, Wade Wolfe, Henry Ellis

thirty-seven B29s and only three in flying status. Could that account for some of the rumors? After some unknown number of flights, we had to shut down for maintenance and repairs. We spent two days and nights on an engine change and inspections. Just got finished and received word from Washington DC they did not want the WASPS to continue flying this ship. Maybe the ladies bolstered the male pilots ego instead of their morale, that's why they complained. So the tour was called off. The ship, Ladybird, was turned over to the base.

We all shipped out in a B17F and landed at Peterson Field, Colorado Springs, in the evening of July 5, 1944. Never heard anymore about the Ladybird. We all went back to our regular jobs with the B29s and bounced around to several air bases, eventually most of us reuniting at Wendover. I don't recall where Didi Moorman went but I made a few more flights with Dora in different aircraft, once in a B26, at different bases, including Wendover. As far as I know, these ladies were the first and probably the last to fly B29s. I always felt confident while flying with them, in any type craft. Eglin Field being a testing and proving ground, my vague recollection is that one or both ladies were flying tow target planes prior to our tour. Seems like flying a B29 was a much safer job!

One day, after the tour ended and they had returned to Grand Island, Dora Dougherty and Bill Knatt were going up in our UC78, so I tagged along. As we reached 500ft off the ground, Dora let Bill take over. He flew about an hour doing banks, turns and stalls. Was a lot of fun. Dora took over for the landing.

Another day Dora, Bill Knatt, Ray Gallagher and I took off in the B34 for Eglin Field. We stopped at Pratt Field, Memphis and Jackson, Mississippi. Had to stay over night because of bad weather out Florida way. Went to Eglin the next day. A few days later, we headed back to Grand Island through Memphis again. After we arrived at Grand Island, Dora got the OK to take the B34 to Chicago, but one engine wouldn't start, so that flight was cancelled.

I don't recall which field it was from but Dora Dougherty, as pilot and I took up a B26 to check it out. She did a really smooth job of takeoffs and landings. The B26 had a bad reputation of being hard to handle. There were some based on the gulf coast of Florida, from where we heard of their accidents. I had also flown with Lt Lewis in one a couple of times; Dora did a smoother job! The purpose of all these flights was to transport personnel, pick up airplane parts from other fields, testing and checkouts after repairs.

September 28, 1944, received good news that Fred Michaels, Prout and I were being shipped out to Wendover Field, Utah. We heard Col Tibbets was forming a new B29 Reconnaissance outfit and we would probably be going overseas soon. A Lt Salman, our officer in charge, said he saw the orders Hap Arnold had signed.

October 4, 1944, we arrived at Wendover for a final regrouping and were told our work was urgent, highly important and secretive. Some of these men went to the Marianas long before the 509th.

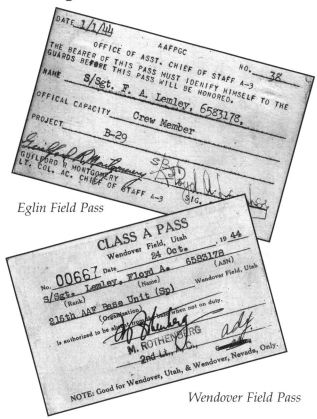

Eglin Field Pass

Wendover Field Pass

November 1944, 3 day pass to Lewiston, Utah, home of Melvin Jones' parents.
Top: Mr. and Mrs. Jones, Ray Gallagher.
Bottom: Abe Spitzer, Floyd Lemley

(L-R): Didi Moorman, Paul Tibbets,
Dora Dougherty, Dean Hudson

LEVY, CHARLES
393rd Bomb Squadron, Bombardier, Crew C-13

On February 1, 1945, our crew was preparing to go overseas for additional training in Cuba . . . (not too far overseas).

As usual, when leaving the States, you are required to take a last stateside physical examination. After being examined by the doctor, the nurse handed me a jar and said, "go in the men's room and fill it up". I went into the men's room and prepared to do as requested,

(L-R): Leonard Godfrey, Charles Levy, Wilbur Lyon - Downtown Havana

when I noticed a bottle of Tincture of Green Soap on a shelf. I said to myself, "what the heck", poured the contents into the jar and gave it to the nurse.

The next day, we left for Cuba. A few days later, I received orders grounding me. When it came time for a mission, I told Captain Young, our Flight Surgeon, who politely told me to get my butt in that plane and go. Soooo . . . I went!

See official copy of the orders grounding me. Translation, more or less, from Latin to English.

"An examination of your urine revealed: Linimentum Saponis Mollis and Tinctura Saponis Viridis. Translation: Tincture of Green Soap in Urine. This is a very rare and unusual disease, etc., etc., etc. You are hereby grounded until further notice."

```
AAF STATION HOSPITAL          GM/PMM/ily
Office of the Surgeon
Wendover Field, Utah

                              2 February 1945.

SUBJECT: Urinalysis Examination.

TO:     Lt. Charles Levy, ASN 0-1296398, 393rd Bomb Group,
        Wendover Field, Utah.

   1. An examination of your urine revealed:

      a. Linimentum saponis mollis.

      b. Tinctura saponis viridis.

   2. This is a very rare and unusual disease. Due to this fact you
will report to the Medical Officer of the Day each evening including
Sunday at 1900 in the Flight Surgeon's Building for further observation
and treatment.

   3. You are hereby grounded until further notice.

                              Philip M. Markle

                              PHILIP M. MARKLE,
                              Major, MC,
                              Surgeon.
```

LYON, WILBUR H.
320th Troop Carrier Squadron, Navigator

At our 509th 50th Reunion, I had a great visit with Fred Bock. He was a great role model for us younger and less experienced officers. Before joining the 509th, he had served a tour as a B24 Pilot in the China Burma India Theater (CBI). One of his stations in India was at Allahabad. While there, he spoke to the students at the university. In 1918, my mother's first assignment was as president of the girl's college in Allahabad where she went as a Presbyterian Missionary.

On a Rest and Recuperation (R&R), he went to Mussoorie in the Himalayas. While there, he talked to the student assembly at Woodstock School. This is the high school I had graduated from in 1940. My two younger sisters' classes were there and heard his talk.

Our 1994 reunion visit to the University of Chicago was very interesting. We had a very informative talk about the initial research and visited the memorial where the first nuclear fission reaction took place in the squash court under the then stadium.

I have had an interesting relationship with the Arthur Compton family for about 60 years so it was meaningful to hear about his involvement with the Manhatten Project again. I met his family first in 1934. We were in Wooster, Ohio on my parent's furlough from India. As a ten year old boy, I had a magazine route. Each week, Arthur Compton's

mother would buy a copy of the Saturday Evening Post, Ladies Home Journal or Country Gentleman, invite me in for an interesting conversation and warm me up with a cup of hot chocolate.

Arthur Compton's sister married a Dr. Rice, who was president of a college in India. They were both long time, good friends of my parents.

After the war, I went to college with Arthur Compton's son.

When my parents retired, they lived for a few years in the same house in Wooster, Ohio where the Compton's were in 1934.

It was interesting to find out that Fred Bock has since communicated with the president of the Toyota Company. His bombs on the Toyota factory after the Nagasaki mission may have been the last bombs of the war since he said he heard of the Japanese surrender over the radio on the way home. He told me that the now president of Toyota told him that if it were not for the atomic bombs, he would no longer be alive. At age sixteen in 1945, his assigned role with others in his age group, was to wrap himself in as much high explosives as he could carry. When the Americans landed, they were to take as many with them as possible.

I have a picture my father took in Nagasaki on his way to India in 1918 aboard the Empress of Japan. It reminded me very much of the fishing boats we saw sailing into the sunset in the bay near the hotel where we stayed in 1945.

During two years I spent as Chief of Surgery in American Samoa from 1959-1961, I got to know well many Japanese with the Nippon and Mitsubishi Companies tuna fishing fleets. I removed US metal fragments from some who had been pilots in the Japanese Air Forces. In discussions with some of their managers, I got the impression they seemed grateful for at least the Hiroshima atom bombing and the end of hostilities.

Base Chapel Bulletin

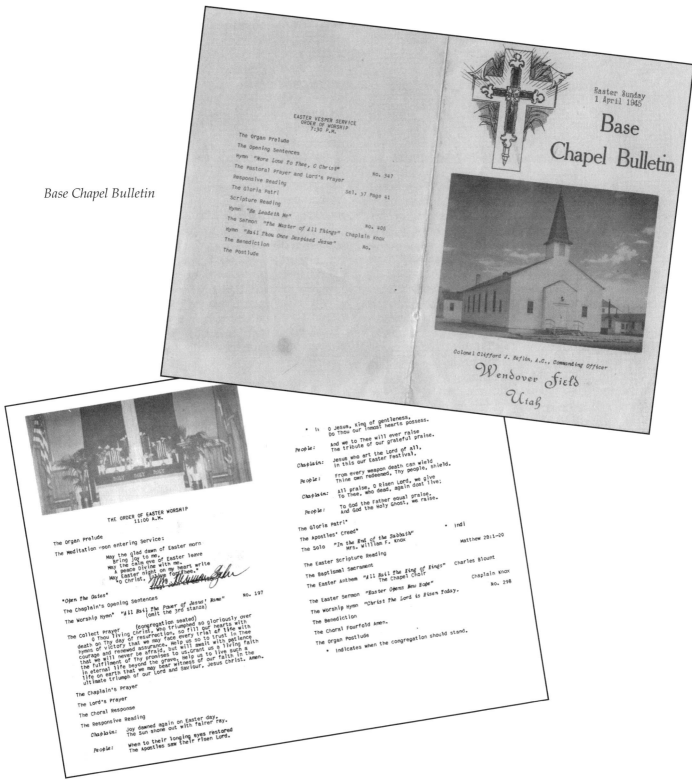

131

MARQUARDT, GEORGE W.
393rd Bomb Squadron, Airplane Commander/Operations Officer, Crew B-10

The 393rd Squadron was pulled out of the 504th Bomb Group in Fairmont, Nebraska, and went to Wendover, Utah, in September 1944. In Wendover, I was assigned to the 509th Composite Group under the command of Col. Paul W. Tibbets. At a meeting, he told us what we were doing could shorten the war. We were all given a ten day leave and told to be ready for work when we returned.

It was at this time, I met my future wife, Bernece. She was private secretary to the owner of the Newhouse Hotel in Salt Lake City. Some of us stayed there on weekends, and I had noticed her in her office located in the lobby. Buck Eatherly and I asked her to type some orders for us to go on leave. She referred us to the public stenographer in the lobby. After finding her busy, we persuaded Bernece to type them for us. After my leave and return to Wendover, we began to date.

In the spring of 1945 prior to our going overseas, I was flying one day with Jim Price and his crew. We had gone to Salton Sea to drop a dummy block buster (10,000 lb bomb). On the way back and in the process of landing, the #2 engine caught fire. I was right over Wendover Air Base. I put the plane in a very steep bank and rang the alarm to alert the crew we were going in for an emergency landing. Before coming to a complete stop, the #2 engine fell off, but all got out safely. The fire trucks put out the fire. I walked over to Col. Tibbets, who had come out to see what the problem was. I said, "Colonel, I'm sorry I burned one of the airplanes". He replied, "George, we're getting new planes next week. They'll have reversible pitch props, one bomb bay, no gun turrets and they're lighter and faster."

In May of 1945, we received our orders to go to the Island of Tinian. Knowing that I would be leaving soon, Bernece and I were married on May 31 in the Presidential Suite of the Newhouse Hotel. We went to Wendover to await my departure. I couldn't tell her anything about our mission except that I knew it would help make the war with Japan end soon and I could return home quickly. Our plane left Wendover for Tinian on June 6, 1945.

Since the food there, mostly mutton, was not the tastiest in the world, fellow pilots, Norm Ray, John Wilson and I chased and caught three chickens. We put them on sticks, built a fire and roasted them. Really had a feast and were envied by many. To this day, I cannot eat lamb, tastes too much like mutton.

When I came back from overseas, and stationed in Roswell, I flew into Wendover one day. They were test hopping the aforementioned plane. It seemed the heat from the fire had shrunk the fuselage, making it fly crooked. It was ultimately destroyed.

George Marquardt at the controls

I had the utmost respect for Classen and Tibbets. I, in turn, was respected by my crew. The airplane commanders cared about each other. At the end of the war, the men of the 393rd had been flying together for two years with no fatalities. I attribute this to good pilots, good crews, excellent maintenance, and double checking!

Marquardt crew after Hiroshima mission.
Back Row, (L-R): James Corliss, Joe DiJulio, Mel Bierman, Anthony Capua, Russell Gackenbach
Front Row, (L-R): James Anderson, George Marquardt, Warren Coble, James Strudwick

MASTICK, DONALD F.
Ensign, USNR, Project Alberta

In 1942, I was a graduate student in chemistry at the University of California, Berkeley working on radioactive carbon studies while the Japanese subs were shelling the coast and blackouts prevailed. Toward the end of 1942, I couldn't stand not being active in the war and told our Dean, Professor Wendell Latimer that I was leaving. He said, "Wait, we have a secret project. You should be part of building a bomb a million times more powerful than the chemical bomb."

Within four hours, I was working with Oppenheimer specifying stock items required to equip the chemical labs at Los Alamos which were then under construction. His office was next door in the physics department and the pressure was on.

I traveled to Los Alamos in early 1943 under rigorous security, being the second technical person in residence there. Those were very active times; the pressure to move ahead was intense and exhilarating.

By 1944, I was doing ultra micro chemical studies on the first few micro grams of plutonium which had been sent from the piles at Hanford, Washington. In late Fall of 1944, a small sample exploded and I ingested about 25 micrograms of plutonium (PU) which the medical group immediately said was 25 lethal doses. Obviously they were wrong since I'm still here and healthy, but no one had any knowledge concerning this matter.

After thorough stomach pumping and recovering the 25 micrograms, it was decided I should no longer work in the laboratory. Of course I was knowledgeable of the growing program to prepare and deliver the bombs so I asked Oppie (Oppenheimer) if I could be assigned to that effort as an assistant to Commander F.L. Ashworth, USN who I knew was very much involved in the program. I reminded Oppie that Latimer in Berkeley had promised me a Navy commission as a result of working in the program.

I was a Los Alamos scientist, chemist, assigned to Wendover in early 1945 as administrative assistant to Commander F.L. Ashworth, USN in charge of ordering equipment and supplies and general coordination as needed by the Project A program. Also, I was part of the Ballistic Test Program dropping Fat Man shapes on a large, white, square float target in the Salton Sea, California. These bombs were appropriately loaded with concrete, called pumpkins as part of the program to develop ballistic tables for the eventual attack.

One real problem was developing a bomb tail configuration that would provide stable and reproductive drop paths. However, there was another problem because of the erratic misalignment of the bomb's steel skin. This skin was fabricated in four sections at locations scattered throughout the country for security reasons. None of the shops had plans or prints for the assembled skin

(L-R): Frederick Ashworth, Donald Mastick, Robert Serber

and made only the quadrant assigned to it. The mandatory reworking carried out at Wendover, grinding, welding, etc, added delays to the test program and some reworking followed through to Tinian.

I recall seeing Art Machen, Project A, sitting on the back of the Nagasaki bomb late at night with a rattail file to align a bolt hole to get a secure fitting of the tail assembly.

Major Stan Sheilds was the test pilot for the B29 making the Salton Sea drops and Dave Semple was the bombardier, the Dave of the Dave's Dream B29 after the war. I'll always remember one round-trip run when the plane threw a collector ring on one port engine, Stan killed the engine and feathered out, grumbling. Then about 100 miles out of Wendover, another port engine went out. With a characteristic remark, Shields killed all remaining engines and settled down to dead-stick that heavy plane to a landing at Wendover Air Field. I was in the bombardier seat and during the last mile it seemed we were cutting off sagebrush. That was my most memorable experience at Wendover.

In late June of 1945, I was commissioned an Ensign, USNR five days before traveling to Tinian with the Project A Group. Commander Ashworth's administrative and planning effort between July and August 5th was intense. I was working constantly with him. A brief respite was when General Farrell directed me to take a message to General LeMay on Guam regarding the timing of our mission and the support we required from his command. As I recall, he wasn't too happy with the 509th rocking the boat.

It was a wonderful experience and I am so proud to have the Bronze Star for Valor from the Atomic bombing of Japan.

McCLARY, ROBERT C.
393rd Bomb Squadron, Armament

After we left the 504th and arrived in Wendover, everyone knew we were in a very remote spot. Those of us who were married and had our wives come there, lived in cement block houses built in tandem. Some with one block, others with two; coal stoves to cook and keep warm; concrete floors and it was very cold. We were there all winter of 1944 and had to buy our coal at the local lumber yard. We had a few stores, a casino and not much else. We went to the PX or theater on the base and walked to work.

I had a couple encounters with security at Wendover. One, when I had to get permission to take my wife home after she had been sick in the hospital. I had a briefing from the security officer not to say anything about what we were doing there. Since I was going back to Iowa, they told me they would be watching closely, so I didn't say anything to anyone.

The other time was when some of us went to Naval Air Station, Inyokern, California, to practice loading and dropping "pumpkins" to test trajectory. It was a restricted base; mostly sailors and marines. I think we were the only Army Air Force there, although there was a lot of experimenting going on. After we loaded the bombs, fat man size, from a pit, we were allowed to go to the drop area, go up a tower with a platform at the top and watch the bomb drop toward the target. The planes flew about 25 or 30 thousand feet so it was hard to see the bomb bay doors open, but radio contact told us when it left the plane and headed for the target area. I remember one bomb coming down end over end,

First 509th compound theater built by 18th Seabee Battalion. June 10, 1945

scared us a little, but hit a good distance from us. We were about to leave there when President Roosevelt died; a very special day; a memorable one.

We were briefed again when we got a weekend pass to Los Angeles. Same story, don't say anything to anyone. After a week or so at Inyokern, we went back to Wendover to prepare for departure to Tinian.

We had loaded TNT bombs at the beginning of our stay on Tinian. An Armorer loaded bombs and ammunition and checked everything that had to do with same. I was on the crew that loaded "Little Boy" into the Enola Gay. We put up our own tent and used 100 pound wooden bomb boxes for the floor. It rained a lot there so that kept us up off the dirt. Activity on Tinian was playing

Bob McClary holding papayas

soft ball, pitching horse shoes, washing our own clothes and reading a lot between bomb loadings. There were several theaters on the Island and we had a Red Cross coffee shop for a while which had caught fire and burned up. We did have some fresh water, from Lake Nagoya in the middle of the island, to take showers. Papayas and bananas grew wild there too.

Bob McClary plays shortstop

The nose art on some of the planes was painted by a tent mate, Bob Wells. He painted Enola Gay, Bockscar, Straight Flush, Next Objective, The Great Artiste, Full House and Strange Cargo. I think the rest were put on after the war. He did a great job.

It was really great to leave Tinian when we did as we got home for Christmas 1945.

Tent mates, 393rd Armament Dept. Tinian 1945
(L-R) Back: Bill Jacks, John Keyser, Bob McClary
(L-R) Front: Joe Clancy, Bob Wells, John Lane

McKNIGHT, CHARLES
393rd Bomb Squadron, Airplane Commander

Written by Mrs. Ruby McKnight

When Pearl Harbor was attacked, Charles McKnight joined the Army Air Corps. We were married in Washington DC in 1943 where we worked for the Department of Justice.

Later, I joined him in Roswell, New Mexico. It was there we bought our first car in the picture. I think it was a Chevrolet but I am not sure of the year.

From there we drove to Fairmont, Nebraska. We found a couple of rooms to rent in York about 45 minutes from the air base. Another couple by the name of Lt. Bill Weber and his wife, Pat, lived there also. We became very close friends.

Our next move was Wendover, Utah. Lt. Weber stayed with another group and we said good-bye.

When we arrived in Wendover in September, we lived in the dorms. Then we were looking to get a small apartment. Lt. Bill Rowe and Betty were close friends and we loved hiking in the hills of Wendover.

In December, we received word Lt. Bill Weber's plane went down over the ocean in Japan. His wife and I still keep in touch.

Charles and Ruby McKnight

Bill and Betty Rowe

Capt. Charles and Ruby McKnight

135

McNARY, SPENCER G.
1027th Air Material Squadron, Signal Supply Officer

In February 1945, I was stationed at Headquarters (HQ) 2nd Air Force (AF) in Colorado Springs as Signal Supply Operator. It was a good job in a nice city, but I felt as signal officer, I wanted to go overseas. My colonel said there was an opening with the 509th Composite Group in Wendover. It was called the "Silver Plate Project". It was a self-contained group that could operate anywhere in the world with little outside help. Rumor was that they were testing a new kind of aviation fuel. In training, the group pilots practiced endlessly on making sharp right and left turns at high speeds. The commander, Col. Paul Tibbets, had a pipeline to Washington and got the group everything they wanted. It sounded like a weird outfit but I took the job to become a member of the 1027th Air Material Squadron (AMS). The sign at the base entrance said, "What You Hear Here, What You See Here, When You Leave Here, Let It Stay Here". The secret was so well kept, that the news on August 6th that the Atom Bomb had been dropped was a big surprise to all group members.

(L-R): Lt. Frank Norris, 320th Pilot, Lt. Spencer McNary, 1027th
Lt. Earl Sands, 1027th

McNITT, DAVID B.
1027th Air Material Squadron

Many of my Wendover memories are of the latrines, since I spent a fair amount of two years time cleaning them.

Shortly after my nineteenth birthday and prior to going into what was then the Army Air Force, my Dad took me aside and solemnly told me that he expected that I would spend some time in the Guard House. This somewhat surprised me, since I had been a relatively easy kid to raise.

One day in Salt Lake City, his prophecy came true when I was unable to convince the MPs that the one hour remaining on my pass was enough time to hitch hike the four hour trip back to Wendover. There were some other prospective Guard House opportunities, but that was the only time that I was caught.

It wasn't until much later in my adult life that I realized why Dad had made that prediction. He recognized the spark that would cause me to resent the loss of individual freedom that we all had to give up to serve our country. Dad should have predicted that I would spend time cleaning latrines. When I did those transgressions, somehow, I was never assigned to guard duty and rarely kitchen police, but mostly "McNitt, go clean latrines"!!

Sometimes they told us that we were being prepared for a job in civilian life. I knew what they had in mind for me, especially after adding to my resume that I had cleaned one of the longest latrines in the world. On board ship, they called it a "head", but I recognized it, and it stretched from Seattle to Tinian.

When we returned from Tinian, a bright omen of my future was when I missed the latrine assignment. That foggy winter morning when we passed through the Golden Gate, past Alcatraz, and saw that huge sign on the hillside "WELCOME HOME - WELL DONE", was the beginning of a happy, new, latrine-free life.

METRO, PAUL
393rd Bomb Squadron, Radar

The Japs attacked Pearl Harbor, Sunday morning December 7, 1941, Hawaiian time. I had been to a movie in Newark and on my way home on #12 Public Service Bus heard people talking about the attack. The next day President Roosevelt came on the radio to announce the declaration of war on Japan. Two days later, Germany and Italy declared war on the US. I had graduated from Linden High School in June and enrolled in a machine shop training course at the Thomas Edison Vocational High School in Elizabeth, New Jersey. Upon completion, they got me a job with the Aluminum Company of America in Garwood. The work involved machine cleaning of aluminum castings. It was predominantly war production and three shifts. I didn't like it but it was defense work and all jobs were frozen. I was stuck. My father let me use his 1938 Oldsmobile to go to work. Because I had a defense job, we had a B gasoline ration sticker which allowed us more gasoline. He used his bicycle to go to work at Bayway Esso.

The Army set up a searchlight antiaircraft battery on a knoll near the intersection of Lower Road and the road leading to the concrete batch plant. The GM automobile plant on US #1 was taken over by Eastern Aircraft to build Grumman Wildcats, Navy fighter planes. A new track was built by the NJ Central from their line in Tremley to GM and a new airfield was built across the highway for testing and flying the planes away. The flight of the Wildcats made me dream of being a pilot but I wore glasses and knew it would not be. It was exciting to see the antiaircraft battery lightup the planes flying to and from Newark Airport. Other evidences of wartime were blackout curtains on house windows, auto headlights and street lights painted half black, service star pendants in windows, food, tire, shoe rationing books and the collection of tin cans, grease, fat, scrap paper, metals, etc. The number of young men hanging out at the candy store was getting smaller and smaller.

On June 30, 1942, I registered for the draft (Selective Training and Service Act of 1940). On January 20,

USO Travelers Aid Lounge, Oakland, California railroad station, October 1, 1944 (L-R): soldiers Cpl. Paul Metro and Cpl. Edmund Hall, 393rd Radar

1943, I received my letter of Greeting from the local draft board to report at the Linden Library on Saturday, January 30. Together with other draftees, I was taken by train to Newark, Prudential Building on Washington Street, given a physical, graded 1A, was sworn into the US Army and sent home.

The next Saturday, February 6, I again reported at the library in the early morning. Our contingent marched down Wood Avenue to the Pennsylvania RR Station where we boarded a southbound train that took us on a slow trip to Fort Dix. We were given a sad sendoff by parents and friends. I didn't see or speak to my family for over 13 months. There were very few people who had telephones and those that did were generally shared party lines.

At Fort Dix, I was assigned to Company G for processing. We lived in rows of four man pyramidal tents which were heated by conical sheet metal stoves in the center. We filled out forms, took aptitude tests, were given smallpox shots, etc. We packed our civilian clothes which were sent home. I was assigned to the Army Air Forces and on February 11 boarded a troop train for an unknown destination.

The train headed southward. I was struck by the shacks along the tracks in which people lived in the southern states. I also remember the colored and whites signs above drinking fountains and on restroom doors at the stations. The Spanish moss hanging from the trees, the cypress swamps, the flat-lands of Florida with the scrubby palmettos and coconut palms were sights from my geography books. We finally arrived at Miami Beach where we

(L-R): Joel Denham, Paul Metro, Andrew Brown after winning game at Enola Gay welcome party. Paul ran backwards while Joel and Andrew ran forward, arms locked together.

Harold Kimme at wheel of ordnance vehicle sometimes used by radar section for transportation

were to have our basic training. The Army Air Forces took over most of the hotels in Miami and Miami Beach.

I was assigned to a room with three other guys in the Grand Plaza Hotel on 31st Street off Collins Avenue. It was a five story building which was stripped bare of all furnishings. The GI bunks had wire springs, without a mattress; we spread out a blanket. All of us were from New Jersey. I remember two guys, Lydecker and McMullen, from Moonachie and Bogota. One of the first things we did was to go to the roof to take snapshots of each other in the different uniforms we were issued.

We were later relocated to another complex known as the Helen-Mars Villas on Collins Avenue and 41st Street. In the backyard was the Atlantic Ocean but we saw very little of it. Here I met Fred Does and Bob Newell, Linden High classmates. We started to live out of barracks bags A and B; we didn't have foot lockers or dressers.

Basic training was a lot of formations in the streets which were closed to traffic. There was a lot of drill, lectures on the golf course and firing of the WWII Enfield Rifle at the range on the beach. We had details such as guard duty outside the hotel, KP and other keep busy activities; more tests, shots and marching. It all seemed pretty disorganized.

I had a pretty good IQ score, so was given an option of three Military Occupation Specialities (MOS) of photography, electrical and radio. I was assigned to radio but didn't know until I reached my next post.

On Thursday March 18, 1943, I boarded another troop train heading north when we learned of our promotion to Private First Class (PFC) effective March 15. I guess it was because we were going to a Technical Training School. Somewhere along the line the train stopped at a station to be serviced. The train commander felt this was a good time to give the troops some exercise. We formed up alongside the train and were marched down the main street of this little town. The townspeople came out to cheer us for this impromptu parade. Just out of basic training and promoted to PFC, we put on a good show. We must have sold some war bonds and savings stamps that day.

Our destination was Scott Field Bellville, Illinois to attend radio operators school where I learned to send and receive Morse Code by radio. I knew the code as a Boy Scout so I was able to receive 3-5 words a minute in short order, but this was slow. The objective was to train radio operators who would be aerial gunners.

After another physical, I was washed out because I wore glasses. All wash outs were sent on to radio mechanics school. When I was at Scott Field, I was assigned to Barrack #323 which was chosen Barrack of the Week for three consecutive weeks.

One mess hall experience I remember was a sign above the serving line "Take all you want! Eat all you take!" The servers didn't ask, they just slapped it on your tray. There was some slop put on my tray which I couldn't eat. The sergeant at the tray cleaning station turned me back to finish what was in my tray. I went back, still couldn't eat whatever it was, so back in line. This time the sergeant took my name, rank and serial number. I never heard a thing; I guess he agreed with me.

On Monday April 19, 1943, we boarded a Milwaukee Road Line troop train for Truax Field Madison, Wisconsin. The coach was built of wood, with oil lamps, wood stoves and cane seats. Truax was a radio mechanics school. I was assigned to the 622nd Technical Training Squadron. We had three of the top ten students of our class, I wasn't one of them. Classes were basic radio theory and building circuitry using breadboards, snap on wiring and components. We learned how to use various meters and read resistor and capacitor codes etc. We graduated August 26, 1943. Our squadron had a movie star celebrity assigned, Edmund O'Brian who was eventually transferred to Special Services, a unit of entertainers, celebrities etc. We also had a mule mascot called AWOL.

The barracks were one story tar papered buildings with a detached latrine serving several barracks. My bunk was at the far end from the latrine. Every morning I would race down the center aisle and hit the bi-parting screen doors with my hands and rush on through. One day, someone hooked one of the doors and when I ran into it, I flew back on my behind. Embarrassed, I quickly got up and continued to the latrine. The damages were bent glasses, which I straight-ened out, and a slight cut on the side of my nose; no damage to the door.

We had a guy who never showered or did his laundry. A group of guys in the immediate area of his bunk carried him out fully clothed into the shower room to teach him cleanliness.

Before getting our weekend passes to Madison, the capital, we had to listen to a talk on morality by

Enos Slaughter, St. Louis Cardinals, autographing a baseball while Paul Metro and H. Kimme watch.

the chaplain. We spent a lot of time at the USO and Tenney Park on Lake Mendota where we went swimming and had lots of fun. One night a group of us were trudging down Main Street singing when we were suddenly surrounded by MPs. None of us had been drinking and we explained we were not looking for trouble, so they let us go. Graduation was in August and on the 30th a group of graduates left again by troop train for Boca Raton. Still no furlough and another winter in sunny climes.

At Boca, we lived in one story wood barracks which were laid out in a haphazard manner, not in the usual military style of rows. They were built on concrete piers with iron anchors as protection against hurricanes. There were none while I was there. The roofs had two or three different colors as camouflage. The ground was sandy so there were boardwalks from the barracks to the streets. We had weekly barracks inspections. I remember being gigged for needing a haircut; they wanted real short hair. We thought they were getting a payoff from the barbers. This was a pretty common demerit. After lining up and reporting to the orderly room, the demerit was removed and your weekend pass was released.

The school buildings were one story concrete block H shaped structures with two classrooms in each leg and a lobby in the center. The buildings were enclosed by a chain link fence with a guard posted at the gate. The instructor would come to the gate and as he called the roll, the students were allowed to enter. Classes were around the clock in three eight hour shifts. We had ten minute breaks every hour and would be marched to and from the mess hall for our meals. We were not allowed to keep notes for study back at the barracks. Posters telling us not to discuss radar outside of class, it was top secret, were everywhere. The FBI conducted background checks on all of us.

Every morning after school, we had to assemble for work details. This included miscellaneous manual labor such as repairing boardwalks, raking sand, KP, moving coal, etc. Hot water was provided by a coal fired boiler in a shed attached to the latrine. Coal was dumped in the road near the latrine and we had to move it into the coal bin. Kitchen police (KP) was from 2 am to 9 pm; it was torture. Those on KP tied a towel at the foot of their bed so that the charge of quarters (CQ) knew who to awaken. KP included washing down tables and mopping the floor after every meal, washing pots and pans, cleaning service trays etc. The garbage was separated into edible and nonedible. The edible was sold to farmers for hog feed. One day while I was on KP toiling over a tub washing service trays, the detail sergeant came through with his tray. He saw the sweat pouring off me and said, "See me in the morning". I did and was assigned to the orderly room as a runner for the remainder of my stay at Boca which wasn't long. A runner is just a messenger boy, but easier to take than KP.

Training included a three day bivouac in the backwoods of the Everglades. We hiked with full packs carrying carbines along dusty dirt roads and trails. We slept on the ground in pup tents and took turns at guard duty during the night. My tent mate scared me when he woke me to take my turn by touching my foot instead of calling my name. I thought it was a snake or other animal. Our meals were K and C rations. I liked the un-meltable chocolate and I gave my cigarettes away. We stopped at a small black community store for cold drinks. Another thing I remember was the chlorine (tear gas) chamber where I couldn't get my gas mask on fast enough and I coughed for hours afterwards. I had a two week Red Cross Water Safety Course at the Boca Club swimming pool. It was enjoyable even though it was about a two mile hike from the field to the pool.

My first airplane ride was a Radar Training Mission. This was an experience because the radar wouldn't work and it turned into a roller coaster ride along the Florida Keys. I got queasy in the stomach but didn't get air sick. The pilot was noted for giving the trainees this kind of fun. The plane was a Lockheed Ventura B34 two engine medium bomber.

It was cool during the winter months, but we had to wear khakis and could not wear a flight jacket. I wore a sweater under my shirt to keep warm, but wore only a T-shirt and shorts during calisthenics. The food was horrible! I ate only the boxed cereals, toast with butter or jam, fruit and milk for breakfast; never the scrambled eggs or coffee, which usually had a greenish tinge. I didn't eat the chipped beef on toast (SOS), although many guys liked it. Other meals I ate at the Service Club and paid for them, it was worth it.

At Boca Raton we saw several USO shows including one with Leo Durocher, manager of the Brooklyn Dodgers and Danny Kaye, a comedian. Another was a variety show featuring Miss Gams, a young lady with pretty legs. At the golf course, Gene Sarazen and a trick shot artist gave an exhibition.

On weekends I went out to US #1, like everyone else, trying to get a ride to one of the towns, north to Delray Beach and West Palm Beach, south to Fort Lauderdale or Hollywood. It was tough getting a ride because there were so many of us and so few cars on this only road out.

On December 6, 1943, I was promoted to Corporal. School was finished in January leaving time for extra details and additional training as well as my first furlough in 13 months from March 6 to 21, 1944. The trip

(L-R): Joe Ross, John Robey, Patrick Robbins pumping gasoline from 55 Gallon drum

home, on a train called the Havana Special that went all the way to Boston, was crowded with servicemen, not everyone had a seat. Sleeping in coach seats or on luggage was not the most comfortable way to travel, but who cared.

On May 12, I shipped out to Lincoln, Nebraska, by a delay enroute, which meant I had another visit at home just six weeks after my furlough. I went to Grand Central Station in New York, then by train to Nebraska, arriving on May 31, 1944.

On June 5, I left for Fairmont B29 Army Air Force Base (AAFB), Geneva, Nebraska, arriving the next day. I was assigned to the 393rd Bomb Squadron, 504th Bomb Group. A squadron was comprised of 15 planes and a group had three squadrons. B29s were designated very heavy (VH) because they were the largest aircraft at the time. Lt. Col. Thomas E. Classen was our Squadron Commander. I was one of the early arrivals; Lt. Jacob Beser arrived a few days later. We had practically no equipment in a small room in the hanger. Even so, radar was top secret so we had restricted posted on our door. We didn't have any airplanes to work on yet.

Some guy on base, an artist, designed the 393rd patch; it was unofficial as were all flight jacket patches and airplane nose art. They were tolerated because they were great morale boosters. I remember buying an unpainted 393rd patch for $5. The design does not reflect the eventual mission of the 393rd even though the B29 does not show any gun turrets. The design carrying two bombs could be misinterpreted as the two atomic missions, but the bomb configurations are conventional and there is no atomic cloud. The official 509th and 393rd patch of later design, including the current ones, do reflect the nuclear capability of the units.

The food here was no better than at Boca Raton. One day, the Inspector General (IG) from Washington conducting an inspection of the base, asked about conditions. An enlisted man could make a complaint without fear of reprisal. We were being fed mashed potatoes three times a day. The potatoes were dehydrated powder. This was my complaint and probably others because we got scalloped potatoes and other variations afterwards.

Weekend passes were spent in York or Geneva. I don't remember them very clearly. On a three day pass, Joel Denham of Texas and I went to Columbus and Omaha. At a country fair in Columbus, we played the horses and got taken for $8.50. Had a thrill in one race when our horse crossed the finish line in first place, but the horses kept running, it was a two lap race. We stayed at the Y in Omaha. We visited Pawnee Park and Father Flanagan's Boys Town. We were escorted by Victor Lange of Wichita, Kansas. The Boys Town Choir performed a concert at the base in Geneva. On our way back to Fairmont, we stopped at B29 Grand Island AAF Base to visit some Boca friends. Upon our return, we learned we were being detached from the 504th and shipping out to Wendover, Utah. The 504th would go overseas with two squadrons. We would meet them later on Tinian.

On Tuesday September 12, we boarded a train for Utah. I don't remember much about the trip except we passed along the shore of the Great Salt Lake and entered barren desolate salt flats. This was to be our home for the next 7-8 months. Wendover was a small com-

munity on the Utah Nevada line about 110 miles west of Salt Lake City and about 110 miles east of Ely, Nevada. Utah is a Mormon state and dry, but there was the Stateline Hotel just across the border in Nevada where the guys could have a drink and play the slot machines. I never got there.

There was a skeleton crew on the base and it looked pretty depressing. The first action after being assigned to barracks was to hold a GI Party. This was scrubbing down the interior of the barracks, rafters, walls, floors and windows. The buildings were one story, tar paper and set in rows. Many are still standing today. There were no trees, shrubbery or grass. The walkways were outlined with stones as was any landscaping. The base had a swimming pool which we didn't have much of an opportunity to use because of the cold. We were issued sheepskin pants and jackets to wear on the flight line. There were bowling alleys which we frequented as well as a PX and Service Club. Also, Saturday night dances with girls bussed in from Salt Lake City and Ely. We saw a lot of movies at the theatre.

The flight line was fenced in with a guard at each gate. We were issued badges which gave us permission to enter. Our planes were Silverplate which meant they were modified to carry an atomic bomb. We didn't know that at the time. The planes were stripped of gun turrets, except for twin 50 caliber machine guns in the tail. Our job, the Radar Section, was to check out the radar sets in the planes and to keep them operable. When the planes were flying, we played a lot of volley ball. We didn't know much about where or what they were doing. Later we found out they were dropping dummy bombs of a special design and practicing a special get away maneuver. However, before we got into anything, Col. Tibbets had us assemble in the theatre where he told us we were embarked on something special and to keep our mouths shut. There were signs posted at the gate saying "What You Hear Here, What You See Here, When You Leave Here, Let It Stay Here!" We radar men were used to this and we didn't know anything anyway, so it was easy to do. Since our planes had not yet arrived, we all got ten day furloughs.

Off base, the only attraction was the State Line Hotel if you wanted to play the slots, or a weekend pass to Elko, Nevada or

Calvin Anstine on Radar Section auxiliary power plant used when preflighting radar in aircraft

Jim Jolly near gravity water tank for showers and washing on Tinian

Salt Lake City, Utah. It was good that the time was broken up by furloughs and a month in Cuba.

On Thursday, September 21, Joel Denham took me to visit his aunt in Mill Valley, California, a small town across the bay from San Francisco. When we arrived at the Oakland train station, they were opening a Service men's Canteen. I was included with Edmund Hall another 393rd radar man, he was shipping out later, and a sailor in a publicity photo for the local paper. I received a copy later in the mail.

Joel and I had a great time seeing everything in and around San Francisco. I don't know how we did it! Golden Gate Park and Museum, the Zoo, Cliff House and the Sea Lions, Lombard Street, the crooked street on Russian Hill, the Top of the Mark! We ate at Alioto's on Fishmen's Wharf near Joe DiMaggio's Restaurant. We helped turn the cable car around, not allowed today, climbed Mt. Tamalpious and visited Muir Woods where the Giant Redwoods grow. We visited two of Father Junipero's Missions, Mission Dolores in San Francisco and Mission of San Rafael. We saw the movie Wilson at the Warfield Theatre. We attended a night baseball game; the Governor's Cup playoff of the Pacific Coast League in which the San Francisco Seals defeated the Los Angeles Angels. On two consecutive Saturdays, we went to Berkeley to see the University of California defeat St. Mary's and UCLA. We did a lot in ten days; Joel's aunt treated us like her sons. My father was disappointed I didn't come home, but I thought six days travel in coach for four days at home was not economical.

On October 13-15, I went on my only visit to Salt Lake City. It was a full weekend of sightseeing, roller skating, lounging at the USO and a football game, Utah 0, Colorado 26. Went to Mass at the Church of the Madeiline; saw the Mormon Temple, the Sea Gull Monument and an exhibit of enemy aircraft, Shot Out of the Sky. The streets are very wide in the city.

On November 17, 1944, I was promoted to Sergeant. We had a pretty good Thanksgiving Dinner. The permanent cooks were a lot better than those in the Technical Training Schools.

On Wednesday December 20, 1944, I got another furlough and went home. Arrived just in time for Christmas Eve. Had a good time. There were free canteens at the train stations where we stopped. I especially remember the North Platte, Nebraska station where the ladies of the region prepared sandwiches, home baked cookies, fruits and other goodies for service men and women. In Union Station, Chicago, Illinois, I got a Catholic New Testament, which I still have. I returned to Wendover on January 7, 1945.

On January 13 we went to Cuba for about six weeks. We left on a C54 four engine transport #019. Our pilot took us to Scott Field, Illinois and we stayed overnight. The next day we flew to Miami, Florida, where we spent another night. When we took off the next day, someone observed an oil leak on the left wing, so we returned to the field. The cap had not been replaced properly. We finally arrived at Batista Field, San Antonio de los Banos near Havana. We could see the whole area around Havana all lit up. We never found out why we had taken this circuitous route.

Batista Field was very nice with palm trees and neatly trimmed lawns. We had chipped in a couple of dollars so the local people could be hired to do KP and other chores for us. This was a life of luxury. The cooks really out did themselves; we even had lobster and filet mignon. It was also a pleasure to be in the sunshine at this time of year.

I was able to visit Havana on three weekends, staying at the luxurious Hotel Nacional overlooking the sea. The first visit was with Wendell Lathrop, Henry Jones and Edwin Bell. It was a festive occasion; Jose Marti Day, was Cuba's Liberator. There was a parade with huge crowds everywhere. We visited some of the tourist spots, had our picture taken at the famous Sloppy Joe's Bar, met a Cuban senator and had a wild taxi ride. I bought souvenirs; a pair of mahogany vases and cheap pair of castanets, saw the sights, took snapshots and had dinner in a restaurant in the Capitolio. Some of the guys went to see the cockfights in San Antonio. I didn't go into town at all.

A B29 crashed in the sugar cane field as it was landing; it was not one of the 393rd's. We had a trio of locals who hung around the radar shack sweeping up and doing odd jobs. I remember one was called Hector. We were learning Spanish and they were learning English.

On Wednesday February 28, we boarded the same plane to take us back to Wendover. This time we flew over the Gulf of Mexico and Texas arriving at Wendover the same day. I think there were three or four planes needed to transport all of us. I learned I was in the ground echelon and we began processing for overseas shipment.

President Franklin Delano Roosevelt died April 12, 1945, at Warm Springs, Georgia and Vice President Harry S. Truman was sworn in as the President. On Thursday April 26, we left the Port of Embarkation (POE) in Seattle, Washington. We stayed at Ft. Lawton in sight of snowcapped Mt. Rainier. I visited Seattle twice. Jack Kennedy reminded me we attended a movie/stage show when I visited him in a Pittsburgh hospital many years later. I vaguely remember that.

On Sunday May 6, we embarked for overseas duty on the USS Cape Victory operated by the Merchant Marines with a Navy gun crew. The voyage to Honolulu, Hawaii, was on a very rough ocean. The bow slammed on the water and the screw popped out of the water causing a lot of seasickness. Fortunately, I was not seriously affected, my meal ticket was punched for every meal. I remember in the head (toilet) one day, two colored soldiers were bent over the bowls. One said, "Lord I's sick!" The one next to him said, "Tell Him you is scared too!"

We finally reached Honolulu on Sunday May 13. We tied up at the pier for a few days. We dropped a rope over the side and bought a few cases of pineapple juice and ice cream before it was stopped. We were treated to a USO Hula Show on the pier. It felt good to be on land for a while; the show was enjoyed.

On Wednesday May 16, we left Hawaii escorted by three destoyer type vessels, albatross (gooney birds) and flying fish. We spent a lot of time on deck watching the flying fish, reading and playing cards. The water was pretty smooth. One day one of our escorts made a fast turn to the rear, the only bit of excitement besides the Navy gunners target practice. We crossed the International Date Line and were able to buy wallet size cards to certify this from the chaplain for ten cents. He also sold us warm cokes for five cents; the officers got cold cokes.

Our ship arrived at Eniwetok on Friday, May 25, to become part of a massive armada of ships. It was an impressive sight; hundreds of ships at anchor. We left the next day, continuing our journey without escort, reaching Tinian one of the Mariana Islands, on Tuesday afternoon May 29 and debarked the next morning. The air echelon was there to greet us. We pitched pup tents on a field on 86th Street. The CBs named the streets they built after the streets of Manhattan. We stayed for three days, eating K and C rations and watching the CBs work day and night improving West Field. We moved to another area where we had pyramidal tents with wood floors and an electric light bulb.

Nine days later June 11, we moved again into Quonset Huts by the 18th CBs at the corner of 125th Street and 8th Avenue. The hut housed the whole Radar Section of 25 men. We slept on cots with mosquito bars which were needed. Our washing facilities were in the open; an elevated tank which was filled daily provided water for a face washing trough and a screened in shower. Our laundry was done for us. We had again chipped in as a group and bought washing machines. We added a wooden porch to our hut where the guys could play cards in the shade. We also did a lot of reading, letter writing and radio listening around the hut. We even tried planting flowers.

We went to the flight line daily to perform our maintenance job of the aircraft's radar equipment. We had the APQ 13 high altitude bombing radar, altimeter, Long Range Navigation (LORAN), IFF and Radar Countermeasures sets to attend to. Our planes were parked on hard

Paul Metro on Tinian with
Windmill washing machine

stands at North Field. Originally our shack was a large tent, later we moved into a Quonset Hut.

Our planes did not join the other groups in the bombing mission on Japan. After orientation training and bombing of Japanese held islands of Rota, Truk and the Marcus, missions to Japan began on July 20. These were special missions with planes carrying a single pumpkin (10,000 pound bomb) to separate targets. They had various wing/tail markings of other groups for deception. The Enola Gay had 313th Bomb Wing (BW), 6th Bomb Group (BG) stationed on Tinian. Bockscar had 58th BW also. All of this was in preparation for the reason the 509th was organized.

In the meantime while our planes were flying, we used our free time to tour the island looking over the remains of Tinian Town, destroyed tanks, planes and some old stone monuments. We went swimming at the beach, played volleyball, softball and pitched horseshoes alongside our hut. When it got dark, we went to their outdoor theatre carrying our raincoat and sun helmet because it was sure to rain. During the daytime, we ignored the rain because we dried off very quickly in the hot sun. We cut off our khakis to be more comfortable in the heat. Dress was very casual.

Our cooks did an excellent job with our meals. But whatever they did, they could not make the mutton we called goat meat very palatable. Many of us swore off lamb for the rest of our lives. One time, they made a valiant effort to make ice cream but it was a great milkshake. This was greatly appreciated anyway. Anything cold was a rare delight. Ice water was a treat when we got it! We were able to buy a weekly ration of two cans of beer and two bottles of coke warm. I traded my beer for cokes. I also gave my rationed cigarettes away.

Besides the movies, we were entertained by USO shows from the states. Eddie Bracken and Peggy Ryan were the only Hollywood stars to visit Tinian while we were there. This Is The Army and Winged Pigeon were two other shows we saw. Touring major league baseball players played exhibition games for us. The field was laid out using camouflage netting for an outfield fence.

Harold Kimme and I attended a game out in right field. Enos "Country" Slaughter of the St. Louis Cardinals played right field and Joe Gordon of the New York Yankees played second base on one team. "Birdie" Tebbets of the Detroit Tigers and other minor league players were on the other team. After a few innings, Enos Slaughter took off his shoes and played in stocking feet. Enos caught the last out of the game. Someone called for him to throw the ball. He did and I caught it. I jumped the fence and got him and Joe Gordon to autograph the ball. The autographs faded and the ball was lost.

To augment my diet, I ventured off the road a few yards to harvest some papayas and wild oranges. We also shared care packages from home. Toll House Cookies were the most popular even though many were just crumbs by the time they reached us.

One night, I had to stand guard duty at the radar tent on the flight line. It was an uneasy night sleeping on a cot under a mosquito bar with my carbine in bed with me. There was also a guard posted at each of our planes. This made me feel more secure, but I was happy to see the sun rise in the morning. There were still Japs on the island.

Things were relatively normal until August 5 when some of us were alerted to be on the flight line at midnight. This was our first clue that what we had been preparing for was to take place. What? We still didn't know. It was a mob scene around the Enola Gay until it took off around 2:45 am August 6, 1945. In the morning, we got the news that Hiroshima was decimated by a special bomb which was later identified as Little Boy, an atomic bomb (uranium). As the Enola Gay was homeward bound, we on Tinian were celebrating the end of the war. We felt sure that Japan would surrender. There was a double ration of free beer, coke, and a flat bed truck with a band where guys could jitterbug with each other since there were no women around. There were pie eating and egg tossing contests. Another contest was a three man race in which the legs of the center man facing backwards were tied to the legs of the outside men. Joel Denham and Andrew Brown were the outside men and I was in the center. We won! The prize was a photo of us, left to right, Joel Denham, Paul Metro and Andrew Brown which they let me keep.

The Enola Gay arrived after 1 pm (1300) with a host of people to greet the crew. General Spaatz was there to pin the Distinguished Service Cross on Colonel Tibbets. Can you imagine all of us in our rags; cutoff shorts, T-shirts, or no shirt at all with so much high ranking brass around?

The next day a crowd was out to watch the newsreel cameras roll as Col. Tibbets, Capt. Parsons USN, the Weaponeer and others were being interviewed. Later, we were also given a briefing on atomic energy.

The Japanese did not concede defeat. So on August 9 around 3 am, Major Sweeney took off in Bockscar for a second atomic mission.

On August 10, Japan accepted unconditional surrender as proposed by the Potsdam Resolution. On September 2, Archbishop Spellman of New York celebrated a Mass of Thanksgiving on our open air theatre. We lined up to shake hands with him. Soon after, we made preparations to return to the USA.

The big day was October 18 when we boarded the Navy Troop Ship USS Deuel. It was crowded, but no one cared, we were headed for home. We arrived in Oakland, California, November 4, 1945. It was an awesome thrill passing under the Golden Gate Bridge. People stopped on the bridge to wave. It was so quiet, everyone must have been saying a prayer of thanks that we returned safely and the war was ended. As we debarked the ship, the Red Cross and Salvation Army were there to serve us coffee and donuts.

A troop train, the last of many for us, was waiting to take us to our next station which was Roswell AAF New Mexico. We arrived November 6. Roswell was a permanent base, not like Fairmont or Truax. We didn't have much to do except go to the gym, relax and wait for our discharge if we had enough points and didn't reenlist. We were awarded two battle stars for our missions against the Japanese Mandates and the Japanese Empire which helped with the points. Some of us visited the Carlsbad Caverns, but when I went, we arrived too late.

Finally my big day arrived, Wednesday November 21, when I received my discharge papers. Joe Ross of Allentown, Pennsylvania and I took the overnight bus to Amarillo, Texas and started to hitchhike on the famous highway Route 66. We had Thanksgiving Dinner at a roadside restaurant on Thursday and spent the night at a YMCA in Tulsa, Oklahoma. On Friday, we were picked up by a sailor's wife traveling from San Diego, California. She was anxious to get home in Bedford, Indiana and drove all the way. She dropped us off at the Bedford Hotel at about 2 am. We hadn't fallen asleep when the telephone rang. It was that wonderful lady calling to tell us that I had left my discharge papers in her car and she would be waiting for us at a particular corner in the morning. We were waiting but when a big tractor trailer stopped, we found out we were at the wrong corner. The driver said hop in, turned the rig around and took us back about a mile to where the young lady was waiting. The driver said he wouldn't mind taking us further but he thought we could get a faster ride. We thanked both and continued on our trip to Pittsburgh, Pennsylvania.

When we got to Pittsburgh, we decided we wanted to get home sooner so we took a train that night. We had some sleep, Joe got off at Philadelphia and I continued on to Newark where I caught some buses to get home at last.

MICKELSON, MONT J.
603rd Air Engineering Squadron, Machine Shop

The infamous events of Pearl Harbor, December 7, 1941, initiated an adrenaline rush to participate, in some way, in the war effort to defend our great country. Subsequent to batteries of aptitude tests, I as a young man, entered and completed the Machinist Learner Program, moved on as programmed to Hill Air Force Base (AFB), achieved the Journeyman Machinist rating, manufacturing various aircraft components and training women to be lathe and milling machine operators. At the end of a one year deferment from the draft, I was offered but declined, another deferment. Hence, requested to be drafted, reported to Ft. Douglas, Utah, one week later transferred to Hill Air Force Base as a GI Machinist, upon induction I failed the vision examination to enter the cadet program which later proved to be a blessing since it was rumored the cadet program suddenly was overloaded and hundreds were transferred to the infantry.

Hill AFB, at the time, had several sub-depots under their jurisdiction in surrounding states which also included Wendover. I was solicited by the personnel office, if I had a choice; I responded no. One week later, I was on orders for Wendover, and would be picked up at a certain point, at a specified time, in Salt Lake City. After some six hours of waiting, the 4x4 truck arrived at midnight, with no heater. The winter day and night was windy and cold with low single digit temperatures. The vehicle also had a governor on the engine so the hours to Wendover seemed endless. Both the driver and I were happy to finally arrive at the base around 0330 hours.

Obviously, I selfishly and silently questioned my decision in leaving the civilian life, an excellent paying job, secure with defense deferments, for this? I was dropped off at transient quarters, a barracks with a large potbellied coal stove in each end. As the door was opened, numerous yelled requests from awakened soldiers were received to shut the door to save what heat remained from the dying fires in the stoves. Shower and toilet facilities were located in a single building about 3/4 block distant. This was a typical arrangement, unless one was lucky to be in a barracks next door, whether it be freezing

cold, blowing sand and salt or whatever the elements were.

I shortly moved to a barracks where machine shop and other technical personnel were quartered, and settled in for work on swing shift. Wendover AFB was a remote base where various aircraft: B17, B24, P47, cargo, and other crews received training. The shops and maintenance facilities were, for the most part, intact and operating. I observed most personnel were proficient, skilled and ambitious in their particular Military Occupational Status (MOS).

The machine shop had new or rehabilitated machinery, lathes, mills, shaper, heat treat ovens, and cadmium plating tank. The stock room was well supplied with various hand precision tools, tool steel, taps and dies, etc. The raw stock of various steels, aluminum, bronze, and brass were properly color coded to assure correct materials were used and which had received the proper heat treat per blueprints and specifications, even quickly drawn sketches.

Suddenly, an air of secrecy filtrated the entire base. B29 aircraft arrived. The 509th Composite Group was formed. I recollect that three of us from the machine shop with an MOS of 114 were asked to volunteer and join the mysterious, newly formed group, the 603rd Air Engineering Squadron in the 509th Composite Group. We were advised the Groups' mission was high risk and top secret and would probably change the tide of the war, if successful. However, we could decline if desired. The three of us, Harold Glick, Farr Hurst, and I volunteered. We were good friends and remain so to this day.

Security of operations was vital, continually emphasized and reemphasized. Machine shop personnel, in support of the 509th, manufactured various components, propeller balancing hubs, brackets, tooling, adapters, specially threaded rods, etc. to close tolerances. On separate occasions, I was met by two fully armed Military Police (MPs), escorted through two security fences with gates guarded with another MP to the flight line and an awaiting B29 aircraft. The guards closely watched my every move as I performed a functional fit of the manufactured part with an interfacing component within the aircraft bomb bay, then escorted back over the return route, outside the highly secured area to the machine shop. It became evident that our 509th Composite Group Commander, extremely bright and intelligent, had chosen the right location for the top secret operations.

Mont Mickelson in machine shop

A few described Wendover as the end of the world in the desert. Though extremely isolated, windy, dusty, and dirty, at times with extreme temperature fluctuations, personnel adjusted to the conditions accordingly. The base had similar amenities, though somewhat austere as other air force facilities: clubs, library, theatre, swimming pool, bowling alley, provisions for your choice of church services, hospital, PX, etc. for off duty utilization. Dances were held on weekends, girls were transported by bus from Salt Lake areas and eastern Nevada for the dances and were returned home the same evening. The Stateline Hotel and Casino was open, and appeared to flourish. There were plenty of hills and mountains and salt flats for hiking and exploring. Three day passes to the cities were provided for off duty personnel as appropriate.

Having dated my girl for several years, we were married in Salt Lake on a three day pass shortly prior to leaving for Tinian in the Marianas Islands. We were very fortunate in renting a two room old frame home with the outside covered with roofing tar paper, located off base close to the railroad roundhouse, a half bath with a coal/wood kitchen range for cooking and heating. The large, high ceiling, wall papered bedroom was too cold in the winter; so we moved the bed in the kitchen leaving about one foot clearance between the range and the bed which also served as a couch. If one should sit on the bed too quickly, the springs and mattress crashed to the floor. This provided much fun as we received guests in our austere, humble, but short lived home.

With off duty hours, I became involved in community and church affairs off base. I express extreme gratitude to many; the residents of Wendover who were good neighbors, who operated the grocery stores, gasoline rationing office, gas stations, fire station, school, etc., who rendered assistance and friendship in so many ways.

Departure preparation date from Wendover Field Utah arrived. I and my bride of some two months evacuated our humble but austere home in Wendover. Good neighbors provided a bedroom for the last night. A friend, remaining with the 216th Army Air Force Base Unit

(AAFBU) drove Ruth home to Salt Lake City the following day. Subsequently, most 509th squadrons, excluding flight crews, boarded the troop train bound for Fort Lawton Washington. Our steam engine train car of early vintage was equipped with few seats and bunked Army cots; heat was minimal, cleanliness in restroom lacking. After two plus days, Fort Lawton Washington was a welcome sight.

Approximately one week later, we boarded Cape Victory, a Victory Class troop ship manufactured by Kaiser Steel. Bunks were layered seven high, canvas roped to steel pipe frames. Needless to say, the environment became extremely smelly and stale. The tranquil trip through Puget Sound was beautiful. Then high Pacific storm seas changed all that. Waves began crashing over the smaller Victory ship's bow. Many personnel became extremely seasick, whether psychological or not. Many relieved stomach contents over the rail for three days before subsiding.

We docked at Honolulu, Oahu, Hawaii for three days, were not allowed to leave the dock but those beautiful and handsome local people entertained us with a typical show of music, singing and dance. Many of us were happy to purchase canned pineapple to enjoy a delicacy eaten without standing upright with the ship heaving and rolling from side to side. The cruise continued to Eniwetok, Marshall Islands for fueling.

At some point in our journey, an enemy submarine alert was sounded. The ship came to a complete stop. Concurrently, we were directed to return to our holds, maintain complete silence, no talking or movement, no smoking or lights. The Navy crews were in their battle positions. Shortly, we heard cans exploding, dropped from our following submarine chaser. Cape Victory's antiaircraft guns and the five inch gun on the fantail remained silent. About thirty minutes later our journey continued. Periodically, we observed possibly fourteen escort ships on the horizon, some followed us into Tinian Harbor. I was highly impressed with most Navy personnel performing their duties during periodic gunnery practices while traveling a zigzag pattern for approximately twenty-four days.

Back view of honeymoon house

Mont Mickelson in front of honeymoon house, 1945

On Tinian, the 603rd Engineering Squadron and others were transferred via truck to a tented area in close proximity to the machine shop and flight line. I with other machinists, Farr Hurst and Harold Glick joined the existing compliment of machinists from other bomb groups. Tents had no floors but huge wooden box sides were obtained for the floor which became a haven and breeding place for huge white rats.

The machine shop, in place, was equipped with mills, lathes, drill presses, adequate hand tools and material stock; also intact was a mobile trailer with generator, air compressor, bench grinder and tool steels. All were primarily for machinists use to drill and remove broken studs and bolts from aircraft engine blocks, landing gears and other support equipment as needed. Because of high tensile strength of bolts and studs used on engines and landing gears etc., frequent sharpening of high speed drill bits was required. Turpentine was used as a coolant. This operation saved time and expense of cylinder or engine replacement, major overhaul of landing gears and other structural components. Off duty hours were spent in the servicedrome outdoor theater conveniently located for movies and infrequent USO shows; also exploration of

2nd front left, back row, Farr Hurst, 2nd from right, back row, Mont Mickelson

bombed out Japanese structures, tanks, guns, caves, negotiating with natives for purchases of shell necklaces and bracelets, hunting for exotic sea life and shells washed into coral pools by ocean waves. Swimming from a sandy beach was popular but frequently risky due to severe riptides and deep channels.

It is believed, Tinian was one of if not the largest airfield in the world though on a small island. Saipan Island shore was about three miles away. The lumbering B29s fully loaded, roaring for takeoff would utilize every yard of runway length. Upon leaving the coral runway shelf, now over water, ripples from the propellers were formed. With baited breath altitude was gained. Too frequently, a B29 would settle in the ocean waters. Patrol boats would pick up those who could exit the plane. After ten to twelve minutes, the plane would no longer be visible. I was always amazed with the ruggedness of the B29s, not our 509th, returning from a mission over Japan badly damaged, even without a major structure or portions thereof, not discounting the crews skill and proficiency. Some upon landing were not so fortunate, but disastrous. Many silent prayers were offered in behalf of those involved.

Subsequent to the August 6th and 9th, 1945 atomic bombings of Hiroshima and Nagasaki, large and small celebrations took place on the island. So at long last, other bomb groups finally recognized the mysterious 509th was present for a purpose, that of turning the tide of the war. Soon the 603rd Air Engineering Squadron (AES) along with other 509th Squadrons boarded the ship USS Deuel for home, picking up other military personnel at Guam. Much faster than the USS Cape Victory, the Deuel cruised around eighteen knots per hour, as told by the crew, reached our United States in approximately eighteen days. The ecstasy of viewing our shores and passing under the Golden Gate could not be surpassed. Headed for Oakland, California, the huge "Welcome Home" appeared on a hill. Subsequent to timely docking and disembarking at Oakland, we boarded a milk run troop train. The ever so frequent stops afforded many personnel a race to liquor stores for refreshments. Needless to say, many became ill with all the symptoms that accompany excessive drinking.

Our destination was Roswell Army Air Force Base (RAAFB) New Mexico. True to form, Col. Paul Tibbets called the group together, expressed appreciation for a job well done, reiterated his previously expressed commitment to take us over as a group and return us home as a group. He made a sincere plea that all who could see fit to reup with him would be appreciated. I believe a goodly number did just that. I elected to return home to a loving family and pursue a college education and so it was.

I was discharged at Fort Logan Colorado. I left Wendover with my loving wife expecting our first child and as a result of Paul Tibbets' commitment, was able to see our first son born into the world. As one of some 1700, a tooth in a gear of multiple gear chains, meshing together into a finely tuned machine, an organization self-sustaining committed to the task at hand, we finished the job.

I express my gratitude to the many service people who became close friends and shared the ultimate goal to restore peace and liberty to our own United States of America.

MILLER, WILLIAM L.
320th Troop Carrier Squadron, Radio Operator

I turned 18 years of age on June 28, 1943, in Provo, Utah. As a high school graduate, I was drafted into the Army in September 1943, reported in at Fort Douglas, Salt Lake City, Utah. I was given the opportunity to choose the US Air Force after completing a battery of examinations at the basic training center at Amarillo, Texas. In addition, I was allowed to enter cadet training as a navigator. After basic training, I left for Cedar Falls, Iowa. This was the location of the 80th CTD (College Training Detachment), Iowa State Teachers College. At this point, I was very pleased at my apparent fortune, as I had entered the Army as a draftee.

There were about 200 Air Force cadets in this program when I arrived. The general plan was to complete the college courses and move on to specific training as a navigator for either troop carrier or bomber aircraft. About half-way through the program at Cedar Falls, we were called into an auditorium and told the program was being terminated, due to an emergency in force structure in Europe. We learned later this was the beginning of the famous "Battle of the Bulge", so called because of the huge effort by the Nazi forces to push the Allied forces back. Apparently there was an emergency call to increase infantry troops in Europe to counter this attack. Men in different Army training branches were funneled into accelerated infantry training at Fort Dix, New Jersey and within a few weeks were actually fighting in battles in Europe. These battles were bloody and intense and in all probability many of my Air Force cadet friends were in this group. Only four of us were singled out and remained in the Air Force at this time. I was extremely lucky and the reason for this follows.

Apparently, the Air Force felt they did not need any more navigators but did need a few more radio operators for crews in the Pacific Theater; more B29 crews anticipated. In order to screen out personnel with a high probability to excel as a radio operator, we all were given a Morse Code type identification test. We sat in a room with headsets on and were required to answer yes or no to identify if two series of Morse Code dits and dahs were yes, the same, or no, different. I remember how easy this was as each series made a rhythm as a unit. It may be that this skill was related to an excellent musical education given me by my father who was a professional violinist in a symphony. I still remember the Morse Code today because of the excellent training I received at the school I was shipped to. The four of us were shipped to the Air Force radio operator, mechanic school at Sioux Falls, South Dakota. I spent the rest of the winter there and graduated in the Spring of 1944. I nearly froze to death at that air base. We were in only tarpaper barracks with a coal stove at each end. Over half of my barracks was in the hospital with influenza at the same time.

As regards to the effectiveness of the training techniques used to prepare personnel to excel as crewmembers, it was outstanding. As I reflect on this as an adult who eventually obtained BS, MS, and PhD degrees from outstanding universities here in the US, this

Air Force school was superb. Many of my Army instructors had combat experience and their attitude was that every individual had to succeed if possible; you were going to be depended on as a crewmember and you better be prepared. I was fortunate to graduate as our class valedictorian. I mention this as it may be related to me getting involved with the 509th.

A few weeks before my graduation at Sioux Falls AAB (Army Air Base), things were happening in my hometown that involved me. Unknown to me, FBI agents were interviewing various people that knew me as I grew up in Provo, Utah. My family told me later that the agents talked to my high school principal, my Boy Scoutmaster, my bishop at church, my family and people that I had worked for. These individuals were asked not to discuss these interviews with anyone at this time. Upon graduation, we were assigned to various air groups, mostly B29 units. I said good-bye to buddies I had gone to school with and shipped off by myself, with a 10 day delay enroute for a little furlough at home. I was to then report for duty at Wendover AAB. Since I was to be at my home first in Provo, Utah, my trip to Wendover was very simple. Forty-five miles north to Salt Lake City and then 127 miles due west to Wendover and the Salt Flats. When I arrived, the base was surrounded by armed guards and who could have known what was about to happen. I was eventually crewed with Russ Angeli (pilot), Ron Adams (copilot), and Virgil Mann (navigator). I cannot remember the names of a couple of flight engineers that completed our C54 crew, flying as part of the 320th Troop Carrier Squadron, 509th Composite Group. This ended up to be quite an experience for a very young man—20 years old, when Colonel Paul Tibbets returned from Hiroshima with Major Sweeney to tell us all, at our Tinian gathering, just what had happened. This initiated the end of the war.

I can remember how unusual it was when we flew to different places within the US. On occasion upon landing, our plane was surrounded by armed guards. This also occurred when we landed at Hamilton Field (north of San Francisco) for refueling before a typical trip to Tinian.

When it was getting close to August 9, 1945, we had some distinguished passengers who were on their way to Tinian. One was Admiral Richard E. Byrd of South Pole exploration fame. He was on the staff of the chief of naval operations for the Pacific area. Other passengers were envoys representing Prime Minister Winston

Churchill. We made five round trips from Wendover AAB to North Field Tinian Island, which were confidential runs with certain personnel and equipment. I used a J38 hand key to transmit messages from my CW (Carrier Wave or so called Short Wave) Transmitter. We used very little voice transmission. For the most part, only the pilots used voice for contacting various towers at the bases when we needed landing instructions or other flight information as we approached or left the airstrips. My various position reports to Island bases were all done in code using my CW Transmitter. The distance this signal could travel compared to voice transmission was much greater.

I can remember the Morse Code totally today as well as many of the Q signals that were 3 letter units meaning certain things. For example, QDM meant a question: "What is my magnetic course with zero wind direction to steer you?" That schooling was so intense you cannot forget it ever! We flew to Atsuki Air Base, near Tokyo, to recover some bodies collected from the Hiroshima area. They were radioactive so their caskets were lined with lead sheets to prevent radiation from escaping. I think they ended up at Walter Reed Hospital in Washington DC for pathological and toxicological studies.

Four other C54s were making trips as well. These trips were intimately involved in the final fabrication of the two atomic bombs, which finally terminated the war in the Pacific.

Lastly, it is rather ironic that a few years later, working as a biological research scientist, I went to Oak Ridge Laboratories for special courses on the use of radio active isotopes in medical research. Some of the instructors were physicists from Vanderbilt University that had worked on the original Manhattan Project (atomic bomb project) helping to develop techniques to purify isotopes to be used for the uranium and plutonium bombs.

MORRISON, LENNIE R.
1395th Military Police Company

Life at Wendover was pretty dull. There wasn't much to see ... a bunch of sand and a few buildings. I don't remember anything about Sloppy Joes ... food was OK. They did have USO dances, but I never attended one. They had a midway gambling place. I had $14, ran it up to $40 ... then I started losing and didn't have better than $4 when I quit. While I was home on furlough before being transferred to Wendover, I had met my future wife at a cafe. She was wearing a fur coat and I thought she had a lot of money. She had $800 more than I did! After I was transferred to Wendover, we corresponded for a while and I asked her to marry me and she accepted. I had her go to my mother's house and while I was on the phone, my mother put an engagement ring on her finger. Alma came out to Wendover to see me and stayed three or four days. It was her first time out of Missouri and her first time on a train. I got a pass, and we went to a Baptist Church north of Wendover and got married, with the pastor and his wife and another older couple to witness. I remember it was while we were there I heard that President Roosevelt had died. Alma didn't believe me at first. We spent one night in Salt Lake City. It was a sad morning the day she left to go back to Missouri. I shed a few tears. It was a lonesome 'hole in the ground'.

I got so sick on the ship over to Tinian Island, I thought I was dead. We had trained for two or three days in Logan, Washington before getting on the (overloaded) ship. When we woke up the next day, we were underway. I think I was already a little queasy and when I went into the dining room, a fellow across the way threw-up into his plate when the ship rolled. I just ran out!

In a few days, by the time we got to Hawaii, I was pretty much okay, but it was rough. Even the crew got sick for part of the trip and they had been on the ship for about six months. They told us the ship actually went backwards a mile or two one day. We stopped at Hawaii for two or three days—couldn't get off the ship—but they put on a big show for us. Pretty girls!

We got to Tinian on 29 May 1945 (easy for me to remember because it was my cousin Dwight Eaton's birthday. He was, at that time, stationed in New Guinea). At first, on Tinian, we slept in tents, then another squadron left and we took over their building. Our shower room was large and had a big tank up high, heated by the sun. I was there about two months, served as MP, guarded the Enola Gay, though I was not on duty at the time of the bombing.

Col. Tibbets
I was an MP guarding the planes at the airport. It was hot there and we would stand in the shade of the planes to get out of the sun. My Commanding Officer was Col. Paul W. Tibbets. He was the nicest, most down to earth person I ever met. He was always dressed so neat and outshined them all. When they returned, Brig. General Davies, Wing Commander, called him to attention. Close behind was General Carl Spaatz, Commander of the USA Army Strategic Air Forces. There was a huge crowd. It became still. General Spaatz faced Col. Tibbets and said a few words of congratulations. Then he pinned the Distinguished Service Cross on his chest, giving special recognition of the great job he and his men had done. I didn't look to see if a button popped off his jacket! I thought he was a wonderful man. I had not known about the reunions, didn't even know that Col. (now General) Tibbets was still living until a couple of years ago when I had the opportunity to see him and talk with him and some of the crew at Branson, Missouri. That was a highlight of my life.

NELSON, RICHARD M.
393rd Bomb Squadron, Radio Operator, Crew B-9

Letters Home

May I, 1945

Dearest Mom, Dad and Loraine,

Mom, the ride home was swell. After I talked to you, we went to another base and then returned to the one we had been to. We picked up a load of freight there and then about 7pm, we took off for Wendover. We arrived at about 9:30 pm and it was a real nice ride, not a bit rough.

Sometime this week, we get our overseas processing. This includes a clothing check, where they take all of the unnecessary clothes away. This will include all of our ODs (olive drabs), blouse, all the OD pants and shirts. Also, they take all of our suntans except one pair, all of our winter underwear and a few other things. We also have to go through another administration check to see that all of our records are in order and also a final medical check.

There isn't much news up here. The weather is really beautiful now, not too hot, but something like California weather. They aren't doing much flying up here, just a couple ships a day are flying. We have almost all of our new planes now and they are really beautiful. I still say that after being in this outfit, I sure wouldn't be happy at or in another one.

Well, you can tell I haven't much of anything to say, so I'll sign off. Take care of yourselves. All My Love, Rich

May 30, 1945

I'm on a fairly long flight with not much to do so thought maybe I'd write a line or two. We are going from Wendover to Roswell, NM, then back to Wendover without stopping. It will take us about seven hours as we have some bombs to drop. It is a beautiful evening, about 9:30 pm. There is a slight haze over the ground but up here at 25,000 feet, the full moon is shining very bright. The haze over the ground isn't enough to cover it, as when we pass over towers you can see the lights easily. We took off around 7 pm and will land around 2 am. This is just a navigational hop so don't have too much to do other than send my reports in every hour and help the navigator. This really is a swell crew I fly with. The bombardier is from California, some town about half way to Frisco. He is fairly young, he and I being the youngest in the crew. His name is Stew Williams. The navigator is a married man who was from Pittsburgh, but wants to live in California after the war. He really likes it out there. He was at Santa Anna so knows what it is like. The copilot is from Seattle and is also a nice guy. Our pilot, Capt. Lewis is a swell egg. He is built about like Dad only quite a bit younger, being about 27. He is really a swell Joe as he doesn't ride us at all. He expects us to do our jobs and at that he doesn't crab at us. The navigator's name is Rider and copilot's is McNamara. The engineer is the oldest man in the crew, he is 32 but really a good guy. His name is Duzenbury and he is from Detroit. Tailgunner is about 24 and was married just last year. He is from New York

and his name is Caron. Our radar man is 30 and also a good Joe. He hails from Texas and his name is Stiborik. That leaves just one more man that is flying with us tonight and he is Shumard. He is about 29 and has been in the Army seven years. The whole crew is darn nice and all real good natured.

The plane is running fine and I just got through sending in a position report. I can hardly hear the ground station because of the interference. They are having a hard time hearing me also, but I finally got it all in. This ground station picked up one of our ships clear in Hawaii. That is really good as that is almost 2600 miles away. It is really smooth up here, hardly any motion at all. Well, can't think of anything else so will put this in my pocket and mail it tomorrow. All my Love, Rich PS: Was glad to hear you got to see a B29 up close and wish you could have gone inside. I guess you got my letter saying to mail my ring and knife here as soon as possible. Love again, R

June 18, 1945

Dear Mom, Dad and Loraine,

Just another little note to let you know what has been happening. Was down to Omaha for two nights last week. Went down Thursday morning to pick up a new B29 and stayed there until Saturday morning. We picked up the first of our new planes and they are really beautiful. They have these new reversible pitch propellers. When you are landing, as soon as your wheels touch the runway, you reverse the props and gun the engines and it really slows the plane down. This is the first B29 to have these props on it, so it was quite a thrill to pick this plane up. It has all our special equipment on it and was known down there as the first of the Silver Plate project and was all very confidential even to most of the employees at the plant.

Because I was down there for two nights, I'm broke again and also owe $10 out, so I guess you'd better send me $20 or $25 as soon as possible. I have to get this letter out right away so I'll close and try to write again tonight. No, it won't be tonight as we are having a squadron party tonight, so I'll write tomorrow night. All my Love, Rich

July 23, 1945 Tinian, Marianas

Dearest Mom, Dad and Loraine,

Just a short note as I haven't much time before briefing. Well, this is to be our first Empire mission. We've picked a pretty tough target, but I'm still very anxious to go. Duzenbury our Flight Engineer has a bad ear so he was grounded. He sure is disappointed; I'm sure glad it wasn't me.

Our plane has really been in tip top condition since we've been here. Some of the other crews have been having trouble, but our baby has really been good to us. We haven't any name for it yet, but I imagine after this raid we'll name it. After tonight it will no longer be a virgin.

There really isn't much for a radio operator to do on these trips. The only time we send anything is just after we drop our bomb. Then it is just a short message. The only time we would do anything was if we were in trouble, then I would really work. I hope I don't have anything to do tonight.

Well time is short. I went to communion tonight so that is why I was a little late on starting this. Take care of yourselves, all of you, and start writing more letters. I got your first one yesterday and it only took seven days to get here. All My Love, Rich

July 27, 1945 Tinian

Dearest Mom, Dad and Loraine,

Just another little note to let you know what is happening. Well I've now finished two missions over Japan. We are really getting our chance now. There really isn't much to tell you about the raids. On the first one, we saw quite a bit of flak, but on the second one, we didn't see any. The first mission we made was when the Navy had so many planes over Japan also. I'll tell you now they are really bombing hell out of Japan. We heard on the Tokyo radio where the Japs are getting really mad. They said they couldn't figure out the American strategy. They said we were making sneak blows against them. We know that it was some of our ships that led them to say this, so we felt pretty proud. This outfit is really showing its' stuff over here. After the second mission, we got a commendation from the Commanding General of this wing because the results were so good.

We got a nice air mattress today. It is nice after sleeping on just a canvas cot for a month. The combat crews really get the gravy over here, and our crew for sure. Our skipper Capt. Lewis has really been decent to us. Some of the other airplane commanders are more worried about themselves than their crews, but not Cap, he really works for us. I even think I'll get a promotion next month.

We only get two bottles of beer every other night, so sometimes after a flight when we can't get beer, the officers on our crew bring us all over a bottle. Not many of the other crews get that. The whiskey we brought over is almost gone now. We brought a case apiece over and I've just a couple bottles left so don't know where I'll get any more. It sells for $30 a fifth over here.

Enola Gay enlisted crew leaves for mission.
(L-R): George Caron, Wyatt Duzenbury, Joe Stiborik, Robert Shumard, Dick Nelson

I've thought of two more things I need. First is clothespins; send some over first chance you get. The second is flower seeds; send a bunch over. Some of everything but I notice Zinias do well over here. We want to make the front of our hut look pretty if we can.

Well can't think of anything more to say except if we keep going like we have been, I'll have my 35 missions in a lot faster than I thought. Take care of yourselves and give my love to everyone. All My Love, Rich

August 7, 1945

Dearest Mom, Dad and Loraine,

Well I've had 4 missions now. The last one was yesterday. It was a good one, just like all the rest of them are. I hope we get the rest of them in fast. I'm already in the mood to come home. I guess we get the air medal after the next mission as you're supposed to get it after the 5th mission. I guess you can see on the envelope they finally made me a Pfc (Private First Class). Two years in the Army and I finally got a promotion. I guess they'll keep coming in now. As a Pvt (Private), I was making about $40 a month and now I'll get about $7.20 more and maybe next month, I'll get Corporal stripes.

Take this money and put it in the bank. I'll send as much as I can home every month. After they take my insurance, bonds and $25 allotment out, it left $50 when I was a Private.

I have so much to tell you but none of it will go through, so I might as well save it until I get home. Part of it you might find out in the newspaper and radio before I'm home but I still have a lot to talk about.

I hope all of you are well and happy. The letters from home sound like you all are. I guess Loraine is really having a good time this summer and that is fine.

Well I'll quit now as I can't think of anything to say. I miss you all. Love, Rich PS Also notice my APO is 336.

August 12, 1945

Dearest Mom, Dad and Loraine,

When we went on the "Big One", it was really something. The plane was right in the center of about a thousand Klieg Lights just like the opening of a supermarket back home. There were about 100,000 people jammed up against the ropes. At least 100 of these people were Generals and Admirals with so many Colonels you couldn't count them.

We finally named our airplane. Colonel Tibbets named it after his mother. It is called "Enola Gay". Perhaps by the time this gets there, you will also have heard of our ship. All of my Love, Rich

August 28, 1945 Tinian

Dearest Mom, Dad and Loraine,

Well, I guess I owe an explanation for not writing for so long. Here is the story. Just after that one flight, we thought we were going to get to go to Washington, that is the crew of our ship. Well they kept detaining us until the next day, etc for almost two weeks. I was going to call you from the States and really surprise you but things changed. I have finally decided it will be a good long time before I'm back, so I'd better start writing again.

We haven't been doing much of anything over here since they stopped fighting, mostly just sitting around. We fly local around here for a few hours twice a week, but that is about all. A lot of the B29 outfits are flying prisoner of war supplies, but we aren't even doing that. The weather has really been lousy around here for the last couple of days. It has rained continuously.

I have received all of your letters and the package with the mirror in it. Also received one letter from Gene. The letter with the article on the front page of the Times was interesting. I was really glad to hear you were both proud of it. That really pleased us as I've always wanted to do something to make you feel that way. When you say that, it makes me feel a lot better than even sending the other articles we've been getting from all over the States. I hope you have been reading all of the magazines.

Well, can't think of much more to say now. I'll be seeing you pretty soon anyway. We won't be over here for more than a year. Did you ever get my Distinguished Flying Cross (DFC) that I sent home? Dad, take care of the car, because when I get back, I want to take it wherever I'm stationed. Tell everyone hello, the Jacksons, Snows and relatives; give them all my love. How are they all, Irving, Grandma and Grandpa and all the rest? Please note the address which means I now get $99 a month. Well, enough for now. All My Love, Rich

September 10, 1945 Tinian, Marianas

Dearest Mom, Dad and Loraine,

Well, there really isn't much to write about but I told myself that I would never let as much time as the last pass between letters.

I guess you know there are no censors reading these letters. That makes me feel a lot better. I never could get used to writing a letter when I knew someone else was going to read it. We are going to school over here again. I know that sounds foolish after the war is over, but that is the way the Army works. It is lead crew school and if the war was still on it would mean every man on the crew could go up one rank over what he could if he wasn't on a lead crew. They have us go to school one day, then on a practice bombing mission two days, then we do it all over again. We're almost through now and so far our crew has been doing fine. This is our old crew; the one without Tibbets, Ferebee and Van Kirk. They just went with us on the big mission. On that mission, our real copilot, navigator and bombardier didn't get to go and these other big shots went in their places.

It still looks like I'll be home pretty soon. I think I'll be stationed at Wendover or maybe Southern California. It looks like it will be one of those. I don't know how soon I can expect to get out of the Army. I haven't been overseas long enough to collect many points. I guess I have a few more than Gene though and also I only need 80 to get out and he needs 85 now.

We, the enlisted men, were very glad when the officers points were raised. I've never in my life been so mad at officers as over here. The discrimination is really something. You find some nice ones, at least you can say most of the flying officers are OK, but I wouldn't give two cents for all the rest put together. If any of them try to get jobs from men who were enlisted men after the war, I'm afraid they'll be out of luck.

Well, nothing more to say and the boys want to play poker on the table so I'll quit. Until Later — All My Love, Rich

NICELEY, GILLON T.
393rd Bomb Squadron, Tail Gunner, Crew C-11

I spent my basic training in the Infantry at Camp Walters, Texas. My Battalion shipped out to Europe and were in the Normandy Invasion. I would have been with them if I had not taken an exam to get into Cadets. I passed it and was shipped to the University of Arkansas to study certain subjects and did some flying there also. Upon finishing, we went to basic flying, etc. Many of us wanted out and were given our choice of Navigation, Bombardier or Central Fire Control School at Lowery Air Force Base in Denver, Colorado. I chose CFC School in Denver. Upon completion, I was sent to Pool at Fairmont, Nebraska, where I changed into the 393rd Bomb Squadron. I knew nothing of what we were to do.

Next to Wendover and overseas, I was very fortunate to have been on such a fine crew.

When we first arrived at Wendover, I thought what a desolate place, but it turned out to be a very warm and caring stay, thanks to all my friends and especially to the fellows on my crew, the Straight Flush, as we were later known by, as that was the name we gave our aircraft.

During our stay at Wendover, we lived in a small two room and bath apartment in a small house off post. We were waiting for an apartment on post which we were eventually assigned. Being a close knit crew, the fellows would drop in from time to time to visit. One evening around 2am, there was a knock at our door and it was Jack Bivans and Al Barsumian out on the town. Of course, I let them in and they stayed for breakfast. That's the way it was with us at Wendover.

I was the only one on my crew who had a car, and shared it with everyone. One weekend, some wives borrowed it for a trip to Salt Lake City and we decided to follow in our B29. It was no problem to catch them as the terrain from Wendover to Salt Lake was open, straight road. After taking off and being in the air for a few minutes, we spotted

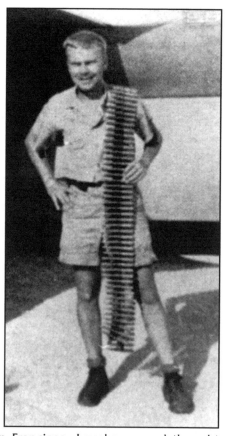

them down below. Someone suggested we say "Hi"– so we dropped down and created quite a large wind which blew the 1941 Plymouth Coupe off the road to open spaces. We continued on with our flight schedule for the morning. We checked to be sure all were safe and sure enough, they got back on the road and continued on to Salt Lake City where we finally heard they had a very enjoyable time.

I recall the day we left Wendover Field, Utah and flew over San Francisco. I woke up and thought someone was shooting at us due to the lights reflecting off the clouds. We flew to Hawaii where we spent some pleasant days. Leaving Hawaii, we landed next at the Island of Kwajalein which was so low the housing was built on stilts to keep it out of water. The one runway began in the ocean and left in the ocean so we were glad to leave there.

Our next stop was Guam. When we taxied to the operations building, the personnel there informed us we were not to be there. So Buck, our Airplane Commander (AC), reversed the props and backed our plane out to the runway blowing gravel and dust all over the place.

We ended up on Tinian, across from Saipan. After landing, we were put in tents but after a few days moved to quonset huts which were comfortable and served our needs. When we were not flying to Japan, we were playing bridge, poker, chess, exploring the island and writing letters back home. Occasionally, we would go to the ocean and catch baby octopuses, as they were supposed to be a delicacy. I never did like them and preferred food I was more familiar with.

The officers' club was down the line of housing from where we were and although we were noncoms, frequented their kitchen often as the food there was better than in the

(L-R), Wendover AAF Pat Baldarsaro, Gil Niceley, Al Barsumian, Jack Bivans

mess hall. Our favorite thing was opening cans of bacon which we fried and ate as sandwiches, quite a treat. To my knowledge, no other crew entered the kitchen, took their rations and ate them except us.

I can recall on return from one trip to Japan, Captain Buck Eatherly called back to me on intercom asking if I'd like to try out my fifties as I had not had an opportunity to fire them. Of course, I answered yes and he dropped down closer to the ocean. I finally spotted a Japanese fishing boat and fired several rounds till he disappeared into the trees on a small island.

I do remember one incident we all laughed about. When Buck Eatherly had a date with a nurse, he borrowed

a jeep and he needed one more thing, a haircut. Though there were no barbers on Tinian, one guy thought he could give him a trim. So we brought him over with his scissors and comb. The more he trimmed, the worse it looked. After awhile, seeing he was not making a good contribution to his evening, he quit. There were no mirrors around, so we were thankful for that. Buck went on his way happily thinking he looked fine.

On our trip to and from Hiroshima, we mostly listened to Tokyo Rose, discussed the mission and I being in the tail, watched for enemy planes or anything that didn't seem natural.

NOLAN, JAMES F. MD
Project Alberta

I went to the Los Alamos site of the Manhattan Project in March of 1943, having been recruited by a classmate and friend, Dr. Louis H. Hempelmann, Professor of Experimental Radiology.

The original plans were for complete seclusion of the scientists and technologists at the site in order to maintain utmost security. Dr. Hempelmann was trained in internal medicine as well as in radiation therapy at Berkeley and I had my training in surgery, obstetrics and gynecology but had some experience with radiation in the treatment of cancer. Since the original plan was to care for only some 250 people, I was to spell him with the radiation safety problems and he, me with the medical problems.

At first everyone concerned was to be in Army service. However, things changed rapidly with an increase in personnel and a separation of the civilian from the military. Dr. Hempelmann remained a civilian employee. I was mustered into the Army in June 1943 and assigned as Post Surgeon since the Los Alamos site was a military post. Because of the great increase in population, it was necessary to recruit other physicians in various specialties to care for the patient load.

In the early part of 1945 when plutonium finally became available, the radiation hazard aspect increased. In the spring of that year, I was replaced as Post Surgeon to work directly with Dr. Hempelmann in the Radiation Health Division of the Scientific Section. I was assigned to set up radiation safety precautions at the Trinity Test Site (Alamogordo) where a calibration shot with 100 tons of TNT was planned. This was carried out in May of 1945. Plans for the explosion of the plutonium bomb were continued at that site.

Dr. Hempelmann's responsibility for the safety phases at the laboratory increased so that I relieved him in preparations for the Trinity Test. It was necessary to ship the uranium bomb, which was not tested, to the Marianas and I was assigned to leave the Trinity Test responsibilities and accompany the active material for this on the Cruiser Indianapolis, after accompanying the material from Los Alamos to Kirkland Air Force Base by motor vehicle and then its transshipment by air to San Francisco where it was loaded at Hunter's Point.

The Indianapolis debarked on the morning of July 17 when the Trinity Test was carried out. I did not hear any news concerning the test until arriving at Tinian Island on

July 27 and my thoughts concerning the first atomic explosion at Los Alamos were those of gratification that the effort had been successful. My duties at the Tinian takeoff point were those of radiation safety for the assembly, loading and takeoff, to ascertain any radiation hazard in case of accident.

After the cessation of hostilities, a larger group of health experts was gathered by Dr. Stafford Warren and were moved on to Okinawa before entering Japan to measure physical and radiation effects. We arrived in Japan on September 5, 1945 and were able to get into Hiroshima by September 9. Two groups of scientists inspected the Hiroshima and Nagasaki sites and about October 6 we left for the United States with the available data.

TOP SECRET
WAR DEPARTMENT
P. O. BOX 2610
WASHINGTON, D.C.
THIS DOCUMENT CONSISTS OF 1
NO. 2 OF 2 SERIES A
17 August 1945.

MEMORANDUM FOR: Admiral W. S. De Lany

    Subject: Transportation of Critical Shipments.

    The U.S.S. Indianapolis departed from San Francisco on 16 July 1945 after picking up the following project cargo at Hunters Point:

    a. 1 box, wt. about 300 lbs, containing projectile assembly of active material for the gun type bomb.

    b. 1 box, wt. about 300 lbs, containing special tools and scientific instruments.

    c. 1 box, wt. about 10,000 lbs, containing the inert parts for a complete gun type bomb.

    The Indianapolis arrived at Tinian Harbor, Marianas on 28 July and discharged the project cargo without mishap.

    3 ATC C-54 airplanes departed from Kirtland Field, Albuquerque, New Mexico, at 1510Z 26 July, with each airplane carrying equal segments of the target assembly of active material for the gun type bomb. The airplanes arrived at Tinian on 28 July (about 48 hours lapsed time) and discharged project cargo without mishap.

    2 ATC C-54 airplanes also departed from Kirtland Field at 1510Z 26 July and carried the sphere of active material and initiator for the implosion type bomb. The airplanes arrived at Tinian on 28 July and discharged project cargo safely.

    3 B-29 specially modified bombers departed from Kirtland Field at 1250Z 28 July and carried 3 HE preassemblies of the implosion type bomb encased in the outer shell. All 3 B-29's arrived at Tinian at 0230Z 2 August and discharged project cargo safely.

    J. A. DERRY,
    Major, C.E.

Last known photo of USS Indianapolis, Tinian Harbor

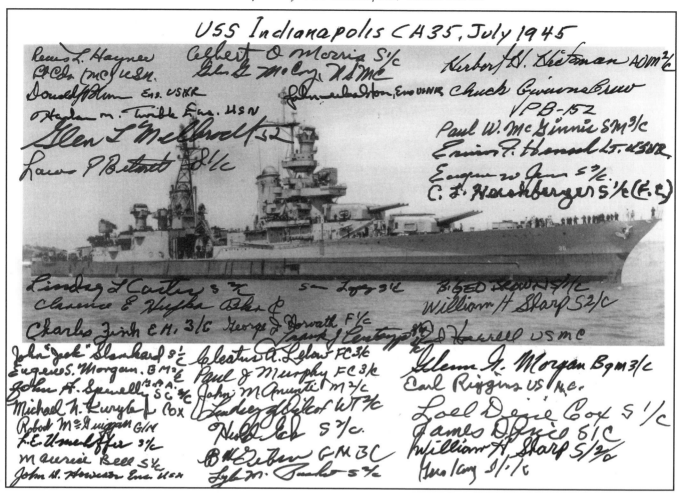

From the end of October until early December, I was assigned to assist Col. Warren in Washington, DC to brief the interested government officials concerning the effects of the bomb. In early January of 1946, I returned to Los Alamos and was discharged from the Army but remained at Los Alamos in a civilian capacity until April. I returned again as a civilian to aid in the radiation safety activities of Operation Crossroads at Bikini in the summer of 1946. Again in the spring of 1948, I served as a civilian consultant in radiation safety at Operation Sandstone at Eniwetok.

FURMAN, ROBERT R.
Manhattan Engineering District

After the two (2) bombs were dropped and the Emperor of Japan declared the war was over, General Groves ordered three (3) investigative teams be formed principally from the personnel already on Tinian. One (1) team went to Hiroshima, one (1) team to Nagasaki and the third team to visit all universities, government bureaus and corporations that might be engaged in nuclear research in Japan or Korea. I headed up the third team consisting of scientists and interpreters. This mission lasted maybe eight (8) weeks, at the end of which I returned to Washington and soon retired.

Accompanied James Nolan on the Indianapolis

154

ORR, LEONARD A.
1395th Military Police Company

In September 1944, I was transferred from Smoky Hill Army Airbase to Salina, Kansas to Wendover Field Utah and assigned to the 1395th Military Police (MP) Company, 509th Composite Group. At Wendover, I trained under the direction of the Provost Marshal learning to fire all types of firearms and did MP duty at the Stateline Hotel. It was our duty to be sure no 509th member got hurt, so when drunk, they were taken by jeep back to the base guard house and held over night to sober up by morning.

My wife Betty and I lived in a one room apartment with sink, running cold water, coal stove for heat and cooking, table and two chairs and one double bed, owned by Millie Lyman, Justice of the Peace in Wendover, who was our neighbor.

I played on the Wendover basketball team made up from all different units of the 509th. We traveled by bus to Ogden Air Depot and Boise, Idaho.

In January 1945, a group of us flew to Havana, Cuba for twelve days where I did MP duty in downtown Havana with Shore Patrol (SP). I had a three day delay in my wife's hometown of Ocala, Florida on my way back to Wendover.

In May 1945, we shipped out for Tinian Island where I was assigned a motorcycle to keep the 509th safe from unauthorized people entering restricted areas. After the Nagasaki bomb was dropped, I volunteered to go to Japan for an indefinite period of time to help provide security.

In September 1945, Colonel Tibbets flew a C54 with five MPs, bags, jeeps and trailers from Tinian to Iwo Jima landing at 2:30 am. Breakfast had been prepared by Marine cooks who had run out of cooking fuel resulting in cold pancakes and coffee. We left Iwo Jima for Japan landing at Atsugi Air Field near Yokohama where the grass along the runway was covered with hundreds of American prisoners

on stretchers with Intravenous (IV) tubes waiting for evacuation. This was one of the most horrible sights in all my time in service. We unloaded our bags, equipment, jeeps and trailers and drove into Yokohama. Our first night we were housed in a silk factory and made our bunks out of raw silk. The next day we proceeded the twenty-five miles from Yokohama to Tokyo on a four lane highway the US Seabees were building. With two Japanese speaking Japanese-American GIs, I drove high ranking officers to all the government buildings in Tokyo. We stayed at the Dai-Ichi Hotel near downtown Tokyo for about a week traveling in all the bombed out industrial areas showing pinpoint bombing was very evident. The War Department was completely bombed out but the banks, on a four lane road just across the street, were never hit.

In October 1945, we left Tinian Island on the USS Deuel for the return trip to the States arriving at Oakland, California nineteen days later. We went by troop train to Roswell, New Mexico where I was discharged November 17, 1945. I returned home to Ocala, Florida, my wife, Betty and our daughter, Wendy who was born August 11, 1945 while I was overseas.

PALMER, DONALD W.
320th Troop Carrier Squadron. Aircraft & Engine Mechanic

I arrived at Wendover, Utah, in June 1943. Of course it was bleak and windy with lots of black smoke coming from train engines passing through. I spent 29 months at Wendover and have pleasant memories. My unit was sent elsewhere and I was to go also. My clothes did, but they had other plans for me, mainly sending me to Roswell, New Mexico.

I was married early and had a young son. After much searching, I found a little two room shack off base, actually had been a coal house. Of course, my wife and son were coming to join me, but this move had to be approved by base inspection. We three moved from Roswell via Greyhound Bus. We took along all our worldly possessions including one gallon of calsomine paint. We were busy painting and had tied our son to a chair with a diaper around his chest so he wouldn't fall out as he was only about nine months old. The inspector came to look us over and said, "Well I guess this will do, but you must get that fly off that baby!"

I stayed in Wendover, serviced the C54s, then went back and forth to Tinian. In late October 1945, all of us that stayed in Wendover received orders to report to Roswell the first of November. I was there about 10 days when I was able to take a discharge; so on November 27, 1945, I left for Roseville, California.

PALMERT, LEE
393rd Bomb Squadron, Radio, Crew A-3

I lived in Canton, Ohio all my life and worked at Diebold as a photographer taking pictures of armor plate after it was tested. When I was drafted into the service in 1943, I was given code and aptitude tests with no idea I would end up in the Air Corps. After induction when they asked what I preferred, I wrote down photographer.

We assembled in Akron, went to Columbus, Ohio then to basic training in Clearwater, Florida. From there, to radio school for thirteen weeks at Scott Field Illinois. After that, I was shipped all over the country; to Richmond, Virginia as a telephone operator; a truck driver to obtain a license to operate a 6x6 and to Pocatello, Idaho for a time. At Wendover, before signing up in the 509th, they had P47s. I was eventually assigned to the 393rd at Fairmont, Nebraska, where I was assigned to a crew. I did not have a car at Fairmont. I remember Glenn Allison replaced a fellow that did not want to fly. I never realized things were that top secret. When the 393rd was pulled out of Fairmont, I thought it was for further training.

I rode by train with the enlisted men to Wendover. I accepted it for what it was. I made friends. I was still classified as a radio operator and did not have much to do. Money was a problem. I never had much in the service. I could not afford to go into town but went to the Stateline a couple of times without gambling. At first, I made $50 a month, then was promoted to Staff Sergeant with an increase in pay to $89 with 50% more for flying and 3% for overseas. Out of your monthly allowance, you had to pay for insurance and I bought War Bonds. When we were paid, we lined up alphabetically, went inside to an officer with cash, sitting at a table, with a soldier on each side with a machine gun. You would salute, the officer would say your name, serial number, count out your money and you would salute, about face and sign the payroll book. If you went below your line and went into another line, you would be "red lined" causing you to miss a payout.

We never had barracks inspection. I would save dimes, put them in my raincoat pocket and never had any stolen. I had a lady friend and on my way home, took the dimes and bought her a bracelet.

Lee Palmert inside V-86

I lived in the enlisted men's barracks. At Christmas, a lot of guys were in the dumps because they could not go home. We had coal burning stoves in the middle and at each end of the barracks. The latrine was at the end of the line that served two rows of barracks. There were only flight crews in my barracks, so I spent most of my time talking with other guys or playing ping pong. Clarence Britt and I were the only enlisted men that went along to pick up our plane in Omaha. Our bombardier, Leon Cooper did not go either.

I did go to Cuba for training and went to Sloppy Joe's, but you can't tell who I am in the picture because I have a drink up to my face. I had a silver dollar with me, the last buck I had; I bought a hat with it.

I had a camera on the base and one day while taking pictures of us in our brand new flight clothing, I saw a jeep go by. I ran into the barracks but he must have seen where we went because he followed us in and took my camera. He took it to the MP Station, said I could have it when I went to town but had to return it when I came back. I was able to take the camera overseas.

On Tinian, we were close to the ocean so we would hunt for sea shells. I remember seeing the windmill washing machines the Seabees built. At first, we did not have a mess hall so we ate our rations. We stayed in tents a short time, then moved into a Quonset Hut we shared with several enlisted men from other crews of which Tom Classen's crew were some of them. I spent a lot of time with the enlisted men from Wilson's crew.

It was hot during the day but cooled off at night. Scott Adams was in charge of Radio Operations. The radio shack had a jeep and I was allowed to borrow it because I had a driver's license. I would pick up the Tinian natives who would clean the latrines and straighten out our camp sites. I imagine the government paid them.

I remember when the Classen crew went back to the States. We never knew why and some of the fellows took what they left behind - their foot lockers were raided.

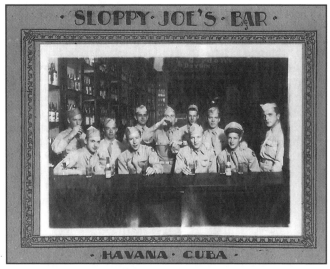
Lee Palmert has a drink a Sloppy Joe's

Lee Palmert and James Davis in Cuba with their dollar hats

PATTEN, DAVID I.
603rd Air Engineering Squadron, 1st Ordnance Welder 256

I worked on the assembly of the bomb at Wendover, particularly the tail fin, etc. to perfect an accurate fall and also to slow the bomb down in its fall, so the plane could get farther away before it exploded. I also was assigned the job of disassembling bomb #3 and disposing of it and all other components after the Japanese surrendered.

My most vivid memory of Wendover was the secret veil, "What You Hear Here, What You See Here, When You Leave Here, Let It Stay Here".

In civilian life, I was elected to the House of Representatives 1964 and 1968. serving eight years.

Working on bomb fins

PATTERSON, JAMES P.
390th Air Service Group

After completion of basic training at Sheppard Field, TX. and release from the Aviation Cadet Program, I was reassigned in January 1945 to Chanute Field, IL., to attend Teletype Operator School. I had been a teletype operator with Western Union in Rocky Mount, NC. prior to being ordered to active duty from Aviation Cadet Enlisted Reserve Corps status in October 1944. I completed the Teletype Operator School as honor student and was interviewed by persons unknown to me and told that I would be "earmarked" for assignment later to an organization that could not be divulged at that time. For an 18 year old private with 5 months Army Air Corps experience, this was quite impressive.

However, I was given a short furlough enroute to my new assignment at Pratt Field, KS. At Pratt Field, I was assigned as a teletype operator working the Base Communications Section night shift. After a very brief tour at Pratt, I was called to the orderly room where the first sergeant told me to pack immediately because I was being "shipped out" that day. I complied, returned to the orderly room, loaded onto a jeep and was driven to the train station where I was given train tickets and a big envelope with my military records. I boarded a Pullman Train Car and traveled unaccompanied to Wendover, Utah. I got off the train and piled onto a jeep that took me to Wendover Field where I was processed in at military personnel, assigned a barracks and unloaded my gear. I was told not to unpack my bag because we were leaving tomorrow morning, which we did. I do remember a sign at Wendover Field that said something to the effect; "What You Hear Here, What You See Here, When You Leave Here, Let It Stay Here".

As far as I have ever known, I must have been either the last or one of the last people to physically join the

509th Composite Group. We traveled by train to the port and boarded the USS Cape Victory for our journey to Tinian.

One last item of interest (to me anyhow) occurred at the completion of our tour of duty on Tinian. I was one of the last of the group to leave Tinian and was assigned to return as a passenger on the B29 piloted by Capt. Lewis which was the Enola Gay. We flew, via Hawaii, to Mather Field, CA, and finally to Roswell Army Air Field, NM (later to become the first USAF Air Base to be designated "permanent" and renamed Walker Air Force Base).

I retired from the USAF as Chief Master Sergeant after 26½ years and my last assignment was at Ramey Air Force Base, Puerto Rico (1967-1970) where, as fate would have it, the Deputy Commander for Maintenance was Col. Thomas Ferebee. As 72nd Bombardment Wing Personnel Sergeant Major and later as Wing Sergeant Major, I frequently had contact with Col. Ferebee.

PETERSON, KENNETH
390th Air Service Group Communications Unit
Headquarters and Base Service Squadron

After completing 2nd Air Force Schools in Salt Lake City and Kearns Air Force Base, I was assigned to 852nd Signal Service Company (Aviation) at Wendover, April 1943.

December 1st, the Signal Service Company was transferred to 305th Headquarters at Wendover. The base Signal Office had TWX, Western Union Telegraph and all telephone operations on the base. All TWX communications in and out went through this office.

In 1944, almost all personnel in the office were transferred to 390th Headquarters Squadron, 509th Composite Group. The group left Wendover for Tinian Island April 1945.

I was a TWX, teletype operator and cryptographer. We handled all communications between General Groves and Colonel Tibbets by radio and TWX. Copies went to 20th Air Force and 313th Bomb Wing. Our radio operators were in contact with every 393rd B29 plane with orders for missions, messages, results of all bombing on both atomic and conventional missions to Japan, also daily reports on aircraft personnel status, all transmitting and receiving in top secret code. We had a telephone switchboard connecting phones to all squadrons and in every officers tent. We also had telephone repair, installation and linemen.

Members of the 390th Air Service Group, Communications Unit, Headquarters and Base Service Squadron were as follows:

Officers	
	W. Bell Jr
	J. Kauffman
	E. Lucke
Enlisted Men	S. Adams
	R. Asseff
	P. Garinger Jr
	T. Gottwig
	P. Grill
	N. Hansen
	R. Heimer
	J. Clemens
	N. Kotoff
	J. Mulligan
	J. Patterson
	K. Peterson
	M. Sanders
	M. Scoggin
	J. Williams

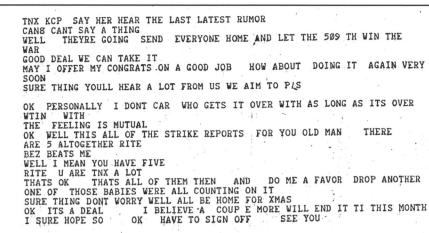

(L-R): Sgt. John Clemens, Cpl. Ken Peterson, Pfc. Maurice Scoggin

```
TNX KCP  SAY HER HEAR THE LAST LATEST RUMOR
CAN8 CANT SAY A THING
WELL  THEYRE GOING  SEND  EVERYONE HOME AND LET THE 509 TH WIN THE
WAR
GOOD DEAL WE CAN TAKE IT
MAY I OFFER MY CONGRATS ON A GOOD JOB  HOW ABOUT  DOING IT  AGAIN VERY
SOON
SURE THING YOULL HEAR A LOT FROM US WE AIM TO PLS

OK  PERSONALLY  I DONT CAR  WHO GETS IT OVER WITH AS LONG AS ITS OVER
WTIN  WITH
THE  FEELING IS MUTUAL
OK  WELL THIS ALL OF THE STRIKE REPORTS  FOR YOU OLD MAN   THERE
ARE 5 ALTOGETHER RITE
BEZ BEATS ME
WELL I MEAN YOU HAVE FIVE
RITE  U ARE TNX A LOT
THATS OK   THATS ALL OF THEM THEN   AND   DO ME A FAVOR  DROP ANOTHER
ONE OF  THOSE BABIES WERE ALL COUNTING ON IT
SURE THING DONT WORRY WELL ALL BE HOME FOR XMAS
OK  ITS A DEAL      I BELIEVE A  COUP E MORE WILL END IT TI THIS MONTH
I SURE HOPE SO    OK  HAVE TO SIGN OFF    SEE YOU



WG SWBD INT K  V AWT  CUT US V35
<<<<(WG SWBD INT K
DID U GET A FLASH ON JAPAN SURRENDERING UP TE THERE
YES WE HEARD THAT THEY ARE WILLING IF THEY CAN KEEP THE EMPEROR BUT IT
IS N'T OFFICIAL AS YET JUST A RUMOR FROMOTHER STATIONS K
OKAY TNX A LOT  K
AR
```

Conversation between TWX operators the day after bomb dropped

390th goes hiking north of Wendover, with Headquarter and Base Service Group

PETERSON, WESLEY P.
390th S/Sgt Air Service Group

I was attending the University of California at Berkeley when I was drafted into the service in September 1942. I was inducted in Monterey, sent to a relocation center in Salt Lake City for a few weeks and then permanently assigned to Wendover Field as a Finance Technician.

When I arrived by rail in either late October or early November, I was a little aghast at what I saw - salt flats, tarpaper barracks, potbellied stoves for heating, crude latrines and privacy and comfort seemed to be nonexistent. As a twenty-one year old, however, I adapted quickly and soon learned there were some real positives. Besides a bowling alley, other improvements on base included an Enlisted Men's Clubhouse and a swimming pool. Girls came out on buses from Salt Lake City for Saturday night dances which helped raise morale.

The finance detachment was small, located in the base headquarters building, but subsequently a separate building was erected. There were only about fifteen men who became a close-knit group that still keeps in touch. There I met Ronald Fredlund, David Chelnik and Arthur Femmel with whom I would spend the rest of my service tenure. Basically, my job during the next three years would involve computing enlisted men's payrolls, processing commercial accounts and keeping War Department accounting records. I spent three months on detached service in early 1944 at the Army Advanced Finance School for enlisted personnel in Fort Benjamin Harrrison, Indiana.

One of the disadvantages of being such a small unit in finance was we were attached to other groups for rations and quarters; the medical corps, quartermaster corps, etc. As those groups gained personnel of their own, we were occasionally forced to move. At one point, we were relegated to some tents that a group of engineers on temporary assignment had erected. One fateful night a rather violent desert windstorm leveled the tents and we resorted to hauling our cots into a nearby latrine where we slept for two nights until more permanent quarters could be found.

When the 509th Composite Group was activated, we three co-workers became members. I believe its activation coincided with the Battle of the Bulge in Europe and a possible threat of being reassigned to the infantry was being rumored. I knew I didn't want that kind of overseas assignment and besides, the 509th was being heralded as a group destined to make history. There were two officers and ten enlisted men that became a part of the finance contingent in the 509th. Ground personnel moved by rail to our port of embarkation at Seattle. Our long voyage to the Marianas in May 1945 was marked by lengthy card games, false submarine sightings, salt water showers and "mal de mer" shortly out of Seattle which kept many of us away from the mess hall and in the head.

Although most of our group was quartered in Quonset Huts on Tinian, four of us in finance slept in a pyramidal tent which was fine except for the night the tail end of a typhoon swept through our area. Since ten enlisted men were not needed on a full-time basis in the finance office,

three of our group ran the Post Exchange and I helped out at Wing Headquarters on several occasions.

As for recreation on Tinian, I remember swimming along with subtropical fish in the warm Pacific waters and trying to avoid getting cut by the coral. I recall outdoor movies, the Eddie Bracken Show and an overseas company production of Irving Berlin's "This is the Army". Always interested in pop music, until hard rock and rap came along, I still remember hearing Doris Day's recording of "Sentimental Journey" for the first time at the Post Exchange. More importantly, I recall the uplift I received at Sunday morning worship services by Chaplain Downey's words of inspiration.

Then came that historic day, August 6, 1945! At the Enola Gay return party, Colonel Tibbet's remarks about "sighting a Japanese city and destroying it; further details will be released from Washington" are permanently etched in my memory. Could this possibly signal the end of the war? We were exhilarated!

Months after August 9, 1945 when the war concluded, another high point for me was sailing back through the Golden Gate, just a few miles from the university I had left three years before and not far from my family home. I was discharged at Roswell, New Mexico on November 21, 1945, returned to college and spent thirty-seven years in teaching and counseling.

Finance Staff (390th)
in front of tent on Tinian (July or August 1945)
(L-R): Jack Gehrken, Dave Chelnik, Wes Peterson, Art Femmel, Ron Fredlund

PETROLLI, ROBERT J.
393rd Bomb Squadron, Navigator, Crew A-2

John Downey and I came from the Lincoln, Nebraska classification center on a train together. We were assigned to the 393rd Bombardment Squadron at Fairmont, Nebraska. I had been through two Radar Schools; Langley, Virginia, and Boca Raton, Florida. I was on Boca Raton with Len Godfrey, Russ Gackenbach and John Dulin. We were supposed to go overseas. I had been married for three days and expected to go to Europe.

Fairmont, Nebraska, was a typical farm town. My wife and I were able to get a room in Geneva. We flew mostly B17s and towards the end maybe 102 flights on a B29. I was in Fairmont for about two months when we received our orders to go to Wendover. Tom Costa had relatives in Chicago and I was going to Chicago to pick up a car so we took a train together.

Our trip was quite an adventure driving from Chicago, falling asleep along the road, going into Grand Island, Nebraska, and our voltage control went out in Cheyenne, Wyoming. We went into a Ford Dealer at five minutes to 5 pm and the dealer said, "we have enough business, we don't need yours". There happened to be a city policeman there who told us to wait outside in the car. He came back later with a voltage control that he had bought for his car earlier in the day. He gave it to us and would not take any money for it.

From there we went to Laramie, Wyoming, slept in the downtown area in the car. We woke up on main street with everyone looking in at us. We finally made it to Salt Lake City. Then our generator stopped working as we drove across the flats. Fortunately, it was a moonlit night and when we saw a car coming towards us, we would turn on our lights.

(L-R): John Downey, Harry Davis, Robert Petrolli at Wendover

My wife had taken a train from Fairmont and when she arrived, we stayed at the Stateline for a week. Fortunately, she got a job at the library and was able to get an apartment. We lived next door to either the Steinkes or Cohens: I can't remember who. The apartments were concrete block with coal burning stoves which we had to get used to. We bought a half ton at a time delivered to our back door. The stove was used for baking, cooking and heating.

We were kept busy with classes every day. Our first set of B29s were converted. The deicers were taken off the edge of the wings and we had to clean the edges with acetone. Every so often the B29 gas tanks would be drained and we added that fuel to our cars for the extra mileage.

I remember the halloween party at the officers club. One of the wives came in a dress made out of newspapers and one of our crew chased her around the club trying to read the papers.

In Cuba, we had a lot of fun. The base had a big party for us. There was a buffet as high as the ceiling. Since we were top secret, they could not touch our planes, so we had no problem flying booze back to Wendover. At the Wendover officers club, you had a locker with a key. You would buy a bottle at the bar and put it in the locker for the next time.

When the officers club burned down, I asked what they were going to do with the slot machines. I was told they were going to take the money out and scrap them. I said I'll take two; took them home, cleaned and rebuilt them.

When our plane "Laggin Dragon" left for Tinian, we had our entire crew, ground crew, a "Fat Man" bomb, a Statue of the Blessed Virgin and the two slot machines. The ground crew played the slot machines on the way to Tinian and I made twenty dollars.

Lt. Petrolli and Lt. Davis in water runabout made from auxiliary gas tanks.

RAMSEY, NORMAN F.
Project Alberta, Scientific/Technical Deputy

History of Project A, Tinian

The Project A organization on Tinian consisted of the following: Officer in Charge (OIC), Captain W.S. Parsons; Scientific and Technical Deputy to OIC, N.F. Ramsey; Operations Officer and Military Alternate to OIC, Commander (Comdr) F.L. Ashworth; Fat Man Assembly Team headed by Roger Warner; Little Boy Assembly Team headed by Comdr. Francis Birch; Fusing Team headed by E.B. Doll; Electrical Detonator Team headed by Lt. Comdr. E. Stevenson; Pit Team headed by Phillip Morrison and C.P. Baker; Observation Team headed by Luis Alvarez and Bernard Waldman; Aircraft Ordnance Team headed by Sheldon Dike; and Special Consultants consisting of Robert Serber, W.G. Penney and Captain J.F. Nolan. The team leaders formed a Project Technical Committee under the chairmanship of Ramsey to coordinate technical matters and to recommend technical actions to Captain Parsons. The following persons were team members: Harold Agnew, Ensign D.L. Anderson, T/5 B. Bederson, Milo Bolstad, T/Sgt. Raymond Brin, T/Sgt. V. Caleca, T/Sgt. E. Carlson, T/4 A. Collins, T/Sgt. R. Dawson, T/Sgt. F. Fortine, T/3 W. Goodman, T/3 D. Harms, Lt. J.D. Hopper, T/Sgt. J. Kupferberg, L. Johnston, L. Langer, T/Sgt. W. Larkin, H. Linschitz, A. Machen, Ens. D. Mastick, T/3 R. Matthews, Lt. (jg) V. Miller, T/3 L. Motechko, T/Sgt. W. Murphy, T/Sgt. E. Nookar, T. Olmstead, Ens. B. O'Keefe, T. Perlamn, Ens. W. Prohs, Ens. G. Renolds, H. Russ, R. Schreiber, T/Sgt. G. Thornton, Ens. Tucker, and T/4 F. Zimmerli. Although not strictly a part of Project A, the following were closely associated with the work of Project A: Rear Admiral W.R. Purnell, representative of the Washington Atomic Bomb Military Policy Committee; Brig. Gen. T.F. Farrell, representative of Major Gen. L.R. Groves; Colonel E.E. Kirkpatrick, alternate to Gen. Farrell and OIC of construction; Colonel P.W. Tibbets, Commanding Officer (CO) of the 509th Composite Group; Lt. Col. Peer de Silva, CO of the 1st Technical Service Detachment, which served as administrative, security and housing organization for Project A; and Major Charles Begg, CO of the 1st Ordnance Squadron, Special.

Although preliminary construction at Tinian began in April of 1945, intense technical activities did not begin until July. The first half of July was occupied in establishing and installing all technical facilities needed for assembly and test work. After completion of these preparations, a little boy unit was assembled and on 23 July, the Tinian base became fully operational for little boy tests with the dropping of unit L1. In this test, the dummy little boy was fired in the air by the radar fuse with excellent results. The second little boy Unit L2 was dropped 24 July and a third Unit L5 on 25 July. The remaining little boy was part of a test to check facilities at Iwo Jima for emergency reloading of the bomb into another aircraft. On 26 July, the little boy U235 projectile was delivered by Cruiser Indianapolis. The three parts of U235 target inserts arrived in three separate, empty Air Transport Command C54s during the evening of 28 to 29 July by 0200. On 29 July a completely successful test of the Iwo facilities was completed. The

plane landed with unit L6 at Tinian so it could be used in the final rehearsal maneuvers. On 31 July, the plane with L6 took off accompanied by the two observation planes, flew to Iwo for a rendezvous, returned to Tinian where the bomb was dropped and observed to function properly. After bomb release, all three aircraft rehearsed turning maneuvers to be used in combat, to clear the area as soon as possible. This completed all preliminary tests with active material to deliver a little boy.

Although the active Unit L11 was completely ready in plenty of time for a 2 August delivery, the weather at the target objective was not. The first, second, third and fourth of August were spent in impatient waiting for good weather. Finally, the morning of 5 August, General LeMay officially confirmed the mission would take place on 6 August.

The first fat man test Unit L13 was made 1 August. This unit used cast plaster blocks, electronic fusing, eight electric detonators, Raytheon detonating X unit, informers and smoke puffs in operation of detonators. All essential bomb components functioned satisfactorily. A second inert fat man F18 was prepared and loaded into a B29 for drop 3 August. Due to lack of Kingman (Wendover) test results for venting adequacy in the sealed fat man, the unit was unloaded and barometric switches modified so this information would be obtained on Unit F18 when dropped 5 August. All components functioned satisfactorily and venting was adequate for internal pressure to close a barometric switch set for 17,000 feet pressure altitude 17 seconds before impact. Closing the barometric switches started the fusing radars to radiate. The only remaining preliminary fat man test was Unit F33, a replica of the active unit except for lack of active material and use of lower quality high explosive lens castings. The components for this unit arrived at 1230 on 2 August and preliminary assembly began. Although it was fully prepared by 5 August, it was not dropped until 8 August due to absence of key crews and aircraft on the hot little boy mission. This final rehearsal

(L-R): Dr. Norman Ramsey, Captain Parsons, General Farrell

Plugs from Hiroshima bomb changed by Morris Jeppson

for the delivery and detonation of the first live fat man unit was completely satisfactory.

The little boy was loaded onto its transporting trailer at 1400 hours 5 August with an accompanying battery of official photographers under G2 security supervision and taken to the loading pit where the B29 backed into position for loading at 1500. The aircraft was then taxied to its hard stand for final testing of the unit and kept under continuous watch by a military guard and key technical group representatives.

After final briefing at 0000 (midnight) of 6 August, the crews had an early breakfast and assembled at their aircraft for pictures, under brilliant floodlights, taken by still and motion picture photographers. For this mission, Colonel P.W. Tibbets pilot of B29 Enola Gay carrying the bomb Little Boy, copilot R.A. Lewis, bombardier Major Thomas Ferebee, navigator Theodore Van Kirk, radio operator R.M. Nelson, radar countermeasures officer J. Beser, radar operator J.S. Stiborick, flight engineer W.E. Duzenbury, assistant flight engineer R.H.Shumard, tail gunner G.R. Caron, bomb commander W.S. Parsons, bomb electronics test officer M.R. Jeppson.

Progress of the mission is best described in Capt. Parsons log kept during flight:

6 August 1945

0245	Take off
0300	Started final loading of gun
0315	Finished loading
0605	Headed for Empire from Iwo
0730	Red plugs in (armed bomb to detonate when released)
0741	Started climb. Weather over primary and tertiary targets good
0838	Leveled off at 32,700 feet
0847	All Archies (electronic fuses) tested OK
0904	Course west
0909	Target Hiroshima in sight
0915	1/2 Dropped bomb. Scheduled time
0915	Flash followed by two slaps on plane. Huge cloud.
1000	Still in sight of cloud which must be over 40,000 feet high
1003	Fighter reported
1041	Lost sight of cloud 363 miles from Hiroshima with aircraft 26,000 feet high

The crews of strike and observation aircraft reported five minutes after release, a low three mile diameter, dark grey cloud hung over the center of Hiroshima with a white column of smoke rising from the middle to a height of 35,000 feet with a large top.

Four hours later, the strike photo reconnaissance planes found most of Hiroshima still obscured by cloud with fires seen around the edges. The following day excellent pictures were obtained showing the tremendous magnitude of power from a single atomic bomb that completely destroyed 60% of the city.

The fat man with active material, unit F31, was originally scheduled for dropping on 11 August but by 7 August it became apparent they could move it up to 10 August. When Parsons and Ramsey proposed this change to Tibbets, he expressed desire to have schedule advanced two days since good weather was forecast for 9 August and five succeeding days were expected to be bad. It was agreed Project A would try to be ready 9 August providing it was understood of the uncertainty in finishing on time. All went well with assembly and by 2200 of 8 August the unit was loaded and fully checked.

The strike plane and two observing planes took off at 0347 local time 9 August. Major C.W. Sweeney was Airplane Commander of B29 Bockscar carrying the fat man bomb, pilot C.D. Albury, bombardier K.K. Beahan, navigator J. F. Van Pelt, flight engineer J. D. Kuharek, Asst flight engineer R.K. Gallagher, radio operator A. M. Spitzer, radar operator E.K. Buckley, tail gunner A.T. Dehart, radar countermeasures officer J. Beser, bomb commander Navy Cmdr F.L. Ashworth, bomb electronics test officer P.M. Barnes. This mission was as eventful as the Hiroshima mission was operationally routine.

Due to bad weather between Tinian and Iwo Jima, a preliminary rendezvous was not planned for the three aircraft at Iwo Jima and instead the briefed route to the empire was from Tinian direct to Yokoshima on Kyushu. The briefed cruising altitude was 17,000 feet. Commander Ashworth's log for the mission is as follows:

0347	Take off
0400	Changed green plugs to red prior to pressurizing
0500	Charged detonator condensers to test leakage. Satisfactory
0915	Arrived rendezvous point at Yakashima and circled awaiting accompanying aircraft
0920	One B29 sighted and joined formation
0950	Departed Yakashima proceeding to primary target Kokura failed to rendezvous with second B29. Radio weather reports good weather Kokura (3/10 low clouds, no intermediate or high clouds forecast improving conditions). Nagasaki weather reports good but increasing cloudiness. For this reason primary target selected
1044	Arrived initial aiming point, started bombing run on target, was obscured by heavy ground haze and smoke. Made two additional runs, but aiming point not visible. Proceeded to Nagasaki after approximately 45 minutes.
1150	Approach to Nagasaki target entirely by radar. At 1158 dropped bomb after 20 second visual bombing run. Bomb functioned normally in all respects.

1205   Departed for Okinawa after circling smoke column. Lack of available gasoline caused by inoperative bomb bay tank booster pump forced decision to land at Okinawa before returning to Tinian.

1351   Landed at Yontan Field Okinawa

1706   Departed Okinawa for Tinian

2245   Landed at Tinian

Due to bad weather, good photo reconnaissance pictures were not obtained until almost a week after the Nagasaki mission. These showed the bomb detonated somewhat north of the Mitsubishi Steel and Arms Works. All other factories and buildings on the Urakami River from the Wakajima Gawa River through the Mitsubishi Urakami Ordnance Plant were destroyed. The distance from the northernmost destroyed factory to the southern boundary of complete destruction was about three miles. Although official record showed only 44 percent of the city was destroyed, this was due to the city's unfavorable shape not to bomb detonation location.

On the day following the Nagasaki mission, the Japanese initiated surrender negotiations. Consequently further activity in preparing active units was suspended. The entire project maintained a state of complete readiness for further assemblies in the event of peace negotiation failure. For the first week, the test program was continued as three dummy fat man units numbers F101, F102 and F103 were prepared. They were not dropped since the Japanese stated their willingness to accept the American terms.

The object of Project A was to assure the successful combat use of an atomic bomb at the earliest possible date after receiving available necessary nuclear material and a field test of an atomic explosion. This objective was very effectively accomplished. The first combat bomb was ready for use against the enemy within seventeen days after the first experimental nuclear explosion at Alamogordo and almost all of the intervening time was spent in accumulating additional active material for making an additional bomb. This atomic bomb was prepared for combat use against the enemy on 2 August within four days of active material delivery needed for that bomb. Actual combat use was delayed until 6 August only by bad weather over Japan. The second atomic bomb was used in combat only three days after the first despite its being a completely different model and much more difficult to assemble.

Originally it was planned to return all Project A technical personnel to the United States on 20 August except for those assigned to the Farrell Mission for investigating the results of the atomic bombing of Japan. On 18 August, a message was received from General Groves stating all key Project A personnel should remain at Tinian until success of Japan's occupation was assured. The scientific and technical personnel finally received authorization for return to the United States on 5 September, departing Tinian 7 September 1945. Although activities of Project A were effectively terminated, Col. Kirkpatrick and Comdr. Ashworth remained behind for final disposition of Project A property.

Project Alberta,
First Technical Service Detachment — Bomb Assembly Group;
Los Alamos, (Manhattan Engineer District).
Group Photo; Tinian, Mariana Islands, Aug. 7, 1945; Marianas Time.

Group Picture, Project A, Marianas Base, August 7, 1945.

Left to right:

Bottom Row: Victor A. Miller, Arthur B. Machen, Roger S. Warner, Harlow W. Russ, Norman F. Ramsey, Edward B. Doll, John L. Tucker, George T. Reynolds, Milo Bolstad, W.R. Prohs.

Second Row: Charles P. Baker, Philip Morrison, W.G. Penney, Theodore Perlman, Thomas H. Olmstead, Francis A. Birch, Adm. W.R. Purnell, Gen. T.F. Farrell, Capt. William S. Parsons, Frederick L. Ashworth, Robert Serber, Lawrence Langer, Bernard Waldman, Luis Alvarez, James F. Nolan, M.D.

Third Row: John D. Hopper, Edward G. Carlson, Leonard Motichko, Henry Linschitz, Benjamin B. Bederson, Raemer E. Schreiber, Walter Goodman, Wm. L. Murphy, Robert P. Mathews, Robert W. Dawson, Harold Agnew, Lawrence H. Johnston, Edward Stephenson, David Anderson, Donald Mastick.

Top Row: Morton Camac, Jesse Kupferberg, B.J. O'Keefe, Eugene L. Nooker, Gunnar Thornton, Wm. J. Larkin, Donald C. Harms, Frank J. Fortine, Frederick H. Zimmerli, Vincent Caleca, Arthur W. Collins.

Missing from Photo: Sheldon Dike

Arthur Josephson takes movie of group

REEDER, LLOYD
393rd Bomb Squadron, Radio, Crew B-8

(From a letter written from somewhere in the Marianas, on July 21).

I am very happy to tell you that, as of yesterday, I have made my first raid over the Jap empire! After all these months of training we are finally paying our respects to the Nips. At eight-thirty the evening of the nineteenth we all attended the general briefing concerning our target over Japan. Although we have gone to many briefings in the past, we were all excited over this one, because this was IT. As in all briefings we were told the course to and from the target, the axis of attack over target, our sea rescue facilities available for our flight in the event that we ran into trouble, etc. The Chaplain gave a prayer for us, and the briefing came to an end. Then the radio operators attended a special briefing to tell us our particular job.

We ate our breakfast meal at 11:45 pm and then we went down to our airplanes to get them ready for the takeoff; our ship was the first to take off. At 2:00 am. we were airborne and enroute to Japan. The trip there is a mighty long hop, longer than you realize. Finally our pilot told us to put on our flak suits as we were over Japan. When you have on all the equipment that is required to be worn over the target you're really uncomfortable. Here's what you wear. The first thing that you put on is a C-I vest, containing the required food and emergency equipment for survival in case you have to bail out or land your ship in water. On top of that goes your life vest, then your parachute harness; then the very important and heavy flak suit, and on top of all that you don your metal flak helmet. Boy, you really weigh a ton!

On this mission we found the Jap mainland completely covered with several layers of clouds. Therefore we had to bomb our targets by radio, and therefore we couldn't see the results, but you can be sure that the Japs did, and PLENTY. We were over the Jap mainland for more than an hour trying to find an opening in the clouds. That is too long for comfort. However, we didn't encounter any Jap fighters or anti-aircraft; where they were I haven't any idea. Here's hoping that they do stay on the ground every mission. Ha Ha!

Needless to say I was really tired on my way back. Incidentally, I sent in a "bombs-away" report in code from the Empire, and the ground station at the base heard me with no trouble at all. That transmitter of ours really puts out! We landed here at 3:25 am, a total of 13 hours and 21minutes in the air. 31 hours without any sleep.

Another letter written on July 30 reads in part as follows:

I wrote my last letter to you just before going on my third mission to the Empire, which made the third mission our crew had flown to Japan in nine days. If we

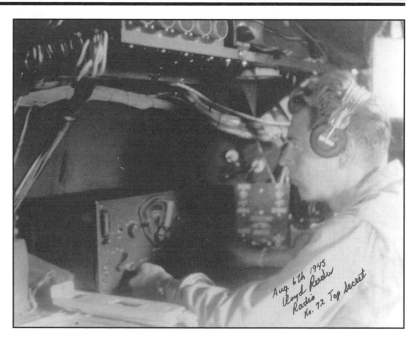

keep on flying Tokyo-way that often, I should be home in good time. Time alone will tell the answer to that last statement. Let's hope that it won't be too far off though.

Our takeoff was 3:00 am this time, which allowed us just that much more time to get a bit of shut-eye. Those missions really tire you out, especially, when you can't catch a bit of sleep in the airplane. Our flight up there was uneventful, as usual; our plane has been flying those long over-water hops like a dream. When we hit our landfall on the Japanese shore line, we saw the usual sight that we had seen previously on our other two missions—by that I mean nothing but clouds and more clouds. At that time McKnight made the remark that it looked like we'd have to bomb without seeing our target again, but luck was with us, for we hadn't flown very far inland before we noticed that the cloud formations were thinning out. By the time we had reached the point where we were to turn into our bombing run the bombardier could see the target clearly. For this mission we had borrowed Lt. Cooper from Lt. Devore's crew, since MacGregor was in the hospital with a very sore throat. Cooper was right 'on the ball' and we did get to see the results of our bomb load this time. It hit within one hundred feet of the center of the target; and all hell broke loose. Almost immediately there appeared a column of smoke ten thousand feet in the air. Boy, am I glad that I'm not a Japanese civilian or soldier! As I said before, the sky was clear that day and we could get a good look at the Jap countryside. Japan is really a beautiful island (I should say islands). It's too bad that the region has to be occupied by such a bunch of fanatics. Anyway our target was destroyed; we had successfully bombed our objective, so without further horsing around we proceeded to get out over the ocean and to safety.

REHL, DONALD C.
Airplane Commander, Crew 123 (Wendover)

After a period as a B24 instructor at Buckingham Field, Ft. Myers, Florida, I was sent to Alamogordo to be assigned to B29 transition and assembly of my crew. On June 30, 1945, we were ordered to Topeka, Kansas, for staging for overseas duty. However, on July 3rd, my crew was ordered to board a train, during the night, for a place called Wendover, Utah. We thought it was very strange that we were the only B29 crew on board but we did notice that most of the other passengers were MPs and civilians. We later learned they were technicians and scientists.

The next day, we got off the train at Wendover and were immediately taken to the base theater for briefing and warned about the level of security we would live with.

We were told we would be training with a huge bomb of approximately 10,000 pounds but, of course, were told nothing about the "nature" of it. There were rumors of men being sent to Alaska by Col. Tibbets for breaching security.

We were puzzled by the fact that we saw no B29s on the base - that was because the 393rd had already moved to Tinian. For the next three or four days, we did very little except swim at the officers club and attend briefings.

Then, very much to our surprise and without explanation, we were granted a ten day leave. I "hitched" a ride on a C54 to Wright Field which was only a few miles from my home in Springfield, Ohio.

On July 16th, I was suddenly ordered back to Wendover. I made it to Salt Lake City by train and arrived early in the morning at the train station. While waiting for a ride to Wendover, I decided to catch breakfast in the station cafeteria. My waitress was overly nice and friendly and asked a lot of questions about where I was going, if I had been there before and what they do there. I guess I was not very "talkative" or gabby because a day or so later, I SAW THAT SAME LADY IN A MILITARY POLICE UNIFORM AT WENDOVER FIELD.

From that day to this, I have never been to Alaska.

RICHARDS, LYNDON
1st Ordnance Squadron, Special Aviation

One of my details was to oversee all the operations of our electrical generating equipment. This instance was on Tinian. We had to generate our own electricity for our headquarters building, our work shops and laboratory. We received two 90 horsepower diesel General Motors Corporation (GMC) engines with a 60 kilowatt (KW) generator mounted to each one. My job was to get them set in place, service them and get them running. Each one had a clock on it that registered the hours each engine ran. The first unit I set up and started, ran 26 hours and stopped with a loud thud. From my past experience with tractor and auto engines, I believed the head of a valve had broken off and went through the piston. I started and put on line the second one. It ran 19 hours and stopped the same way as the first one. All the officers took to the belief that some way I had sabotaged the engines. There was no way two new engines could have the same thing happen to them at nearly the same running time. So, I was locked in the building with the generators and an MP guard while my fate was being decided.

The next morning, they brought in a Navy diesel expert from a ship near Tinian. We discussed what had happened and what I thought it was. He said, "It could be possible, but not very probable". He said, "Let's you and I take the head off unit 1 and have a look". So we did. Sure enough, the exhaust valve head in number 3 cylinder had come off the stem and went through the piston as the picture shows. The Navy man had a new head assembly, a piston and connecting rod on the ship. He had them delivered to me and told me to put that engine together, get it running and ordered transportation to take the other unit to the ship for repairs. I put it together and it ran perfectly for as long as we were on Tinian. The report from the overhaul of unit 2 showed the problem was the same as unit 1 except the valve head broke off in number 5 cylinder.

Lyndon Richards with broken valve head

RICHARDSON, PORTER A.
393rd Bomb Squadron, Radar Countermeasures Line Chief

After spending a couple of years in the Aleutians, Airborne Radar, I was sent back to radar school in Boca Raton, Florida for advanced training. While in radar school, I met my wife who lived in Hollywood, Florida. I married her while on furlough from the 393rd. From Boca Raton, I was sent to Wendover. Upon arrival, the radar section was set up and I was on the table of organization as Countermeasures Line Chief. The responsibility of our section was to ferret and log enemy radar frequencies and characterists as well as our own, so that clear channels with no interferences could be related to operate and record the atomic bomb. There were only five or six of us in countermeasures and since we did not have a lot to do, we helped the radar section maintain the radar equipment, absolute altimeter, loran, sharan and IFF.

Lt. Jacob Beser was the only countermeasures equipment operator. We had a one on one communication with him which made maintenance easy. Regular radar operators would "red line" their equipment and list problems with a "won't work right".

One of the radar bunch said he was going to build a radio and get Tokyo Rose on it. Of course, we all snickered and I can't remember which guy it was. As far as I

Porter Richardson, Wendover, 1944

know, he was the only one of us who had any prewar electronics experience. He was a radio ham and had built his own rigs etc. Anyway, he built the short-wave radio, wound the RF and LF coils on wooden dowels, used tin cans for part of it and it had a loudspeaker. I was there when he first turned it on. After a bit of squealing and static, the very first thing it said was, "Hello boys, this is Tokyo Rose!" Needless to say, I was amazed. Throughout our tenure, I turned to him many times to get me out of a radar maintenance dilemma.

When we arrived on Tinian, we set up temporary tents for a few days. We were a considerable distance from the flight line. We would catch a ride in a group

393rd Radar Men at Wendover

(L-R): **Front Row:** *Porter A. Richardson, Patrick C. Joyce, Stanley A. Kiedrowski, Henry I. Jones, Patrick C. Robbins, Royal H. Mohr, Calvin C. Anstine, Glenn A. Baugh, John B. Kennedy, Aubrey Pair, Lt. Elroy Homa*
Back Row: *Lt. Jacob Beser, James W. Jolly, Norman B. McIntosh, John D. Robey, Harold E. Kimme, John H. Harrington, Marvin O. Beatty.*
Missing: *Paul Metro, Warren Best, Andrew A. Brown, John E. Collins, Joel S. Denham, Grover C. Cooper, Joseph L. Ross, Wendell B. Lathrop, Edwin M. Bell*

jeep, weapons carrier or truck belonging to the 509th or sometimes went down to the road and hitchhiked. The 509th was enclosed by a barbed wire fence with machine gun equipped sentries. There were still Japanese soldiers hiding on the island.

Most of us stayed in pyramidal tents. The Seabees had framed the sides and made the floors from 100 pound practice bomb wooden boxes laid against each other. Normal rains they handled nicely, however, we were in the side winds of a hurricane one time when tent, floor and all washed away. We were alerted

Hitching a ride at Broadway and Canal

in time to grab our duffle bags, etc. and went to the mess hall.

ROSS, JOSEPH
393rd Radar Countermeasures

I remember my first view of Wendover as the troop train arrived at the base; it didn't look like much of an oasis at the end of the Salt Flats but it was our new home. Gradually, we settled into barracks life and began to get acquainted with the new base. Our work area was in one of the hangers and while most of the Radar Section worked on the APQ13 navigational/bombing equipment, five of us with Radar Countermeasures Military Occupational Status (MOS) learned about some gear designed to search and record enemy radar signals.

I was close with Porter Richardson and got to know him very well. Wendell Lathrop, our master sergeant and group leader, was also a great guy to talk with.

Some of us were assigned to a portion of the 393rd that went to Cuba for special training. This turned out to be an eye opening experience to get to visit Havana.

Finally, the 509th was assigned over seas. A portion of the radar section traveled by ship; I was assigned to fly over with the B29s. The long flight from Wendover to Oahu, Kwajalein and Tinian was somewhat boring; I was able to nap in the padded tunnel.

A bit of excitement occurred as our plane started to land at Kwajalein in a rain squall. Suddenly, we banked hard to starboard. Looking out our port side, we saw a C54 banking hard to his starboard, away from us. It looked a bit close.

On Tinian, we continued to train and even enjoy our new base. Though we were separated from all the other groups, we seemed to be quite self-sufficient.

Finally, we got a hint that something "big" was about to happen when early in the dark of August 6, 1945 a large assembly of "brass" appeared at the Enola Gay. Lt. Beser instructed me to install a special voice recorder in the bombardier position and connect it to the intercom circuit. As I left the cockpit area, I looked into the front bomb bay to see what all the furor was about; just a dirty bomb I thought; how wrong I was.

Then it was back to California by slow boat; train to Roswell, New Mexico; discharge and a glorious trip home with Paul Metro; by thumb.

RUSS, HARLOW
Project Alberta

Quoted From: Project Alberta Exceptional Books and Personal Letters to the Editor

Although I heard W47 (Wendover) mentioned frequently and knew it was the Base of Operations for flight and drop test programs for the bombs, I had no idea as to its location and never saw or heard its real name mentioned during my first visit there. At Albuquerque airport, we loaded boxes and luggage into an Army C47 and all passengers climbed aboard. The C47 was arranged so the passengers sat on bench type rows of bucket seats designed for use with a parachute seat pack with seat belts, no cushions or arm rests with their backs to the windows. The cargo was stacked and strapped down in the middle of the floor.

Among the 20 or so passengers, four were Army officers in uniform. Shortly after takeoff, I noticed all of these officers removed the Engineering Corps Insignia from their jackets and shirts and replaced them with Air Force Insignia.

After we landed, the few of us making our first trip to W47 were taken to the Base Security Office to obtain our passes and be briefed by Major William Uanna, who had been sent by General Groves to command the Manhattan District Security Group.

Major Uanna explained that his security group, Col. Tibbets, his Deputy, Lt. Col. Classen, and Executive Officer, Lt. Col. Bean, a few electronics officers in the B29 Flight Crews and the First Ordnance Squadron Special (Aviation) were the only people in the 509th Composite Group that knew of the existence and purpose of the Manhattan Engineer District and the location and purpose of Site Y, Los Alamos.

All Site Y personnel, military or civilian at W47 were required to stay in a special Transient Officers Quarters (BOQ) immediately adjacent to the Officers Club, and must take all of their meals in the Officers Club. They were prohibited from visiting any other quarters or barracks.

Site Y personnel could leave the base on foot to visit the nearby town of Wendover only in groups and only if accompanied by a security officer or agent. The location of W47 was classified and was not to be mentioned at Site Y.

All incoming and outgoing telephone calls were monitored by the security group and would be chopped if mention of classified information appeared imminent.

The project technical operations were conducted in an isolated, fenced and guarded area some distance south of the main landing runway and flight line area. Admission to this technical area was by special pass only. Access to the base was by base pass only.

The Officers Club next door to the BOQ was a large building with large dining hall and bar room that served as a recreation center. The meals served in the dining hall were very good. In order to have a drink at the bar, one purchased a bottle, to which the bartender attached a tape showing the owner's name. When not in use, the bottle was stored until called for. All the transients'

bottles were stored in a separate area. Utah State Law permitted one bottle per week per person. My first bottle lasted through the rest of my visits to the base.

One of many advantages for using W47 as base of operations for 509th and drop test programs was its location on a main railroad line with a spur running directly into the base. Sealed carloads of classified bomb parts, pumpkins and equipment could be delivered on the base, unloaded and moved to storage areas without security risk.

During a two week stay at W47, we participated in some of the evening social activities, such as bingo parties and other functions the wives attended a couple nights each week in the dining hall at the Officers Club. The bingo parties were popular and drew large crowds. The winners' prizes were either cash or whiskey, with the latter being most popular. The 509th had trained in Cuba and bought up a couple C54 loads of scotch at a dollar a bottle, so they had a good supply of these prizes. On other nights, if nothing special was scheduled, people gathered in the bar to drink and talk. One officer was a good piano player and the crowd enjoyed singing popular songs with his accompaniment.

Main attractions in Wendover were the State Line Hotel and Spikes. The hotel rooms and restaurant were in Utah. The State Line passed through a hallway connecting the bar and gambling hall in Nevada. Spikes was entirely in Nevada. It was a restaurant, bar with music and dance floor and was very popular with enlisted men from the base. On some Saturday nights, an Army Bus would bring USO girls from Salt Lake City for dances at the club. The bachelor officers enjoyed these occasions. Major Uanna's Agents kept a watchful eye on Site Y personnel to insure we only viewed these affairs from the sidelines and did not participate or converse with these visitors.

Once, I witnessed an interesting "it's a small world" encounter at the bar. Brode and some of his fusing people always occupied a booth and with their own kit and materials would go through the ritual of making martinis during cocktail hour. Henry Silsbee, one of Brode's principal assistants, always participated in these sessions. Henry was part of Special Engineering Department (SED) from Site Y and of course wore civilian clothes. On this particular occasion, another civilian, a stranger we did not know, approached Henry and greeted him effusively. Apparently, he had known Henry for a long time. Almost immediately he said in effect, "Henry, I thought you were in the Army; what are you doing here"? In about fifteen seconds, the stranger was surrounded by Major Uanna's Agents and was ushered into a side room. After a conference that lasted about thirty minutes, they all emerged. The stranger was completely intimidated and from that time on accompanied by an agent, he kept his distance from Henry and the other civilians.

First Tech
Service Detachment

Project Alberta was code name and location code was Destination O (Tinian). The group shown in the photos is about 1/3 Army, 1/3 Navy and 1/3 civilian. Captain Parsons USN, was officer in charge (OIC) of the group with Commander Frederick Ashworth Naval Aviator, the Deputy OIC. Brig. Gen. Thomas Farrell was Gen. Groves personal representative of the Manhattan Engineer District. Rear Admiral W.R. Purnell represented the Military Policy Committee. W.G. "Bill" Penney, was a British Observer and Scientist. There was also a British Royal Air Force observer, Group Captain Cheshire. who went on some practice and other flights.

Commander Ashworth who was Capt. Parsons assistant at Los Alamos, Ordnance Div, went to Guam in early spring 1945 to brief Admiral Nimitz (CINC PAC) about the project and get permission to establish our base and facilities at Tinian. Ashworth selected locations for 509th and Project A and Col. Kirkpatrick was sent by General Groves in April 1945 to direct construction of site facilities by the Seabee Battalion.

The large enclosure was occupied for work, not living quarters and maintained by the First Ordnance Squadron. It was a secured area under guard 24 hours per day and required a pass and badge to enter. The First Ordnance Area was located near the northwest corner of North Field runway. The final bomb assembly work was done in three areas; one was for Little Boy, one for Fat Man and one for Pumpkins, high explosive but non-nuclear bombs the same size as Fat Man. Pumpkins were used for practice on combat areas Rota and Truk Atolls and finally on Japanese home islands.

The First Ordnance Squadron enclosure contained seven large metal quonset type buildings and other facilities. One was the Project Office and Headquarters with administration offices for Major Begg, Commander of the First Ordnance Squadron and Captain Combs, office manager and custodian of all classified papers. He stored all Los Alamos, Project Y, drawings and specifications in safes and furnished office space for Captain Parsons and other administrative people.

One large quonset with no windows, was used for opening crates with bomb parts and other material sent by ships and for preliminary bomb assembly work. Five large quonsets were warehouses for bomb parts, equipment, small parts and tools storage. There were four, small, air-conditioned quonsets for use by fusing, firing, pit and observation teams.

In essence, everything that was shipped to Tinian from Los Alamos, Wendover, the Navy at San Francisco and all other sources, wound up in storage in that enclosure. The whole setup was built by Seabees under the direction of Colonel Kirkpatrick who worked for General Groves.

The Indianapolis arrived in the afternoon July 26, 1945 Tinian time. There was no dock so it was anchored inside the antisubmarine net in the harbor area. A small Navy boat went out to the Indianapolis to pick up cargo from Los Alamos Site Y. It had made the voyage in a lead lined bucket type container bolted to the deck in Captain's quarters. It was escorted by three Site Y secu-

July 1945. Tinian, Marianas, 509th Composite Group, First Ordnance Sqdn. First Ord. Sqdn Transportation & Repair Station, Facing Philippine Sea. Paved with Coral sand, watered daily with seawater. First Tech. Svc. Detachment. Harlow W. Russ

rity agents, Manhattan District, and one medical doctor Capt. James F. Nolan, US Army Los Alamos, a radiation expert. One of the security agents Charles O'Brien, moved into our tent with Art Machen, Vic Miller and Harlow Russ. The Indianapolis was at Tinian about 3 1/2 hours, then left for Guam to refuel and give the crew a day of freedom.

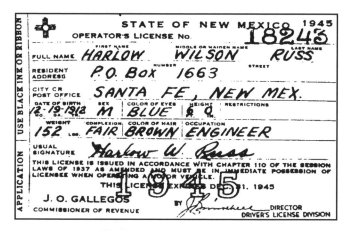

P.O. Box 1663 was the postal code for the secret city of Los Alamos

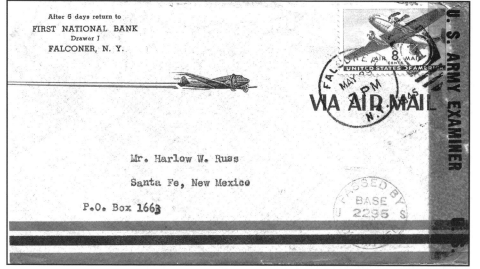

July 1945
Tinian, Marianas Islands
509th Composite Group
First Ordnance Squadron Enclosure
N.W. Coast of Tinian, Facing Philippine Sea,
Security Area, Bomb Components Storage Area.
Harlow W. Russ
1st Tech. Svc. Detachment.

SCHAFHAUSER, PAUL C.
Asst. Crew Chief, Ground Crew V-91

December 2, 1942, at age 18, I enlisted in the Army Air Corps as a cadet, spent three months in basic training, six months in a College Training Detachment (CTD), from there went to classification where I was washed out for pilot training, and offered a bombardier position which I turned down. I asked for mechanic training and was shipped to B17 mechanic school in Amarillo, Texas. After five months, I was sent to Chanute Field, Illinois graduating as an engine specialist (MO 684) on Wright R3350 18 cylinder double row radial engines. I was transferred to Walker Field Kansas and put into a filler pool for the 58th Wing located in India. That was disbanded two or three months later and I was shipped to the 393rd Bomb Squadron 504th Bomb Group at Fairmont, Nebraska.

In September 1944, the 393rd Bomb Squadron was transferred to Wendover, Utah and assigned to the 509th Composite Group. When the B29s started arriving, we were busy keeping them flying. I was a 20 year old Private First Class (PFC) and the 44 year old crew chief was given a choice of going overseas or staying in the States so he chose the latter.

In January 1945, I and other mechanics flew to Cuba for three months to maintain aircraft while flight crews

Paul Schafhauser celebrates V-J Day in #3 engine air scoop

flew training missions over water. Upon returning to the US, we had an inflight engine failure causing us to land in Galveston, Texas where we had to wait until an engine could be shipped to us.

A short time after arriving in Wendover, a crew of us mechanics flew to the Naval Ordnance Test Base at Inyokern, California. They test dropped the Fat Man bomb at targets in the Mojave Desert and made necessary adjustments to the problem with the way it descended. Six of us mechanics had a barracks to ourselves with one aircraft to maintain. Our time was mostly spent loading the bomb, fueling the aircraft, wiping oil from the engine nacells and cleaning the windshield. There were no engine changes and we didn't see any of the bomb drops. One weekend, we hitched a ride to Los Angeles and back. I remember on the return trip to Wendover, we received a radio message that President Roosevelt had died April 12, 1945.

Shortly after arriving in Wendover, we were given thirty days furlough. I took a train back home to Appleton, Wisconsin unaware if I was being watched by Security People. I never had a problem with them. I do recall people in our barracks who were very pleasant to be around, but you didn't dare ask any questions.

Back in Wendover after furlough, we received new B29s that had Curtis Electric reversible propellers and a pneumatic system that operated the bomb bay doors. In the rear bomb bay, three fuel cells were installed and the front bomb bay was a platform where baggage and equipment was placed for travel overseas. I did not take part in picking up the new aircraft or manuals, but I'm sure we received new instruction and tools for removing and reinstalling the propellers.

Before we shipped overseas, we had to turn in all our winter uniforms and received summer clothes. Each mechanic had their own tool kit. Engines, other equipment, everything we needed was delivered by cargo ship, even the pit and hydraulic lift were available upon arrival. When the aircraft traveled, I and several other main-

Paul Schafhauser cutting Woitto Laine's hair on the field near plane and equipment tent.

tenance people were fortunate to be included in the Air Echelon. We took our small hand tools as all the airbases would have necessary equipment. Engines were not overhauled in the field, replacements were shipped in.

Upon arrival at Tinian, we were kept busy maintaining aircraft after every flight by checking oil sumps for metal, cleaning the interior, refueling, changing cylinders and engines when necessary which took probably 12 hours or so, plus routine aircraft and engine inspections. We did not overhaul or rebuild engines.

Each time before the engines were started, the propellers had to be pulled through about eight to ten blades. On radial engines the lower cylinders can accumulate oil causing an hydraulic lock when the engine is turned over. If this happens when the starter is used, it can cause engine damage. When the engine is turned over by hand, the prop will suddenly stop. The cure for this is to remove the spark plug of the cylinder affected and let the oil run out.

When the aircraft flew bombing missions, they usually took off early morning one to two am and returned early to midafternoon. We had to be there both times. It was a good thing they didn't have to fly everyday. When they returned, we guided them into and around the revetment until it was facing outward. While parked, wheel chalks were placed fore and aft of the wheels so wind would not move the aircraft.

Celebrating V-J Day... Note 6th Bomb Group emblem painted on airplane commander's side of plane.

#2 engine change, Ship V-91

Taken from the wing tip of Ship V-91

SERBER, ROBERT
Project Alberta, Letter Written by Fred Bock

Copy Given to Editor by Fred Bock

Reaching back more than half a century, I well remember when we were both on Tinian Island; you as a civilian scientist in Project Alberta (Project A) and I as an Airplane Commander in the 509th Composite Group. I recall having numerous conversations, at that time, with you and other scientific members of Project A, particularly Luis Alvarez, Philip Morrison and Lawrence Johnston, concerning the atomic initiative and other matters.

The reason for writing now is to ask if you can clarify some aspects of the second atomic strike on 9 August 1945. On that mission, with Kokura as the primary and Nagasaki as the secondary target, the intended strike formation consisted of three Silverplate B29s manned by regular crews and others of the 509th plus members of Project A and official observers.

(1) V-77 Bockscar carried the Fat Man Plutonium Bomb
(2) V-89 The Great Artiste was equipped with instruments to detect and record the shock waves from the explosion
(3) V-90 Big Stink was equipped with a special Fastax Camera for photographing the detonation of the bomb and the early growth of the fire ball.

My crew of nine men C-13, of which I was the Airplane Commander, flew V-89 on that occasion, though the B29 we regularly flew was V-77. On board with us were Lawrence Johnston and Walter Goodman of Project A, Also William Laurence, science writer for *The New York Times* and special consultant to the Manhattan Project. There were three instrument canisters containing pressure gauges and radio transmitters in the bomb bay of V-89 to be dropped with deployable parachutes at the same time

as the Fat Man Bomb. Equipment was installed on V-89 to receive signals from the three canisters (transmitted on different frequencies), display the shockwave profiles on cathode-ray tubes and make photographic records. Johnston and Goodman, supplemented by my Radar Operator, William Barney, monitored the three sets of equipment.

I know that you, Alvarez and Morrison prepared a letter to Professor Ryokichi Sagane of the University of Tokyo warning of the dire consequences if Japan did not surrender immediately and urging him to convey this message to the Japanese General Staff. Copies of the letter were taped inside the covers of the three canisters before loading on V-89. (The canisters and letters were later recovered by Japanese military personnel. In 1989, I saw one of the canisters and a large blowup of the letter in the Nagasaki International Culture Hall.)

The questions I have relate primarily to the planned operation of the Fastax Camera on V-90 and what actually occurred prior to and after takeoff.

My understanding is that those scheduled to fly on V-90 consisted of: nine men of Crew C-14 except James Hopkins was the Airplane Commander in place of Norman Ray who was ill; two official observers from Britain, Group Captain G. Leonard Cheshire of the RAF and Dr. William G. Penney of London University and Project A; and yourself as operator of the Fastax Camera.

From Berlyn Brixner of Los Alamos National Laboratory, I have learned the Fastax was a special type of ultra-high-speed camera, capable of taking as many as 4000

Robert Serber on Tinian

frames per second (fps) on 16mm film, which was rolled continuously. A rotating prism was used in place of a shutter. Loaded with 100 feet of film, the running time was about 1.25 seconds at a speed of 4000fps, 5.0 seconds at a speed of 1000fps, etc. Several had been used successfully by Brixner to photograph the explosion of a device of Fat Man type at the Trinity Test on 16 July 1945 from fixed positions at ground level. For use in a B29, the camera was swivel-mounted in the nose section in place of the bombsight.

On the Hiroshima mission of 6 August 1945, one of the three B29s in the strike formation had been equipped with the Fastax Camera, that is (ie) V-91 Necessary Evil flown by Crew B-10, George Marquardt Commander. Bernard Waldman, one of the civilian scientists in Project A, was on board to operate the camera. The camera plane made a circle just before reaching the target vicinity so the plane was at a safe distance from, but headed toward, the aiming point at the moment of detonation. For some reason no images of the explosion or aftermath were found when the film was developed, although the camera had presumably been aimed correctly and turned on at the proper time.

A couple of accounts of the Kokura/Nagasaki mission of 9 August 1945 (in which he did not directly participate) were written by Luis Alvarez. For a long time I supposed the paragraphs pertaining to your involvement were correct. However, recently I have corresponded with the three surviving members of Crew C-14 and they raise doubts as to the accuracy of some of the statements made by Alvarez. These men are: Richard Cannon, Radar Operator; Stanley Steinke, Navigator and George Brabenec, Flight Engineer. Cannon was stationed in the rear compartment of V-90 while Steinke and Brabenec were stationed in the nose section.

The mission of 9 August 1945 is described in considerable detail in a letter from Alvarez to General Leslie Groves of the Manhattan Project, dated 5 May 1965. A verbatim excerpt dealing with the planned utilization of the Fastax Camera and what actually happened is as follows.

"On the Nagasaki mission, the job of official Fastax Cameraman was assigned to Dr. Robert Serber, a Theoretical Physicist from Los Alamos. (Bob is now professor of physics at Columbia University.) He obtained his permission to fly on the mission just about a day before the planes took off, so Dr. Waldman spent a good deal of that time instructing him in the use of the camera. Before the final briefing for the mission, I helped Bob assemble his flying gear, which had to be checked out of various storerooms. We piled it all in one corner of the ready room - flak proof armor, parachute, one man life raft, etc. - so it would be ready to pick up just before the flight. We went to the briefing, then picked up Bob's gear and the two of us carried it out and boosted it through the escape hatch leading into the bombardier's compartment.

I then drove in my jeep up to the top of the cliff overlooking the airfield and watched the three planes take off. You can imagine my surprise when I returned to my tent and found my tentmate, Bob Serber, sitting dejectedly on the doorstep. It turned out that after his plane had taxied down to the end of the runway, preparatory to taking off, the pilot called for a parachute check. Everyone on the plane had a parachute except Bob; he had two one-man life rafts! Apparently, one of us had mistaken a life raft for

a parachute in the darkened ready room. (Tinian was in a state of blackout because radar had detected Japanese planes heading toward the island.)

So we had the ironical situation that the only man who could not be spared from that plane was unceremoniously dumped off just before takeoff. The only reason that plane was in formation was it carried the Fastax Camera and the only person who had been trained to operate the camera was Bob Serber. Bill Penney (later Sir William) was familiar with the operation of a Fastax Camera, but he wasn't familiar with the sequence of timing signals between the lead plane and the camera plane, so he wouldn't have been able to start the camera at the proper instant. Since the film ran so fast through the camera, the exact timing of the start-up of the camera was essential."

The story is also told, more briefly, on pages 144-145 of Alvarez' autobiography, *Adventures of a Physicist* (Basic Books, 1987) published the year before his death.

What prompts my inquiry to you is none of the surviving Crew C-14 men remembers you were on board V-90 or when the plane taxied to the end of the runway, a parachute check was made and you were ordered to leave. It seems likely to me that such an unusual incident would be remembered, particularly since two of the men were in the nose section of the plane, where according to Alvarez, your gear was stowed. However, it may be that the events occurred as related but did not make an impression strong enough to last 52 years.

Other accounts of the mission have it that, after V-90 took off, you reported to General Thomas Farrell, who was on Tinian as second in command to Groves, and he authorized breaking radio silence in order to communicate instructions on the operation of the Fastax Camera to one or more men in the airplane. A paragraph on page 30 of the book *Nagasaki: The Forgotten Bomb* by Frank Chinnock (World Publ. Co. 1969) reads as follows.

"In the third plane, the one carrying the photo equipment, Major Jim Hopkins was trying to absorb the instructions he had received a little while earlier. Just before takeoff, Dr. Robert Serber, the expert in high-speed photography, had turned up without his parachute. Hopkins had ordered him to get it, but the plane was already airborne when he returned with his chute. Crestfallen, Serber had reported to General Farrell, who decided to break radio silence. For some twenty minutes after Farrell got through to Hopkins, Serber had given radio instructions to him on the proper use of the special photo equipment. Hopkins hoped he had it all straight in his mind."

As it turned out, for some reason V-90 did not make the planned rendezvous with V-77 and V-89 over Yakushima Island off the south coast of Kyushu, so the Fastax Camera could not have been used for the intended purpose even if you had been on board.

With the aim of achieving historical accuracy, so far as possible, concerning the climactic events at the close of World War II, I would greatly appreciate any information you can provide as one of the eminent scientists who were on Tinian and a direct participant in the run up to the mission of 9 August 1945.

Editor's Note - Robert Serber died 1 June 1997 without responding to this letter. The contents of the letter is believed to be what actually happened. Copy of this letter was supplied by Fred Bock.

SHADE, ROBERT L.
1st Ordnance Squadron, Special Aviation

I entered service February 1, 1943 and was employed by the Waco Aircraft Company in Troy, Ohio as a tool and die maker. Waco was building aircraft to train pilots for the Air Force and gliders for the invasion of Europe.

I was given basic training in Miami Beach, Florida, then assigned to Armament School at the Aberdeen Proving Grounds. After finishing school, I was sent to Ardmore Army Air Base in Oklahoma to train heavy bomber crews for the war over Europe.

In September of 1944, I was moved in the first group to Wendover Field Utah, reporting to Major Begg and assigned to 1st Ordnance. After a few days, we were put to work in an Ammunition Storage Area isolated away from the main base. The building had no chains to lift the bomb so we moved a C2 Wrecker in to move and lift the bomb as needed.

My first job on the bomb along with Lyndon C. Richards was to install a set of baffle plates in the tail section because the bomb was so large the tail assembly could not make the bomb fall true. At this time, the bomb was just a steel ball the size and weight of the final product.

After several weeks, all components of the Fat Man Bomb arrived and it was our duty to assemble and make sure all parts fit. We had to bolt together the five sided plates to make the large ball inside the bomb. Next came the five sided powder blocks with the large end to fit the outside radius of the ball and the small end to fit the radius of the small end of the steel ball in the center called the pit which contained the ball of plutonium. At this time these blocks were made of concrete.

The next step was to assemble the two (2) outer ellipsed shell that enclosed and completed the weapon. Since the shell parts were only partly finished, we had to hand drill and tap a series of holes for the bolts to fasten the shell to the large ball inside.

The nose section contained the lens mounts for the trigger that would start the nuclear reaction. The Los Alamos laboratory shipped a fixture that properly located the tubes containing the lens. I had to burn holes in the nose shell to locate and weld the tubes in place. The tail section contained the controls, installed by personnel from other laboratories, for firing of the bomb.

Next we had to dig and construct a pit so 1st Ordnance could make a cradle to hold the bomb in a stable position as it was raised into the aircraft standing over the pit. Another 1st Ordnance detail headed by 1st Sergeant Rzepinski was to manufacture a shackle to hang the bomb in the bomb bay. We were working two shifts to complete the bomb as soon as possible. Some of the men decided to paint the bomb to look like a shark. I never did learn what happened to this prototype we finished at 2am.

(L-R): Robert Shade, David Patten

In the meantime, we were in the process of constructing an assembly building outside Wendover in the Salt Flats. I was given the job of welding the steel I beams that formed the rails for the ten ton overhead traveling crane. I was working night shift on a platform twenty feet up and the coyotes would come in close and howl. Before we could complete this project, we received orders to move to Tinian Island via the Transport Squadron.

Upon arrival, I was assigned a 6x6 truck containing a welder, compressor, drill press, lathe and shaper as my portable machine shop. Then I was assigned to fence in the work area with barbed wire. The Seabees had erected a large Quonset Hut to house a central machine shop and assembly building. Once again I welded the steel girders and I beams forming rails in the ceiling center to hold the traveling crane that moved the heavy bomb parts.

While the bombers were getting into routine raids over Japan, we watched with binoculars as they made test drops over our area coast to perfect the delivery. The Japanese radio noted some of our planes were dropping one large bomb.

After the war, 1st Ordnance disassembled, destroyed and sunk into deep water some of the bomb stockpiles.

I received my discharge at Dayton Air Base Ohio and returned to work at Waco Aircraft developing a new radical commercial plane with propellers in the tail to push it forward. Waco had 400 orders but the government cancelled price controls and the planes could not be delivered at a profit so the project was terminated.

Some months later, I worked one of three shifts seven days a week machining the fuel and oxygen valves for the Jupiter and Redstone Guided Missile Program that put John Glenn into orbit.

SHAMLIAN, ARMEN
390th Air Service Group Photographer

My interest in photography began at an early age. I was a member of the Camera Club at Kearney High School, Kearney, New Jersey. I graduated in 1940 and started working for two ex-news photographers in Newark while on Christmas vacation. I was hired at $8 a week doing darkroom work. By May, I was doing all black and white printing; there was practically no color work done at the time.

I worked for them until I was drafted in April 1943. I had basic training in Atlantic City, New Jersey and went to Lowery Army Air Force (AAF) Denver, Colorado Technical Training School for photography. I went home on furlough for Thanksgiving. Upon return was sent to Salt Lake City, Utah and was assigned to the Wendover AAF Base Photo Unit.

On arrival, the first thing that caught my eye was the sign on the mountainside, "Kill or be Killed" and the desolate surroundings. My job was darkroom work in printing photos of airplane crashes, morgue photos and general events photographs. For recreation we played basketball, went to the movies and spent a few weekends with my buddies on trips to Twin Falls, Idaho or Salt Lake City, Utah. In calisthenics, I was able to do 110 sit-ups; I thought it was a record.

In September 1944, the 393rd Bomb Squadron arrived at Wendover from Fairmont AAF Nebraska. We learned it was to be the nucleus of a top secret operation that would bring the war to an end and we should not talk to anyone about what we were doing or where we were going. Some of us were separated from base photo and we moved into a luxurious building, becoming part of the 390th Air Service Group which was officially formed in December of 1944.

Six of us were chosen to do motion picture work; the rest of us did still photo and lab work. Our work now was mainly processing photos of practice bomb drops made at Salton Lake. It was a special design and

Alex Schiavone with camera equipment, Wendover 1944

we asked no questions. We did this until the 509th was ready for combat.

In April, all but six of the photo unit boarded a train for the port of embarkation, Fort Lawton, Seattle, Washington. The remaining six, including me, were to fly over on a C54 piloted by Colonel Tibbets stopping at Hamilton Field, California, Hawaii, Johnston Island and Kwajalein taking two and a half days to arrive on Tinian June 8, 1945. On Tinian,

Armen Shamlian

we lived in Quonset Huts and used the 313th Bomb Wing laboratory. Our planes went on separate missions from the other groups dropping one bomb over Japan and returning. We developed and printed the strike photos; some of which were displayed in the mess hall. The other guys were curious about what we were doing; we ignored their questions.

On August 5th, we were told the mission that would end the war was on. I took photos of loading "Little Boy" into the bomb bay of "Enola Gay", with top brass looking on. As the photos were developed, I had time to relax and be ready to shoot the take-off at 2:45 am August 6th. The scene at the hardstand was like a Hollywood Premiere; scientists, generals and GIs all around. I took photos of the crew etc. with the final shot being Colonel Tibbets looking out the window from the cockpit. I called out to him, "Colonel, please wave", so he did with a smile and the plane started rolling away to take off for Hiroshima.

I went back to the photo lab to develop and print the negatives. They looked good so I went to bed. I woke up about 7 am wondering about the mission. Later, we heard it was a success. Most of the 509th were celebrating with a "The End of the War" picnic, with some photo guys shooting the activities. I had to be at the hardstand to shoot the return of Enola Gay at about 2:45

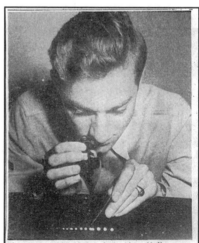

Hits Jackpot Of 11 Pearls, In Mess Hall

'Bingo . . . Keno . . . small time stuff! Eat at the Consolidated Mess and come out with a handful of pearls, advises Pfc. Armen Shamlian of Kearney, N. J. It happened on Friday, May 25, according to the records, when Shamlian sat down to a supper of fried oysters.

As he bit into an oyster, he felt something grinding against his molars . . . and extracted 11 pearls from the bivalve. Witnesses to the event were Pvt. Al Schiavone, Cpl. Paul Lentz and S-Sgt. Al LeMay.

pm which was crowded with brass and others. I photographed General Spaatz pinning the Distinguished Service Cross on Colonel Tibbets flight suit along with photos of the debriefing at the Officers' Club. I developed the

100 exposure roll of film taken by the tail gunner, Bob Caron, of the Enola Gay. Back at the lab, everyone crowded around to see the awesome shot of the atomic cloud over Hiro-shima. Later that evening, the Recon photos were received, developed and printed. Everyone was amazed with disbelief at the bombing results.

Our jubilation was short-lived; Japan did not surrender. On August 9th, Bockscar went on a second atomic bomb mission, target being Nagasaki, diverted from Kokura because of cloud coverage. We did our "shooting" duties as before, with the hope this would be the last. IT WAS!

Inside Wendover photo lab – Note poster on wall of German spies landed by submarine on Long Island, NY

When it was time to go home, I went by troop ship with the rest of the guys arriving in Oakland, California on November 4, 1945 and went by troop train to Roswell, New Mexico. Several of us drove to Santa Ana, California, where I was discharged on February 6, 1946. I bought civilian clothes and stayed with relatives until May, after which I took a train for Newark, New Jersey and a bus home to Kearny.

Paul Lentz, Armen Shamlian - Wendover, 1944

SLABY, JOSEPH
320th Troop Carrier Squadron, Technical Supply Sergeant

When I enlisted in the Air Force May 18, 1942, in Lincoln, Nebraska and inducted at Omaha, I had no idea so much packing and being transferred would involve serving at so many bases during my enlistment. I received my basic training at Jefferson Barracks, Missouri, transferred to Leavenworth, Kansas; from there to Minter AFB near Bakersfield, California, a base for basic pilot training. After some time, I was transferred to Camp Pendleton near Stockton, California; then on to Pendleton AFB in Oregon to train as an airplane mechanic for a P38 Fighter Squadron. I didn't like being a mechanic so I spoke to my Squadron Commander and since I had quite a bit of office experience, asked for a transfer to some base where I could receive administrative training.

I was sent to Camp Stockman in California for a short time, then received orders for assignment to Chaffey Jr. College at Ontario, California for a course in administration. Upon completion of the six weeks course, I was transferred to Camp Tan Foran, a staging area near San Francisco where I was assigned to the squadron as a clerk. After a few short weeks, I was transferred to Wendover Field AFB, Utah. What a surprise to see miles and miles of Salt Flats, sheep trails leading into the hills and an old dilapidated grocery store as I disembarked from the train. Looking off to the south, I saw the base, a sprawling range of barracks, runways, etc. I was assigned to Headquarters Squadron to work in the Sub Depot, a distribution center

for airplane parts for all planes on the base. I was in charge of eight civilian women employees comprising the billing department who maintained a perpetual inventory of all items issued to all airplane squadrons at all times.

In December 1944, a new group was activated called the 509th Composite Group comprised of seven squadrons. I was assigned as Tech Supply Sergeant to the 320th Troop Carrier Squadron located in our hanger. My assistant John Fisher and I were to maintain all the supplies and equipment for our C54 planes. When the 320th Troop Carrier Squadron was transferred to Tinian AFB to bring wounded soldiers from overseas to hospitals in the states, seventeen men including myself were left stateside. On their return trips, it was my duty to fulfill the planes supply needs.

On August 9th, the day the Atomic Bomb was dropped on Nagasaki, the war ended and Colonel Tibbets ordered all overseas duty cancelled. I remained at Wendover AFB a short time thereafter. My final transfer came through to Roswell AFB New Mexico where I received my honorable discharge on November 16, 1945.

Memories of Wendover
Written by Ruth Slaby

Some of my fondest memories include my two and a half years at Wendover. Joe and I had just been married six months when he enlisted in the Air Force. Little did we know how an interruption in our lives could possibly grant us so much happiness and leave us with so many fond memories. We corresponded daily but one day his letter suggested I join him in Ontario, California where he enrolled in an Administration course at Chaffey Jr. College for six months. What a welcome idea! My father warned me against going since I had only been out of Nebraska a time or two. He said, "Joe will probably be shipped out soon and then what will you do?" At age twenty-two, I was determined to go, so I quit my secretarial job at the State House Game and Parks Commission, borrowed some money for four new tires on our '37 Chevy and off I went to be with my husband. Little did we know the day after I arrived in Ontario, Joe would be transferred to Camp Tan Foran, a Staging Area.

I was befriended by another Army wife from Texas named Joanne. Together we rented a room in a home. The second night at 3 am, we heard a loud knocking on our door to find Joe and Joanne's husband, Art. After a short discussion, we were enticed into going with them in Art's Ford Convertible to Camp Tan Foran where they were stationed. Of course we went! Upon arrival, we learned our husbands could not live with us so we rented a room a mile from camp and shared expenses. The landlady informed us no soldiers were allowed to sleep there. The following night Joe and Art appeared after dark to stay. There was one bed with two mattresses and an old Army

Official 216th AAF - BU
Air Inspector's Office, 1943
Lt. Webb, Sgt Bob Conley, Ruth Slaby

cot. We drew straws to determine who would get the bed while the other couple slept on a mattress on the floor. Joe and Art always left before dawn so the landlady wouldn't catch them.

With only $6 a month from Joe's pay, it was necessary for me to get a stenographer's job at the shipyards. After only two weeks, the fellows were transferred to Wendover AAF Base Utah. I followed by train and as it rounded the mountains I saw a sheep trail to the right, Base off to the left, no sign of main street businesses except a little old grocery store. I was elated to see Joe waiting for me. His first words were, "Honey, you can only stay if you work on the Base".

The housing consisted of a fifteen foot trailer two wives shared. Servicemen weren't allowed, so Joe left before dawn with me hoping no shots would be fired from the water tower.

I became a secretary to Lt. Lowe, head of civilian employees, as a Civil Service Clerk in the Civilian Personnel Office located on the Base. A few days later, a WAC contingent was assigned to us but didn't like working for civilians so were deployed.

After six or seven months of trailer life, I was privileged to rent one of the newly constructed block apartments available for officers and noncom wives. I painted the two room floors and made pillows for the iron cot to resemble a sofa.

Colonel Dippy, the Base Commander's secretary left so I filled her position. When the 509th was activated, the Air Inspectors Office had several office positions available so I was assigned as Secretary and Chief Clerk with Pauline Bysom and Ruth Russell assisting. What an enjoyable assignment working for the Air Inspector, Major William N. Vickers; Tactical Inspector, Capt. Andrew DeMelik; Technical Inspector, Lt. Charles P. Walker; Communications Inspector, Lt. Don Niffenegger and Administrative Inspector, Lt. William F. Webb; and those great enlisted men who were like brothers to me, Tech/Sgt Robert Hannah; Tech/Sgt John Garrison; Sgt Robert Conley; Sgt Nutting; Cpl John Fisher; Cpl John Witherell and Cpl Red Timmerman.

Sgt Joe Slaby - 3rd from right, 1st row
T/Sgt Bob Hannah, end one on the right, 1st row
Cpl John Witherall, 2nd from right, 1st row
Pfc John E. Fisher, end one on the right, 2nd row
Sgt Clarance Hull , 4th from right, 1st row

Joe and I enjoyed celebrating Sundays and Holidays with enlisted men serving home cooked dinners and reminiscing about their lives back home. In our '38 Chevy Coupe, we invited other couples to Salt Lake City to dance at Covey's Little America Ballroom to Tommy Dorsey, Glenn Miller, Guy Lombardo and others. Sleeping in on Sunday morning was a real treat before going back to Wendover.

In December 1944 while pregnant, I continued working to remain on base though Joe's transfer to Tinian was imminent. An order from Colonel Tibbets for seventeen men including Joe to remain stateside was a terrific relief!

Our first son was delivered by Captain Boccardi, in the Base Hospital, on August 9th. The temperature outside and in the west wing for wives of noncoms was around 100 degrees. Major Vickers came to visit, noted the extreme temperature, went to Captain Boccardi and ordered I be placed in the officers' wives air-conditioned east wing rooms.

Joe received his orders to Roswell AAF Base, New Mexico for his Honorable Discharge in December 1945.

SMITH, ELBERT B.
393rd Bomb Squadron, Airplane Commander

"Wendover Memories" conjured up a veritable flood of memories of that barren Army Air Force Base, the living conditions, the parties we had, the constant training and the flights that I made all over the country at all hours of the day and night and in all kinds of weather.

Wendover was a never-to-be forgotten experience and memories of all of those experiences will stay with me as long as I live. My first wife, Anita, was with me the whole time and our first child, Stephanie, was born at Wendover on March 25, 1945.

I haven't seen Bill Rowe since the war ended, but over the years, I've had a couple of phone conversations with him. In the course of the last one, several months ago, we were reminiscing about the mission we flew out of Tinian on July 29, 1945.

I had arrived on the island on June 19 as Operations Officer of the 320th Troop Carrier Squadron and early in July had transferred over to the 393rd Bombardment Squadron to fly with Tom Classen's crew. The way I understood it at the time, Tom had been restricted to two missions a month because he'd been briefed on the nuclear bombs, but they wanted his crew flying more frequently than that.

So, I moved into the Quonset Hut with the other officers on Tom's crew; Bill Rowe, Bill Wright, Bobby Chapman and Floyd Kemner. We shared that Quonset with the officers from Fred Bock's and Buck Eatherly's crews.

We made a few local flights while I got reacquainted with the B29. I'd flown with the 393rd from the time it was activated until after we'd all transferred to Wendover. On July 26, with Tom Classen in command, we flew to Japan and dropped a "pumpkin" on a copper mine outside Hitachi.

We were then scheduled for another "pumpkin" mission to a target in the vicinity of Osaka and took off on that flight at some ungodly hour the morning of the 29th. It was sort of a learning experience, at least for me. There were two things our Intelligence Officers had told us, which gave us a fairly comfortable feeling. First, that Japanese fighters, if they were lucky enough to make a pass at us at 30,000 feet, would never be able to catch us for a second pass. Their planes didn't perform that well at that high an altitude. Second, they didn't have anti-aircraft guns that could reach us at 30,000 feet.

Somewhere between Iwo Jima and Japan, Al Lewandowski (our tailgunner) came on the intercom to

Elbert Smith on Tinian

advise that an unidentified fighter plane was climbing up behind us. As it closed in, he said it looked like a US Navy Fighter and, sure enough, a few minutes later, he pulled up off our left wing, as I remember it was a Corsair. We waved to each other and he dove off. The thought went through my mind that maybe the Japanese didn't have fighters that could perform well at 30,000 feet, but our Navy sure did.

When we got over Japan, as happened so often, our primary target was obscured by haze, as was the first secondary target we tried to bomb. So I headed down toward Kobe. We had a secondary target in that area, but again that haze made it too difficult for Bobby Chapman to line his bombsight up on it. We had cleared the shore line and were over Kobe Harbor when Lewandowski got on the intercom again and said somebody down there was shooting at us. He first announced the flak bursts were well below and behind us and then they seemed to be coming higher and closer. Suddenly, "Boom - Boom", two deafening bursts went off in quick succession. It sounded like they were right inside the plane.

I started taking evasive action, checked that everyone on the plane was OK and headed down the bay. We soon passed out of range of the unfriendly anti-aircraft guns. Lewandowski had announced they had stopped firing, when the bombardier suddenly shouted, "Hey, look at that", and there dead ahead of us was what looked like a large power plant, sitting out in the clear, right on the edge of Kobe Bay. We agreed this was a great "target of opportunity", so he lined up his bombsight on it, kicked out the bomb, and with that loss of weight, the plane instantly gained about a thousand feet of altitude. We continued down the bay, snapping pictures of our bomb as it dropped toward the target. But, then, as it was approaching the point of impact, a low layer of clouds drifted in below us and we were unable to bring back a picture of the explosion.

When we got back to Tinian, we found a couple of holes in the wing of our plane to support our story that, "They do have anti-aircraft that can reach you at 30,000 feet". I brought it up at our debriefing and one of the Intelligence Officers asked, "Where were you?" When I told him we were over Kobe Bay, he said, "Oh, that was the Japanese Navy".

So, we learned a few lessons on that mission, fortunately, we never had to use since that was the last combat mission this crew ever flew. A few days later, along with Bob Lewis', George Marquardt's and Don Albury's crews, we were called in by Intelligence and started studying the four nuclear targets; Hiroshima, Kokura, Nagasaki and Niigata. Those four crews were restricted from combat until the nuclear missions and, luckily, two of those were enough.

July 26, 1945 – Hitachi bomb cloud is circled

Unless I'm mistaken, we had the distinction of flying the only 509th mission that suffered any "battle damage", if that's what you can call a couple of holes in the wing. To this day, I don't know whether that's good or bad. But ever since then, I haven't believed everything I've been told, until I could check it out myself.

STEWART, FRANK
Navigator, Crew 123 (Wendover)

It was late October and still mild weather. Our Tail Gunner, Harrison Vail (now deceased) lived in the Enlisted Mens (EM) Barracks which is customary. He liked to go to the State Line Hotel and get loaded. On the way back to his barracks he had to pass the Officers' Barracks.

At first, he was content to scoop up a couple handsful of pea gravel and put them in my bed. An aggravation, but nothing serious and easy to dispose of. Next, he emptied bottles of catsup and chili sauce at the foot under the covers where I would put my feet in the mess when I got in bed. It worked. It was not funny.

But the climax came when he was assigned to a task force to go in the mountains and throw dirt over a very old B24 wreck in which there were obviously no bodies; they had long since been removed. However, he came upon an old spinal column, later determined to be from an antelope, according to the base vet. Enough is enough—but this was too much.

As fate would have it, I happened upon a huge tarantula slowly making its way out of a hangar on the warm concrete. I found a cardboard box and with a stick, I whacked him inside and taped it shut. When I got back to barracks, the crew said it had to go even though I volunteered to pitch it, box and all, into the glowing hot coals in the pot bellied stove.

So I took it down to the vet. He was delighted. He took it out with some hemostats which the critter didn't particularly like. He became active, to put it mildly. The vet put it back in the box with some cotton soaked with chloroform and left him for one minute. Then he dumped it back out on the table. Almost immediately it began to show signs of life. This time, back in the box overnight to make sure.

I returned the next day. He had pinned it to a piece of corrugated cardboard to dry. He pinned it in such a position that it appeared ready to jump. These critters can jump three feet, I'm told. Later that day or the next, I took the spider to the EMs barracks. I unscrewed the hinges from Vail's foot locker and placed the spider on top of his toothbrush and shaving items. The crew said I should have stayed around for the fun. It had the desired results. Vail never said a word to me about it, but he never bothered me again. Score one for the officers. I still get a chuckle out of it as I write.

SULLIVAN, JAMES B.
393rd Bomb Squadron, Engineering Clerk

I enlisted in the Air Corps in December, 1942, at the age of 19, in California. In Los Angeles, I graduated from Engineering Clerical School in April, 1943. I was assigned to the B29 Airbase in Fairmont, Nebraska. When the 393rd Bomb Squadron was activated in late 1943, I was made a part of that unit. Following that, the 393rd was made a part of the 509th Bomb Group and I found myself transferred to Wendover Field in late 1943. I knew nothing about the unit or about being followed at any time by agents. Perhaps this was because I never discussed what I was doing with anyone at any time I was in the 509th, as per my original instructions upon arrival at Wendover. I found it to be a very large airbase in a very desolate desert. During the next thirteen months, I performed my duties as an engineering clerk; recording all air time on all fifteen planes and up-dating entries in the tech manuals. To accomplish these jobs, it was necessary for me to contact all crew chiefs for each of the 15 planes.

My favorite memory of life at Wendover is of the weekly dances, where young women from Salt Lake City arrived by bus to dance with us in the enlisted men's center. At an early dance, I met a red head, who remained in contact with me until I returned to Salt Lake City after my discharge from service. We became engaged but never married and when we broke up, I returned to California. I began college and while there, I met the lady I married.

On January 13, 1945, I left Wendover in one of our B29s in the midst of a bad snowstorm, for a non-stop

flight to Batista Field in Cuba. We arrived in very humid, hot weather and I still remember most of us heading for the PX for a banana split. While I continued my regular duties, our air crews were practicing their navigational skills over open waters. I signed up to represent our 509th Unit in a tennis exhibition doubles match with S/Sgt. Andrew Demo. Our opponents were Pauline Betz, at that time, current Women's US National Singles Champion and Dorothy Bundy, ranked 5th in Women's tennis. I won the serve and served three straight aces. The final score of our match was 6 Love, with the women winning, because we never won another point. I still don't know why!

We left Cuba on February 28, 1945, and returned to Wendover. On June 29, 1945, I left for Tinian, courtesy of a Green Hornet C54, feeling sorry for the guys in the unit who would be making the trip to Tinian by ship. I arrived on Tinian July 3, 1945, and three of us, Sgt. Hyatt Norman, Pfc. Tom Weimer and I was the Cpl., began our same duties for our 15 planes. I lived in a tent, with a nice wooden floor. My favorite memories there include having my picture taken with me in the window of the Enola Gay; playing 10 man softball on the flight line and being in the work crew assigned to clean out the Red Cross tent as we prepared to leave the island. Imagine my surprise when I tried to kick a large box and it barely moved. I immediately had lots of friends as it contained 180 beautiful English Ping-Pong balls. I was one of the lucky ones who left Tinian November 4, 1945, flew in one of our B29s to Roswell Field, New Mexico, arriving November 7, 1945.

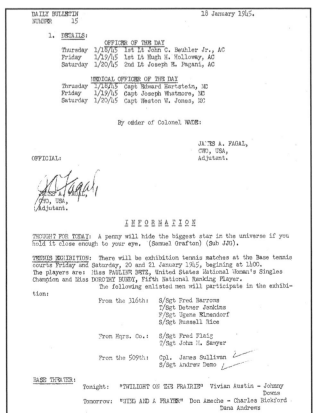

"Free Cocktail" card

183

SULLIVAN, MAURICE C.
1395th MP Company, Criminal Investigation

Early in 1944, I was an enlisted clerk in the Wendover Base Intelligence Office. I was classified as a GI 4F and was resigned to spending the duration at Wendover.

Suddenly, the base was flooded with all types of strangers working on various secret surveys. The 509th was also being formed. The Base Intelligence Office cooperated closely with the strangers. After a while, I, being an avid science fiction fan, began to form a minuscule idea of the mission of the 509th. To learn more of atomic theory, I checked a book from the base library entitled, "Atoms in Action". Shortly thereafter, I was visited by a very curious CIC Agent in my quarters. I played it cool. Later I was interviewed by his superior and others.

To make a long story short, I was immediately qualified for overseas service, my MOS (Military Occupational Status) number was changed, and I realized my hope of transferring into the 509th. The only conditions were to keep quiet and do my job.

MPs on Tinian
(L-R): Maurice Sullivan, Philip Matranga, Earl Thorstrom, Louis Hefferman, Winton Bagley, Ray Jensen, Harry Herman, Natalie Reale

SWASEY, HERBERT D.
603rd Air Engineering Squadron

Enlisted in the Army Air Corps October 16, 1942 in San Francisco, California and was sent to Presidio of Monterey for one week to received shots and other procedures. From there, went to Air Cadet Advance Training Center at Stockton Field California to work on AT6s, advanced single engine planes. It was cold working on them at the flight line. Also did Kitchen Police (KP) duty for the mess hall. Reported for duty at 4:30 or 5 am and worked steady until 7 or 8pm.

Left Stockton Field June or July 1943 for Chapman College, Los Angeles for Army Specialized Training Program Unit 3937 to start August 9, 1943. This was an accelerated program needing education etc to qualify for Officers' Candidate School (OCS). I didn't make it! I was transferred to Army Air Force Redistribution Center, Kerns, Utah. Left Kerns, via train en route to sheet metal school at Chanute Field, Rantoul, Illinois, 150 miles south of Chicago. Unfortunately, while on the train, I fell asleep next to an open window in the Pullman car. The temperature was very cold and I developed an earache which stayed with me to Chicago where I was admitted to USA Gardiner General Hospital October 6, 1943 for evaluation. My ear was infected needing a mastoid operation which prevented me from taking the train to Chanute Field.

After almost four months of being observed, I left the hospital January 30, 1944 for Chanute Field to work with sheet metal, power machines, mechanical drawing and airplane metal. Upon completion of training was transferred to Army Air Base (AAB) Lincoln, Nebraska for a short time then to AAB McCook, Nebraska to work in sheet metal shop.

I left there November 1944 for Wendover Air Base to join the 509th Composite Group, 603rd Air Engineering Squadron. While there, I had a three day pass to Salt Lake City that was good until 12am Sunday night. However, if you passed through the MP Gate to enter the Base by 8am Monday, you were OK. I was waiting in the bus station to leave Salt Lake City at 2am when in comes an MP who checked my pass. Because the pass

left: Cpl Herbert D. Swasey
right: Sgt Kenneth C. Ferst

was up at midnight, he immediately took me to MP Headquarters for questioning and to empty my pockets. I was taken back to the station to catch a later bus arriving in Wendover about 10 am reporting to the First Sergeant. He must have heard from the MPs because he didn't seem too disturbed by my late arrival.

Wendover Field was very desolate as were most Air Force Bases in the US. The Western Pacific Railroad ran through Wendover and the station was close. One time, some coaches were deadheading empty to Salt Lake City; I was in uniform and the conductor told me to take a free ride to Salt Lake City, but warned me to duck and cover when going through the switching towers in the Salt Lake rail yards.

I had a three day pass to visit my hometown of San Francisco 650 miles away. A friend had a Lincoln at Wendover Field so three of us

Rail tickets to Wendover

took the journey leaving at 5 pm, driving all night and arriving on the San Francisco Bay Bridge at 8am! This was pretty amazing considering there were no freeways, two lane roads all the way, Sierra Nevada Mountain roads and one had to go through all towns and cities. We stopped in Reno, Nevada forty-five minutes.

On another three day pass from Wendover, I wanted to visit Salt Lake City. A friend and I were in his car and we took turns driving. The trip to Salt Lake City went without incident and we had a great time. However, we stayed in SLC as long as possible before starting the 125 mile drive before dawn knowing we had to be through the gate at 8am. While driving, I fell asleep crossing the Salt Flats and was awakened by the sound of running over gravel! Fortunately, we missed hitting telephone poles and who knows what else! That did it for me. I turned the wheel over to my friend and we made it through the gates before 8am.

About midway through my stay at Wendover, my buddy received orders for transfer to other duty. Next day he was gone! No word of why, how or where he went.

I remember going to the PX and buying cigarettes for five cents a pack, fifty cents a carton. I didn't smoke so gave them to a girlfriend.

We left Wendover headed to Seattle, Washington for Pacific deployment. On May 6, 1945, we boarded a troop transport Victory Ship named Cape Victory with crowded bunks in the hold where it became too hot to

sleep. Many times I left my bunk to sleep on deck which was OK until it rained.

On May 29, 1945, we arrived on Tinian, an island six miles wide and twelve miles long of white coral as that is what the North Field runways were made of. There were four parallel runways; largest air field in the world guarded with Military Police. The fifteen special built B29s and Headquarters were located on the northwest corner of the runway. Security was very tight with the 509th. I never saw the Enola Gay or visited 509th Headquarters.

Our groups were living in tents on the northeast corner of the island two or three miles apart from North Field. We worked in sheet metal shops repairing planes hit by flack over Japan. None of the 509th was battle damaged due to flying at altitudes over 30,000 feet. We made our own diving masks, in metal shop, to see a lot while swimming in the warm, clear water at the beaches. It was a very pretty place with lots of sugar cane fields and coral caves.

We left Tinian via ship for San Francisco October 17, 1945, arriving November 4, 1945, then were sent to Roswell Air Base, New Mexico. While driving from Roswell to be honorably discharged as a Sergeant from the US Army Air Force at Santa Ana Air Base in Riverside, near Los Angeles in February 1946, we filled the gas tank along with two five gallon cans for the small sum of five or maybe ten cents per gallon!

TUCKER, JOHN L.
Project Alberta

Just a few words concerning my short Naval career. I was sent to Oak Ridge along with 150 other Navy Reserve Officers in March 1943 to help get the place operational. They were not able to recruit enough civilian personnel to get the place up and running. In late February 1945, Lt Commander Norris Bradbury, and a Dr. Brode (the Spectroscopist at Ohio University) came out from Los Alamos and recruited 50 us of to come to Los Alamos. Norris recruited me to be a member of the "Destination Team". I was the only one so recruited from Oak Ridge of those that went to Los Alamos. I jumped at the chance and got to Los Alamos in late March of 1945. I was assigned to the Firing Unit Team, with Lou Fussell, the Group Leader and Lt Commander Stevenson as the Assistant Group Leader.

I helped build the first X-Unit Bread Board Prototype before shipping it off to Raytheon for making of the Mark I which was shortly thereafter upgraded to the Mark II. As a designated Destination Team member, I spent my time back and forth to Wendover where I worked with our assembly people there, members of the First Ordnance Squadron. When we left Los Alamos, we could not tell people where we were going and when we arrived, we could not tell people where we had come from. When at Los Alamos, I helped design X-Unit handling equipment, wrote X-Unit disassembly, inspection, test and assembly check sheets. I also worked on getting materials ready and shipping them to Trinity.

In late June 1945, three of us Buck Ensigns, Bill Prohs, Barney O'Keefe and myself were selected to go to Tinian and get our facilities ready. Our people of the 509th had already preceded us to Tinian. Before leaving, I asked "What if our tools, etc. that had been sent by boat earlier did not arrive, or got lost"? I was allowed to make up a box of supplementary tools, miscellaneous meters, etc. I put a big wooden box on a push cart, pushed it up and down the warehouse isles, and threw in all the tools, etc. I thought might be needed if our regular tools did not arrive. These I had sent to Tinian by a Green Hornet plane.

We three left San Francisco on July 4, 1945 along with Capt. Parsons to go to Tinian. On arrival at Guam, Capt. Parsons took us with him up to Admiral Nimitz' Headquarters where he briefed the Admiral on what was about to happen. The three of us waited in the outer office during this time and were entertained by three Navy Captains. Parsons then took us to Tinian where we were billeted with the Sea Bees until our regular facilities were completed. After his inspections and meetings, Parsons immediately left to return to Los Alamos and Trinity. Unknown to me, Harlow Russ and Lt Victor Miller had preceded us there, however, I did not know this until after we came home.

O'Keefe and I went about getting things set up for the Firing Unit Section. Prohs was with the Radar

Section and did the same with them. Our assembly site was shortly thereafter completed and we began moving into our assigned Quonset Assembly buildings. We could not find our tools, inspection and test equipment sent by ship, but the tools I had sent by Green Hornet were there, and that is what we used. I set up a small open Quonset Hut just back of our main assembly building to house the Bowen Rotating Mirror Camera where I did the final acceptance testing of the X-Units for Fat Man. I found one that was better than the other two and that was the one used.

After Trinity, the rest of the Alberta people jumped on a plane and came to Tinian. We then did our thing and subsequently came home.

After VJ Day, the lost tools and equipment were found very neatly packaged and cosmolined. They were beautiful kits, but our job was over and we had no use for them then. Before we went home, we loaded these kits and most of the other tools and equipment we had brought over, into a Landing Ship Tank (LST), took it out to sea and dumped it overboard.

Orders to establish laboratory at destination (Tinian)

186

VAN PELT, JAMES F., NAVIGATOR
ALBURY, CHARLES D., AIRPLANE COMMANDER
393rd Bomb Squadron, Crew 15, Unpublished Manuscript 1946

Our group was originally designed to be self-sustaining. This was one of the main reasons we went to Batista, to test our ability to move quickly. We designed the group in such a way that we had our own service groups. We had our own metalsmiths. We could make a complete repair and almost build a ship; also had quite a few technicians. Everything was moved from Wendover to Batista. We carried the equipment in our airplanes, B29s and C54s. We moved in two days carrying crews, spare parts, crewchief stands, engines, bombing and navigating equipment, etc.

When we first arrived in Batista, we were the only outfit there. The Gypsy Task Force moved in later. It was a B29 outfit with P51s attached to it. Their type of training was mostly made up of long missions, very light bombardment. We didn't have much to do with them. The Gypsy Task Force lost about five or six airplanes and crews. One was when a B29 caught fire on takeoff and exploded. Another one was coming in low on gas and ran out just on the edge of the runway about two feet in the air and burned when it hit the ground. It killed everybody. The other three went down in the Atlantic.

Our crew (C15) was only there about two weeks. The group was at Batista for two months and their training was just about over when our crew arrived. We were doing text work in Wendover when the group moved to Batista. Tibbets, Ferebee, Beahan, Van Kirk, Luetcke, Col. Payette, Jim McFall and I went down to Batista to see what they had to offer us as a training school, practice bombs, medical assistance, etc. and to see what we would have to take with us. We went back to Wendover and finally decided to take everything down with us. We used C54s mostly for handling cargo, but the B29s took everything they could, passengers, spare parts, engines. Col. Classen was in charge down there to fly familiarization flights.

The bombing range was southeast of Cuba in the middle of the Caribbean Ocean and was a perfect radar target. The uninhabited island had a lagoon in the center. They picked this point because water is so easy to pick up in the radar scope. The target was in the middle of the lagoon. On the first flight, you had to be at least 20,000 feet above the terrain. We were using regular 100 lb. practice bombs. The island was about a mile long and one-fourth mile wide.

On these radar bombing missions, we briefed about 6 am and took off about 7 am. We had 20 practice bombs, one half to be dropped by radar and one half dropped visually. We were over the target by 9:30 am. In Cuba, we used the left hand traffic pattern. It was a triangular course. The airplanes would be so spread out that it took two runs to drop one bomb. You could drop one about every fifteen minutes. We had to leave the range about 12pm and then the Gypsy Task Force took over. That put us in the air from 7 am until 12 pm. We carried about 4000 gallons of gasoline. We tried to save our engines as much as possible. We had to change five engines

Charles Albury (left) and Jim Van Pelt (right)

while we were down there. They were the old type B29s with Curtis Wright engines. The reason for the engine failures was the low octane fuel we were buying from the Cuban Government. We had pretty good luck, managing to keep about 95% of our planes in the air. The other groups averaged about 50%.

We were to have 10 missions of radar bombing and to have four long-range, over water, cross country flights. One from Havana to Bermuda, from Havana to Bermuda to Richmond and return, making no landings. The weather used to be so bad that the Richmond flight was cut out. They decided Bermuda was hard enough to find. One of them was a radar mission that we would fly an archipelago down there. It went all the way to Puerto Rico and back. It was a very good radar drop. Navigation was done mostly by the radar operator. The navigator would use celestial navigation to be sure we didn't get lost. The flights were made at night. It was about 1500 miles, taking around seven hours. As far as our crew was concerned, we didn't go on any of these cross countries.

Sweeney got his nickname in Cuba. On our first trip to Cuba, we went over to Havana one night. We got into Havana about noon, giving us the afternoon for shopping. They have a "Siesta" in Cuba every afternoon, so when we got there everything was closed.

We went to the Hotel National and got rooms. There was Sweeney, Beahan, McFall, Col. Payette, Van Pelt and myself. We had three rooms. We took baths and got dressed. By that time, the "Siesta" was over so we all went shopping. Beahan wasn't in a hurry to do any shopping so he left us. Most of the boys were looking for shoes, silk hose, alligator purses, etc. Beahan went into a bar and we were to meet him later. Col. Payette, Sweeney, Jim and I started a little bit of shopping. Col. Payette dropped out, so that left the three of us. Our taxi driver, named Jocko, was taking us around. We decided that every time we passed a bar, we would take a drink. Finally, we had made our purchases and were in a little curio shop buying some liquor to take back to the hotel. We were sampling the Cuban Rum, very good rum. The clerk gave us about four samples of the stuff; so we were really lit up. It was about five in the afternoon, none of us could see very well. We picked up Beahan and decided to go back to the hotel. Sweeney was in a very loving mood whenever he got tipsy. He was telling everybody he loved them. He was putting his arms around the cab driver and said "Jocko, I love you". That's when we started calling him Jocko. We found out later that the taxi driver got a percentage on everything we bought. He was telling another cab driver that he had made about $80 on us that trip. Beahan could understand enough Spanish that he knew what he was telling the other cab driver. This occurred on our second trip to Cuba. Beahan and I actually walked into a bar that Jocko was in and Bee heard him talking to another driver.

On February 1st, our crew flew three crews to Batista Field in Cuba for training. We arrived in Cuba and spent four or five days, most of it in Havana, where we stayed at the Hotel National. In Cuba, they had taxicabs waiting at the gate at Batista Field. We hired them for the weekend. They would drive you to Havana, some 16 or 20 miles to the hotel, and after we rested at the hotel, they would drive you to the various shopping places in Havana all during the day and take you to the various places at night. On our first trip, we did a lot of shopping in the afternoon and didn't take anything to drink until 6 o'clock, and finally stopped at Sloppy Joe's and got started. Everyone who goes to Havana visits Sloppy Joe's. The result is we got started before sunset and all got drunk before dinner. Colonel Payette was with us on this trip. Sunday, we visited Morro Castle and many historic points of interest. Sunday night we took in a jai alai game, which is quite impressive the first time you see it. We came back to the States on Tuesday, and in a few days packed our bags, and went down to Cuba ourselves for two or three weeks training.

Sweeney was unable to go with us as he was the Commanding Officer of a Troop Carrier outfit at that time. Don took the crew down with Russ Angeli as copilot because, at that time, Olivi had not been appointed to our outfit. Spitzer was home on furlough, so we took another radio operator. We went down to Cuba on Thursday morning, started flying the following day, and did not miss a single day flying while we completed our training. Colonel Tom Classen took Beahan and me out the first day. He taught us how to bomb by radar. I dropped several bombs, but couldn't hit anywhere near the island. We were bombing Cayo Travesia, which is about 186 miles southeast of Batista Field. The next day, we took our own crew out but we didn't do much better. After many days of bombing, we increased our efficiency in radar bombing to the point where we got very accurate. In the evening, around five, the bar opened. We could get a scotch and soda for around 25 cents, so it was only natural for many of the boys to do a lot of drinking. We had to be up at 5 am for 7 am take off. We wouldn't be down from our bombing mission until 1 or 2 pm.

Our crew was living in the same Bachelor Officers Quarters (BOQ) as Colonel Classen. Colonel Leutcke, who was our Deputy Commander at this time, flew down to see us. He landed about 1 am and was going to stay in our BOQ. He missed the party and decided that he

would start a party of his own. We had all just gotten into bed. The Colonel came and got me up; he had a bottle. We were going down to the next room to get Beahan up. Apparently, we woke Colonel Classen up and he gave me heck for being up. He told me to go back to bed. This other colonel gave me heck for being in bed and told me to get up. There I was in the middle of it. Anyway, I finally went to bed, but the colonel couldn't get a room, so he had to sleep in the hall right next to my room, so I might as well have been up.

We had bought a lot of stockings, shoes for our children and ourselves, clothes, and other items of that nature, which we were going to bring back in our B29s when we came back to the States. We were very worried about customs people because we had to stop at Galveston, Texas, and stand a customs inspection. Actually, there were about 12 B29s at the same time and we all landed at Galveston. The customs people checked the first one and took so long to check the airplane and all the personal belongings of the various men and the ground crews that they gave up and let the other planes pass through.

One morning, we were to be on a test mission calibrating our airspeed indicator on the calibration course in Wendover. We had been out with the group the night before for a party. Dickinson, who was the chief engineer for Douglas Corporation was checking us. We got home about 1 or 2 am and managed to get to bed about 3am. We had to get up at 4 am in order to take off at 5 am. The reason we had to take off so early was that once the sun was up, you get a lot of thermals which made the air bumpy and made it hard to hold a true, steady speed. The velocity of the winds is less also. (Bea and Albury were living together as Albury's wife had gone home.) I called Beahan at 4 am and he was grouchy and feeling bad. He said, "A great artiste like me doesn't have to get up this early". He lets the other boys take care of that. It was all in a bragging manner, so after that we called him "The Great Artiste". We used to kid him a lot in Cuba.

When we went overseas, the personal affairs officer wanted to know the name of our plane. The boys submitted a lot of names. I think every member of the crew put the name "The Great Artiste" in at least once. After the process of elimination, "The Great Artiste" was unanimously chosen. It was named just before our first mission.

June 1st we flew to Omaha, Nebraska in a C54 to pick up our B29 The Great Artiste, serial number AC 44-27353. We checked it out at Omaha, took it to Wendover Field Utah, where the ground crew checked the airplane for three weeks before we left for Mather Field Sacramento, California, June 21, 1945.

Spent two days at Port of Embarkation (POE) in classroom being indoctrinated in over water training under the direction of the Air Transport Command. We left Mather Field June 23rd, 3 am on a perfect flight to John Rogers Field, Oahu Island, approximately 2400 miles, arriving there the same day in time to go downtown and have our last fling at civilization before leaving the next morning. The entire crew hit all the bars. It was real warm when we arrived in Oahu and we proceeded to Waikiki Beach to find it very short, very narrow and stopped to ask where it was because this was too small. Bea,

Albury, Olivi, Sweeney, Van Pelt had a few drinks, a big dinner and turned in early for a good night's sleep.

We took off the next morning about nine o'clock, proceeded 750 miles from Hawaii over a speck in a great big ocean called Johnston Island without stopping.

We were passing another airplane of our group commanded by Lt. Col. Tom Classen who was Deputy Commander of the 509th Composite Group. We were following radio compass but missed the Island of Kwajalein under a 300 foot ceiling because of a thunderstorm. Albury immediately cut our power setting down through the overcast on top the water and into Kwajalein some distance behind Classen. We were supposed to miss Woje Island because that point was being held by Japs and planes that flew over were fired upon. It is said but not authenticated, that General Harmon was shot down here. This was in a direct line from Johnston Island to Kwajalein.

We had to wait 1 1/2 hours for transportation to our quarters consisting of old Japanese barracks which were two story, frail, flimsy construction, stairs on front and back outside, sides run up 3/4, then ceiling to roof with no windows. The officers were sleeping upstairs and enlisted men downstairs. During the night, a rat bit into Sgt. Buckley's toe causing it to bleed freely. Kwajalein was hot, close, sultry, food was poor, conditions were terrible. It was the kind of place you didn't want to stay in long. The quicker you could get out the better and you wouldn't care about getting back.

Tinian

We left there the next morning, flying 1200 miles West Northwest enroute to Tinian, which was to be our new home. The weather was beautiful the last 200 miles into Tinian as we let down right over the water, we could see the line of Mariannas Islands. It is really beautiful from the air. It is approximately 1000 statute miles south of the Japanese Empire, three miles south of Saipan, 70 miles north of Rota and 155 miles north of Guam. It is approximately 12 miles long, 5 miles wide and shaped like South America. It is built up on coral, primarily a rock. The water surrounding the island is said to have the greatest depth in the world. The climate is typical of all tropical climates. The temperature never rises as high as some parts of Texas, but there is so much moisture that it is always close, during the months of July and August becoming almost unbearable. During the rainy season, some parts of the island are swamped 24 hours a day to exceed 120 inches a year. It pours to such an extent that raincoats are useless. Sweeney contacted our home base tower at North Field, supposedly the largest air field in the world.

We arrived at noon June 27, 1945 and went to lunch. We were greeted by friends who immediately told us about Japs killing island personnel and scared us all. Gives you quite a feeling to look at this beautiful island of mostly white coral, covered with thick, green foliage and wonder how many Japs were looking at or drawing a bead on you, but after 24 hours, you had forgotten all about this. Albury had heard so much about wandering Japs that he slept with his gun right beside him the first night, saying at the first sound, I'm going to shoot. I was afraid to go

to the latrine for fear he would mistake me for a Jap and shoot.

The Seabees constructed the buildings, landscaped and cleared foliage. The roads were asphalt, laid out on the same plan as the streets in New York City, thus we had Broadway, 42nd Street, Boston Post Road, etc. They constructed the roads with such speed, you could go out in the morning on a dirt road, returning the same evening on a completed asphalt highway.

The natives on Tinian were Korean laborers resembling Japanese in stature and appearance, speaking Japanese and having most of their customs with respect to religion and living conditions. The Japs brought laborers from other islands, Okinawa, Korea, Iwo, etc. These people were used in sugar cane fields and mills to produce much of Japan's sugar.

Tinian Town was their local city located on the south end of the island. When the island was invaded, the Navy bombarded the town, composed of concrete structures housing a population of about 8000 people, to rubble. All during the air offensive, our infantry troops were capturing Japanese prisoners who had infiltrated the mountains. Some of our souvenir hunters went out and were later found by search parties sometimes cut into pieces. The native men were used as laborers and cleanup details around camp, while the women were used in laundries. They were afraid to have their pictures taken because we couldn't convince them the Japanese were defeated and not coming back.

The method of capturing Japanese prisoners was quite unusual. They would form search parties with a couple Japanese trustee prisoners; go into the hills and while they lay on their stomachs with guns down, the trustees would try to convince the die hards to surrender. Some wouldn't until they killed a Yankee and would go back into the hills; others that did would keep their word. This was Jim McFall's experience.

Our camp was situated on the northwest side of the island, approximately 300 yards from the waterfront. It had been a Seabee camp consisting of quonset huts and tents. The flying officers of our group had about seven of these huts in which they and three crews all lived together. Between our camp area and the ocean was the American grave yard which was kept in perfect condition. No mother need fear her son's grave would be mistreated in any US cemetery. The casualty rate for the flying crews was so great they had to keep 15 of these graves open at all times. A disheartening sight to pass every time you went on a mission.

In every camp area, we had a theatre that showed the latest pictures released, free to GIs. It consisted of a screen, approximately 40 or 50 rows of wooden benches, no roof or sides, open skies and we had to sacrifice dry clothes to watch during the rainy season.

Tinian had two fields: North Field belonged to the 313th Bombardment Wing where our group was located, with a runway east and west, 9000 feet long; West Field, located in the center of the island, was used exclusively by the 58th Wing who was the first B29 outfit to go overseas. They operated out of China and India during 1944 with a very high casualty rate.

There was another small island about five miles south of Tinian, to which many Japanese swam when

Tinian fell to our troops. After their town was completely demolished, our Government turned a large number of packing cases over to them for constructing homes consisting of one room with floor. As far as I know, about 8000 lived in one area as large as five square city blocks, although some committed suicide by jumping off the rocks located on the northeast side.

The natives were checked by MPs every morning when they went out and every evening when they came in. The harbor was located on the south side of the island. It was impossible to go swimming anywhere without wearing some type of shoes as coral existed everywhere on the ocean bed. A coral foot cut caused swelling within 12 hours, redness, throbbing and the person being subject to a nasty infection.

The Route to the Japanese Empire

It was standard operating procedure to fly first to Iwo Jima, on to Japan and return the opposite way. The reason was long distance using Iwo as a check point for the navigator and as an auxiliary field in case of any flight problems. On take off from Tinian, it was necessary to fly parallel to the island of Saipan for five minutes to avoid Saipan's field of heavy air traffic. Usually, we would course over the north tip of Saipan where our navigation aids, radio range and radar beacons were located, also on Iwo, with loran stations located on Guam, Ulitha, Okinawa, Philippines and China.

Weather

Europe, the Aleutians etc. all have their peculiarities, but in the Pacific, it is quite different than anywhere else. The Cumulus Clouds build up to such an extent that it makes island recognition almost impossible since they look like small islands themselves after flying for many hours. The weather over Japan was roughest during the winter when the Empire was overcast at times up to 30,000 feet or higher approximately 75% of the time, causing us to use radar a great deal. The wind velocity at high altitudes would be as strong as 200 miles per hour causing one B29 flying over a target to actually go backwards. During the summer months when the 509th Composite Group was operating, the winds averaged between 25 and 60 miles an hour, resembling that of the US.

Air Sea Rescue

The Army and Navy working together perfected a plan that saved many flyers after they ditched in the broad Pacific Ocean. No one can realize the vast size of the Pacific until they have seen it. You can fly for hours without seeing a single island, then see a small uninhabited coral island about one mile square. Imagine yourself downed a thousand miles from your home base in this vast ocean. To combat this, the Army and Navy perfected an excellent air sea rescue system consisting of; first, radio contact between headquarters in the Marianas with all airplanes flying over water; second, destroyers and submarines were placed along the route so they could bail out as close to them as possible. Nothing can be said that would be enough to credit the work these unsung heros did during the latter days of the air offensive against Japan. The Air Force sent out B29s called Super Dumbos while the Navy sent smaller Dumbos to fly the route and stay in certain positions until every airplane had been accounted for (Catalina PBYs were Dumbos).

Over water navigation is quite different than over land. A typical mission would consist of taking off, caging your gyro fluxgate compass, turning your drift meter on, turning your loran set on, calling the radar operator to turn radar set on. After five minutes, the pilot turned on course as previously explained climbing to prescribed altitude to conform with flight plan drawn up by group operations. During this time, the navigator was taking drift readings (the effect of wind on the airplane that needs correcting to keep the plane on prescribed true course), observing altitude, airspeed, computing true airspeed, determining deviation of gyro fluxgate compass by means of Astro Compass, an instrument that determines deviation by observing the sun, stars or planets. He is also determining ground speed, checking compass to see that pilot is on course, taking radar readings on a radar beam, reading loran set, taking radio bearings for radio station if available, sun lines and IOPs if one is in an overcast. Usually 30 to 45 minutes is allowed to elapse before any celestial observations are used. Climb is 30 minutes to an hour depending on what altitude is desired. Censorship prevents our giving accurate figures on the B29 climb.

Being in the test crew, we had always known something big was up. After arriving overseas and flying missions with another type of bomb, we

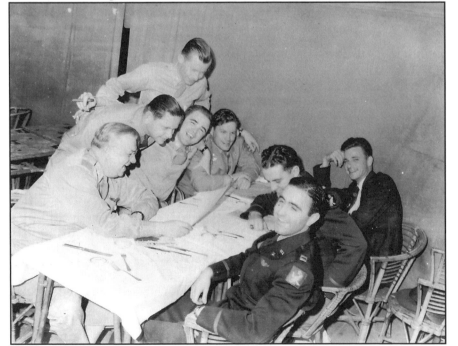

Standing: Jim McFall
Top Row, (L-R): Hazen Payette, Don Albury, Charles Sweeney, Kermit Beahan. Looking at camera: Jim Van Pelt, Capt. Ed Lucke, Security Man

lost some of the strain of flying an atomic bomb. Around August 1st, six crews were called into our camp area Intelligence Room. Our Intelligence Officer, Lt. Col. Payette, showed us three atomic bomb targets, Hiroshima, Kokura, and Nagasaki to memorize backwards, forwards, and in our sleep. I remember my reaction when I first heard these were the targets. In all our briefings, Capt. Joe Busher, our Intelligence Briefing Officer, told us not to drop bombs on any of the named targets because of Prisoner of War (POW) camps located there. That was a sure way to keep us away from assigned atomic targets.

In our operations over Japan, we flew each mission individually with a special assigned target to test radar bombing. If there were both mountains, a river running through, or harbor, we could proceed; but one without the other would cause interference with radar and we would go on to another target.

The intelligence obtained detailed pictures of the three targets from the 20th Air Force with all the important information as to population, industries, harbors, shipping, and military fighter strength. For one solid week these six crews spent three or four hours a day in the Intelligence Library studying these charts with MPs guarding the building. Our camp was situated away from the others, so there was little contact with other personnel.

The day before the early morning takeoff of the Hiroshima mission, we had a special briefing with pictures, about the atomic bomb test in New Mexico, which had taken place July 16, 1945. Rear Admiral Parsons, then Captain, gave us correct information of how much shock to expect, what the cloud and flash would be like down to the smallest detail. The other crews studying these three targets were Major George Marquardt, Major Fred Bock, Major Buck Eatherly and Captain McKnight. This specialized briefing took place from 3 to 4pm, we returned to our quonset huts to relax and weather permitting, we would take off early the next morning. Col. Tibbets had obtained permission to drop the first bomb two days earlier from General Arnold, who didn't want him to because of his knowledge of the bombing mission. In case something should happen, they didn't want him hurt or captured. Otherwise, Sweeney's crew would have gone.

All time throughout the story is on 24 hour basis: 6 pm is 1800, etc.

At 1800, we had a briefing which lasted two hours. We were then instructed to go back to bed and relax. Things were really quiet around camp. We could feel the tension knowing this particular mission was different. We all realized the importance the outcome would have on the whole world.

At 2200, we had another briefing at which time we were given the weather report, flight plans, air/sea rescue communication, charts, intelligence reports, special briefing and speech by Col. Tibbets. He only made three speeches the entire time on Tinian. One was before our first mission, one before the first atomic bomb mission, and one before the Nagasaki mission. We finished our briefing about 2400 at which time we had a late snack at the mess hall including fried eggs, a rare occasion in the Pacific. After eating, we loaded into waiting trucks, stopped by the quonset hut to pick up our chutes and navigation equipment and had a quiet ride to the parking ramp. It was a beautiful night with stars out and weather reports indicating the Japanese Empire would be clear the next morning.

The 509th had their own parking area with the Enola Gay next to the Great Artiste. They had two big sets of Hollywood studio lights consisting of a steel rack with about thirty lights on wheels so it could be moved around. They were positioned around the Enola Gay while photographers were taking pictures of Col. Tibbets and his crew. Captain Parsons was to accompany Col. Tibbets on this mission as a Naval Ordnance expert. Admiral Purnell, in charge of this project was there with General Farrell plus many

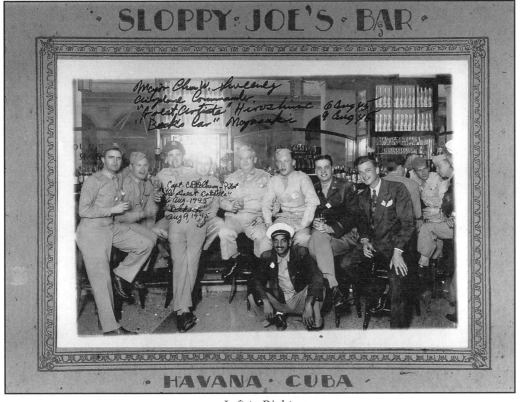

Left to Right:
Jim VanPelt, Kermit Beahan, Charles Sweeney, Charles Albury, Hazen Payette, Jim McFall, Capt. Ed Lucke, Security Man, "Jocko" kneeling

scientists and officials. Chaplain Bill Downey came to wish us good luck and he would see them upon their return. Captain Mel Irwin, our assistant intelligence officer, was always there to write something on our bomb and instruments regardless of takeoff time.

Our three weather ships commanded by Eatherly, Taylor and Willson took off an hour ahead of us, each to one of the three targets, Hiroshima, Kokura and Nagasaki. Complete radio silence was essential so we could listen to their radio broadcasting frequency. An hour from our turning point, we would receive weather reports from these three ships telling us which target was clear.

The ground crews as well as some officers helped pull the props through, which on the B29 required the efforts of both. Chuck Sweeney went over to bid the Colonel good luck and good bye. At 0200 Col. Tibbets started his engines; a minute later, we started ours. At 0210, the Colonel started taxing with us following shortly thereafter. At 0315, the Colonel took off on runway A (Able). We could see the Colonel taxing, gaining flight speed and finally airborne with the world's first atomic bomb. Two minutes later, we took off on runway B (Baker). Just about the time we hit the end of the runway, Chuck

pushed throttles forward, released brakes and we were off. Takeoff was to the east so we circled around Saipan across the northern tip and proceeded on course to Iwo Jima. We were flying formation with George Marquardt in the photo plane on Colonel Tibbets left wing, while we were on his right wing with the instruments. Chuck Sweeney stayed in the first pilot seat with Don Albury flying in the copilot seat. John Kuharek kept checking instruments and gasoline consumption, while Beahan relaxed in a reclining position with his feet resting on one side of his bomb sight with his pillow he carried on all missions for comfort. Chuck and Don would take turns waking Bea, making him very unhappy. Once he was up, he would call me asking a thousand questions about position, altitude, time of day, weather, anything to annoy me. If I seemed to disregard it, he would make a special trip back to my compartment to talk to me. Sweeney came back to see how we were doing and check the charts so if anything came up he would have a thorough knowledge of the mission navigation.

We had a scientist on board explaining many things about the bomb to Chuck and Don. The enlisted men chattered over innerphone for a while after takeoff, but

(L-R): Marquardt Crew; Sweeney Crew
having all received Air Medal for Hiroshima mission

soon all but one scanner were asleep. Pappy was not in his tail gunner's position so there were three in the rear compartment. We reached Iwo right after daylight and could see Colonel Tibbets ahead of us. It looked to be a beautiful day, the weather was almost perfect. There were a few clouds over the water but I can't remember any day I spent in the Pacific when it was more perfect for flying than it was on August 6th. We could see boats around Iwo with their hulls sticking out of the water, airplanes were taking off and landing. Chuck was still in radio contact with the Colonel submitting position reports to aid the operator every hour and a half in case of a ditching. We could see a few ships we had to classify, record their position, speed and direction of travel in the navigator's log. At 2030 hours, we sighted the Japanese coast. Colonel Tibbets contacted the weather planes and Buck Eatherly, who was flying over Hiroshima, told the Colonel the weather was perfect at the primary target. The Colonel called Chuck and said, "Chuck, it is Hiroshima". Our three plane formation turned course to fly across the island of Shikoku, that looked like a dark green mass, to our initial point (IP) 60 miles east of Hiroshima. There were a few clouds, radar reception was perfect, the crew had grown very quiet and were alert. Within a half hour of the coast, the crew put on their parachutes, C1 vests and flak suits except those moving around too much. We wore our May Wests at all times. The Colonel turned on course for a bomb run on Hiroshima. We were all getting very tense. The minutes seemed like hours. Finally, the Colonel opened his bomb

bay doors. We could see Hiroshima ahead and below us. It is located on the water front of Honshu Island with seven rivers and an old castle in the center very near our target. A bombardier could not ask for a more perfect day. We put on our welder's goggles. Finally, Beahan called "bombs away". Chuck threw the plane into a steep left turn about 180 degrees and got out of there. Even with our goggles on, we could see a brilliant flash said to be brighter than the sun. We removed our goggles to see the entire city of Hiroshima covered with dust and debris. The smoke cloud had already built up to about 15,000 feet and looked like a big mushroom head. It was at least five miles in circumference. After leaving the coast of Japan, we removed all our equipment for the return trip.

We flew back to Iwo Jima arriving about a half hour after Colonel Tibbets. After landing, he adjusted his flying equipment, completed Form 1, and checked with the engineer before departing the aircraft. General Spaatz, accompanied by many high officials and dignitaries, presented Colonel Tibbets with the Distinguished Service Cross and congratulated him for a job well done.

We started briefing for the flight on 8 August 1945, a dummy drop test. We were supposed to go to Iwo but the weather got bad so Commander Ashworth decided, before the flight, we could fly out between two submarine lanes, which were 180 miles apart, approximately 300 miles east of Tinian where we dropped the test bomb. When we returned about 2pm, in interrogation we found out we were going to fly the next morning. We had a

Don Albury receives congratulations for receiving Air Medal from Gen Davies for Hiroshima mission

Gen Davies, 313th Wing, congratulates Maj Sweeney for Hiroshima mission. Maj Sweeney has just received the Air Medal. James Van Pelt and Kermit Beahan are next.

test from Hazen Payette, map study, etc. Beahan and all of us had to study the target and learn it by heart. They started briefing us about 4pm to go over the target and course again with Payette. They briefed us until 6pm and after supper we went to the show. They had everybody working on the planes. We had specialized briefings until 9pm, then went back to the Quonset hut and ate at 11pm. When we had our final briefing, we found out there was a typhoon hitting Iwo, so we were going to have to fly through to Yakashima.

The final briefing was about the same as the first. The Colonel got up, gave a little speech; in a general way said this was something new, not dangerous; it was going to make the first one obsolete; Washington was watching along with General LeMay and we would have to do a good job because of that. The briefing was secret with guards outside the door. They didn't show us any pictures as they were all shown before the Hiroshima mission. About 1am, Gallagher went to the mess hall for food, we got into trucks and went to the airplane. There were Hollywood flood lights around the lane when we arrived. The procedure for going to the airplane early was to check all their equipment and be sure the plane was completely overhauled and ready for operation before takeoff; including preflight fuel inspection, gas lines leading from gas tanks through nacelles to the engines, check shimmy damper for right amount of fluids, tires for proper inflation pressure, brake lines for hydraulic fluid, gear motors for pulled plugs for traction and landing gear operation, make sure there were no broken, cracked or frayed cables, no excessive oil in the cells. Also, check inspection plates underneath your wing that unscrew to check flight control cables, check ailerons, elevators and rudder for tears, go around fuselage making sure there are no holes doing same procedures on the right wing. We looked over the maps while they took pictures.

Everybody came to the hard-stand to say good-bye along with Rear Admiral Purnell, General McFarley, Colonel Tibbets, Ted Van Kirk, and Tom Ferebee. Mel Irwin was the only one to write on our bomb. This time they knew what was going to happen; the first time, they didn't.

Bob Lewis made me uneasy because he scared me about what would happen if we had a salvo (bomb release) on takeoff.

We had two bomb bays, forward and aft, where the two fuel tanks were located. The upper bomb bay

Hazen Payette

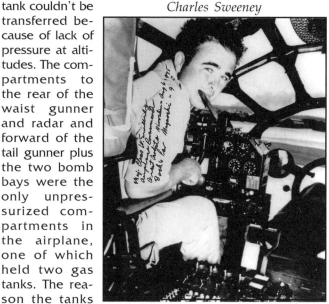

Charles Sweeney

tank couldn't be transferred because of lack of pressure at altitudes. The compartments to the rear of the waist gunner and radar and forward of the tail gunner plus the two bomb bays were the only unpressurized compartments in the airplane, one of which held two gas tanks. The reason the tanks were in back was the plane was stripped of all armor from behind the engineer's panel and bomb bay. They left it behind the pilot and copilot's seats and bullet resistant glass in front on top of the instrument panel. The only guns we had were two 50 caliber machine guns in the tail. They took out four 50 caliber from the upper fore turrets and two from the lower rear turrets along with the central fire control system. Taking out all this armor made the airplane nose heavy. The reason the gas tanks were in the rear bomb bay was to equalize the weight and balance to the center of gravity.

Before each flight, if the airplane has been on the ground more than an hour, we always pull the props through. The crew gets together and pulls each of the four blades through four times making sixteen pulls. It is quite a bit of compression. It takes two men to pull one blade through. When the airplane stands for any length of time, the oil leaks through the bottom cylinders of the engine and when you pull the blade through, it releases this oil if you have an oil lock. When you get too much oil in the cylinders, the pressure is so great it will break the crank shaft or bend or burst the cylinder head.

John Kuharek couldn't transfer 300 gallons of fuel from the lower tank. When he went to see if the valve was stuck, he found the transfer motor was inoperative. He told Sweeney and Sweeney asked the Colonel what to do. We figured it would be all right to go ahead. It was time to start the engines, so we climbed into the airplane about 2:46am. First the pilot unlocks his controls, makes sure his turbo control is turned down to zero, puts his brakes on and makes sure the chocks (wedges of wood that keep the wind from moving the airplane) are under the wheels. He makes sure his props are in low pitch or high rpm. The pilot calls out his window, "ready on one". The fire guard, with the fire extinguisher, calls back "ready on one". The pilot tells the engineer to start one. By this time, there is so much confusion, noise and smoke from the engine, you just hold out two fingers for "ready on two". Then the copilot holds out three fingers, gets acknowledgment from the fire guard and tells the engineer "ready on three",

Charles Albury

doing the same with four. The engineer checks his engines by letting them warm up and idle until the oil temperature rises and the cylinder head temperatures rise so there is enough heat to go through the engineer's flight check. Then he calls to the pilot he is ready for an engine check.

The Curtis electric propeller, used strictly for our group in the Pacific, is a four bladed, paddle an inch longer than the usual B29 two paddle Hamilton standard hydraulic propeller. You have toggle switches for increasing and decreasing RPMs (rotations per minute) and feathering the engines. A synchronization knob controls all four engines to the same RPM and pitch at the same time. If the engines are not synchronized, it causes a throbbing sound and heavy vibration throughout the airplane. If you look between two blades when in sync, there is a steady shadow; if not in sync, the shadow keeps rotating. After waiting for cylinder and oil temperatures to go up by engine idling, you throttle up to 1500 RPMs. You check all four engine propellers by using the toggle switch to decrease and increase RPMs, then switching it back to automatic position. In check-

Fred Olivi

ing the feathering mechanisms switches, you decrease RPMs to about 400 then back to normal and it automatically goes back to 1400 RPMs. To check the propellers reverse, there is one switch to operate the outboard engines #1 and #4 and another switch to operate the inboard engines #2 and #3. You throw your reverse switch, hit the actuating button to reverse the propellers. When you switch it back, it automatically returns to normal.

When these checks are completed, you turn everything over to the engineer who increases the power of the engines to 2000 RPMs to check the left and right magnetos. If you get over 100 drop in RPMs, there is something wrong in the engine and takeoff is terminated. He also checks the power and generators.

At about 2:56am, we taxied to runway Able taking off toward the west due to direction of the wind. This was the first westerly takeoff; winds usually predicted an easterly takeoff. The pilot calls for wheels up and the copilot throws the switch. We had complete radio silence so the Japanese couldn't pick up any tower instructions. These were given to us during briefing. The 20th Air Force procedure, for takeoff through the tower radio, is to lock your brakes at the end of the runway, push throttles full power, release brakes at time of takeoff and control the airplane by pulling less power off one engine as you move right or left going down the runway. In a B29, your rudder doesn't come in to effect until the airplane is moving 60-70 miles per hour. If your airplane weighed 130,000 pounds, you would hold it on the runway until 130 miles per hour, pull the nose up and she would take right off.

It is absolutely tense in the cockpit with no lights. It is hot and sultry with everybody sweating. Before takeoff, you need twenty-five degrees of flaps down and after takeoff the pilot calls for flaps up at five degrees at a time to continue lifting the airplane The copilot is so busy on takeoff you don't have time to think, except do your job on hand. The navigator doesn't have anything to do until you get off the ground. They have a very powerful spotlight the plane stays on top of all the way out the runway so they don't go into the water. They held a steady level course about fifty feet above the water carrying an Atomic bomb. On this particular night there was no spotlight, about 4/10 cumulus cloud cover, not leaving much light as we used up the whole 9,000 feet of runway. There is always a crash boat in the harbor to keep the waterways clear.

We went out five minutes, turned on a northerly course for Hakashima, Japan, approximately 800 miles away. We were climbing 195 miles per hour (MPH) when the pilot called for power number two climbing power increasing 43 ½ feet and 400 RPMs which means approximately 25 minutes to climb 7,000 feet at 150 to 200 feet per minute showing about 206 MPH. During the climb, I had checked the airplane compass with my astro compass, caged my flux-gate compass, while the radar operator collaborated and checked the radar set. I was using my indicated air speed, free air temperature and average altitude to compute my true air speed, plus computing the wind and climb. On a flight like this, it was important to keep accurate position reports available at all times in case of forced landing on water to notify the air/sea rescue of our position. A matter of ten miles may mean the difference between spending a day or a week on the water, or life and death. We leveled off at 3:22am. We always flew at the odd altitudes and they always tried to put us just above the clouds. We went through several thunderstorms when we got near Iwo and couldn't see around or below us. They had a recording machine attached to our inter phone system to record all conversations. Beahan was giving a description of takeoff, climb and how everything was going. He called all the different members of the crew to say who they were, their hometown etc. After that, he went to sleep.

We didn't see land until we got to Yakashima, a little island in the Ryuki chain. Don had changed his power settings, Sweeney and Olivi were asleep, and Commander Dick Ashworth couldn't sleep the whole trip. At that time, it was clear enough to navigate by celestial means. If the stars were out, Venus was like a big spot light. We were still at 7,000 feet. It was rough that night. We started running into weather at approximately 4:45 am and I didn't have but a few celestial shots. The radar wasn't too sharp that night either. I worked harder that mission than on any other. On the others, we had Iwo or Saipan to get a fix. I got an occasional shot from a star and near Iwo I got several radar beacons and a radio check but they weren't too accurate because the thunder attracted the radio compass. I used the Loran secondary to celestial and radar. We passed Iwo Jima at 6:04am, got a radar, loran and radio check 200 miles west of it. The sky cleared up on one side of the airplane for a few minutes and I got a shot of a star off our left wing, then we went back into rough weather. The plane was bumping all over the sky.

At twenty hours, 7:10, we started our climb to 31,000 feet. It took us one hour to climb and leveled off at 8:05, one o'clock in the morning in daylight that started about 5:30. We were still in bad weather and didn't break out until almost to the coast. At 8:45, reported an island straight ahead. At 9:20 it started coming into view. We saw a four engine super dumbo (a B29 rigged like a PBY for rescue work), airplane on the water along with two US submarines off the coast of Japan. There was also a dumbo Catalina circling off Yakashima that carried a lot of supplies, receiving set and more radar than we did.

We circled the island for forty minutes, twenty-five minutes too long, looking for Major Hopkins who never arrived because they were circling the wrong place. After the mission, he swore he was there. When we arrived in Okinawa he said, "Where were you?" I answered, "I was at Yakashima waiting for you." He said, "We and the other plane were there, but you weren't." To the right was a long skinny island and further on was a circular island. The camera ship was there. Sweeney had sent Fred Olivi back to the navigator hatch in the astrodome (a clear circular dome in the tunnel, something like a blister) to look for enemy fighters or other airplanes. The weather was clear, about 2/10ths coverage. We could see the water way below us along with Japan. The islands looked black on both sides; Kyushu on the left and on the final bomb run, the island of Honshu on our right. Our previous course to the Initial Point (IP), we had flown between them.

Prior to our takeoff, back on Tinian, there were two weather ships that took off; one went to Kokura, the

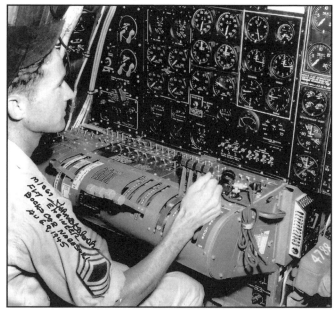

John Kuharek

other to Nagasaki. An hour before we were supposed to drop the bomb, we got the first weather report on Kokura that it was hazy, one to two tenths coverage, wind at 250 degrees, 60 knots and clearing rapidly. We got the same report from Nagasaki, but both targets were supposed to be open and clear for bombing. Our first run on the target, it was quite hazy with one to tenths coverage, but we couldn't pick up the target or the aiming point because of heavy industrial smoke. So Beahan, the bombardier, told us we might as well turn around and try again. So we went back to our IP and made another run without success in seeing the target. We all knew where to drop it, but we were under orders to drop our bomb visually. So we decided after the second run to go towards Yawata in the Shimonoseki Straights.

On the first flight, you didn't see the other two ships until they met you at the target, then we flew in formation, the camera ship on the left to make a left turn, we

Ray Gallagher

Jim Van Pelt

were on the right, with complete radio silence. We carried juice and sandwiches and the bread was very dry. We flew to Kubora our turning point (TP), then turned to fly over Mitusukue our initial point (IP). While passing between these two points, the crew put on their flak suits, studied their charts, etc. Except Beahan, Sweeney and Van Pelt, all were watching for the turning point to notify Van Pelt. Ed Buckley was watching the radar scope. We were briefed by the group navigator to fly about ten miles east of the point to ensure a proper radar turn. We turned again for a radar run on Kokura. We were fifty nautical miles out so the bombardier picked up our target on radar. I was giving lateral corrections to bring the ship over the city so the bombardier could do a visual drop through the bomb sight. After thirty miles, we made a 180 degree turn, came back towards the target, but it was the same heavy industrial smoke, so we decided to go back to our TP for a run to Nagasaki.

Sweeney said the gas was too low to go back, so he and Commander Ashworth decided to turn directly west to Nagasaki. They talked more about the gas situation and Commander Ashworth decided we were to go ahead and drop the bomb by radar if we couldn't see the target visually. Ed Buckley and I really went to work. I headed for the center of Nagasaki that appeared rounded, lighter, bluer center as an outline of a city with a darker background surrounded by water and mountains, making it a difficult target. I looked at my map, estimated the coast line with my radar scope and flew with my heading marker between two land reference points which apparently was a good course from Kokura. While debating, we weren't paying attention to our altitude. We had reduced our power and had seen three fighters take off from Ashiya, an airfield west of Yawata. By the time we reached Nagasaki, we had lost 3,000 feet, giving us an indicated altitude of 26,000 feet, going over the target at 28,000 feet.

We had polaroid glasses with density control to make them too dark to see your hand when the bomb flash came. The last ten seconds of the bomb run, Beahan found an opening in the Cumulus clouds right over the aiming point, shouted to Sweeney, "I have it". He made a two degree correction and at 11:58 Beahan shouted "Bomb Away". The airplane was supposed to turn left at a sixty degree bank but it was a slower forty-five degrees making it unable to clear the danger area specified by the scientists. There was a brief interval before we saw a purplish, white, brilliant flash the scientists claim is nine times greater that the intensity of the sun. Before we rolled out of our turn, we felt the first shock wave, then shortly after, the second which were much more intense than over Hiroshima. When the third one hit, I thought something was wrong. When the fourth one hit, I was really worried. The fifth one I didn't know what to think. They seemed very close together. I looked out my navigator's window, left side of the ship and could see the mushroom head building up underneath us rapidly. At the end of our turn, our assistant engineer, Ray Gallagher, called up informing us the cloud was coming up under us. After describing what it looked like, they decided it was the shock waves. The first time I saw the cloud, it was about 20,000 feet with a deep salmon color around the edges with a white top. Even with split second glances by various people, the mushroom changed color. It was pink or almost red. It wasn't as bright at 20,000 feet as at 30,000 feet. Below the stem, it was dark, black or grayish color. Even with minimal gas, we did circle the cloud once, getting close enough that it looked like it could envelop us. Fortunately, our altitude was so great and our speed so fast, we outdistanced the mushroom head that looked to be about 3,000 feet across. We could see fires burning on both sides of the mountains.

Abe Spitzer

As we left the target area, Beahan started working on his strike report which is sent back to the ground station on radio strike frequency. It contained information on 9/10s cloud coverage, altitude 31,000 feet and heading of the drop was visual, time 11:58 am and damage assessment classified as excellent, good or fair. Captain Beahan classified this drop as good due to seeing the target during release of the bomb but 9/10s cloud cover obscured its impact. Immediately, Abe Spitzer sent the strike report on the strike frequency. As we were leaving the coast, the crew took off their flak suits, goggles, parachutes and C-1 vests. I then realized I was thirsty and none of the crew had eaten or drunk anything for hours before arriving on the coast of Japan. The canteens were all very cold from being on the floor. Then the crew went into a relieved, happy, carefree mood, laughing and congratulating everyone else.

I called Sweeney to give him the magnetic heading for Okinawa. Sweeney called John Kuharek to ask how much fuel was left. John had to calculate so we started our descent. John called back with 300 gallons available, but the bomb bay tanks were of no use. First we cut back on power and lowered the nose. At 1400 RPMs and twenty-eight inches of manifold pressure, you are using approximately 78 gallons of gas an hour. Sweeney told me to be especially careful as to our latitude and longitude for a position report because there might not be enough gas to reach Okinawa. As we crossed the southern coast of Japan, Sweeney called air/sea rescue with our position, altitude, speed, destination and estimated time of arrival (ETA). He called for about fifteen minutes but received no answer. We thought the coast of Japan had been alerted after the bomb, so the air/sea rescue facilities had gone, submarines submerged, superdumbos and dumbos met with opposition and left the area. This supposition was substantiated by the radio operator being in contact with the ground station on strike frequency through the entire mission.

Sweeney attempted to contact Okinawa tower about an hour out. We were to land on Yantan Island. Okinawa was surprisingly large about 60-75 miles long and 10-15 miles wide. By the time we were in sight of the field, we were at 2000 feet. Since he couldn't contact the tower, he called back to Spitzer and me to shoot flares. Colors of the day were red and green of which we had four in the kit. After shooting them, we proceeded to use everything in the kit consisting of about 24 flares even into final approach. We never did receive any recognition from the tower by radio or biscuit gun which is a light signal for visual morse code. We landed approximately halfway down the 6000 foot runway, about 120 miles per hour, bounced about thirty feet in the air, bouncing again, settling, then immediately put the Curtis Electric Propellers into reverse, applied the brakes and came to a safe, slow, roll stop in about 1500 feet. Evidently, the tower had seen our flares or heard our radio because there was a crash wagon (fire truck) and meat wagon (ambulance) waiting. A jeep led us into a taxi strip and on to a hardstand. Abe Spitzer, the radio operator, checked the radio when we landed. As Sweeney departed the plane to radio Tinian, the whole crew hugged the ground. Fred Bock landed his instrument ship right behind us. In about forty-five minutes, Major Hopkins landed the camera plane wanting to know where we were.

James Hopkins

Someone decided it was time to eat, so we left John Kuharek and Ed Buckley to gas the plane while we went to find a mess hall in Air Transport Command (ATC) base. They gave us peanut butter, jelly, hardtack (biscuit) and coffee. One of the men stationed there sat at our table to tell us about the Atomic Bomb, dropped by parachute, on Hiroshima by a P38 stationed on Okinawa. Due to security, we listened attentively and remarked "Is that right." We walked back, noticing Okinawa's terrain was a lot of foliage, rolling hills, valleys and high cliffs. The plane had taken 4000 gallons of gas and was ready to go. Sweeney had talked to General Doolittle. We took off to the northwest at five o'clock, climbed to 10,000 feet altitude and passed three islands before dark. All was going smoothly until we were within 200 miles of Tinian where we ran into a treacherous storm. We landed on Tinian worn out and exhausted. We piled out of the airplane and removed our gear. We were met by Admiral Purnell who said after the bomb drop, they thought something had happened to us since there was no news. Colonel Tibbets was pretty worried, but never gave up hope.

Trucks took us to Colonel Payette who interrogated the crew. We were sitting around a table when the *Stars and Stripes* reporter came in who was stationed with me in Walla and had previously worked for *Time Magazine*. We made records later broadcast over hookups to the US. After interrogation, we went to medical detachment who set up a bar in the Officer's Club for the whole crew to drink from twelve to five AM. Tom Ferebee and I were the only two left when the whiskey gave out and the bartender went home. We went to Jim McFall's and pulled him and Stanley Crouse out of bed. Then we swiped the General's jeep and tried to drive it through my quonset hut. Then I went in and pulled Beahan and Albury out of bed.

In early September, Colonel Tibbets invited us to go with him to Japan. We were some of the first Americans to land. We were to take the medical men to Nagasaki. We landed at Atsugi Air Field in Tokyo. Due to crowded conditions at the airfield, we were forced to move our C54 to Chofu Field, a small grass field outside the city.

In Tokyo, we stayed at the Dai Ichi Hotel, one of the few remaining structures still standing. Our facilities were neat, clean and undersized. The Army had taken over the hotel and dining facilities. The next day we took a jeep and trailer filled with C-rations sight seeing with the idea of bartering with our rations. We ended up giving them to a priest running a Catholic School for distribution to his parish. We left our jeeps and trailers with Marines in Tokyo and flew to Kobe. We looked at our bomb damage at the Imperial Government railroad shipyards on "Our practice mission". From there, we flew to Hiroshima. At a distance, it looked completely white. We flew very low to see only five or six concrete buildings standing with everything else flat. We circled a few times and saw people walking on the roads.

We were the first Americans to land at Omura Naval Base. The Japanese Commander of the base came up and surrendered his sword to Colonel Kirkpatrick. He had been waiting for someone of his own rank to surrender it to. We waited for about one and a half hours until we finally got five charcoal burning trucks and buses. We hadn't gone a half mile when the first bus broke down. Immediately the driver jumped out, threw up the hood and examined the engine. We waited about an hour to see if he could repair it, decided he couldn't, so we all piled into the rest of the trucks and buses. We had only gone about a quarter of a mile when another truck broke down. That driver jumped out and started tinkering with the carburetor, could not repair it, so they piled into another truck. We had gone about another five miles when the third bus broke down and we didn't even wait to see what happened. We all jumped out and got into the two remaining trucks. Another broke down about one mile from there, so we decided to two it. We were climbing up a mountain and half way up, the last one broke down. We finally got to town, with one load and coming back for another, by commandeering a truck that was passing by. They were all Chevrolet trucks.

We went to Nagasaki passing through a very long divided tunnel. One way traffic on one side and machinery and manufacturing equipment on the other. We were taken to a schoolhouse, one of the few buildings standing, where they were still having school. The school had Prefectural Police, who were in command of the town until someone came to take over. There were quite a few troop ships in the harbor waiting for us to come with medical men to check for radioactivity. We arrived in town very late and went to a little place, located in the mouth of the harbor on the other side of the island from Nagasaki, called Mogi. We stayed at a home, turned into a hotel, that had been an American Resort before the war. We had very delicious jumbo, saki and we brought our own coffee.

The next morning, we went by truck, through the whole town of Nagasaki where there was nothing but wreckage. The first real destruction we saw was the over a mile long frame and steel, twisted, knocked down, completely demolished Mitsubishi Steel Mill. The only part not damaged was the dock area. In Tokyo, people were friendly, waving and smiling at us. They did not know we were the people who dropped the bomb. In Nagasaki, they did not turn and look at you. They were sober and did not look friendly at all. We then went to

Nagasaki cloud
Photo taken by Len Godfrey from Great Artiste

the wooden structured Munitions Factory (torpedoes) that was completely demolished with the help of the munitions inside. From there, we went to the Medical School, a seven or eight story concrete building that did not look damaged from the outside, but inside was completely charred and burned. You could see people who had been operating with a skeleton on the table, some lying around the room and some in beds. The elevator was not running, the stairs were burned out and safes were blown.

There were skulls along the roads. The Japanese people had built air raid shelters (a hole about five or six feet deep with sandbags around it) in front of their houses, where you could look down and see skeletons. The medical officers, with us, checked the whole area in the vicinity of the bomb blast and found very few places of radioactivity enough to injure anyone.

In the southern parts of town, toward the docks, about ten miles from the center of the actual bomb destruction area, you could walk along see one house standing and next door be caved in. The scientists claimed the hills and mountains and the echo of shock waves returning, caused the skip and hit, not the direct result of the explosion. We had an English Professor at the University, guide us, that lived twenty miles away, heard noise like thunder, felt the ground shaking and saw the blinding light of the explosion. He told us the Japanese people would probably never forget the great, sorrowful loss to them. You could see the sadness on their faces and they felt revengeful toward us.

Charles W. Sweeney
Aircraft Commander

M/SGT John D. Kuharek
FLIGHT ENGINEER

Harold M. Agnew
Scientific Field Observer

Lawrence H. Johnston
Scientific Observer

Lt. Fred J. Olivi
Copilot - "Bockscar"
Nagasaki - 9 Aug. 1945
Al Moon Mack #89

Sgt. Ray Gallagher
Assistant Flight
Engineer
Hiroshima aug. 6
Nagasaki aug. 9
1945

Capt. C. Dohlen
Pilot "The Great Artiste"
Aug. 6, 1945 Hiroshima
Pilot Bocks Car
Nagasaki aug. 1945

Kim Van Pelt
Navigator

Plane flown by Crew C-15 to Hiroshima.
Note: Olivi was a regular crew member but was pre-empted by a scientist

WAINSCOTT, JAMES J.
393rd Bomb Squadron, Sgt/Major Administrative Specialist

I was in the 9th Bomb Group when I was sent to Fairmont, Nebraska to become part of the 393rd Bomb Squadron. My job was Sgt/Major Administrative Assistant. When Colonel Tibbets took command, the squadron became part of the 509th Composite Group.

At Wendover, I was an Administrative Specialist with several people working with me. I worked closely with Colonel Tom Classen and Lt. Roy Edwards.

On Tinian Island, my duties were about the same as Wendover. I did a lot of coordinating with the Commanding Officer (CO) and Adjutant.

Top row: Tom Classen, Edwards, Tillman, King, Wainscott, Tigner
Bottom row: McBride, Bennett, Biggio, Dramby, Hesse, Goldberg

WESTCOTT, KERMIT F.
509th Headquarters, Line Chief

I was stationed at Ardmore, Oklahoma, Air Base, when the "Silver Plate Project" was formed. This air base was a training school for B17 combat crews for England. We had about ninety B17s for training these crews. My job was NCOIC of the aircraft maintenance inspection and test flight of the aircraft after maintenance of them. I had twelve assistant inspectors. I and twelve other maintenance personnel volunteered for the "Silver Plate Project" and were shipped to Wendover Air Force Base. In the fall of 1944, I was assigned to the 320th Troop Carrier Squadron as maintenance inspector.

Shortly thereafter, in January, 1945, I was sent to Batista, Cuba, with five maintenance men to take care of the maintenance of the 509th B29s that flew through here on their training missions. I was in charge of eight aircraft mechanics. Our duty was to maintain the 320th and 393rd aircraft that stopped over there. I would like to add that the maintenance people of the 393rd and 320th Squadrons were excellent in maintaining their aircraft.

About a month later, we returned to Wendover. I was reassigned to Group Headquarters of the 509th. I was then assigned to the Air Inspectors Office as chief maintenance inspector under Major Darby. I held this position for the duration of the war. While in Wendover, we set up our needed technical orders and AF Regulations, plus required equipment for shipment overseas.

Also while at Wendover, I enjoyed the Spike Jones music at the Nevada Club.

WEY, FRANKLIN K. (KEN)
393rd Bomb Squadron, Bombardier, Straight Flush, Crew C-11

This is the first I have known of this crew picture without me taken at Wendover. Evidently, it was made in November 1944 while I was on leave for the birth of my first daughter "Bomsa" Wey. This is a typical picture of Baldy and Barsumian. Reminds me of Barsumian wearing my Lieutenant bars on his Private first Class (PFC) shirt to get into the Officers' Bar at a hotel in Omaha, Nebraska, when we went to pick up The Straight Flush. As for naming The Straight Flush, I recall the painter had drawn a number of pictures and since Buck and I played a lot of poker, he offered the name to us. The Straight Flush crew was recognized as the most "unmilitary" crew in the 509th. We tended strictly to business when on duty, but off duty we saw to it that our enlisted men were taken care of, airmen and ground crew alike. We were all the best of friends.

Buck and I were the closest of friends. We roomed and flew together for some thirty months from the day the 509th was formed until the completion of the Bikini Bomb tests in December 1946. When not on duty, we went to the bar, played golf, dice, cards and traveled; you name it, we did it.

As for the passing of the bottle between cars, it was done more than once. Buck always had a supply of liquor. He was caught by Utah authorities with a dozen or more ration cards. The secret operations at Wendover kept him out of trouble when he gave up all but one card. Marquardt's home was in Utah and was usually the other car in the "speeding transfer". There was a speed trap between Wendover and Salt Lake City and after the second or third ticket Buck received, the officer would stop him, call him by name and hand him a ticket already made out. Buck would thank him for saving time.

In Utah, they used silver dollars instead of paper bills. We bought all the silver dollars from the other crews, before they learned better. In Havana, with those round dollars, we were the "cocks of the walk" and the bartenders and girls would almost fight for our attention.

We didn't fly many hours while at Batista Field. We were free to go into Havana when not flying. We made the Nacional Hotel our "Headquarters". I went to the Havana Golf and Country Club the first trip into town, met the golf pro, he loaned me clubs and shoes, introduced me to the members and I had a foursome every time I went out there, four or five times a week. Only the very wealthy could afford the club, so I had a big time. They wouldn't let me spend a dime. I was a guest at someone's dinner party every night after a round of golf. When I left the club, I would go back to the Nacional Hotel to find some of our crew at the bar and usually end up at Casa Marinas with the rest of them. It was a hotel with the finest bar and dance floor in Havana even though they didn't cater to luggage carrying guests. Of course, Buck was the one who discovered Casa Marinas on his first trip into town and made us swear we wouldn't tell any of the other crews about it.

As far as I can remember, Lefty Grennan was the only one of our crew that was approached by his security people. It was around Christmas 1944 when we were all on leave, for the last time, until we came back after the war was over. It was in the Chicago Railroad Station and all he told a friend was his training was secret. He had to report to Paul Tibbets when he returned to Wendover for a tongue lashing and last warning.

Some of our escapades like giving the Seabees on Tinian two quarts of Early Times to build us a private tent house with a shower and steal us a Jeep from Saipan. We didn't let them know we kept the good stuff, Jack Daniels, to drink ourselves.

On the August 6th mission, the ground crew, as usual, loaded a case of beer on the catwalk in the bomb bay so it would be cold when the plane returned. Fred Krug was a weatherman from the briefing team and a close friend to Buck and me. He wasn't scheduled to fly a mission and since we weren't carrying a bomb, we smuggled him aboard so he could tell his grandchildren he flew a mission over Japan.

I made two bomb runs over the target, on the same heading they would fly to drop the bomb, to make sure cloud cover would not interfere with the sighting. My message to the Enola Gay was 2/10ths cloud cover at 15,000 feet bomb primary. It was coded and radioed and

Crew of Straight Flush

Back row (L-R): Ira Weatherly, Claude Eatherly, Francis Thornhill, Eugene Grennan
Front Row (L-R): Jack Bivans, Pasquale Baldasaro, Gil Niceley, Al Barsumian.
Ken Wey not in photo

35 to 40 minutes later Ferebee dropped the bomb right on target. As for watching the Hiroshima bomb drop, we were 35 minutes ahead of the Enola Gay. We did talk it over among ourselves, but we had been ordered beforehand not to stay. When we returned to Tinian, we used a poker game Eatherly had to play as an excuse for not staying.

Claude "Buck" Eatherly

V-85 in flight August 8, 1945 - Hiroshima markings on plane

"Buck" Eatherly waves from plane on Tinian

WHEELER, SAM R.
393rd Bomb Squadron, Assistant Flight Engineer, Crew A-4

In September 1941, I went to work in engine service on the Santa Fe Railroad.

In September 1942, I left this good job to do something in the war effort.

I enlisted in Phoenix to be an aircraft mechanic, the recruiter said "great". I was sent to Ft. McArthur, California, then to Merced Army Air Base. Lo and behold, they had me typing in a Basic Flying School (BT13s). I soon got bored with that and took the officers candidate exam. I was interviewed by a group of officers and OKd for Officers Candidate School. They put me on a list for over a year, so I decided to take the Army Air Corps exam and be a cadet. I passed and since I was a year short of having my degree, they sent me to Pilot Training School at Butler University in Indianapolis, Indiana, for a year. They taught me how to fly a small plane and I was appointed a flight leader of about 50 men (in their every Saturday parade).

I graduated and was sent to San Antonio for assignment to Pilot, Navigator, Bombardier School. All schools were filled and after 30 days of waiting, they sent me to Gunnery School at Harlington, Texas. I graduated and got my wings.

Then they sent me to Fairmont, Nebraska, and assigned me to a B17 Bomber Crew. After a short while, I was picked by the 509th and assigned to a B29 Crew at Wendover. By this time, they had taken all the turrets off our B29 to save four tons of weight and allow us to fly 400 miles per hour. So here I am, a gunner and no guns - so they gave us some on the job training as an Assistant Flight Engineer plus classroom instruction at Wendover for six months. Then to Cuba for the twelve hour long flights up the east coast and back. After about a month, we were back at Wendover with my lovely wife at the Stateline Hotel.

One day at Wendover, I stood on the bomb drop reviewing stand watching an unarmed Block Buster Bomb fall from one of our planes about 10,000 feet up. The stand was only about a half mile from target. If I hadn't had complete confidence in the crew flying that plane, I wouldn't have been there. The sound I have never forgotten - like 20 freight trains all together and I know that sound from experience running trains. Anyway, the bomb drop was perfect in the circle and made quite a crater.

In late July 1945 while stationed on Tinian Island with the 509th Composite Group, we were called on a mission to bomb targets in Japan with three other B29s. All the planes had armed, 10,000 pound bombs in their bomb bays. My B29 Strange Cargo was to fly 3,000 miles nonstop, a 12 to 14 hour flight. We had done this with our 10,000 pounder before. This morning was different. As we were preparing for the bombing mission, still parked with the bomb bay doors open, I, as Assistant Flight Engineer, was checking the right landing gear wheel well for leaks while John Dulin, Navigator checked the left. All of a sudden, the pumpkin bomb dropped onto the asphalt just ten feet from where I stood. I ran out into the night till I was out of breath. I stayed there fifteen minutes, decided if the thing was going to get me it would have had me by now, so I walked back to the plane to find Col. Tibbets and others in shock. The mission was aborted because the plane couldn't be moved until the pumpkin was removed; which took some very careful maneuvering.

Crew of Strange Cargo on Tinian

*Top (L-R): Lou Allen, John Dulin, Maj. James Hopkins Jr.,
Bill Desmond, Bobby Donnell*
Front (L-R): Jim Doiron, Sam Spradlin, Sam Wheeler, Bill Cotter

WIDOWSKY, JACK
393rd Bomb Squadron, Navigator, Crew B-8

How could I ever forget the first time I set foot in Wendover after the long ride from Salt Lake City past the Bonneville Salt Flats. I said to myself, "Where the hell am I?" It got better later. We got a two week leave before we came back for our special mission training.

Who could ever forget the trip to Cuba and other destinations.

If you ever felt like gambling, we had the casino at the Stateline Hotel right outside the camp. However, there were always enough poker games at the Officer's Club to satisfy your desires.

How can I ever forget the problem our crew encountered on a training flight to the West Coast. As we were flying over San Francisco Bay at about 30,000 feet, the cover to the lower turret blew out due to explosive decompression. Because of where I was standing, at the time, a piece of flying equipment hit me on the side of my head knocking me unconscious, also due to the lack of oxygen. Jake Bontekoe, George Cohen,

and Don Cole, after a long struggle, placed an oxygen mask on my face and revived me.

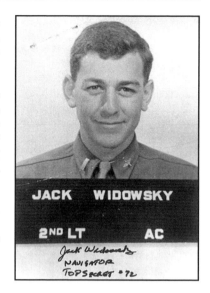

Our Airplane Commander, Charles McKnight, and Jake Bontekoe had a very difficult time keeping the airplane on a steady course. We finally landed at a field in the San Francisco area, where I received medical attention for the cuts I had on my scalp.

The next day, we returned to Wendover after the cover was replaced. All's well that ends well.

Most important of all, the friendships that were made at Wendover that have endured through the years.

V-72 Returns to Roswell
Back row (L-R): Jacob Bontekoe, Jack Widowsky, Charles McKnight, Lloyd Reeder, Roderick Legg
Front row (L-R): George Cohen, Franklin MacGregor, William Orren, Donald Cole

WORLEY, HOWARD C.
603rd Air Engineer Squadron, Armament

I arrived at Wendover Field in September of 1944, after two years of overseas duty in Africa, Sicily and Italy. At a group meeting, we were informed a new group was being formed to operate anywhere in the world and we would go overseas again. I was assigned to the 603rd Air Engineer Squadron, in the armament section.

When assigned to the shop, we were split into two sections, one to take care of the guns, the other to take care of the bombs. I was one of the first four armament men to be taken out at night to work on the plane at the pit. Here we loaded the bomb and during the day, altered the bomb bay on the planes.

In the early spring of 1945, we loaded a bomb on a plane and flew it to Offutt Field at Omaha, Nebraska. We unloaded the bomb into a pit which they had ready for us, and then loaded it into a plane which was right off the assembly line and built to our specifications. Later in the spring, I was sent to the Island of Tinian, where I spent the summer of 1945 working on bombs and guns. I was on the Island of Tinian when the bomb was dropped.

I was to go to Iwo Jima, with another armament man, where they had put a pit and had a plane ready in the event that it would be needed should the first mission not be successful. At the last minute, only one man was sent to Iwo Jima, not two.

After the bomb was dropped, they called me to the orderly room and told me I had more points than anyone in the squadron and I could go home by boat or plane. I chose to go by plane and was discharged from the Army Air Force at Fort Douglas, Utah, on September 30, 1945.

WRIGHT, JOHN W. "JACK"
393rd Bomb Squadron, Armament Officer

At Wendover, my time was spent loading practice bombs in planes for aiming at our target which was in the desert 100 miles south of Los Angeles. Many bombs were loaded, different shapes and sizes before the basic shape for Little Boy and Fat Man were firmed up. As Armament Officer, I was involved with all the bombs at Wendover and Tinian. I have no memory of a bomb named Thin Man although among the shapes I handled was a long thin one that extended across the two bomb bays.

The OSS (Offices of Strategic Services) wanted it to drop on the tunnel that runs under Tokyo Bay. At Wendover, the stripes and white paint were for photographic purposes of the practice bombs (armament) when it was in flight. Planes were backed over the pit which contained an hydraulic piston lift, similar to an automotive lift found in garages. Once it was positioned in the cradle on the lift, the bomb was raised so its lug fitted into a bomb shackle, a British make. The steadying bolts were positioned, the arming pin was activated and all was ready. At Inyokern, a miserable spot out in the desert, the bombing (gunnery) range had large slabs of battleship armor plate propped up; these were targets. Very few had holes in them due to bombs or gunnery. I was with Col. Tibbets before Wendover - I ran a B29 gunnery test at Eglin Field.

A 10,000 pound bomb loaded with high explosives can make a mess. We were getting ready for take-off on a mission early in the morning around 4am. My section chief and I were on the line when one of the armorers ran up and said, "Captain, the arming light is on in my plane". Having the arming light on means the bomb is ready to drop. Ed, my section chief and I went up into the bomb bay very cautiously. The bomb lug is precisely made, so we got on our hands and knees and crept on top of the bomb to put the device back in place. As I reached over to the top of the bomb to do it, the bomb fell.

My legs were going forty miles per hour and Ed's were doing the same thing. We were not moving an inch. The only guys that really got hurt were a group of guys around the plane waiting to see what was going to happen. They dove off the hardstand onto the hard, sharp coral. There were about twenty people in the first aid tent that day. The ordnance crew was right there and disarmed the bomb.

ZAHN, HERMAN STAN
393rd Bomb Squadron, Airplane Commander, Crew C-12

There are so many memories: the many friends, the Stateline Hotel, the concrete block apartment with the brand new electric refrigerator, water heater, and a coal-fired cooking stove, (we never needed the space heater all winter long).

Saving food stamps, so we could buy a steak.

Climbing up to the eye of the needle in the mountain north of Wendover. A jeep ride up the same mountain with a tank of gas for the beacon on top.

An outing across unmarked desert to a grove for a picnic with Ed and Jo Costello.

Saturday night dancing at the Officers Club. The USO show where one of the dancers was a classmate from middle school in Philadelphia.

My three day pass to Salt Lake City with four wives (including my own).

The flight from Inyokern to Wendover in an AT11 when we couldn't pull full power and used the air currents to get high enough to cross the mountain ridges. (We had a weekend leave to see our wives.)

The training flight from Batista Field in Cuba that was planned to fly at 10,000 feet through a 12,000 foot mountain on the Island of Hispaniola. The mountain was shrouded in clouds so everyone climbed above them and safely passed the mountain except one. He flew around the mountain in the clouds on radar. He also returned last and Batista was fogged in, so he got to spend some time in Jamaica. (Just compensation).

I could go on and on, but have exhausted my space.

ZIMMERLI, FRED H.
Project Alberta, Technician 3rd Grade (T3)

Several GIs from West Virginia University, went to Los Alamos as a group. Fred Adams was in charge. Others were William Cocke, Arthur Collins, Ted Felbeck and another. We had been told we would go to Fort Campbell in Kentucky. This was near Oak Ridge, Tennessee. We were the first group to be sent directly to Santa Fe instead of going to Oak Ridge first. We were riding together in the second section of the Santa Fe train "California Limited". This train had only military personnel with orders, but were traveling on their own.

Our orders were to get off at Lamey, New Mexico. Six of us got off. There was only the station and one house—the rest was almost all desert. Others on the train asked us what we had done to deserve being dropped off in no where. We were then picked up by bus and taken to Santa Fe. The orders said to report to an address on Baker Street. We were greeted by a military policeman. We were told to wait for transportation to "The Hill". The station wagon took us to Los Alamos, but no one called it Los Alamos.

We were part of the SED (Special Engineering Department). I was assigned to Dr. Brode's group on ballistics. It took until February before I realized what was being made. We were involved with a distance radar to be used to trigger the bomb 2,000 feet above the ground. It was a modified "Tail Gun Charlie" radar used on fighter planes to warn of the enemy behind the plane. It is referred to as "Archie".

In spare time, I played on the "west mess" basketball team. William Locke was manager and Art Collins was the star and spent a lot of time in the lab experimenting with electronic circuits. Fred Adams bought a good Jansen loudspeaker and we listened to one of the first Hi-Fis.

Several of us, can't remember who, were sent to Wendover Field, Utah to work with equipment to put on "Fat Man" bombs that were tested for ballistics. We were supplied with civilian clothes and given a letter authorizing us to wear them. I remember having gone with an officer to a men's shop on the square in Santa Fe to get the suit, shirt, tie, socks and probably shoes. We lived in the BOQ (Bachelor Officer Quarters) at Wendover. Several of us went to the Salton Sea Naval Air Station where we operated radio telemeter equipment that gave information on the trigger operation during actual dummy bomb drops. I remember that the dummy bombs landed in the sand several hundred feet from our testing site and eating with Navy personnel, who were there to observe low level bombing practice by Naval Aviators. There were movie cameras to record the drop.

We had several days without tests and were allowed to go to Los Angeles. We went by air to Inglewood. I remember oil wells nearby. Since this was before the summer season, we found a hotel in Hermosa Beach.

One of our group came from Los Angeles and took us to the Palladium Ballroom. I never felt so embarrassed, being a civilian who didn't look like 4F. I think we had a meal at the fellow's home. We went back by bus, through Palm Springs, Indio. I remember the fig trees, found horned toads at the edge of Salton Sea, went swimming, very salty. I remember watching the bomb doors open and the bomb drop. Even at 30,000 feet, it was visible.

At Wendover, I was not busy one day when several airmen had to calibrate altimeters and said I could go along. I did go but got air sick because they went up and down checking the calibration. I had to clean the can coming back from Wendover to Los Alamos. The pilot took us over the Grand Canyon—beautiful! I remember also, Mount Taylor near Gallup, New Mexico. The only mountain west of Albuquerque. We flew from Kirtland Field in Albuquerque.

Went to Albuquerque several times. Stayed overnight in a private barracks type lodging; had bed bugs.

When we were ready to go with the bomb, we had to go in uniform. People at Wendover were surprised. They knew then that we had been in the service all the time because Larkin was a Sergeant.

We had the last laugh on the officers there. Their officers club burned down in June. So we had the tail non com club but they had a makeshift club. I was transferred to the 509th Composite Group on June 29, 1945. On July 1, I was supposed to be promoted to a technician T4, but because of the transfer, it was disallowed. We all got a blanket promotion on Tinian.

206

SHORT TAKES

Harold Agnew recounted why the bomb core is scratched out in this snapshot: I was in Chicago after the war in 1946. The FBI came and said they believed I had some secret pictures. They went through my pictures and found nothing. Then like a fool I said, "Maybe this one is secret". They wanted to know what that thing was. I told them and then they said that must be secret and wanted the picture. I wanted the picture so they agreed if I scratched out the thing I could keep the slide.

AGNEW, HAROLD M.
Project Alberta Scientist

My assignment to Don Albury's crew was always just for the training period in Cuba. Major Sweeney was unable to make the trip for some reason and Don needed a copilot. I was flying regularly with the 320th at the time but there were no extra pilots in the 393rd. I had been pilot (copilot) in the 393rd and prior to that trained as first pilot in B17s. I was well qualified to serve as Don's copilot.

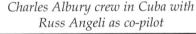

Charles Albury crew in Cuba with Russ Angeli as co-pilot

ANGELI, RUSSELL PILOT
320th Troop Carrier Squadron

My function in the crew was Assistant Flight Engineer/Scanner. We each had a role in preflighting the airplane. I always checked the fuel and oil tanks for capacity and did a visual check of the complete airplane. During the actual flight, I would relieve Rod Arnold at the Flight Engineer's panel.

On August 9th, this was my role except at the time of the bombing I recorded the Atomic blast and cloud on an 8mm movie camera for the Los Alamos Group, Lawrence Johnston in particular. On return to Tinian, all of us were debriefed about what we had seen and felt during the mission.

As to my thoughts on the mission, I felt it was necessary and have not changed my mind since.

BELANGER, RALPH D.
Asst Flight Eng / Scanner, Crew C-13

There are two things I will never forget about Wendover and Wendover Airbase.

One was the Stateline Hotel, Bar and Casino. Two or three times a week, when my work was done in the evening, I would walk across the field, out the West gate into the Stateline which was in Nevada. I would stay until about eleven pm playing blackjack, I would win a bundle and lose a bundle. In the end, I just about broke even but I had a great time. I remember behind the bar were stacks of silver dollars on the wall.

The other thing was the midnight Christmas Service, December 25, 1944, at the base chapel. Most of my friends had gone home for the holidays. When I came out of the chapel, it was a very cold and crisp night and I took a walk. As you know, the airbase was surrounded by mountains. They were playing Christmas Carols and the music was reverberating off of the hills. It was beautiful, but this was one time I was really homesick in the service.

BERGER, RALPH C.
603rd Engineering Squadron
Aircraft Engineering Technician

The last fifteen seconds over Nagasaki I heard the bombardier say, "I've got a hole, I've got it". The bomb had three shock waves. It cleaned out every cloud in the sky. After the bomb was dropped, we notified Air Sea Rescue and headed for Okinawa.

Sweeney told the navigator to fire the flares, there was so much smoke, I thought some of my equipment was on fire. We came in long and hot. Just as we landed, two inboard engines stalled, starved, out of fuel. At the end of the runway, we were pulling one hundred miles per hour. Sweeney did a ninety degree turn without warning anyone and I was thrown into the side of the plane.

BESER, JACOB
Radar Counter
Measures Officer

My first view of Wendover was in September 1944, transferring from Nebraska by car with three other 393rd Engineering Squadron members. My first thought of Wendover was a place of little activity; I very soon learned the opposite.

Soon after the arrival of the entire squadron, our commander called us together and told us we would be working "bankers hours" at Wendover. All of us enjoyed that!

My wife soon arrived by train from Illinois. She was a former officer in the Army Nurses Corp and soon found employment in the base hospital. We enjoyed the company of many friends and the available base activities.

I had the experience of flying to our destination, the Island of Tinian, in the very famous Enola Gay. I found our former training very valuable.

BISHOP, WILLIAM E.
393rd Engineering Squadron
Tech. Inspection

I was NCOIC of the Armament Section at Wendover Field. I also had the Gunners and Ordnance personnel until the ordnance section moved to the secret compound to work on the atomic bomb.

The wind blew so hard, gravel would fly up in one's face, the streets were gravel and no grass on lawns.

Housing was made of blocks. Our quarters consisted of two bedrooms, combination kitchen and dining, and the one bathroom door opened into the dining room. Our living room was quite small and had a small stove heated with coal. Our kitchen stove was also coal burning and the only hot water came from a reservoir on the stove. The floors were cement covered with linoleum and very cold! We shared our quarters with another couple, as there was no other available housing.

I walked to work, about half a mile. One thing I shall never forget was a sign that read like this: "What you hear here, What you see here, When you leave here, Let it stay here". These signs were posted everywhere and close together.

Shopping was very limited; one drug store, one mercantile store and one small meat market; one theater on base.

There are lots of memories, some good, some bad, some happy, and some sad, but the best memory of all was the time our family spent together.

BLACK, NORMAN E.
393rd Armament

V-77, the "Bockscar" was the second of the fifteen modified Silver Plate Planes to be built at the Martin Plant in Omaha. There were several modifications, fuel injection instead of carburetion so the fuel would be evenly distributed, no severe overheat and the reversible propellers for stopping. The lack of armament improved the speed of the airplane so we could fly higher and faster.

Over Nagasaki, we observed from the Great Artiste, the boiling mass rise up. Our tail gunner, Robert Stock, took many photos as well as a movie. Within two minutes, the cloud was beyond our altitude of 30,000 feet. In three to four minutes, it was beyond 50,000 feet.

BOCK, FREDERICK C.
Airplane Commander Crew C-13

I was a T/SGT with the 393rd Bombardment Squadron on arrival. Lt. Colonel, Thomas J. Classen was commanding officer then. I was their Ordnance NCO.

Shortly after arrival, I was transferred to the First Ordnance of the 509th Group. Major Charles Begg was CO. There I trained on an inert bomb that was to hit Nagasaki when fully loaded. Winters were cold at Wendover, but I enjoyed passes to Salt Lake City for R and R.

BONJOUR, GLENN
1st Ordnance Squadron
Special Aviation

On April 29, 1943, I was assigned to Herington Army Air Force Base (AAFB) Herington, Kansas as Ordnance Property Officer. That was where I first met Major Begg. He was the Wing Ordnance Officer at Topeka AAFB which controlled most of Herington's ordnance supplies.

On March 31, 1945, I was assigned to Wendover Field and thence to the 509th Group and First Ordnance Squadron where I worked in the ordnance supply section. I am not sure how I was selected for assignment to First Ordnance. It may be that I worked with Major Begg while at Herington.

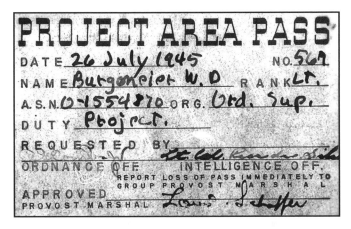

I am not aware of any encounters with security while with the First Ordnance. Security agents did do a check on me before. They checked with several people in my home town.

I went to Tinian by air via the Green Hornet line. Colonel Tibbets was the pilot on that trip. On Tinian I was responsible for supplying various equipment and tools used in the assembly area. We had a large amount of non-sparking tools.

My Project Area Pass allowed me access to all restricted areas. I did not actually work with the atomic or conventional bombs.

I returned to the US via ship, a slow and tedious journey.

BURGMEIER, WILLIAM
1st Ordnance Squadron
Special Aviation

Letter to Parents Aug. 7, 1945

Hi Folks,

How you all be today? I got seven letters of yours to answer. There were five waiting here when I got back last evening and two the day before. We had a beer celebration last night but all we could get were four beers and a couple of sandwiches.

It was supposed to be for our crews but all the pencil pushers and clerks were bartenders so we got gypped. The combat crews in this outfit really take a rooking. All the pencil pushers really are the big gears around here and get all the ratings. I was hoping to make Technician but it is beginning to look hopeless.

I've been a Staff so long, I've grown to like it. Oh well, there are guys worse off.

Bye Now, Love, Bob

PS: Another new APO number, please note APO 336

CARON, GEORGE
Enola Gay Tailgunner, Crew B-9

I was a member of the base Service Squadron of Wendover before I was transferred to the 390th Air Service Squadron. While at Wendover, I worked in the 509th post office, and filled in with the base band on occasion. Also, played on the 390th softball team with some excellent ball players. Enjoyed the passes I had to visit Salt Lake City and the beautiful cities of Utah, such as Provo. My fondest memories are of the wonderful life style and high caliber of the people I met in Utah. I will never forget this. It gave me a lifetime of respect for Utah.

CARROLL, WILLIAM E.
390th Air Service Squadron

Jim Connally was Commanding Officer (CO) of the 9th Bomb Group (BG) in charge of training cadres for the 8th Air Force. I was CO of the 1st Bomb Squadron (BS) assigned to Brooksville Army Air Force (AAF). After this job was done the 9th was disbanded and transferred into the B29 program where Jim Connally was given the 504th BG and I the 393rd BS destined for future assignment to Tinian. James Hopkins also a former 9th member in a different squadron, became my operations officer in the 393rd, built such a good outfit, the squadron was picked for assignment to the 509th Composite Group. Jim Connally was the best boss I ever had.

During our trip to Cuba, there was another outfit called the Gypsy Task Force operating on the same field. They were having such a hard time getting an airplane in the air that Headquarters (HQ) sent an Inspector General (IG) team to find out what was wrong. While there, they came to see what we were doing and found not one single abort had taken place. The result was a letter of a commendation from Air Force HQ praising our operation.

Our success in this venture was due to one man and his bunch of GIs, Cecil King. He did a great job and deserves a lot of credit. The crews by this time were well developed into teams and could do anything they were told to do. They needed to have a good airplane and Cecil saw that they had it.

I don't believe I ever heard the word atomic until after the initial test. We had the photos on Tinian a couple days later and then everyone knew. However, we knew we were going to drop a big bomb after one look into the bomb bay - the hook told the whole story.

CLASSEN, COL. THOMAS J.
509th Deputy Commander

Tom Costa outside nurses' quarters entrance, Wendover (back of photo was censored by Base Examiner)

In front of nurses' dorm, Wendover: Bob Wasz, Nurse Campbell (Cambie), Stu Williams

In front of nurses' dorm, Wendover: Top row, (L-R) Nurse Gosney, Tom Costa Front row (L-R) Jane Pajak (nurse), Lt. Stewart Williams, Nurse Campbell (Cambie), Bill Collinson

I knew the nurses very well and hung out with Jane Pajak whenever we were off duty. We dined together every chance we could at the Officers' Club special events. I believe we were the best baby sitters for the Perry's when they were free to attend a base movie. My Navigator, Bill Collinson squired Nurse Gosney around and we had fun at "Spikes" in town or at the State Line Hotel.

COSTA, THOMAS
393rd Bombardier

Soon after arriving at Wendover from Fairmont, four of us borrowed a jeep, sneaked off the base by driving over the railroad tracks, and went deer hunting in the mountains. It was still winter, so we wore our sheepskins including the boots. Late in the afternoon, our driver (nameless of course) hit a large rock and broke a tie rod. We were about ten miles from the base so we walked about five miles in those outfits, then reached a road and eventually a ride back to the base. We and the jeep had been missed by now so there was a welcoming committee.

I think the penalties would have been so severe that the brass decided to pretend it did not happen. Our good luck followed us the rest of the time we were in the 509th.

DELANEY, J. SLADE
320th Troop Carrier Squadron
Pilot

I was a member in the 393rd Bomb Squadron. My Spec. #932 is in the Refueling/Engineering Department and Heavy Equipment operator. I went where our squadron went to Cuba and Pacific Tinian Island. I remember a lot of Wendover Field, especially the old CCC barracks. I had never used coal for heat before and have a lot of other memories.

DEPRANG, RALIGH, K.
393rd Bomb Squadron
Refueling/Engineering Dept.
Heavy Equipment Operator

When our squadron was restricted to the base - shortly before leaving for overseas - Major Geller decided it would be fine if the EM had a party. But where would money come from. He instructed all officers in the squadron to kick in so much for the party. We dispatched one of our guys to pick up half barrels of beer at Elko, Nevada. I remember this guy's name as well as my own but think it best not to mention it.

He must have had a few too many at the watering hole in Elko because on the way back, he ran off the road and damaged the truck. Luckily, he was not hurt, nor the barrels damaged.

We borrowed a field range, got some ground beef from somewhere and had hamburgers and beef for our party. A real treat for Wendover.

FELLWOCK, ROBERT A.
1027 Air Material Squadron

I designed and painted the first C54 with a green wing and stripe on the fuselage. Col. Tibbets flew it to Washington the next day for approval.

We spent many 12 to 14 hour days keeping five C54s flying. A few of us never got to Tinian, due to the "Mad Scientists" and "High Priority Freight". Our aircraft would come back from Tinian with an odd engine and we would wind up changing all four engines due to different Dash Numbered Engines available.

We knew it was a hot project but we didn't know what. President Roosevelt passed away during this period, but no one seemed to know who the Vice President was.

Harry Truman took over very effectively. The bombs were dropped and the war ended abruptly. I feel we who never left Wendover contributed in a small way to the effort.

FITHIAN, THOMAS H.
320th Troop Carrier Squadron
Aircraft Inspector

I was newly married and wrote a letter every day. I worked in an office and had access to a typewriter. Since I ran a teletype, I was pretty accurate and could type 60 words a minute. We had an APO, San Francisco Post Office address and most of the mail was sent airmail.

We sent mail free for a while. William Carroll would arrive in a jeep, yell "mail call" and we would all gather around. Sometimes I would receive six letters a day, but there were periods when mail would not come through. It could take a week to ten days or it would get lost and you would receive it a month later.

Every letter was not sealed. It went to the censor. He went through it and would cut out passages. Some of my mail was pretty cut up. I was trying to indicate where we were as my wife did not know. She just assumed we were in the Pacific somewhere.

At times, we would do things that were not so smart. Maurice Scoggin and I would take a jeep and go into the jungle. There were roads and trails. We knew that guys were being shot at by the Japanese, but we were young, only 22.

GRILL, PATRICK
Base Signal Office

A portion of the ground crews in our squadron were assigned to the 15 planes of the 509th Composite Group. Three prop specialists from the 393rd Bombardment Squadron, Norman Carson, Bill Stuewe and myself, Harter, were responsible for all 15 planes in the 509th Group. We went where the planes went because they didn't want other ground crews working on these planes for security reasons. I inspected the props of the Enola Gay in the early morning hours of August 6, 1945.

HARTER, CLEO
393rd Prop Specialist

Arrived in Wendover in December 1942 and was assigned to the Bombing and Gunnery School back in the hill one mile from base. There is probably still lead in the surrounding hills and target wood on the flats. When Gunnery School closed, I was assigned to Base Headquarters and with exception of four months, stayed there until the 509th went overseas.

Due to the ruggedness of the Wendover area, friendship was very important. As Ground Troop Commander, I remember the beautiful train trip from Salt Lake to Seattle even if it was a troop train leaving for overseas.

I worked at the docks long hours before embarking, and had the dubious honor of being the first to get seasick even while we could still see land.

HOLMES, JAMES F.
390th Air Service Group
Adjutant

I worked for Jim Hinchey and Joe Buscher in the Intelligence Office. When we were on Tinian, Jim was the Air Sea Rescue Officer. We prepared all the information for the crews in case they had to ditch. We knew where the fleet was, the submarines, at all times so we could make up the folders in case you had to bail out.

JERNIGAN, NORRIS
Intelligence Office Clerk

211

We had just flown in to Batista Field, Havana, Cuba from Wendover. After we unloaded, we sat around on our bags in the tropical sunset waiting for something to happen. We finally hailed a busted down '36 Plymouth Taxi. A happy little Cuban, glad to get a fare, insisted our whole crew and luggage would somehow fit in. It would be a profitable trip for him. We passed sugar fields, banana plantations and then those narrow street villages. We made good time until a noise beneath the car indicated the drive shaft was trying to drive itself into the bottom of the car. As we traveled, the noise changed from an annoying vibration to a thumping. The once happy Cuban began to mumble something over and over. One of our crew understood Spanish. He told us he was reciting the Rosary over and over praying the taxi would make it to our destination. Just as we rounded the corner to the hotel driveway, the drive shaft gave a final thump. We walked the few steps further. The little happy Cuban was now elated as we each paid the taxi fare. His prayers had been answered. Maybe ours had been too, as we left the smoking antique.

KRAUSE, EUGENE
320th Flight Engineer

On we went to Nagasaki, a prayer in everyone's heart for a change in luck. Our radar soon told us we were approaching the city and the nearer we came, the greater grew our dejection. Like my friend Luis Alvarez, I had an Adjutant Generals Office (AGO) card on my person specifying it was valid only if captured by the enemy and informing the enemy I was entitled to the privileges of a colonel. I said to myself, any minute now, you may become a colonel.

LAURENCE, WILLIAM A.
New York Times Science Reporter
Observer on board Great Artiste
August 9, 1945

What did I think of Wendover? I didn't think there were places like that in the USA. But, being at war, we all had a job to do.

As for being inducted into the 509th, we, of the medical group, were not picked until the group came to Wendover. We were attached to the base hospital at that time. All of the groups needed medical personnel. It took all different technicians from medical, surgical, laboratories, dental, etc. I went as a surgical technician.

As it all turned out, I will say, I was lucky to be in a group such as the 509th. Security was tight but you learned to keep your mouth shut. As the sign said at the gate: "What You Hear Here, What You See Here, When You Leave Here, Let It Stay Here".

There was a large group out at 2 am to watch Col. Tibbets wave as he taxied to the runway for take off to Japan

MALONEY, ANTHONY J. JR.
509th Headquarters

At Eglin Field with The Ladybird, Ray Gallagher told me, "If you want to ask Paul Tibbets a question, wait till he is smoking his pipe. Don't ask him a question when he is smoking a cigarette".

McKEOWN, DORA DOUGHERTY
WASP Pilot B29 "Ladybird"

My stay at Wendover was only a couple of days. I kept to my Los Alamos Group mainly on the grounds of being secretive. All I can recall of Wendover is the amazing Salt Flats with the steady thermal mirage of hot air above them. I flew to the Pacific from Wendover by 509th Transport.

MORRISON, PHILIP
Project Alberta Scientist

The first day I visited the Flight Line to see the aircraft which I was assigned to, I decided to take a picture of it. As luck would have it, a guard was present and quickly informed me that NO Pictures were allowed on Wendover's Flight Line and he proceeded to take my camera which I never saw again. Thus, I am in no position to supply you with any photos you requested.

NORRIS, FRANK W.
320th Pilot

For lowly 2nd Lieutenants, at the low end of the pecking order, it seemed like we inherited the worst sleeping accommodations on the base. The one story, tarpaper shacks, not far from the Officers Club had no central heat but were heated by a pot bellied, coal stove, at each end of the barracks and attended by enlisted men assigned to keep the fires going and generally clean up the sleeping quarters. The centrally heated, comfortable Bachelor Officers Quarters (BOQ) buildings were assigned to the higher ranks (what else is new!). Along with nice rooms, beds and good furniture, instead of bunk beds like we had in our tarpaper suites, but we endured!

Many were the times we awoke in the morning to find it was darn cold, our coal stoves out, and a layer of black soot laying all over our beds and belongings because the stoves had backed up and gone out, causing one big messy clean-up job. Yes, one of the happy memories of our stay at Wendover during WWII.

OLIVI, FRED J.
393rd Bombardment Squadron
Crew C-15
Pilot

It is a very hard task to go back forty-five years and pick out the highlights of ones achievements.

The time spent at Wendover Air Base will never be forgotten. There were good times and times that were not so good, but I am thankful that most of my times were good ones.

It would be impossible to tell the whole story of my duties as a flight chief for the Enola Gay and the other six aircraft in the flight.

I would say one of the most memorable times was going to Omaha, Nebraska, to watch the seven aircraft I had, being built. The airplanes were special built and had equipment the other B29s did not have. To me, this was quite an honor.

OWENS, ELBERT CHRISTMAN
393rd Bombardment Squadron
Flight Chief

Arrived in Wendover on September 3, 1943, from Atlantic City, New Jersey, and was assigned to the 521st Service Squadron which was deactivated, and then assigned to the 401st Service Squadron which was also deactivated. I was then assigned to the 216th Base Unit until transferred to the 1027th Air Corps Supply of the 509th. All duties were in Air Corps Supply. My wife, Mary and I lived in a trailer off base. There were two couples to a trailer and only one door.

OXLEY, CHARLES R.
1027th Air Material Squadron
Air Corps Supply

My friend, Gerald Corcoran, and I were returning to Wendover after a furlough in Philadelphia. We boarded the Rio Grande and Western train at Denver. While taking on coal and water at the Moffitt Tunnel, we were talking to the locomotive engineer and he invited us to ride in the steam locomotive with him. We left the train at Wendover which was another coal and water stop.

To a couple of young fellows, it was a thrill to be in the locomotive with him.

I was assigned to B29 named "The Big Stink".

Francis Pellegrino

Gerald Corcoran

PELLEGRINO, FRANCIS A.
393rd Bombardment Squadron
Ground Crew

I was a member of the First Ordnance Squadron. Our primary responsibility was to assemble the atomic bombs on Tinian. This was accomplished in thirty-three days after the arrival of all organizational equipment. My job description was to load and drive the BST (Bomb Service Trailer). I only stayed at Wendover Field three days. I met Daisy, my wife of 54 years, there.

PEPE, HENRY J.
1st Ordnance

I remember arriving with our two month old son before our belongings did. "Cappy" slept in a bureau drawer, his diapers were attached to the clothes line with safety pins.

Many, many times the washings had to be redone due to the soft coal that was in the air.

One day, I looked out and sheep were everywhere. They were coming down from the mountains.

PERRY, CHARLES A.
393rd Bombardment Squadron
Mess Officer
Submitted by Evelyn Perry

I vividly remember being temporarily quartered in some pyramidal tents and when a heavy windstorm leveled our tent one night, we hauled our cots into the nearest latrine and spent the rest of the night there. We spent the following night there as well until we could be assigned new accommodations.

Then, of course, I remember those often greasy eating utensils and the divided metal trays, that periodically gave us a case of the "GIs". The coal burning, pot bellied stoves in the barracks that blew up occasionally also came to mind.

But, most memorable of all is the camaraderie that we enjoyed in the finance department; in fact, bonds developed that have lasted, in some cases, until the present.

PETERSON, WESLEY P.
390th Air Service Squadron
Finance Clerk

We were dropping 10,000 pound bombs. They were called "pumpkins". That was one reason I named my airplane "Some Punkins". The Salt Lake City newspaper had a cartoon about two long legged girls. They were called "some punkins" and they looked like one of the girls we had painted on the airplane.

PRICE, JAMES
Airplane Commander Crew B-7

I went into the service July 1942 and received eight weeks of basic training at Mineral Wells, Texas. Next stop was Salt Lake City, Utah but was not assigned to any crew there. About a month later, I went by train to Wendover Field, Utah. There I was assigned to the Motor Pool and became a truck driver for sometime. Then they assigned me as dispatcher.

Later I was approached to join this special group no one knew anything about. The transportation officer asked if I would like to join. He said there would be many promotions working in the new company. I don't think I had any choice, so I was assigned to the 390th Air Service Group.

When we were shipped to Tinian, I was one of the lucky ones to go by air. My return to the States was much longer as I was aboard ship.

I arrived the last part of October 1945. Was transported to Roswell, New Mexico by train. I was discharged November 1945.

PRINCE, R. L.
390th Air Service Group

Among my many memories of Wendover include: The day Whitey Fellwock pulled me off the drill field to report to First Sgt. Robert Kelley. He asked me if I could be on the flight-line for departure to Los Angeles (home) in one hour. I was there in 45 minutes to board the C54 piloted by Col. Tibbets. The mission was to pick up some aircraft parts and attend the Nelson Eddy Radio Program to introduce the 509ths official song "Silver Wings".

Standing on the dock of Warehouse Building 2224 watching the Western Pacific Rail Road's United Nations Special, slowly pass through Wendover enroute to the May 1945 conference in San Francisco, California.

SHEPHERD, HARRY G., JR.
1027th Air Material Squadron
Tech Supply Clerk

I got a kick out of seeing the Fairmont Army Air Field News with the picture of my crew as "Crew of the Week". It brought back memories of one of those marathon flights that we were "awarded" for. We could take a B17 any place we wanted to go in the US for a weekend. Takeoff Saturday morning and be back in time for duty Monday morning.

SMITH, ELBERT B.
Airplane Commander Crew A-5

"I've looked at you. You have looked at me. I'm not going to get stuck with all of you, but those of you who remain are going to be stuck with me. You have been brought here to work on a very special mission, those who stay will be going overseas. You are here to take part in an effort which could end the war. Don't ask what the job is. That's a sure fire way to be transferred out. Do exactly what you are told, when you are told, and you will get along fine. Never mention this base to anybody. This means your wives, girls, sisters, family. It's not going to be easy for any of us but we will succeed by working together. However, all work and no play is no fun. So as of now, you can go on furlough. Enjoy yourself."

TIBBETS, PAUL W.
1st Meeting with 509th

On July 20, 1945, we had to fly over the emperors palace to bomb our assigned target, a Tokyo Railroad Station. We dropped the bomb just as the train came in. I'll bet the locomotive spun 100 feet in the air.

THORNHILL, FELIX
Navigator Crew C-11

At Wendover, P47s, B17s then B29s. Engine changes, fences, security. No air conditioning, no television, lousy food and a place to lose your money.

After my basic training in Miami, Florida, I went to B17 Mechanic School. I was sent to Wendover, Utah, from Lincoln, Nebraska, only to find P-47's with Pratt Whitney engines. Soon after, 15 new B29s came in and I was in the Engine Buildup Department. I was a grease monkey, crew chief, etc.

With a 3 day pass, I went to Salt Lake City. When I returned, the PV Marshall called me in his office. He told me exactly who I was with, what I ate, what I smoked, and everything I did, etc. Little did I know what top-secret we were under. Walter Winchell called Wendover "The concentration camp of America". Then the day came that we knew what we were doing (bombing).

After the war was over, we were changed to ATSC (Air Tech. Service Command), all experimental stuff.

On February 22, 1946, I was discharged from Fort Dix, New Jersey. I hitchhiked home - about 70 miles and 30 rides.

TYNAN, EDWIN
216th Base Unit
Engine Buildup Department

I remember "Spikes" great food at great prices. How can you sell a steak during wartime for $2? I remember Lou Schafer lining up all the MPs at Batista Field and marching them through the terminal. Paul Tibbets, Tom Ferebee and I were the first to arrive in a C54 in Cuba. It was the middle of the night and Paul told Tom and me we could not go to bed until everyone in the 509th was fed. Tom had to pull his .45 on the cook.

I remember the great people. Not any individual, but the people as a group (and not as in Air Force Group). A few of the individuals were to put it kindly, forgettable and have been forgotten. But the vast majority were what the young generation classifies as "neat". They were competent, professional, friendly and had class. It was enjoyable being around them both at work and at play. Wendover didn't have much to offer but the people made it memorable.

VAN KIRK,
THEODORE J.
"DUTCH"
Headquarters
Group, Navigator

Ted Van Kirk's meal ticket for Dai Ichi Hotel

1st Individual Air Force patch, presented to Ted Van Kirk at Wendover before formation of the 509th

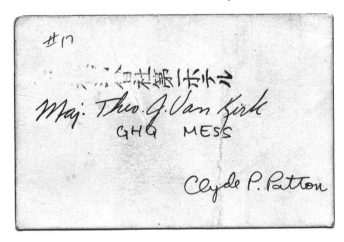

215

Wendover Field

Pre-war Wendover had a population of 103. Approximately one person per slot machine. Spike Birdsell, the Mayor of the town, went out of his way to make the soldiers at home in Wendover. He reasoned "the boys went out of their way to get to Wendover".

Spike had his own place of business called "Spikes", always having good food and drinks on hand. For those who liked to dance, he had a dance floor and the music.

All that was needed were the girls. For additional entertainment, there was the Stateline Hotel with its western style bar and casino.

If a soldier didn't leave base, there were weekly dances at the service club. Girls came by bus from Salt Lake City, Utah, Ely, Elko, Wells and McGill, Nevada and other settlements within a radius of 150 miles. There were two post theaters and an outdoor swimming pool.

Near the base hospital was the library. It was furnished with comfortable lounge chairs and the soldiers could speak to friends without receiving the "hush-hush" look from the librarian. The library had a music room and a collection of records.

393rd Patch

Tom Classen briefs 393rd crews

393rd Crews listening to Tom Classen
Front row: Charles McKnight; 2nd row: Ira Weatherly,
Claude Eatherly

Jacob Beser, 393rd Radar

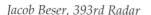

216

Processing at Wendover

Code training at Wendover

Major George W. Wescott

Clothing display

AFBU 28FEB.45 857-2 218CLOTHING DISPLAY

*Billy Burns,
Armament*

*William Wright,
Navigation*

*Fred Krug,
Weather*

*Thomas Karnes (right)
with his look-alike*

*V-2 test rocket
being fired at
Wendover*

Crew A-1

(L-R)
Nat Burgwyn, Radar
*Ralph Taylor, Airplane
Commander*
Mike Angelich, Bombardier
Ray Biel, Pilot
Robert Valley, Tail Gunner
Theodore Slife, Radio
Fred Hoey, Navigator
*Richard Anselme, Assistant
Flight Engineer*
Frank Briese, Flight Engineer

Crew A-2

Top Row, (L-R)
*Edward Costello, Airplane
Commander*
Harry Davis, Pilot
Tom Brumagin, Flight Engineer
Bob Petrolli, Navigator
John Downey, Bombardier

Front Row, (L-R)
James McGlennon
Unknown
Carleton McEachern, Tail Gunner
David Purdon, Radio
*Maurice Clark, Assistant
Flight Engineer*
James Bryant, Radar

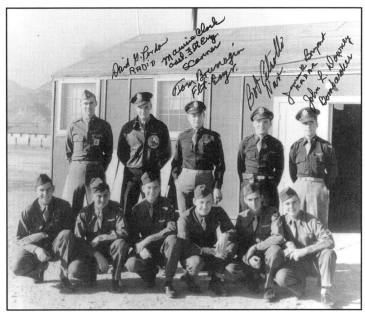

Crew A-3

Top Row, (L-R)
Ralph Devore, Airplane Commander
William Easton, Pilot
Leon Cooper, Bombardier
William Hulse, Flight Engineer
Frank Wimer, Navigator

Front Row, (L-R)
Clarence Britt, Assistant Flight Engineer
Glenn Allison, Tail Gunner
Michael Bohon, Radar
Lee Palmert, Radio

Crew A-4

Top Row, (L-R)
William Desmond, Pilot
Robert Donnell, Engineer
Louis Allen, Bombardier
John Dulin, Navigator
Joseph Westover, Airplane
Commander

Front Row, (L-R)
Walter Spradlin, Tail Gunner
James E. Doiron, Radio
Sam Wheeler, Assistant Engineer
William Cotter, Radar

Crew A-5

Top Row, (L-R)
George Weller, Radar
Lee Caylor, Assistant Engineer
Alfred Lewandowski, Tail Gunner
William Rowe, Pilot
Omar Strickland, Radio

Bottom Row, (L-R)
Lt. Col. Thomas Classen, Airplane Commander
William Wright, Navigator
Floyd Kenner, Engineer
Bobby Chapman, Bombardier

Crew B-6

Top Row, standing
James Duva, Navigator
James Davis, Engineer
Ellsworth Carrington, Pilot

Front Row
Unknown
John Wilson, Airplane Commander
Vernon Rowley, Radar
Donald Rowe, Assistant Engineer
Paul Gruning, Bombardier
Chester Rogalski, Tail Gunner
Glen Floweree, Radio

Crew B-7

Top Row, (L-R)
James Price, Airplane Commander
Everist Bednorz, Pilot
Thomas Costa, Bombardier
William Collinson, Navigator
James Adkins, Engineer

Front Row, (L-R)
Clyde Bysom, Tail Gunner
Robert Byrd, Radio
Frederick Brown, Assistant Engineer
John Britt, Rear Gunner
Adam Castellitto, Gunner

Crew B-8

Top Row, (L-R)
Charles McKnight, Airplane Comander
Jacob Bontekoe, Pilot
Jack Widowsky, Navigator
Franklin MacGregor, Bombardier
George Cohen, Engineer

Front Row, (L-R)
PFC Sherman, Radar
Donald Cole, Waist Gunner
Lloyd Reeder, Radio
PFC Cordiere, Waist Gunner
PFC Corliss, Tail Gunner
Sgt. Pasternick, Central Fire Control
"Monty" the dog

Crew B-9

Top Row, (L-R)
Richard McNamara, Pilot
Harold Rider, Navigator
Stewart Williams, Bombardier
Robert Lewis, Airplane Commander

Bottom Row, (L-R)
Richard Nelson, Radio
George Caron, Tail Gunner
Robert Shumard, Assistant Engineer
Wyatt Duzenbury, Engineer
Joseph Stiborik, Radar Operator

221

Crew B-10

Top Row, (L-R)
George Marquardt, Airplane Commander
James Anderson, Pilot
Russell Gackenbach, Navigator
James Strudwick, Bombardier
James Corliss, Engineer

Bottom Row, (L-R)
Joseph Dijulio, Radar
Dobson, dropped from crew
Anthony Capua, Assistant Engineer
Warren Coble, Radio
Melvin Bierman, Tail Gunner

Crew C-11

Top Row, (L-R)
Claude Eatherly, Airplane Commander
Ira Weatherly, Pilot
Frank Wey, Bombardier
Francis Thornhill, Navigator
Albert Barsumian, Radar Operator

Front Row, (L-R)
Jack Bivans, Assistant Engineer
Gillon Niceley, Tail Gunner
Pasquale Baldasaro, Radio Operator
Eugene Grennan, Engineer

Crew C-12

Top Row, (L-R)
Herman S. Zahn, Jr., Airplane Commander
Gilbert B. Dickman, Pilot
Henry Deutsch, Navigator
Francis R. Ormand, Bombardier

Front Row, (L-R)
James Elder, Engineer
Neil R. Corey, Assistant Engineer
Leander J. Baur, Radio
Raymond E. Allen, Tail Gunner
Gerald F. Clapso, Radar

Crew C-13

Top Row, (L-R)
Frederick Bock, Airplane Commander
Hugh Ferguson, Pilot
Charles Levy, Bombardier
Leonard Godfrey, Navigator
Robert Stock, Tail Gunner

Bottom Row, (L-R)
Ralph Belanger, Assistant Engineer
William Barney, Radar
Ralph Curry, Radio
Roderick Arnold, Engineer

Crew C-14

Top Row, (L-R)
Stanley Steinke, Navigator
Myron Faryna, Bombardier
John Cantlon, Pilot
Norman Ray, Airplane Commander

Bottom Row, (L-R)
George Brabenec, Engineer
Francis Dolan, Radio
Richard Cannon, Radar
Martin Murray, Tail Gunner
Thomas Bunting, Assistant Engineer

Crew C -15

Top Row, (L-R)
Fred Olivi, Pilot
Kermit Beahan, Bombardier
Charles Sweeney, Squadron Commander
James Van Pelt, Navigator
Charles Albury, Airplane Commander

Bottom Row, (L-R)
Albert Dehart, Tail Gunner
John Kuharek, Engineer
Edward Buckley, Radar
Raymond Gallagher, Assistant Engineer
Abe Spitzer, Radio

223

Crew 123 - Wendover

Top Row, (L-R)
Don Rehl, Airplane Commander
Frank Stewart, Navigator
Raymond Diering, Radar
Richard Sands, Pilot
Chris Turoff, Bombardier
George Gregovich, Engineer

Front Row, (L-R)
Ralph Jensen, Radio
Bob Dempsey, Assistant Engineer
Harrison Vail, Tail Gunner

*Orders to Rehl crew to look for radiation clouds
with scientists on board*

Army Shifts Commanders At Wendover Air Base

Tribune Intermountain Wire

WENDOVER—Col. Clifford C. Heflin, Fresno, Cal., has been appointed commanding officer at Wendover field, succeeding Lt. Col. Charles E. Trowbridge, public relations officers announce Tuesday.

Col. Heflin, who returned recently from the European theater of operations, where he served with the Eighth air force, was commanding officer of a Liberator bomber group and served with the royal air force coastal command.

Promoted to a colonelcy in May, 1944, he holds the distinguished flying cross with oak leaf cluster, the air medal with five oak leaf clusters, the French legion of honor and the croix de guerre with palm.

Col. Heflin was commissioned with the air corps reserve in 1937 and in the regular army in 1939. He attended Fresno State college and Santa Clara university, where he participated in three sports. He was tackle on the Santa Clara football team and competed in basketball and boxing.

He holds a senior pilot rating.

Mrs. Heflin and their two children joined him recently at Wendover.

RESTRICTED

HEADQUARTERS WENDOVER FIELD
Wendover, Utah

SPECIAL ORDERS   11 Aug 1945
NUMBER   223

1. Fol named EM, Sq A 216th AAFBU (Sp), WP on TDY to Ft Douglas Utah o/a 11 Aug 45 by Govt MT for purpose of picking up vehicles and upon compl this TDY will ret this sta. In accordance with AR 35-4610,FD will pay in advance the prescribed monetary alws in lieu of rat a/r $1.00 per meal for 2 meals to 2 EM each. TDN. 601-29 P 432-02 212/60425. Auth 2AF Ltr 35-30 11 Jan 45.

Cpl Robert H Lasher   13134479   Cpl Cornelius A Talsma   37280012

2. The VOCO 8 Aug 45 directing the fol named AC O and EM,Sq A 216th AAFBU (Sp), to proceed on TDY to Seattle Wash by mil acft to perform routine tng flt and upon compl this TDY to ret this sta is hereby confirmed and made a matter of record, the exigencies of the sv having prevented issuance of orders in advance. In accordance with AR 35-4610,FD will pay EM the prescribed monetary alws in lieu of rat and qrs a/r $5.00 per day for period of TDY at destination where rat and qrs were not available. TDN. 601-29 P 432-02 212/60425. Auth 2AF Ltr 35-30 11 Jan 45.

2D LT GEORGE W GREGOVICH   0709129   2D LT DONALD C REHL   0828527
FO   RAYMOND J DIERING   T138923   FO   FRANK B STEWART   T142706
S Sgt Ralph L Jensen   36332617   S Sgt Harrison A Vail 12027271
                           Sgt William R Horton   34737145

3. Permission previously granted the fol named EM, Sq A 216th AAFBU (Sp), to rat separately and reside off the Base is hereby withdrawn:

Sgt Edward E Booker   18046372   Sgt Calvin H Lengel   13008827

4. S Sgt Wilbert P Koenig 36317679, on DS this sta from 4000th AAFBU Wright Fld Dayton Ohio, is atchd Sq A 216th AAFBU (Sp) for rat, qrs and adm eff 10 Aug 45. (Confirming VOCO 10 Aug 45).

5. Fol named EM,Sq A 216th AAFBU (Sp), are granted permission to rat separately and reside off the Base:

T Sgt Harold F Morris   15017013   S Sgt Harvey Fullerton   36459134
Sgt Montfort L Clark   31358565   Sgt Carl W Culver   36215348
Sgt Emanuel Sharoff   32241355   Cpl Ralph E Mieland   36696468
Pfc Robert J Smith   36641989   Pvt Eugene J Hernandez 39590821

6. Pfc (747) James O Miller 13089583 (Col K) AC (W),MOO 590,Sq A 216th AAFBU (Sp) 2AF, is trfd and WP Project REB-13 232nd AAFBU Dalhart Tex 2AF o/a 14 Aug 45. In accordance with AR 35-4810,FD will pay in advance the prescribed monetary alws in lieu of rat a/r $1.00 per meal for 5 meals to 1 EM. TDN. 601-31 P 431-02 212/60425. Auth TWX 2AF GB5883 23 July 45. EDCMR 17 Aug 45.

BY ORDER OF COLONEL HEFLIN:

                                      CLAYTON A PEARSON
                                      CAPT, AC
OFFICIAL: Actg Adj

CLAYTON A PEARSON
CAPT, AC
Actg Adj

DISTRIBUTION
A   -1-

SO 222 this Hq cs contains 19 pars.

RESTRICTED

Records and Investigation Section, 1395th MPs

1395th MPs at Wendover

509th Photo Section, December 1944

Left to Right: 1st Row: Robert L. Wells, Alexander G. Schiavone, Domonick Osoco, Jerome J. Ossip, Harold L. Weiss, Robert E. Mulvey, John H. VanderVoort, Floyd E. Ross 2nd Row: Frank McMillan, Adolph Gasser, Ed C. Berg, Harold W. Dube, Edward A. Burgess, Joseph Gayeski, Allan L. Karl, Arthur E. Josephson, William H. Reimers Missing from Photo: Paul Lentz, Armen Shamlian (both on furlough)

320th Emblem and Patch

320th Flight Line, Wendover

320th Crew #2

(L-R)
John Casey, Squadron Commander
Arthur Henderson, Pilot
Deane Churchill, 3rd Pilot
Robert Ames, 2nd Pilot
Wilbur Lyon, Assistant Navigator
Wilbur Waggoner, Navigator
Frank Carlo, Radio
John Williams, Engineer
James Babcock, Assistant Engineer

320th Crew prior to Tinian Flight

(L-R)
1st Lt. Gold
2nd Lt. Bruenger
2nd Lt. Briggs
1st Lt. Lyon
F/O Castater
Pfc. Doubeck
Sgt. Smith
T/Sgt. Miller

320th Crew prior to Tinian Flight

(L-R)
Col. Tibbets
Col. Fisher
1st Lt. Gold, Pilot
2nd Lt. Briggs, Pilot
1st Lt. Lyon, Navigator
F/O Castater
Pfc. Doubek
T/Sgt. Miller
Sgt. Smith

320th Crew
prior to Tinian Flight

(L-R)
T/Sgt Robert Hannah, Engineer
Lt. Loren Mills, Pilot
2nd Lt. Russell Angeli, Pilot
2nd Lt. Frank Griffin, Pilot
2nd Lt. Virgil Mann, Navigator
Sgt. William Boles, Engineer
Cpl. Robert Felblinger, Radio
Cpl Paul Marcello, Radio
2nd Lt. George Scheer, Navigator

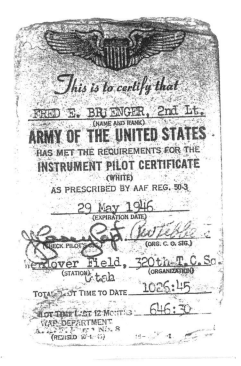

Fred Bruenger, Pilot
Stephen Briggs, Pilot
320th Headquarters,
Wendover

320th Operations
Office at Wendover.
S/Sgt. Mark Bayuk
is on left.
John Cloepfil on
right. John was
always promoting a
ride to Omaha to
visit his folks... he
would check opera-
tions to see who was
nearby and could
pick him up for the
return trip.

C54 on autopilot,
pilot resting

C54 49007 (#4)
at Tinian with Saipan
in background, July 1945

C54 49007

Col. Tibbets boards plane

Col. Tibbets

*1395th M.P.s and Photo Unit
board plane for Tinian*

Ready for takeoff

320th Ground Crew

(L-R)
Parke Miller
Fox
Rowland Robinson
Arthur Stein
Victor Lange

**320th
Maintenance
Crew Group
Photo**

**320th Ground
Crews**

**320th Ground
Crew**

320th Troop Carrier Squadron Group Photo

Orders for first two 320th crews to go to Tinian

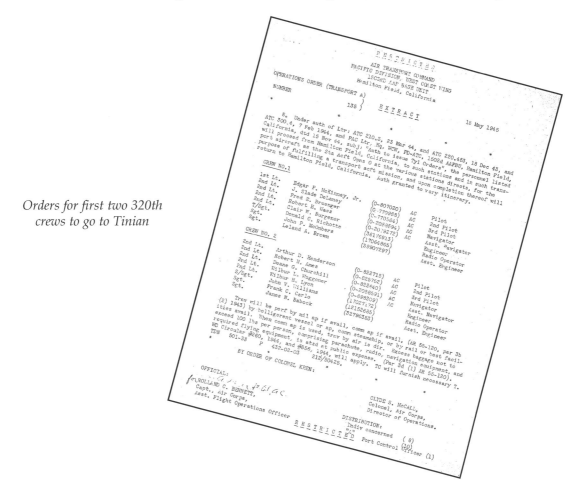

We Trained in Cuba

On January 7, 1945, an advance party of six officers and twenty-six enlisted men of the 393rd Bombardment Squadron, together with other personnel of the group, left Wendover for temporary duty at Batista Field Cuba. This was the beginning of a period of extensive training which was to last until the end of February. By the 14th of January, ten B29s with combat and ground crews were at Batista Field ready for specialized training operations.

The training was divided into two parts. The first part consisted of radar bombing from altitudes of 20,000 to 30,000 feet. Gunnery was also practiced on these flights. Briefing was held at 0600, takeoff scheduled for before 0800 and landing at approximately 1400.

The second part was a simulated combat mission with formal briefing and a simulated enemy target. At a joint staff meeting, the day previous to the missions, due consideration was given to the course of, over and returning from the target, enemy situations and capabilities, the target itself, communications, operational data, weather and all other information to make the mission both plausible and successful. From the 15th to the 31st of January, the crews averaged 42 flying hours in training missions.

In February, the necessary additional crews were blended into the training program; at the end of February, training was completed. The average number of simulated combat missions flown was approximately 3½. The average time flown by each crew, for the period of temporary duty, at Cuba was 66 hours.

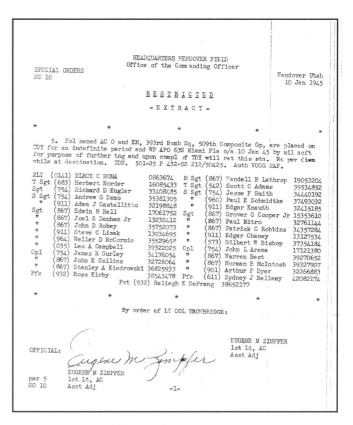

Orders for 393rd Radar to go to Cuba

Orders for 393rd, 216th B.U., 1395th MPs, and 1027 to go to Cuba

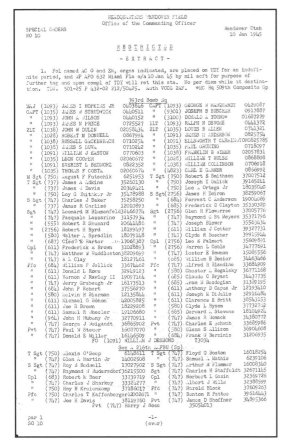

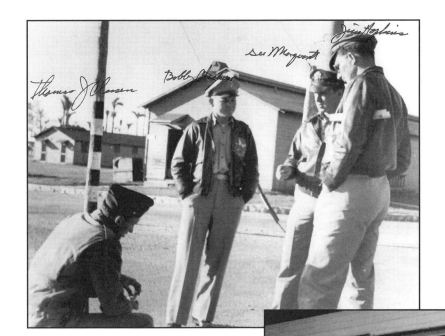

Batista Field
(L-R)
Thomas Classen
Bobby Chapman
George Marquardt
James Hopkins

393rd Radar — "Chow Hounds",
February 6, 1945
Facing camera: (L-R): Denham,
McIntosh,
Metro, Robbins, Baugh

Batista Field kitchen

Batista Field kitchen workers

*Officers Club,
Batista Field*

*Barracks,
Batista Field*

*Barracks,
Batista Field*

Basketball and baseball at Batista Field

Control Tower, Batista Field

Barracks, Batista Field

Barracks, Batista Field Note Cuban and American flags

C54 at Batista Field before nose art was painted

Servicemens Club and Gym
Batista Field

Batista Field Paper

SLOPPY JOE'S BAR

Batista Field was located near Cayuga, Cuba, 30 miles Southwest of Havana. Sloppy Joe's Bar was located on Animas Street between Prado and Zulueta. Mr. Jose Abeal (Sloppy Joe) bought a small grocery store at that corner and was visited by several friends who said, "Joe, this place is sloppy." From then on the name "Sloppy Joes" stuck to Jose Abeal. Later his bar business, at the same address, became famous and internationally known.

Back Row (L-R)
Jim Duva, Don Rowe, Unknown,
Bob Shumard, Unknown,
Ellsworth Carrington,
Chet Rogalski, Wayne Gruning,
Glen Floweree

Front Row (L-R)
Unknown, Jim Davis, John Wilson, Unknown,
Unknown, Unknown

(L-R)
Franklin MacGregor, Donald Cole,
Lloyd Reeder, Charles McKnight,
Roderick Legg, Jacob Bontekoe,
George Cohen, Jack Widowsky

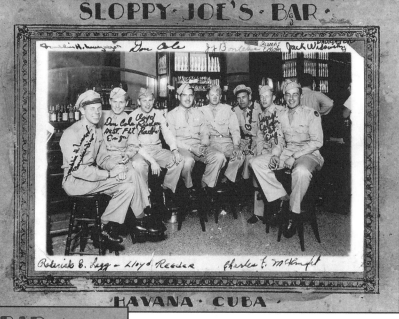

This photo contains crew from B29 "City of Omaha" on February 15, 1945. The 330th Bomb Group was training at Batista Field the same time as the 509th. The 330th were told not to mix with the 509th.

Top Row (L-R)
Milt Leibowitz, Bombardier (330th);
Glen Jensen, Co-Pilot (330th);
Howard McClellan, Pilot (330th)

Middle Row (L-R)
Tony Ruggeri, Radar (330th); Tony Capoccia, Gunner (330th); Ernie Brock, CFC Gunner (330th); Jane, Charles, and Gloria Goldman (from Chicago area); Gilbert Arce, Tail Gunner (330th)

Front Row (L-R)
Sgt. Campbell & Cp. Chester Hammond (both 509th); Lyle Thomas, Flight Engineer (330th); Joe Cermeno, Radio (330th); Chuck Wassum, Gunner (330th); and Sgt. Steve Kinosh (509th)

240

(L-R)
Fred Bock, Charles Levy,
Len Godfrey

Front Row Seated, (L-R)
John Dulin, John Hubeny,
James Hopkins, Robert Donnell, William
Cotter, Loy Whitaker

Second Row Standing (L-R)
Cleo Harter, James Womak,
William Desmond, Charles Baker, Samuel
Wheeler, Louis Allen,
James Doiron, Robert Smithson

Third Row (L-R)
Charles Schwab, Deward Stevens

Identified on photo

(L-R)
Unknown, Unknown,
Pasquale Baldasaro
Albert Barsumian,

(L-R)
Frank Wimer, Wilbur Lyon,
Leon Cooper, Locke Easton,
Fred Bruenger

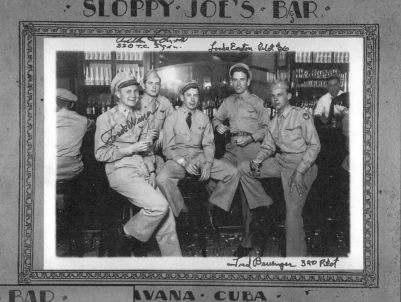

Back Row (L-R)
Sid ?, Dick Cannon, Rod Arnold,
Tom Bunting, Hank Elder, Francis Dolan,
Mike Bohon, Bill Barney

Front Row (L-R)
Martin Murray, Fred ?, Joe ?
Clarence Britt, Verne Holmes

242

SLOPPY · JOE'S · BAR ·

Tom Brumagin, Flti Engr. #95

Robert Petrolli Nav.

· HAVANA · CUBA ·

(L-R)
Cuban Guide, Bob Petrolli,
Tom Brumagin, Harry Davis,
Ed Costello, John Downey

(L-R)
Arthur Stein, Victor Lange,
Alfred Norris, Robert Davenport, William
Cain, William Anderson, Robert Hensler

· SLOPPY · JOE'S · BAR ·

· HAVANA · CUBA ·

SLOPPY · JOE'S · BAR

· HAVANA · CUBA ·

(L-R)
William Miller, John Williams
Robert Ames, Unknown
George Sheer, Loren Mills
Russ Angeli

243

(L-R)
Wendell Lathrop,
Edwin Bell,
Melvin Jones,
Paul Metro

(L-R)
Stanley Kiedrowski,
John Robey

Front Row (L-R):
Unknown, Joseph DiJulio, George
Marquardt, Warren Coble, Unknown,
Unknown

Back Row (L-R):
Russell Gackenbach, Joseph Gulick,
James Anderson, Unknown, Fred
Clayton, Unknown, James Strudwick,
Melvin Bierman

We Leave for Tinian

The main ground echelon, having completed all required training and processing, received orders to depart on Thursday morning April 26, 1945 from Wendover Field, Utah. For the purpose of traveling by rail, this group was divided into two sections; one, totaling 36 officers and 532 enlisted men, boarded the train at Wendover Station and pulled out promptly at 0800 April 26, 1945; two, totaling 8 officers and 283 enlisted men repeated the process several hours later. Major George Wescott, the Troop Commander, reported the trip by rail would have been uneventful had not a formidable siege of dysentery overtaken about 60 personnel.

On Saturday morning April 28, both sections arrived at the Seattle, Washington military terminal. A convoy of trucks from Fort Lawton drove the group to the Fort. Within two hours after leaving the train, all personnel were fed and assigned to barracks.

On Saturday May 5, the main portion of the group was conveyed to the port and there put aboard the ship "Cape Victory". The next morning the remaining personnel followed and at 1220 May 6, 1945, all passengers were advised by the ship's captain to wear or have at hand at all times, their life jackets. Each soldier on board had been issued motion sickness tablets at Fort Lawton.

On the latter part of the second day out, the ship encountered a storm, the severest reported in eight months, which upset many a stomach. On Sunday May 13, just one week after leaving the States, the troopship sailed within sight of the Hawaiian Islands and dropped anchor that evening in Honolulu Harbor, Oahu.

The men were restricted to the ship the following day until early in the evening. Mail call, the first since leaving the States, kept everyone in high spirits, during the day, as did frequent musical sessions by a five piece combination organized within the group.

A representative of Army Special Services, having heard the group had docked, arranged to bring a troupe of native singers and dancers to the warehouse adjoining the pier to present an evenings entertainment. The men aboard ship enjoyed two hours of unique and colorful songs and dancing.

On the morning of May 15, a mobile Post Exchange Unit pulled into the adjoining warehouse which by now was being used as a recreation and exercise area. The men were now able to purchase food, toilet articles, stationary and other necessities.

The "Cape Victory" left Honolulu Harbor as one of a convoy of three troopships at 1830 May16. After nine days of travel, the ship entered the Atoll at Eniwetok, stayed for a little more that twenty-four hours and proceeded on the final leg of her journey accompanied by a single Patrol Craft.

The ship docked at Tinian in the afternoon of May 29, 1945. A total of twenty-three days was required for the voyage. The personnel debarked at 0815 Memorial Day, May 30 and were met by acting Commanding Officer, Lieutenant Colonel Hazen Payette.

Leaving Wendover

Overseas Movement, Advanced Air Echelon

The advanced Air Echelon was commanded by Lieutenant Colonel Hazen J. Payette. It consisted of twenty-nine officers and sixty-one enlisted men. Three C54s were furnished by the 320th Troop Carrier Squadron to transport these individuals from the States to Tinian. The first two planes departed Wendover Field, Utah, May 15, the third plane did not depart until May 19, the delay being occasioned while awaiting the arrival of the pilot from his familiarization flight over the route with the Air Transport Command.

A total of 520 officers and enlisted men made up the advance, main and rear air echelons, transported quickly and efficiently by planes of the 320th Troop Carrier Squadron. By the end of May, after enjoying leave and furloughs, the 393rd Squadron had nine new modified B29s, each having been flown by one of the Squadron's crews from Omaha, Nebraska to Wendover Field, Utah. Then began acceptance checks and shakedown missions before leaving the States. Each aircraft put in from 25 to 40 hours

Hurry up and wait

flying time during these missions, which consisted of bombing, calibration of instruments and cruise control practice.

The first of the fifteen crews, Lt. Westover, Lt. McKnight and Capt. Wilson departed from Wendover on June 5. Three days later the crews of Capt. Price and Capt. Eatherly departed. In another three days Capt. Bock, Capt. Taylor, Capt. Marquardt and Lt. Devore and their crews took off. Lt. Col. Classen left on June 19. Maj. Sweeney (Lt. Albury's crew), Captain Lewis and Lt. Ray left Wendover on June 27. This brought the total number of crews en route overseas to thirteen and left two at Wendover, Captain Zahn's and Captain Costello's who at this time had not yet received their planes from Omaha.

Upon arrival at Tinian, all combat crews spent seven days in the Wing Lead Crew Ground School. Subjects covered included, theatre history, air/sea rescue, ditching and bail outs, survival, Japanese people, radar bombing methods, Wing and Army Air Force regulations, weather, cruise control, emergency procedures, camera operation, dinghy drill and other classes bearing directly on combat operations.

1st Ordnance Squadron, Special (Aviation) Movement Overseas

While many of the 1st Ordnance Squadron were undergoing an intense schedule of training at Wendover Field, movement to the overseas destination had begun. Three officers and seventy enlisted men left Wendover Field for the Seattle Port of Embarkation on June 4, 1945 and then to Tinian on June 15.

During the same period, six officers and fifty-six enlisted men departed by air on June 5, 6 and 7, 1945. One officer and forty-six enlisted men comprised the Second Airborne contingent which departed Wendover Field on June 16 and 17, 1945.

As the remainder completed their required training, they left a few at a time with flights of the 320th Troop Carrier Squadron.

Tinian

The greater part of the 509th arrived in May 1945, but it is important to note that from June 1st until the first week in August, both individuals and equipment arrived almost every week from the States by C54 or B29. In June 1945, the 1st Technical Service Detachment, War Department Miscellaneous Group became attached to the 509th.

This technical service detachment had been activated for the purpose of administering a variety of scientists, security officers and naval personnel needed in the Atomic Bomb Project. Among these personnel were physicians whose assignment was to examine the physiological effects of the Atomic Bomb upon crew members and the enemy. There were Navy Officers who aided in designing the bomb, Counter-Intelligence Officers, fuse experts, radar specialists and scientists who contributed to the development and perfection of the Atomic Bomb and bombing techniques.

During the first part of June, all available personnel were busy unloading group equipment from ships. The "Cape Victory" was unloaded by June 5, 1945. Five days later the "Emile Berlinger" docked. The bulk of its cargo, the Groups' organizational equipment was unloaded in five days.

Large Quonset Huts were utilized as storage warehouses and items needed for immediate use were issued from them. On June 11, the complete organization, with exception of the 603rd Engineering Squadron and the 1027th Air Material Squadron, moved to the 18th Naval Construction Battalion (NCB) Area. A large empty warehouse was discovered in this area and put to use as Group Supply Headquarters. The Groups' property was transferred from the Quonset Huts, which would belong to the 1st Ordnance, to the new area. A total of eleven B29s arrived in June. The Maintenance Unit immediately began to conduct one hundred hour inspections on each aircraft, required after an overseas flight. On July 8, 1945, the Group moved to the 13th NCB Area, where they acquired eighty-nine Quonset Huts, a consolidated mess hall, a large warehouse with sizeable fenced area, and sufficient latrine, shower and water facilities to accommodate the Group.

An attractive headquarters area of Quonset Huts arranged in a unique and symmetrical fashion furnished the Group with a pleasant area in which to work. A chapel modest and simple was centrally located for everyone's convenience. An open air theatre was named "Pumpkin Playhouse" with a seating capacity of approximately 1000 persons.

July was a busy month for aircraft maintenance men. There were no major problems as most of the missions flown were training missions, no aircraft sustained any

battle damage. During July, the permanent maintenance area was completed and turned over to the Group.

It included hardstands, taxi strips and twelve Quonset Huts. The entire maintenance section, including technical supply, began the work of moving all shops and equipment to this area. The twelve Quonset Huts were found to be sufficient only for the housing of the shops. It therefore became necessary to set up part of the combat line maintenance section in squad tents. The tents were used for the protection of equipment, not as work shops.

The Group motor pool and motor pool maintenance shops were also moved into the new area. The 603rd Air Engineering Squadron and 1027th Air Material Squadron were to continue working in the service centers. They

remained in their assigned areas and made necessary arrangements for permanent quarters there.

Training Missions

Required training missions in the 313th Wing were as follows; 4 ½ hours instrument calibration and orientation flight; 8 hour navigational flight to Iwo Jima, returning to Rota for bombing with four (1000 pound) high explosive; a two hour local night mission; two (4 hour) radar and visual bombing missions on Rota with eight (500 pound) high explosive and a shakedown bombing mission on Truk with eight (1000 pound) high explosive.

The first group overseas training mission was flown, on June 30, with nine aircraft airborne after a briefing at 0430, takeoff at 0700 and landing at approximately 1200 hours. On July 1, training mission number two was flown; nine aircraft scheduled and completed the mission as briefed to Iwo Jima and then to Rota to drop two (1000 pound)

Boarding train

high explosive from 25,000 feet. Six of the bombs were dropped by radar, twelve visually with excellent results.

Crews participating were Capt. Wilson, Lt. McKnight, Lt. Westover, Capt. Price, Capt. Eatherly, Lt. Devore, Capt. Bock, Capt. Marquardt and Capt. Taylor. Briefing for these missions and all subsequent missions were held in the theatre with interrogations in the intelligence lounge.

Training mission three was flown July 3 with nine aircraft participating. Takeoff at 1230 and estimated time of arrival at Rota was 1630. Fifty-four bombs were carried, forty-six dropped on Rota, seven salvoed, one hung up and later pried loose. V2 returned early with high oil temperature on engine #1; overall results were recorded as good to excellent.

Training mission four, July 4, with same nine aircraft repeated bombing of Rota. Fifty-two bombs were released on target, two jettisoned because of a shackle malfunction; results were recorded as good to excellent.

Training mission five was July 5 with nine crews scheduled. Five were scratched and four flew completing the mission with Capt. Bock, Capt. Wilson, Lt. Westover and Lt. McKnight. The bomb load was six (1000 pound) general purpose (GP); briefing at 1530, takeoff at 1800, estimated arrival of 2400. The target was Moen Airfield in the Truck Islands. All four aircraft bombed by radar from 25,000 feet through cloud coverage ranging from one tenth to eight tenths with unobserved results. No fighters were encountered and only three bursts of antiaircraft shells were reported. For training mission five, the scratching of five planes was because the squadron was about to fly combat missions.

July 6, the target was both runways on Marcus Island; briefing was at 1530, takeoff at 0800, arrival at 1500. The bomb load was twenty (500 pound) GP bombs. Altitude was 20,000 feet and 20,500 feet. Capt. Taylor, Capt. Marquardt and Lt. Devore bombed the runway. Results were good to excellent with the majority of bombs hitting Marcus; one salvoed and one hung up. No enemy aircraft were encountered and flak amounted to several inaccurate bursts. All crews commented on difficulties locating the target.

July 7, the same mission was flown to Marcus by Capt. Wilson, Lt. Westover, Capt. Taylor, Capt. Bock and Lt. Devore with good to excellent results. July 8, again Capt. Eatherly, Lt. McKnight, Capt. Marquardt, Capt. Price and Capt. Bock bombed Marcus with the same good to excellent results. July 9, Lt. McKnight, Lt. Westover, Capt. Wilson, Lt. Devore and Capt. Taylor bombed Marcus this time with delayed action 500 pound GP bombs. Four planes bombed by radar with unobserved results; the fifth having excellent results visually.

Then followed a series of practice bombing missions on Rota and Guguan interspersed with the usual orienta-

tion and training missions for the other crews who had finished ground school in the meantime.

July 21, Lt. Ray and Capt. Lewis flew the Marcus mission which was now classified as only a training mission. Both planes bombed visually from 25,000 feet through five tenths to eight tenths Cumulus Clouds over the target. By this time, combat strikes against the Japanese Homeland had gotten under way. Training became a place of secondary importance, but continued throughout the Groups period of overseas operations in the form of practice bombing missions to unoccupied islands north of Tinian.

Operations

On July 19, 1945, Field Order #104 announced the 313th Wing will attack Empire targets with ten aircraft of the 509th Group. Target study classes were again conducted. Last minute questions from the crews were answered. Special briefings were held by staff.

At the general briefing, Col. Tibbets wished the crews well reminding them the eyes of the 313th Wing were upon them. At 0200 July 20, 1945, the first 509th aircraft were airborne en route to the Japanese Homeland. All ten aircraft bombed their primary targets; three visually and two by radar. Four dropped their bombs on secondary targets of opportunity (other than primary) by means of radar. The tenth aircraft was forced to jettison its bomb at sea, en route to the target, due to an engine failure. The results were officially reported fair to unobserved.

One aircraft, V-85, piloted by Claude Eatherly, found its primary target completely obscured by clouds. The crew decided to drop their bomb on the Emperor's Palace. Because of clouds over Tokyo, the bomb was dropped by radar missing the palace and hitting a railway station.

Some hours later, Tokyo radio had this to say, "The tactics of the raiding enemy planes have become so complicated, they cannot be anticipated from experience or the common sense gained so far. The single B29 which passed over the Capitol this morning dropping bombs on one section of the Tokyo Metropolis, taking unaware slightly the people of the city, are certainly so-called sneak tactics aimed at confusing." (the minds of the people)

July 23, 1945, ten crews prepared for the second combat mission over the Japanese Homeland. Each crew was assigned a specific target and aiming point and briefed accordingly. Strike reports and interrogation afterward, disclosed the weather was clear. Nine planes bombed visually, one by radar, seven bombed their primary targets and three their secondary targets. The results were recorded as effective and successful.

The mission of July 26 saw ten 509th aircraft airborne. The targets attacked were in the Nagaoka and Toyama areas. Not one plane bombed its primary target. Of the ten secondary targets bombed, seven bombs were dropped visually, three were dropped by radar. There was ten tenths cloud coverage over the primary targets. The results were recorded as successful, but fair as to effectiveness.

The mission of July 29 put eight 509th "pumpkin" carrying aircraft over the Japanese Homeland; nine planes were scheduled to participate. Shortly before takeoff, however, the "pumpkin" carried in the plane under the command of Maj. Hopkins with Lt. Westover as copilot, suddenly broke loose and thudded into the asphalt hardstand. Fortunately, none of the flying or ground personnel were under the plane at the time, although a few minutes before, Maj. Hopkins had been under the plane.

The weather was more favorable for this mission; four planes bombed their primary targets, four found breaks in the weather over secondary target areas. All aircraft bombed visually. The results were recorded as effective. As July drew to a close, comments were rampant from other units located on Tinian, the gist being "Well, the 509th and their fifteen planes don't seem to be winning the war yet".

The first Atomic Bombing mission was carried out August 6, 1945. Several days prior to this, the six crews concerned were instructed in target studies and were given special instructions on the actual bomb dropping procedure. Briefing was in two parts; the first part conducted two days before takeoff, included a disclosure of the targets, explanation by Navy personnel of the immediate effect of the bomb and an overall listing of operational data; the second part of the atomic briefing, held just before takeoff, included air/sea rescue and weather details.

It was emphasized, at this briefing, that under no circumstances were aircraft to go within fifty miles of the target four hours prior to strike time and six hours after. In the case of distress rescue, facilities would not venture within the forbidden area for the prescribed length of time. Special air/sea rescue facilities were provided for this mission by planes of other groups and by Navy planes and submarines.

On the same day, other 20th Air Force aircraft were attacking targets in Japan in the hope of diverting any enemy defensive action which would deter the atomic mission. The primary target was Hiroshima with Kokura and Nagasaki as alternates. The aiming point was just below Army Division Headquarters at the tip of the island on which the Hiroshima Airfield was located.

Seven of the Groups B29s participated in this mission. One deployed to Iwo Jima to be used as a spare in case of emergency. Three "weather planes" were to proceed to their specifically assigned targets, appraise the weather over it and relay the information to the strike plane. The remaining two were to escort the strike aircraft; one with special camera equipment, the other with special instruments.

At least four hours after the bomb was released, two photo ships from the 3rd Photo Reconnaisance Squadron were to make photo coverage of the Hiroshima area. The two photo crews were to be briefed by 509th Intelligence Officers and given all necessary information to carry out their mission.

On August 8, the 509th sent six B29s to targets in Yokkaichi, Uwajima, Tsuruga and Tokushima. Each plane carried a "pumpkin". Two aircraft bombed their primary targets; poor weather conditions forced three to seek secondary targets and one aircraft was forced to abort and returned with its bomb load intact. The five bombs were dropped by visual means, with results officially designated effective.

August 9, the 509th prepared for its second Atomic Mission. The general plan was the same as the first, with the following exception. In the first mission, there were three targets designated; in the second mission, there were two. Accordingly, two weather aircraft, one standby and two escort planes; one with camera equipment, the other with scientific instruments and one strike aircraft participated in this mission. The primary objective was Kokura, Nagasaki was secondary.

During the last several days of the war, the 509th carried out its last strike against the Japanese Homeland. On August 14, seven of the Groups planes bombed targets in Koromo and Nagoya with seven "pumpkins". All bombed their primary targets by visual means with observed results ranging from poor to excellent. These were probably the last bombs dropped by the 20th Air Force bombers in World War II.

Wives wave goodbye

B-29 Airplanes of the
393rd Bombardment Squadron (VH)

509th Composite Group, Based On Tinian In 1945,
In Order Of The Army Air Forces Serial Numbers,
With The Combat Crews That Regularly Flew Them, The Number Of Combat Sorties Of The
Planes To Japan, And The Letters Substituted For The Arrow On The Tail

Data supplied by Dick Campbell and Fred Bock

Block and Serial No.	Victor V-	No	Name	Regular Crew and Commander		Plane Sorties	Sub Tail Mark
36 44-27296	4,	84	Some Punkins	B-7	Price	5	A
44-27297	7,	77	Bockscar	C-13	Bock	4	N
44-27298	13,	83	Full House	A-1	Taylor	6	P
44-27299	6,	86	Next Objective	A-3	Devore	3	N
44-27300	3,	73	Strange Cargo	A-4	Westover	4	A
44-27301	5,	85	Straight Flush	C-11	Eatherly	6	N
44-27302	2,	72	Top Secret	B-8	McKnight	6	A
44-27303	1,	71	Jabit III	B-6	Wilson	5	A
44-27304	8,	88	Up an' Atom	B-10	Marquardt	5	N
40 44-27353	9,	89	The Great Artiste	C-15	Albury	4	R
44-27354	10,	90	Big Stink	C-12	Zahn	3	R
45 44-86291	11,	91	Necessary Evil	C-14	Ray	4	R
44-86292	12,	82	Enola Gay	B-9	Lewis	4	R
50 44-86346		94	Luke the Spook	A-5	Classen	0	P
44-86347		95	Laggin' Dragon	A-2	Costello	1	P

NOTES:

1. All 15 of these Silverplate B-29 Superfortress airplanes were assembled at the Omaha plant of the Glenn L. Martin-Nebraska Company (code MO), AAF Project No. 98228-S, production blocks 36, 40, 45, and 50.

2. The Victor (tactical) numbers were prominently painted on both sides of the fuselage, behind the AAF emblem and on the nose section. The first 13 planes were given Victor numbers 1 to 13; these were changed to higher numbers, in the range 71 to 91, before 6 August 1945.

3. Unless circumstances dictated otherwise, which happened about 30% of the time, a crew flew missions in its "own" airplane.

4. Not counted in the combat sorties are two aborted Pumpkin missions; in one case the bomb was dropped in the ocean; in the other it was returned to base. Also not counted are the backups to Enola Gay and Bockscar on the two atomic missions.

5. The original tail mark, painted on after the planes arrived at Tinian, was a forward-pointing arrow in circle. Tail marks of other Marianas-based bomb groups (letters) were substituted prior to 6 August to avoid easy recognition of 509th planes, as indicated in the last column of the table:
   "A" no border, 497th BG, 73rd Wing, Isley Field, Saipan
   "N" in triangle, 444th BG, 58th Wing, West Field, Tinian
   "P" in square, 39th BG, 314th Wing, North Field, Guam
   "R" in circle, 6th BG, 313th Wing, North Field, Tinian

Summary Data on the 15 Airplanes
in Order of Production

The 15 planes are first listed on one page in the order of their USAAF serial numbers, which provided permanent and unique identification. All the planes were assembled at the plant of the Glenn L. Martin-Nebraska Co. in Omaha. There were four production blocks, the first and largest being 36 with nine planes, followed by 40, 45, and 50 with two planes each. The block number, acronym MO for Martin Omaha, and the AAF serial number were stenciled at the factory on the fuselage below the airplane commander's window. The last three digits of the serial numbers were different on the 15 planes and were used in place of the 5-digit or complete serial numbers in many of the operations orders (e. g., 296 in place of 27296 or 44-27296). The planes were flown from Offutt Field in Omaha, adjacent to the factory, to Wendover by 393rd crews after acceptance by the AAF.

The Victor (V), i. e. tactical, numbers were assigned by Group Operations and painted in black on the airplanes. The placement and size of the numerals made these highly visible in the air and on the ground. They could be, and were, changed to help confuse the enemy: the V numbers originally assigned to most of the airplanes were superseded by higher numbers before the atomic missions (e. g., "5" was altered to "85" by prefixing the "8"). The V numbers were used in radio communication with the control tower at North Field and other ground stations, and between airplanes.

The tail marks were also changed prior to the atomic missions. The original tail mark of the 509th on Tinian was a forward-pointing arrow within a circle. Tail marks of other B-29 groups in the 20th Air Force were substituted (see last column and footnote of the airplane summary). The arrow-in-circle was eventually restored.

Airplane names and associated nose art were informal additions to the ID numbers, chosen by the crew members and painted to order by men having the required skills. Most were put on after the cessation of hostilities. Also added, below the left cockpit windows, were symbols for the combat sorties by the primary crews (not necessarily the airplanes): profiles of fat men representing bombs dropped or participation in an atomic mission. The name Jabit III has been variously spelled Jabbit III and Jabbitt III but the first version is now known to be authentic.

The name Luke the Spook was evidently chosen after V-94 returned to the U. S., and not by crew A-5.

For each B-29 the. primary or regular crew and airplane commander are identified, and the number of combat sorties by that plane is given, as explained in a footnote.

Summary Data on the 15 Crews

The crews of the 393rd Bomb Squadron, which were numbered 1 through 15, with five in each of three flights (A, B, and C), are listed in that order in the one-page summary that follows together with the airplane commander or commanders of each crew, the assigned B-29, and the number of combat sorties to the Japanese home islands of Honshu, Shikoku, and Kyushu.

Four of the 15 crews had two airplane commanders on different sorties. Smith took over from Classen (509th Deputy Group Commander) as airplane commander (AC) of crew A-5 after two sorties. Hopkins (509th Group Operations Officer) flew with Crew C-14 as AC after their first three sorties, due to illness of Ray. Tibbets (509th Group Commander) was AC of crew B-9 on the first atomic mission, flying the Little Boy bomb plane (Enola Gay) to Hiroshima. Sweeney (393rd Squadron Commander) was AC of crew C-15 on both the Hiroshima and Nagasaki atomic missions, flying the instrument plane (The Great Artiste) on the first and the Fat Man bomb plane (Bockscar) on the second.

The total number of combat sorties per crew includes participation in the two atomic missions as well as sorties in which Pumpkin bombs were dropped. The number of sorties flown in other than the assigned B-29 is also given. The overall total number of combat sorties was 60, of which 19 were flown in substitute airplanes of the squadron.

Detailed Information on Each Crew and Assigned B-29

Detailed information concerning each crew (in order from A-1 to C-15) and, on a facing page, detailed information concerning the B-29 assigned to that crew, with a photograph, follow the airplane and crew summaries.

Newly Arrived Silverplate Planes on Tinian

Ellsworth T. Carrington
Co-Pilot

1st Lt. Paul W. Groening
Bombardier
Kobura Weather Plane
August 6, 1945

James W. Davis
Flt. Eng.

Glen Flowerree
Radio Opr.

Joe Westover
Capt. Airplane Commander

John McClellin
Lt. Navigator

Lloyd Reeder
Radio

Lt. George H. Cohen
Flight Engineer

Lt. Jack Widausky
Navigator

Donald Cole
Asst. Flt. Eng./Scanner

Lt. Jacob Bontekoe
Pilot

Oscar J. Sheffer
A&E Mechanic

Frank Achramke
A&E Mech.

Thomas F. Costa
Bombardier

James N. Price
Airplane Commander

Jim Westbrook
Pilot

Eugene "Lefty" Thomas
Flt. Engr.

Jack Beam
Asst. Flt. Eng./Scanner

Ken Wey
Bombardier

Ic Nicoley
Tail Gunner

Lt. W. Locke Easton
Pilot

Thomas John B. Brunner
Navigator

Gilbert B. Dickman
Pilot

Jim Frank Eder
Flight Eng.

Neil Corey
Asst. Flt. Eng./Scanner

Arthur (Vern) Holmes - Eng. Mech

Herman S. Zahn Jr.
Airplane Commander

The name and duty of each of the nine regular flight-crew members, and also the name of each ground-crew member (where known), are given on the crew pages.

Specific information on each of the combat missions of each flight crew consists of the number of the Special Bombing Mission directive (issued by Headquarters Twentieth Air Force), the Operations Order (issued by 509th Group Operations), the date of the mission, the B-29 flown, and a description of the mission. The targets are those actually attacked, which number of instances are different from the briefed primary target due to unfavorable weather conditions encountered.

The first part of the historical record for each airplane consists of the delivery date at Omaha, ranging from 19 March to 15 June 1945, and the month it was flown to Wendover and then to Tinian. Next is the record of its sorties against Japan: date, crew, airplane commander, type of bomb and the target attacked or the plane's role in an atomic mission.

The postwar history of the airplanes was provided by the records kept at Maxwell Field and furnished to Richard Campbell. All except Jabit III went to Roswell AAF, NM, where the 509th was stationed after departure from Tinian. Several saw extensive service. Laggin' Dragon and Luke the Spook, the two airplanes of block 50, the last to be delivered from the factory, were not dropped from inventory until July 1960, at Naha Air Base on Okinawa.

Just two of the 15 Silverplate Superforts have escaped salvage: Enola Gay, now on display at the National Air and Space Museum of the Smithsonian Institution in Washington DC, and Bockscar, which has been in the U. S. Air Force Museum near Dayton OH for many years.

The pictures included here show how all 15 planes looked on Tinian, or shortly after return to the U. S. Nearly all the photographs are zeroed in on the nose sections, on which Victor numbers, names, art, and symbols for the combat sorties of the regular crew were painted. Color photos of the nose art are featured in the color section.

Flight Line (L-R): Up an Atom, Great Artiste, Enola Gay

CREW A-1
393rd Bombardment Squadron (VH), 509th Composite Group

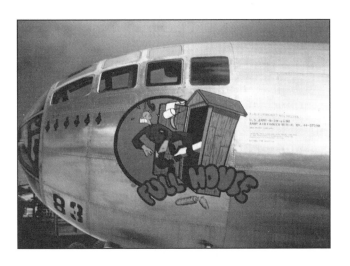

FLIGHT CREW

Airplane Commander ....Ralph R. Taylor Jr
Pilot ....Raymond P. Biel
Navigator .... Fred A. Hoey
Bombardier ....Michael Angelich
Engineer.. Frank M. Briese
Radio Operator.......................................Theodore M. Slife
Radar Operator................................ Nathaniel T. Burgwyn
Tail Gunner .... Robert J. Valley
Asst Eng./Scanner ....Richard B. Anselme

GROUND CREW

Glen Mahugh
Chester A. Hammond
Steve J. Kinosh Jr
William B. Reedy
Donald D. Fockler
Mario A. Litterio

ASSIGNED SILVERPLATE B-29 SUPERFORTRESS
Serial No. 44-27298, Victor No. 83, "FULL HOUSE"
CREW COMBAT MISSIONS

Mission No. / Opns Order	1945 Date	B-29	Description of Mission	Notes
4 / 20	20 Jul	V-83	Pumpkin, Toyama (Aluminum plant)	
5 / 24	24 Jul	V-83	Pumpkin, Niihama (Sumitomo Copper Refining Co.)	
9 / 27	26 Jul	V-83	Pumpkin, Yaizu (Railroad yards)	
10 / 30	29 Jul	V-83	Pumpkin, Ube (Nitrogen Fertilizer Plant)	
13 / 35	6 Aug '	V-83	Advance weather recon, Nagasaki.FIRST ATOMIC MISSION	
16 / 39	9 Aug	V-83	Backup for "Bockscar", Iwo Jima. SECOND ATOMIC MISSION	

HISTORICAL RECORD OF PLANE

Dates		Key Events
20 Mar	45	Delivered to USAAF by Martin Aircraft Co., Offutt AAF, Omaha, NE
Apr	45	To 509th Composite Group, Wendover AAF, UT, and to Crew A-1 (Taylor)
Jun	45	To Tinian North Field
COMBAT MISSIONS		
20 Jul	45	Crew A-1 (Taylor), Pumpkin, Toyama (Nichiman Aluminum Co.)
24 Jut	45	Crew A-1 (Taylor), Pumpkin, Niihama (Sumitomo Copper Refining Co.)
26 Jul	45	Crew A-1 (Taylor), Pumpkin, Yaizu (Railroad yards)
29 Jul	45	Crew A-1 (Taylor), Pumpkin, Ube (Nitrogen fertilizer Co.)
6 Aug	45	Crew A-1 (Taylor), Weather recon, Nagasaki. 1st ATOMIC MISSION
9 Aug	45	Crew A-1 (Taylor), "Bockscar" backup, Iwo Jima, 2nd ATOMIC MISSION
14 Aug	45	Crew C-13 (Bock), Pumpkin, Koromo (Toyoda Auto Works)
POSTWAR		
Nov	45	To Roswell AAF, NM
Apr	46	To Task Force 1.5 (Operation Crossroads)
Aug	46	To 509th Bomb (VH) Group (SAC), Roswell AAF
Jun	49	To 97th Bomb (M) Group, later Wing (SAC), Biggs AFB, TX
Apr	50	Converted to TB-29 at Tinker AFB, OK
Aug	52	To Sioux City AFB, IA; Radar Calibration units
Dec	53	To Hill AFB, UT; Radar Evaluation unit
Mar	55	To Nashville, TN; Mobile Air Materiel unit
Jun	55	To Yuma County Airport, AZ; Tow Target & Air Defense units
Nov	56	To Navy (China Lake, CA ?)

CREW A-2
393rd Bombardment Squadron (VH), 509th Composite Group

FLIGHT CREW

Airplane Commander ....Edward M. Costello
Pilot .... Harry B. Davis
Navigator .... Robert J. Petrolli
Bombardier ....John L. Downey
Engineer..Thomas H. Brumagin
Radio Operator...David Purdon
Radar Operator...James R. Bryant
Tail Gunner.....................................Carleton C. McEachern
Asst Eng./Scanner ....Maurice Clark

GROUND CREW

John C. Hansen
Robert J. Dowling
Robert E. Holse
Robert R. Garn
Fred D. Butler
James W. McGlennon
Charles W. Rich

ASSIGNED SILVERPLATE B-29 SUPERFORTRESS
Serial No. 44-86347, Victor No. 95, "LAGGIN' DRAGON"

CREW COMBAT MISSIONS

Mission No. / Opns Order	1945 Date	B-29	Description of Mission	Notes

Notes

No combat missions were flown by Crew A-2 due to late arrival on Tinian.
This crew and airplane transported a Fat Man bomb assembly (one of three) from Kirkland Field, Albuquerque NM, to Tinian North Field, arriving there on 1 August 1945.

HISTORICAL RECORD OF PLANE

Dates		Key Events
15 Jun	45	Delivered to USAAF by Martin Aircraft Co., Offutt AAF, Omaha, NE
Jul	45	To 509th Composite Group, Wendover AAF, UT, and to Crew A-2 (Costello)
1 Aug	45	To Tinian

SPECIAL MISSION

1 Aug	45	Delivered Fat Man assembly to Tinian, flown by Crew A-2 (Costello)

COMBAT MISSIONS

9 Aug	45	Crew B-8 (McKnight), Weather recon, Nagasaki. 2nd ATOMIC MISSION

POSTWAR

Nov	45	To Roswell AAF, NM
Apr	46	To Task Force 1.5 (Operation Crossroads)
Aug	46	To 509th Bomb (VH) Group (SAC), Roswell AAF
Jun	49	To 97th Bomb (M) Group, later Wing (SAC), Biggs AFB, TX
Apr	50	Converted to TB-29 at Tinker AFB, OK
Sep	52	To Yokota AB, Japan; Radar Calibration & Evaluation units
Jul	56	To Johnson AB, Japan; Pacific Air Forces
Jul	58	To Naha AB, Japan (Okinawa)
Jul	60	Dropped from inventory as surplus (scrapped)

CREW A-3
393rd Bombardment Squadron (VH), 509th Composite Group

FLIGHT CREW

Airplane Commander	Ralph N. Devore
Pilot	William J. Easton
Navigator	Franklin B. Wimer
Bombardier	Leon Cooper
Engineer	William T. Hulse
Radio Operator	Lee E. Palmert
Radar Operator	Michael B. Bohon
Tail Gunner	Glenn S. Allison
Asst Eng./Scanner	Clarence E. Britt

GROUND CREW

Forrest C. Anderson
Marion C. Fowler
Mack Newsom
James R. Womack
Jerry Grubaugh Jr
Charles E. Schwab

ASSIGNED SILVERPLATE B-29 SUPERFORTRESS
Serial No. 44-27299, Victor No. 86, "NEXT OBJECTIVE"
CREW COMBAT MISSIONS

Mission No. / Opns Order	1945 Date	B-29	Description of Mission	Notes
4 / 20	20 Jul	V-86	Pumpkin, Toyama (Nippon Soda Co.)	
5 / 24.	24 Jul	V-86	Pumpkin, Niihama (Sumitomo Rayon Co.)	
9 / 27	26 Jul	V-71	Pumpkin, Osaka (Urban area)	
14 / 38	8 Aug	V-86	Pumpkin, Aborted (Bomb returned to base)	
17 / 44	14 Aug	V-86	Pumpkin, Nagoya (Arsenal factory)	

HISTORICAL RECORD OF PLANE

Dates		Key Events
20 Mar	45	Delivered to USAAF by Martin Aircraft Co., Offutt AAF, Omaha, NE
Apr	45	To 509th Composite Group, Wendover AAF, UT, and to Crew A-3 (Devore)
Jun	45	To Tinian North Field

COMBAT MISSIONS

20 Jul	45	Crew A-3 (Devore), Pumpkin, Toyama (Nippon Soda Co.)
24 Jul	45	Crew A-3 (Devore), Pumpkin, Niihama (Sumitomo Rayon Plant)
14 Aug	45	Crew A-3 (Devore), Pumpkin, Nagoya (Arsenal factory)

POSTWAR

Nov	45	To Roswell AAF, NM
Apr	46	To Task Force 1.5 (Operation Crossroads)
Aug	46	To 509th Bomb (VH) Group (SAC), Roswell AAF
Apr	49	To 97th Bomb (M) Group (SAC), Biggs AFB, TX
Jul	49	Dropped from inventory as salvage (scrapped)

CREW A-4
393rd Bombardment Squadron (VH), 509th Composite Group

FLIGHT CREW

Airplane Commander .... Joseph E. Westover
Pilot .... William J. Desmond
Navigator .... John W. Dulin
Bombardier .... Louis B. Allen
Engineer.................................... Robert M. Donnell
Radio Operator.......................... James H. Doiron
Radar Operator.......................... William J. Cotter
Tail Gunner............................... Walter A. Spradlin
Asst Eng./Scanner .... Samuel R. Wheeler

GROUND CREW

Robert E. Smithson
Clyde R. Beecher
Cleo E. Harter
Filbert Reynolds
Derward A. Stevens
John H. Hubeny Jr
Francis J. Merry

ASSIGNED SILVERPLATE B-29 SUPERFORTRESS
Serial No. 44-27300, Victor No. 73, "STRANGE CARGO"
CREW COMBAT MISSIONS

Mission No. / 1945 Opns Order	Date	B-29	Description of Mission	Notes
6 / 24	24 Jul	V-73	Pumpkin, Kobe (Mitsubishi Heavy Industries)	
8 / 27	26 Jul	V-72	Pumpkin, Taira (Industrial area)	1
14 / 38	8 Aug	V-73	Pumpkin, Tsuruga (Chemical Plant)	
17 / 44	14 Aug	V-73	Pumpkin, Nagoya (Arsenal factory)	

Notes: 1.   The B-29 was "Top Secret"

HISTORICAL RECORD OF PLANE

Dates		Key Events
2 Apr	45	Delivered to USAAF by Martin Aircraft Co., Offutt AAF, Omaha, NE
Apr	45	To 509th Composite Group, Wendover AAF, UT, and to Crew A-4 (Westover)
Jun	45	To Tinian North Field

COMBAT MISSIONS

20 Jul	45	Crew C-13 (Bock), Pumpkin, Fukushima (Light industries)
24 Jul	45	Crew A-4 (Westover), Pumpkin, Kobe (Mitsubishi Heavy Industry)
8 Aug	45	Crew A-4 (Westover), Pumpkin, Tsuruga (Chemical plant)
14 Aug	45	Crew A-4 (Westover), Pumpkin, Nagoya (Arsenal factory)

POSTWAR

Nov	45	To Roswell AAF, NM
Apr	46	To Task Force 1.5 (Operation Crossroads)
Aug	46	To 509th Bomb (VH) Group (SAC), Roswell AAF
Jun	49	To 97th Bomb (M) Group (SAC), Biggs AAF, TX
Aug	49	Converted to WB-29 at McClellan AFB, CA
Dec	50	To Tinker, McClellan, Hickam, Warner Robins, Eielson, Tinker Fields; Weather Reconnaissance units
Apr	55	To Nashville (converted to TB-29)
Jun	55	To Wheelus and Nouasseur Fields; Tow Target, Maintenance & Support unit:
Jul	57	To 3920th Air Base Goup (SAC), RAF Brize Norton, UK
Aug	57	Dropped from inventory as salvage (scrapped)

CREW A-5
393rd Bombardment Squadron (VH), 509th Composite Group

FLIGHT CREW

Airplane Commander	Thomas J. Classen
	Elbert B. Smith
Pilot	William M. Rowe
Navigator	William E. Wright
Bombardier	Bobby J. Chapman
Engineer	Floyd W. Kemner
Radio Operator	Omar G. Strickland
Radar Operator	George A. Weller
Tail Gunner	Alfred A. Lewandowski
Asst Eng./Scanner	Lee E. Caylor

GROUND CREW

Claude E. McLenon
Roy K. Balliet
Donald E. Piehl
Calvin B. Popwell
Hinginio A. Baca

ASSIGNED SILVERPLATE B-29 SUPERFORTRESS
Serial No. 44-27354, Victor No. 90, "BIG STINK"
CREW COMBAT MISSIONS

Mission No. / Opns Order	1945 Date	B-29	Description of Mission	Notes
3 / 20	20 Jul	V-90	Pumpkin, Nagaoka (Tsugami-Atagi Manufacturing Co.).	1
8 / 27	26 Jul	V-90	Pumpkin, Hitachi (Copper Refinery)	1
12 / 30	29 Jul	V-88	Pumpkin, Wakayama (Oil refinery)	2
/ 41	9 Aug	V-94	To U. S. to get Fat-Man components; no return to Tinian due to war's end	3

Note 1.   Classen was Airplane Commander; the B-29 was "Big Stink".
Note 2.   Smith was Airplane Commander; the B-29 was "Up an' Atom"
Note 3.   Classen was Airplane Commander. V-94 was named "Luke the Spook" some time after the airplane returned to the U. S.

HISTORICAL RECORD OF PLANE

Dates			Key Events
20	Apr	45	Delivered to USAAF by Martin Aircraft Co., Offutt AAF, Omaha, NE
	May	45	To 509th Composite Group, Wendover AAF, UT, and to Crew A-5 (Classen), then to Crew C-12 (Zahn) in early August 1945
	Jun	45	To Tinian North Field

COMBAT MISSIONS

20	Jul	45	Crew A-5 (Classen), Pumpkin, Nagaoka (Tsugami-Atagi Mfg Co.)
26	Jul	45	Crew A-5 (Classen), Pumpkin, Hitachi (Copper Refining Co.)
6	Aug	45	Crew B-8 (McKnight), "Enola Gay" backup, Iwo Jima. 1st ATOMIC MISSION
9	Aug	45	Crew C-14 (Hopkins), Cameras, Nagasaki. 2nd ATOMIC MISSION

POSTWAR

	Nov	45	To Roswell AAF, NM
	Apr	46	To Task Force 1.5 (Operation Crossroads). Renamed "Dave's Dream" after bombardier David Semple, killed in a B-29 crash
1	Jul	46	Dropped a "Fat Man"-type bomb at Bikini in a test against ships
	Aug	46	To 509th Bomb (VH) Group (SAC), Roswell AFB
	Jun	49	To 97th Bomb (M) Group, later Wing (SAC), Biggs AFB, TX
	Apr	50	Converted to TB-29 at Tinker AFB, OK
	Oct	52	To Sioux City AFB, IA; Radar Calibration units
	Dec	53	To Hill AFB, UT; Radar evaluation units
	Jun	59	To Davis-Monthan AFB, AZ; Aircraft Storage unit
	Feb	60	Dropped from inventory as salvage (scrapped)

CREW B-6
393rd Bombardment Squadron (VH), 509th Composite Group

FLIGHT CREW

Airplane Commander .... John A. Wilson
Pilot .... Ellsworth T. Carrington
Navigator .... James S. Duva
Bombardier .... Paul W. Gruning
Engineer.. James W. Davis
Radio Operator.. Glen H. Floweree
Radar Operator...Vernon J. Rowley
Tail Gunner .... Chester A. Rogalski
Asst Eng./Scanner ....Donald L. Rowe

GROUND CREW

Charles J. Baker
Kenneth L. Baxter
Pasquale Lazzarino
William F. Jellick
George I. Schreffer

ASSIGNED SILVERPLATE B-29 SUPERFORTRESS
Serial No. 44-27303, Victor No. 71, "JABIT III"
CREW COMBAT MISSIONS

Mission No. / Opns Order	1945 Date	B-29	Description of Mission	Notes
3 / 20	20 Jul	V-71	Pumpkin, Taira (Urban area)	
10 / 30	29 Jul	V-71	Pumpkin, Ube (Nippon Motor Oil Co.)	
13 / 35	6 Aug	V-71	Advance weather recon, Kokura. FIRST ATOMIC MISSION	
14 / 38	8 Aug	V-71	Pumpkin, Uwajima (Assembly plant)	
/ 41	9 Aug	V-71	To U. S. to get Fat-Man components; no return to Tinian due to war's end	

HISTORICAL RECORD OF PLANE

Dates		Key Events
3 Apr	45	Delivered to USAAF by Martin Aircraft Co., Offutt AAF, Omaha, NE
Apr	45	To 509th Composite Group, Wendover AAF, UT, and to Crew B-6 (Wilson)
Jun	45	To Tinian North Field

COMBAT AND SPECIAL MISSIONS

20 Jul	45	Crew B-6 (Wilson), Pumpkin, Taira (Urban area)
26 Jul	45	Crew A-3 (Devore), Pumpkin, Osaka (Urban area)
29 Jul	45	Crew B-6 (Wilson), Pumpkin, Ube (Nippon Motor Oil Co.)
6 Aug	45	Crew B-6 (Wilson), Weather recon, Kokura. 1ST ATOMIC MISSION
8 Aug	45	Crew B-6 (Wilson), Pumpkin, Uwajima (Assembly plant)
9 Aug	45	Crew B-6 (Wilson), To U.S. to get Fat Man components, no return to Tinian due to war ending

POSTWAR

Oct	45	To 4200th AAF Base Unit, Chicago Municipal Airport, IL
Apr	46	Dropped from inventory as salvage (scrapped)

CREW B-7
393rd Bombardment Squadron (VH), 509th Composite Group

FLIGHT CREW

Airplane Commander .... James N. Price
Pilot .... Everist L. Bednorz
Navigator .... William J. Collinson
Bombardier .... Thomas F. Costa
Engineer.. James A. Adkins
Radio Operator... Robert H, Byrd
Radar Operator... Joe R. Brown
Tail Gunner.. Clyde L. Bysom
Asst Eng./Scanner .... Frederick E. Brown

GROUND CREW

Russell D. Carrigan
Raymond G. St. Myers
William R. Compronio
William R. Crotty
Joe M. Madrid
Edward M. Josefiak
Donald E. Miller

ASSIGNED SILVERPLATE B-29 SUPERFORTRESS
Serial No. 44-27296, Victor No. 84, "SOME PUNKINS"
CREW COMBAT MISSIONS

Mission No. / Opns Order	1945 Date	B-29	Description of Mission	Notes
4 / 20	20 Jul	V-84	Pumpkin, Toyama (Fujikoshi Steel Products)	
7 / 24	24 Jul	V-84	Pumpkin, Ogaki (Urban area)	
9 / 27	26 Jul	V-84	Pumpkin, Shimoda (Urban area)	
15 / 38	8 Aug	V-84	Pumpkin, Yokkaichi (Converted textile mill)	
17 / 44	14 Aug	V-84	Pumpkin, Nagoya (Arsenal factory)	

HISTORICAL RECORD OF PLANE

Dates		Key Events
19 Mar	45	Delivered to USAAF by Martin Aircraft Co., Offutt AAF, Omaha, NE
Apr	45	To 509th Composite Group; Wendover AAF, UT, and to Crew B-7 (Price)
Jun	45	To Tinian North Field

COMBAT MISSIONS

20 Jul	45	Crew B-7 (Price), Pumpkin, Toyama (Fujikoshi Steel Products)
24 Jul	45	Crew B-7 (Price), Pumpkin, Ogaki (Urban area)
26 Jul	45	Crew B-7 (Price), Pumpkin, Shimoda (Urban area)
8 Aug	45	Crew B-7 (Price), Pumpkin, Yokkaichi (Converted textile mill)
14 Aug	45	Crew B-7 (Price), Pumpkin, Nagoya (Arsenal factory)

POSTWAR

Nov	45	To Roswell AAF, NM
Mar	46	To Task Force 1.5 (Operation Crossroads)
Apr	46	To 428th AAF Base Unit (SAC), Kirtland AAF, NM
Aug	46	Dropped from inventory as surplus (scrapped)

CREW B-8
393rd Bombardment Squadron (VH), 509th Composite Group

FLIGHT CREW

Airplane Commander ....Charles F. McKnight
Pilot .... Jacob Y. Bontekoe
Navigator ....Jack Widowsky
Bombardier .... Franklin H. MacGregor
Engineer.. George H. Cohen
Radio Operator...Lloyd J. Reeder
Radar Operator.. William F. Orren
Tail Gunner.. Roderick E. Legg
Asst Eng./Scanner .... Donald O. Cole

GROUND CREW

Arnold E. Sleipnes
Carmine A. Genova
Chester J. Krajewski
Oscar J. Thigpen
Francis J. Schramke
Frank E. Sutton

ASSIGNED SILVERPLATE B-29 SUPERFORTRESS
Serial No. 44-27302, Victor No. 72, "TOP SECRET"
CREW COMBAT MISSIONS

Mission No. / Opns Order	1945 Date	B-29	Description of Mission	Notes
1 / 20	20 Jul	V-72	Pumpkin, Otsu (Urban area)	
7 / 24	24 Jul	V-72	Pumpkin, Yokkaichi (Harbor, heavy industry)	
10 / 30	29 Jul	V-72	Pumpkin, Ube (Industrial soda Co.)	
13 / 35	6 Aug	V-90	Back-up for "Enola Gay", Iwo Jima. FIRST ATOMIC MISSION	1
16 / 39	9 Aug	V-95	Advance weather recon, Nagasaki. SECOND ATOMIC MISSION	2
18 / 44	14 Aug	V-72	Pumpkin, Koromo (Toyoda Auto Works)	

Notes:
1. The B-29 was "Big Stink".
2. The B-29 was "Laggin' Dragon".

HISTORICAL RECORD OF PLANE

Dates		Key Events
2 Apr	45	Delivered to USAAF by Martin Aircraft Co., Offutt AAF, Omaha, NE
Apr	45	To 509th Composite Group, Wendover AAF, UT, and to Crew B-8 (McKnight)
Jun	45	To Tinian North Field
COMBAT MISSIONS		
20 Jul	45	Crew B-8 (McKnight), Pumpkin, Otsu (Urban area)
24 Jul	45	Crew B-8 (McKnight), Pumpkin, Yokkaichi (Harbor, heavy industry)
26 Jul	45	Crew A-4 (Westover), Pumpkin, Taira (Industrial area)
29 Jul	45	Crew B-8 (McKnight), Pumpkin, Ube (Soda plant)
8 Aug	45	Crew C-11 (Fatherly), Pumpkin, Yokkaichi (Harbor, heavy industry)
14 Aug	45	Crew B-8 (McKnight), Pumpkin, Koromo (Toyoda Auto Works)
POSTWAR		
Nov	45	To Roswell AAF, NM
Apr	46	To Task Force 1.5 (Operation Crossroads)
Aug	46	To 509th Bomb (VH) Group (SAC), Roswell AFB
Jun	49	To 97th Bomb (M) Group, later Wing (SAC), Biggs AFB, TX
Apr	50	Converted to TB-29 at Tinker AFB, OK
Mar	53	To Elmendorf AFB, AK; Radar Calibration & Maintenance units
Sep	53	To Davis-Monthan AFB, AZ
Jul	54	Dropped from inventory as salvage (scrapped)

CREW B-9
393rd Bombardment Squadron (VH), 509th Composite Group

FLIGHT CREW

Airplane Commander .... Robert A. Lewis
Pilot .... Richard McNamara
Navigator .... Harold J. Rider
Bombardier .... Stewart W. Williams
Engineer .... Wyatt E. Duzenbury
Radio Operator .... Richard H. Nelson
Radar Operator .... Joseph S. Stiborik
Tail Gunner .... George R. Caron
Asst Eng./Scanner .... Robert H. Shumard

GROUND CREW

Steve C. Lizak
Leonard W. Markley
Jean S. Cooper
Winfield C. Kinkade
John E. Jackson
John J. Lesniewski
Harold R. Olson

ASSIGNED SILVERPLATE B-29 SUPERFORTRESS
Serial No. 44-86292, Victor No. 82, "ENOLA GAY"

CREW COMBAT MISSIONS

Mission No. / Opns Order	1945 Date	B-29	Description of Mission	Notes
6 / 24	24 Jul	V-82	Pumpkin, Kobe (Steel works)	
9 / 27	26 Jul	V-82	Pumpkin, Nagoya (Urban area)	
11 / 30	29 Jul	V-89	Pumpkin, Koriyama (Marshalling yards)	1
13 / 35	6 Aug	V-82	"LITTLE BOY" bomb, Hiroshima FIRST ATOMIC MISSION	2
14 / 38	8 Aug	V-88	Pumpkin, Tokushima (Light industry)	3

Notes:
1. The B-29 was "The Great Artiste".
2. Paul Tibbets was Airplane Commander, Lewis was Pilot, Theodore Van Kirk was Navigator, and Thomas Ferebee was Bombardier. William Parsons of Project Alberta was Bomb Commander and Morris Jeppson of 1st Ordnance Squadron was Electronics Test Officer for the bomb. Jacob Beser was Radar Countermeasures Officer.
3. The B-29 was "Up an' Atom".

HISTORICAL RECORD OF PLANE

Dates		Key Events
18 May	45	Delivered to USAAF by Martin Aircraft Co., Offutt AAF, Omaha, NE
Jun	45	To 509th Composite Group, Wendover AAF, UT, and to Crew B-9 (Lewis)
Jun	45	To Tinian North Field
COMBAT MISSIONS		
24 Jul	45	Crew B-9 (Lewis), Pumpkin, Kobe (Steel Works)
26 Jul	45	Crew B-9 (Lewis), Pumpkin, Nagoya (Urban area)
6 Aug	45	Crew B-9 (Tibbets), "LITTLE BOY" bomb, Hiroshima. 1st ATOMIC MISSION
9 Aug	45	Crew B-10 (Marquardt), Weather recon, Kokura. 2nd ATOMIC MISSION
POSTWAR		
Nov	45	To Mather AAF, CA
Dec	45	To Roswell AAF, NM
Mar	46	To Task Force 1.5 (Operation Crossroads)
Jun	46	To Pacific Area via Hamilton AAF, CA
Jul	46	To Fairfield-Suisun AAF, CA
Aug	46	To 4105th AAF Base Unit (AMC), Davis-Monthan AAF, AZ
		Dropped from inventory by transfer to the Smithsonian Institution, DC. Now on display there

CREW B-10
393rd Bombardment Squadron (VH), 509th Composite Group

FLIGHT CREW

Airplane Commander	George W. Marquardt
Pilot	James M. Anderson
Navigator	Russell E. Gackenbach
Bombardier	James W. Strudwick
Engineer	James R. Corliss
Radio Operator	Warren L. Coble
Radar Operator	Joseph M. DiJulio
Tail Gunner	Melvin H. Bierman
Asst Eng./Scanner	Anthony D. Capua

GROUND CREW

Joseph I. Gulick
George J. Brown
Matthew W. Huddleston
George P. Hammons
Frank W. Berzinis
Aram E. Bezdegian
Carl C. Mason

ASSIGNED SILVERPLATE B-29 SUPERFORTRESS
Serial No. 44-27304, Victor No. 88, "UP AN' ATOM"
CREW COMBAT MISSIONS

Mission No. / Opns Order	1945 Date	B-29	Description of Mission	Notes
1 / 20	20 Jul	V-88	Pumpkin, Taira (Urban area)	
9 / 27	26 Jul	V-88	Pumpkin, Hamamatsu (Urban area)	
13 / 35	6 Aug	V-91	Cameras, Hiroshima. FIRST ATOMIC MISSION	1
16 / 39	9 Aug	V-82	Advance weather recon, Kokura. SECOND ATOMIC MISSION	2

Notes:
1. The B-29 was "Necessary Evil". Bernard Waldman of Project Alberta operated the Fastax camera.
2. The B-29 was "Enola Gay".

HISTORICAL RECORD OF PLANE

Dates		Key Events
3 Apr	45	Delivered to USAAF by Martin Aircraft Co., Offutt AAF, Omaha, NE
Apr	45	To 509th Composite Group, Wendover AAF, UT, and to Crew B-10 (Marquardt)
Jun	45	To Tinian North Field

COMBAT MISSIONS

20 Jul	45	Crew B-10 (Marquardt), Pumpkin, Taira (Urban area)
26 Jul	45	Crew B-10 (Marquardt), Pumpkin, Hamamatsu (Urban area)
29 Jul	45	Crew A-5 (Smith), Pumpkin, Wakayama (Oil refinery)
8 Aug	45	Crew B-9 (Lewis), Pumpkin, Tokushima (Light industry)
14 Aug	45	Crew C-14 (Hopkins), Pumpkin, Nagoya (Arsenal factory)

POSTWAR

Nov	45	To Roswell AAF, NM
Apr	46	To Task Force 1.5 (Operation Crossroads)
Aug	46	To 509th Bomb (VH) Group (SAC), Roswell AFB
Aug	49	To 97th Bomb (M) Group (SAC), Biggs AFB, TX
Apr	50	Converted to TB-29 at Tinker AFB, OK
Oct	51	To Hamilton AFB, CA; Radar Calibration & Evaluation units
Mar	55	To Nashville, TN; Mobile Air Materiel unit
May	55	To Yuma County Airport, AZ; Tow Target unit
Nov	56	Transfer to Navy (China Lake, CA ?)

CREW C-11
393rd Bombardment
Squadron (VH),
509th Composite Group

FLIGHT CREW

Airplane Commander	Claude R. Eatherly
Pilot	Ira C. Weatherly
Navigator	Francis D. Thornhill
Bombardier	Frank K. Wey
Engineer	Eugene S. Grennan
Radio Operator	Pasquale Baldasaro
Radar Operator	Albert G. Barsumian
Tail Gunner	Gillen T. Niceley
Asst Eng./Scanner	Jack Bivans

GROUND CREW

Donald D. Beaudette
Howard A. Thompson
Yive J. H. Ping
William E. Smith
Chester S. Chudy
Harold E. Knisley
William J. Jacks

ASSIGNED SILVERPLATE B-29 SUPER FORTRESS
Serial No. 44-27301, Victor No. 85, "STRAIGHT FLUSH"
CREW COMBAT MISSIONS

Mission No. / Opns Order	1945 Date	B-29	Description of Mission	Notes
1 / 20	20 Jul	V-85	Pumpkin, Tokyo (Railroad station)	
7 / 24	24 Jul	V-85	Pumpkin, Otsu (Toyo Rayon Factory)	
8 / 27	26 Jul	V-85	Pumpkin, Tsugawa (Unidentified target of opportunity)	
12 / 30	29 Jul	V-85	Pumpkin, Maizuru (Naval base)	
13 / 35	6 Aug	V-85	Advance weather recon, Hiroshima. FIRST ATOMIC MISSION	
15./ 38	8 Aug	V-72	Pumpkin, Yokkaichi (Harbor area, heavy industry)	1

Notes: 1. The B-29 was "Top Secret".

HISTORICAL RECORD OF PLANE

Dates		Key Events
2 Apr	45	Delivered to USAAF by Martin Aircraft Co., Offutt AAF, Omaha, NE
Apr	45	To 509th Composite Group, Wendover AAF, UT, and to Crew C-11 (Eatherly)
Jun	45	To Tinian North Field
COMBAT MISSIONS		
20 Jul	45	Crew C-11 (Eatherly), Pumpkin, Tokyo (Railroad station)
24 Jul	45	Crew C-11 (Eatherly), Pumpkin, Otsu (Toyo Rayon plant)
26 Jul	45	Crew C-11 (Eatherly), Pumpkin, Tsugawa (Target of opportunity)
29 Jul	45	Crew C-11 (Eatherly), Pumpkin, Maizuru (Naval base)
6 Aug	45	Crew C-11 (Eatherly), Weather recon, Hiroshima. 1st ATOMIC MISSION
14 Aug	45	Crew C-15 (Albury), Pumpkin, Koromo (Toyoda Auto Works)
POSTWAR		
Nov	45	To Roswell AAF, NM
Apr	46	To Task Force 1.5 (Operation Crossroads)
Aug	46	To 509th Bomb (VH) Group (SAC), Roswell AAF
Jun	49	To 97th Bomb (M) Group (SAC), Biggs AFB, TX
Apr	50	Converted to TB-29 at Tinker AFB, OK
Apr	53	To Elmendorf AFB, AK; Radar, Calibration & Maintenance units
Dec	53	To Davis-Monthan AFB, AZ; Storage unit
Jul	54	Dropped from inventory as salvage (scrapped)

CREW C-12
393rd Bombardment Squadron (VH), 509th Composite Group

FLIGHT CREW

Airplane Commander .... Herman S. Zahn
Pilot .... Gilbert B. Dickman
Navigator .... Henry Deutsch
Bombardier .... Francis R. Ormond
Engineer.. James K. Elder
Radio Operator.. Leander J. Baur
Radar Operator... Gerald F. Clapso
Tail Gunner .... Raymond E. Allen
Asst Eng./Scanner .... Neil R. Corey

GROUND CREW

Elbert E. Owens
Carl W. Rein
Gerald J. Corcoran
Francis A. Pellegrino
Lavern L. Holmes

ASSIGNED SILVERPLATE B-29 SUPERFORTRESS
Serial No. 44-86346, Victor No. 94, "LUKE THE SPOOK"
CREW COMBAT MISSIONS

Mission No. / Opns Order	1945 Date	B-29	Description of Mission	Notes

No combat missions were flown by Crew C-12 due to late arrival on Tinian.

This crew, flying airplane V-94, "Luke the Spook", transported a Fat Man bomb assembly (one of three) from Kirkland Field, Albuquerque NM, to Tinian North Field, arriving there on 1 August 1945.

HISTORICAL RECORD OF PLANE

Dates			Key Events
15	Jun	45	Delivered to USAAF by Martin Aircraft Co., Offutt AAF, Omaha, NE
	Jul	45	To 509th Composite Group, Wendover AAF, UT, and to Crew C-12 (Zahn) then to Crew A-5 (Classen) in early August 1945
1	Aug	45	To Tinian North Field

SPECIAL MISSIONS

1	Aug	45	Delivered Fat Man bomb assembly to Tinian, flown by Crew C-12 (Zahn)
9	Aug	45	To U. S. to get Fat Man components, flown by Crew A-5 (Classen). No return to Tinian due to war ending. Airplane named in U. S.

POSTWAR

Nov	45	To Roswell AAF, NM
Apr	46	To Task Force 1.5 (Operation Crossroads)
Aug	46	To 509th Bomb (VH) Group (SAC), Roswell AAF
Jun	49	To 97th Bomb (M) Group, later Wing (SAC), Biggs AFB, TX
Apr	50	Converted to TB-29 at Tinker AFB, OK
Aug	52	To Yokota AB, Japan; Radar Calibration & Evaluation units
May	57	To Johnson AB, Japan; Pacific Air Forces
Nov	58	To Naha AB, Japan (Okinawa)
Jul	60	Dropped from inventory as surplus (scrapped)

CREW C-13
393rd Bombardment Squadron (VH), 509th Composite Group

FLIGHT CREW

Airplane Commander	Frederick C. Bock
Pilot	Hugh C. Ferguson
Navigator	Leonard A. Godfrey
Bombardier	Charles Levy
Engineer	Roderick F. Arnold
Radio Operator	Ralph D. Curry
Radar Operator	William C. Barney
Tail Gunner	Robert J. Stock
Asst Eng./Scanner	Ralph D. Belanger

GROUND CREW

Frederick D. Clayton
Robert L. McNamee
John L. Willoughby
Robert M. Haider
Rudolph H. Gerken

ASSIGNED SILVERPLATE B-29 SUPERFORTRESS
Serial No. 44-27297, Victor No. 77, "BOCKSCAR"

CREW COMBAT MISSIONS

Mission No. / Opns Order	1945 Date	B-29	Description of Mission	Notes
2 / 20	20 Jul	V-73	Pumpkin, Fukushima (Light industry)	1
5 / 24	24 Jul	V-77	Pumpkin, Niihama (Sumitomo aluminum plant)	
11 / 30	29 Jul	V-77	Pumpkin, Tokyo-Musashino (Nakajima aircraft engine factory)	
16 / 39	9 Aug	V-89	Instruments, Nagasaki. SECOND ATOMIC MISSION	2
18 / 44	14 Aug	V-83	Pumpkin, Koromo (Toyoda Auto Works)	3

Notes:
1. The B-29 was "Strange Cargo".
2. The B-29 was "The Great Artiste". Two members of Project Alberta, Lawrence Johnston and Walter Goodman, monitored the three sets of instruments (blast gauges), assisted by William Barney of this crew. William L. Laurence was an observer as Special Consultant to the Manhattan Engineer District and Science Writer for The New York Times.
3. The B-29 was "Full House".

HISTORICAL RECORD OF PLANE

Dates		Key Events
19 Mar	45	Delivered to USAAF by Martin Aircraft Co., Offutt AAF, Omaha, NE
Apr	45	To 509th Composite Group, Wendover AAF, UT, and to Crew C-13 (Bock)
Jun	45	To Tinian North Field
COMBAT MISSIONS		
24 Jul	45	Crew C-13 (Bock), Pumpkin, Niihama (Sumitomo aluminum plant)
26 Jul	45	Crew C-15 (Albury), Pumpkin, Toyama (Urban area)
29 Jul	45	Crew C-13 (Bock), Pumpkin, Tokyo area (Nakajima A/C engine plant)
9 Aug	45	Crew C-15 (Sweeney), "FAT MAN" bomb, Nagasaki. 2nd ATOMIC MISSION
POSTWAR		
Nov	45	To Roswell AAF, NM
Jun	46	To Task Force 1.5 (Operation Crossroads)
Aug	46	To 509th Bomb (VH) Group (SAC), Roswell AAF
Sep	46	To 4105th AAF Base Unit (AMC) Davis-Monthan AAF, AZ
		Dropped from inventory by transfer to the U. S. Air Force Museum, OH
22 Sep	61	Flown from Davis-Monthan via Wendover to the AF Museum for permanent display there

CREW C-14
393rd Bombardment Squadron (VH), 509th Composite Group

FLIGHT CREW

Airplane Commander	Norman W. Ray
	James I. Hopkins Jr
Pilot	John E. Cantlon
Navigator	Stanley G. Steinke
Bombardier	Myron Faryna
Engineer	George L. Brabenec
Radio Operator	Francis X. Dolan
Radar Operator	Richard F. Cannon
Tail Gunner	Martin G. Murray
Asst Eng./Scanner	Thomas A. Bunting

GROUND CREW

William E. Egger
Richard E. Blouse
Woitto T. Laine
Paul C. Schafhauser
Barton B. Crespin
Edgar A. Poe
Troy B. Scott

ASSIGNED SILVERPLATE B-29 SUPERFORTRESS
Serial No. 44-86291, Victor No. 91, "NECESSARY EVIL"

CREW COMBAT MISSIONS

Mission No. / Opns Order	1945 Date	B-29	Description of Mission	Notes
6 / 24	24 Jul	V-91	Pumpkin, Kobe (Kawasaki Locomotive and Car Co.)	1
8 / 27	26 Jul	V-91	Pumpkin, Kashiwazaki (Urban area)	1
11 / 30	29 Jul	V-91	Pumpkin, Koriyama (Light industry)	1
16 / 39	9 Aug	V-90	Cameras, Nagasaki. SECOND ATOMIC MISSION	2,3
17 / 44	14 Aug	V-88	Pumpkin, Nagoya (Arsenal factory)	2,4

Notes:
1. Ray was Airplane Commander.
2. Hopkins was Airplane Commander due to illness of Ray.
3. The B-29 was "Big Stink". Two observers on board, representing Great Britain, were Leonard Cheshire and William Penney.
4. The B-29 was "Up an' Atom".

HISTORICAL RECORD OF PLANE

Dates		Key Events
18 May	45	Delivered to USAAF by Martin Aircraft Co., Offutt AAF, Omaha, NE
Jun	45	To 509th Composite Group, Wendover AAF, UT, and to Crew C-14 (Ray)
Jun	45	To Tinian North Field

COMBAT MISSIONS

24 Jul	45	Crew C-14 (Ray), Pumpkin, Kobe (Kawasaki Locomotive & Car Co.)
26 Jul	45	Crew C-14 (Ray), Pumpkin, Kashiwazaki (Urban area)
29 Jul	45	Crew C-14 (Ray), Pumpkin, Koriyama (Light industry)
6 Aug	45	Crew B-10 (Marquardt), Cameras, Hiroshima. 1st ATOMIC MISSION

POSTWAR

Dec	45	To Roswell AAF, NM
Apr	46	To Task Force 1.5 (Operation Crossroads)
Aug	46	To 509th Bomb (VH) Group (SAC), Roswell AFB
Jun	49	To 97th Bomb (M) Group (SAC), Biggs AFB, TX
Apr	50	Converted to TB-29 at Tinker AFB, OK
Sep	52	To Biggs AFB, TX; Tow Target unit
Mar	53	To Griffiss AFB, NY; Radar Calibration & Evaluation units
Mar	55	To Nashville, TN; Mobile Air Materiel unit
Jun	55	To Yuma County Airport, AZ; Tow Target & Air Defense units
Nov	56	Dropped from inventory by transfer to Navy (China Lake, CA ?)

CREW C-15
393rd Bombardment Squadron (VH),
509th Composite Group

FLIGHT CREW

Airplane Commander	Charles D. Albury
Pilot	Fred J. Olivi
Navigator	James F. Van Pelt
Bombardier	Kermit K. Beahan
Engineer	John D. Kuharek
Radio Operator	Abe M. Spitzer
Radar Operator	Edward K. Buckley
Tail Gunner	Albert T. Dehart
Asst Eng./Scanner	Raymond G. Gallagher

GROUND CREW

Chester V. Pawiak
Charles B. Rinard
Claude C. Gilliam
Allan L. Moore
James J. Reilly
Theron L. Blaisdell
Robert E. Davenport

ASSIGNED SILVERPLATE B-29 SUPERFORTRESS
Serial No. 44-27353, Victor No. 89, "THE GREAT ARTISTE"
CREW COMBAT MISSIONS

Mission No. / Opns Order	1945 Date	B-29	Description of Mission	Notes
2 / 20	20 Jul	V-89	Pumpkin, Aborted (Bomb dropped at sea)	
6 / 24	24 Jul	V-89	Pumpkin, Kobe (Railroad yards)	
9 / 27	26 Jul	V-77	Pumpkin, Toyama (Urban area)	1
13 / 35	6 Aug	V-89	Instruments, Hiroshima. FIRST ATOMIC MISSION	2
16 / 39	9 Aug	V-77	"FAT MAN" bomb, Nagasaki. SECOND ATOMIC MISSION	3
18 / 44	14 Aug	V-85	Pumpkin, Koromo (Toyoda Auto Works)	4

Notes:
1. The B-29 was "Bockscar".
2. Charles Sweeney was Airplane Commander, Albury was Pilot. Three members of Project Alberta monitored the instruments (blast gauges): Luis Alvarez, Lawrence Johnston, and Harold Agnew.
3. The B-29 was "Bockscar". Charles Sweeney was Airplane Commander, Albury was Pilot, Olivi was Co-pilot. Frederick Ashworth of Project Alberta was Bomb Commander and Philip Barnes of the 1st Ordnance Squadron was Electronics Test Officer for the bomb. Jacob Beser was Radar Countermeasures Officer.
4. The B-29 was "Straight Flush".

HISTORICAL RECORD OF PLANE

Dates			Key Events
20	Apr	45	Delivered to USAAF by Martin Aircraft Co., Offutt AAF, Omaha, NE
	May	45	To 509th Composite Group, Wendover AAF, UT, and to Crew C-15 (Albury)
	Jun	45	To Tinian North Field
COMBAT MISSIONS			
24	Jul	45	Crew C-15 (Albury), Pumpkin, Kobe (Railroad yards)
29	Jul	45	Crew B-9 (Lewis), Pumpkin, Koriyama (Marshalling yards)
6	Aug	45	Crew C-15 (Sweeney), Instruments, Hiroshima. 1st ATOMIC MISSION
9	Aug	45	Crew C-13 (Bock), Instruments, Nagasaki. 2nd ATOMIC MISSION
POSTWAR			
	Nov	45	To Roswell AAF, NM
	Apr	46	To Task Force 1.5 (Operation Crossroads); deployment overseas
	Aug	46	To 509th Bomb (VH) Group (SAC), Roswell AFB
	Sep	48	To 538th Air Base Group (MATS), Goose Bay AB, Labrador
	Oct	48	To 1227th Air Base Group (MATS), Goose Bay AB
	Sep	49	Dropped from inventory as salvage (scrapped) after damage due to a crash landing at Goose Bay AB

1st Atomic Mission

Reason for Selection of Target

Hiroshima was highly important as an industrial target. Prior to this attack, Hiroshima ranked as the largest city in the Japanese Homeland, except Kyoto which remained undamaged by B29 incendiary strikes. In 1940, the city had a population of 344,000.

Hiroshima was an Army city, headquarters of the 5th Division and a primary port of embarkation. The entire northeastern and eastern sides of the city are military zones.

Prominent in the north central part of the city are the Army Division Headquarters (Hiroshima Castle) with numerous barracks, administration buildings and ordnance storage houses. In addition, there were the following military targets: Army reception center, military airport, ordnance depot, Army clothing and food depot, large port and dock area, several shipyards and ship building companies, the Japan Steel Company, railroad marshaling yards and numerous aircraft components parts factories.

The fact that Hiroshima was undamaged made it an ideal target which was necessary to assess correctly the damage which could be inflicted by the Atomic Bomb. According to preliminary data, it was believed the radius of damage which could be inflicted by the Atomic Bomb was 7500 feet. By placing the aiming point in the center of the city, the circle of prospective damage covered almost the entire area of Hiroshima with the exception of the dock area to the south.

L-1 test unit on Tinian

(above right) Hiroshima Bomb inside Tinian Assembly Building connected to monitoring equipment

(below right) Navy Commander Francis Birch, in charge of Little Boy assembly, paints L-11 on bomb case as Norman Ramsey, Deputy Director Project Alberta, looks on.

L-11 arrives at loading pit

Removing canvas

Above, (L-R): Rear Admiral Purnell, representative of the Military Policy Committee and Commander in Chief, U.S. Fleet; Brig. Gen. Thomas Farrell, Deputy Director of the Manhattan Project; Captain William Parsons, Officer in Charge of Project Alberta; and Dr. Norman Ramsey, Deputy Director, watch loading of bomb

Backing Enola Gay over bomb pit

270

Enola Gay is now over the bomb – the
three green plugs can be seen.

Another view of bomb
in pit

Enola Gay ground crew poses for photo after
backing plane over pit.
Back, (L-R): John Lesniewski, John Jackson,
Leonard Markley, Harold Olsen
Front: Jean Cooper, Winfred Kincaid

L-11 being raised into the Enola Gay

Bomb being raised into the Enola Gay

(L-R): George Reynolds, Billy Burns, William Parsons, Norman Ramsey confer as bomb is being raised

Norman Ramsey watches

*George Reynolds standing
on trailer watches work on
L-11*

Sheldon Dike studies bomb before positioning sway braces

The bomb is now inside the plane

*Hiroshima Briefing
(L-R): Charles Begg, Commander First Ordnance
Joe Buscher, Public Relations Group Combat
Hazen Payette, Intelligence Officer*

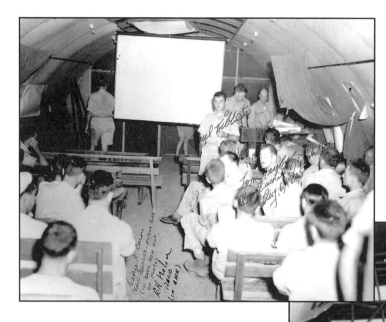

*Briefing for the Hiroshima
mission*

*Captain Parsons and
Morris Jeppson
being interviewed before mission*

*Morris Jeppson before
mission*

*New York Times William L. Laurence
with Public Relations Officer,
Maj. George Monyhan*

(L-R): Dr. Norman Ramsey, Capt. William Parsons, Col. Tibbets, Edward Doll, Ensn. George Reynolds

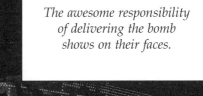

The awesome responsibility of delivering the bomb shows on their faces.

(L-R): Ted Van Kirk, Tom Ferebee, Sheldon Dike, Paul Tibbets, Bob Lewis

(L-R): Hazen Payette, Tom Ferebee,
Paul Tibbets, Ted Van Kirk

Enola Gay crew prepares to have photo
taken. Adolf Gasser behind lightstand

CREW OF THE ENOLA GAY

Standing: *Lt. Col Porter (Ground Officer, not on crew)*
                      Capt. Theodore J. Van Kirk, Navigator
                      Maj. Thomas Ferebee, Bombardier
                      Col. Paul W. Tibbets, Pilot
                      Capt. Robert A. Lewis, Co-Pilot
                      Lt. Jacob Beser, Radar Countermeasure Officer

Kneeling: *S/Sgt. Joe A. Stiborik, Radar Operator*
                      T/Sgt. George R. Caron, Tail Gunner
                      Sgt. Richard H. Nelson, Radio Operator
                      Sgt. Robert H. Shumard, Asst. Flight Engineer
                      M/Sgt. Wyatt Duzenbury, Flight Engineer

Missing from picture: Navy Capt. William S. Parsons, Lt. Morris Jeppson

Col. Tibbets waves before takeoff

I did a photo of the crew, I turned around and they were gone. The next thing I knew Col. Tibbets was in the cockpit. I saw Col. Tibbets, "Colonel would you please wave". I photographed the event. Before I knew it, the window closed, the engines were revved up, it slowly moved down the runway. You could see the blue flames coming out of the engines as it slowly rose.

ARMEN SHAMLIAN
509th Photographer

Hiroshima cloud taken from Enola Gay

Hiroshima cloud taken from
Navigator's window of V-91
by Russ Gackenbach

200 miles later

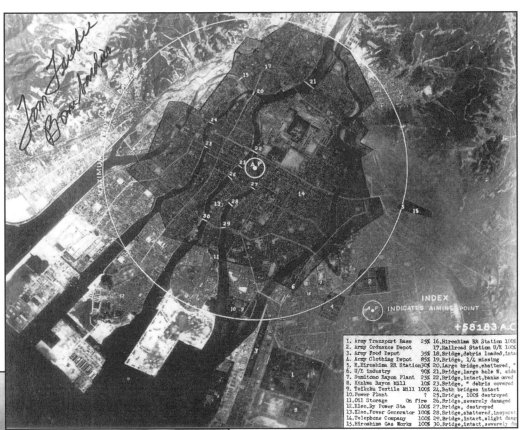

Hiroshima aiming point

INDEX
④ INDICATES AIMING POINT

+58183 A.C

1. Army Transport Base	25%	16. Hiroshima RR Station 100%
2. Army Ordnance Depot		17. Railroad Station U/E 100%
3. Army Food Depot	25%	18. Bridge, debris loaded, inta
4. Army Clothing Depot	85%	19. Bridge, 1/4 missing
5. E.Hiroshima RR Station	90%	20. Large bridge,shattered, "
6. U/E industry	90%	21. Bridge,large hole W. side
7. Sumitomo Rayon Plant	25%	22. Bridge, intact,banks cave
8. Kinkwa Rayon Mill	10%	23. Bridge, " debris covered
9. Teikoku Textile Mill	100%	24. Both bridges intact
10. Power Plant	?	25. Bridge, 100% destroyed
11. Oil Storage	On fire	26. Bridge,severely damaged
12. Elec.Ry Power Sta	100%	27. Bridge, destroyed
13. Elec.Power Generator	100%	28. Bridge,shattered,inopera
14. Telephone Company	100%	29. Bridge, intact,slight dam
15. Hiroshima Gas Works	100%	30. Bridge, intact,severely da

Enola Gay returns

*Awaiting the return of
the Enola Gay
(L-R):
Frederick Ashworth, USN
Sheldon Dike,
Francis Birch, USN,
Rear Admiral Purnell,
Norman Ramsey,
Gen. Giles, Brig. Gen. Farrell,
Gen. Twining,
Gen. Spaatz, Gen Davies*

279

The Enola Gay returns

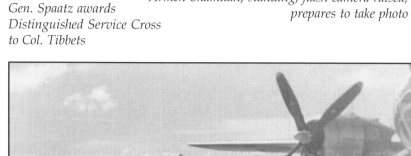

Armen Shamlian, standing, flash camera raised, prepares to take photo

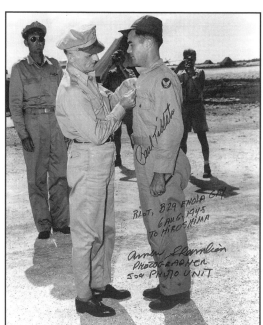

Gen. Spaatz awards Distinguished Service Cross to Col. Tibbets

Brig, Gen. Farrell runs to greet William Parsons

Heading toward hardstand

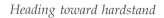

Flight and ground crew pose for picture

Crowd watching ceremony

Rear Adm. Purnell, Gen. Spaatz. Gen. Giles, Gen. Twining at interrogation

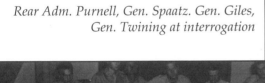

Captain Parsons makes a point

Ted Van Kirk goes over navigational charts while tired crew members look on.

Back (L-R): Gen. Davies leans on counter, Tom Classen, John Porter, and James Hopkins

Col. Tibbets smiles at Enola Gay return party

509TH
FREE BEER PARTY TODAY 2 P.M.
TODAY—TODAY—TODAY—TODAY—TODAY
PLACE—509TH BALL DIAMOND
FOR ALL MEN OF THE 509TH COMPOSITE GROUP
FOUR(4) BOTTLES OF BEER PER MAN
NO RATION CARD NEEDED
LEMONADE FOR THOSE WHO DO NOT CARE FOR BEER
ALL-STAR SOFT BALL GAME 2 P.M.
JITTER BUG CONTEST
HOT MUSIC
NOVELTY ACTS
SURPRISE CONTEST—YOU'LL FIND OUT
EXTRA—ADDED ATTRACTION, BLONDE, VIVACIOUS,
CURVACIOUS, STARLET DIRECT FROM ???????
PRIZES—GOOD ONES TOO
AND RATION FREE BEER
FOOD GALORE BY PERRY & CO. CATERERS
SPECIAL MOVIE WILL FOLLOW AT 1930, 'IT'S A PLEASURE'
IN TECHNICOLOR WITH
SONJA HENIE AND MICHAEL O'SHEA
- - - - - - - - - - - -
CHECK WITH YOUR ORDERLY ROOM
FOR MORE DETAILS
- - - - - - - - - - - -
WEAR OLD CLOTHES   WEAR OLD CLOTHES
6 AUGUST 1945
WELCOME PARTY FOR RETURN OF
ENOLA GAY
FROM
HIROSHIMA MISSION

Party after return of Enola Gay ... pie eating contest

Announcing the winner

282

Daily MISSION

- VOLUME 1. No. 145 - - TINIAN, MARIANAS - - - WEDNESDAY 8 AUGUST -

ATOMIC FURY HITS JAPAN
JAPS ACKNOWLEDGE HIROSHIMA BLAST

TRUMAN MAKES ANNOUNCEMENT TO WORLD SAYS JAP WAR MACHINE TO BE OBLITERATED

The United States unleashed the most terrible weapon in history--an atomic bomb carrying the destructive power of 20,000 tons of TNT.

President Truman made the initial announcement that the US and British scientists had won the race to unlock the power of the atom, saying the 1st atomic bomb had been dropped on the city of Hiroshima 16 hrs before.

One bomb alone carries more wallop than 2,000 B-29's carrying high explosives, and Secy Stimson said that the blast has stirred such a cloud of smoke and dust that observation was impossible. He said the power of the bomb was such as to stagger the imagination, and would prove a tremendous aid in shortening the war.

The Jap Radio said "Considerable damage was caused at Hiroshima as a result of an attack made by a small number of B-29's. The enemy appear to have employed new type bombs in this attack, however details are now under investigation."

President Truman said the surrender ultimatum had been issued in an effort to spare the Jap people from utter destruction. "Now," he said, "they can expect a rain of ruin the like of which has never been seen on this earth."

The President said the bomb draws its power from the same source as the sun, and has 2,000 times the blast power of the 11-ton "grand slam" bomb. It was the result of an Anglo-American victory in the feverish battle of the laboratories. Germans were reported working steadily on the weapon in the closing months of the European war.

The size of the bomb has not been revealed, except to say that the explosive charge is exceedingly small. All that is known is that the bomb involves the use of radioactive uranium.

The bomb was previewed by the Army in the Arizona desert July 16 when the test bomb was set off from a steel tower. Explosions there sent a huge ball of fire brighter than the midday sun billowing skyward and set off a blast which rattled windows 250 miles away. The test bomb was set off at 0530 in the morning, and accounts said there was a blinding flash brighter than the day, then came a sustained roar and heavy pressure waves. Immediately after, a huge surging cloud boiled up to an altitude of over 40,000 feet.

Truman said the monster could wipe out civilization, and that some defense against it must be found before the secret is released. He said "We are now prepared to obliterate completely every productive enterprise the Japs have above ground in any city. Let there be no mistake--we shall completely destroy Japan's power to make war."

THE ABOVE STORY CONTAINS ALL OFFICIALLY RELEASED INFORMATION ON THE NEW ATOMIC BOMB. WHATEVER ELSE YOU MAY HEAR IS RUMOR, UNLESS A FURTHER RELEASE IS MADE BY THE PRESIDENT OR ANOTHER OFFICIAL SOURCE. THE DAILY MISSION HAS GIVEN FULL PLAY TO THIS STORY, AS A SERVICE TO ITS READERS AT THE EXPENSE OF OTHER NEWS. --ed.

THE MEN THAT DID IT

THE CREW THAT DROPPED THE BOMB THAT SHOOK JAPAN IS WELL-TRAINED, HOT OUTFIT

Col Paul W. Tibbets, the man who piloted the ship that dropped the first atomic bomb, declared to be the most powerful weapon in the world, enlisted in the Army Air Forces in 1937 and was commissioned a 2nd Lt in February, 1938. In June, 1942, as a Major, Tibbets was sent to England with the Eighth Air Force, and began an outstanding war record when he piloted the first B-17 to cross the English channel on a mission against Germany.

A trusted pilot was needed to fly General Mark Clark and General Eisenhower to Gibraltar for the conferences that led to the N. African invasions. Young Major Tibbets was selected. Later he flew Canada's Gen MacNaughton to Algiers, where he landed on a field that was under attack by German bombers.

In 1943 after service on the staff of the 12th Air Force, he was assigned to the AAF Tactical Center at Orlando, where he was among the first pilots to fly the experimental models of the new B-29, and then was transferred to Grand Island, Nebraska, and was put in charge of the 17th Wing, a B-29 training outfit.

In September of 1944, he was put in command of the as yet unnamed and unformed 509th Composite Group. He took charge of the operational end of the program, and has remained with it ever since that time.

He holds, in addition to the Distinguished Service Cross which he was awarded on the completion of the historic mission to Hiroshima, the DFC with one cluster, the "Air Medal" with three clusters; the Purple Heart, the European Theater ribbon with three battle stars, and the American Theater ribbon.

The bombardier who let loose the greatest destructive force in warfare was Major Thomas J. Ferebee, who has been with Col Tibbets since 1942. He is from Mocksville, N.C. The navigator was Capt Theodore J Van Kirk, of Northumberland, Penna. and has also been with Col Tibbets since 1942. His co-pilot, was Capt Robert A Lewis.

Enlisted men in the crew are S/Sgt Wyatt E. Duzenbury, S/Sgt George R. Caron, Sgt Robert R Shumard, PFC Richard Newson, Sgt Joe E Stiborik.

The ship is the "Enola Gay", according to reports from the 509th Group the boys are mighty happy over their first successful run -- they are on the front pages of the world's newspapers for their pioneering with this new, highly secret, and terrible weapon. Hats off to the Colonel and his crew!

ACTIVITIES

MOVIE SCHEDULE FOR WEDNESDAY, 8 AUG.
AVENGER(504th) "Mr. Emmanuel"
    Felix Aylmer, Greta Gynt, Ursula Jeans
THOR(504th) "Captain Eddie", story of Eddie Rickenbacker, plus "G.I. #96"
RENDEZVOUS(9th) "Valley of Decision"
    Greer Garson, Gregory Peck
STARLIGHT(6th) "Pillow To Post"
    Ida Lupino, Sidney Greenstreet
LITTLE THEATER IN THE WOODS(313th) "Keep Your Powder Dry"--Lana Turner, Laraine Day, Susan Peters plus "Captain Eddie", story of Eddie Rickenbacker
SERVICEDROME "Bullfighters"
    Laurel and Hardy
CAH#2 "Delightfully Dangerous"--Jane Powell, Connie Moore, R. Bellamy
PUMPKIN PLAYHOUSE(509th) "Crime Doctor's Courage" - Warner Baxter
CORAL GABLES(Chem. Co#) "G.I. #95"

BASEBALL
Yesterday's postponed game between the 313th FLYERS and 73rd BOMBERS will be played today at 1500 at THOR (504th) Field.
CAH ALL-STARS vs. NAB Team at 1430 at 17th A.A. Field.

GROUP STUDY CLASSES
RIVERSIDE UNIVERSITY "Review Arithmetic" at 1930 hours.

Officers of Enola Gay pose for photo
(L-R): Thomas Ferebee, Paul Tibbets, Ted Van Kirk, Robert Lewis

Hiroshima Damage
Photos

Gen. Davies presents the Silver Star to crew of the Enola Gay.

Crowd watches presentation, mostly Project A people. Harlow Russ can be seen with FM emblem on his shirt.

Morris Jeppson and the Enola Gay flight crew displaying their medals, the Distinguished Flying Cross

Tom Ferebee with his bombsight

Removing circle R tail marking
from Enola Gay

2nd Atomic Mission

Reason for Selection of Target

Kokura and Nagasaki contained essentially the same characteristics for a good target as Hiroshima, with the exception they both had Prisoner of War Camps nearby. Nagasaki was the poorest of the three targets as to situation and overall construction and for those reasons was made the third target.

Kokura had a 1940 census population of 168,000 inhabitants. The target was three miles by two miles in area with many industrial targets. The Kokura Arsenal was one of the largest Japanese Arsenals and the most important in Japan for the manufacture of light automatic weapons, smaller type antiaircraft and anti-tank guns as well as combat vehicles. Production rates were unknown because of such a diversity of activities, but probably was several thousand machine guns of all types per month.

Fat Man test unit 3 on Tinian

The arsenal is known to produce 6.5 millimeter (mm) and 7.7mm light machine guns, 7.7mm heavy machine guns, 20mm antiaircraft, anti-tank guns and ammunition. It was reported to be equipped to mix poison gas, to load gas shells and store these shells underground. The most essential processes of this plant are the mailing and assembly of ordnance, forging and pressing.

Nagasaki, one of Japan's leading shipbuilding and repair centers, was also important for its production of Naval Ordnance and its function as a major military port. Primary objectives were the concentration of Mitsubishi Heavy Industries Shipbuilding and Repair Facilities, comprising a shipyard, dockyard and marine engine works. Located on the western side of the harbor within an area measuring approximately 6500 feet by 2000 feet.

The Mitsubishi Steel and Arms Works, with its new rolling mill, located along the Urakami River in northern Nagasaki was integrated with the shipyards that produce ship plate, castings, forgings as well as Naval Ordnance the majority of which is torpedoes. A wood working plant, with extensive timber and lumber stor-

ages, was located just to the south of the rolling mill and supplies lumber and wooden fittings to the shipyards.

The Kawanami Industry Company Shipyard located on Koyagi Island to the south of the harbor entrance was an important producer of medium sized vessels, marine engines and boilers.

The eastern side of Nagasaki Harbor contained loading and storage facilities. Nagasaki's southwest location made this city a primary embarkation and supply port for operations on the mainland and the docks and freight yards were believed to be congested with military supplies. Numerous reports referred to large scale expansion of dock and storage facilities and the entire waterfront was lined with small shipyards, equipped with shops, foundries and slipways. These yards build small wooden cargo and shipping vessels as well as lifeboats. Three unidentified factories are located along the railway to the north of Mitsubishi Steel and Arms Works. Of these, the northernmost appeared significant comprising of some eight or ten shop type buildings, the largest measuring approximately 900 by 400 feet, a power plant and several storage buildings. The plant's general appearance suggested a very large textile mill or major assembly plant.

Intelligence reports mentioned new munitions plants, in this area, and an aircraft engine factory was also reported. In Nagasaki proper, commercial and public buildings were concentrated along the eastern and central parts of the city. Densely grouped houses crowd the buildings and extend in an almost solid mass to the hills. All important industrial installments are located outside the city proper.

The city was virtually untouched by previous bombings enabling accurate damage assessment. The city was the third largest on the Island of Kyushu with a population of 235,000. The city measured approximately five miles north to south and five miles east to west. It was believed that an accurate drop would destroy the bulk of the city east of the harbor and possibly carry across to the western shore.

Final preparations to Fat Man Unit F31 prior to mission

*Outside bomb
assembly building*

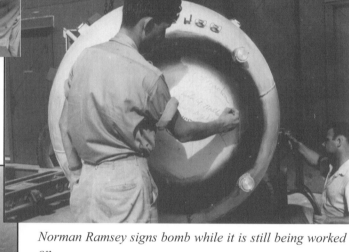

Applying tape to nose seam

*Norman Ramsey signs bomb while it is still being worked
on*

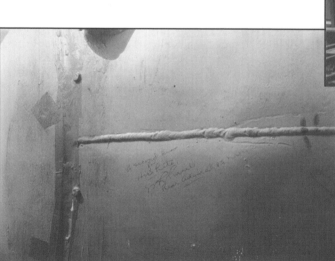

Side view showing signatures

Side view of tail

F31 loading onto transport trailer. Signatures can be seen on tail.

Loading pit for Fat Man F31

Being transported to loading pit

Pushing bomb towards pit while Norman Ramsey (left) looks on

289

Removing rails

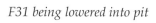

F31 being lowered into pit

Working on bomb shackles

Bob Haider towing
V-77 Bockscar.
V-77 backed over pit
using reversable
props.

Maj. Charles Sweeney doing
pre-flight check

Ray Gallagher
checking fuel level

(L-R):
Charles Albury, Co-Pilot
Charles Sweeney,
Airplane Commander
Ed Buckley, Radar
Abe Spitzer, Radio
Mel Irwin, Intelligence
Ray Gallagher, Asst.
Flight Engineer

Philip Barnes, 1st Ordnance
Weapon Test Officer

Maj. Charles Sweeney holding flashlight
2nd Lt. Fred Olivi holding map.

Reviewing map (L-R):
Lt. James Van Pelt,
Navigator
Maj. Charles Sweeney,
Airplane Commander
2nd Lt. Fred J. Olivi, co-
Pilot/Observer on
mission

Flight Engineer John Kuharek
checks load/fuel calculator. His
flight gear next to him includes
variable density goggles in can.

Lt. Jacob
Beser, Radar
Counter-
measure
Officer,
watches
John
Kuharek
calculate.

292

(L-R):
Fred Olivi, Norman
Ramsey, Charles Albury,
Charles Begg, Tom
Ferebee, Sheldon Dike,
Charles Sweeney

(L-R): Kermit Beahan, Jim McFall

(L-R): Norman Ramsey, Kermit Beahan, Frederick
Ashworth, Sheldon Dike

(L-R): Ralph Devore, Charles Sweeney

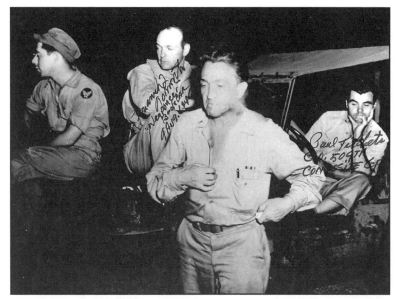

(L-R):
Jacob Beser, Radar
Countermeasure Officer
Frederick L. Ashworth, USN,
"Weaponeer"
William Laurence, Science
Reporter, New York Times,
Col. Paul Tibbets, Commanding
Officer, 509th Composite Group

(L-R): Edward Buckley, Radar
Abe Spitzer, Radio

(L-R):
Maj. Charles Sweeney,
Col. Paul Tibbets,
Rear Adm. William Purnell, USN,
Capt. William Parsons, USN,
Cmdr. Frederick Ashworth

(L-R):
William Laurence,
holding goggles in can
Col. Paul Tibbets
Rear Adm. Purnell
Lt. Charles Albury

(L-R): Charles Albury, Ray Gallagher, John Kuharek, Ed Buckley
(far right)
Rotating props before starting engines

The Sweeney/Albury crew arrived at the plane a little after 0200. It wasn't raining, but every few minutes there was a flash of lightning or bolt of thunder.

The order to climb aboard came at 0330. At 0335, John Kuharek yelled "Major", advising Sweeney that one of the instruments showed that he might not be able to get the gas stored in the bomb bay tank.

Major Sweeney stepped out, talked to Col. Tibbets, then stepped back into the plane at 0345. The brakes were released and throttles advanced.

Nagasaki photo taken by
Navigator Len Godfrey
on board the Great Artiste

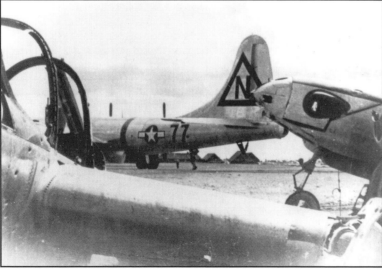

Photo of Bockscar taken after emergency
landing on Okinawa. There was only enough
gas left for 5 minutes of flying.

Crew photo taken upon arrival on Tinian

515 TH COMBAT BOMB WING - - - INFORMATION AND EDUCATION OFFICE

Daily MISSION

VOLUME 1, NO. 145 - - - TINIAN, MARIANAS - - - FRIDAY 10 AUGUST - - -

RUSSIA AT WAR WITH JAPAN
SECOND ATOMIC BOMB DROPPED!

NAGASAKI SECOND VICTIM OF NEW WEAPON AS W.D. DENIES LENGTH OF BOMB EFFECTS

Japan's twelfth largest city, with a population of about 230,000, became the second area to feel the awful might of the new atomic bomb at noon yesterday. Crew members of the Marianas-based B-29 which carried the bomb reported good results, but no details have thus far been released. Nagasaki is an important seaport on Kyushu and is the site of three Mitsubishi aircraft plants.

Meanwhile, the War Department denied reports that areas devastated by the atomic bomb would continue radioactive for years, and said that rays which are emitted are fatal only when a person is subjected to them at close range for a long time. They said publicity reports of 70-year devastation of a bombed area were without foundation and completely unauthorized.

JAP RADIO REPORTS ON HIROSHIMA DAMAGE

A Jap broadcast at 0200 Marianas-time Thursday spoke of the effect of the atomic bomb on Hiroshima, saying in part "practically all living humans and animals were seared to death."

B-29'S HIT FOUR JAP CITIES FOR 3RD DAY

Fire and demolition bombs rained on Yawata, steel city, Nakajima A/C plant Tokyo arsenal, and Fukuyama, chemical center, from nearly 400 B-29's Wednesday in the 3rd day of massed attack.

THIRD FLEET RETURNS TO HIT N. HONSHU

Admiral Halsey's Third Fleet moved into action again Wednesday, throwing hundreds of carrier planes against northern Honshu, hitting shipping, airfields, and military targets.

JAPS REPORT MANCHURIA FIGHTING BEGUN TRUMAN ANNOUNCES STARTLING DEVELOP

Japan today was facing annihilation by strong Russian forces, as firebombs, atomic bombs, fleet strikes and naval shelling. The Russians announced early yesterday that they were at war with Japan.

Foreign Commissar Molotov declared to the Russian people and to the world that "true to her duty as an ally, Soviet government had joined in Allied war against Japan." He pointed out that Japan was the only great power that stood for continuation of war. He said that US and Britain had asked Russia at Potsdam to join the war against Japan and thus "shorten the war, reduce the number of victims, and facilitate restoration of a universal peace."

President Truman announced the Red declaration in a simple statement and newsmen rushed out to give it to the startled world. Secy of State Byrnes said there is still time—but little time—for the Japanese to save themselves.

Feeling in Washington was that the length of the war has been shortened immeasurably by the developments of the last few days.

Although Russia had still made no announcement at 0100 today, the Japs claimed that the Russian armies had attacked on a 300 mile front in Manchuria in a vast pincers movement against the Jap Kwantung Army there. Japs said the blow was loosed early yesterday morning with bombers in direct support.

HONORS GO TO NAVAL OFFICER AND CREW OF SHIP THAT TOTED FIRST ATOMIC BOMB

By direction of President Truman, it was announced that Naval Captain W. S. Parsons, the Senior Military Technical Advisor on the historic mission to Hiroshima, was awarded the Silver Star, and the crew of Col. Paul Tibbets plane have all been presented with the Distinguished Flying Cross.

Capt. Taylor's citation reads in part, "After take off in the early morning hours the plane set course as planned. Captain Parsons then climbed into the bomb bay to personally load the charge, which had been postponed until after take-off to assure the safety of the island from which they had departed....accompanying the mission to assure correct use (of the bomb), and rendering of a decision in event deviation from the planned tactical employment of the bomb was necessary; Captain Parsons kept careful watch until the plane was in its position and then approved release. At 0915 the switch was pressed, the bomb cleared safely."

The Crew members, Maj T W Ferebee; Capt. R A Lewis, Capt T J Van Kirk, 1st Lt J Beser, 2nd Lt M R Jepson, S/Sgt W E Dusenbury, S/Sgt G R Caron, Sgt J S Stiborik, Sgt R H Shumard, Pfc R H Nelson, were awarded the DFC for the extraordinary risk taken, and skill shown in the first mission of its kind in the history of war.

Weather: Thursday's high; 81; low 76; humidity, 84%. Today: partly cloudy, scattered showers in afternoon.

Daily MISSION

This paper is published by the Wing Information - Education Office, and receives ANS and CNS material. Republication of credited matter prohibited. STAFF: Editor, Cpl R B Luce; Assistant Editor, Cpl Bill Lauten; Code Man, Cpl Al Southard. Production and Circulation: Pfc. Harold Hopper; Artist: Pfc Henry Shore.

PHONE - CLEAR HEEL 5834

POSTMARKED USA

IT LOOKS AS IF THIS men's "panties" situation is the real McCoy. The men, in desperation, have taken to buying dainty canary yellow, pink, and blue silk panties. The salegirls are beginning to get used to the idea, and smile condescendingly at their red-faced male customers.

ATTENTION MASSACHUSETTS MEN: Here's the way you'll pay back that 100 dollars bonus. If a veteran and his wife smoke a pack of cigarettes a day, the tax they pay will be $87.64 in six yrs and if they buy a quart of whiskey every three weeks, the other tax on whiskey will cost them $13. So if you want to get the benefit of your bonus the idea is to lay off whiskey and cigarettes.

A MOVIE YOU'LL WANT TO SEE— Fred Astaire dancing while Judy Garland sings in "Belle of New York."

LONG POOP FROM HOLLYWOOD says that Cary Grant has signed with an English producer and will go to London to do a picture with Alfred Hitchcock.

THE NEW KAISER-BUILT automobile is likely to be on the market within the next six months. It will be built of magnesium and aluminum. New features that it is rumored to have: rear engine mounting a new power plant, elimination of the old conventional carburetor, fuel to be piped directly into the cylinders, and a new individual wheel suspension system.

IN WASHINGTON it was announced that Tokyo Rose won a citation from the United States Navy "for meritorious service contributing greatly to the morale of American troops in the Pacific." As a further tribute, the Navy granted her permission to broadcast a description of Admiral Halsey riding the Emperors White Horse.

THE 1944 CITATION FOR SPORTSMANSHIP has been awarded posthumously to Sgt Torger Torkle, the champion ski-jumper who was killed in action in Northern Italy last spring, the Sportsmanship Brotherhood announced.

Nagasaki Damage Photos

Damaged Mitsubishi Steel and Armament Works on east bank of Urakami River south of hypocenter by 3/5 of a mile.

Damage further south of Mitsubishi Steel

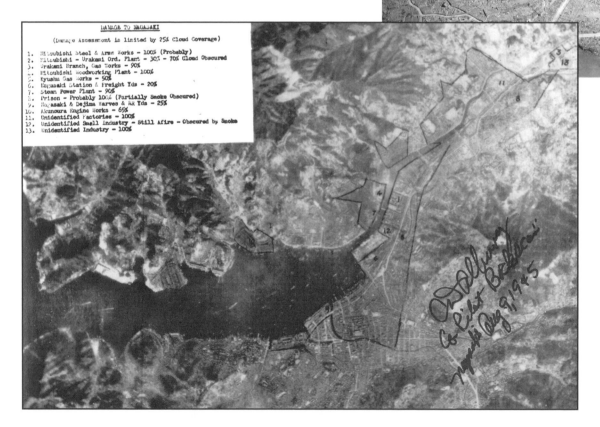

DAMAGE TO NAGASAKI

(Damage Assessment is limited by 25% Cloud Coverage)

1. Mitsubishi Steel & Arms Works - 100% (Probably)
2. Mitsubishi - Urakami Ord. Plant - 30% - 70% Cloud Obscured
3. Urakami Branch, Gas Works - 90%
4. Mitsubishi Woodworking Plant - 100%
5. Kyushu Gas Works - 50%
6. Nagasaki Station & Freight Yds - 20%
7. Steam Power Plant - 90%
8. Prison - Probably 100% (Partially Smoke Obscured)
9. Nagasaki & Dejima Warves & RR Yds - 25%
10. Akunoura Engine Works - 65%
11. Unidentified Factories - 100%
12. Unidentified Small Industry - Still Afire - Obscured by Smoke
13. Unidentified Industry - 100%

ATOMIC BOMB PRESS CONFERENCE
509TH COMPOSITE GROUP

A press conference, the subject of which was the Atomic Bomb, was called on 11 August 1945 at the Briefing Room of the 509th Composite Group. Beginning at 1000 and ending four and one half hours later, the meeting was presided over by Brigadier General Thomas W. Farrell. Also in attendance were Rear Admiral Purnell, Major John F. Moynahan, and Major Finney, PRO for the 20th Air Force.

The press and radio network representatives were given brief historical sketches which included the military backgrounds of all crew members participating in the first two drops of the Atomic Bomb. The crews were then introduced and questioned by the Press. Following this, certain of the scientists closely connected with the project were called upon to introduce themselves, and they in turn were questioned by the correspondents.

Press and radio were represented as follows:

United Press	Hazel Hartzog
Associated Press	Bonnie Wylie
International News Service	George McWilliams
Time	Bill Howland
Saturday Evening Post	Richard Tregaskis
N.Y. Herald Tribune	Homer Bigert
Newark N. J. News	Bob Taylor
Still Picture Pool	Max Desfor
Impact	Capt. T. Prideaux
Brief	Sgt. Bob Speer
Farm Journal	Robert Manus
Yank	Y2/c Bob Schwartz
National Broadcasting System	Ray Clark
Mutual Broadcasting System	Sgt. Mike Cassidy
Central Broadcasting Company	Jack Shelley

After this interrogation, the meeting turned into an informal discussion during which the Press interviewed the crew members and technicians at will. Pictures of the crews and other persons were then taken as requested by the Press. The representatives of the broadcasting networks made recordings of Colonel Tibbets and members of his crew, and of Major Sweeney and members of his crew. Other interviews were recorded for use by the several networks in the States.

The Twelve Men Who Flew on "Enola Gay" to Hiroshima 6 August 1945

Both photos taken August 11, 1945 by Max DesFor, still picture pool, Associated Press

Front row, L to R: Lt Jacob Beser, 393rd Bomb Squadron, Radar Countermeasures Officer; Lt Morris R. Jeppson, 1st Ordnance Squadron, Bomb Electronics Test Officer; Capt. Theodore J. Van Kirk, 509th Headquarters, Navigator; Major Thomas W. Ferebee, 509th Headquarters, Bombardier; Navy Capt. William S. Parsons, C. O., Project Alberta, Bomb Commander; Col. Paul W. Tibbets Jr, 509th Headquarters, Airplane Commander; Capt. Robert A. Lewis, Crew B-9, 393rd Bomb Squadron, Pilot *Back row, L to R:* Sgt Robert H. Shumard, Crew B-9, 393rd Bomb Squadron; Ass't Engineer Cpl Richard M. Nelson, Crew B-9, 393rd Bomb Squadron, Radio Operator; S/Sgt Joseph S. Stiborick, Crew B-9, 393rd Bomb Squadron, Radar Operator; T/Sgt Wyatt E. Duzenbury, Crew B-9, 393rd Bomb Squadron, Engineer; T/Sgt George R. Caron, Crew B-9, 393rd Bomb Squadron, Tail Gunner

The Thirteen Men Who Flew on "Bockscar" to Nagasaki, 9 August 1945

Front row, L to R: Lt Philip M. Barnes, 1st Ordnance Squadron, Bomb Electronics Test Officer; Lt Jacob Beser, 393rd Bomb Squadron, Radar Countermeasures Officer; Lt Fred J. Olivi, Crew C-15, 393rd Bomb Squadron, Co-pilot; Capt. Kermit K. Beahan, Crew C-15, 393rd Bomb Squadron, Bombardier; Capt. Charles D. Albury, Crew C-15, 393rd Bomb Squadron, Pilot; Capt. James F. Van Pelt, Crew C-15, 393rd Bomb Squadron, Navigator; Major Charles W. Sweeney, C. O., 393rd Bomb Squadron, Airplane Commander; Navy Cmdr Frederick L. Ashworth, Opns Off., Project Alberta, Bomb Commander *Back row, L to R:* M/Sgt John D. Kuharek, Crew C-15, 393rd Bomb Squadron, Engineer; Sgt Abe M. Spitzer, Crew C-15, 393rd Bomb Squadron, Radio Operator; Sgt Raymond K. Gallagher, Crew C-15, 393rd Bomb Squadron, Ass't Engineer; S/Sgt Edward K. Buckley, Crew C-15, 393rd Bomb Squadron, Radar Operator; S/Sgt Albert T. Dehart, Crew C-15, 393rd Bomb Squadron, Tail Gunner

509TH MOVIE INTERVIEWS, AUGUST 14, 1945
Conducted and Introductions by
Major George Monyhan, Public Relations Officer

Transcript:

We are standing in front of the first Atomic Bomber, the Enola Gay, a storied B29 which carried the revolutionary Atomic Bomb to the enemy. Gathered here are a group of key men representing both the project personnel in the theater and the Air Corps. It was this group and this airplane which outmoded present warfare.

Brigadier General Thomas F. Farrell of Albany, New York, Theater Commander of the Atomic Bomb Project

I know I speak for every man and woman of the huge throng who worked so long and so faithfully on this great fantastic fairyland project which has had such a tremendous impact on the war against Japan. So much credit is due to so many that it would be difficult to properly apportion that credit. We have, however, a sense of great moral responsibility because this great power has been given to us and we should be ever humble and grateful that it was given to us rather than to our enemies. All of us who have had a part in it's development and in carrying out it's use should dedicate our strength, our wealth, our brains and even our very lives to see that it is always used for good and never for evil.

Captain William Sterling Parsons, United States Navy, Fort Sumner, New Mexico, Scientific Head of the Atomic Bomb Project

After a photographing session that made us feel like a Hollywood Premier, we got off at about three o'clock in the morning darkness, headed for Iwo Jima which we reached about sunrise, made certain adjustments and tests on the bomb during that flight, then headed for the Empire. The weather improved as we went along and we felt it was our lucky day and we knew it was as we made the final approach toward Hiroshima which the Navigator hit right on the button. The Bombardier took over, identified the target and everything went with perfection not approached in the rehearsals. A bomb was finally released exactly at the designated hour and the explosion occurred as planned.

Colonel Paul Tibbets of Miami, Florida, Commander of the Atomic Bomb Group

Well, as the bomb left the airplane, we took over manual control, made an extremely steep turn to try and put as much distance between ourselves and the explosion as possible. After we felt the explosion hit the airplane, that is, the concussion waves, we knew that the bomb had exploded, everything was a success, so we turned around to take a look at it. The sight that greeted our eyes was quite beyond what we had expected because we saw this cloud of boiling dust and debris below us with this tremendous mushroom on top. Beneath that was hidden the ruins of the city of Hiroshima.

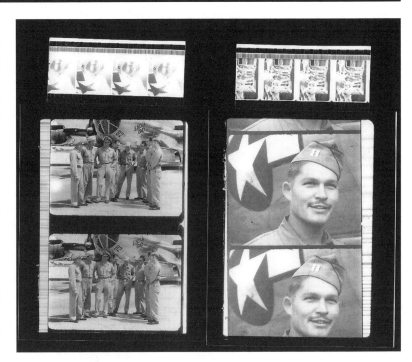

Commander Frederick L. Ashworth, United States Navy, of Wenham, Massachusetts, Technical Member of the Crew in the Second Atomic Bomb Raid

There was a tremendous suspense and tension as we approached the target as we had just failed to be able to bomb our primary target. We made our test and as we proceeded into the dropping point, I knew that everything was functioning perfectly. At that time, the Bombardier took over. For some, as the bomb was released, was considerable relief and I knew when I saw the flash of the explosion that the second Atomic Bomb had been successfully delivered to the enemy.

Major Tom Ferebee of Mocksville, North Carolina, Bombardier of the First Atomic Bomber

My Navigator had me perfectly lined up with the target. When I touched down with my sight, I could clearly see the city of Hiroshima within my bombsight. Then I touched down and took the run; I felt the bump of the airplane; I was greatly relieved 'cause I knew the unit had gone from the airplane; that we had successfully delivered; that meant so much to the Army Air Forces, American Science and Industry.

Major Charles W. Sweeney of Quincy, Massachusetts, Pilot of the Great Artiste

We were briefed on, of course, the primary and secondary target. As usual we took off and the flight was uneventful except for some weather on the way up. The primary target was located and we made three runs on it but were unable to get into it. Commander Ashworth and I held a little conference with the Bombardier and the Navigator. We started for the secondary target which was Nagasaki at which time, the Flight Engineer told us we had just 1300 gallons of gasoline left. We picked our route into the secondary target and dropped it on Nagasaki. We were very relieved to have it go, much more relieved when we saw the tremendous flash and knew that it had functioned. At that point, we hit the road for Okinawa, the first petrol station.

Captain Kermit K. Beahan of Houston, Texas, Bombardier of the Great Artiste

I suppose it was in the clouds on the way up over the target, Nagasaki. The target was as pretty as a picture. I made the run; let the bomb go; that was my greatest thrill.

Captain Theodore J. Van Kirk of Northumberland, Pennsylvania, Colonel Tibbets' Navigator

I knew when we hit the coast of Japan that we were well on the way to completing a successful mission and that the new bomb, we carried, would be a great help in shortening the war.

(L-R):
Brig. General Farrell
Capt. Parsons
Comdr. Ashworth
Thomas Ferebee
Theodore Van Kirk
Paul Tibbets
Charles Sweeney
Kermit Beahan

Capt. Parsons,
George Monyhan

Paul Tibbets, Pilot to Hiroshima 6 Aug. 1945

Dutch Van Kirk Navigator Enola Gay

Maj. Chas Sweeney A/c Bockscar 8/9/45

Maj. Chas W. Sweeney A/c Bockscar 9 Aug 45

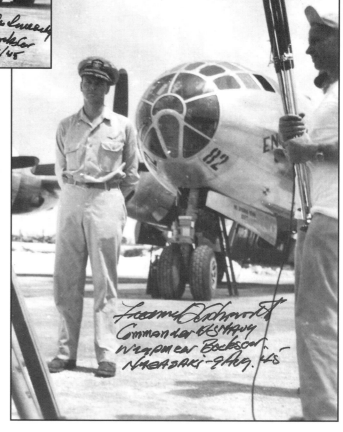

Fred Ashworth Commander U.S. Navy Weaponeer Bockscar — Nagasaki - 9 Aug. 45

Tom Ferebee being introduced by George Monyhan

304

Charles W. Sweeney
Commander
"Bockscar" 9 Aug '45

Daily MISSION

VOLUME 1 - NO. 150 - - - TINIAN, MARIANAS - - - WEDNESDAY 15 AUGUST

EXTRA EXTRA EXTRA
WAR ENDS

JAPANESE HAVE ACCEPTED UNCONDITIONAL SURRENDER

HERE IS THE TEXT OF JAPAN'S ACCEPTANCE MESSAGE OF THE POTSDAM DECLARATION UNCONDITIONAL SURRENDER TERMS:

"With reference to the announcement on August 5 regarding the acceptance of the provisions of the Potsdam Declaration and the reply of the Governments of the United States, Great Britain, the Soviet Union and China, sent by American Secy. of State Byrnes on August 11, the Japanese Government has the honor to communicate to the Governments of the Four Powers as follows:

1. His Majesty, the Emperor, has issued an Imperial Rescript regarding Japan's acceptance of the provisions of the Potsdam Declaration;

2. His Majesty, the Emperor, is prepared to authorize and ensure the signature by his Government and Imperial General Headquarters of the necessary terms for carrying out the provisions of the Potsdam Declaration;

3. His Majesty, the Emperor, is also prepared to issue his commands to all the Military, Naval, and Air authorities of Japan and all forces under their control, wherever located, to cease active operations, to surrender arms and to issue such other orders as may be required by the Supreme Commander of the Allied Forces for the execution of the aforementioned terms."

Signed: — TOGO, Foreign Minister of Japan.

THE DAILY MISSION WILL NOT BE PUBLISHED TOMORROW MORNING, AS WE HAVE BEEN AUTHORIZED TIME OFF THIS EVENING FOR CELEBRATION OF JAPAN'S DEFEAT AND THE END OF THE WAR.
THE STAFF

Japan surrendered unconditionally this morning, Tuesday, August 15th, Marianas Time. History's most destructive war is now over except for the formalities of signing surrender documents and carrying out their terms. President Truman released the stirring news at 7 O'Clock Tuesday night, Washington Time. The Wareary world also received announcements simultaneously from Moscow, London, and Chungking. Arrangements still must be made for the signing of formal surrender terms. President Truman said that General Douglas MacArthur has been appointed Supreme Allied Commander to receive the Jap surrender. The V-J Day will be proclaimed. The President announced that advancing Allied armed forces have been ordered to suspend offensive action.

While the world celebrated with unrestrained joy, President Truman ordered the Jap government which once had promised to dictate peace terms in the White House to stop war on all fronts. Through Secretary of State Byrnes and the Swiss Legation, Mr. Truman did the dictating. He decreed that the Jap government: 1. Direct prompt cessation of hostilities by Jap forces. 2. Notify General MacArthur of effective date, and hour of cessation of hostilities, and send emissaries to General MacArthur to arrange formal surrender. In addition, Mr. Truman announced plans for slashing Army draft calls from 80,000 to 50,000 per month. He said the draft would continue since now the question is one of getting men with long and arduous

(Continued on back page, Col. 1.)

JAP SURRENDERS (Contd.)

...ize out of uniform. The draft will continue to provide replacements for veterans. Mr. Truman predicted return of 5 to five and a half million soldiers to civilian life within 12 to 18 months. Mr. Truman summoned reporters to the White House executive officer Tuesday and read statement which the Japanese had replied to Allied surrender demands.

Said Mr. Truman: "I deem this reply full acceptance of the Potsdam declaration which specified unconditional surrender of Japan. In reply there is no qualification." The President said he had been informed that Emperor Hirohito is prepared to authorize and ensure signature by the Japanese Government, and Japanese Imperial Headquarters to necessary terms for carrying out the Potsdam Declaration. Mr. Truman said also that Emperor Hirohito is prepared to issue commands to all Japanese Military Naval, Land, Sea and Air authorities to cease operations.

Thus was the sneak attack on Pearl Harbor fully avenged three years, eight months, and seven days after Jap planes struck the United States without warning. Japan had paid the full penalty for the treachery which plunged the United States into a 2-front war, the costliest and bloodiest conflict in all human history. The great conflict cost the U.S. in blood and treasure more than one million casualties, and 300 billion dollars. The cost to the world is estimated at more than 55 million casualties and one trillion dollars in money, material, and resources. For Japan it meant the end of savage conquest, dismemberment of the Japanese Empire, and disarmament and occupation by Allied forces. Once Japan kept half-billion people enslaved under iron rule, and threatened to engulf another half billion.

Japan was defeated without invasion but at terrific cost. For the moment, all the world forgot the horrors of

CONTINUED IN NEXT COLUMN

JAPAN SURRENDERS (Conclusion)

conflict which had its seeds in the Jap grab of Manchuria in 1931. In Washington and the rest of the nation, screaming, whooping throngs let off steam in joyous celebration, but other thousands thronged to the nation's churches for prayer and thanksgiving.

President Truman spoke to thousands of Washingtonians massed before the White House.

Said the President — "This is a great day. This is the day we have been waiting for since Dec. 7, 1941. This is the day when Fascism and Police Government ceases in the world."

Activities

MOVIE SCHEDULE THURSDAY 16 AUGUST

NGFR (505th) "Power Of The Whistler"
Richard Dix - Janis Carter

OR (504th) "Eadie Was A Lady"
Ann Miller - William Wright

RENDEZVOUS (9th) "The Affairs Of Susan"
Joan Fontaine, George Brent, Dennis O'Keefe, Walter Abel

STARLIGHT (6th) "GI Movie # 97"
LITTLE THEATER IN THE WOODS (313th)
"Gentle Annie" - Donna Reed, Marjorie Main

SERVICEDROME "That's the Spirit"
Jack Okie, Peggy Ryan

CAH #2 — "Bring On The Girls"
Eddie Bracken, Veronica Lake

PUMPKIN PLAYHOUSE (509th)
"Diamond Horseshoe" - Betty Grable, Dick Haymes

CORAL GABLES - "Mr Emmanuel" Greta Gynt, Felix Aylmer

RELIGIOUS THANKSGIVING SERVICES WILL BE HELD THIS EVENING: ----

Catholic High Mass of Thanksgiving: C.H Chapel #2, 1700

Protestant Service, CAH Chapel #. 1830

**Parade for
General LeMay**

"Surrender on Broadway"

Vol. VII, No. 5   PUBLISHED DAILY AT ISLAND COMMAND, TINIAN   **5 SEPTEMBER 1945**

YANKS EXPANDING GRIP ON JAPAN

MacARTHUR HALTS RADIO TOKYO ENGLISH LANGUAGE BROADCASTS

TOKYO:--Japan's Domei news agency in a broadcast Tuesday said Gen. MacArthur had ordered Radio Tokyo off the air except for Japanese language broadcasts. Domei's English language broadcast said all foreign language broadcasts would be ended and all future broadcasts would be in Japanese.

Diet Convenes

Radio Tokyo had the last word, however. It said the Imperial Diet had convened yesterday in the presence of Emperor Hirohito but that the session was concluded swiftly. It did not say what went on in the Diet.

Earlier Tokyo Radio reported that the Emperor, accompanied by the Empress, had donned classic ceremonial robes and visited shrines on Imperial palace grounds. There he solemnly informed his ancestors that the empire they had handed down to i lost the war.

'Solemn Ceremony'

The Domei agency, in an FCC recorded dispatch, said the Imperial ancestors were advised of the situation at a "most solemn ceremony," Hirohito worshipping at three sanctuaries in the palace.

BRITISH TASK FORCE IN SINGAPORE HARBOR

RANGOON:--Commander in chief of the British East Indies Fleet, Admiral Arthur Power, triumphantly entered Singapore harbor yesterday aboard the cruiser Cleopatra, accompanied by minesweepers that had cleared the Strait of Malacca. British transports have not yet arrived, but arrangements will be made for the quick occupation of Singapore.

KYUSHU LANDINGS SLATED TODAY; TROOPS CROSS RIVER BELOW TOKYO

YOKOHAMA (ANS VIA RADIO):--American occupation forces expanded their holdings yesterday as seaborne units moved into Kagoshima Bay at the southern tip of Kyushu island to start landings in force there today. Airborne troops are also slated to land in Kyushu today, the United Press reported last night.

On Honshu, 8th Army forces continued to pour ashore in the Tokyo area while

WAR CRIMINAL LISTS

YOKOHAMA:--Four Army teams began plowing through records, questioning liberated war prisoners and compiling a list of Japanese war criminals to be held responsible for brutality in internment camps. This loomed as the first war criminal list for the Japs, since no Allied pronouncements have been made against any Japanese war leaders.

other U.S. troops moved across the Tama river south of Tokyo and took over control of four airfields to bring some 720 square miles of Japan under occupation.

Gen. MacArthur, meanwhile, has not yet issued orders for an Allied march into Tokyo itself. He warned Allied troops not to molest Jap soldiers, saying they would be disarmed by Jap police, who are the only uniformed Japs now allowed to bear arms.

While Japan was being given stark evidence of the cost of losing a war, Tokyo reported that Premier Higashi Kuni had selected five "noted intellectuals" to assist him in constructing a new Japan. His five advisers were not immediately identified.

---

5 SEPTEMBER 1945   THIS SMALL WORLD   **PAGE 3**

— BATTLE LINES —
TWO AGUIJAN JAPS VISIT TINIAN UNDER TRUCE

TINIAN:--Although living within sight of Tinian's busy B-29 base, several hundred Japanese military, civilians, holding out on the by-passed island of Aguijan, five miles south of here, had had no news of the outside world for nearly a year until negotiations for their surrender began last week.

While the island's commander appeared credulous when Lt. John G. Reifsnider, Naval Intelligence officer, told him of the Emperor's capitulation order, he declined to sign formal surrender documents until he had heard news from Japanese sources. Lt. Reifsnider landed on Aguijan from an LCM for his talks with the Japanese officer.

As a result, under a flag of truce, two Japanese non-coms boarded a Coast Guard cutter which brought them to Tinian where, after a six-hour vigil, they heard a Radio Tokyo broadcast of the Emperor's instructions to his troops.

These preparations for the surrender

negotiations were under the direction of Col. Robert C. Pixton, Iscom G-3.

*   *   *

GUAM (ANS):--Group by group Japan's war-torn island empire shrunk today as Jap officers yielded in separate surrender ceremonies to Fleet Admiral Chester W. Nimitz's subordinate commanders.

Surrender of the Bonins, north of bloody Iwo Jima, was signed yesterday; the Truk and Palau groups in the Carolines, and Pagan and Rota in the Marianas.

Bypassed Japs in the Marshalls had surrendered even before the formal signing on the U.S.S. Missouri Sunday.

*   *   *

YOKOHAMA (ANS):----The first United States servicewomen arrived yesterday in Japan. 85 army nurses and four Red Cross workers, all members of the 42nd General Hospital staff, landed here to assist in operation of the hospital which eventually will have a staff of 400. The 42nd opened in June, 1942, at Brisbane.

Investigative Mission To Nagasaki

On August 24, 1945, Major General Groves authorized teams of investigators headed by General Farrell to go to Japan to make sure there were no ill effects from radioactive materials on our troops. General Groves also authorized Colonel Nichols at Oak Ridge to assemble survey parties.

The investigators entered Nagasaki on September 17, 1945, a week before the occupying Army. The group included Scientists and Air Force personnel. Colonel Tibbets had asked for and received permission to go. Atomic Flight Crew members who went were Paul Tibbets, Tom Ferebee, Ted Van Kirk, Charles Sweeney, Don Albury and Kermit Beahan. Bob Lewis went with them as far as Tokyo, then returned to Tinian. The Pilots and 320th Navigators traveled with them also.

To quote Ted Van Kirk, "The 509th was sitting on Tinian with no missions to fly; to be offered the chance to visit a foreign country and see the people, assess what we had done, was a matter of great interest to me".

Since there was no place to land in Hiroshima, they could only fly over that city. They landed at Tokyo on September 15th. Taking two days to make the round trip to Nagasaki, they traveled via the 320th's C54 "The Green Hornet" to Omura, an airport near Nagasaki and on September 17th were transported by charcoal burning trucks into the city. They encountered many Japanese along the way who merely glanced at the Americans and returned to their work as if they had seen nothing unusual.

When they arrived, they observed the ground surface was still distorted from the pressure of the explosion waves. The group walked through the Urakami District trying to locate ground zero.

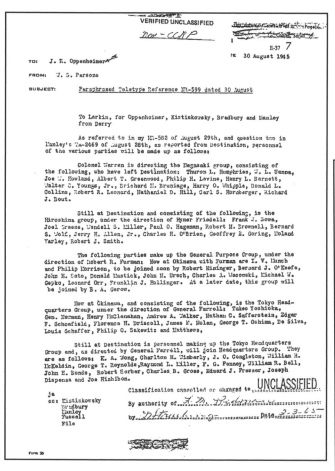

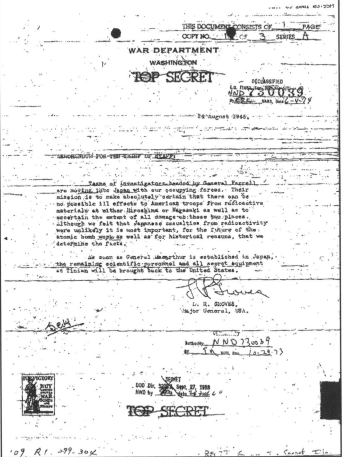

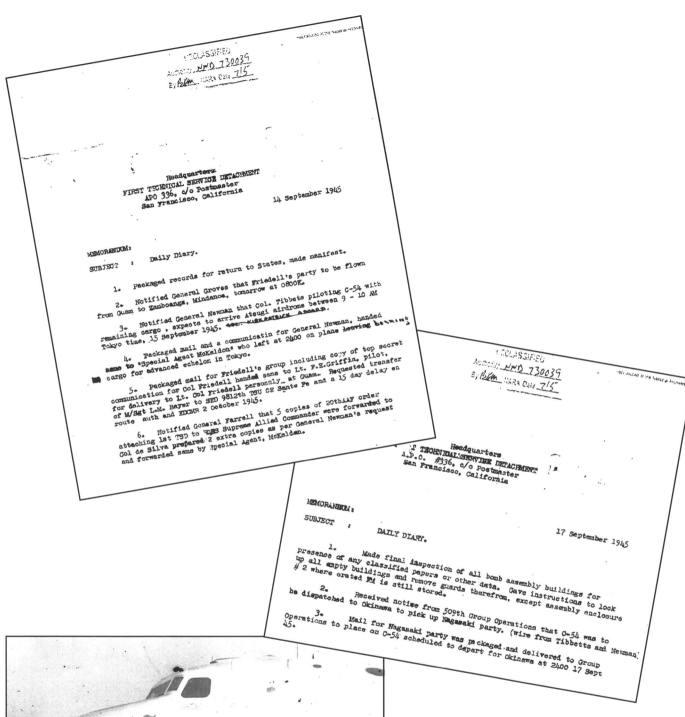

Headquarters
FIRST TECHNICAL SERVICE DETACHMENT
APO 336, c/o Postmaster
San Francisco, California

14 September 1945

MEMORANDUM:

SUBJECT : Daily Diary.

1. Packaged records for return to States, made manifest.

2. Notified General Groves that Friedell's party to be flown from Guam to Zamboanga, Mindanao, tomorrow at 0800K.

3. Notified General Newman that Col. Tibbets piloting C-54 with remaining cargo, expects to arrive Atsugi airdrome between 9 - 10 AM Tokyo time, 15 September 1945. Sent communication, aboard.

4. Packaged mail and a communicatin for General Newman, handed same to "Special Agent McKeldon" who left at 2400 on plane leaving beams, and cargo for advanced echelon in Tokyo.

5. Packaged mail for Friedell's group including copy of top secret communication for Col Friedell handed same to Lt. F.E.Griffin, pilot, for delivery to Lt. Col Friedell personally, at Guam. Requested transfer of M/Sgt L.M. Bayer to SED 9812th TSU CE Sante Fe and a 15 day delay en route auth and EDCMR 2 October 1945.

6. Notified General Farrell that 5 copies of 20thAAF order attaching 1st TSD to the Supreme Allied Commander were forwarded to Col de Silva prepared 2 extra copies as per General Newman's request and forwarded same by Special Agent, McKelden.

Headquarters
FIRST TECHNICAL SERVICE DETACHMENT
A.P.O. #336, c/o Postmaster
San Francisco, California

MEMORANDUM:

SUBJECT : DAILY DIARY.

17 September 1945

1. Made final inspection of all bomb assembly buildings for presence of any classified papers or other data. Gave instructions to look up all empty buildings and remove guards therefrom, except assembly enclosure #2 where crated FM is still stored.

2. Received notice from 509th Group Operations that C-54 was to be dispatched to Okinawa to pick up Nagasaki party. (wire from Tibbetts and Newman.

3. Mail for Nagasaki party was packaged and delivered to Group Operations to place on C-54 scheduled to depart for Okinawa at 2400 17 Sept 45.

Gen. MacArthur's plane with Green Hornet in background

309

Omora Airport Naval Offier who provided truck transportation.

(L-R): Louis Schaffer, Paul Tibbets, Steve Briggs, Henry McClenahan Sleeping under Green Hornet

Louis Schaffer, Paul Tibbets

Ted Van Kirk loading jeeps

A flat tire in Tokyo
Bob Lewis lifts jeep

On the way to
Nagasaki

311

The Japanese charcoal burning trucks broke down frequently

Mogi Beach Hotel where group spent the night before going into Nagasaki

School children planting potatoes

312

Lone Japanese soldier returns home. Mitsubishi Steel and Armament in background

750 meters from hypocenter. Nagasaki University Hospital in background

Mitsubishi Steel and Armament Works

Damage to Mitsubishi Steel and Armament Works — Note safes in wreckage

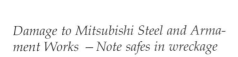

313

Worth the Damage, Miamian Says

Atomic Bombers Inspect Targets

By United Press

TOKYO — The men who dropped the atomic bombs on Nagasaki and Hiroshima returned Thursday from a tour of the devastated areas and reiterated their belief that the goal achieved was worth the terrible results.

One of the airmen said "the dropping of a third atomic bomb or 30 bombs would have been worth it to save our marines and soldiers from fighting on the beachheads."

Maj. Charles W. Sweney of North Quincy, Mass., pilot on the Nagasaki raid, said, "I'm sorry so many people were killed in order to get the Mitsubishi planes but we got the minimum in order to hit the factories—which were worth the cost."

Col. Paul W. Tibbets of Miami, Fla., pilot of the superfort which bombed Hiroshima,

TIBBETS   ALBURY

led the fliers in a low-level flight over Hiroshima and later on an expedition afoot through Nagasaki in order to see the final results of their missions.

Tibbets said the industrial area in Nagasaki was the target "and it was worth the damage to wipe that out."

The pilots had expressed the

same feeling after the bombings —before they had seen the destruction.

The airmen said they were struck by the "dumbfounded looks" of the people of Nagasaki and the hatred displayed for the American party.

Maj. Tom W. Ferebbe of Mocksville, N. C., the Hiroshima bombardier, said:

"It was a completely different attitude than the people of Yokohoma or Tokyo showed, understandable considering the bomb. But we still feel it was better that one bomb should remove the agony and misery than months of consecutive bombing by hundreds of superforts in order to wipe out war machinery."

Also in the 33-man party was Capt. Charles D. Albury of Miami, Fla.

Miami Atom Bomb Pilot Says Secret Must Be Kept

The Miami pilot of the second B-29 to drop an atomic bomb on Japan declared last night this country should keep its bomb a secret.

Albury

"It would be a terrible thing for another country to drop one on us," said Capt. Charles Donald Albury, 25, of 252 NW Fourth st. "It's hard to realize what it can do. Just one bomb would take all of Miami right away."

"From 400 miles away we could see the cloud over Nagasaki. You wouldn't believe it if you hadn't seen it."

Interviewed by The Miami Daily News by telephone at his brother's home in Jacksonville, Capt. Albury revealed he accompanied Col. Paul W. Tibbets of Miami in an escort plane when Tibbetts' plane dropped the first bomb on Hiroshima.

Of the two, the Nagasaki explosion was far more powerful, he said.

"Over Hiroshima we felt two distinct shock waves that felt like somebody slapped our whole plane all over," he said. "Over Nagasaki we felt three or four heavy shock waves."

Just back in the United States from the Mariannas from which the atomic bomb missions were flown, Albury

disclosed he and other members of the special flight crews that carried the bombs made an inspection tour of Nagasaki after the bombing.

He described Nagasaki as "an awful thing to see." On the controversial question as to whether after-effects caused by radio-activity continued to kill people long after the bomb explosion, Albury quoted physicians at a Nagasaki hospital.

"They told me people died several days afterwards and sometimes two or three weeks later," he said. "One girl, they told me about, went to the hospital two or three days after the bombing. She didn't have any injuries, but she had lost her appetite. Ten days later she died."

Physicians told him white blood corpuscles of victims were destroyed and they died.

His conscience, he declared was clear when he dropped the bomb, and, after touring Nagasaki, it still was.

"It was my job and I didn't mind doing it. After all, it ended the war and saved other lives. We used to kid the bombardier (Capt. Kermit K. Dehan) about having destroyed a city, but he said that as long as it ended the war he didn't mind."

Albury is one of three officer sons of Mr. and Mrs. Joseph Leonard Albury.

RATION CALENDAR

SUGAR—Stamp 38 good through Dec. 31 for five pounds.

Wilbur Lyon stands on wrecked steam engine

A Tinian Picture Portfolio

North Field Runway

North Field, Tinian

Flight Line

Aerial view
North Field

Entrance to Navy Base

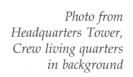

Headquarters

*Photo from
Headquarters Tower,
Crew living quarters
in background*

509th area off of 8th Ave. and 125th St.

Living quarters

Living quarters

Mess Hall on left
Living quarters across street

Chapel with theatre behind

Orderly Room
1st Technical Service Detachment

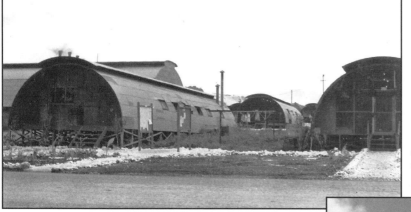

393rd Sqdn
Orderly Room

Group Mess Hall

Group Hospital

Tent area

509th Compound

Crash on Tinian

Asphalt plant

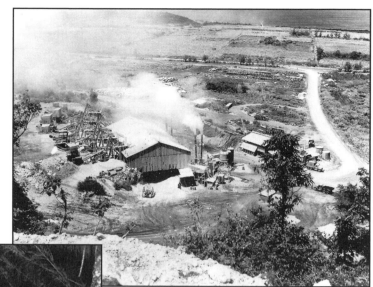

Japanese cave

American cemetery

JAPANESE
WAR DEAD
CEMETERY Nº2

Japanese cemetery

Sign reads: "Prehistoric ruins
left by unknown race which
inhabited Tinian many
centuries ago, probably
formed first floor of temple or
house for chieftan."

Fueling plane

Bombed out Japanese
Administration building

Japanese Shrine

Danger, Japanese still hiding

Caves where Japanese hid

Native camp

Dock area

Scrap yard

Officer's beach

Dock area,
southwest coast

Armament area

Weld Shop

Motor Pool

Tinian Tavern
"Longest bar west of
Oahu"

Toilet Area

Briefing Room

Bomb Assembly Building

Officer's Club
(L-R): Fred Hoey, John Cantlon,
Raymond Biel, Francis Thornhill,
William Downey, Joe Busher

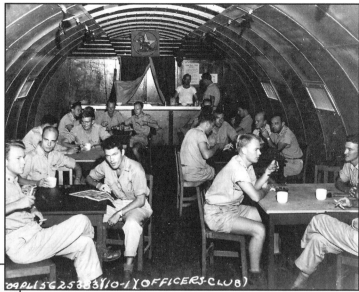

Officer's Club

Enlisted Men's PX

Enlisted Men's Club burns

Enlisted Men's Club after the fire

326

Outdoor Theatre
Chaplain Downey
conducts service

320th heads
towards Tinian

320th Operations Tent

E.E. Kirkpatrick
In charge of establishing 509th facilities on Tinian
Reported directly to Leslie Groves

Lt. Col. Pere DeSilva, Intelligence Officer, Los Alamos
Reported to William Parsons
He was part of Project Alberta Administrative Unit
On July 11, 1945 he interviewed all 509th pilots to see
what they knew about the bomb

Lt. Harley Grimm (left) and
Lt. James B. Price, Jr. (right)

Joe Buscher conducts lecture

Combat Crew study class

First Ordnance Capt.
Charles F. H. Begg at his
desk on Tinian

Father Toomey celebrates mass,
August 16, 1945

Leon Smith stands at
42nd and Broadway

Windmill washing machine

Formation

Washing utensils
after dinner

Painting circle arrow
back on tail

Boarding the USS Deuel for trip home

Above deck on trip home

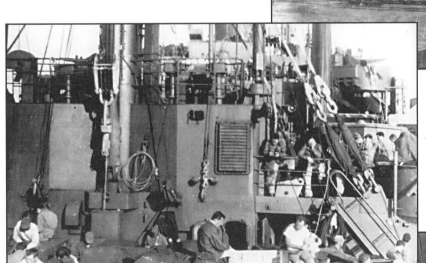

Playing cards

A band played upon arrival
Oakland, CA

At return to Roswell, the 509th new home

Some Punkins became victim
of collision with another B-29
at Roswell

Photo with J. Edgar Hoover, F.B.I. Chief, Leslie Groves, Charles Albury. Gen. Groves took several atomic crew members on speaking tours

Charles Albury and Charles Sweeney photo that appeared in the Saturday Evening Post, June 8, 1946

After the war, officers of both atomic crews visited New York and the office of the president of Curtiss-Wright Corporation

At the Stork Club, (L-R): Charles Albury, Kermit Beahan, Tom Ferebee, James Van Pelt, Charles Sweeney

Chaplain Downey

It has been a long road that we traveled — one of grief, heartbreak, and sorrow — one of blood, devotion, and consecration, but under God we have persevered and, at long last, have gained the victory. Now we find stretched before us another highway, which, if followed to its end, will lead us and all humanity to a new birth of peace and good will. It is a vision that men a long time past have glimpsed when they wrote,

"And a highway shall be there and a way, and it shall be called the way of holiness . . . no lion shall be there, nor shall any ravenous beast go up there on."

With hearts humble, yet somehow uplifted, we gird ourselves for the task which is set before us. Let no man give us stay; let no man hinder us in our appointed duty — for as others have in other days worked for their own noble ends, so will we now, under the grace of God, put our hands to the task of our generation — the task of peace on earth, goodwill toward men.

We have seen in our days of trial and tribulation, great and awful things; we have seen man's entry into the storehouse of Nature and his harnessing of the greatest source of power in the universe. We have within our hands one of God's tremendous secrets. The responsibility which is now ours is clear — our purpose is set before us. There is a stirring in our soul and we hear whispered, "And He showed me a pure river of water of life, clear as crystal, proceeding out of the throne of God. In the midst of the street of it, and on either side of the river there was the tree of life, and the leaves of the tree were for the healing of nations." And we pray with the airmen, "Lord grant us Thy peace. Amen."

334

TAIL GUNNERS

I was shipped from Peterson Field, Colorado Springs to Wendover in March 1945. Joined the 1st Ordnance Squadron as a clerk. June 16, a few of us boarded a C54 and flew to Tinian. I was attached to the bomb squad for per diem. Another soldier and I spent over 2 weeks at a Seabee Carpenter Shop making desks, file cabinets and a few wardrobes for some of the higher brass.

The main group of the 1st Ordnance went over by boat. After they got settled in, I was put in an office with a Tech Sergeant that I later found out was one of the 22 Secret Service men in the 509th. We picked up the mail from Headquarter Squad and the classified mail went to the Commanding Officer or the Executive Officer. They read it and sometimes took it to another office or two. It was then locked up in the safe.

Even though I saw those letters, I did not know we had an Atomic Bomb until after the first one was dropped.

DUGGER, JAMES M
1st Ordnance Squadron
Special Aviation

I had a brother-in-law, Paul Podish, who served on the USS Indianapolis. When I learned of the sinking, I heard that Paul had survived and was in a hospital on Guam. I asked Captain King in Headquarters for a three day pass to go to Guam to see Paul. Captain King said, "Can't do it, there's a war going on."

Sam Weintraub was a Major in the Island Command Intelligence Division. He was my wife's cousin through marriage. I asked him if he could help. Later I was paged to the orderly room where Captain King handed me a three day pass. I went to Guam on a 320th plane loaded with mailbags. After arriving on Guam, I was told by MPs I could not be on the Navy Base. I managed to obtain Navy clothes which I stashed under mail bags on the return trip.

HAIDER, ROBERT
393rd Bombardment Squadron
Ground Crew C-13

I was one of the team that went to the Tokyo area in early September – before the peace treaty signing.

Our original mission was to dash to the 42nd Parallel of the Korean Peninsula to inspect reported rich uranium deposits there. That was quickly canceled after we landed at a small, bomb-cratered airport outside of Tokyo because the Russians had quickly moved down to the 38th Parallel!

I was teamed up with a 2nd Lieutenant, Irving Munch from Brooklyn. He had gone through the Army's Japanese language school. First night, sleeping in Army barracks in a low-sided coffin with a wooden block for a pillow and

the next night in the Dai Ichi Hotel.

Then followed many adventures for us as we poked around the devastated city. Popped in the Naval base at Yokosuka to see the airplane carrying submarines, the inner decks covered with rice and dead fish for food. The commanding Admiral surrendering the base and his jeweled ceremonial sword to Munch.

Visiting the office of the Japanese Nobel-Laureate Physicist who told me he once had a cyclotron out his window, now nothing but rubble. That he had run cross-sections on some sodium uranyl nitrate salt crystals and was able to calculate the critical mass of the Little Man Bomb–he had it to within one percent! That startled me and emphasized that security in purely scientific matters was not to be obtained.

Then raw-silk hunting twenty or thirty miles out of town (I'll never know why) and running into two armed, 6'2" Royal Japanese Marines in a cul-de-sac. Reverse, 4 wheel drive back to Tokyo! The peace accord wasn't effective as yet.

Invited to the home of a physicist (ex UCLA) for dinner, touring the house into his office where a huge German Swastika sat menacingly on the wall. And the lights went out, me with a .38 revolver in a stupid shoulder holster. Mere power failure.

MASTICK, DONALD F.
Ensign USNR, Project Alberta

In June 1996 issue of Air Classics Magazine, a letter to the editor caught my attention. The reader was trying to contact survivors of a B24 that crashed near Miles, Montana; one name mentioned was Stanley L. Kieltyka. I asked myself how many Stanley L. Kieltykas could be in this country. I knew one and I had his 1945 home address.

I responded to the writer's letter who now lived in Illinois. A short time later, I received a note that it was one of the men he was trying to contact. He gave me Stan's current address, still in Detroit, and his phone number. He also told me the story of the crash, which he remembered as a six year old kid, supported by recent searching of old newspapers and inquiries with the Air Force.

The crash occurred about 2 a.m. on 13 May 1944. The B24 was based at Casper, Wyoming and was on a training flight to Western South Dakota with 11 crewmen, Stan was the Radio Operator. During the flight, the plane lost power in two engines. In trying to make an emergency landing at Miles Airport, a wing clipped the ground causing the plane to cart-wheel. Five crewmen were killed instantly and two later died of injuries. Stanley sustained severe injury to his arm, nearly wrenched out of the socket. He was treated at the local hospital. He was one of the four survivors.

Stanley had joined the 393rd at Wendover as a Radio Mechanic. We became good friends, spent a lot of time playing cards and doing other things, when we weren't on the line. Stan never mentioned he had flown as a Radio Operator or been in an airplane crash. He showed no physical signs of injury.

I telephoned Stan and we exchanged a few letters. Stan got married in 1947, had 4 children and 10 grandchildren. He had been retired for 17 years and said he was feeling good. He also sent me some photos, including the windmill washing machine in the 509th Remembered Book. I told Stan about the 509th Reunion to be held at Dayton, Ohio in 1997 and hoped to see him there. Unfortunately, Stan died before the reunion.

This was a great "reunion" for me and I think Stan felt good about regaining contact with someone from the "good old days."

METRO, PAUL
393rd Bombardment Squadron
Radar

My life as a military wife started April 17, 1943. Charles A. Perry was in Miami Beach, Florida at an Officers' Training Center. He was one of the instructors and had a nice apartment. His civilian job in Massachusetts had been at the Boston State Hospital in Mattapan, Massachusetts where he was the Steward, which meant he was in charge of everything that wasn't medical. I also worked at the hospital as an occupational therapist.

Because the superintendent didn't approve of the staff going out with each other, Charlie and I met outside the grounds of the hospital. I would take a streetcar to Mattapan Square and Charlie would meet me there. After a certain time at night, the watchman would lock the area where I lived. When we returned from our date, the watchman was around and would let me in. However, once he wasn't there and I climbed up on a rubbish container to reach a window.

Charlie and I were engaged before he joined the Air Force and attended the Military Training School in Florida. After he finished the school and because of his prior experience as a Steward, he was assigned as General Mess Subsistence Supply Officer at Miami's Air Force Technical Training Command. He traveled around the bases and cooked for the other Air Force men wherever he went. He was so good at what he did and was so well liked that he was promoted to Captain. We were married in

Florida on April 17, 1943. I flew to Miami with my wedding gown in a suitcase. My sister went with me. After our wedding in the chapel, we had a nice reception at a nearby hotel. Charlie's brother and my sister were there for the ceremony.

We lived in an apartment in Miami near Charlie's base and enjoyed it very much. I would walk to the training area where the men did their daily physical training. Soon I was joined by other wives. After asking permission from the instructor, we began doing some of the physical training at the side of the field. It was great fun. The fellows marched in formation and sang songs as they marched from one area to another. It sounded wonderful.

Soon after I became pregnant with our first child, Charlie was ordered to Combat Training School in Pueblo, Colorado. We decided I should return to New England and my family in Connecticut. Our son, Cappy (Charles Jr) was born

on 21 August 44 in Hartford, Connecticut. On August 24, Charlie flew from Nebraska to Connecticut to see our new son. He was able to spend four days with us. Then he went on to begin his tour of duty with the 509th Fighter Wing. He was later sent to Wendover Field, Utah.

At first, no families were allowed in Wendover, Utah where Charlie was assigned as the Mess Officer of the 393rd Special Squadron, commanded by Colonel Tibbets. Soon, however, to make it look like a normal Army Base, families were permitted to live there. With my two month old son, I left from New York and flew to Salt Lake City. Charlie borrowed a car from the chaplain to pick us up at the airport. Cappy slept in a dresser drawer in the hotel that night. The next day it was a long ride to Wendover and our cabin.

Many necessary items needed for the baby had not arrived and I remember hanging the diapers on the clothes line with safety pins until our clothes pins arrived. Cooking in our cabin was with coal. But since I was brought up on a farm in Connecticut where we had a wood stove, the coal wasn't that different. It was just much dirtier. One time, I got Cappy up from his nap and he had a real black eye (from the soot).

The cabin actually was too big for a family of three so

we shared the second bedroom with another couple. Baby sitters were never a problem. There were many volunteers from the men who worked with Charlie. They also offered to push Cappy around the base. Maybe it was because I always had a "home cooked" meal for them and they were welcome to bring their towels and use our private shower after Cappy went to sleep. We had to be very careful with the shower because it was very narrow and it was easy to hit your arms on the sides.

We could walk to the State Line House on Saturday night where there was a band. Charlie and I would go most Saturdays. When the music started, someone would ask me to dance and I never sat out a number and hardly saw Charlie until it was time to leave. That was Saturday night at Wendover.

Mornings I would bathe Cappy and do his washing. The clothes pins and baby carriage had finally arrived. Sometimes we would walk around our section of the base. One morning I met Enola Gay Tibbets pushing a baby carriage too. She was at Wendover for a short visit and was out walking with her grandson. A few times we stopped and had coffee together. She was the mother of Colonel Tibbets, Charlie's commanding officer.

Living in Utah was quite a different experience. One morning I looked out the window of our cabin and all I could see was sheep everywhere. The were being brought down from the mountains into a warmer place as the weather was turning cold. The men on the base also hunted deer. There was no other place to keep the meat, so Charlie kept it in the coolers at the dining hall. We all could have venison anytime we wanted.

Charlie was the Chief Steward at the base and the men were very appreciative of the food they received. Commander Tibbets told him that he could request anything he wanted for the mess hall because he wanted his men to have the best. When it came time for the crew of the Enola Gay to go to Cuba to train in an area where the conditions would be similar to those flying to and over Japan, Charlie went as well. So the men had the good food they were used to. He told me he would be gone a week or less. He thought he would just set up the facilities and then come back to Utah. Although I had letters from him, I did not see him again for several months. I guess they wouldn't let him go because he provided such good food for the crew of the planes.

This was a very exciting and interesting part of my life as an Army wife. However, it did not stop there. After World War II, Charlie became a member of the National Guard. In the early 1960s he was called to active duty and served in France. By that time, we had three children and we did not go with him overseas. Although he was away, my life did not change much from our civilian routine except that he was half a world away and I was home raising the children. Our whole family is very proud that Charlie served our country in both the Army and National Guard.

PERRY, CHARLES A.
393rd Bombardment Squadron
Mess Officer
Submitted by Evelyn Perry

I was born and grew up at Bishop, Texas, 35 miles Southwest of Corpus Christi. I graduated from high school and worked in the drug store and as a bank teller. My father was a cotton farmer so I grew up on a farm. Went to 2 years of college which I needed to become an Aviation Cadet. I almost didn't get into the Air Corps but some major at the school of Aviation Medicine at Randolph Field decided to give me ½ pound after I had eaten all I could to meet the required weight. A friend of mine and I were sworn in at Fort Sam Houston.

They had no uniforms for us so we drove, in his car, to Ontario, California in civilian clothes. When we arrived at Calaero Academy, we had to start drilling. The drill sergeant told me, "If you can't drill better, I don't know how you will learn to fly an airplane." I had a private pilots license before joining the service.

I graduated from there with no trouble. Then I went to Victorville, California in the Mojave Desert for advanced flying school. We flew twin engine AT9 planes. They had very short wings. They said they took off at 120 miles per hour (mph) and landed at 120mph.

From Victorville, I went to Sebring, Florida where I did nothing for 6 weeks. I was on a skeleton (parts) crew. We were shipped to a field at Boise, Idaho. As soon as our squadron got there, they shipped all of our first pilots out to Florida to develop a skip bombing technique. All we had was a lot of copilots. I was the first to be checked out to land a B17 plane. After 4 landings, they issued orders making me an instructor. I instructed for 2 days and was given a crew and sent overseas to Guadalcanal in the South Pacific. I checked out a B17 in California and we got down there with the help of a Ferry Command Pilot and Navigator.

Guadalcanal was a tough place. I didn't think I would live to get back to the States so I started smoking. My Radio Operator refused to fly anymore after our first combat mission. Our one plane was attacked by 8 Japanese Zeros. I was there for about 7½ months. I received a Distinguished Flying Cross and an Air Medal.

We went back to Alexandria, Louisiana to a Combat Crew School. Our squadron was training 36 combat crews going to Europe. We would train 36 B17 crews for 3 months. When I left there, I was Operations Officer in one of the 3 squadrons. I had 75 B17 instructors and office clerks working for me.

A military telegram (TWX) came from the Air Force asking if I was available for B29 training. The people at Base Headquarters told me, "If I didn't want to go, they would report I was not available." I agreed to go even if it meant I would probably have to go overseas again.

I went to a field in West Texas and then to Fairmont, Nebraska where I joined the 393rd Squadron - later to be in the 509th Bomb Group. I was checked out there in a B29 and given a crew. The 393rd Commanding Officer, Thomas F. Classen was at Guadalcanal where I was. He was shot down there. The crew given me at Fairmont was a group of nice, smart people. We dropped practice bombs and went on training missions.

Colonel Tibbets said that General Ent told him the 393rd Squadron had the best training record of any in the 2nd Air Force so he took us to Wendover, Utah. I was impressed with what I saw at Wendover. The Air Force would not send a person overseas the second time unless they signed a Waiver and Go (permission to go). I did this because I wasn't about to get out of this outfit.

We trained at Wendover and dropped several 10,000 pound bombs for Los Alamos. They had to change the tail fins so the bombs would not tumble. There is no accuracy with bombs that tumble.

Captain Norman Ray and I were in Wendover Officers Club. Ray told me a man standing at the bar was a physicist named Ernest Lawrence who had a cyclotron and had been splitting atoms. I then knew we were going to drop Atom Bombs.

My second year physics book had said that Atomic Energy would be used in warfare some day. This was in 1938. I was afraid the club was bugged, so I took Captain Ray out in the street and told him we were going to drop Atomic Bombs. I didn't tell anyone else. He later took credit for thinking of it.

We acquired new planes and flew over to Tinian. I didn't try to make many friends in the 393rd because when we changed stations, they would always get lost.

I say we dropped the last 10,000 pound bomb on Japan and Fred Bock said he dropped the last one.

I stayed in the Air Force Reserve for about 15 years and retired a Lieutenant Colonel. I also attended the Naval Reserve Officers School for 7 years. That was where I met my wife.

While at Wendover, my copilot and I went with 2 sisters in Salt Lake City. He had a car. My girl friend had a new Pontiac convertible. I drove it around Salt Lake City most every weekend for about 6 months. I have never owned anything but a Pontiac.

PRICE, JAMES N. JR.
393rd Bombardment Squadron
Airplane Commander, B-7

To this day, we don't know who was doing surveillance on our family in our small town with 300 population. After my father died in 1995, the elderly man who was the rural mail carrier in 1944 told me he and the postmaster had been questioned by an FBI agent about Dad and all of his family shortly after Dad was drafted at age 33. They were told to never relate this incident and he had never even told my father.

This is what my father wrote about my mother coming to Wendover, Utah in 1944.

We were told we would all get a 15 day leave over Christmas. Then we would go on alert to move overseas, somewhere in the Pacific area. Then, all at once, they canceled the leaves. I wrote Vienna and told her my leave was canceled. A few days later I was doing some welding on one of the bomb tail assemblies, when one of the Intelligence Officers tapped on my shoulder and said, "Turn over what you are doing to someone else, get ready and take the train into Salt Lake City. Your wife and little son got on a train at Creston with a ticket for Wendover. (I had never told Vienna that I was going overseas–she said she knew–I never wrote it as it would have been censored anyway. This made me a firm believer they had me locked up.)

We don't have any place on this base for them to stay.

They are coming into the Salt Lake City Train Station tomorrow. You get them off the train and you have reservations now at the Hotel Salt Lake. It's right downtown. We will contact you when we work something out. Stay in the hotel and eat your meals in your room. I could hardly believe they knew that much and was looking after them all the way–and unknown to Vienna!! When the train pulled in, I went up to the conductor and told him who I was, that my wife and little boy were on this train with a ticket to Wendover and I had to get them off now. He took me right to them. We stayed at the hotel 2 nights before I got a call from the base to come on out as they had something worked out for Vienna and Melvin to stay there. I have often wondered how they kept track of our families but imagine the phones were tapped, etc.

Wendover is 125 miles west of Salt Lake City. We got on the train and went to Wendover. There was only a depot, a big restaurant, casino, and a few houses at Wendover and of course, the Air Base a mile to the south. In one of the houses, an approximately 50 year old couple lived. Mr Wiley worked on the base. McComas, who was with my group, was from Los Angeles, California and his wife had done the same thing, but they let her get to Wendover. The McComas were staying with the Wileys and they had offered to take us in also. They had one spare bedroom that McComas had taken and a closed in porch with a wood heat stove, a bed and a cot for us. They had plenty of blankets from the base. We all shared the bath and cookstove. Actually, McComas and I showered and shaved at the Base. The nights were really cold but the wood heater kept us pretty comfortable. The seven of us got along great and had some fun. It was only a few days until the orders were changed and we got our 15 day leave. Vienna, Melvin and I got on the train on my birthday December 15 and headed for Tingley. But now, I knew we were being closely monitored and weren't traveling alone.

RICHARDS, LYNDON
1st Ordnance Squadron
Special Aviation
Submitted by Daughter, Sue Richards

The 509th 1027th Air Material Squadron was assigned to other departments on the Island. Five of us were to haul oxygen cylinders and store them between the warehouses close to our living area. Each morning we would go to the Navy, 9 miles to the harbor. We would pick up 100 large oxygen cylinders, bring them to the warehouses, unload and after chow, we would do the same thing. Our B29s didn't need many cylinders as they were partly pressurized but the other B29s used them daily. Our five were Hartley, Shryer, Stevenson, Whitaker, Wyatt and the truck driver, McDonald from another squadron.

SHRYER, WILLIAM G.
1027th Air Material Squadron

All the B29s in the Air Force were equipped with Curtis Wright Engines with standard aircraft carburetors. They were the same as a car carburetor introducing gasoline into the induction system. However, on an aircraft engine the induction system is so large that when you have a backfire, the mixture catches fire in the induction system and causes engine failure. It was decided this was unacceptable for the airplanes carrying the "new" bomb. It was decided that a direct injection system should be developed to put the fuel directly in the cylinders. Bosh and Bendix were asked to develop a system to accomplish this direct delivery of fuel.

In 1938, I was working for TWA as a mechanic. Bendix was testing a 9 cylinder fuel injection pump on a Northrup Gamma single engine that was owned by Howard Hughes. It worked well but was too expensive for commercial application. Therefore, two of the pumps were installed on the 18 cylinder Wright Engine. Bosh also had a similar system.

Boeing supplied a B29 and Bendix had two engines equipped with their system. Bosh also had two engines equipped with their system. By this time, I was Tech Rep for Bendix and was assigned to the 150 hour test run at Boeing. Bendix won the competition and all of the 509th Group airplanes were equipped with fuel injection by Bendix. Only 14 airplanes in the Air Force had this system at that time.

I was sent to Wendover, Utah to be with the 509th Group until we were sent to Tinian in May 1945 and stayed until October 1945.

As a Tech Rep, I was required to wear an officers uniform. However, it had no identifying marks on the jacket sleeve. The shirt pocket stated "US Tech Rep." All Tech Reps were considered officers but only with regard to meals and housing privileges. It should be noted the same mess hall was used by officers and enlisted persons on Tinian.

Before I left for Tinian, I bought a used 35mm Leica Camera and purchased several rolls of color slide film which was a new development from Kodak.

My job as Tech Rep was to help out with any problems with the fuel injection system and to train the Air Force in the maintenance and operation of that Bendix Fuel System. I taught classes where I explained to mechanics and pilots, including Colonel Tibbets, the workings of the fuel system.

All the while, I was with this group, I never heard the word "Atomic." We all knew this bomb was bigger than normal bombs being dropped because the bomb bay was bigger than any other B29 in service. The bomb was so big it would not fit under the plane and had to be lowered into a pit on an elevator and then raised into the airplane.

I first heard about the Atomic Bomb an hour or so after it was dropped in an airwave speech delivered by President Truman. Five or so hours later, the Enola Gay landed back on Tinian. I had my camera and assigned Jeep which was allowed down at the flight line. I took the

Tom Ferebee with Norden Bombsight Tech Rep

color pictures of General Spaatz pinning the Distinguished Flying Medal on Colonel Tibbets. I kept those slides in my basement for 50 years and then presented them to the Smithsonian Air and Space Museum. The slides may be the only color still photos of the return of the Enola Gay.

There were several other Tech Reps assigned to the 509th on Tinian. One was from Curtis Wright Propellers, one was from Curtis Wright Engines, one was from Collins Radio and one was from Norden Bombsights and there were a couple of others that I do not recall at this time. I was one of the last Tech Reps to leave Tinian in October 1945–two months after the bombs were dropped and the war was over.

Tech Reps were paid by their companies and the companies were given a monthly flat rate amount contracted between the military and the companies.

STALEY, GEORGE
Bendix Aviation Tech Rep

As I recall, we reached the Initial Point (IP) cruising at 30,000 feet. We were on radio silence so there was no way of communicating. We did not make visual contact so we were not in formation. We cruised the IP for 15 or 20 minutes. During that time, I spotted a B29 at our altitude flying in the opposite direction to ours. Our Tailgunner also reported the sighting but no one else in the crew made the sighting.

Sometime after that, it was decided to head toward

the primary target to make contact. I don't know the time frame when the Radio Operator intercepted the message the drop had been made. We made a quick visual check of the results and headed for Okinawa as radio contact had been established and those were the orders.

STEINKE, STANLEY
Navigator, Crew C-14
Letter written to Fred Olivi in response
to questions about Nagasaki

INDIVIDUAL FLIGHT RECORD

WAR DEPARTMENT
AAF FORM NO. 5
APPROVED DEC. 7, 1941

(1) SERIAL NO. 16036015 (2) NAME BRABANEC, GEORGE L. (3) RANK M/Sgt (4) AGE 19¼
(5) PERS. CLASS 3S (6) BRANCH Air Corps (7) STATION APO 336
(8) ORGANIZATION ASSIGNED 20th 313th 509th 393rd
(9) ORGANIZATION ATTACHED
(10) PRESENT RATING & DATE
(11) ORIGINAL RATING & DATE
(12) TRANSFERRED FROM
(13) FLIGHT RESTRICTIONS
(15) TRANSFERRED TO
(14) TRANSFER DATE

(17) MONTH August 19 45

DAY	AIRCRAFT TYPE, MODEL & SERIES	NO. LANDINGS	FIRST PILOT	NON-RATED
2	B-29	1		2:05
9	B-29	2		15:55
14	B-29	1		12:20
18	B-29	1		1:55
22	B-29	1		2:05
24	B-29	1		2:10
25	B-29	2		1:45
29	B-29	2		1:55
31	B-29	1		2:10

CERTIFIED CORRECT:

George W. Marquardt
GEORGE W. MARQUARDT,
Captain, Air Corps,
Operations Officer

COLUMN TOTALS 12 40:20

(37) THIS MONTH
(38) PREVIOUS MONTHS THIS F.Y.
(39) THIS FISCAL YEAR
(40) PREVIOUS FISCAL YEARS
(41) TO DATE

George Brabanec's Flight Record Illustrating Flight Hours for Aug. 9th Nagasaki Mission

Ralph came back to Monroe, Louisiana from Tinian in November 1945 on a 30 day leave. He was then going back to Roswell, New Mexico and, when released from service, would return to Monroe where we would live in an apartment. After his 30 day leave, he went to Roswell. At the end of January, he called and said, "Hey, come on out here. They will not let me out yet." There was just no place to live in Roswell. It was a tiny little town. It was filled with service people. He finally found a place to stay so I headed in that direction.

We landed at Roswell at about 8 p.m. in the middle of a dust storm and it was horrible. The plane ride was rough. One lady's head dented the airplane luggage rack. The wind was blowing sand / dust so heavily that you could not see your hand in front of your face. Everyone had to wrap something around their heads to protect their faces from the blowing sand. The airport workers who came out to meet us had goggles on and led us to the terminal by holding one of our arms because we could not open our eyes. They led us back into a little shack that was the airport terminal. We simply could not see. The sand would just absolutely blast your eyes away.

Ralph had a taxicab waiting. The taxi only went about three blocks from the airport, turned left, and went up an alley. There were big rocks in the road and that little old dumpy taxicab really bumped around. Our place was down the alley about half way. Garbage cans were sitting out in the alley and the cats were sitting all around meowing. They scattered as we drove up. Our apartment was in an old stucco building on an alley. We got out of the taxi and Ralph got my suitcases and everything.

When we went inside, I saw an old couch that Ralph had made into a bed with an Army colored comforter on it. No sheets or anything. In the bedroom, there was an old iron bed with a little thin cotton mattress on it. There was an Army comforter on top of that also. We had to make down the couch at night for the kids. Those were our quarters. I thought we also had access to the upstairs area but the apartment upstairs had nothing to do with our one bedroom little dinky thing downstairs. Upstairs was another deal (another apartment). We had one bedroom, one bath, no lavatory or place to wash our hands. The bathroom had an 8 foot long bathtub and a "Johnny." The kitchen was about 14 feet long but it was only three feet wide–like a hallway. There was a different kind of linoleum in every room: the bedroom; living room; breakfast room; kitchen; hall; and bathroom. It was all so grease covered you could not tell what color it was. You could just see the pattern was not the same.

The dishes and all the pots and pans that were furnished consisted of four plates with chips out of them, two cups, one had no handle, and one cereal bowl. There was a cardboard icebox–actually made out of cardboard (war time stuff). It was painted white enamel and looked like it could be a refrigerator. However, it was a real icebox–you put a block of ice in the upper part to cool the lower part.

The entire apartment building was made of two by fours and old car parts (fenders and hoods) that had been hammered out straight (flat) and nailed onto those two by fours. Chicken wire had been nailed over the flattened car body parts. Stucco was plastered over that. The walls inside the apartment still had some of the chicken wire ends sticking out about 4 inches. I had to go along the walls and either bend the chicken wire over or cut it off so the kids would not scratch themselves.

When we had a sandstorm, the blowing sand was so thick you could not see across the alley (10 feet). The windows had no weather stripping or anything–they would just rattle as the wind blew and the sand hit the glass. My little kitchen sink would have enough sand in it to plant geraniums. Sand also made its way inside the icebox.

In order to get ice delivered, you had to put a card in the window for the iceman when he came up the alley, specifying whether you wanted 5, 10, 25 or 50 pounds. There was a different number on each side of the card. You would indicate the number of pounds you needed by placing that number at the top of the card. You'd put the ice in the icebox and chip it up. If you wanted any ice, you had to get the ice pick and chip off a hunk.

There was a little grocery store about 3 blocks down the street from our rented apartment. I'd put my kids in a little wagon and walked to that grocery store. We would all walk back because the wagon was full of groceries. The first time I went to the grocery store (I know this was a standard joke for any yokel that went in there), I said, "Boy this is dry country. My skin is just dying and flaking off. I am just not use to this. I am from Louisiana and it is wet country." He said, "Yeah, I heard that a year or two back they thought it was gonna rain but it never did. I don't mind so much for myself as I do for my boy here. He is seven years old but he has never seen rain." It is really dry country. It is beautiful in the mountains but it was dry and dusty where we lived. You could look out at the horizon and see dust coming that would not arrive until the day after tomorrow. Well, it did rain occasionally but not very much.

Our landlady was a redheaded lady barber and her husband was an alcoholic painter. Apparently, he lived elsewhere. Every now and then he would run out of money and would try to slip back into the house to have a place to sleep. She would meet him at the door or window (sometimes he would climb a ladder to an upstairs window). Whenever he tried to sneak in, she would hit him over the head with an iron frying pan. She really did.

During WWII, the OPA controlled housing rent. They seemed to control/regulate everything. Many things were rationed and we were issued ration books. The OPA only allowed the landlady to charge $42.50 per month for that apartment. However, she charged $50. When you paid your rent she put her Bible on her back porch. You gave her a check for $42.50 and the rest in cash in the pages of her Bible.

The fence around our small yard had a white picket gate.

PX at Roswell

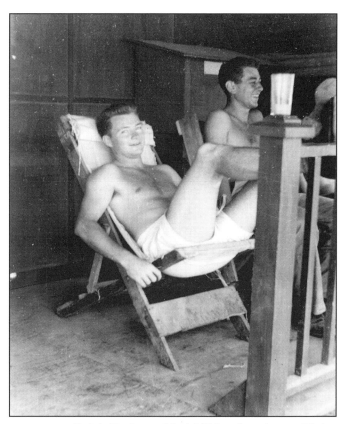

Ralph Taylor and Jack Widowsky relax on Tinian

We actually lived in the landlady's backyard on the alley. There was a one car, white garage just outside of her white picket gate–it belonged to Mrs. Brown, our landlady.

At that time, Roswell was a very small place. There were a lot of service people in the Roswell area. The community did not think well of military service people. If you were in the military, it was a strike against you. If you had children, that was two strikes against you. They just did not want to rent to you. They sometimes spat on the soldiers that were in the downtown area. The Commanding Officer at Roswell Air Force Base had a brilliant idea. He said, "We will make the next payroll in $2 bills and let the people of Roswell see where their money is coming from." They paid the whole base, civilian and military, in $2 bills (cash), no government checks or anything–just cash. When the people of Roswell saw all they had were $2 bills, they changed their minds about liking the military. Everything was OK after that. Contractors began building houses and other things to accommodate the service people.

We were at Roswell for 4 ½ years. Eventually, we found a new house to live in. Brand new house–just finished. When we moved into the new house, we bought furniture and twin beds for the kids. We even connected the washing machine. I had that washing machine shipped all the way from Monroe, Louisiana but it just sat there in the crate at the rented apartment. It was a Bendix Washing Machine but the landlady in our previous apartment, would not allow it because it ran her water bill up. I had to wash all the diapers (2 kids) in the bathtub on a washboard. So, it was still in the shipping crate when we moved to the new house. Six weeks later we were transferred.

While we were in Roswell, we had to deal with some hard water. I have forgotten the grain measurement of the water. When you used soap to wash your hands, it would flake off in little pieces and fall into the sink. When we first got to Roswell, I tried to cook a pot of beans. They were in boiling water cooking for 4 days but they never did cook. Nobody ever told me we were at high altitude and you needed to soak them all night and all the next day before you could cook them. You also had to adjust cake recipes for high altitude or it would never get off the bottom of the pan. I did not know any of that kind of stuff.

TAYLOR, RALPH R.
Airplane Commander Crew A-1
Submitted by Marcelena Taylor

Beginning with Cuba early in 1945 at Batista Field where our Sixth Bombardment Group was also training, my curiosity got the best of me and one day while working in the photo lab, I asked one of your photographers, who was working alone, if I could help him develop the aerial film they had been shooting. His prompt reply was, "No thanks." When asked why their B29s were different than ours, he indicated they were "a photo recon outfit and needed additional speed to fly at a higher altitude."

It wasn't until I came to Tinian and the flights were flown dropping the Atomic Bombs that I put two and two together. I took a photo of a C54 and the crew chief, one of your Green Hornets at Batista Field.

WEBSTER, WILLIAM
6th Bomb Group
Photography

I was married in 1944 after I graduated from Gunnery School at Harlington, Texas. My wife and I traveled with another couple all the way from Fairmont to Wendover. We lived at the Stateline Hotel for a short time, then my wife returned to Prescott, Arizona. We were on a training mission in May 1945 when I was informed of the birth of our daughter.

I got a 3 day pass and hitch hiked to Prescott to see them. I knew I would be going overseas. I got to Hoover Dam and the nice guard there stopped a salesman passing through. He took me all the way to the Prescott Hospital. I barely saw them both for about thirty minutes, then I had to go back to Wendover. We shipped to Tinian shortly after I returned.

WHEELER, SAM R.
393rd Bombardment Squadron
Assistant Flight Engineer / Scanner
Crew A-4

William Webster photo of Green Hornet at Batista Field

ONE LAST LOOK

A Scientist's Reflection

I left Los Alamos in June 1945 for Albuquerque, New Mexico and then to Wendover, Utah where I was given a uniform, dog tags and a duffle bag filled with Army clothes. My own civilian clothes were put in a cardboard box and returned to my wife in Los Alamos.

We flew from Wendover to San Francisco to Hawaii to Johnston Island to Quad (Kwajalein) and then finally to Tinian on the Green Hornet a C54. The first thing I remember seeing on Tinian and still have that picture in my mind was the cemetery with all the white crosses. I thought about all the Marines and Seabees who lost their lives taking that island and building the facilities while there were still Japanese soldiers on the island.

I was sent as part of a small team led by future Nobel Laureate Luis Alvarez to attempt to measure the yield of the nuclear bombs we were planning to employ. My first task was to start installing the equipment required in the back section of the plane assigned to us, The Great Artiste and was told our pilot would be Chuck Sweeney.

Installing the equipment in the daytime inside that aluminum fuselage was a very very sweaty job. Our plan was to follow alongside the Enola Gay and when the bomb was dropped, release our blast gauges which were suspended by parachutes and receive a signal of the blast pulse and its duration and record it on film using standard gun cameras hooked up to an oscilloscope.

We flew alongside the Enola Gay and over Hiroshima dropped our gauges with 2 out of 3 working perfectly and determined the yield was about 15 kilotons. We had worried about the effect of the explosion on us. When the Little Boy went off our little enclosed place lit up with a really bright white light. Then a few seconds later we felt a sharp slap and then another. We realized the second slap was the reflection of the shock from the ground. I wrote in my notebook, "It really went off, it really did."

Our return to Tinian was uneventful, but we were not allowed to land until Tibbets and his crew were royally received and given medals. We just landed and gave our film to be processed and went to our quarters. One experience on the island made me decide if I had to join the military, I would join the Navy as an officer.

With the 509th we ate outside using metal trays and were served cafeteria style. Then sloshed our trays in a 50 gallon drum filled with boiling water. I had a high school friend who was a JG (Junior Grade Navy Officer) stationed in the middle of the island and he invited me for dinner. First he shared quarters with another guy and they had a refrigerator in their room with stacks of cokes alongside. With the 509th cokes were rationed and considered a treat.

When we went to dinner, we ate inside a building with white tablecloths and white napkins; they even had napkin rings. We were served by Navy personnel and ate off chinaware. We had lettuce! Never had lettuce with the 509th. Be an officer in the NAVY.

When the USO came, we attended their show and

Harold Agnew holding the Nagasaki bomb core
Tinian, August 1945

once a major league pickup group came and I saw Pee-wee Reese and other major league stars. These visits were great. We were not allowed to return stateside until the treaty was signed. When it was, we returned using the Green Hornet to get to Albuquerque and then by car to Los Alamos.

I had arranged to take a movie of Hiroshima myself which didn't turn out very well but it is the only movie of it that exists.

Set up cameras with the tail gunners for the Nagasaki flight and they got great movies. Had a very hard time keeping the film out of General Groves' clutches but was able to get them back to Los Alamos where I handed them over to Oppenheimer not knowing whether we had anything on the film at that time. After the war, I gave my film to the Hoover Institute at Stanford where copies can be obtained for a nominal fee.

We all did our jobs and should be proud of our collective efforts. The Los Alamos group, called "Project Alberta" while on Tinian and the 509th did an outstanding job overseas.

AGNEW, DR. HAROLD
Project Alberta Scientific Observer
For the Hiroshima Mission
Aboard "The Great Artiste"

Flight Of Three B29s To Tinian With Fat Man Bomb Assemblies

Overview By Frederick C. Bock, 393rd Bomb Squadron, Airplane Commander, Crew C-13

In late July 1945, three Silverplate B29 airplanes, piloted by Captains Herman Zahn, Edward Costello and William Hartshorn, transported three Fat Man Bomb Assemblies from Kirtland Field, Albuquerque, New Mexico, to North Field, Tinian Island in the Marianas, where the 509th Composite Group of the Army Air Forces and Project Alberta from Los Alamos National Laboratory were based. The starting point for this flight, the overseas portion of which was classified secret, was Wendover Army Air Field (AAF) Utah, where the crews and airplanes were stationed at the time of departure.

The B29s first went from Wendover to Kirtland, where the planes were moved to an outlying area and the bomb assemblies were loaded in the forward bomb bays. Some boxes were also loaded. The planes then proceeded from Kirtland to Mather AAF, Sacramento, California, the port of Aerial Embarkation for the trans-Pacific segment of the journey. Under the jurisdiction of the Air Transport Command of the Army, they then continued via John Rogers Field on Hawaii and Kwajalein Island in the Marshall Islands to Tinian, arriving on 1 or 2 August where the assemblies and boxes were unloaded.

Two of the planes and the men on them, commanded by Zahn and Costello, remained at Tinian in the 393rd Bomb Squadron. The third plane and its crew, commanded by Hartshorn, returned to Wendover and continued to serve in the Flight Test Section of the 216th AAF Base Unit (Special).

The men were not allowed to see the loading of the bomb assemblies at Albuquerque and were not informed as to the nature or intended use of the casings and contents. Observations made by the crews after the planes were loaded, together with evidence from other sources, provided strong indications as to the critical items in the cargo delivered to Tinian only a few days before the Atomic Missions to Japan.

The Airplanes

The USAAF serial numbers of the three airplanes reveal they were among the Silverplate B29s produced at the Martin Factory in Omaha, Nebraska, specially designed and constructed to be capable of combat delivery of the Atomic Bombs. Numbers 44-86346 and 44-86347 were the newest and the last to arrive of the 15 that were in the 393rd on Tinian at the close of the war. They were delivered to the USAAF by Martin-Omaha on 15 June 1945 and were then flown from Offutt Field, adjacent to the factory. to Wendover. On reaching Tinian, they were assigned tactical (Victor) Numbers 94 and 95, respectively. The third B29 on the flight, No. 44-65386 on delivery to the AAF was assigned to the Flight Test Section of the 216th Base Unit and presumably had dropped numerous bombs in tests conducted before the trip to Tinian. It was not given a tactical number or name.

The Men on Board

Crews C-12 (Zahn) and A-2 (Costello) of the 393rd each consisting of 9 men, flew 44-86346 and 44-86347 respectively from Wendover to Tinian. Additional men brought the final number on Zahn's plane to 18 and on

Costello's to 19. Some of these were in the ground crew, some were security personnel and the duty of others is not known. On Zahn's plane, the security officer was 2nd Lt. Vaughn Richardson from Santa Fe, who boarded at Albuquerque. The names of the security personnel (probably 2) on Costello's plane are not known.

Hartshorn's crew, which flew 44-65386 to Tinian and back, included as known members Capt. William Hartshorn Pilot, David O'Hara Copilot, Walter Stevens Jr. Navigator, Arthur Yoder Flight Engineer, Carl Holz Radio Operator and seven others including security personnel. The final number on board when the plane went from Kwajalein to Tinian was 12.

Sequence of Events

22-23 July. Special Orders Number 203 and 204 are issued by Headquarters Wendover Field, Utah for 2 crews and B29s with pilots Captain Herman Zahn and Captain Edward Costello to proceed on or about 24 July to Kirtland Field, Albuquerque, New Mexico and thence to Port of Aerial Embarkation (POAE) at Mather Field Sacramento, California for temporary duty with the Air Transport Command (ATC). Similar special orders are presumably issued by Headquarters Wendover Field o/a these dates for one crew and B29 of the Flight Test Section, Captain William Hartshorn Pilot to proceed o/a 24 July to Kirtland Field and thence to POAE at Mather Field for attachment to the ATC. Silverplate B29s having AAF serial numbers 44-86346, 44-86347 and 44-65386 are assigned to Zahn, Costello and Hartshorn, respectively.

26 July. The three crews and airplanes proceed from Wendover Field to Kirtland Field with no bomb assemblies on board.

26 July. Three bomb assemblies F31. F32 and F33 are loaded into the three airplanes concealed behind revetments at Oxnard Field (Sandia Site) adjacent to Kirtland Field. Boxes of parts are loaded on Costello's and Hartshorn's planes. Crew members can see the bomb casings are of the Fat Man not the Little Boy type. Crews begin posting sentries at all times while the planes are on the ground.

27 July. The three loaded airplanes proceed from Kirtland Field to Mather Field with security personnel now on board in addition to the men who had come from Wendover.

28 July. Operations Orders Number 187 are issued at Mather Field by the ATC for movement overseas of two crews and B29s with Pilots Zahn and Costello. Similar orders are presumably issued at Mather Field by the ATC for movement overseas of the crew and B29 with Pilot Hartshorn.

28 July. The three crews and airplanes proceed from Mather Field to John Rogers Field Hawaii. On takeoff from Mather, a large life raft on Costello's B29 releases from its storage bay, apparently due to not having been properly secured after inspection by ground personnel at Mather, causing damage to the empennage and requiring an emergency landing at Mather. Costello and Davis have to wrestle with the controls in making the approach and landing. Repair of the tail surfaces by the ground crew delays departure of this airplane for several hours.

29 July. All three planes are at John Rogers Field early on the 29th.

30 July. The three crews and airplanes proceed from John

Rogers Field to Kwajalein Island crossing the International Date Line. However, Kwajalein appears to have been on Hawaiian time so the skip to the next calendar day did not occur until the leg from Kwajalein to Tinian.

30 July. Orders for departure on 31 July are issued by ATC, Central Pacific Wing at Kwajalein for the three crews and airplanes.

31 July. The three crews and airplanes proceed from Kwajalein to North Field Tinian Island advancing the date from 31 July to 1 August while doing so.

1 August. The planes arrive at Tinian North Field. The three bomb F31, F32 and F33 assemblies and parts are off loaded from the airplanes.

2 August. Hartshorn's Crew and B29 leave Tinian returning to their unit at Wendover. The crews and B29s with ACs Zahn and Costello remain at Tinian in the 393rd Bomb Squadron.

The Bomb Components Used

The precise use made on Tinian of the three Fat Man Bomb Assemblies and boxed items that were delivered on 1 August 1945 by the three B29s and crews is not certain, but it seems very likely that what occurred is generally in accordance with the following chain of events.

First, the fissionable material (plutonium core or pit) for the Fat Man Bomb (Unit F31) that was dropped at Nagasaki was transported by C54 airplanes of Air Transport Command or the 320th Troop Carrier Squadron of the 509th, not by B29s. The C54s carried the core hemispheres from Kirtland Field to Tinian North Field in the care of couriers, arriving on 28-29 July.

It does appear that critical items were transported to Tinian on the B29s and used, namely, the high explosive blocks (lenses) that were essential to the implosion method for detonation of the Plutonium Bomb. According to Harlow Russ Project A, "On August 2nd, three sets of HE components for Fat Man Bombs were delivered to Tinian by three B29 airplanes that had flown the sets from Albuquerque. When unpacked, one set of HE blocks was found to be badly cracked and was not usable. The best set was reserved for the combat Fat Man unit (ie F31, dropped on 9 August from Bockscar) and the second best was assigned for use in a complete dry run full function test drop unit (ie F33, with an inert core, dropped on 8 August from Bockscar)." The bracketed comments have been added.

It is plausible, but not certain, that the sets of HE lenses were inside the casings of the Fat Man Assemblies on the way to Tinian and were unpacked when the assemblies reached the Tech Area north of North Field on 1 or 2 August. Two of the three sets of lenses were then used in the final preparation of (1) the last pre strike test unit, dropped at sea near Tinian on 8 August and (2) the Fat Man Bomb dropped at Nagasaki on 9 August.

BOCK, FREDERICK C.
393rd Bombardment Squadron
Airplane Commander, Crew C-13

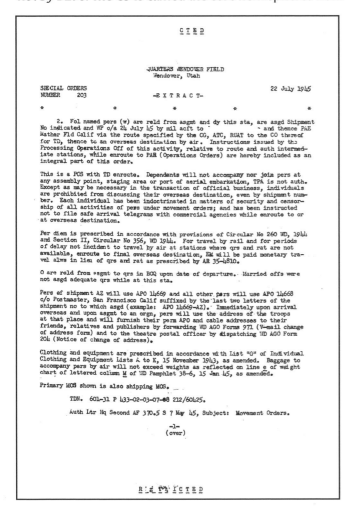

Life at Wendover

In 1944, my husband, Albert Bartlett, and I were living in Geneva, Nebraska. He was with the 393rd Bomb Squadron at Fairmont Air Base. Sometime in September of that year, word came down the outfit was going to move to Wendover Field, Utah. I was grateful to learn the families would also be allowed to go, just not on the troop train. So I purchased my bus ticket, packed my bags and was able to leave earlier than the troops. Even with a change of buses in Salt Lake City, I arrived 6 hours before the train.

My first stop at Wendover was at the housing office. There I was informed that in order to be eligible for housing, I needed to get a job. So off I went to the PX to apply for a job, after figuring out how to get a pass to get on base. Luckily I was hired on the spot and was able to return immediately to the housing office with the required paperwork. I got to the station as the train was pulling in with my husband. Some of the other soldiers saw me and quickly told Albert that "his wife was already there!" I felt very proud of myself that by the time he arrived, I had a job and we had an apartment. Our life in Wendover had begun.

Bright and early the next morning I began serving donuts and coffee at the PX. I learned how to make the batter and fry donuts. Empty coffee cups went into the dishwasher. Each night I went home smelling of fried dough and coffee.

The apartments had coal stoves with a water closet to heat water. We washed our clothes by hand in the shower and hung them to dry on any and every surface inside as it was impossible to hang anything outside due to the coal dust. It was necessary to keep the stove burning at all times to have hot water for baths. We were fortunate that my family sent us extra ration stamps to use for meat and sugar.

L-R: Patrick Robbins, Lawrence Strasburg, Albert Bartlett, Patrick Joyce, Joel Denham

We settled into our new location and got to know our roommates Fran and Bob McClary. In December of 1944, we got leave and used the time to visit my family in Brooksville, Florida.

In January 1945, Albert and his crew were sent to Batista Field in Cuba for 4 to 6 weeks of further training. His letters told of the hard training they were doing. But pictures of Albert and his friends at Sloppy Joe's Bar proved they had at least one night of fun! During this time, planes flew back and forth carrying supplies to Cuba. In one of his letters, Albert told me they couldn't get any sweets. When I learned that a friendly face, Frank, was to make a round trip supply run, I decided to send a cake back as a surprise. I later heard that when Frank entered the barracks he called out to Albert, "Your wife sent you a cake!" Albert said he was lucky to get one slice.

In March, families were sent home. Albert and I took a train trip to western New York to visit his family before he was scheduled to leave for Tinian. I spent some time there before returning to Brooksville to await his return to the States.

BARTLETT, ALBERT
393rd Bombardment Squadron
Submitted by Esther Bartlett

Destination I

During our stay at Wendover, periodically one of the flight crews would be conspicuous by their absence from the base. After a few weeks they would reappear and when they were queried as to where they had been, the answer was "Destination I." What were you doing there was always the next question and the answer was always the same "can't say."

When it was our turn to visit the mysterious "Destination I," we found it was the Naval Ordnance Test Station, located at Inyokern, California. Mystery solved. The station had instrumented bomb ranges and we were there to experience flying with and dropping the bomb as well as to help in the development of the aerodynamic characteristic of the "Fat Man" bomb. Various tail configurations were tried in an effort to extend the distance from the release point to impact, thus providing a greater time period for the crew to execute the tight right hand diving maneuver known as "Gett'n the heck outta there" to lessen the bomb blast impact on the aircraft.

We replaced the crew that was on site and over the next few days flew 3 missions dropping the inert sand-filled bombs with fairly good results considering everything was experimental and we were using the standard bomb tables for the 500 pound General Purpose Bomb to set up the Norden Sight for a 5 ton bomb with unknown characteristics.

We were then notified the next drop would be with a

John L. Downey
Bombardier "Laggin' Dragon"

live bomb, at least one with the explosive blocks installed and fused to explode on impact. Now if you will, remember everything was secret and none of us peons knew what the end product was to be, so naturally we were concerned at being so honored as to drop the first one.

To alleviate our concern, we were taken to a remote part of the field to a bomb-proof igloo and were shown a "Fat Man" under assembly with the ball shaped core being enclosed in the explosive blocks each of which was individually, electrically, fused to explode simultaneously. All of this was to be enclosed in the outer iron shells with the tail fin attached. We were permitted to ask questions and the only unanswered one was posed by our Radio Operator, David Purdon when he asked, "What happens if we are struck by lightening?"

The first 3 bombs we dropped were at low altitude, 10 to 12 thousand feet, and the bombing tables we used were satisfactory. When we were told we were to drop the first "live" bomb and it would be from 30,000 feet, the whole picture changed as the bomb tables for the 500 pound GP were only calibrated to 20,000 feet.

These tables present the required values for setting up the bombsight including the altitude disc speed, trail distance, bombing altitude as affected by temperature, airspeed and actual altitude above ground. I spent several hours searching out constants in the progression of values

as related to altitude of each criteria and once determined, applied these factors to the required altitude to arrive at the bombsight settings for next days mission.

Our airplane had been modified to the extent that a bracket to hold a small movie camera had been fastened to the underside of the left outboard wing aimed at the bomb bay to photograph the bomb as it exited the airplane. The trigger for the camera was installed on the bombardier's panel and I was to actuate it just before bomb release. Sounds OK in theory but in practice the wings of the B29 flex up a considerable distance during flight. Even in consideration of this, when the bomb is released and the airplane sheds over 5 tons of weight in a mille-second and the airplane jumps straight up about 100 feet, the wings tend to flex downward. Don't believe the camera got anything but empty space.

The next morning, the bomb which had been painted in black and white quadrants around the circumference of the body with the rear half colors reversed from the front for a checkerboard display to aid in tracking the trajectory, was loaded in the front bomb bay. With preflight completed, the engines were started and we taxied to the active runway for take-off. On the way my conservative side said to me "Wouldn't it be better to remove the four nose fuses from the bomb and reinstall them after we got airborne?" Just in case something unexpected occurred. So I did. We took off with the fuses laying in my lap, on a short runway, got airborne and were gaining altitude as I went into the bomb bay and reinstalled the fuses. When I tried to open the hatch to the cockpit area, it felt like it was stuck so I applied my foot to it and kicked it open. It was then I found out the Flight Engineer, Thomas Brumagin had started to pressurize the airplane and he was upset because I had dumped the pressure.

When we reached bombing altitude, we were joined by a Navy Pilot in a Grumman Hellcat setting a few yards off our wing, flying formation with us. We could see him sitting in a cramped cockpit, bundled up in a heavy flying suit with oxygen while we were in shirt sleeves, smoking cigarettes and enjoying the spaciousness of our quarters. His job was to, at bomb release, dive after the bomb and photograph it on the way down.

We picked up the target, made our bomb run, released the bomb and as was hoped for, the bomb fell true and the explosion was of the desired high-order class which made all the scientists happy. We asked for and received permission to make a low pass over the impact point and descended to about 100 feet over the desert. As we passed over the bomb crater, we could see the bomb had hit directly in line and only about 100 feet short of the target. It was gratifying to know we had helped move the development phase one step forward.

DOWNEY, JOHN L
393rd Bombardment Squadron

The Cuban Mission

The Laggin' Dragon was placed on temporary duty in January of 1945 and with three other aircraft and crews of the 393rd flew the right wing position of a 4 plane formation flight to Batista Field just outside Havana, Cuba from Wendover Air Force Base. Some say the training was to see if our group could operate as an individual entity, like being on a small island all by ourselves, others say it was to develop over water mission capability, maybe both.

The flight training in Cuba was conducted in two phases, one consisted of both radar and visual bombing from 20,000 to 30,000 feet altitude. Gunnery practice for the tail gunner was included during these flights. Mac (Carlton McEachen, Tail Gunner) almost shot up a small fishing vessel that was in our flight path, since no one told him it was coming up while he was busy shooting at white caps.

The second part was simulated combat missions, with formal briefings, against a simulated enemy target. All facets of planning and conducting a very realistic combat mission were followed. From the 15th to the 31st of January, the participating crews averaged 42 flight hours each in these training exercises. By the end of February, the average number of simulated combat missions per crew was 3 1/2 with average time flown at 66 hours.

On one of these missions, we encountered a rain squall en route and were pretty much flying blind at a low altitude over the ocean heading east toward the island of Bermuda. Without any warning we broke out of the storm and thanks to Pete's (Bob Petrolli, Navigator) navigation we were right over the bay at Bermuda; it was late in the day and just getting dark. From the nose position, I could see a large ship below us that was busy turning on all their large red crosses, a hospital ship. At the same time, there was a Navy Destroyer along side the hospital ship and they were busy turning on their searchlights and illuminating us. Seems like they were as surprised as we were and weren't taking any chances on us being unfriendly. Captain Eddy (Ed Costello, Airplane Commander) got on the radio quickly and identified us and all was well. Would have been embarrassing, to say the least, to be shot down by our own folks.

Side Notes: Visiting Havana was quite an experience starting with riding the local bus from the base; people, animals, packages and a whole lot of etcetera. This combined with a rickety vehicle, a narrow road in serious need of repair and a devil may care driver made for a real experience. Harry Davis, Ed Costello and myself visited Havana and started to tour the capitol building, however on each floor of the building was a guard with his hand out for a payoff so we didn't get very far. We did tour Moro Castle on the bay, our guide was an ebony black man who spoke clipped British English, rather unexpected. In the old days, a ship would carry a chain from the castle across the bay to opposite land to secure the harbor each

Laggin' Dragon
Bob Petrolli, Navigator
John L. Downey, Bombardier

evening and open it up in the morning. On the parapets of the castle were mounted several cannons on swivel bases pointed out to sea to ward off pirates. The cannons had a range of 1/4 mile. We stayed at the Hotel National over night, had an impressive view out the windows which were wide open, no glass, only shutters to close if the weather demanded. While touring the hotel gift shop the next day, we met and chatted with Edward G. Robinson of Hollywood fame.

It was a common practice to hire a driver for an evening who would tour you around the hot spots in town. Tom Brumagin, Flight Engineer, Harry Davis, Copilot, Pete (Bob Petrolli), Navigator, Ed Costello, Airplane Commander and myself did so one night and had quite a time. We visited a number of bars and in each one the driver would cash a 10 or 20 dollar bill for smaller bills. We finally caught on that he was getting a kick back for bringing us to the bar since he would get more back then the cash value of the bill. The popular drink at that time was Cuba Libre, Rum and Coke. Rum was plentiful but Coke was in short supply so the drinks were powerful; I always had to ask the bartender for more Coke. Drivers in the town had quite a system, when approaching an intersection they would blow their horn and if no one responded with their horn, it was full speed ahead; if they did get a response, they blew their own horn again and went full speed ahead; seemed like the loudest horn won. Narrow and dark streets made this great fun. It was on this trip that we visited the world famous Sloppy Joe's Bar and had our picture taken with an old fashioned flash powder camera.

Returning from one of our flights, we were landing at Batista Field and had touched down, still rolling at a good speed when another B29 (not one of ours) came directly over us in an attempt to land in front of us. I could count every rivet in the belly of that plane as he passed over us. He finally decided he couldn't make it and put on power to go around. He had one propeller feathered and must have been really anxious to get back on the ground.

When we finished up our tour, we flew back to the states and had to land unexpectedly at Galveston as a Port of Entry to have our planes and cargo inspected for contraband by the Customs Department. We had all bought things not available or rationed in the States at that time. We were the 3rd in line and everyone had to put all their luggage out on the tarmac for inspection. It took the inspectors about 3 hours to barely get started to examine the 1st plane and it was getting late in the day, so they gave up the inspection and had us all sign statements that we were not bringing in contraband. We loaded back up and headed for Wendover.

DOWNEY, JOHN L
393rd Bombardment Squadron

Tinian's Wildlife

Tropical Islands in the Pacific all suffer or benefit (depending on your outlook) from an over abundance of rainfall, generally at night, followed by days of intense heat, all of which resulted in lush vegetation and a unique form of wildlife, at least it did on Tinian.

The flora on Tinian was no exception. The fast growing plant life reclaimed cleared areas almost as you watched, so fast that it was somewhat hazardous to stand in one spot too long. (It was rumored that a small group to Seabees, who were preparing an area for runways, slipped off in the jungle to take a smoke break and a nap, were overtaken by the growth and it took about a week for their complexion to return to normal from green.) The fauna, the only specie I personally observed on the island, reproduced at about the same speed, even when you weren't watching.

As part of the effort to provide some of the niceties of home for the troops, the 509th boasted an outdoor movie theater, which presented a Hollywood epic each evening. The main feature started at 1900 hours and the daily rain started at 1930 hours. The choice of uniform for movie going was a plastic helmet liner and a waterproof poncho.

The consistent rainfall also produced permanent pools of water in every low spot on the island, some small, some large. It was in these pools the most prominent animal life form of Tinian was to be found by the thousands, small black aquatic forms, wriggling and darting around in the water. As time passed, they grew in size, lost their tails, grew legs and transformed from tadpoles into frogs.

At nightfall, when the island cooled off, the frogs would congregate on the roadways where the coral based blacktop still retained the warmth of the sun that the frogs seemed to take great delight in absorbing by body contact.

Driving a vehicle on the roads at night, in addition to the sounds of the tires on the wet pavement and the exhaust, another sound was to be heard and I can still hear it in my head. It was the splat, splat, splatter splat of countless numbers of those amphibians becoming casualties of progress. Rather than feeling sorry for them, consider it a population control means, without which the island would have soon been overpopulated and the frogs would have starved to death. One way or another, they would have croaked.

DOWNEY, JOHN L
393rd Bombardment Squadron

Train To Roswell

When I think of Capt. Siegle, I am reminded of the following. Returning to the United States from overseas, we landed near San Francisco, California. A train was quickly formed and we were soon on our way to Roswell, New Mexico.

On the second day of our trip, we were told we would stop at the next town for about 1/2 hour for railroad maintenance. 1st Sgt. Kelly and I went to Capt. Siegle and asked for permission to leave the train while work was being done. He said, "OK, but there better not be anyone missing when the train pulled out."

The train stopped right along the town's commercial district where taverns, liquor stores and groceries were located. A lot of us came back from there carrying whatever we could. Some had 3, 4 or 5 bottles of beer to take back onto the train. On our train, the drinking water tank already had ice in it but not the water, so we put our beer in the tank. The steel tank was elevated so you could not see into it. When the railroad attendant came aboard with his water hose, he reached up to add water, but the hose was hitting something! I wonder what it could be? When he reached up to see, behold there were the beer bottles. Then he realized there were guys watching, so he sheepishly looked at us and said, "I don't think you guys will need any water."

We had a great evening and no one missed getting back onto the train.

FELLWOCK, ROBERT A. "Whitey"
1027th Air Material Squadron

Whitey Fellwock at Wendover March 1945
2nd from bottom row–2nd person from right

A Veteran Remembers

A few crew members went to a Naval Base at Inyokern, California to work on loading and dropping the "pumpkins." We, Joe Clancy, Bill Jacks and I, got a weekend pass to go to Los Angeles. We were ground crew but they flew us down to Burbank after our security briefing and were supposed to be back there by midnight on Sunday for our ride back to Inyokern. We missed our ride and had to hitch hike back. We got a ride from an old guy in a brand new 1942 Buick Road Master. He asked if one of us could drive and I volunteered. He said he would take us as far as the Sansalito turn off. It was dark and I missed the sign and went about 50 miles past his turnoff. He woke up and said "Where are we?" I said I wasn't sure and when he saw the next sign, he was a little annoyed that I missed the turnoff. So we got out and started hitching again. This time we got a ride with 2 women and 1 guy who had been celebrating all weekend and were pretty well smashed. They took us all the way back to the base and the Navy passes were good till 7am. We got back there at 6:30am so we didn't get in any trouble, but never got much sleep until the next night.

While we were at Inyokern, President Roosevelt died before we left to go back to Wendover and Harry Truman took over. We left for Tinian a short time later but were amazed at the things going on at Inyokern, a Naval testing base. We saw one of the first night fighter planes as well as working on the future first "Atomic Bomb." We had to have various security badges for different parts of the base and got a little extra money for being there. We were supposed to pay for meals but the sailors let us eat for nothing.

MCCLARY, ROBERT
93rd Bombardment Squadron
Aircraft Armorer

L-R:
Bob McClary, Joe Clancy, Bill Jacks

THEIR BOY DROPPED IT

Mr. and Mrs. W. F. Ferebee, Route 1, Mocksville, parents of Maj. Thomas Wilson Ferebee, who dropped the atomic bomb on Hiroshima, Japan. At left is Miss Maxine Ferebee, their daughter. They were Charlotte visitors yesterday, and after a radio broadcast over WBT, had luncheon with M. S. Ward, Mrs. Ferebee's brother, at 1208 East Fifth street. At bottom is picture of Major Ferebee, the boy who dropped the first atomic bomb on Japan.

Hero's Parents Visit Charlotte

Ferebees Now Hope Son Will Come Home

A father and a mother who love their son deeply, slowly beginning to realize that the son has participated in a shattering, epochal history-making event, want nothing more now than for him to come home safely to them.

"He has flown 61 missions in the North African and Italian campaigns," said W. F. Ferebee, the father. "He has known all the perils of such missions, flying over Ploesti oil fields and over the aircraft factories in Austria.

"Now that he has been privileged to drop the atomic bomb that has startled the world—we just want him home again."

"And Tom always hoped he would make his mark in the world," said the mother. "I guess we never dreamed that would be accom-plished by dropping the world's most awful explosive."

Tears were in their eyes, but they were not ashamed. They had just come from station WBT, where they were guests, and where they had broadcast an interview. Now they were at the home of Mr. and Mrs. M. S. Ward, 1208 East Fifth street—and out on the porch. Mr. Ward is a brother of Mrs. Ferebee. They told of Major Thomas Wilson Ferebee's

(See FEREBEE, Page 7, Col. 4.)

MORE ABOUT FEREBEE

STARTS ON PAGE ONE.

boyhood days, of his ambitions and his love for airplanes.

"BOMBED" CHICKENS.

Often when Tom went to the store, the country store, with a basket of eggs, he'd destroy several by "bombing" chickens or rabbits or fenceposts along the way. In those days Tom didn't know that on Monday, August 6, 1945, he would toss upon the soil of Japan the greatest explosive power in human history—a power that would destroy in one fell blow multiple tens of thousands of people.

But Mr. and Mrs. Ferebee are not sorry their son destroyed the Japs. Somebody had to do it, they contend. If the Lord willed it for their son, then so be it—and they are happy about it.

The Ferebees live on a farm six miles from Mocksville. Tom was reared there; and so was his sister, Maxine, who also came to Charlotte yesterday. Maxine thinks her brother is pretty fine, and handsome, and she's tremendously proud of him. He weighs 180 pounds, has brown hair and blue eyes, is five feet eleven inches tall—and he's good natured, gallant—and, well, a swell brother.

WITH DOOLITTLE.

He was with General Jimmy Doolittle in Africa, and he's now with the Ninth Air Force in Pacific. After 23 months in Europe, he came home, and then went on some mysterious mission to the West.

"My work is sacred," he told his parents. "I can't discuss it with you. Someday you'll maybe hear about it through the newspapers."

Major Ferebee is a graduate of Lees-McRae college, class of 1940, where he was outstanding in football, basketball and track, and he was a member of the student council and of the Demosthenes club, men's leadership organization.

His parents had a letter from him dated July 25, and mailed from Tinian, near Saipan. He spoke of a good setup for his outfit, and his hope to be home reasonably early.

The Ferebees left yesterday afternoon for Mocksville, which is about 65 miles from Charlotte.

On August 7, 1945, the day after the bomb was dropped, my father, mother and I were invited by Grady Cole, WBT Radio Announcer in Charlotte, North Carolina for a live interview. Since we had no car, a neighbor, Cleo Tutterow, drove us. Numerous news people came to our home as we had no telephone. I shall never forget this special day.

MAXINE FEREBEE PRUIT
Sister of Thomas Ferebee, Bombardier

Incident On Tinian

In early August 1945, I was an Army Air Corps Captain on Tinian Island as a member of the 509th Composite Group of B29s, Colonel Paul Tibbets commanding.

I was routinely assigned as Island Officer of the Day (OD) an overnight security tour. After routine inspecting, I returned to my quarters with a field phone. About 9:30-10:00pm, I received an urgent alert from Military Police Headquarters (MPHQ) advising an Army Engineer Soldier had "gone berserk with a machete." I told the MP who called to contact the medical OD and send a vehicle for me.

Speedily, an MP jeep took me to the detached engineer area. There, at a brightly lighted Quonset Barracks, were 30 to 40 soldiers gathered outside. I asked the soldier's name and what caused the uproar, but they only knew his nickname and there had "been no trouble before," so I'll call him Jim. Then I entered the Quonset. The soldier with the machete was standing at the far end – a big fellow, in his shorts, very agitated. I slowly advanced toward him, about 15-20 feet and called, "I am Captain Siegle, Officer of the Day and I am here to help you."

Slowly, I moved in closer; he pointed at the machete and said, "Don't come any closer – you have a gun," referring to my holstered Colt sidearm. By then, I was closer to a point of no return. I replied that I would not use the gun, but if I was to help him, he would have to drop the machete on the closest bunk. He hesitated and dropped the machete. Whew! His bunk was nearby with a shelf showing a leather framed picture of his wife and

two small children. He was no school boy. I asked what caused his outbreak and he said, "The daily insults of hick, stupid, ignorant by his bunkmates and others." His Arkansas background was alien to the majority of his unit who were mostly city boys.

I had him dress, get his photo and stationary together, and we exited through a greatly subdued group at the doorway. I told his Charge of Quarters

(CQ) to advise his commander and send his footlocker to the hospital. He gave no trouble and asked me to visit him, which I did the next day. He was heavily sedated. The following day he was "transported" off the base.

On September 1, I became Squadron Commanding Officer (SCO) of the 1027th Air Material Squadron and in early October our entire group returned stateside.

The acronym (CQ) refers to the position of "Charge of Quarters." Every squadron or Army unit designated an officer or noncommissioned officer (NCO) to take charge of the unit – usually during the off hours of night time and functioning as the one "holding down the fort" on behalf of the Commanding Officer (CO) and the day duty staff.

The dog in the photo is a former Japanese mascot who wisely changed sides.

SIEGLE, CALVIN G.
1027th Air Material Squadron
Captain

I graduated from Chemical Warfare School, Officer Candidate School, Edgewood Arsenal, Maryland, May 1943. After serving at several different bases, I was transferred to Wendover Field, 216th Base Unit as chemical officer. On August 12, 1944, I was granted a 21 day leave of absence at which time, I went fishing with my parents at Sparrow Lake Canada.

During my stay at Sparrow Lake, I saw Anne and told my mother that was the girl I was going to marry. I proposed 3 days later and we were married at Salt Lake City in an Episcopal Church. We moved into the State Line Hotel and lived on the second floor. I remember there was a slot machine at the bottom of the stairs and each time I went by I put in a quarter.

Each day I went to my office on the base, Anne worked on the base also. When groups went on maneuvers, I was the enemy. I had the tear gas grenades. I put the men through gas chambers – they hated me. I remember Anne took bridge lessons from Mrs. Tibbets. One time I skinned my knee playing touch football. They gave me sulfa, which turned out I was allergic to it and my knee swelled up. My fellow officers enjoyed dancing with Anne at the Officers Club.

On Tinian, one of the fellows in our Quonset Hut had decided to grow a moustache. It was curled up on the ends. One night when he had too much to drink, someone clipped off half his moustache. I never saw anyone so mad in my life.

Being the Fire Marshal on Tinian and in charge of the decontamination truck, I had access to fire extinguishers and tanks of various gasses. We would open the oxygen tank, fill it with water 3/4 full, then charge it with carbon dioxide. This made our mix for drinks in our Quonset. All we had to do was add lime and liquor.

I had a chemical warfare class on Guam the day the bomb was dropped. A captain in the class knew I was in the 509th and asked me to talk to the class about the bomb. I knew nothing about it, but stood up and said, "I'm sorry I don't want to divulge any secrets." I received applause.

I returned to the states by ship on the USS Deuel. Somehow Ida Young, Aitken Young's wife found out when the ship was to arrive and there was Ida on the dock yelling and screaming and we were yelling back "Hello Ida."

While overseas, Anne saved my allotment. I went to Canada to get Anne. Then we both went to Roswell. Each day I waited for them to cut orders for me, if they did not, I went and played golf.

SPRAGUE, WILLIS N. JR.
390th Air Service Group
Base Chemical Officer

Card for crossing equator on Cape Victory

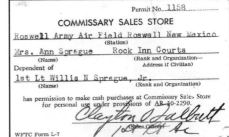

Commissary sales store identification card

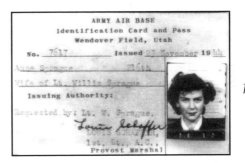

Anne Sprague's pass to get on base

State Line Hotel, where you could rent a room for $1.00/ day.

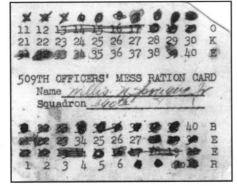

Coke and beer ration card – Tinian

Large 8x10 V-Mail given to Willis Sprague signed by all in his Quonset Hut. Hung on wall of hut.

At the beginning of June 1945, our crew was told we would be going overseas very shortly; Destination Tinian. We were all ready because I think we were tired of the intense training we received the past 8 months. We were issued side arms and left about June 5, 1945 for our first destination, Sacramento, California, a staging area. We were there a day or so. Then left on the next leg of our journey, Honolulu, Hawaii, where we spent 1 day. We enjoyed the sights of downtown Honolulu where this picture was taken. We also visited Waikiki Beach.

The next day we left for Johnston Island, a small dot in the middle of the Pacific Ocean, for an overnight stay. From the barracks, we were quartered in, we stepped out the back door for a swim in the ocean. The next day we took off for our final destination, Tinian. On arrival, we were temporarily quartered in tents, later moving into our permanent area which was quite nice. My first impression of Tinian – I couldn't believe so many planes and the large runways could be on such a small island. The rest of our stay until we left in October 1945 is history.

WIDOWSKY, JACK
393rd Bombardment Squadron
Navigator, Crew B-8

L-R Hugh Ferguson, Fred Hoey, Jack Widowsky

Since the IFF (Identification Friend Foe Signal) told our own ground radar that we were friendly, the upkeep of the IFF also was carried out by the 393rd Radar section. The IFF was so greatly classified that its wiring and components were not color coded or numbered. It contained a magnesium bomb which would explode it if the plane should crash and fall into enemy hands. Exploding it was a device called the crash switch. It was located on one of the bulkheads in a bomb bay. As part of a radar preflight one could lay on ones back on the side of the bomb bay and kick the bulkhead smartly to attest that the crash switch would trip. This was of course, to be done with the power disconnected from the IFF. I did this once when I had failed to pull the plug! The inside of the IFF was just a wad of molten metal. I don't remember if everyone could or not, but Wendell Lathrop and I could go to air corps supply, sign our name and the word "SILVERPLATE" and get anything we wanted, no questions asked. I took the belated IFF to air corps supply and swapped it for a new one and nobody said a word. If I had had to sign a statement of charges, the thing listed for almost $1000.

RICHARDSON, PORTER A.
393rd Bombardment Squadron
Line Chief Radar/Countermeasures

Members of 393rd Radar Section
Standing on back of jeep, L-R: Calvin Anstine, Aubrey Pair, John Harrington, John Robey
Back of jeep with legs hanging out: Joseph Ross
Passenger side, L-R: Porter Richardson, Patrick Joyce, Wendell Lathrop, Grover Cooper
Leaning against windshield: John Kennedy
Holding radar flag and wearing pith helmet: Andrew Brown
Sitting on hood: Norman McIntosh
Sitting on bumper: James Jolly

Sketch done on Tinian by Porter Richardson of 393rd Radar Shack

507th Radar Shack

14 AUG 1945
TINIAN, MARIANAS

Quarry for road building

Unloading Fat man housings on Tinian

WINGMEN VERSUS FLYERS

General Roger Ramey,
Commanding

58th Bomb Wing 7 RUNS

General John Davies,
Commanding

313 Bomb Wing 10 RUNS

AUGUST 14, 1945

Chuck Stevens (Browns)	1B	Johnny Sturm (Yankees)
Art Lilly (Hollywood)	2B	Bob Adams (Reds)
Bill Hitchcock (Tigers)	3B	Lou Riggs (Dodgers)
Joe Gordon (Yanks)	SS	Nan Fernandez Braves)
Al Lang (Reds)	LF	John Jenson (San Diego)
Joe Marty (Phillies)	CF	Max West (Braves)
Enos Slaughter (Cards)	RF	Walter Judnich (Browns)
Birdie Tebbetts (Tigers)	C	Bill Leonard (Oakland)
Tom Gabrielli (Pirates)	C	Bud Storie (Tigers)
Howie Pollett (Cards)	P	Rugger Ardizoia (Yanks)
Chubby Dean (Indians)	P	Stan Goletz (White Sox)
Roy Pitter (Yanks)	P	Eddie Chandler (PCL)
Ed Kowalski (AFF)	P	Carl Derose (Yanks)
George Gill (Indianapolis)	P	Al Olsen (San Diego)
Vic Wertz (Tigers) (OF)		Don Loeser (AFF)
Pete Layden (Red Sox) (OF)		

58th Bombardment Wing Diamond
TINIAN

New York Yankee 2nd baseman Joe Gordon signs baseball for 509th men

Dock Area

Fat Man housings on Tinian dock

Japanese tanks destroyed during invasion

Cletrac tractor in front of Bockscar

509th Headquarters

*Building coral runways on
Tinian–pre-509th*

509th Composite Group and Project Alberta Roster (Tinian, 1945)

This roster of the men of the 509th Composite Group and Project Alberta who were based on Tinian in July-August 1945 was originally prepared by Fred and Helen Bock in 1995. Their primary source of data was the collection of unit photographs and accompanying captions included in the 509th Pictorial Album. The names of the men who came to Tinian from the Los Alamos Laboratory of the Manhattan Project were taken from Harlow Russ's Project Alberta: The Preparation of Atomic Bombs for Use in World War II. Minor editing of the original roster has been accomplished to eliminate some duplication of names.

The number of men in each unit of the 509th Composite Group and in the Project Alberta contingent is given in the "Size" column. The Washington Representatives were Brigadier General Thomas F. Farrell (deputy to General Groves) and Rear Admiral William R. Purnell (Navy member of the Military Policy Committee). Other than the listing of the Commanding Officers of the nine units, no attempt was made by Fred and Helen Bock to include rank, duty, or other information in this roster. Ranks were not given in many of the unit photographs in the source material and promotions did occur while the 509th was on Tinian.

The unit abbreviations, full names, number of men assigned, and the unit Commanding Officers are as follows:

	Unit	Size	Commanding Officer
509HQ	Headquarters, 509th Composite Group	98	Col. Paul W. Tibbets, Jr.
393rd	393rd Bombardment Squadron (VH)	535	Major Charles W. Sweeney
1St	1St Ordnance Squadron, Special Aviation	296	Major Charles F.H. Begg
320th	320th Troop Carrier Squadron	149	Capt. John J. Casey, Jr.
390th	390th Air Service Group	189	Lt. Col. John W. Porter
603rd	603rd Air Engineering Squadron	227	Capt. Earl O. Casey
1027th	1027th Air Materiel Squadron	141	Major Guy Geller
1395th	1395th Military Police Company (Aviation)	133	Capt. Louis Schaffer
Proj A	Project Alberta	51	Capt. William S. Parsons (U.S. Navy)
HQ	Washington Representatives	2	
	Total	**1,821**	

Roster

Abraham, Sheffe	1st
Acker, John G.	320th
Ackerman, Carl.	393rd
Adams, Bob	1395th
Adams, L.J., Jr.	390th
Adams, Ronald K.	320th
Adams, Scott C.	390th
Adams, Vernon	1395th
Adkins, James A.	393rd
Agnew, Harold	Proj A
Albright, Lee S.	1027th
Albury, Charles D.	393rd
Alexander, Adair M.	603rd
Alexander, Albert D.	1st
Alexander, John	1st
Alger, Frank A.	509HQ
Aljian, Edward	390th
Allen, Louis B.	393rd
Allen, Raymond E.	393rd
Allen, Sam, Jr.	320th
Allison, Glenn S.	393rd
Allison, Noah C.	1027th
Allshouse, Dorsey	1st
Almon, Jabez W.	320th
Alvarez, Luis	Proj A
Amentt, Michael J.	603rd
Ames, Robert N.	320th
Anderson, David	Proj A
Anderson, Edsel	1395th
Anderson, Forest C.	393rd
Anderson, Howard J.	390th
Anderson, James F.	393rd

Anderson, James J.	393rd
Anderson, James M.	393rd
Anderson, Jonie	603rd
Andrews, Lester W.	1395th
Andrews, Sam G.	509HQ
Andritsis, Harry D.	393rd
Angeli, Russell F.	320th
Angelich, Michael	393rd
Anselme, Richard B.	393rd
Anstine, Calvin C.	393rd
Anthony, Michael A.	1027th
Apgar, Stanley C.	393rd
Arena, John L.	393rd
Armijo, Cicilio	603rd
Armstrong, James S.	1027th
Arnold, Alvin R.	1027th
Arnold, George L.	393rd
Arnold, Marvin H., Jr.	320th
Arnold, Roderick F.	393rd
Arnson, Robert J.	1st
Artripe, Asper A.	603rd
Ashworth, Frederick L.	Proj A
Asseff, R.T.	390th
Astarita, Thomas	1st
Atkielski, Joseph R.	393rd
Aungst, Sharon	1st
Ayers, Robert L.	393rd
Babock, James W., Jr.	320th
Baca, Hinginio A.	393rd
Back, Lawrence L.	393rd
Bacon, Charles E.	1st

Bagley, Winton	1395th
Baiago, Joseph	1027th
Bailey, Kenneth E.	393rd
Baker, Charles J.	393rd
Baker, Charles P.	Proj A
Baker, Delbert R.	320th
Baker, George S.	393rd
Baldasaro, Pasquale	393rd
Baldwin, Robert F., Jr.	1027th
Ball, Walter A.	1027th
Balliet, Roy K.	393rd
Bandick, R.N.	390th
Bandy, Ray C.	509HQ
Bankoski, Edward	603rd
Barbera, James J.	320th
Bardecker, Irving E.	393rd
Barker, Curtis T.	1st
Barker, John O.	320th
Barnard, Harry N.	320th
Barnes, Philip M.	1st
Barney, Arthur G.	393rd
Barney, William C.	393rd
Barrett, Orin R.	393rd
Barsumian, Albert	393rd
Barthelomew, Stanley M.	603rd
Bartholomew, W.E.	390th
Bartlett, Albert L.	393rd
Bateman, Rao H.	603rd
Batt, Kenneth L.	320th
Baugh, Aaron C.	393rd
Baur, Leander J.	393rd
Baxter, Kenneth L.	393rd

Baxter, Marcus W.	393rd
Bayrik, Mark L., Jr.	320th
Beahan, Kermit K.	393rd
Bean, Bernard H.	1027th
Bean, Gerald E.	509HQ
Beatson, James A.	1st
Beatty, James A.	320th
Beaty, Marvin O.	393rd
Beaudette, Donald D.	393rd
Bederson, Benjamin B.	Proj A
Bednorz, Everist L.	393rd
Beebe, Vernon C.	393rd
Beecher, Clyde R.	393rd
Beeler, Kenneth E.	1st
Bega, Joe	1027th
Begg, Charles F.H.	1st
Begnoche, Raymond	1st
Behr, R.B.	509HQ
Belanger, Ralph D.	393rd
Belasco, Daniel M.	1st
Belcher, Ray	1395th
Bell, Edwin M.	393rd
Bell, Francis III	509HQ
Bell, W., Jr.	390th
Bellamy, Sidney J.	393rd
Benbrook, Robert E.	393rd
Benenati, Frank J.	393rd
Benjamin, Farron P.	1027th
Bennett, Cecil	390th
Bennett, Ralph M.	393rd
Benson, Bernard F.	320th
Benson, Robert A.	603rd

Berardo, D.J. ... 509HQ
Berg, E.C. ... 390th
Bergamo, Frank ... 1395th
Berger, Ralph C. ... 603rd
Berkanholtz, I. ... 390th
Berkeley, Theodore ... 1395th
Berkoff, Louis ... 603rd
Bernath, Glen A. ... 393rd
Berry, Kenneth E. ... 1st
Berzinis, Frank W. ... 393rd
Beser, Jacob ... 393rd
Best, Warren ... 393rd
Betes, Manual ... 393rd
Betts, Loyal E. ... 1st
Bever, Theodore G. ... 603rd
Bezdegian, Aram E. ... 393rd
Biel, Raymond P. ... 393rd
Bierman, Melvin H. ... 393rd
Biggio, William D. ... 393rd
Bingman, Sandy M. ... 603rd
Birch, Francis A. ... Proj A
Birkenkamp, Allen A. ... 1st
Bishop, Gilbert W. ... 393rd
Bishop, William E. ... 393rd
Bissonnette, George ... 390th
Bivans, Jack ... 393rd
Black, Norman ... 393rd
Black, Richard ... 1395th
Blaisdell, Theron L. ... 393rd
Blakely, Earl ... 1st
Blakney, Earl J. ... 603rd
Blandine, Alfred H. ... 393rd
Blankenship, Vester ... 1395th
Blasingame, Thomas E. ... 1027th
Bloam, James C. ... 1st
Block, George ... 1st
Block, Otto C., Jr. ... 393rd
Bloomfield, Ralph ... 603rd
Blouse, Richard E. ... 393rd
Blower, Joseph, Jr. ... 393rd
Blum, J.E. ... 509HQ
Blumenfeld, Leonard M. ... 393rd
Blyler, Ernest J. ... 509HQ
Bobinson, J.R ... 509HQ
Bock, Frederick C. ... 393rd
Boehm, W.A., Jr. ... 390th
Bohine, S.H. ... 509HQ
Bohon, Michael G. ... 393rd
Bolles, William H. ... 320th
Bolstad, Milo ... Proj A
Bonadies, Anthony ... 393rd
Bonczek, Walter J. ... 393rd
Bonds, John E. ... 390th
Bonjour, Glenn ... 1st
Bontekoe, Jacob Y. ... 393rd
Borger, Joseph B. ... 603rd
Borgerson, William H. ... 393rd
Borgstadt, William C. ... 393rd
Born, W.R ... 509HQ
Bossert, Frederick ... 1st
Bost, Avery C. ... 320th
Boucher, Charles E., Jr. ... 393rd
Bourre, John P. ... 393rd
Bowen, H.D. ... 390th
Bowen, Harry ... 393rd
Bower, Robert ... 603rd
Bowman, Lester E. ... 393rd
Boyle, Ray N., Jr. ... 393rd
Brabenec, George L. ... 393rd
Bradley, Guy C. ... 603rd
Bradley, James H. ... 1st
Bradley, Max W. ... 320th
Brady, Frank J. ... 320th
Bramer, Bill ... 1395th
Branfeld, J.G. ... 390th
Breeding, William ... 1st
Brending, Edward ... 1395th
Brevelle, Curtley, J.B. ... 1027th
Brewster, Leon J. ... 1027th
Brice, George F. ... 393rd
Bridges, James H. ... 393rd
Briese, Frank M. ... 393rd
Briggs, Stephen W., Jr. ... 320th
Bright, J.L. ... 509HQ
Brightman, Stanton H. ... 1395th
Brin, Raymond ... Proj A
Brininger, Ralph A. ... 1st
Brinkley, Raymond ... 1st
Britt, Clarence E. ... 393rd
Brooks, Charles W. ... 603rd
Broussard, V. ... 509HQ
Brower, V. ... 509HQ
Brown, Andrew A. ... 393rd
Brown, Asa H. ... 1st
Brown, Dale M. ... 320th
Brown, David S. ... 1st
Brown, Frank S. ... 1st
Brown, Fred E. ... 393rd
Brown, George J. ... 393rd
Brown, Joe R. ... 393rd
Brown, Leland A. ... 320th
Brown, Richard ... 1st
Brown, Venard ... 1027th
Brown, William E. ... 393rd
Bruenger, Fred E. ... 320th
Brumagin, Thomas H. ... 393rd
Brumfield, Abram A. ... 1027th
Bruno, N.F. ... 509HQ
Bryan, John C. ... 1st
Bryant, Claude E. ... 393rd
Bryant, James R. ... 393rd
Buchner, Charles ... 1st
Buckley, Edward K. ... 393rd
Budai, Stephen ... 1st
Budmen, Bernard H. ... 1st
Bunting, Thomas A. ... 393rd
Burford, Kermit ... 1st
Burgener, Fred E. ... 320th
Burgess, E.A. ... 390th
Burgmeir, William D. ... 1st
Burgwyn, Nathaniel T.R. ... 393rd
Burns, Billy B. ... 509HQ
Burns, Ernest C. ... 393rd
Burns, James A. ... 393rd
Burris, Donald E. ... 1st
Busang, Joseph S. ... 320th
Buscher, Joseph D. ... 509HQ
Bush, Neal W. ... 1395th
Bushee, Joseph C. ... 1027th
Butensky, S.J. ... 390th
Butler, Fred D. ... 393rd
Butterfield, Harold ... 1st
Buxton, Carl E. ... 1st
Byczynski, Edmund S. ... 393rd
Byler, George G., Jr. ... 1st
Byrd, Robert H. ... 393rd
Byrnes, William ... 1st
Bysom, Clyde L. ... 393rd

Caddell, Curtis W. ... 1st
Cagle, Howard L. ... 1395th
Cain, William R ... 320th
Caleca, Vincent ... Proj A
Callahan, Cordell W. ... 1st
Camac, Morton ... Proj A
Camden, Paul M. ... 1027th
Campbell, John M. ... 393rd
Campeau, Edward J. ... 603rd
Canby, Joel S. ... 509HQ
Cangilla, Maurice C. ... 1st
Canjar, Mathew H. ... 320th
Cannon, Richard F. ... 393rd
Cantlon, John E. ... 393rd
Capua, Anthony D., Jr. ... 393rd
Carling, Francis A. ... 320th
Carlo, Frank C. ... 320th
Carlon, Earl L. ... 603rd
Carlson, Edward G. ... Proj A
Carlson, Per E. ... 603rd
Carlson, Russell R. ... 1027th
Carmichael, D.D. ... 390th
Carol, Andrew ... 393rd
Caron, George R. ... 393rd
Carpenter, Charles E. ... 320th
Carr, Charley C. ... 393rd
Carrasco, T. ... 390th
Carrigan, Russell D. ... 393rd
Carrington, Ellsworth T. ... 393rd
Carroll, William E. ... 390th
Carter, Malla ... 1395th
Carwile, William M. ... 1027th
Cary, Delbert P. ... 1st
Casci, Peter ... 1st
Casey, Donald M. ... 603rd
Casey, Earl O. ... 603rd
Casey, John J., Jr. ... 320th
Cash, Bertram S. ... 393rd
Castater, John W. ... 320th
Castellitto, Adam J. ... 393rd
Catt, Grover H. ... 393rd
Gaughey, Glenn ... 1395th
Caylor, Lee E. ... 393rd
Cetti, Bob ... 1395th
Chadwick, B. ... 509HQ
Chambers, C.F. ... 390th
Chaney, Edgar ... 393rd
Chapman, Bobby J. ... 393rd
Chapman, Elzie ... 1395th
Chase, Ralph E. ... 320th
Chatt, John O. ... 509HQ
Chaussy, Pern J. ... 1st
Chavez, Alfredo ... 1395th
Chavez, Henry G. ... 320th
Cheek, Ples M. ... 1st
Cheeseman, John L. ... 1027th
Chelnik, D. ... 390th
Childs, Raymond ... 1395th
Chisom, R.C. ... 509HQ
Chiuchiolo, Michael ... 320th
Christensen, John E. ... 1027th
Christie, D.T. ... 509HQ
Chudy, Chester S. ... 393rd
Churchill, Deane G. ... 320th
Ciaccio, B.P. ... 509HQ
Cirami, Salvatore P. ... 1027th
Clancy, Joseph L. ... 393rd
Clapso, Gerard F. ... 393rd
Clark, C.C. ... 390th
Clark, Ernest K. ... 1st
Clark, Joe L. ... 1st
Clark, Maurice J. ... 393rd
Classen, Thomas J. ... 509HQ
Clay, R.L. ... 393rd
Clayton, Frederick D. ... 393rd
Cleary, John P. ... 1027th
Clemens, J.C.W. ... 390th
Clement, Jackson M. ... 393rd
Clements, William M. ... 393rd
Clifton, Robert L. ... 1st
Clifton, Robert R. ... 603rd
Cloepfil, John K. ... 320th
Coble, Warren L. ... 393rd
Codatta, Antonio, Jr. ... 393rd
Coffman, Lynn P. ... 1st
Cohen, George H. ... 393rd
Cole, Donald O. ... 393rd
Cole, Gerald F. ... 1st
Cole, Leon ... 393rd
Colella, Joseph, Jr. ... 1st
Collins, Arthur W. ... Proj A
Collins, John E. ... 393rd
Collins, Kenneth ... 603rd
Collins, William Q. ... 509HQ
Collinson, William ... 393rd
Collinsworth, James ... 603rd
Combs, Archie G., Jr. ... 1st
Compronio, William R. ... 393rd
Conkle, Arthur R. ... 393rd
Conley, Robert C. ... 393rd
Connaughton, Joseph L. ... 393rd
Conner, Lloyd G. ... 393rd
Cooke, R.K. ... 390th
Cooper, George ... 1395th
Cooper, Grover G., Jr. ... 393rd
Cooper, Hubert L., Jr. ... 1395th
Cooper, Jean S. ... 393rd
Cooper, Kenneth J. ... 1st
Cooper, Leon ... 393rd
Cooper, W.J. ... 509HQ
Cope, Curtis ... 1395th
Coppola, Jack J. ... 393rd
Corcoran, Gerald J. ... 393rd
Corey, Neil R ... 393rd
Corliss, James R. ... 393rd
Cornett, Pearl ... 320th
Corrigan, Bruce G. ... 1st
Corson, Norman O. ... 393rd
Cortez, Leonides C. ... 1027th
Cortez, Louis Y. ... 1st
Cosimano, Anthony ... 393rd
Costa, Thomas F. ... 393rd
Costello, Edward M. ... 393rd
Cothran, J.G. ... 390th
Cotton, Ira J. ... 393rd
Cotter, William J. ... 393rd
Cottrill, Harold W. ... 1027th
Coury, Harry J ... 603rd
Covatto, Armand C. ... 603rd
Covington, Guy ... 1st
Coy, Seth ... 320th
Cozad, Ellis E. ... 1st
Craft, Cecil W. ... 1st
Crawford, William D. ... 1027th
Creed, J.D. ... 320th
Crespin, Barton B. ... 393rd
Crisp, George W. ... 393rd
Crotty, William R. ... 393rd
Crouse, Stanley, Jr. ... 509HQ
Crow, Harvey J. ... 603rd
Crusenberry, L. ... 390th
Csome, Andrew, Jr. ... 1027th
Cullom, Homer L. ... 603rd
Cummins, Joseph H. ... 320th
Cunningham, Loren L. ... 393rd
Curry, Ralph D. ... 393rd
Custer, Glen L. ... 603rd
Cybert, E., Jr. ... 390th
Czaja, Leo J. ... 603rd

D'Alessio, L.M. ... 390th
Dacorte, Antone M. ... 1st
Daggett, Ralph ... 603rd
Dahl, Newell E. ... 603rd
Daloisio, Albert R. ... 603rd
Daly, James R. ... 1395th
Damask, Arthur C. ... 603rd
Damron, Chester ... 603rd
Danahy, James C. ... 603rd
Danby, Jack I.H. ... 509HQ
Daniel, James ... 390th
Darby, G.C., Jr. ... 509HQ
Darre, Eugene W. ... 603rd
Davenport, Robert E. ... 393rd
Davidson, James E. ... 1027th
Davis, Albert ... 1st
Davis, Grover ... 1st
Davis, Harold ... 1st
Davis, Harry B. ... 393rd
Davis, James W. ... 393rd
Davis, Robert K. ... 320th
Davis, Wiley H. ... 1st
Davis, William J. ... 1027th
Davison, Benjamin D. ... 393rd
Dawson, Robert W. ... Proj A
Day, Joe B. ... 509HQ
Deacon, Richard S. ... 1st
Deal, S.J. ... 390th
DeCuir, Laurence E. ... 1st
Dehart, Albert T. ... 393rd
Deis, Bert ... 1st
DeLaney, J. Slade ... 320th
Delehanty, James F. ... 1395th
Delmar, John C., Jr. ... 603rd
DeLong, E.E. ... 509HQ
Deming, R.O., III ... 509HQ
Demo, Andrew G. ... 393rd
Denham, Joel S., Jr. ... 393rd
Denman, Howard B. ... 393rd
Denton, Freddie ... 1st
Depner, Michael ... 393rd
Deprang, Raleigh K. ... 393rd
Desmond, William J. ... 393rd
Deutsch, Henry ... 393rd
DeVito, J. ... 390th
Devore, Ralph N. ... 393rd
DeWoody, Bill J. ... 603rd
Dhonau, John E. ... 393rd
Dial, Walter E. ... 1st
Dickman, Gilbert B ... 393rd
DiJulio, Joseph M. ... 393rd
Dike, Sheldon ... Proj A
DiLeonardo, J.J. ... 390th
Dillinger, Dwight ... 1st
Dillman, Richard J. ... 393rd

Dimoush, Melvin E. 1395th
DiPalantino, Dominic J. 603rd
DiRienzo, Vito 1st
Disparti, Joseph C. 1st
Dispensa, Joseph S. 393rd
DiTullio, Arthur J. 1027th
Doane, Philip E. 1st
Dodge, William W. 1027th
Dodgen, Roy E. 393rd
Doine, Harold G. 603rd
Doiron, James H. 393rd
Dolan, Francis X. 393rd
Dolan, John J. 393rd
Doll, Edward B. .... Proj A
Donnell, Robert M. 393rd
Dorsch, Allen R. 1027th
Dorsey, Alan G. 320th
Doss, Maxie H. 393rd
Doss, Victor H. 393rd
Doty, Wayne 1st
Doubek, Van, Jr. 320th
Dowling, Robert J. 393rd
Downey, John L. 393rd
Downey, William B. 390th
Downs, T. 390th
Drag, John W. 1st
Drainer, William C. 393rd
Dramby, Arthur E. 393rd
Dreckshage, Charles 603rd
Driesel, Joel 1st
Dube, H.W. 390th
Duffy, Frank K. 393rd
Duga, Paul 1st
Dugger, James 1st
Dulin, John W. 393rd
Dunlap, Harold T. 603rd
Dunnagan, William 603rd
Dunsing, Leonard W. 393rd
Duquette, Ovila J. 320th
Duran, Jewel 1395th
Durey, Dale H. 603rd
Durham, Francis 1st
Durrum, Robert C. 1st
Duva, James S. 393rd
Duzenbury, Wyatt E. 393rd
Dyer, Arthur F. 393rd

Easterly, Elliott 1st
Easton, William J. 393rd
Eatherly, Claude R. 393rd
Eberle, R G. 390th
Echert, John P. 393rd
Eckley, James N. 1st
Edgecomb, Jesse 1395th
Edwards, James 1395th
Edwards, Roy R., Jr. 393rd
Edwards, William, Jr. 320th
Egger, William E. 393rd
Eidnes, Kenneth L. 393rd
Eilers, Herbert 1395th
Elam, Robert 393rd
Elder, James K., Jr. 393rd
Elder, Stanley P., Jr. 393rd
Eley, John F. 1st
Ellerman, Leslie A. 603rd
Elliott, Merle E. 393rd
Ellis, George W. 1st
Ellis, Lloyd F. 393rd
Ellis, Roger J. 603rd
Ellison, Jackson V. 1027th
Ellison, O.J. 390th
Ellison, Tom G. 1st
Elvidge, Russell P. 320th
Emerson, Clarence G. 320th
Ender, Kenneth A. 1027th
Engle, John P. 1st
Ensle, Cecil H. 603rd
Epperson, Silas M. 1395th
Erickson, Carl R. 320th
Esposito, Ignatius J. 393rd
Esten, Edward T. 1st
Evans, William P. 1st
Ewell, Leighton B. 393rd

Fabinack, Charles C. 603rd
Faidley, Clarence A. 1st
Faist, Leonard W. 1st
Faith, Randal L. 603rd
Falks, Albert L. 1st
Farmway, Edgar F., Jr. 1027th
Farrell, Thomas F. .... HQ
Faryna, Myron 393rd
Faucitano, J.N. 390th
Fawcett, Jay W. 1395th
Feally, Frank J. 1st
Feiler, Edgar 603rd
Felblinger, Robert J. 320th
Felchlia, Albert O. 320th
Fellwock, Robert A. 1027th
Femmel, A.H. 390th
Ferebee, Thomas W. 509HQ
Ferguson, Hugh C. 393rd
Ferguson, William N. 393rd
Ferre, Keith W. 603rd
Ferst, Kenneth C. 603rd
Fetterman, R.A. 509HQ
Field, J. 390th
Filichia, Joe L. 603rd
Firneno, Michael J. 1st
Fischer, Karl R. 393rd
Fish, Anthoney J. 390th
Fisher, Earl W. 603rd
Fisher, John E. 320th
Fisher, William T. 603rd
Fithian, Thomas H. 320th
Flanagin, Rollin L. 1st
Fleischman, Howard A. 390th
Fletcher, J., Jr. 390th
Florer, Darrell W. 1st
Flournoy, Cecil B. 603rd
Floweree, Glen H. 393rd
Flowers, C.L. 390th
Fockler, Donald D. 393rd
Fogarty, George R. 393rd
Forman, Glenn 1027th
Fortine, Frank J. .... Proj A
Foss, Richard H. 1st
Foster, Clifford E. 603rd
Foster, Wallace A. 320th
Fowler, Calvin B. 1st
Fowler, Curtis P. 1027th
Fowler, Marion C., Jr. 393rd
Fowler, Percy 1395th
Fox, James L., Jr. 320th
Fox, Lawrence 1395th
Fox, Miles V. 1st
Francis, R.E. 390th
Franckowiak, Aloysious L. 603rd
Frank, Joseph J. 603rd
Frank, Meyer 1st
Franz, Paul J. 1st
Fredlund, Ronald D. 390th
Freet, Robert 1395th
French, L.C. 390th
Frese, Gilbert S. 320th
Frey, Ernest W. 393rd
Fricker, Glen E. 320th
Friedman, Robert A. 603rd
Frisbie, George 603rd
Frohn, Charles E. 1027th
Fry, Ralph D. 603rd
Frye, Thomas 1395th
Fuller, Willis E. 320th
Funwela, Pasquale E. 393rd
Furman, Ralph A. 603rd
Futschik, August F. 393rd

Gabor, John 1395th
Gackenbach, Russell 393rd
Gagnon, Joseph A.R. 320th
Galati, V.G. 390th
Galbreath, James E. 390th
Galdarisi, Joseph, Jr. 1st
Gallagher, Raymond G. 393rd
Galusha, Howard J. 393rd
Gamelier, Michael J. 603rd
Ganley, John H. 603rd
Garinger, P.L., Jr. 390th
Garman, Kenneth J. 1st
Garn, Robert R. 393rd
Garner, Carl M. 393rd
Garner, R.E. 390th
Garrett, John E. 1027th
Gaskins, W.E. 390th
Gaskins, Willard E. 509HQ
Gasser, Adolph 390th
Gayeski, J.S. 390th
Gehrke, V.P. 509HQ
Gehrken, J.S. 390th
Geller, Guy 1027th
Genova, Carmine A. 393rd
Geren, Theodore R. 603rd
Gerken, Rudolph H. 393rd
Gerster, Clarence W. 320th
Gibavitch, Albert J. 1st
Gibbs, Charlie L. 1027th
Gibson, Adam L. 393rd
Giguere, William C. 603rd
Gilbert, Charles M. 390th
Gililland, Cecil C. 1st
Gilliam, Claude C. 393rd
Gilliam, Claude W. 393rd
Gills, Rodney L. 393rd
Gilmet, James H. 393rd
Giroux Joseph W. 1st
Gitnick, Edwin I. 320th
Glanz, Arthur 1395th
Glazer, Sam 1027th
Gleason, George D. 393rd
Gleneski, John 320th
Glick, Harold B. 603rd
Glore, Ralph A. 1027th
Glore, Charles E. 1395th
Glosser, Saul H. 393rd
Gmach, Edward J. 1st
Godfrey, Leonard A., Jr. 393rd
Godfrey, Paul E. 1st
Goff, Stanley P., Jr. 393rd
Gold, Oliver W. 320th
Goodman, Walter .... Proj A
Goodwin, Alvin P. 1st
Gorecki, Walter M. 390th
Gosnell, Samuel, Jr. 603rd
Gostovich, Mike 1st
Gottwig, T.P. 390th
Gowans, Daniel M. 1st
Grady, James E. 1st
Green, Clifford O. 1st
Green, Fred 1st
Green, George W. 1395th
Grennan Thomas 393rd
Griebe, Norman 1395th
Griep, Hugo 1395th
Griffin, Francis E. 320th
Griffin, Michael F. 1027th
Griffin, Thomas R., Jr. 393rd
Grill, I.P. 390th
Grimes, James B., Jr. 1027th
Grimm, Harley L. 320th
Grossman, Elmer G. 1027th
Grosso, Josepf P. 393rd
Groves, Elery M. 1027th
Groves, Paul P. 393rd
Grubaugh, Jerry, Jr. 393rd
Gruning, Paul W. 393rd
Grzywinski, Edward 1395th
Gulick, Joseph I. 393rd
Gunderson, Rex E. 603rd
Gurly, James R. 393rd
Guszak, Matthew A. 1395th

Hagan, Ralph V. 1st
Hagar, Nelson F. 393rd
Haider, Robert M. 393rd
Halbur, Edwin 1395th
Halden, Kermit W. 603rd
Hale, Samuel E. 393rd
Halein, Floyd 393rd
Hall, Norman 1395th
Haluska, Michael J. 1027th
Hamilton, LeRoy 1395th
Hammond, Chester A. 393rd
Hammons, George P. 393rd
Hancock, Lonnie B. 393rd
Hannah Robert D. 320th
Hannert, William J. 393rd
Hanse, Eugene L. 1st
Hansen, James T. 393rd
Hansen, John C. 393rd
Hansen, N.B. 390th
Hanson, Arthur R. 320th
Hanson, James H. 603rd
Harbuck, Atward J. 1027th
Hardin, Glen G. 1395th
Harding, Lonnie T. 1027th
Hardy, Leonard 603rd
Harman, Billy J. 603rd
Harms, Donald C. .... Proj A
Harrigan, Cornelius 603rd
Harrington, John H., Jr. 393rd
Harris, Brooks H. 603rd
Harris, Jack E. 393rd
Harris, James M. 320th
Harris, Peter T. 393rd
Harter, Cleo E. 393rd
Hartley, Granville K. 1027th
Hartman, Clarence W. 393rd
Hartnick, Milton 603rd
Hartpence, Jack 1395th
Harty, Frank R. 393rd
Harvey, Leonard 1027th
Harwell, Leon 1395th
Hassel, Robert T. 1st
Hatch, Floyd L. 1027th
Havekotte, Curt J. 1st
Hayes, Robert R. 320th
Headrick, A.L. 390th
Heath, Robert F. 393rd
Heathcote, Kenneth S. 393rd
Heddy, Thomas L. 320th
Hefferman, Louis J. 1395th
Heideman, Melville 1st
Heimer, R.K. 390th
Hemmel, C.H., Jr. 390th
Henderson, Arthur D. 320th
Hendren, Charles H. 603rd
Hengen, James F. 1395th
Hennes, Robert J. 509HQ
Henze, Wilbur S. 393rd
Herbert, Maurice D. 1395th
Herman, Harry 1395th
Hess, C.W. 509HQ
Hess, D.A. 509HQ
Hesse, Richard M. 393rd
Higgins, Thomas L. 320th
Hill, C.F. .... 509 HQ
Hill, James 1st
Hill, Thomas P., III 393rd
Hill, Thomas 1st
Hillhouse, Murray M. 1027th
Hills, Clayton 1st
Hinchey, James J. 393rd
Hintz, Norman S. 603rd
Hochlerner, Arnold H. 1027th
Hodson, Carl 603rd
Hoey, Fred A. 393rd
Hofstede, John C. 393rd
Hogan, Patrick J. 603rd
Hogg, Rudolph W. 1st
Hogue, Melvin L. 1st
Hollinger, Frank 1395th
Hollis, Fontaine O. 603rd
Holmes, James F. 390th
Holmes, John G., Jr. 1st
Holmes, Lavern L. 393rd
Holse, Robert E. 393rd
Holub, E.J. 509HQ
Homa, Elroy C. 393rd
Homer, Michael 390th
Hooker, James A. 393rd
Hopkins, James I., Jr. 509HQ
Hopkins, Melvin G. 1st
Hopkins, Vincent P. 603rd
Hopper, John D. .... Proj A
Horn, Bobby E. 1st
Hornicak, Joseph A. 1st
Horton, Leon 393rd
Hoss, H.L. 509HQ
Houser, Loy F. 393rd
Hovsepian, David P. 1027th
Howard, Jim D. 393rd
Howle, B.A. 509HQ
Howley, Daniel J. 1st
Hubbs, J.H. 390th
Hubeny, John H., Jr. 393rd

Hubly, James W.	509HQ
Huddleston, Matthew W.	393rd
Hudgens, Edwin C.	1st
Hudson, Ernie	1395th
Hudson, Jack	1st
Huey, Lankford	603rd
Hull, Claud E.	320th
Hulse, William T.	393rd
Hunt, Robert L.	603rd
Hurst, Farr L.	603rd
Hutnick, Paul G.	603rd
Hylton, William H.	1st
Inaprucker, Raymond	1395th
Inzer, Luke	1395th
Iorio, Joseph	1st
Iosco, D.	390th
Irick, Edward B.	320th
Irwin, Ted C.	393rd
Jacks, Robert B.	320th
Jacks, William J.	393rd
Jackson, A.D.	390th
Jackson, D.M.	390th
Jackson, Goble	603rd
Jackson, John E.	393rd
Jackson, Severn A.	1st
Jacobson, I.H.	390th
Jacobson, Q.L.	390th
James, David B., Jr.	1st
Jameson, D.L.	390th
Jay, Edward	1395th
Jellick, William F.	393rd
Jenceleski, William J.	603rd
Jenkins, William, Jr.	603rd
Jensen, Maurice	1st
Jensen, Ray	1395th
Jensen, W.F.	390th
Jeppson, Morris R.	1st
Jernigan, Norris N.	393rd
Johanson, Ross H.	603rd
Johnson, A.J.	390th
Johnson, Arthur J.	390th
Johnson, Frankie R.	393rd
Johnson, Howard V.	1st
Johnson, James J.	603rd
Johnson, M.	390th
Johnson, Willard	1395th
Johnston, Lawrence H.	Proj A
Johnston, William J.	1027th
Jolly, James W.	393rd
Jones, Charles C.	393rd
Jones, Dale W.	603rd
Jones, Glenn E.	1027th
Jones, Henry I.	393rd
Jones, Melvin A.	320th
Jones, Paul W.	1st
Jones, Weston W.	320th
Jones, William A.	1st
Josefiak, Edward M.	393rd
Josephson, Arthur E.	390th
Joyce, Patrick J.	393rd
Juchno, Joseph	1395th
Judkins, Gordon D.	393rd
Juntti, Melvin W.	603rd
Kaddatz, Carl	1st
Kade, Bertram J.	393rd
Kainz, Frank C.	603rd
Kamla, John L.	320th
Kammerer, Philip E.	1st
Kanapaux, Eugene F.	393rd
Kandel, Edwin	393rd
Kansella, Howard R.	1st
Kapitz, Richard J.	1st
Kaplan, S.	390th
Kapral, Andrew	603rd
Kapusta, M.	390th
Karl, Allan L.	393rd
Karnes, Thomas L.	509HQ
Kasalek, Carl	1st
Kasik Joe	1395th
Katlarz, Bruno A.	393rd
Katz, Seymour S.	603rd
Kauffman, John R.	509HQ
Keene, Francis W.	603rd
Keister, Robert E.	393rd
Kelleher, John R.	1st
Keller, John E.	603rd
Kelly, Daniel J.	1027th
Kemner, Floyd W.	393rd
Kennedy, John B.	393rd
Kern, F.	390th
Keyser, John H.	393rd
Kiedrowski, Stanley A.	393rd
Kieltyka, Stanley L.	393rd
Kimber, Charles E.	390th
Kimme, Harold E.	393rd
King, Cecil N.	393rd
King, Herbert L.	1st
King, Horace	1395th
King, J.T.	509HQ
King, J.W.	509HQ
King, John A.	393rd
King, Joseph R.	603rd
Kingston, Earl, Jr.	603rd
Kinkade, Winfield C.	393rd
Kinnaman, John	1395th
Kinosh, Steve J., Jr.	393rd
Kirby, Harold W.	1st
Kirby, Wesley	1st
Kirk, Dixon P.	1st
Klement, Edmund M.	393rd
Kling, Werner	1395th
Kloss, Emil	1027th
Knapp, Raymond G.	1st
Knaub, Baird D.	603rd
Knauth, Edgar	393rd
Knisley, Harold E.	393rd
Knowles, Rellie R.	1st
Knox, Edward S.	320th
Knox, Willard G.	603rd
Koester, George A.	1st
Kogler, L.F.	390th
Kohn, Armine E.	320th
Kolasinski, Peter P., Jr.	1395th
Kolesky, Leonard	390th
Konkle, Edwin W.	320th
Koons, William W.	603rd
Kopka, Frederick D.	1027th
Koplets, Theodore F.	1st
Korthals, Ernest W.	1027th
Kosh, Stephen	603rd
Kotoff, Nick G.	390th
Kotzian, Francis S.	1st
Kowalski, Frank V.	1027th
Kozlowski, Charles	393rd
Krajczynski, Chester S.	603rd
Krajewski, Chester J.	393rd
Krause, Eugene H.	320th
Krauss, Roy H.	390th
Kregar, Edward E.	1st
Kroes, John J.	1st
Kruba, J.	390th
Krug, Frederick C.	393rd
Krug, Robert E., Jr.	393rd
Kuck, Leslie C.	603rd
Kugler, Richard D.	393rd
Kuharek, John D.	393rd
Kuhlman, M.	390th
Kuhn, Howard L.	1395th
Kuhner, Roy D.	1st
Kupferberg, Jesse	Proj A
Kurowski, Adam	1st
Kushner, Theodore	393rd
Kvam, Dale D.	1st
Kwiatkowski, John	603rd
Kwiatokowski, B.F.	390th
LaCombe, Henry R.	1st
LaCroix, Russell J.	393rd
Laine, Woitto T.	393rd
Laitala, Harold M.	393rd
Lambert, Rufus J.	1027th
Lane, John H.A.	393rd
Lang, Chester	1395th
Lang, William O., Jr.	1st
Lange, Victor W.	320th
Langer, Lawrence	Proj A
Lanuti, Carl A.	393rd
Largur, Joseph	603rd
Larkin, William J.	Proj A
Lathrop, Wendell B.	393rd
Lauer, Ronald C.	603rd
Laurino, J.	390th
Lawler, James A., Jr.	603rd
Lawrence, Albert B.	1st
Lawrence, Kenneth	1395th
Lawrence, Virginia	390th
Lazzarino, Pasquale	393rd
Leach, Paul E.	393rd
Leazer, Chloe S., Jr.	393rd
Lee, Jimmie F.	393rd
Lee, Louis M.	390th
Leffler, Raymond W.	1395th
Legg, Roderick E.	393rd
Lemley, Floyd A.	603rd
Lentz, Paul	390th
Leon, Diego	393rd
Lesniewski, John J.	393rd
Levy, Charles	393rd
Lewandowski, Alfred A.	393rd
Lewandowski, S.R.	390th
Lewinson, R.J.	509HQ
Lewis, Darwin C.	509HQ
Lewis, Henry E.	1027th
Lewis, Joseph R.	603rd
Lewis, Robert A.	393rd
Lincoln, Drexel	1st
Lindau, Harold F.	393rd
Lindemann, Herbert E.	509HQ
Lindsay, Harold J.	393rd
Lindsey, Charles, Jr.	603rd
Lindsey, Jack D.	320th
Linschitz, Henry	Proj A
Linton, John T.	1395th
Lipschitz, Max	393rd
Liptak, August S.	1027th
Litowitz, M.M.	390th
Litterio, Mario A.	393rd
Littlejohn, William	603rd
Liukkonen, William	603rd
Lizak, Steve C.	393rd
Locke, Buford L.	1st
Loden, Charles A.	603rd
Loder, Burnell M.	1027th
Long, William G., Jr.	1st
Longwell, B.R.	390th
Lonnquist, Vincent	1st
Lonsinger, G.W.	390th
Loomis, John F.	603rd
Lovstad, Stanley	1395th
Lowder, James L.	603rd
Loyacono, Patsy	1395th
Luccioni, Anthony	393rd
Lucero, Mauricio G.	1027th
Lucke, E.G.	509HQ
Luckert, Alton L.	1027th
Ludwig, Melvin R.	1st
Luguet, G.A.	509HQ
Lundgren, John L.	393rd
Lunn, Ralph W.	603rd
Lyberger, George N.	1st
Lydon, John C., Jr.	603rd
Lynch, James R.	393rd
Lynch, Laverne L.	1st
Lyon, Wilbur H.	320th
Maas, Robert H.	603rd
MacGregor, Franklin	393rd
Machen, Arthur B.	Proj A
Madden, Joseph H.	603rd
Maddux, Emos E.	1st
Madrid, Joe M.	393rd
Magby, Charles H.	393rd
Mahon, Newton R.E.	320th
Mahugh, Glen, Jr.	393rd
Malcolm, L.R.	390th
Maling, A.S.	509HQ
Mallory, K.L.	509HQ
Malnek, Edward	1395th
Maloney, Anthony J., Jr.	509HQ
Manganielo, R.R.	509HQ
Mann, Virgil I.	320th
Manning, Glenn B.	1027th
Manuel, Howard G.	1027th
Marcello, Paul L.	320th
Marchese, James R.	603rd
Marchlewski, Raymond A.	1st
Markley, Leonard W.	393rd
Marks, Marvin	603rd
Marmolejo, R.	390th
Marquardt, George W.	393rd
Marshall, Stanley J.	1st
Marstellar, John	603rd
Martin, Herbert L.	1st
Martin, John B.	1st
Martinez, Juan	1027th
Mason, Carl C.	393rd
Masoner, Lee R.	603rd
Massengill, Joe M.	603rd
Mastick, Donald	Proj A
Matheny, C.S.	509HQ
Mathews, Robert P.	Proj A
Mathison, Clarke C.	320th
Matranga, Phil	1395th
Matson, Lee W.	1st
Matson, Thomas C.	393rd
Matthews, Malcom E.	1027th
Mauldion, Don A.	393rd
Maynard, Thomas C.	393rd
Mazuco, N.E.	509HQ
McBride, Chester G.	393rd
McCabe, Edward	603rd
McCain, Clarence D.	1027th
McCaleb, Walter F.	393rd
McCall, Ivan J.	390th
McClary, Robert C.	393rd
McClung, Samuel A.	1st
McComas, Wayne L.	1st
McCoy, Earl W.	1st
McCoy, Ralph R.	393rd
McCright, H.S.	390th
McCullough, J.B.	509HQ
McCurley, Robert E.	320th
McCutcheon, Clifford C.	1st
McDivitt, John V.	390th
McDuffie, Lewis W.	603rd
McEachern, Carleton A.	393rd
McFall, J.	390th
McFarland, Clyde R.	1st
McGlennon, James W.	393rd
McGurrin, Francis J.	393rd
McIntosh, F.D.	509HQ
McIntosh, Norman B.	393rd
McKee, Dean W.	1st
McKenny, Charles A.	393rd
McKey, Irvine	603rd
McKinney, Edgar P., Jr.	320th
McKnight, Charles F.	393rd
McKnight, Walter A.	1027th
McLachlan, G.E.	390th
McLaughlin, Frank	1st
McLaury, William J.	1st
McLenon, Claude E.	393rd
McMahan, Allen P.	320th
McManus, John J.	603rd
McMillan, F.E.	509HQ
McNamara, Richard	393rd
McNamee, Robert L.	393rd
McNary, Spencer G.	1027th
McNaught, Joseph	603rd
McNeely, Richard	1395th
McNeiece, Robert L.	320th
McNitt, David B.	1027th
McOmber, John P.	320th
McQueen, D.L.	390th
McVay, Burdette R.	320th
McWherter, Ned	1st
Meeson, Phip	1395th
Melton, Linton W.	320th
Mendl, John J.	1st
Merkle, William R.	603rd
Merry, Francis J.	393rd
Mersky Jacob	603rd
Metcalf, Bob	1395th
Metro, Paul	393rd
Meyer, Dale R.	603rd
Meyer, Morris	603rd
Meyers, Gene H.	393rd
Meyers, Jack	1027th
Michaels, Fred H.	393rd
Mickelson, Mont J.	603rd
Migneco, Victor	1st

Mikulenka, J.E. 390th
Miller, A. 509HQ
Miller, Arthur, Jr. 603rd
Miller, Donald E. 393rd
Miller, Lawrence J. 393rd
Miller, Leon R. 1027th
Miller, Parke N. 320th
Miller, R.P. 509HQ
Miller, Raymond L. 390th
Miller, Robert C. 1st
Miller, Victor A. .... Proj A
Miller, William L., Jr. 320th
Milligan, Harvey R. 1st
Mills, Gordon W. 1st
Mills, Loren W. 320th
Mingin, Lester W. 1st
Mitchell, Robert W. 393rd
Mize, Charles E. 603rd
Mize, Earney 1395th
Mockler, Bernard W. 1027th
Moe, Robert 603rd
Mohr, Royal H. 393rd
Moore, Allan L. 393rd
Moore, Billy 1395th
Moore, Everett L. 1st
Moore, Jesse 1395th
Moorehead, Harold 603rd
Moorehead, Ralph 603rd
Moose, Dewey H. 603rd
Morawa, Leo P. 393rd
Moreau, William A. 603rd
Morrison, Lennie 1395th
Morrison, Philip .... Proj A
Morton, Hector 1st
Moseley, Clarence T. 320th
Motichko, Leonard .... Proj A
Mullany, Gerald 603rd
Mulligan, J.J. 390th
Mullins, Bob B. 603rd
Mullins, Clyde 393rd
Mullins, D.J. 390th
Mulvey, R.E. 390th
Munivez, S. 509HQ
Muretic, Matthew S. 320th
Murphy, James H. 1395th
Murphy, William L. .... Proj A
Murray, Herman C. 603rd
Murray, Joseph, Jr. 1027th
Murray, Martin G. 393rd
Muscolo, Annibale 1st

Nabors, Robert C. 393rd
Nagy, John P. 1st
Napier, Omar E. 1st
Napoli, Louis J. 1027th
Nardi, Flavio H. 1027th
Nash, William L. 603rd
Naughton, R R. 509HQ
Neas, Harry C. 1027th
Nelson, Emmert L. 603rd
Nelson, Frederick H. 1st
Nelson, Lloyd H. 320th
Nelson, Richard M. 393rd
Nesseth, Arvid T. 1027th
Newman, Jack E. 603rd
Newsom, Mack 393rd
Nicely, Gillon T. 393rd
Nichols, Cecil C., Jr. 393rd
Nicholson, Oscar C. 1st
Nicklaus, Roy C. 1st
Nicola, Frank E. 603rd
Nieme, Eugene E. 320th
Noble, Frank N., Jr. 1st
Nolan, James F. .... Proj A
Nolte, Harry W. 603rd
Nooker, Eugene L. .... Proj A
Norder, Herbert 393rd
Norman, Hyatt D., Jr. 393rd
Norman, Thomas W. 390th
Norris, Francis W. 320th
Nottingham, Lee F. 393rd
Nowels, A.Wilson, Jr. 390th
Nunnemaker, Earl R. 393rd
Nyhan, Dennis J. 1st

O'Callaghan, Homer M. 1st
O'Hara, Clement J. 1027th
O'Hara, Franklin B. 1st
O'Keefe, B.J. .... Proj A
O'Neal, Gail 1395th
Oakley, Eldridge W. 603rd
Oakley, Terry D. 1027th
Olin, H.F. 390th
Olivi, Fred J. 393rd
Olmstead, Thomas H. .... Proj A
Olson, Harold R. 393rd
Olsson, Frank A. 603rd
Opsahl, Arthur S. 603rd
Ormond, Francis R. 393rd
Orr, Leonard 1395th
Orr, Wilford A. 320th
Orren, William F. 393rd
Ortega, Leo A., Jr. 393rd
Ortiz, Frank E. 603rd
Osborne, James 1395th
Ossip, Jerome J. 509HQ
Overman, Robert 603rd
Ovesey, Lionel 390th
Owen, H. 390th
Owens, Elbert E. 393rd
Owens, Owen 1027th
Oxley, Charles R. 1027th

Page, Joseph G. 1027th
Painter, Earl 320th
Pair, Aubrey 393rd
Pake, Tom T. 603rd
Palmer, Donald W. 320th
Palmert, Lee E. 393rd
Parker, Edison, Jr. 603rd
Parr, Howard T. 603rd
Parson, Q. 390th
Parsons, Earnest C. 603rd
Parsons, William S. .... Proj A
Paschall, R.L. 509HQ
Patrick, James 1st
Patten, Davis I. 1st
Patten, George A. 320th
Patterson, Archie 1395th
Patterson, J.P. 390th
Patusch, Eric P. 320th
Paulauskas, John 1395th
Paulikonis, Peter P. 320th
Pavone, Theodore C. 320th
Pawiak, Chester V. 393rd
Payne, James H. 1st
Payne, Kenneth 603rd
Payton, Lawrence S. 320th
Pearson, Morris J. 1st
Pegram, James I. 393rd
Pellegrino, Francis A. 393rd
Pellow, W.J. 390th
Pembroke, Milo E. 603rd
Penney, W.G. .... Proj A
Penninger, Harry 393rd
Pepe, Henry J. 1st
Perez, J.M. 390th
Perez, Jacob 1395th
Perlman, Theodore .... Proj A
Perry, Charles A. 393rd
Pescho, M. 390th
Peters, John G. 393rd
Peters, O.H. 390th
Peterson, Clarence 603rd
Peterson, Kenneth C. 390th
Peterson, Wesley P. 390th
Petrolli, Robert J. 393rd
Petroski, John H. 603rd
Pettengill, Leland F. 393rd
Pettigrew, Elliott, Jr. 603rd
Pettit, Paul R. 390th
Pfaff, Thomas J. 1395th
Pfeiffer, John C., Jr. 393rd
Pfister, Kurt 1395th
Pharr, Gordon C. 1st
Phillips, William S. 320th
Phipps, John E. 393rd
Piehl, Donald D. 393rd
Piepho, Harvey L. 1st
Pierce, K.L. 390th
Pilgrim, Audave C. 603rd

Pinchot, Albert 1st
Ping, Yive J.H. 393rd
Pirkle, Chester G. 1027th
Plato, Peter P. 393rd
Podolsky, Richard J. 1st
Poe, Edgar A., Jr. 393rd
Poehls, I.H. 390th
Poehls, Irvin F. 390th
Pogue, Charles E. 1st
Polakowski, Joseph 603rd
Poli, A.J. 509HQ
Politi, Carmine V. 393rd
Polito, John 1st
Poole, Quinton 1027th
Popp, George F. 603rd
Popwell, Calvin B. 393rd
Porter, George A. 1st
Porter, John W. 390th
Poslof, Anton 1027th
Pratt, Robert H., Jr. 393rd
Prebel, Edward 393rd
Presser, E.J. 390th
Price, Edward A. 603rd
Price, James B., Jr. 320th
Price, James N., Jr. 393rd
Prince, R.I. 390th
Pringle, John C. 603rd
Prohs, W.R. .... Proj A
Prout, Charles H. 603rd
Puckett, D.W. 509HQ
Puckett, James A. 393rd
Pugh, Charles J. 320th
Pugh, Lyle E. 390th
Pulfer, Carl A. 603rd
Purdon, David 393rd
Purdum, John M 603rd
Purnell, W.R .... HQ
Putsch, Charles P. 1027th

Quartana, Oakley P. 1st
Quiggin, Edward R. 1027th
Quigley, Wilbur W. 393rd

Raffel, LeRoy R. 603rd
Rainey, Milton F. 1027th
Ramsey, Norman F. .... Proj A
Rara, Edward J. 320th
Raub, Leo G., Jr. 1st
Ray, Norman W. 393rd
Rayome, Clayton J. 320th
Reale, Natalie 1395th
Reames, D.G. 390th
Rebol, R.R. 509HQ
Reed, Vestle O. 393rd
Reeder, Lloyd J. 393rd
Reedy, William B. 393rd
Reese, Thaddeous L. 320th
Reidelbach, Stanley F. 1395th
Reilly, James J. 393rd
Reimers, W.H., Jr. 390th
Rein, Carl W. 393rd
Renfro, Floyd K. 1st
Rentschler, Stanley 1395th
Repko, Mike 1395th
Reynolds, Clarence 1027th
Reynolds, Filbert 393rd
Reynolds, George T. .... Proj A
Reynolds, Grover 1st
Rice, William H. 1st
Rich, C.D. 390th
Rich, Charles W. 390th
Richard, G.W., Jr. 509HQ
Richards, Lyndon 1st
Richardson, Harold H. 1027th
Richardson, Porter A. 393rd
Richardson, Willard H. 1st
Richardson, William H. 320th
Richotte, Donald C. 320th
Rider, Harold J. 393rd
Rigby, Henry 1395th
Rigler, Robert B. 1st
Rinard, Charles B. 393rd
Rissbacher, Frank 1027th
Ritchie, Floyd J. 1027th
Ritchie, M.E. 390th
Rivera, Trinidad 1395th

Roark, F. 390th
Robbins, Patrick J. 393rd
Robertson, R.F. 390th
Robertson, Robert D. 1st
Robey, John D. 393rd
Robinson, Aubrey C. 1st
Robinson, George F. 393rd
Robinson, Rowland E. 320th
Rodolico, Thomas A. 393rd
Rodriguez, B.R. 390th
Roebuck, Kenneth O. 1st
Rogalski, Chester A. 393rd
Rogers, Clarence E. 1st
Rogers, Joel B. 1st
Rogers, Rudolph E. 1st
Roland, Whitney G. 603rd
Romine, Kermit H. 1027th
Ronfeld, B.H. 509HQ
Ronk, Edwin A. 1st
Rosenberger, Earl E. 603rd
Rosenthal, Howard 1st
Rosenthal, Hudson D. 1st
Ross, Floyd E. 390th
Ross, Frederick 1395th
Ross, Joseph L. 393rd
Ross, Kirby 393rd
Rothenberg, Meyer 603rd
Rothschild, John A. 393rd
Rotunno, C. 390th
Rouse, Berndon N. 390th
Rovello, A.J. 390th
Rowe, Donald L. 393rd
Rowe, Glenn O. 1st
Rowe, William M., Jr. 393rd
Rowley, Vernon J. 393rd
Roy, Carl R. 393rd
Rubis, Andrew 1st
Rudgers, M.T. 509HQ
Ruscio, John L. 320th
Rush, R.B. 390th
Russ, Harlow W. .... Proj A
Russell, John 1st
Russell, Paul V. 1027th
Russell, Vernon 1st
Russo, John A. 1st
Ruzzo, Pasquale C. 393rd
Ryan, Edward A., Jr. 1st
Ryder, Roland E. 603rd
Rzepinski, Marshall 1st

Sabatura, Harry 1395th
Salyer, Everett L. 320th
Sanborn, P., Jr. 390th
Sanders, David M. 603rd
Sanders, Jason E. 603rd
Sanders, M.A. 390th
Sanders, Ray 1st
Sanders, Rex 1395th
Sands, Earl E. 1027th
Sanfratello, Salvatore S. 1027th
Sapunka, Joseph S. 393rd
Sarni, Tony 393rd
Saunders, Charles O. 509HQ
Saunders, Harold N. 1st
Savage, Evell G. 603rd
Savage, Frank L. 1027th
Schaffer, Louis 1395th
Schafhauser, Paul C. 393rd
Schaller, J.G. 390th
Scharf, S.W. 390th
Schauer, L.M.E. 390th
Scheer, George F. 320th
Scheuern, John A. 1st
Schiavone, Alexander G. 390th
Schick, John A. 320th
Schiller, William 1st
Schlesinger, Edward P. 393rd
Schlessel, Walter 320th
Schmidtke, Paul C. 393rd
Schneider, Sidney S. 1027th
Schramke, Francis J. 393rd
Schreffer, George I. 393rd
Schreiber, Raemer E. .... Proj A
Schrodt, Sterling F. 603rd
Schultz, William T. 1st
Schwab, Charles E. 393rd

Schwab, Charles W. ... 393rd
Scoggin, Maurice L. ... 390th
Scott, John B. ... 603rd
Scott, Troy B. ... 393rd
Scott, W.T. ... 390th
Scott, Wilbur G. ... 603rd
Scully, Charles H. ... 1027th
Scully, J.B. ... 390th
Seaman, Harold F. ... 603rd
Seay, M.L. ... 393rd
Sedor, Joseph ... 390th
Seely, R.L. ... 509HQ
Sekeres, E.J. ... 509HQ
Sekeres, Elmer C. ... 393rd
Selander, Walter ... 1395th
Sells, Robert M. ... 1027th
Sensibaugh, William P. ... 1027th
Serber, Robert ... Proj A
Serrietella, Rocco F. ... 393rd
Severinsen, Leslie A. ... 1395th
Seweryniak, Thaddeus J. ... 1st
Shackelton, LeRoy ... 1st
Shade, Robert L. ... 1st
Shakespeare, Howard V. ... 1027th
Shaller, Joseph G. ... 393rd
Shamlian, Armen ... 390th
Shaw, Earl ... 1395th
Sheehan, William P. ... 509HQ
Sheets, Donald L. ... 603rd
Shepherd, Harry G. ... 1027th
Shepler, Clarence M. ... 393rd
Sherwood, John J. ... 603rd
Shields, Wilson D. ... 320th
Shmiske, Paul C. ... 603rd
Shofield, Edgar F. ... 393rd
Showalter, Frederic ... 1st
Shropshire, William O. ... 1st
Shryer, William G. ... 1027th
Shuhmaker, I. ... 390th
Shults, John H. ... 1027th
Shumard, Robert H. ... 393rd
Shvegel, Edward P. ... 603rd
Sibulski, George P. ... 603rd
Sidebottom, Mobly A. ... 1027th
Siegle, Calvin G. ... 1027th
Simanovich, Nicholas ... 393rd
Simon, Stanley ... 1st
Simpson, Leonard ... 1395th
Skaggs, Glen F. ... 393rd
Skidmore, George A ... 1st
Skora, Walter, J. ... 393rd
Skrupsky, Metro ... 509HQ
Skull, William G. ... 1027th
Slaby, Joseph ... 320th
Sleipnes, Arnold E. ... 393rd
Slife, Theodore M. ... 393rd
Slusky, Joseph ... 509HQ
Slussar, Walter J. ... 1st
Smallwood, E.R. ... 509HQ
Smiley, Doyle C. ... 1st
Smith, Albert E. ... 509HQ
Smith, Charles W. ... 393rd
Smith, Earnest P. ... 1027th
Smith, Elbert B. ... 393rd
Smith, Harry D. ... 393rd
Smith, Henry L. ... 393rd
Smith, J.I. ... 390th
Smith, Jesse F. ... 393rd
Smith, John ... 1395th
Smith, Leon D. ... 1st
Smith, Newton R., Jr. ... 320th
Smith, Paul C. ... 1st
Smith, Robert C. ... 393rd
Smith, Roger M. ... 1st
Smith, Sawdon S. ... 603rd
Smith, Seth I. ... 1st
Smith, William E. ... 393rd
Smith, William, Jr. ... 393rd
Smithson, Robert E. ... 393rd
Snider, Glasgow ... 1st
Snyder, Frank E. ... 393rd
Snyder, Murray ... 1027th
Snyder, W.W., Jr. ... 509HQ
Sorci, Anthony J. ... 320th
Sosna, A.B. ... 390th
Sowers, Wilson C. ... 393rd
Sparrow, Jimmie ... 390th
Spiker, Chlorus M. ... 603rd
Spitzer, Abe M. ... 393rd
Spradlin, William J. ... 393rd
Sprague, Willis N., Jr. ... 390th
Sprouse, Milton C. ... 393rd
Spurling, Harold M. ... 320th
St. Myers, Raymond G. ... 393rd
Stafford, James, Jr. ... 603rd
Staley, Clifford L. ... 1027th
Standholm, H.S. ... 390th
Stanek, Frank ... 1st
Stankevitch, Robert ... 1st
Stasiak, Lawrence J. ... 509HQ
Stasink, Thomas J. ... 390th
Staton, Raymond ... 1395th
Stein, Arthur C. ... 320th
Steinke, Stanley G. ... 393rd
Stephenson, Edward ... Proj A
Steur, Paul W. ... 393rd
Stevans, Howard H. ... 390th
Stevens, Derward A. ... 393rd
Stevens, George E. ... 1st
Stevenson, Robert L. ... 1027th
Stewart, F.H. ... 509HQ
Stewart, Ivan H. ... 393rd
Stiber, Andrew J. ... 1027th
Stiborik, Joe S. ... 393rd
Stiegman, John L. ... 1st
Stillwell, B. ... 390th
Stinnette, William S. ... 1st
Stock, Robert J. ... 393rd
Stockwell, Vaughn ... 603rd
Stolsonburg, William G. ... 393rd
Stone, Charley L. ... 603rd
Storey, James M. ... 393rd
Stough, Harold L. ... 390th
Stradford, Leroy ... 1st
Strasburg, Lawrence F. ... 393rd
Strayer, C. ... 390th
Streaker, Frederick H. ... 1st
Strickland, Omar G. ... 393rd
Stringfellow, William ... 1st
Strudwick, James W. ... 393rd
Stuewe, William C. ... 393rd
Sullivan, Charles ... 1st
Sullivan, James B. ... 393rd
Sullivan, Joseph G. ... 320th
Sullivan, Joseph M. ... 1st
Sullivan, Maurice ... 1395th
Supienko, Joe ... 1027th
Sutton, Frank E. ... 393rd
Swafford, H. ... 390th
Swasey, Herbert D. ... 603rd
Swatha, E.J. ... 390th
Sweeney, Charles W. ... 393rd
Sweitzer, Lawrence J. ... 1027th
Switalski, Leonard ... 1st
Switzer, Carl ... 1st
Sylvia, Michael H. ... 393rd
Szczepanik, Eugene F. ... 1027th
Szczuka, Mitchell S. ... 393rd

Taeger, Glenn M. ... 1027th
Tagliabue, Richard F. ... 320th
Tardiff, B.A. ... 390th
Taylor, George E. ... 1027th
Taylor, John B. ... 509HQ
Taylor, Jack ... 1395th
Taylor, James R., Jr. ... 393rd
Taylor, Ralph R., Jr. ... 393rd
Teckentien, W.R. ... 390th
Teel, James E. ... 1st
Tenzer, Harold N. ... 603rd
Teuton, Edwin ... 1395th
Theno, J.B. ... 390th
Thetford, Oscar L. ... 1027th
Thigpen, Oscar J. ... 393rd
Thomas, Leslie ... 1395th
Thompson, Howard A. ... 393rd
Thompson, Howard B. ... 393rd
Thompson, John M. ... 1395th
Thompson, Virgil ... 1395th
Thornhill, Francis D. ... 393rd
Thornton, Gunnar ... Proj A
Thornton, Robert E. ... 1027th
Thorstrom, Earl ... 1395th
Tibbets, Paul W., Jr. ... 509HQ
Tigner, Richard O. ... 393rd
Tijerina, Thomas T. ... 393rd
Tilley, James P. ... 393rd
Tillman, Paul L. ... 393rd
Timberly, Harold E. ... 603rd
Tippett, Clarence E. ... 1395th
Tirabassi, Louis ... 1395th
Tison, Ralph R. ... 393rd
Tobias, Joe P. ... 1395th
Toldness, Robert H. ... 320th
Tortosa, Aubrey ... 393rd
Trainer, Jesse W. ... 1027th
Travis, Frank H., Jr. ... 1st
Travis, William ... 1st
Troutner, Leon C. ... 603rd
Truhlar, Lewis ... 393rd
Tucker, John L. ... Proj A
Tuggle, Thomas E. ... 1027th
Turner, Claude A. ... 603rd
Turner, John M. ... 320th
Turner, Merle C. ... 320th
Tuttle, Donald D. ... 393rd
Twork, Chester ... 393rd
Twyford, William ... 603rd

Ursch, John ... 1395th
Utley, Arthur M., Jr. ... 1st

Valley, Robert J. ... 393rd
Van Pelt, James F. ... 393rd
Vanderhoof, Ronal ... 1st
VanDerHom, H. ... 390th
Vandermale, Carl A. ... 1st
VandeVoort, John H. ... 390th
VanKirk, Theodore J. ... 509HQ
VanMeter, Glen ... 1395th
Varga, Charles A. ... 603rd
Vavro, J.A. ... 509HQ
Vedder, Spencer ... 393rd
Valazquez, Edward G. ... 1027th
Vella, James ... 603rd
Vernon, Chester ... 1st
Vertz, Richard W. ... 1st
Vester, Donald W. ... 1st
Villarreal, Marion M. ... 603rd
Vitale, L.W. ... 390th
Vrana, Leon J. ... 320th

Wacowski, Charley ... 1395th
Waggoner, Wilber L. ... 320th
Wagner, Edgar G. ... 393rd
Wainscott, James J. ... 393rd
Waldman, Bernard ... Proj A
Walgamotte, N.L. ... 390th
Walk, Paul W. ... 393rd
Walters, Aaron ... 1395th
Walz, Jack ... 1st
Ward Elvern ... 1395th
Ward, George T. ... 1st
Warga, Edward ... 1st
Warner, Roger S. ... Proj A
Warner, Stanley ... 1027th
Wasz, Robert H. ... 320th
Wayland, Clarence R. ... 320th
Wayland, R.C. ... 390th
Weatherly, Ira J. ... 393rd
Weaver, Alvin O. ... 393rd
Webb, E.W. ... 390th
Webb, William F. ... 320th
Weeks, Alfred R. ... 1st
Weichel, Edgar ... 603rd
Weigandt, George J. ... 393rd
Weimer, Thomas J. ... 393rd
Weiner, M.B. ... 390th
Weiss, Harold L. ... 509HQ
Welle, Raymond ... 1395th
Weller, George A. ... 393rd
Wellman, Merl L. ... 1027th
Wells, James L. ... 1027th
Wells, Robert L. ... 393rd
Wendlandt, L.W. ... 390th
Werney, Morris ... 1027th
Wertz, Keith ... 603rd
Wertz, Kenneth ... 390th
Wescott, George W. ... 509HQ
West, Billy A. ... 1st
Westcott, Kermit F. ... 509HQ
Westmark, Robert J. ... 1st
Westover, Joseph E. ... 393rd
Wey, Franklin K. ... 393rd
Whan, Orval ... 603rd
Wheeler, Samuel R. ... 393rd
Wheelock, Phillip T. ... 1st
Wherland, E.J. ... 390th
Whitaker, Baxter L. ... 393rd
Whitaker, Loy G., Jr. ... 393rd
Whitaker, W.M. ... 390th
White, Charles ... 603rd
White, Clifford C. ... 393rd
White, Everett E. ... 603rd
White, James H. ... 1395th
White, William J. ... 393rd
Whitehead, R.H. ... 509HQ
Widowsky, Jack ... 393rd
Wierenga, Russell G. ... 1395th
Wierman, F.C. ... 509HQ
Wilbur, John A. ... 1st
Wilkerson, Fred ... 1395th
Williams, Albert J. ... 320th
Williams, Andrew ... 603rd
Williams, J.C. ... 390th
Williams, John O. ... 603rd
Williams, John V. ... 320th
Williams, Marion L. ... 603rd
Williams, Perry O. ... 1st
Williams, Ray ... 1st
Williams, Stewart W. ... 393rd
Willis, John W. ... 1st
Willis, Robert D. ... 603rd
Willison, Clifford E. ... 1027th
Willoughby, John L. ... 393rd
Wilson, John A. ... 393rd
Wilson, Robert ... 393rd
Wimer, Franklin B. ... 393rd
Winslow, Warren W. ... 1027th
Wisnewski, Joseph A. ... 1st
Witherell, John H. ... 320th
Wlodarski, John ... 603rd
Wolf, Donald L. ... 603rd
Wolfe, Charles R. ... 603rd
Wolfe, Theodore E. ... 393rd
Wolff, Russell R. ... 390th
Womack, James R. ... 393rd
Wong, Patrick P. ... 393rd
Woodard, Carlie, Jr. ... 603rd
Woodbury, J.K. ... 390th
Worley, Howard C. ... 603rd
Worthington, Clark ... 320th
Wrede, William L. ... 1st
Wren, William H. ... 603rd
Wright, Alex V., Jr. ... 393rd
Wright, David B. ... 603rd
Wright, John W. ... 393rd
Wright, Philip L. ... 393rd
Wright, R.M. ... 390th
Wright, William E. ... 393rd
Wrzesienski, Alfred ... 1st
Wysocki, Thaddeus ... 603rd

Yeager, Homer L. ... 1027th
Yeagley, Clyde ... 1395th
Young, A.F. ... 509HQ
Young, Donald A. ... 393rd
Young, William E. ... 393rd

Zachary, James ... 1395th
Zafonte, A. ... 390th
Zahn, Herman S., Jr. ... 393rd
Zammarrelli, N.J. ... 390th
Zangre, Joseph A. ... 390th
Zauratsky, Joseph F. ... 1st
Zechman, George ... 1395th
Zeinfeld, V.W. ... 509HQ
Ziegler, Arthur B. ... 1395th
Zimmerli, Frederick H. ... Proj A
Zimmerman, Harry ... 320th
Zozom, Frank, Jr. ... 1027th
Zweber, Emmery H. ... 1395th

Index

365

366

Fred Bock,
Robert A. Krauss,
Robert W. Krauss

Forest Dunes,
Lake Michigan
August 1990

Robert and Amelia Krauss
509th Composite Group Reunion,
Seattle, Washington, 1992

(L-R): Ted Van Kirk, Mary
Ann Ferebee, Robert W.
Krauss, Amelia Krauss
Dayton, Ohio

Acknowledgments

Much of the information contained in this book was provided with the help of many individuals. The editors would like to thank all those who contributed their stories and photo collections and the following individuals:

Richard Campbell for providing the 509th Roster, the summary data on the 393rd crews and planes, and photos from the Air Force historical Research Agency along with Leon Smith's collection. John Coster-Mullen for providing photos from the National Archives and Dr. Frank Shelton for providing photos from the Harold Agnew Collection.

To Leon Smith for taking so many wonderful photos of crews, planes and Tinian scenery. Mark Natola for providing much historical footage, interviews and for archiving the Charles Perry collection. To the family of Jack Wright who never received the credit he so deserved for the color photo of the Enola Gay with the Bockscar in the background used on the cover of this book. Dave Serikaku for the Nagasaki damage photos; Armen Shamlian for Wendover photos; Wilbur Lyon, Nagasaki trip photos; Carl Garner, 393rd plane photos; and Elbert Smith's photo collection.

We also wish to thank John Harsh of CBI Graphics for quality negatives and prints; Joe Littleton for his prints and Dave Olson, owner of Printers Press. And most of all Erin Howarth of Wilderness Books who spent many hours correcting problems and putting together a quality book.

If we missed anyone, please forgive the oversight, it was unintentional.

Epilogue

by Robert Krauss

Fred Bock

I remember the many summers I spent with Fred Bock at his summer home "Forest Dunes" on Lake Michigan and the hours he spent assisting me in the identification of photos in my collection and the activities contained within them.

I would like to thank my wife, Amelia and my son, Robert, who have had to put up with my passion for collecting 509th photographs and autographs; and to the members of the 509th and their families who through their generosity have made this book possible and gave us 58 years of peace.

Ray Gallagher

I also remember Ray Gallagher, a veteran of the B29 testing program at Eglin Field, a member of the Tibbets' trained "Ladybird" crew and as Assistant Flight Engineer on Crew C-15 participated in both Atomic missions : First on the Hiroshima instrument plane and second on the Nagasaki strike plane.

We first met Ray at the 1990 reunion in Wendover. He observed we were trying to preserve the history of the 509th composite Group and was helpful to us in locating other crew members. It was Ray who spoke of war being a monster on the loose and someone had to stop the monster. He told me and others that to fully understand you had to put yourself into those times.

To The Members of the 509th Composite Group:

At the September 2000 Kansas City reunion, I volunteered that if there was to be another reunion and if you would hold it in Wendover, I would be your chairman. I wanted to give back to you, as my way of saying "Thank You" for what you did as a combined effort to help win the war and for your kindness and generosity in sharing your time, photos and memorabilia with me.

Special Thanks:

I would like to quote Mont J. Mickelson, who said: "I express profound appreciation for many friends, fine leadership exhibited by enlisted and officer personnel alike. Of the many, George and Bernice Marquardt who championed the 1990 509th 45th Anniversary Reunion at Wendover under extreme extenuating circumstances, for the monument erected in West Wendover, Nevada, in honor of all 509th Composite Group, and James S. Petersen, President of Wendover Historic Airfield to generate and enlarge a museum to preserve the history and provide an emblem for peace for present and future generations to enjoy, endear and remember."

This says it all.

George Marquardt

To Bob From Sgt. Ray Gallagher

ATOMIC MIGHT

The Japs well knew, they had been warned
Of the Allied might that was being formed.
But they chose to die for the Rising Sun
And proudly stuck to their ill made gun.
But a thunderous blast, a blinding light,
Brought the 509th atomic might.

It was the 6th of August, that much we knew
When the boys took off in the morning dew,
Feeling nervous, jumpy, sick and ill at ease
They flew at the heart of the Japanese,
With a thunderous blast, a blinding light,
And the 509th's atomic might.

Below like a miniature checker board
Lay a Japanese town in one accord,
Unknowing the might that lay in store
It went to the shelters, the rich and poor,
That's when the thunderous blast, and blinding light
Came from the 509th's atomic might.

From out of the air the secret fell
And created below a scene of hell;
Never before in times fast flight
Has there been displayed such at sight,
As the thunderous blast, the blinding light,
Of the 509th's atomic might,

From ear to tongue, from tongue to press
The story spread — stupendous — nothing less!
From pole to pole, around the earth,
Folks knew now of our powerful worth,
With the thunderous blast, the blinding light,
Of the 509th's atomic might.

Oh, God! -- that when this War doth cease
And again we turn our thoughts to peace
That you will help us build, -- not devastate,
A life of love and truth, -- not hate,
Without the thunderous blast, the blinding light
Of the 509th's atomic might.

Sgt. Harry Bernard

CREW A-1
393rd Bombardment
Squadron (VH),
509th Composite Group
flight history on page 254

CREW A-2
393rd Bombardment
Squadron (VH),
509th Composite Group
flight history on page 255

CREW A-3
393rd Bombardment Squadron
(VH),
509th Composite Group
flight history on page 256

**CREW A-4
393rd Bombardment
Squadron (VH),
509th Composite Group**
flight history on page 257

**CREW B-7
393rd Bombardment
Squadron (VH),
509th Composite Group**
flight history on page 260

**CREW B-8
393rd Bombardment Squadron
(VH),
509th Composite Group**
flight history on page 261

CREW B-9
393rd Bombardment
Squadron (VH),
509th Composite Group
flight history on page 262

CREW B-10
393rd Bombardment
Squadron (VH),
509th Composite Group
flight history on page 263

CREW C-11
393rd Bombardment
Squadron (VH),
509th Composite Group
flight history on page 264

CREW C-12
393rd Bombardment
Squadron (VH),
509th Composite Group
flight history on page 265

CREW C-13
393rd Bombardment Squadron
(VH),
509th Composite Group
flight history on page 266

CREW C-14
393rd Bombardment
Squadron (VH),
509th Composite Group
flight history on page 267

CREW C-15
393rd Bombardment Squadron (VH), 509th Composite Group
flight history on page 268

Leather jacket patch worn by JABIT III Crew

Leather jacket patch worn by Straight Flush Crew

Leather jacket patch worn by 393rd Bomb Group

Emblem and patch of the 320th

A Tinian Picture Portfolio

Col. Tibbets salutes Gen. Spaatz after receiving Distinguished Service Cross Gen. Davies watches, Armen Shamlian takes photo

Paul Tibbetts still clasping his pipe in his hand after medal award ceremony as Ted Van Kirk walks behind.

North Field, Tinian

(L-R): Fred Bock, Dr. Young, Lou Allen, Franklin MacGregor

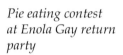

Pie eating contest at Enola Gay return party

Caution, Japanese still hiding

Tinian Harbor

*320th C-54
"Green Hornet"
on Tinian*

North Field, Tinian

Wendover postcard

509th Headquarters–Tinian

509th living area

509th Compound–Tinian

American cemetery

American cemetery–Tinian

American cemetery–Tinian

Japanese headquarters Ushi Point

*Japanese headquarters
Ushi Point*

Swim area–Tinian

Officer crews of "Strange Cargo" and "Top Secret"– See page 72

*Early photo of
"Big Stink" on
Tinian*

*Early photo of
L-R "Bockscar"
"Great Artiste"*

*Flight
line–Tinian
L-R "Up
an Atom"
"Great
Artiste"
"Enola
Gay"*

Engine change–Tinian

"Green Hornet" on Tinian

Loading "Green Hornet" on Tinian

Loading "Green Hornet"
on Tinian

Little Boy L-11 leaves Bomb
Assembly Building

photo courtesy John Coster-Mullen

Fat Man F-31 leaves Bomb Assembly
Building

photo courtesy of John Coster-Mullen

Refueling "Green Hornet" on Tinian

"Enola Gay" returns to Tinian after Hiroshima   *George Staley photo*

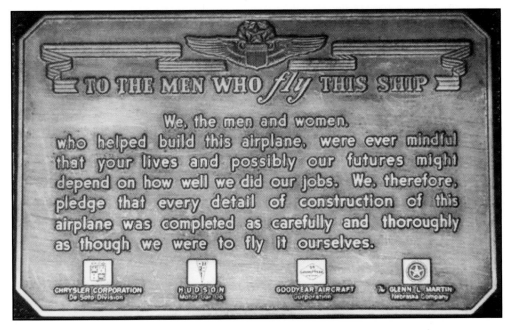

Plaque placed inside each 509th B29

Enola Gay on Tinian

"Enola Gay" on Tinian

"Enola Gay" on Tinian; "Bockscar" in background